بسم الله الرحمن الرحيم

IN THE NAME OF ALLAH, THE MOST GRACIOUS AND MOST MERCIFUL

MUQADDAMA-E-SIRAJUL ABSAR

Volume 1

BY
Haz. Syed Yaqoob Bazmi(Rh)
S/o. Haz. Syed Mustafa Tashreefullahi(Rh)

Translated by
Syed Sharief Khundmiri
S/o Haz. Syed Qasim Khundmiri(Rh)

American Edition

MUQADDAMA-E-SIRAJUL ABSAR

(3RD. EDITION, INCLUDING THE SUPPLEMENT)

URDU EDITIONS

First Edition:1365 Hijri   Second Edition: 1382 Hijri, (22nd. February 1965 AD)
        Third Edition : 26th.Ramzan, 1410 Hijri, (23rd. April 1990 AD)

AUTHOR

HAZRAT SYED YAQOOB BAZMI (RH)

PUBLISHER OF URDU EDITION

SYED MAHMOOD TASHRIFULLAHI (B.Tech.Osmania)

s/o late HAZRAT SYED ASHRAF TASHRIFULLAHI(Rh)

URDU EDITION PUBLISHED ON

26TH. RAMZANUL MUBARAK/23RD.APRIL 1990

PRINTED BY AI'JAZ PRINTING PRESS, CHATTA BAZARHYDERABAD, ANDHRA

PRADESH

3

بسم الله الرحمن الرحيم

In the name of Allah, the most Benevolent and most Mercifull

For the Benefit of English Knowing Generation of Millat-e-Mahdavia

MUQADDAMA-E-SIRAJUL ABSAR

BY

ALLAMATUL ASR, MUHAQQIQ-E-MAHDAVIA

HAZRAT SYED YAQOOB BAZMI (RH)

TRANSLATED BY

SYED SHARIEF KHUNMIRI

Order this book online at www.trafford.com
or email orders@trafford.com

Most Trafford titles are also available at major online book retailers.

Printed in the United States of America.

ISBN: 978-1-4669-8688-6 (sc)
ISBN: 978-1-4669-8687-9 (e)

Because of the dynamic nature of the Internet, any web addresses or links contained in this book may have changed
since publication and may no longer be valid. The views expressed in this work are solely those of the author and do
not necessarily reflect the views of the publisher, and the publisher hereby disclaims any responsibility for them.

Any people depicted in stock imagery provided by Thinkstock are models,
and such images are being used for illustrative purposes only.
Certain stock imagery © Thinkstock.

Trafford rev. 10/18/2013

 www.trafford.com

North America & international
toll-free: 1 888 232 4444 (USA & Canada)
fax: 812 355 4082

BOOKS AVALABLE AT:

CHANCHALGUDA: Br. Syed Sultan Naseer Ph: 903-0048-309,Br. Maqsood Ali Khan Ph: 9885237858,Br. Syed Isa Ph: 9959912642,

MUSHIRABAD: Br. Syed Ishaq Ph: 9866344800, Hz. Faraz Miyan Mushtahedi Ph: 9949113612

CHANNAPATNA: Abid Masjid Ph: 9611213519

BANGALORE: Br. Syed Tashrif Ullah Ph: 9481036300

PALANPUR: Br. Salaam Ullah T. Syed Ph:2742 246 382

BURBANK: Br. Syed Shahabuddin Ph:818-736-6250, Br. Syed Ziaullah Ph: 818-557-1345

CHICAGO: Br. Noor Mohammed Ph: 773-764-5707,Br. Rahmath Alik Khan 773-743-4329

ATLANTA& N.Carolina: Br. Syed Rashid-ul-haq Ph: 704-709-7144

LONDON: Haz. Syed Khudmir Sahib, Ph: 44894466402

PAKISTAN: Br. Rahman Farid Ph:3333093234T:

List of Contents
VOLUME ONE

Title 2
Books Available 4
Translator's Note 14
Acknowledgement 19
Dedication 20
Publisher's Note on Urdu Edition 21
Impressions 24
Dedication 29
Submission by Allama 30
Preface 31
Eulogy in Urdu by Dr.Athar 32
Appreciation 33
Allamatul Asr 35
Abdul Malik Sajawandi 38
Shaik Ali Muttaqi 40
Abu Rija Mohammed Zaman Khan 41
Submission in Urdu by Allamatul Asr regarding Muqaddama Nigari 55
Translation of the above Urdu version 55
Arrangement of the "Muqaddama-e-Siraj-ul-Absar" .65

Part One

Chapter One—Geneology and Early Life of Imamana (AS) 74
(Note regarding Juanpur) 74
Imamana's early life 82
City of Juanpur 83
Importance of Juanpur 85
Juanpur became famous for learning 87
Juanpur and Indian scholars 91
Juanpur's excellence 92
Battle with Raja Dalpath (875 H) 93
Successors of Sultan Naseer 94
Raja Kauns 95
Land lords of Juanpur 96
Imamana's period of Trance 96
Sultan Hussain Sahuaqi 100

Chapter Two—Migration and Proclamation of Mehdiath 101
Importance of migration 101
Invitation to Mahdaviath 104
Emergence of Mehdi from Yemen 108
(Note regarding karara) 109
Invitation for witness 111

Witness by Contemporaries 113
Witness by Indian Historians 114
Imamana's ancestors 114
Witness of Arabic History 115
Explanation about Azhra shams 116
Basics of the mission of Imamana (as) 118
Discussion between Herql and Abu Sufyan 119

Chapter Three—Proofs regarding Mehdiath 119
Prophecy of Torah 121
Daniel Asha 2:44 122
Safar Habqooq Asha 3:34 122
Bible Luga 24:49 123
Bible Yuhoma 15:26 123
Bible Yuhuma 12:14 123
Tradition for Advent of Mahdi 124
Descension of Bounty 130
(Note again – Beads counting) 132
Abu Yada Moosli's narration 136
Meanings of Yadi Rujl 144
Mehdi, Descendant of Imam Hassan also. 145
Imamana's name was Muhammad 145
Characters resemble to that of Holy Prophet 145
La Yasbahu fil Khulqi 145
Another objection 147
Book 2—Mehdi to live for 40 years 160
Mahdi to die on his bed. 160
After Mahdi (as)Man emerges from Qahtan. 160
He too had characters of Mahdi (as) 162
Signs of Allah 162
Characters of Mahdi (as). 170
Attributes of Imamana (as) stated by— 171
    •   Mulla Abdul Qader Badyuni 171
    •   Abdul Qalam Azad 172
    •   Ali Sher Khane 172
    •   Maulvi Khairuddin 173
    •   Shah Waliullah 173
    •   Professor Shirani 173
Public Recognition of Beneficence 173
Splendor of facial complexion. 174
Beneficence from his company 175
Efficacy of Narration. 177
Asceticism. 178
Comparative Study between the Holy Prophet and Imamana 180
Generosity 180
Bravery 183

Patience. 183
Surrendering to the will of Allah 184
Affection. 185
Tolerance. 186
Forgiveness 187
Trust in Allah 188
Social Etiquette. 189
Humility 189
Humor. 190
Instruction for peace 191
Renounce the lower self 191
Following of Shariath 192
Plenty of Worship 192
Emphasis on practice 193
Preference to Divine Law 194
Revival of Divine Law 195
Completion of Deen 199
Completion of Divine Blessings 203

Chapter Four—Companions of Imamana Scholars, Kings, Nobles and Ministers 205
Companions of Imamana:. 205
Bandagi Miran Syed Mahmood (Rz):. 205
Bandagi Miyan Syed Khundmir (Rz.):. 205
List of pamphlets of Bandagi Miyan (Rz):. 206
List of Books written on martyrdom of Bandagi Miyan (Rz):. 206
Bandagi Miyan Shah Nemat (Rz):. 208
Bandagi Miyan Shah Nizam (Rz):. 209
Bandagi Miyan Shah Dilaware (Rz):. 210
Bandagi Malik Ilahdad, Khalifa-e-Giroh (Rz):. 210
Bandagi Malik Burhanuddin (Rz.): 211
Bandagi Malik Gauher (Rz):. 212
Bandagi Malik Ji, governor of Nagore (Rz):. 212
Bandagi Shah Abdul Majeed Noori (Rz.): 212
Bandagi Malik Ma'roof (Rz): 212
Bandagi Miyan Yousuf (Rz.): 212
Bandgi Miyan Shah Ameen Mohammed (Rz): .212
Other Pious people (From Sindh-Pakistan) 213
Pir Aasaat (Rz) : 213
Shaikh Jhanda Panti (Rz):. 213
Miyan Abu Bakar(Rz):. 214
"Shaik Daniyal" (Rz) : 214
Qazi Sheik Mohammed Oucha (Rz): 215
Sheik Sadruddin (Rz):. 215
Qazi Qadan (Rz): 216
Mohammed Taj (Rz): 217
Companions of Prophet Isa (As). 218

Scholars of Herat: 219

Prophets Ibrahim and Rasoolullah as being Witnesses: 223

Significance of Questions of the scholars of Herat: 226

Kings who accepted Imamana (As) as True Mahdi: 230

Sultan Husain Sharqi: 230

Sultan Ghiasuddin Khilji 230

Sultan Mahmood Beghda: 231

Ahmed Nizam Shah of Ahmed Nagar: 232

Burhan Nizam Shah: 232

Mirza Sultan Husain, Ruler of Khurasan: 233

Difference of date of Sultan's demise: 234

Holy Prophet's Age?: 234

The Karbala Episode: 235

Mistakes of Indian Histories: 235

Imamana's Date of Demise as per encyclopedia: 239

"Baber Nama": 240

"Rouzatus Safa": 240

Nobles And Ministers who became Devotees: 241

Zubdatul Mulk 241

Darya Khan (Rh) 241

Shah Baig (Rh): 242

Mir Zanoon (Rz), Ruler of Farah: 243

Fahaadul Mulk And Saleem Khan: 244

Mubarizul Mulk (Rz): 244

Chapter Five—Daira-e-Mahdavia, Mahdavis, Mahdavi Faith and Mahdavi Preachers 245

"Sheik Abdullah Niyazi (Rz): 245

Mahdavi Dairahs and "Muntakhabatut Tawareekh': 246

Mahdavi Dairahs And "Ma'asira-e-Raheemi": 249

Mul lah Abdul Baqi Nihavandi had written about Description of Ushr. 250

Dairah-e-Mahdavia & Socialism: 252

Distribution of Wealth And The Holy Prophet (Slm): 253

Booty from Bahrain: 254

Distribution during the period of Khulfa-e-Rashedeen (Rz): .254

Abu Zarr Gifari's Faith: 254

Alamgir And Mahdavi Faith: 258

Farhang-e-Asafia And Mahdvia Faith. 260

Mahdavia Faith and Syed Abu Zafer Nadvi: 261

Mahdavi And Mahdavi Faith: 261

Mahdavi Predecessors: 262

Middle Order Mahdavis: 267

And Their Followers: 267

Distinctive features of Mahdavis: 268

Dairah-e-Mahdavia and propagation of Quran and traditions: 268

Harmony between practice and knowledge: 269

Daira-e-Mahdavia and Aaliat (Adopt most preferable): 270

Distinct Mahdavi Preachers:. 271
Miyan Sheik Alaai (Rh):. 271
Miyan Sheik Mustafa Gujrati (Rh): 276
Miyan sheik Mubarak Nagori (Rh): 279

Chapter Six—Dissemination and Propagation of Mahdavi Faith. 282
Mahdavi Faith And Moderation:. 282
Spread of Mahdavi Faith: 284
Bengal to Turkistan: 284
   1.   Goud—Portion of Bengal: 285
   2.   Bihar: 285
   3.   Juanpur: 285
   4.   Allahabad: 286
   5.   Jaais-Lukhnow: 287
   6.   Amethi:. 288
   7.   Muradabad:. 288
   8.   Sumbhal: 289
   9.   Badayun: 289
  10.   Agra: 289
  11.   Biyana: 291
  12.   Bisawer: 292
  13.   Delhi: 293
  14.   Sar-e-Hind- Punjab: 294
  15.   Bunn (Punjab): 294
  16.   Lahore: 295
  17.   Jah'ni: (Lahore) 295
  18.   Shergadh: 295
  19.   Saamana: 295
  20.   Narnole: 296
  21.   Multan: 296
  22.   Dhamtod: 296
  23.   Dera Ismail Khan: 297
  24.   Dera-e-Ghazi Khan, where many Madavis were residing. 297
  25.   Kabul: 297
  26.   Badakhshan: Turkistan, Persia upto Raskumari (India) 298
  27.   Ghor 298
  28.   Balakh: (Turkistan). 298
  28.   Maroojaaq: 298
  29.   Undkhud: 298
  30.   Herat: 299
  31.   Farah Mubarak: 299
  32.   Khurasan: 303
  33.   Qandhar: 303
  34.   Kashikor of Iran: 304
  35.   Kashaan of Iran: 305
  36.   Baluchistan 306

37. Isfahan:. 306

38. Ferat:. 307

39. Keech 307

40. Makran: 307

41. Qallat: 308

42. Lasbela:. 308

43. Sindh: 308

44. Lukki of Sindh:. 309

45. Thatta 309

46. Bhakker, ...309

47. Mukalli: 309

48. Moorbi: (Khatiawar). 310

49. Gujrat:. 310

50. Palanpur:. 310

51. Khambayet:. 311

52. Khanbel: 312

53. Surat 312

54. Bombay: 312

55. Poona:. 312

56. Shakkar War Pet 315

57. Belgaum:. 315

58. Ahmadnagar: 315

Sherza Khan: (of Adil Shahi Period):. 315

59. Bijapur:. 316

60. Gokak: 319

61. Dharwad: 319

62. Mysore:. 319

63. Kirgawal: 322

64. Channapatna: 322

65. Malabar: 323

66. Palghat: Palghat 323

67. Kochin:. 323

68. Travencore: 323

68. Pangudi. 323

69. Tichnalore: 324

70. Trichnapalli: 324

71. Chittor: 325

72. Coimbatore: 325

73. Salam 325

74. Sidhot 325

75. Cudapah 325

76. Kurnool. 325

77. Machli Bander 325

78. Adhoni:. 325

79. Pindyal: 326

80. Fursat Patan: 326

81. South of Deccan 326
82. Chanchalguda: 332
    Battle of Chanchalguda 333
    Discussion between Abdul Karim and Miyan Yaseen Khan 335
    Munirul Mulk's order Involvement of Mahdavis 337
    Demand to produce Yaseen Khan 338
    Mahdavia Army 343
    The Stampede 345
    Arab's defeat 345
    Pursuing the fleeing Army 346
    English Army Called For Help 346
    Exodus of Mahdavis From Hyderabad 347
    Conspiracy of Izzat Yar Khan 348
    Nawab Sikander Jah And Mahdavis 350
    Nawab Naasirud Dowlah and Mahdavis 351
    Fate of Izzat Yar Khan 352
83. Episode of Saidabad 354
84. Berar: (Khandes) 356
85. Balapur: 356
86. Jalgaon jamood: 356
    Beliefs of Tashrief-e-Haq (Rz) and Imamana's Companions: 358
87. Burhanpur: 359
88. Khandes: 359
89. Borkheda: 359
90. Suhagpur 360
91. Ajmir 360
92. Nagore 360
93. Khawaspur (Jodhpur): 360
94. Jodhpur 362
95. Jalore 362
96. Dongerpur (Mewad) 362
97. Udaipur: 362
98. Jaipur 362
99. Khandela. 364
100. Belikhun (Jaipur): 364
101. Kalpi: 364
102. Fath-e-pur Saikri: 366
    Mahdavi faith in cities of of India: 367
103. "Bahut" 367
104. Makkah-e-Moazzamah 367
105. Madinah-e-Munawwara 368
    Different Cities And Shah Burhan (Rh): 368
    Peoples of different cities: 369
106. Qabchaq: 370
107. Khattah: 371
108. Sherwan: 371

109. Shiraz: 371
110. Gazron: 371
111. Hamdan: 371
112. Mazandran: 371
113. Bukhara: 372
114. Baghdad: 372
115. Rome: 372
   Spread of Mahdavia Faith And Khaja Hasan Nizami 372
   Spread of Mahdavia Faith and Mahmood Shirani Spread of
   Mahdavia Faith and Mahmood Shirani. 372

Chapter Seven—Traditions About Mahdi And Ibn Khaldun And Others 374
Margalit said that: 374
Period of Bani Abbas. 380
Authors of Sihah 382
Imam Bukhari (Rh) and Prophet's traditions: 382
Imam Bukhari (Rh) & Narrators of Mahdi's Traditions: 383
Ibn Khaldun: 387
Traditions of Mahdi (As) and Hafiz Ibn Timia (Rz): 390
Cross Examination of the Traditions: 390
Badruddin Aini says that: 395

Chapter Eight—Confirmation of obligation 400

Part Two

Chapter One—Doubts of Fault Finders about Imamana's Characters & Their Answers. 426
   1. Performing Migration, Punishment for Turning back from migration: 428
   2. Kisan-e-Mahdi to meet Jesus Christ: 433
   3. Descending of Esa (As) is near: 435
   4. Imam's Prophecy and His Demise: 436
   5. Day of Imamana's Demise: 438
   6. Nasikh-o-Mansookh. 439
   7. Accusation of Tampering Qur'an: 439
   8. Ta'iyyeyun is Layeen: (Fixation is disgraceful) 451
   9. Earning for Livelihood is Lawful-Kasab is Halal: 454
   10. Relinquishing Worldly Affairs: 455
   11. Invitation for Feast: 455
   12. General Dinners (not the valima): 457
   13. Attainment of Learning: 457
   14. Performance of Hajj and Not Visiting the Grave of the holy Prophet (Slm): 463
   15. Naubat-e-Izbeaj: 469
   16. Takfeer-e-Munkereen: 474
   17. Leadership (for prayers) of Non Believers: 485
   18. Difference In Precept And Practice: 487

19. Friday Prayer and Conditional Obligations:.................................493
20. Idolatary and Hypocrisy- Clarified:.....................................494
21. Jinn Became Dog, as per tradition:.....................................496
22. Obligation of Hajj - Capacity to Perform:...............................506
23. Jinn and Punishment:...510
24. 1. Previous Learning 2. Sikander's Episode:............................510
25. After Farz, Lifting Hands for Blessings: Against tradition:...............510
26. Mairaj of Imamana (As):..516
27. Tradition of Grazing Goats:...517
28. Last Prayer of Imamana (As) in a Masjid:...............................519
29. Description of the Verse of Holy Qur'an:...............................521
30. Glad Tidings to Bandagi Miyan (Rz)...................................525

Chapter Two—Imamana's Commands About the Saints.......................527
   • Imamana (As) at the grave of Khaja Gaysoo Daraz (Rz) (Gulbarga)............527
   • Ranks of Seven Saints:..530
   • Saints Supported Pilgrims' Ship:.....................................532
   • Legs of Abdul Qader Jeelani on the Necks of All Mystics:................532
   • Sheik Akber's Manifestation:...537

Chapter Three—Imamana's Commands about his Companions.....................538
Caliphs of the Prophet (Slm) and Khalifatullah:..............................555

Chapter Four—Imamana's Assertions And the Prophets.........................556
Born in the Heart of Ibrahim (As):...557
Disappearance of camel of the Holy Prophet.................................574

Chapter Five—Imamana's Assertions About Monotheism and Its Interpretation.........582
Explanation of Old God..586

Chapter Six—Commands Of Imamana(As) Regarding Qur'an's Consistency...........596
Qur'an and Parenthetical Clauses:...599
Jumla-e-Mustanifa:..603
Qur'an and Snapped Qualification:...606
Qur'an and Omission:..608
Qur'an and Extra Words:...608
Qur'an and Repetition of Verses..609
Qur'an and Abrogated Verses:..610
   1. Legacy:..611
   2. Jihad:...611
   3. Matrimony (Nikah):...612
   4. Najwah (privacy):..613
   5. Tahajjud:..613
      Remembrance of Allah...614

Translator's Note

Shaik Ali Muttaqi, a contemporary of the companions of Imamana Mahdi Alaihis salaam had written a derogatory booklet against Imamana (As) in 960 H. under the title "Al Rudd" in Arabic. When it reached Hazrat Aalim Billah Miyan Abdul Malik Sujawandi (Rh) he took it to Hazrat Syed Shahabuddin Shahabul Haq(Rz), son of Hazrat Bandagi Miyan Syed Khundmir Rz. who read it and asked Aalim Billah (Rh).to write a rebuttal with a befitting reply to this unscrupulous and baseless booklet. On the orders and guidance of Bandagi Miyan Syed Shahabul Haq,(Rz) Hzt.Aalim Billah Rh)Rh. wrote a befitting rebuttal under the title "Sirajul Absar"("Al Raffauz Zulm Un Ahl-e-Inkaar"- "Under the light of the Vision to lift the curtains of the Darkness") in Arabic . This book was translated in Urdu by Hzt. Syed Mustafa Saheb Tashrifullahi Rh. under the title "Muqaddama-e-Sirajul Absar" along with an exhaustive preface published in 1945 AD.

It is necessary to write about Aalim Billah Bandagi Miyan Abdul Malik Sujawandi Rh. who comes from the lineage of Hazrat Imam Ali (Rz) ibn Abi Talib. His forefathers belonged to a city known as Sujawand in Khurasan they migrated to India and settled down in Gujrat. They were very religious and were attached to the court of the Sultans of Gujrat for their bravery, command and proficiency in religious knowledge. His father had two sons: Miyan Abdul Malik Sujawandi, author of "Sirajul Absar" and Miyan Abdul Ghafoor Sujawandi who wrote about eighteen verses of the Holy Qur'an which Imamana Alaihis Salaam had asserted that these verses pertain to him and his Ummah. This book is known as "Hazhdah Ayath".

Miyan Abdul Malik Sujawandi Rh. was a very intelligent scholar of his time, had learned fourteen branches of religious knowledge and became known as a proficient Mahdavi Scholar in Gujrat. The king of Gujrat granted him a village, Budhasan, as his jagir. He became the disciple of Hazrat Bandagi Shah Dilawer Rz in the beginning.

It is said that once he was passing through a jungle where some kids of the dairah of Hazrat Shah Dilawer (Rz) were gathering some woods. Suddenly, the time for Asr prayer came and the kids offered prayer under the leadership of an elder one among them, who, after the prayers, gave a sermon on Qur'an which Abdul Malik Sujawandi (Rh) heard with interest and was astonished to hear such a sermon. He asked the kids from where they learnt such a superb knowledge of the Holy Qur'an. The kids led him to the dairah where he met Hazrat Shah Dilawer (Rz) and at the very first sight he offered his allegiance on the hands of Hazrat Shah Dilawer and became Mahdavi. He relinquished his wordly life and lived in the company of Hazrat Shah Dilawer (Rz).

It is said that Shaik Ali Muttaqi, who wrote "Al Rudd" afterwards, was also living in this Dairah. During a sermon Bandagi Shah Dilawer (Rz) said that an eunuch would not enter the Heaven. Shaik Muttaqi took these words as to have been directed towards him, and left the Dairah and went to Makkah. Hazrat Shah Dilawer (Rz) passed away in the year 944 H. Shaik Ali wrote "Al Burhan" in 952 H. and the "Risalatur Rudd" in 960 H. It was a period when Aalim

Billah Abdul Malik Sujawandi(Rh) Rh., after the demise of Bandagi Shah Dilawer (Rz), came to Bandgai Miyan Syed Shahabul Haq (Rz) in Khanbail and became his disciple. When "Al Rudd" reached him, he read it and took it to Bandagi Miyan Syed Shahabul Haq (Rz)., as has been stated above, who also read it and became very agitated and asked Aalim Bilah Rh. to write a befitting rebuttal against the "AL-Rudd".

Surprisingly it is narrated in some of our books that during the lifetime of Hazrat Shah Dilawer Rz. this "Al Rudd" was read by Bandagi Shah Dilawer (Rz). who asked Aalim Billah Rh. to write against it. Historically it seems to be a wrong version since Bandagi Shah Dilawer Rz. died in 944 H, while "Al Rudd" was written in 960 H, and on the advice of Hazrat Bandagi Miyan Syed Shahabul Haq (Rz), according to Hazrat Bazmi, Hazrat Aalim Billah wrote his befitting reply "Sirajul Absar" during the period between 964 H to 972 H. Bandagi Miyan Syed Shahabul Haq(Rz) read the reply and praised Aalim Billah (Rh). for his befitting rebuttal in Arabic language. Bandagi Miyan Syed Shahabul Haq Rz. died in 972. Thus the legend that under the advice of Bandagi Shah Dilawer (Rz), Aalim Billah(Rh) wrote "Sirajul Absar" is utterly wrong which requires serious research and correction.

Another book under the title "Hadia-e-Mahdavia" was written by Abu Rija Zaman Khan Shahjehanpuri in 1285 H, and was published in 1287 H, in north India. This book also was against Mahdavia faith and Imamana (As) as well. It was covertly and dubiously circulated in Hyderabad to incite Mahdavis not only against Zaman Khan, but against Sunni Muslims, just to create enmity between these two sects who were living together in peace. Thus it resulted in a tragic death of Zaman Khan by Hzt. Abji Miyan (Shaheed) and the exodus of Mahdavis from the Nizam's Dominion for a second time in a Century.

Thus "Muqaddama-e-Sirajul Absar" not only deals with the objections of these two Books but also with other objections raised by so many opponents like Ibn Hajr Makki, Mulla Ali Qari, Asad Makki, Ibn Khaldun,Margoliath,Sayeed Ahmad Bejnuri and Abul Aalaa Moudodi. Hazrat Syed Yaqoob Bazmi's father was the author of the above said "Preamble on the Urdu translation of "Sirajul Absar. After the demise of his father, Allama Bazmi(Rh) became enthusiastic to finalize the job left incomplete by his late father, he took up the job seriously as a challenge by reading and collecting relevant references from hundreds of related classical and other concerned Mahdavi and Non Mahdavi literature by studying minutely in many libraries, day in and day out. Whenever he got some doubt about any Tradition, he wrote to eminent universities and Darul Qaza and even to Al Azhar University of Cairo, Egypt and other prominent Islamic Institutions of different Islamic countries. After obtaining authentic replies only, he incorporated in his "Muqaddama-e-Sirajul Absar" providing all references in order to substantiate his arguments about the proof of Mahdiath. On account of which the second edition became double in size comparing to the first edition which was published by him in 1965 AD.

During the life time of Hazrat Bazmi Rh. some more opponents like Aamir Osmani editor of Tajalli and Niyaz Fathepuri editor of Nigar, A.S.Ansari author of Shiraz-e-Hind etc wrote against Imamana(As). He wrote a supplement against their objections which was published in 1975 after his demise.

When the second edition was completely sold out, in order to meet the demand, his younger brother the late Hz. Syed Ishaq and his nephew, Br Syed Mahmood Tashrifullahi took interest to merge the supplement to the relevant subjects of the original book and, in 1990 published the third edition which contains 1036 pages. This voluminous book is like an encyclopedia that provides befitting replies to any and all unscrupulous and unwanted objections against not only Imamana (As), but against Mahdiat itself.

Every now and then every Tom and Harry tries to spread anti Mahdi propaganda by jetting down useless and unworthy objections among the masses require to be dealt with spontaneous replies to negate these unholy remarks against Imamana (As) and our Faith. In this connection Haz. Syed Abid Miranji, other Murshideen and prominent scholars are able to write befitting answers to such biased and unholy objections.

It is also important to mention that our new generation is dangerously ill equipped with religious information on account of lack of basic knowledge about our faith which is available in Arabic, Persian and Urdu languages that are alien to the new generation. This Translation is presented in English for the benefit of young generation. Our Murshideen are doing their best by educating and providing religious information to the new generation, but unfortunately, and hopelessly our young generation has no understanding about Urdu, in which our history and religious information is available. It is, therefore, felt necessary to translate this book which pertains for complete education and information about the basics of our religious beliefs and provides complete historical facts and teachings of Imamana (As), his companions and Tabay Tabayeen. This book teaches with material and knowledge how to reply to the objections if raised by opponents. Apart from this, the "Muqaddama" is a complete, exhaustive and comprehensive guide to anyone who really wants to understand about our Faith. It is suggested, that in order to inculcate basic knowledge, constructive planning of Tableegh and Seminars must be arranged every week, better, rather every day and of course in every Masjid.

About the "Muqaddama"

The late Allama Syed Yaqoob, Bazmi (Rh) displayed a profound mastery about the proofs of our faith based on Qur'an and the traditions, pertaining to the Sunnat-e-Mustafavi(Slm) by writing in an elaborate, systematic and logical style, thus making his manuscript like an encyclopedic type of treasure of knowledge which provides befitting replies to so many allegations by many decliners of our Faith. He had divided his book in four parts, and each part contains many related topics, and every topic is self explanatory in the sense that each topic has been clearly elucidated by facts and figures, complete with historical background which cannot be rejected.

The author was brought and bred by his father by infusing in him the zeal to understand how to refute allegations of the decliners, by refuting in a scientifically and logically convincing style which cannot be repudiated by any one. For that purpose he learned Arabic, Persian and English languages first, when became proficient, he concentrated minutely on the Arabic Text of "Sirajul Absar", then he studied the allegations made in the "Al Rud" by the Shaikh and Hadai-e-Mahdavia by Zaman Khan and other allegations by so many decliners. Then he collected references against allegation-wise and decliners-wise. Then, he minutely studied those classical and relevant books which provided him proper guidance to elaborate his logical approach to refute one and all biased and baseless allegations in a befitting manner that whoever read them would become fully satisfied.

I would like to suggest the readers to go through the chapter "Arrangement of the Muqaddama" which will pinpoint the subjects dealt in each chapter of four parts and guide you to find out your selected topic.

The beginning of the book deals with his thesis on how to write "muqaddama" on any book by devising three kinds of "Muqaddamas" and by providing references of the books, then he had elaborated upon his own "Muqaddama" by mentioning how he had kept in view those peculiarities in writing his book. His thesis in this respect is first of its kind.

Part one deals with the historical background of Juanpur, the place of birth of Imamana (As) which was known as "Shiraz-e-Hind", par with "Shiraz-e-Persia, a Learning capital of the Shah Husain's Sharqi Dynasty in the Eastern part of India.

As the legend goes,Prophet Ibrahim (As) was born in Urr, the most famous capital of the kingdom of a mighty ruler, Nimrod. Prophet Musa(AS) was born in Egypt, the capital of the first civilized nation of the Pharaohs. Prophet Jesus Christ(As) was born in Jerusalem, the most important town of the Roman Empire. The Holy Prophet was born in "Ummal Qur'a, Makkah, the center of the worshipping place of the pagan area. Thus, there must not be any doubt that as to why Juanpur, a literary capital of Sharqi Dynasty, known as "shiraz-e-Hind" or "Second to Delhi "for its becoming the sacred birth place of a commissioned personality of Imamana(As)?

The author has rejected allegations of the decliners who had gone out of bound in condemning Imamana (As) and his companions on the question of declaration of Mahdiat in the Tenth Century, since they are of the view, based on their unfounded belief, that Imam Mahdi (As) shall appear along with prophet Jesus Christ on the Doomsday.!!

The author's mastery over his, to-the-point writing, based on logically woven fabric and his peculiarly crafted sense of maintaining balance in moderation and his exemplary conclusions brought the book to an undisputed place among the scholarly written manuscripts of the modern times.

Chapters of the first part deal with historical facts about Imamana (As) and his migration to many places of India, pilgrimage to Makkah and back to India and to Farah Mubarak. Chapter 7 deals with those important traditions regarding advent of Mahdi about which the opponents, particularly Ibn Khaldun, had raised doubts about their reliability. Author's deliberations regarding these allegations are not only convincing, but also educative on how to refute them, and also provide ample material to understand the factual background of those traditions.

In Part Two, Chapter One deals with deals with characters of Imamana (AS) in comparison with that of the Holy Prophet (Slm) who had prophesied that Mahdi would carry his own characters by saying "Khulquhu Khulqi"(meaning, Mahdi's characters shall be like mine) which became the criterion for the Holy Prophet (Slm) as the "Rahmatul Lil Aalameen", then why the like Characters of Imamana (As) should not be treated Imamana (As) as the "Mahdi-e-Akhiruz Zaman". Thus through his logical arguments, he correctly emphasized to count characters as a criterion for commissioning of the designated personality of Imamana (As).

Chapter 8 is based on the assertion of Imamana (As) that the holy Qur'an is consistent from inception to its end. It is a very masterly written chapter, rather a commendable thesis, must be read minutely to refute unscrupulous remarks that the Qur'an has become inconsistent in view of the so called abrogation of some verses. The author has shown his skills by his befitting arguments to nullify that no verse of the Holy Qur'an was abrogated.

Part 3 deals with the biographies of Imamana's caliphs in detail by refuting the allegations made by Zaman Khan on their characters and sayings.

Part four deals with the concluding chapters regarding befitting answers to every allegation raised by decliners, name by name. It furnishes all the required material which teaches us the basics of our sublime Beliefs with complete elucidation with convincing arguments. In short, entire Part 4 deals with the befitting answers to the unholy and biased allegations, hence it is the most challenging part which must be read again and again to grasp the crux of the problems enunciated by the author and opens the dialogue how to refute those allegations in a logical and convincing manner not found in any book.

Answers to the main allegations made by Ibn Khaldun, Sir Syed Ahmed Khan and Margouliat, are given in Part One, Chapter 7, and that of Mahmood Shirani is given in chapter One of Part One.

And, of course, the most important are the befitting answers for the unholy, biased and cunning allegations raised by so many decliners, starting from the beginning to this date. Thus, it is a book having lucidity in understanding the crux of the problems in a very simple language, understandable by each and every reader which is written in a very laudable and convincing style.

To glorify venerable personalities, I have used just (Slm) for "The Holy Prophet Anhazrat Mohammed salle alaihi wassallam, and (As) for "Imamana" for our beloved Mentor, Mahdi-e-Akhiruz Zaman", "(As)" also for all prophets, (Rz) for both companions of the holy Prophet (Slm) and Imamana (As), and (Rh) to the Descendants and eminent followers.

Finally, wherever the word came as" Rudd", it may be taken for the pamphlet "Risalthul Ruddel Mahdi" written by Sheikh Ali Muttaqi, and wherever the word "Hadia" has come, it may be taken for the book "Hadiya Mahdavia", written by Zaman Khan Shahjehanpuri.

In the original Text, there are many repetitions particularly in verses and the traditions. These repetitions are necessary but some people who had reviewed my Translation asked me to delete such repetitions. But I am not agreeable to such remarks, since a translator should not do so. I have tried my best to translate the correct meanings and the sense of what is written and mentioned in "Muqaddama-e- Sirjul Absar". I hope it shall never transgress from what has been subscribed by the Author; Insha Allah.

I am preparing a Supplement to provide the references of the books given at the end of each page as the Foot Notes, in the Urdu Manuscript, which shall be published in due course of time, after publication of this book. It will be useful for those who desire for their research work in writing.

To err is human. I do not boast that I have not committed any mistake in translation by omission or commission, in spellings, in the style and its elegance etc, therefore I request the readers to pardon me and to inform me about such lapses for necessary record for the future.

***

ACKNOWLDGEMENT

I am highly thankful to Br. Syed Shafeeq Mahdi, who after reading my English book "Qur'an and Science: Their implications on the mankind" published by E.Amazan, in USA,became impressed and suggested me to undertake translation of "Muqaddama-e-Sirajul Absar" of Hazrat Syed Yaqoob Bazmi (Rh) which is the need of the day to inculcate our young generation, who like to read and understand, in English, about the Sublime Mission and Faith as presented by Imnamana Hazrat Syed Mohammed Juanpuri, Mahdia-e-Mauood Alaihis Salam. Of course I too had the same desire, since long, to translate this voluminous book into English, but its bulkiness was challenging. However, Br. Shafeeq's timely suggestion gave me strength and I could not postpone my own ambition. For that reason, I consulted with my well wishers and members of my family, who encouraged me propfusely.

I am highly thankful to Br. Syed Mahmood Tashrifullahi alias Saidanji Miyan, who on my request, after appreciating my desire to undertake translation of this exhaustive, rather a reference book, whole-heartedly gave his permission for the English Tranlation and had invested his time and energy in going through all the pages of the book and final proof reading along with his wife by vetting and in completion of this voluminous book and provided his commendable coopeartion in bringing the book in the present shape.

I am very much oblidged to the zeal and enthusiasm showed by my wife, Sabiha Saleem Khundmiri in undertaking the Translation Work of this voluminous book during her life time, and had established a TRUST in her name for its publication, but unfortunately she passed away in 2010 AD. "Inna-Lillahi wa-Inna Ilaihi Rajeuon".I am on the job for the last five years, now it is completed after her death.

I am highly grateful to Moulana Syed Abid Miranji who had taken much pain in vetting the entire thousand pages of this Muqaddama by going through word by word, line by line and paragraph by paragraph to correct the typing mistakes in Arabic and Persion versions. Particularly with regard to "Consistency in Qur'an"his guidance is examplary.

I am highly grateful to my friend Syed Noorul Arifeen for his valuable services by typing all Arabic, Persian and Urdu quotations and the verses of the holy Qur'an properly on the right side margin of the book. He very expediciously completed the text on INPAGE Format, which was converted to PDF, "Print Ready" by Syed Wasim Mahdi, my grandson.

Let me add some more names, my son Syed Shahabuddin, my grandson Syed Wasim Mahdi, Syed Nematullah and my granddaughters Syeda Saheba Mahdi and Syeda Aeysha Fatima who helped me in proof reading and in correcting spelling mistakes, to make this Translation error free from all aspects, still, I am not so sure that it does not carry any mistake. For which I beg your pardon.

Jazakallahu Khairun

Dedication and Humble Request

I humbly "DEDICATE" this Translation to the Mahdavia Community particularly. And also to the Muslim Ummah generally since this book is a commendable source of exhaustive knowledge and voluminous religious and fiqh curriculum. It provides treasure of general knowledge of academic value which is "food for thought" for the research scholars as well.

Lastly, I humbly request to my every Mahdavi brother to keep this book in his or her library as a guidance, not only for present generation, but also for the future generations to come, as a permanent source of guidance and instruct them to read, chapter by chapter, for making themselves perfect in understanding the Mission of Imamana (As) to its entirety and to study biographies of the prominent personalities and get guidance for their future life and also the history of Mahdavi Ummah to familiarate themselves as to how our Ummah suffered so many obstacles and hardships, still got its prominent position in the Muslim Ummah.

About the Trust:

From, the Sale Proceeds of this Book:

The Trust is meant for assisting:

1. To eliminate illiteracy, the Trust shall provide assistance to achieve the Goal: "No Child Left Behind."

2. Assisting poor families for marrying their girls to the extent possible;

3. For publication of religious pamphlets and books.

Further details about the Trust may be obtained by writing to the Trustees:

1. Syed Shahabuddin. (001-818) 736-6250,

2. Syed Sultan Naseer 903 0048- 309

3. Syed Wasim Mehdi (001-818) 434-8180.)

I, the translator, Syed Sharief Khundmir, son of Haz. Syed Qasim Saheb Tashrifullahi Alias, Shah Saheb Miyan (Rh), maternal grandson of Hazrat Shah Saheb Miyan (Rh), the elder brother of Hazrat Syed Mohammed Abjee Miyan Saheb,, Shaheed (Rh), humbly submit this "Muqaddama" in English, as a comprehensive encyclopedic guide for those who really have a genuine desire to become well versed in the Mission of our Mentor, Hazrat Imamana Syed Mohammed Juanpuri, Khalifaullh, Muradullah, Mahdi-e-Maood, Alaihis salato wassalaam.

Wama Alaina Illal Balagh.

Faqeer Syed Sharief Khundmiri

*****

Publisher's Note about the third Urdu Edition:
BROTHERS OF THE MILLAT!

The first edition of "Muqaddama-e-Sirajul Absar" was published in 1365 Hijri/ 1945 AD, and the second one in 1382 Hijri (22nd. February 1965 AD) at Hyderabad, Andhra Pradesh.

A period of 48 years has passed after the publication of the second edition. During this period a new young generation had emerged. Most of the youths and even elders are unaware of the discussions contained in the second edition, since the book is unavailable.

Meanwhile, the opponents and mischievous persons have been busy in creating ambiguities and doubts against the personality of Imamana Alaihis Salaam and Mahdavia beliefs. The cure for such unwanted remarks is available in the "Muqaddama-e-Sirajul Absar."

The Second edition of "Muqaddama-e-Sirajul Absar" contains replies in the light of the holy Qur'an and the Traditions to the objections made by opponents of Mahdi Alaihis Salaam, like, Ibn Hajr Makki, Shaik Ali Muttaqi, Mulla Ali Qari, Asad Makki, Ibn Khaldun, Margouliat, Sir Syed Ahmed Khan, Zaman Khan Shahjahanpuri author of "Hadia", Najmul Ghani Khan author of "Mazahab-e-Islam", Sayeed Ahmad Bijnouri author of "Tazkeratul Ulema", Rafeeq Dilawari author of "Ayamma-e-Talbees", Nazeerul Haq author of "Kitabul Islam", Niyaz Fateh puri, Editor of "Nigar", Abul Aala Moududi, etc.

During the life period of Allamatul Asr Muhaqqiq-e-Mahdavia, Miyan Syed Yaqoob Bazmi Tashrifullahi(Rh), some more objections were made by the opponents like Aamir Osmani, editor of "Tajalli, Devband", A.S.Ansari of Pakistani Asiatic Research Academy, author of "Shiraz-e-Hind". Replies to their objections have been (simultaneously) given in the pamphlets. Those replies were compiled in a book as the Supplement to the "Zamima of Muqaddama-e-Sirajul Absar", but this book was not published during the life time of Haz. Bazmi. After his demise, the Supplement was published in the year 1975 AD. The second edition of "Muqaddama-e-Sirajul Absar" and the "Supplement" both became unavailable in a short period.

Mahdavis from various parts of India were demanding for publication of the third edition by merging the supplement.

In short, Allamatul Asr, Muhaqqiq-e-Mahdavia Miyan Syed Yaqoob Bazmi, Tashrifullahi,(Rh) had performed a magnificent job of a religious and academic nature which shall be remembered till the Doomsday.

This memorable work is not only a treasure of knowledge for the Mahdavia community, but of the entire Muslim world. Every learned man had acknowledged his academic excellence, may he be a Mahdavi or a Sunni, or a Shia, Asna-e-Ashri or even an Ismaili, everyone had praised his academic excellence.

When I expressed my desire for publication of the third Edition to my venerable father, Hazrat Syed Ashraf, Razmi Tashrifullahi and my uncle Hazrat Syed Ishaq, they agreed to my proposal. When the time came to start the work, we planned for merging the Supplement in appropriate chapters of the second edition which needed ample time. Since my father and my uncle, the Allama had expired. However, my second uncle, Faqeer Hazrat Syed Ishaq Tashrifullahi, the second son of Hazrat Syed Mustafa Tashrifullahi, took this responsibility in-spite of his old age.

Then, we were in search of a Mahdavi caliographer. By Allah's grace we found out Alhaj Syed Ashraf Saheb, editor of "Naiy Nukat" a weekly paper, s/o the late Hzt. Syed yahiya alias Khajazade Miyan Saheb (Rh), who accepted this responsibility in-spite of his ill-health. He did this job with great devotion perfectly well. By Allah's grace and the beneficence of Khatemain(ahs) while the calligraphic work was going on properly, proof reading was being done by my uncle so perfectly well that there arose no need to give the list of corrections.

I am highly grateful to my brother Syed Hasan Tashrifullahi who took the difficult responsibility of the publication of this book, in my absence and completed the work with great diligence. May Allah (swt) shower His mercy and reward to him, since he tried his best by working day and night to present this venerable book to Mahdvi brothers as the 3rd. edition in 1990 AD.

******

Impressions

(of different persons about the author as stated above)

1. Epic writer, match-less orator, **Allama Hazrat Moulana Abul Aayez Syed Ahmed Saheb, Munawari** (Rh)

In the remote past, Hzt. Bandagi Abdul Malik Sujawandi had written 'Sirajul Absar" in reply to a pamphlet by name "AL RUDD": by one Shaik Ali Muttaqi, which was hidden in heaps of dust. Janab Muhaqqiq-e-Mahdavia, Allamatul Asr Syed Yaqoob Saheb Bazmi cleared the book from the dust, translated in Urdu and printed it and wrote a detailed preamble to it.

Muhaqqiq-e-Millat had discussed about the art of "Muqaddama Writing" which has no example in any literature of any language.

He searched for "Juanpur Nama"and through its writings he introduced Mahdiat of Imam-e-Huda. Apart from "Juanpur Nama" he had submitted proofs of Mahdiat from various classical sources of Persian and Arabic languages. This is the first attempt by him by publishing "Muqaddama". This Muqaddama presents philosophical discourses on the objections of the opponents regarding Mahdavia faith and its founder. Its language is simple, understandable by each and every one; its style is arguable from the beginning to the end. It has poetic taste as well, has no lengthy passages having a bitter taste.

Ibn Khaldun, Sir Syed Ahmed Khan,Marguliet (German Philosopher) had discussed about the correctness of the traditions regarding Imam Mahdi(As), as if the holy Prophet (PBUH) had never informed about the advent of Mahdi.

Janab Muhaqqiq-e-Mahdavia had presented true and correct traditions relating to Advent of Mahdi based on literary, historically, characteristically, biographical record of the Traditions and argued on the basis of principles and art of traditions. Thus he had correctly tried to present the proof of the advent of Mahdi (As) on the basis of the classical sources about character, art, history and Rijal. This is the first attempt in view of the history of the art of tradition not only in the Mahdavia community, but also the entire Muslim world. It is a fact that Ahmed Bin Mohammed Damishqi had tried to reply to Ibn Khaldun in the year 1344 H. but it was incomplete since his discussion is one sided only.

Muhaqqiq-e-Mahdavia had presented the obligations of Vilayet in the light of the Holy Qur'an, and the discussion he had advanced in this respect is first of its kind in the Islamic literature.

The Author had elucidated the characters of Imam-e-Huda elaborately.

On one hand he had resembled the attributes of bravery, trust in Allah, patience, forgiveness, tolerance and graciousness and a long list of attributes to that of the holy Prophet (PBUH) and through scholastic arguments he had proved the characters of the Imam-e-Huda which were truly matching to that of the holy Prophet as prophesied by the Prophet himself by telling "Khulquhu Khulqi".

Secondly, the author of Hadia and other opponents had discussed about certain traditions and submitted them as if they were against Imam Mahdi (As), but Muhaqqiq-e-Mahdavia had refuted their allegations from the same traditions which were presented by the opponents in their books.

In the Muqaddama, Janab Muhaqqiq-e-Millat had a firm belief that the Holy Qur'an has consistency and continuity. According to Imamana's assertion, he had arguably discussed and maintained with his befitting academic arguments in the light of Imam-e-Huda (As). Thus he correctly proved that no verse of the Holy Qur'an is annulled. It does not have parenthetical clauses, it does not have any mustanifa clauses, it does not pertain extras and there are no omissions. This discussion, regarding the Holy Qur'an, is the first of its kind in the Islamic literature.

The author of Hadia had created objections by wrongly translating some excerpts from the books of Mahdavia literature to suite his arguments. Janab Bazmi Saheb had correctly translated actual documents and refuted his wrong claims.

The Muqaddama presents the elucidation about the propagation of our beliefs in a unique style which is new of its kind.

The author of Hadia and Mahmood Shirani had objected on the history of Mahdavia, whose answers are correctly elaborated in the Muqaddama. In this connection he presented Tareekh-e-Rasheeduddin Khani and Gulzar-e-Asafia, written by the non Mahdavi historians, thus he correctly refuted their objections. He, even by presenting some more references of the classical and authentic record, already accepted by those who are well versed in history. The author of Hadia had tried to mislead the public by neglecting the historical facts with regard to their battles of Poona, Sri Ranga Patnam, Battle of Chanchalguda, the episodes of Sayeedabad and martyrdom of Hzt. Abjee Miyan (Rh). But Moulana did a wonderful job by minutely researching the facts of those tragedies and presented correct historical undeniable record.

The Muqaddama presents the proofs regarding the advent of Imam Mahdi in the light of the

Holy Qur'an and traditions and submitted irrefutable arguments about the sanctity of the Mahdavia beliefs and about the advent of Imam Mahdi (Ahs). Thus, in the light of the above arguments presented by Moulana Bazmi, anyone who had a little spark about the sanctity of Mahdiat, would whole-heartedly accept Imam (Ahs) as true Mahdi (As).

Thus Muqaddama had presented irrefutable answers to the filthy remarks made by Ibn Hajr Makki. Shaik Ali Muttaqi, Assad Makki, Zaman Khan Shahjehanpuri.

Further, the Muqaddama presents the grandeur of Imamana's characters through befitting replies to the malicious objections. Thus Muqaddama records correct biography of Imamana (As) and proved Imam's Mahdiat by pinpointing Qur'anic verses and traditions of the Holy Prophet (Slm). The biography of Imamana (Ahs) would have become incomplete if it did not possess befitting replies of the biased objectors. Thus Muqaddama is not only the complete biography, but arguably proves Imam's Mahdiat.

Characters of Imam (As) would have become questionable if the answers to the biased objections on the characters of Imamana (As) were not properly given by undeniable facts. The reality is that the bats are deprived of the brilliance of the light, therefore how can they tolerate the illumination caused by the coming of the commissioned personality?

It is but natural to wait for the coming of the moonlight in a pitch dark night and when it rises the mercurial restlessness gets complete satisfaction.

Rahnuma-e-Millat,Muhaqqiq-e-Mahdavia Janab Syed Yaqoob Bazmi's magnificent work in the shape of "Muqaddama" is just like a moon arising in the dark pitch night.

The devoted lovers of Imam-e-Huda (Ahs) were restlessly waiting for the "Muqaddama" to come, and when it appeared, it became the cause for enjoyment as an Eid to them.

Still let me say that had Janab Bazmi Saheb not helped (In presenting this voluminous Muqaddama) the ignorant persons would be deprived of from finding the reality of the real Mahdi.

Lastly, May the Almighty Allah grant His retribution for my humble prayer to Muhaqqiq-e-Mahdavia who had presented this Muqaddama which is an embodiment of "(AMAR BIL MAROOF (ENJOIN WHAT IS RIGHT)" Jazakallahu Khaira. Aameen.

2. Sahebzada Dr.Mir Taher ALi Khan Muslim Retd. Director, Nazm-e-Jamiat (Army), Private Secretary and Asst. Controller for the Heir Apparent.

Sahebzada was a professor for Persian language in the Nizam college. He was also a professor for German and Persian languages in the Night College. He was a real scholar of Persian, Arabic and many European languages. He was also an accredited Urdu and Persian poet too. He had addressed in one of his letters to Hazrat Muhaqqiq-e-Mahdavia in the following words as a gratitude to Bazmi Saheb:

"For the Review by the Highly Respected Janab Moulvi Syed Yaqoob Saheb Bazmi"

My writing although had no value by itself, but your kind affection helped it to reach to an exalted position. During the friendly moments, petty items amassed to a heap of mountain for which I was so overpowered by acute madness that I was subdued by mischievous energy and still I am in its grip. In such circumstances people waste their money, but I had just jotted down on some white papers. In short, I am much anxious for your kind courtesy. If you come, it will be a great relief and solace to me otherwise, I would have to take the blame for the blood of an innocent. Further nothing to say, except waiting for you today (To come).

Yours faithful servant
Signed, (Taher Muslim)

3. Moulvi Masood Ali Mahvi:

Retired Sessions Judge, Member Board of Translation, acclaimed learned translator of Persian and Arabic languages; belongs to the initial period of Shibli as his student. He wrote on the front page of his Devan by stating: "A humble gift to my honourable friend Moulvi Syed Yaqoob Bazmi" from: Masood Ali Mahvi.

4. Dr. Zahed Ali:

Madras University printed a book "Kanzul Fawaed". Dr. Zahed Ali who was a professor and Vice Principal of the Nizam College presented one of its volumes to Muhaqqiq-e-Mahdavia, by writing on its first page:

"A Gift to an acclaimed scholar Moulvi Syed Yaqoob Bazmi".
From: Zahed Ali, Professor of Arabic language, Nizam College.

5. Aaqa Syed Mohmmed Ali:

Aaqa Syed Mohammed Ali is well known as an Islamic preacher all over India, Pakistan and Iran. Before becoming professor for Persian language at the Nizam College, he had been a dialectic speaker against Christian missionaries; on account of it he was called the Preacher of Islam. He had compiled five voluminous volumes of "Farhang-e-Nizam". While offering one of its volumes to Muhaqqiq-e-Mahdavia as a Gift, he subscribed on its front page:

"A memorable gift" to my excellent student Aaqa Syed Yaqoob Bazmi".
Signed (Syed Mohammed Ali, Author).

6. Begum Saheba Qaed-e-Millat Bahadur Yar Jung:

She wrote in favour of Muhaqqiq-e-Mahdavia that:

"Allamatul Asr Muhaqqiq-e-Mahdavia Moulana Syed Yaqoob Bazmi is the patron of the"Muhaqiq"magazine". His patronage is a pleasure for the Mahdavia community. An excellent and well acclaimed scholar in oriental and occidental sciences, therefore he is an asset for the community; just like a shot in the blue."

7. Hazrat Allama Mohammed Sadatullah Khan Mandozai:

Moulvi Kamil; Scholastic professor, retired Principal of Darul Uloom, Hyderabad. He had subscribed an Arabic Ode in the Dairatul M'uarif which is in reference to the research work done by Muhaqqiq-e-Mahdavia:

"Yaqoob Bazmi Ghaas fi baharal Kitab Aati Bi Zalik Al Dar Bil Ailan."

يعقوب بزمى غاص فى بحر الكتاب   اتى بذاك الدربالاعلان

Allama had himself translated this Ode in Urdu. While translating he had subscribed the words "Allamatul Asr, Muhaqqiq-e-Mahdavia" preceding the name "Yaqoob Bazmi".

8. Recognition of cooperation by Moulvi Masood Ali Mahvi:

Some 57 (now 110) years ago, Sir Kishan Prasad, Prime Minister of the Nizam's Dominion had published a Persian volume of "Diwan-e-Hasan Sanjari". In its compilation Hazrat Muhaqqiq-e-Mahdavia had assisted Moulvi Masood Ali Mahvi. Therefore Mahvi himself had written in its preface that:

"First was the job to collect different volumes then to select one diwan as a base, and to complete it with reference to other poetic books was not an easy job. For that we have to scrutinize all other volumes. It is an accepted fact that, had my young friend Syed Yaqoob Bazmi not assisted me, this job would not have been completed in such a limited time. (A group photo was taken at the opening ceremony of the "Diwan-e- Hasan Sanjari" in which Muhaqqiq-e-Mahdavia also has taken part).

From the above mentioned references it is proved that what status Hazrt Bazmi had in the academic circle of Hyderabad.

Syed Mahmood Tashrifullahi (B.Tech)

s/o Haz. Syed Ashraf Tashrifullahi (Rh)

☆☆☆

DEDICATION

TO MY BELOVED SON
MIYAN SYED MOHAMMED TASHRIFULLAHI
ALIAS MIRANJI MIYAN SALLAMAHU (RH)
ON WHOSE PERSUATION THIS MUQADDAMA WAS GOT PUBLISHED

(RAHNUMA-E-MILLAT, MUHAQQIQ-E-MAHDAVIA
ALLAMATUL ASR SYED YAQOOB)

BAZMI TASHRIFULLAHI

DATED 22ND. SHABANUL MOAZZAM 1382 HIJRI (19TH. JANUARY 1963 AD).

At the time of publication of the 2nd. edition of Muqaddam-e-Sirajul Absar, my son was alive.

IN THE NAME OF ALAH, THE MOST BENEVOLENT AND THE MOST MERCIFUL.

SUBMISSION (By Allama)

I had given answers in the second edition of "Muqaddam-e-Sirajul Absar" regarding the criticism against the traditions pertaining to Imam Mahdi(As): on his personality, Mahdavia beliefs and historical facts, raised by the decliners (of Imam Mahdi(As), for example Ibn Hajr Makki; ShaikAli Muttaqi; Asad Makki, Mulla Ali Qari, Ibn Khaldun,Margouliat, Zaman Khan, author of Hadia-e-Mahdvia,Najmul Ghani Rampuri author of "Mazaaheb-e-Islam", Sayeed Ahmed Bijnouri author of "Anwarul Bari" and "Sharhul Bukhari", Syed Abdul Hai, director of Nadwatul Ulema, Lukhnow and author of "Nuzhatul Khawatir", Rahman Ali author of "Tazkeratul Ulema", Rafeeq Dilaweri author of "Aiymma-e-Talbees", Nazeerul Haq author of "kitabul Islam",Niyaz Fathepuri Editor of Nigar, Abul Aala Moudodi etc, upto the year 1343 Hijri/22nd. February 1963 AD.

Now, after 1383 Hijri. some more decliners like, A.S.Ansari of Islamic Research Studies, Karachi (In English Language),author of Tareekh-e-Shiraz-e-Hind, Juanpur; Editor of Monthly Magazine Tajalli(Devband),Tayyab Qasimi Superintendent, Nadwatul Ulema, Lukhnow,etc; had raised objections against Hazrat Mahdi-e-Maood Alaihis Salaaam and on Mahdavia Beliefs whose answers are given in the Supplement to the "Muqaddama-e-Sirajul Absar.

Bazmi Tashrifullahi (Rahmatullahi Alaih)
18th. Ramazanul Mubarak 1385 Hijri (11th. January 1966 AD)

This was his last writing under the title "Submission" which was written on 11th. January 1966 AD at the completion of the Supplement to the "Muqaddama-e-Sirajul Absar" by the Author.

Publisher

IN THE NAME OF ALLAH THE MOST BENEVOLENT AND THE MOST MERCIFUL.

PREFACE

My pious father, Allamatul Asr Muhaqqiq-e-Mahdavia Miyan Syed Yaqoob Bazmi Tashrifullahi, had given answers in the second edition of "Muqaddama-e-Sirajul Absar" in the light of the holy Qur'an and Traditions, to the objections raised by the decliners not only against Mahdiat of Imam Alaihias Salaam, but also raised against his undeniable and auspicious biography and sublime characters.

In short, "Muqaddama-e-Sirajul Absar" presents not only the complete biography of Imam Alaihis salato wassalaam, but also the complete proof of his Mahdiat in the light of Qur'an and the traditions.

Hazrat Muhaqqiaq-e-Mahdavia Rahmatullahi Alaih had enlarged the Muqaddama-e-Sirajul Absar (Second Edition) under the title "Supplement" which is wonderful, the same is now being published after his sad demise.

Submitted by:

Syed Khundmir, Azmi.
12th Rabiul Awwal, 1395 Hijri
26th March, 1975 AD.

The Supplement was separately published on 26th. March 1975 Ad.
Now it is being published in the 3rd. edition after merging into the Second edition. (Publisher)

32

IN THE NAME OF ALLAH THE MOST GRACIOUS AND MOST MERCIFUL.
EULOGY COMPILED BY DR.SYED ALI ATH'HER, YADULLAHI

پیکر علم و یقین

بزمِّ اعلٰی نظر اے پیکر علم و یقیں   عالم دیں عاشق زار رسول آخریں

تیری نظروں میں سدا تھا جلوۂ نورِ مبیں   عشق مہدیؑ نے تجھے بخشا تھا عزم آہنیں

روز و شب صبح و مسا تھا کارِ دیں پیشِ نظر

خدمتِ دیں سے عبارت زندگی کا تھا سفر

تیرے نورِ علم سے کرتا ہے عالم اکتساب   کر نہ ڈالے تیری جہل تا دل کو خراب

دوست دشمن سب ہیں تیری تحریروں سے فیض یاب   صَرف راہِ حق میں تو نے کر دیا زور شباب

عشق و علم و فضل میں کوئی تیرا ہمسر نہ تھا

کسب میں بھی تیرا تقویٰ فقر سے کم تر نہ تھا

اہل حق کو ہے مقدم بس رضائے کردگار   عیش و راحت ہو انھیں یا رنج دور و انتشار

ہے یقیں مردِ خدا کو کچھ نہیں یاں پائندار   جادۂ عمر گریزاں کا ہے سب گرد و غبار

مردِ حق اہلِ وفا تھا تو! نہیں اس میں گماں

سر خوشِ صہبائے عشق و بے نیاز ایں و آں

موت کر سکتی نہیں اس زندگی کا اختتام   علم دیں کا ہر زمانے کو جو بخشے فیض عام

عاشقِ ذاتِ امام مہدیؑ گردوں مقام   روز فردا بھی رہے گا زیر دامانِ امامؑ

موت کیا ہے عالم دیں کی نوید زندگی

شام غم کے بعد گویا صبح عید زندگی

عشق مہدیؑ نے کیا تھا تجھ کو خود سے بے خبر   دل کی ہر دھڑکن میں تھی آواز "یا مہدی" مگر

خوب تو نے طے کیا اس زندگانی کا سفر   خوب ہی تو نے گذاری یہ حیات مختصر

تیرے عشقِ مہدیؑ موعود کی ہے یاد گار

تیری تصنیفِ وقیع اثباتِ دیں کا شاہکار

(Note:Apology by the Translator who is unable to translate the poetic phraseology.)Nahmadahu Wa Nusalli Alaa Khatimul Karimain.

APPRECIATION

(In Arabic Language - Translated in English)
Presented by

Mashaeq Alhajj the Late Syed Mahmood Akailvi, Moulvi Kamil, Sajjada-e-Daira-e-Akaili Kalan (Zaheerabad), president "Tanzeem-e-Anwarul Huda", Malakpet, Hyderabad. A.P.

TRANSLATION:

"Muqaddama-e-Sirajul Absar" is highly desired by the Seekers of Divine knowledge and is well appreciated by the research scholars. This Muqaddama was written by Muhaqqiq-e-Mahdavia, the eminent scholar, Allamatul Asr Hazrat Syed Yaqoob Bazmi(Rh). I had gone through the Muqaddama from the inception to its end. I have found in it the unfathomable raging ocean of the righteousness of the Mahdiat of Hazrat Imamana Mahdi Alaaihis Salaam. Author of "Kanzul Ummal" known as Shaik Ali Muttaqi had vehemently objected to the claim of Mahdiat by Imamana Mahdi Alaihis Salaam. Likewise, author of "Hadia-e-Mahdavia" known as Zaman Khan also had raised objections in his book on the proclamation of Mahdiat by Imamana Alaihis Salaam. He had criticized on the very personality of Imamana with mischievous motives and thus both of them had strained their every nerve to nullify the acclaimed traditions in respect of Imamana Alaihis Salaam.

On the same line, Aamir Osmani, Editor of Tajalli of Devband also had in his monthly magazine criticized on the traditions regarding Imamana and had maliciously opined his own misconceptions. In this manner they have deprived themselves to be authoritative and reliable persons for the seekers of the Divine Knowledge. Thus Allama Muhaqqiq-e-Mahdavia Syed Yaqoob Bazmi Rh. presented real facts (about Mahdiat) in his "Muqaddama-e-Sirajul Absar". Then he tried to answer the criticism of Ibn Khaldun and refuted his malicious pretension in his famous book known as "Muqaddama-e-Ibn Khaldun". Against suchcores of malicious allegations, Allama Bazmi rightly pinpointed the traditions in respect of Imam Mahdi Alaihis Salaam. Thus his detailed research got the exalted position and reached to the highest level of understanding. In view of those taunting remarks of the fault finders on the traditions regarding Imam Mahdi (Ahs), Allama Bazmi tried to present and prove Imamana's righteousness in the light of the Islamic thinking. Then he had rightly argued about the verses of the Qur'an and various commentaries pertaining to the advent of Imam Mahdi (Ahs).Thus in this manner Hazrat Bazmi had done justice by arguing correctly about the advent of Imam Mahdi (As) in the light of the Qur'an and its commentaries. When I have gone through the reasoning and the cause and effect presented in the Muqaddama, I found it on the divine path upon which no evil could effectuate on it. Thus after reading it carefully I put the seal of its sanctity and stability.

The "Muqaddama" along with its supplement is being arranged to be published for the third time by his nephew Janab Syed Mahmood Tashrifullahi for the people.

Summary of the discussion:

The Muqaddama purifies and brightens the heart and soul and strengthens the faith of those who ponder on the proofs regarding Mahdiat (of Imam-e-Huda). It provides perfect and genuine remedy to the fault finders who object on the sublime characters of Imam-e-Huda (As), the seal of the vilayet-e-Mohammedia, thus it becomes a voluminous guide for the research scholars as well.

I pray the Almighty Allah to grant His Blessings to the author of this "Muqaddama" and also to those who are assisting in its safeguarding and publishing. May Allah Make this "Muqaddama" an eternal source of guidance to the followers of the holy Prophet Hazrat Mohammed Rasoolullah (PBUH) till the Doomsday. Ameen.

Syed Mahmood Akailvi
(Sajjada Daira, Zaheerabad, A.P.India)

The Translator feels it necessary, before going to the text of the book, to provide with short sketches of those who are involved in it: They are:

1. Allamatul Asr Hzt.Syed Yaqoob Bazmi, (Rh) author of "Muqaddanma-e-Sirajul Absar" in Urdu

2. Aalim Billah Hzt. Abdul Malik Sujawandi (Rh), author of "Sirajul Absar" in Arabic

3. Shaikh Ali Muttaqi, author of "Al Rudd" in Arabic

4. Abu Rija Zaman Khan Shahjahanpuri, Author of "Hadia-e-Mahdavi" in Urdu.

1. Allamatul Asr Hzt. Syed Yaqoob Bazmi (Rh)

Allamatul Asr, Muhaqiq-e-Mahdavia, Hazrat Syed Yaqoob Bazmi(Rh), alias Dada Miyan, was born in 1903 in a highly well-educated and learned atmosphere. His father, Hazrat Syed Mustafa Tashrifullahi, was well versed in Persian and Urdu and was an accredited poet under the pen name Khurshidi. His mother was a pious lady of noble characters, came from a very religious family. Hazrat Bazmi was born and bred under such a religious and academic background. He had religious affiliation with his cousin Hazrat Syed Naseeruddin Tashrifullhi, a well-known religious guide of his period with a highly religious background, always busy in religious discussions with who ever visited him. The same was the case of Allama Syed Yaqqoob Bazmi (Rh) who displayed a profound mastery by presenting his arguments based on Qur'an and traditions with respect to Imamana's proclamation of Mahdiat in his masterpiece "Muqaddama-e-Sirsajul Absar. After minutely scrutinizing scores of allegations against our Mentor(As) and our sublime Faith, He declared correctly that the non-mahdavi scholars have gone out of the bound in condemning Imamana(As) and his companions for the declaration of Mahdiat in the Tenth Century Hijri, and arguably condemned them by presenting reliable and unquestionable proofs based on Qur'an and Sunnah.

Being born in a very religious atmosphere, he too had an inclination to attain religious knowledge also along with worldly education. He had God-Given inclination towards learning from the very child-hood. He was brought and bred by his father in understanding the need to refute scientifically and logically the un-warranted allegations of the non mahdavi scholars by quoting proper references from the original classical manuscripts to substantiate correctness of our answers which could not be refuted by any decliner and opponent of our venerable faith..

He graduated from the Nizam College with merit. He gained mastery in Arabic and Persian languages too. Although he had chances to get employment in other departments, but he selected Teaching Profession as his career. And circumstances also helped him to attain his ambitions. His elder brother Hzt. Syed Zainullabuddin was a teacher in the Government High School, Chaderghat, but unfortunately died at an early age, on which occasion, Mr. Shaker, Principal of the High School visited the bereaved family for offering condolences, and meanwhile, after knowing Hazrat Bazmi's credentials, offered the post of a teacher became vacant on the demise of his elder brother. After consultation with his elders, accepted the offer and thus joined the Teaching Profession and started his career from the Chaderghat High School, Abids. He got his pension by serving a long academic service of 55 years. Then he joined the Asafia High School at Malakpet. He was acclaimed as a well-disciplined teacher, who invested his energies in providing highly educative skills to his pupils. Although he was known as a very strict and a desciplined teacher, still he used to have lively jokes every now and then to make the thick atmosphere light, on account of which he was very famous among his pupils and staff, on account of which his pupils used to attend his classes regularly without being absent.

As regads his academic and literary calibre, he pragmatically devised his unique way of criticism. He used to study the allegations first, then studied the sources from which he could deduce the befitting answers to a particular allegation. Being proficient in all languges he concentrated minutely on the Arabic text of "Sirajul Absar" along with his father's Urdu translation to understand the nature of the objections and then studied the allegations initiated by Shaik Ali Muittaqi in his derogatory Arabic pamphlet "Al-Rudd", then studied "Hadia-e-Mahdavia written by Abu Rija Zaman Khan and also gone through scores of allegations from hoards of unscrupulous non mahdavi writers. Then he took up each and every allegation by listing topical wise and also author wise, then he systematically studied those classical books which gave him proper guidance, then only he jotted down his refutation in such a way that whoever read it may become satisfied.

His mastery over his peculiar writings based on logically woven fabric, his specially crafted sense of balance in moderation and his brilliant philosophical conclusions enhanced his voluminous book on an undisputed place among the scholarly written manuscripts in the modern times. May Allah, the Almighty Grant His approval to his masterpiece which proves the correctness of the proclamation of Mahdiat by Imamana(As).

In view of the dictates of Imamana(As), Allama Bazmi(Rh) had elaborately presented by pinpointing some obligations which are mentioned in the Holy Qur'an, known as Fara-e-ze Vilayet. He has correctly named them that these are the Obligations pertaining to Vilayet-e-Mustafavi(slm). His convincing approach in presenting them is very understandable and laudable for the readers.

With reference to the holy Prophet's prophecy that Imam Mahdi shall carry character as his own by telling "Khulquhoo Khulqi"(meaning:His-(mamana's),shall be of mine(the Holy Prophet's). Allama Bazmi had ventured to present a detailed comparative study on at least 25 aspects relating to characters of the Holy Prophet (Slm) and of Imamana(As). Thus, with this comparison, he has successfully proved that Imamana(As) was the true follower of the holy Prophet in all respects, not only on Shariat but also on the day to day problems. Such a comparison also is first of its kind, which is not available in any book to our knowledge. That is the beauty of his caliber which penetrates into the depth of a problem.

Allama also had a poetic taste and his poetry got befitting appreciation from the audience. On account of which he came in the good books of the Maharaja Kishan Prashad, the then prime minister of the Nizam's Dominion, who used to arrange periodically poetic gatherings (Mushaeray) in which the Allama also used to take part.

One of Allam's well recognized work was the compilation of the collection of the poems of Amir Hasan Sanjari (b.653, d.738 H.) a highly respected Persian Poet, who was a contemporary of Hzt. Amir Khusro. In order to preserve his Persian compilation, the Maharaja appointed Masood Ali Mahvi (Alig), retired Session Judge, and a famous Urdu and Persian poet of that period, for compilation of Hasan Sanjari's poetry from inception to the last couplet. Mr. Mahvi would not have been able to complete it without the active cooperation provided by Allama Bazmi. This compilation became one of Maharaja's academic service, which was printed on about 633 pages, in the Ibrahimia Printing Press, Hyderabd Deccan in 1352 H. This compilation brought fame to both Masood Ali Mahvi and to Allama Bazmi.

His main life project was printing and publishing of "Muqaddam-e-Sirajul Absar" in which, the proofs regarding Mahdiat and answers to the decliners, on the basis of Qur'anic Dictates and the Traditions are given.

He lived a life mostly in seclusion and invested his time and energy in different libraries. He had studied some 412 Classical Books in compiling the said Muqaddamah, whose workmanship points out that how much talent and skill, Allama, might have invented in writing such a comprehensive, an encyclopedic book which is not only exhaustive, but a self-educative book on Mahdaviat with no parallel.

Apart from this voluminous book, Allama had written a detailed treatise under the name and title "Biyan-e-Qur'an" which contains references of the objections raised by some commentators, about whom Imamana(AS) pointed out that some of them were trustworthy, who asserted correctly. This book, unfortunately is missig, otherwise had it been published, it would have brought another feather to his cap by enhancing his fame among the Islamic literary circle.

Allama's Persian poetry, together with its Urdu translation shall be published shortly. One of his another exemplary treatise on the life and work of the 17th. Century's well known Persian-Uzbek poet Mirza Abdul Qader Baydil, although he was born in India, latter on migrated to Uzbekistan. This Treatise also was not published due to his early demise. In completion of this book, his nephew, Dr. syed Ali Ather, had volunteered his services, which is commendable.

Allama never wished for worldly fame and egotism. He spent his whole life in reading and in research and led a very religious life. His Muqaddamah is well known and appreciated among the Mahdavia community and hopefully it would remain famous till the Doomsday, Insha Allah.

On the successful completion of his famous Muqaddamah, he had compiled a Persian couplet offering his humble gratitude to the Almighty Allah; whose translation is given hereunder:

" I had spent all of my life to follow the way of my Beloved, Allah. And I am highly satisfied that I had accomplished my desire."

Finally let me subscribe that all his life was filled with love of Allah suhana o ta Allah, the holy Prophet(Slm) and Imamana(As), as an example to others. A week before his demise, he had a little pain in his thumb of his right leg, which was treated well, still he surmised Allah's Will, therefore, two days earlier to his demise, he invited his Murshid, Abul Hadi Syed Mahmood Akhailvi and proclaimed before him the religious obligation of Worldly Renunciation; and finally on 12th. Rajjab 1386 H./ 27th. October 1967 AD, passed away at his age 63. His survivors were his widow, one son and three daughters. He was buried beside his father's grave at Chanchalguda, in the Hazeera-e-Hzt.Syed Raje Mohammed (Rh). -

With courtesy from Br. Syed Mahmood Tashrifullahi

(Note: at the time of this writing, his son and wife also passed away leaving daughters alive.)

2. Hz. Abdul Malik Sujawandi (Rh), Author of "Sirajul Absar", a befitting Rebuttal to the "Al Rudd" of Shaik Ali Muttaqi.

Aalim Billah's father, Younus Sujawandi, was from Sujawand, a hilly village in Khurasan near Kabul. After migrating to India his descendants settled down in Gujarat. The king of Gujrat had high regard for Hz. Abdul Malik Sujawandi (Rh) for his high caliber and proficiency in Arabic language. The King welcomed him and granted a village Budhasan as his jagir. Hz. Malik accepted the Mahdavia faith at the hands of Hz. Bandagi Miyan Shah Dilawar (Rz), the fifth Khalifa of Imamana Mahdi Alaihis Salaam in the year 919AH.

Hzt.Shah Dilawar (Rz) had established his Dairah at Radhanpur, in Khandes. At his demise there were 1400 Fuqaras, (seekers of Allah) in his Dairah who were divided into two groups of 700 each. One group was attached to Hz. Abdul Kareem Noori (Rh) and the other was with Hz. Abdul Malik Sajawandi (Rh). He left Shah Dilawer's Dairah along with 700 Seekers and established his own dairah in his jagir, Budhasan village of Gujarat. He engaged himself in propagation of the Faith and had several meetings with the non-Mahdavi scholars of Gujrat and explained them the fundamentals of our Faith in a very laudable and convincing manner. He had also written several books. A few of them are:

1. "Siraj-ul-Absaar" (Arabic) an answer to "Risala Al Rudd" of Shaik Ali Muttaqi and against the Fatwah of Ibn Hajr Makki which was given by him against Mahdavis.

2. "Khasayes-e-Imam Mahdi" - This booklet was written to show the status of Imam Mahdi (As) among the Ummah which is above the Khalifas of the Prophet (Slm) and equal to him.

3. "Fazilat-e-Imam Mahdi Alal Shekhayn" (Arabic) - This booklet is also on the same topic as that of "Khasayes". It was not published so far.

4. "Sab'abul Islam Min Al-Sahabatal Ikram" (Arabic)

This topic is "the reason for accepting the Prophet (Slm) by his companions was his sublime "Characters" but not the "miracles."

5. "Sirajul Millat" (Arabic) - its second name is "Minhaj-ut-Taqveem."

6. "Minhaj-ut-Taqveem" (Arabic) (Reply to the questions by Shaik Mubarak Nagori on the Mahdiat of the Imam-e-Huda (As).

7. "Makateeb" (letters) (in Persian - On different topics of the Faith to different persons).

8. "Khutba-e-Nikah" (The marriage sermon) (in Persian) (This sermon is commonly used for marriages in the community even today. This khutbah includes a unique condition which is very helpful to the Bride. It gives the authority to woman to go free from her husband in case of non fulfillment of the conditions prescribed in khutbah. It is generally felt that woman should also have right to divorce her husband. This right is given to Muslim women long back.

There are some more books written by Hz. Bandagi Mian Abdul Malik Aalim Billah (Rh), but such books are not available now.

The book "Sirajul Absar" was originally written in Arabic language in reply to Shaik Ali Muttaqi, on his "Risala Al Rudd". This book was written on the advice of Hz. Bandagi Miyan Syed Shahabuddin Shahabul Haq, the eldest son of Hz. Bandagi Miyan Syed Khundmir Siddiq-e-Vilayat(Rz). It was written somewhere in between 964AH and 972AH. This book is much popular in the Mahdavia community, hence in every period it was translated or its topics were explained in books like "Sharah"(Clarification). Some of such books are mentioned hereunder: -

1. "Sharah" - written by Miyan Syed Husain who is the author of the book of "Naqliat", titled as "Tazkiratul Saleheen".

2. "Zia ul Quloob" - Sharah by Hafiz Mohammed Qasim Bin Shaik Abdul Lateef Farooqi. He accepted Mahdavia Faith only after reading this venerable book. It is a bulky work covering almost 1133 pages in the script.

3. "Hashiah Ziaul Quloob" - It contains the footnotes on the book "Zia ul Quloob". Hz. Syed Fazalullah (d 1160AH) has given 86-footnotes on "Ziaul Quloob."

4. "Sharah" by Hz. Malik Sharfuddin the grandfather of the author of Khatim-e-Sulemani.

5. "Suboot-ul-Mahdi" By Miyan Hz Syed Ibrahim alias Badey Miyan. He passed away in 1297 H. at Pindiyal near Vijayawada in Andhra Pradesh. It is the first Urdu translation of "Sirajul Absar."

6. "Misbah ul Anwaar" - It is the translation of "Sirajul Absar" in Persian language by the well-known scholar of the community, Hz. Syed Isa alias Aalim Miyan. He has written several booklets in reply to "Hadia-e-Mahdavia" of Zaman Khan Shahjahanpuri. He is also the author of several books on the Faith. The book "Misbahul Anwaar" was published from Madras. (At that period Books on Mahdavi Faith were prohibited to be published in Nizam's Dominion)

"Hashia Misbahul Anwaar" In the margin of "Misbahul Anwaar" Urdu translation of "Sirajul Absar" also has been provided.

8. Urdu translation of "Sirajul Absar": This translation was done by Hz. Syed Ashraf Ali alias Achcha Miyan Palanpuri.

9. "Sharah-Ahadith-o-Ayat" which were used in "Sirajul-Absar" by Hz. Syed Nusrat (Rh), author of "Kohlul Jawahar".

10. "Siraj-ul-Absar Mai Muqadamah-wa-Tarjumah" by Hz. Moulana Syed Mustafa Tashreefullahi (Rh). It was published in 1365 A.H./1945 AD, along with Arabic text and Urdu translation. The book contains a bulky foreword in Urdu which covers all topics relating to the Faith and also covers answers of objections against Mahdavia Faith. The second Edition was published in 1382 H. under the title "Muqqadama-e-Siraj-ul-Absar." In this edition the text and its Urdu translation were omitted, but the answers to all objections against our Faith from any opponent were given in detail. It covers (1020) pages. Its third Edition was published in the year 1410 A.H. i.e. 1990AD by Br. Syed Mahmood Tashrifullahi, which contains (1036) pages. The additions were inserted by Muhaqiq-e-Mahdavia, Hzt. Syed Yaqoob Bazmi (Rh), the eldest son of the Author, in the original "Muqadamah" in the second and the third editions. It has become an exhaustive, comprehensive and an encyclopedic type "Reference Book" of Mahdavia Faith, furnishing history, biographies of eminent personalities and also provides befitting replies to the unholy objections and allegations against our Faith.

3. **Shaik Ali Muttaqi** (born in 885 H.) Author of "Al Rudd" The Arch Rival of

Imamana (As).

His forefathers migrated from Juanpur to Burhanpur. In those days, Shah Bajan was a popular priest of the Chishtia order of Sufism. He was not only a religious guide but a well known Unani Hakeem and a Deccani (Urdu) Poet also. Shaik's father Abdul Malik S/o Qazi Khan was a disciple of Shah Bajan. The Shaik (Sheikh Ali) was made a disciple of Shah Bajan at his age 8 years and was given the costume of the priest of the silsila by the son of Shah Bajan, Shaik Abdul Hakeem after many years.

The Shaik was not satisfied with this order of Sufia therefore he left the Chishti Silsila. While wandering he came to know about Mahdvia Dairah of Hz Shah Dilawer (Rz), 5th Khalifa of Imamana Mahdi Alaihis Salaam. He joined the Dairah with a hope that the seekers of the Dairah would welcome him. But he came to know about the many restrictions in making the effort for worldly gains by depending totally on Allah for everything including the sustenance, which became out of his reach, since the Shaik had altogether a different worldly approach to these things.

It is saids that on account of some physical weakness, he did not marry and was living alone. Unluckily, one day, he heard Hzt. Shah Dilawer (Rz) was giving a sermon in which he, without pointing towards any person, informed that an eunuch would not enter the paradise. The Shaikh took it as if it was directed to him. Thus became furious, left the Dairah and migrated to Makkah for ever. Apart from this episode, he could not bear the hardships of the Dairah, thus, for no reason, he cultivated bias and enmity against Mahdvia Faith and became a bitter critic of Imamana (As) as well.

Thus the Shaik became an arch rival of Imamana (As). As a scholar, he has written more than (100) booklets on different topics on religion, traditions, fiqha, and also against Imamana (As). The well known book "Kanzul A'amal" written by him became very famous. Another Risala "Al Burhan" also became very famous in the Muslim Ummah. Being heartened by the popularity of those books, he ventured wrongly to write "Al Rudd" in 960 H. against Imamana (As) and Mahdavia Faith and circulated it in India and other Islamic countries for unholy propagation against our Faith. He obtained many Fatwas against us from scholars of Makkha and brought personally to Gujrat and poisoned the ears of the king against Mahdavis.

4. Abu Rija Mohammed Zaman Khan: Author of "Hadia-e-Mahdavia"

He was born in Shahjehanpur in 1242 H. and died in 1292 at Hyderabad. He was very much interested in studying about religion, Qur'an, traditions and Fiqh. After studying his preliminary education in Shahjehapur, he went to Kanpur in 1262 H and became the pupil of Moulana Salamat Ali Shah. After three years of learning he went to many places like Farukhabad, Rai Barieli, Rampur, Akberabad, Dholpur, Gawaliar, Jhansi, Bhopal, Hoshangabad, Amrawati, Nanded and finally to Hyderabad, where he settled down. He studied Traditions under the guidance of Moulvi Karamat Ali Dehlavi. Slowly he cultivated friendship with the elites of Hyderabad and tried to have an audience of Nizam Nasiruddowla. With the help of Hakeem Mohiuddin Ahmed Yar Khan, he got the chance to have the audience of the Nizam, who became impressed by his academic caliber, granted him a mansub of Rs. 60/- per month and was appointed as the teacher of the Heir Apparent Nawab Afzaluddowlah.

After some time, Nawab Mukhtarul Mulk appointed him as the Principal of Darul Uloom in 1273 H. Mukhtarul Mulk, who was a Shia, instructed him to write down two curriculums for the school, one for the Sunnis and the other for the Shias. Although he completed a curriculum for the Sunnis but declined to write for the Shias. This was the beginning of the rivalry between Abu Rija and Mukhtarul Mulk, which resulted in Abu Rija's resignation as the principal of Darul Uloom in 1277 H.

After the demise of Nasiruddowla, Nawab Afzaluddowlah became the Fifth Nizam, and his son, Nawab Mir Mahboob Ali Khan became the Heir Apparent. Thus he was appointed as teacher for the Heir Apparent on a monthly salary of Rs.1000/-. This appointment gave phillip to the rivalry between Mukhtarul Mulk and Abu Rija further.

Abu Rija had opened a school by name "Mahboobia School, where he started teaching students. After some time he went on a journey to Islamic countries and returned after five years in 1282 H. When he returned to Hyderabad, one of our Mahdavi Preachers, Hz. Aalam Miyan Saheb met Abu Rija. It seems they might have discussed about Mahdiat and Abu Rija might have asked Moulana to provide some books on Mahdiat. Among those books he gave a recently published book "Shubhaatul Fatwah" which was printed in Bangalore.

After receiving the books, it seems Abu Rija, instead of having a dialectical dialogue with Aalim Miyan Saheb, he consulted Mukhtarul Mulk and requested him to get Aalam Miyan Saheb exiled from Hyderabad, so that he could study the books peacefully and write a book about his impressions on Mahdiat.

It was an opportune time for Mukhtarul Mulk, being a shia, to cultivate friendship with Abu Rija by accepting his request for the exile of Aalim Miyan Saheb, and on the other hand, to flare up the classic rivalry between Sunnis and Mahdvis by a covert plan to involve Abu Rija to write against Mahadavis. Thus he ordered Aalim Miyan Saheb for the exile on one hand, and financially helped Abu Rija in writing and publishing a book against Mahdavis on the other hand. In this way, Mukhtarul Mulk was sure that such a derogatory book shall cause much havoc in which Abu Rija would be murdered by Mahdavis as a revenge. Aalim Miyan left Hyderabad and reached Pindyal. Thus his exile gave ample time to Abu Rija to scrutinize the books with an anti Mahdi point of view and after carefully studying the books along with a group of scholars, Abu Rija finally completed his "Hadia-e-Mahdavia" with financial help from Mukhtarul Mulk. The book was ready in 1285 H. and was printed in 1287and circulated in Hyderabad, which opened a Pandora Box. Ultimately it resulted:

(1) The murder of Abu Rija Zaman Khan by Hz. Abji Miyan Shahaeed. Thus Mukhtarul Mulk's covert plan became successful, since his rival Abu Rija was no more.

(2). Second exodus of Mahdavis from the Nizam's State in 1293. First exodus was after the Chanchalguda Battle of 1238H.

****

Note: on suggestion by Br. Syed Mahmood Tashrifullahi, publisher of the third edition of "Muqaddama-e-Sirajul Absar" I happily provide hereunder the original Urdu Text of Hazrat Bazmi's "Arz-e-Hal" (Submission) from pages 22 to 33 of the Urdu Edition, and its English Translation follows just after it. ....

بسم الله الرحمن الرحیم

بعد حمد خدا وتحیت محمد مصطفیٰ وصلوٰۃ وسلام برامام ہدیٰ

عرض پرداز

سید یعقوب بزمی بن میاں سید مصطفیٰ المعروف بہ خوب صاحب میاں (مدفن حیدرآباد) بن میاں سید یعقوب (حیدرآباد) بن میاں سید نور محمد (حیدرآباد) بن میاں سید اشرف (کرگاول میسور) بن میاں سید عبداللطیف (ترچنا پلی) بن میاں سید راجے محمد (چن پٹن علاقہ میسور) بن میاں سید عبداللطیف (سورت علاقہ گجرات) بن بندگیمیاں سید جلال شہید (برہان پور) بن بندگیمیاں سید عبداللطیف اول (بیجاپور) بن بندگیمیاں سید شریف تشریف تشریف لاگاؤں (جامودجلگاؤں علاقہ مہاراشٹرا ابن سید الشہد أحضرت بندگیمیاں سید خوند میر صدیق ولایت رضی اللہ عنہٗ (سدراس،ن پٹن چاپانیر علاقہ گجرات) از اولا دامام موسیٰ کاظمؓ وخلیفہ حضرت سید محمد جونپوری مہدی موعود علیہ الصلوٰۃ والسّلام (فراہ مبارک علاقہ افغانستان)

مقدمہ سراج الابصار کا پہلا ایڈیشن (جو پانچ سوانتالیس ۵۳۹ صفحوں پر مشتمل تھا) ۱۳۶۵ھ میں شائع ہوا تھا۔

حضرت والد ماجد کے ارشاد کی تعمیل میں،ٔ میں نے مقدمہ سراج الابصار میں تقریباً دو گنا اضافہ کر کے مقدمہ کو چار حصوں میں تقسیم کیا ہے اور ابواب کی ترتیب بھی بدل دی ہے،ٔ فرزند عزیز سید محمد تشریف اللہی عرف میر انجی میاں سلمہ اللہ کے اصرار پر اس کی طباعت کا آغاز کیا گیا۔

مقدمہ کی ضخامت کم کرنے کے لئے میں نے موجودہ ایڈیشن میں کتاب کو کراؤن سائز پر رکھا اور مسطر پچیس ۲۵ سطری کر دیا (پہلے ایڈیشن میں طباعت رائل سائز پر ہوئی اور مسطر اکیس ۲۱ سطری تھا) اور اسی لئے متن کو بھی مقدمہ سے الگ کرنا پڑا لیکن مباحث کے سلسلے میں متنِ سراج الابصار کی عبارت یا اس کا ترجمہ ناظرین کی سہولت کے لئے بقدر ضرورت پیش کر دیا گیا ہے۔

مقدمہ نگاری سے متعلق ذیل میں تفصیلی بحث کی جاتی ہے۔

مقدمہ کی قسمیں : مقدمہ کی تین قسمیں ہیں۔

(١) ایک وہ مقدمہ جو کتاب کی حیثیت رکھتا ہے، یہ کسی کتاب کا جزو نہیں ہوا کرتا، اس کو اسی فن کی مناسبت سے مقدمہ کہتے ہیں جس فن کے باب میں لکھا گیا ہے، اس نوعیت کی ایک قدیم کتاب کا بیان یہاں ذکر کیا جاتا ہے تا کہ یہ معلوم ہو کہ عربوں میں اس نوع کی تصنیف کس زمانہ سے متعارف تھی۔

مقدمہ الجرمی، یہ عمرو ابن صالح بن اسحق الجرمی البصری ہیں المتوفی ٢٢٥ھ یہ مقدمہ نحو میں ہے، اس کی شرح ابوالحسن محمد بن عبداللہ المعروف ابن الوراق النحوی المتوفی ٣٨١ھ نے لکھی ہے اور اس کا نام ہدایہ رکھا ہے۔	المقدمة الجرمی (المقدمة الجرمی) و هو عمر ابن صالح بن اسحق الجرمی البصری المتوفی سنه ٢٢٥ خمس و عشرين و مائتين و هی فی النحو شرحها ابو الحسن محمد بن عبدالله المعروف با بن الوراق النحوی المتوفی سنه ٣٨١ احدی و ثمانين و ثلثماية و سماه بالهدايه

مذکورہ عبارت سے ظاہر ہے کہ اس قسم کی مقدمہ نگاری تیسری صدی ہجری کے اوائل میں متعارف تھی، بعد کو بھی اس قسم کے مقدمہ لکھے گئے، اس نوعیت کا مشہور مقدمہ وہ ہے جو ابن صلاح نے لکھا ہے۔

مقدمہ ابن صلاح: اس مقدمہ میں علم الحدیث سے متعلق جملہ اصول و فروع پر بحث کی گئی ہے اور حدیث پڑھنے والے کیلئے اس کی

حیثیت ایک مقدمہ کی ہے، اس کو پڑھے بغیر حدیث رسول اللہ صلعم کو اصول حدیث کے مطابق نہیں سمجھ سکتے، ابن صلاح کا سن وفات ٦٤٣ یا ٦٤٦ھ ہے۔

(ب) دوسرا وہ مقدمہ ہے جو کسی کتاب کا جزو ہوتا ہے اور مولف اس میں ایسے امور درج کرتا ہے جن کے پڑھنے کے بعد کتاب کے مندرجات سمجھنے میں آسانی ہو جاتی ہے، اس قسم کے مقدمہ کی ابتداء محدثین نے کی۔

مقدمہ صحیح مسلم: مسلم (المتوفی ٢٦١ھ) نے اپنی کتاب کے آغاز میں ایک مقدمہ لکھا ہے، اس میں وہ اصول و شرائط بیان کئے ہیں جن کے تحت انہوں نے حدیثیں لیں یا ترک کر دیں، علماء حدیث نے اس مقالہ کو مقدمہ تسلیم کیا ہے۔ نووی نے شرح مسلم میں یہ لکھا ہے۔

ذکر کیا مسلم رحمہ اللہ نے اپنی صحیح کے مقدمہ کے شروع میں کہ انہوں نے حدیثوں کی تین قسمیں کی ہیں۔	ذکر مسلم رحمه الله فی اول مقدمة صحیحه انه یقسم الاحادیث ثلاثة اقسام الی آخره

مولوی وحید الزماں نے "المعلم ترجمہ صحیح مسلم" میں یہ لکھا ہے

"تمام ہوا مقدمہ کتاب مسلم کا اب شروع ہوتا ہے بیان ایمان کا الی آخرہ"

مقدمہ سنن ابوداؤد : ابوداؤد (المتوفی ۵ے۲ ھ) نے اہل مکہ کے نام ایک خط لکھا ہے' اس میں سنن ابوداؤد کی مندرجہ روایتوں کے خصوصیات بیان کئے ہیں' اس خط کو ابوداؤد نے اپنے سنن کے آغاز میں بطور مقدمہ درج کیا ہے ابوداؤد کی عبارت یہ ہے۔

مقدمہ قال ابوداؤد فی رسالتہ الی اہل مکہ سلام علیکم مقدمہ کہا ابوداؤد نے اپنے خط میں جو اہل مکہ کے نام ہے سلام علیکم
فانی احمد الیکم اللہ الذی لا الہ الا ہو الی آخرہ ھ میں تمہارے نزدیک اللہ کی حمد کرتا ہوں جس کے سوا کوئی معبود نہیں۔

بعد کو مورخین اور محدثین نے اس مقدمہ کو ترقی دی' ذیل میں اس کی چند مثالیں دی جاتی ہیں۔

مقدمہ ابن الطقطقی : محمد بن علی بن طباطبا المعروف بابن الطقطقی نے ایک تاریخ لکھی ہے موسوم بہ کتاب الفخری فی الا داب السلطانیہ والدولۃ الاسلامیۃ'' یہ کتاب دو فصلوں میں منقسم ہے' فصل اول کی حیثیت ایک عام مقدمہ کی سی ہے اور فصل ثانی میں خلافت راشدہ سے خلافت عباسیہ کے خاتمہ تک تمام حالات اجمالاً بیان کئے گئے ہیں۔ یہ کتاب ۷۰۱ھ جیسا کہ خود مصنف نے کتاب کے آخر میں بیان کیا ہے۔

ابن الطقطقی نے اس امر کی تصریح کر دی ہے کہ فصل اول میں کن کن امور سے بحث کی گئی ہے' ابن الطقطقی کی عبارت یہ ہے۔

فالفصل الاول تکلمت فیہ علی الامور السلطانیۃ و فصل اول میں' میں نے ان امور کے باب میں گفتگو کی ہے' امور سلطانی اور سیاست ملکی' بادشاہ کے خصوصیات جن کی بناء پر وہ

السیاسیات الملکیۃ و خواص الملک التی یتمیز عوام الناس سے ممیز ہوتا ہے اور وہ خصوصیات جن کا بادشاہ میں
بہا عن السوقۃ والتی تجب ان تکون موجودۃ او ہونا یا نہ ہونا ضروری ہے اور وہ امور جو اسکی رعیت پر واجب ہیں
معدومۃ فیہ و ما تجب علی رعیتہ و ما یجب لہم اور رعایا کے وہ امور جو بادشاہ پر واجب ہیں' اس میں' میں نے
علیہ و رصعت الکلام فیہ بالآیات القرآنیۃ کلام کو آیات قرآنی احادیث نبوی عمدہ حکایتوں اور اچھے اشعار
والاحادیث النبویۃ الحکایات المستظرفۃ والاشعار سے متحکم کیا ہے۔
المستحسنۃ [۷]

ظاہر ہے ابن الطقطقی نے فصل اول میں امور سلطانی اور سیاست ملکی سے بحث کی ہے اور ان تمام امور کا ذکر کیا ہے جن کا ہونا اور نہ ہونا بادشاہوں کے لئے ضروری ہے اس میں ان امور سے بھی بحث کی گئی ہے جن کا رعیت میں ہونا ضروری ہے۔ اس کے ذیل میں آیات قرآنی' احادیث نبوی حکایات اور اشعار سے بھی استدلال دیا گیا ہے۔

اس مقدمہ سے متعلق جرجی زیدان (المتوفی ۱۳۳۳ھ) نے یہ لکھا ہے۔

46

و فـی صـدر الکتـاب مقدمة طویلة فی الامور
السلطانیة و السیاسیات الملکیة و هی من قبیل
فلسفة التاریخ او فی اسباب الحضارة نحو ما فعل
ابن خلدون فی مقدمته مطولا[١]

کتاب کے شروع میں ایک طویل مقدمہ ہے امور سلطانی اور
سیاست ملکی کے باب میں اور یہ ازقبیل فلسفہ تاریخ ہے یا تمدن
کے اسباب کے باب میں' قریب قریب اسی کے ہے جو ابن
خلدون نے تفصیل سے لکھا ہے۔

جرجی زیدان نے اسی کتاب الفخری کے مقدمہ سے متعلق یہ بھی بیان کیا ہے۔

فمقدمة الفخری هذه من قبیل الانتقاد التاریخی
لکن ابن خلدون خطا فی مقدمتة خطوة اخری[٢]

پس مقدمہ فخری' از قبیل انتقاء تاریخی ہے لیکن ابن خلدون
نے اپنے مقدمہ میں ایک اور قدم آگے بڑھا دیا۔

جرجی زیدان کی مذکورہ عبارت سے ثابت ہے کہ کتاب الفخری کا مقدمہ جو ابن الطقطقی نے لکھا ہے نقش اول ہے اور ابن خلدون کا
مقدمہ نقش ثانی ہے۔

مقدمہ ابن خلدون : ابن خلدون (المتوفی ٨٠٨ ھ) نے جو تاریخ لکھی ہے وہ ایک مقدمہ اور تین 'کتابوں' پر مشتمل ہے' مقدمہ میں علم
تاریخ کی فضیلت بیان کی گئی ہے اور اس فن کی تحقیق کی گئی ہے۔ کتاب اول میں تمدن اور عوارض تمدن کا ذکر کیا گیا ہے۔ عام طور پر جب مقدمہ کہا
جاتا ہے تو اسی مقدمہ اور کتاب اول دونوں پر اس کا اطلاق ہوتا ہے۔ بیروت کا مطبوعہ ایڈیشن ہمارے پیش نظر ہے یہ ٥٥٢ صفحوں پر مشتمل ہے۔

کتاب دوم میں اخبار العرب کا بیان ہے اور کتاب سوم میں اخبار البری دیار العرب کا ذکر ہے۔
ابن خلدون نے مقدمہ کا اس طرح ذکر کیا ہے۔

المقدمة فی فضل علم التاریخ و تحقیق مذاهبه
و الماع لما یعرض للمورخین من المغالطه و الاوهام
و ذکر شئی من اسبابها[٣]

مقدمہ علم تاریخ کی فضیلت' تاریخ کے مختلف مذاہب کی تحقیق'
مورخین کو مغلطے اور ابہام پیش آتے ہیں ان کی جانب اشارہ
اور اس کے کسی قدر اسباب و علل کے بیان میں۔

کتاب اول کا اس طرح ذکر کیا گیا ہے

الکتاب الاول فی طبیعة العمران فی الخلیقة وما
یعرض فیها من البدو الحضر و التغلب و الکسب
والمعاش و الصنائع والعلوم و نحوها و مالذلک
من العلل والاسباب[٤]

پہلی کتاب مخلوقات میں انسانی آبادی کی طبعیت' مزاج اور ان
کے عوارض کے باب میں جو اس پر طاری ہوتے ہیں مثلاً بدویت'
شہری زندگی (تمدن) جابرانہ غلبہ اور اکتساب اور معاشی زندگی'
مصنوعات' علوم وغیرہ اور اس کے جو اسباب و علل ہیں۔

مقدمہ ابن خلدون میں تین امور سے خاص بحث کی گئی ہے' ایک تاریخ کی تحقیق اور فضیلت' دوسرے امور اور وہ تمدن کی

تعمیر اور تخریب میں ممد و معاون اور اثر انداز ہوتے ہیں' تیسرے علوم و فنون اسلامیہ کی حقیقت۔

جرجی زیدان نے مقدمہ ابن خلدون سے متعلق یہ لکھا ہے۔

فمقدمة ابن خلدون خزانة علوم و اجتماعیة و   پس ابن خلدون کا مقدمہ اجتماعی' سیاسی اقتصادی اور ادبی
سیاسیة اقتصادیة و ادبیة ـ[۱]   علوم کا خزانہ ہے۔

مقدمہ ابن خلدون کا ترجمہ ترکی' فرانسیسی' انگریزی اور جرمن زبان میں بھی ہوا ہے۔ حاصل یہ کہ ابن خلدون نے اپنے مقدمہ میں
جن امور کو بیان کیا ہے اس کا مقصد یہ ہے کہ آئندہ ''کتاب'' دوم اور ''کتاب'' سوم کے مندرجات سمجھنے میں سہولت ہو۔

مقدمۂ فتح الباری: محدثین کے ہاں مقدمہ فتح الباری کو خاص اہمیت دی جاتی ہے جو کئی جلدوں میں لکھی
گئی ہے' شارح یعنی ابن حجر عقلانی (المتوفی ۸۵۲ھ) نے ''صحیح'' بخاری سے متعلق وہ تمام امور جو شرح کے ذیل میں نہیں آ سکتے تھے مقدمہ
میں علحدہ بیان کئے ہیں' یہ مقدمہ' شرح بخاری کا مقدمہ کہا جاتا ہے حقیقت یہ ہے کہ اس کا راست تعلق اصل کتاب سے ہے اس کو ''مقدمہ صحیح
بخاری'' کہنا ہی زیادہ مناسب ہے' مقدمہ فتح الباری' فتح الباری کے ساتھ مصر سے شائع ہو گیا۔ بڑی تقطیع کے ۳۴ سطری چار سو چورانوے ۴۹۴
صفحوں پر مشتمل ہے۔

مقدمہ فتح الباری میں دس فصلیں ہیں اور اس کے مندرجات کو اصولاً تین حصوں میں تقسیم کیا جا سکتا ہے۔ ایک حصہ میں ''امام بخاری''

کے حالات' ان کی تصانیف' ان کے شیوخ وغیرہ کا حال آ جاتا ہے دوسرے حصہ میں ''صحیح بخاری'' کے خصوصیات بیان کئے گئے ہیں۔
تیسرے حصہ کا تعلق مشتملات کتاب سے ہے اس کے چند عنوانات ذیل میں درج کئے جاتے ہیں۔

(۱) **الفصل الخامس فی سیاق ما فی الکتاب من**   پانچویں فصل ان لغات غریبہ کے باب میں ہے جو بخاری میں آئے
الالفاظ الغریبة علی ترتیب الحروف مشروحها[۲]   ہیں' بترتیب حروف تہجی درج کر کے ان کی شرح کی گئی ہے۔

مذکورہ عبارت سے ظاہر ہے کہ ''صحیح بخاری'' میں جو لغات غریبہ آئے ہیں اس کی شرح مقدمہ میں کی گئی ہے۔

(۲) **الفصل السادس فی بیان المؤلف و المختلف**   چھٹی فصل ان ناموں' کنیتوں' القاب' و انساب کے باب
من الاسماء والکنی والالقاب والانساب مما وقع   میں ہے جو مماثل یا مختلف ہیں اور صحیح بخاری میں آئے ہیں'
فی صحیح البخاری علی ترتیب الحروف[۳]   بترتیب حروف تہجی درج ہیں۔

مذکورہ عنوان بتلاتا ہے کہ صحیح بخاری میں جو اسماء' کنیتیں القاب اور انساب مذکور ہیں ان کی حقیقت مقدمہ میں بیان کی گئی ہے۔

(۳) **الفصل الثامن فی سیاق الاحادیث التی انتقد علیه**   آٹھویں فصل ان حدیثوں کے باب میں ہے جن پر محدث
حافظ عصره ابو الحسن الدارقطنی وغیره من النقاد   عصر ابو الحسن دارقطنی وغیرہ نے انتقاد کیا ہے' ایک ایک
و ایرادها حدیثا حدیثا علی سیاق الکتاب و سیاق   حدیث کر کے ان پر جو اعتراضات وارد ہوئے ہیں وہ پیش
ماحضر من الجواب عن ذلک[۴]   کئے ہیں اور ان کا جواب دیا ہے۔

اس عبارت سے ظاہر ہے کہ مقدمہ میں دارقطنی وغیرہ کے اس انتقاد کا جواب دیا گیا ہے جو بخاری کی حدیثوں سے متعلق ہے۔

(۴) الفصل التاسع فی سیاق اسماء من طعن فیہ من   نویں فصل اس کتاب کے ان رجال کے باب میں ہے، جن

رجال ھذا الکتاب مرتبالھم علی حروف المعجم   پر طعن کیا گیا ہے بترتیب حروف تہجی اور ہر مقام پر جو

والجواب عن الاعتراضات معضا موضعا ⁵   اعتراضات وارد ہوئے ہیں ان کا جواب

رجال بخاری سے متعلق ہے جو طعن ہے، وہ سب مقدمہ کی اس فصل میں دفع کئے گئے ہیں۔

(ج) مقدمہ کی تیسری قسم یہ ہے کہ ایک عالم دوسرے عالم کی کتاب پر لکھے، اس کی ابتداء دیباچہ، شاہنامہ سے ہوئی۔

مقدمہ شاہنامہ: شاہنامہ کے دو دو دیباچے مشہور ہیں، ایک قدیم دیباچہ جس کے متعلق مرزا عبدالوہاب قزوینی نے یہ خیال ظاہر کیا ہے کہ وہ چوتھی صدی ہجری کی تصنیف ہے، اس دیباچہ کا ترجمہ مستشرق ویلن برگ (Wellen Bourg) نے ۱۸۱۰ء میں وائنا (علاقہ آسٹریا) سے شائع کیا۔

دوسرا دیباچہ مرزا بایسنقر کا ہے۔ مرزا بایسنقر (التوری ۸۳۷ھ) بن شاہرخ بن تیمور کے ایما پر شاہنامہ کا ایک نسخہ مرتب کیا گیا اور اس پر ایک دیباچہ بھی لکھا گیا۔ یہ واقعہ ۸۲۹ھ کا ہے جیسا کہ ٹرنر میکان (Turner Macan) نے بیان کیا ہے۔

" *The first public attempt to correct the Shah Nama was made by order of Baysinqhur, grandson of Timur, and has already been appended to in a note in its preface. The editor in his preface states that Baysinqhur Khan took great delight in reading the Shah Nama but found the text was curruputed and filled with errors of every kind, thererfore he directed to collect all copies of Shahnama in his library and to correct the errors nd prepare a corrected one to be written. This was accordingly done and the copy completed in A.H. 829 (AD 1425)* "

یعنی صحیح شاہنامہ کی پہلی عام کوشش بایسنقر نبیرہ، تیمور کے حکم سے ہوئی جیسا کہ اس دیباچہ کے ایک نوٹ میں اس کی طرف اشارہ کیا گیا ہے، ایڈیٹر اس دیباچہ میں بیان کرتا ہے کہ بایسنقر کو شاہنامہ پڑھنے کا بہت شوق تھا لیکن اس نے شاہنامہ کے متن کو مسخ اور غلطیوں سے معمور پایا، اس نے حکم دیا کہ اس کے کتب خانہ میں شاہنامہ کے جتنے نسخے تھے ان سب کا مقابلہ کرکے صحیح نسخہ مرتب کیا جائے، اس کے حکم کی تعمیل میں یہ کام کیا گیا اور یہ نسخہ ۸۲۹ھ میں مکمل ہوا (جو مطابق ہے ۱۴۲۵ء کے)

دیباچہ مرزا بایسنقر اپنی نوعیت کے اعتبار سے پہلا مشہور مقدمہ ہے۔

اس سے قبل بیان کیا گیا ہے کہ ویلن برگ نے ۱۸۱۰ء میں شاہنامہ کے قدیم دیباچہ کا ترجمہ شائع کیا ہے خود اس نے بھی فرانسیسی زبان میں شاہنامہ پر ایک مقدمہ لکھا ہے۔

اس کے بعد ۱۸۳۷ء میں جولیس موہل (J.Mohl) نے فرانسیسی ترجمہ کے ساتھ شاہنامہ کی طباعت شروع کی، اس نے بھی اس کی ابتدا میں ایک مقدمہ لکھا، جس میں شاہنامہ کے عہد تصنیف اور اس کے ماخذوں پر بھی بحث کی ہے۔

ٹرنر میکان نے جب شاہنامہ ۱۲۴۵ء میں کلکتہ سے شائع کیا تو اس پر دو مقدمہ لکھے، ایک فارسی میں دوسرا انگریزی میں۔ فارسی مقدمہ

میں دیباچہ، مرزا ابوالسفر درج ہے اور اس کے ان تاریخی مندرجات سے جو اس کے نزدیک صحیح نہ تھے حاشیہ میں تعرض کیا ہے۔ انگریزی میں جو مقدمہ لکھا گیا ہے اس میں فارسی مقدمہ کا تمام مواد نہیں لیا گیا کیوں کہ اس میں خاص طور سے انگریزی داں طبقہ سے تخاطب ہے

شاہنامہ کے دیباچہ کے بعد مستشرقین نے عام طور پر عربی اور فارسی کتابوں پر مقدمہ لکھنا شروع کیا۔

مقدمۂ تاریخ طبری وغیرہ: بطریق مستشرقین جو مقدمے لکھے گئے اور یورپ سے شائع ہوئے۔ ان میں دو مقدمے ضخیم ہیں ایک مقدمہ تاریخ طبری جو لیدن (لندن) سے شائع ہوا ہے، یہ ۸۰۳ صفحات پر مشتمل ہے، اس میں فرہنگ لغات اور ایک ضمیمہ بھی شامل ہے، طبری کے تاریخی حالات بھی بیان کئے گئے ہیں۔

دوسرا وہ مقدمہ جو عوفی کی کتاب ''جوامع الحکایات'' پر لکھا گیا ہے، اس پر پروفیسر نکلسن Nicholson نے ایک دیباچہ بھی لکھا ہے۔ عوفی کی کتاب جیسا کہ اس کے نام سے ظاہر ہے حکایتوں کا مجموعہ ہے، اس کا مقدمہ چوالیس (۴۴) سطری بڑی تقطیع کے تین سو سولہ (۳۱۶) صفحوں پر مشتمل ہے۔ اس میں مصنف، تصنیف کے ماخذ، مختلف ترجموں اور حکایتوں کی تاریخی تقسیم وغیرہ سے متعلق بحث کی گئی ہے۔

مولوی عبدالحئی فرنگی محلی نے ہدایہ دو حصوں میں شائع کی تو اس پر مقدمہ بھی لکھا اور حاشیہ بھی، مقدمہ کے چند عنوانات ذیل میں درج کئے جاتے ہیں۔

(۱) هداية فى ترجمة مؤلف الهداية و ذكر تصانيفه[۲]   مؤلف ہدایہ اور ان کی تصانیف کا تذکرہ

(۲) هداية فى عادات صاحب الهداية فيها[۳]   مؤلف ہدایہ کی عادتِ ہدایہ میں (یعنی ان کا اسلوب)

(۳) هداية فى ذكر بعض اسانيد الىٰ مؤلف الهداية[۴]   مؤلف ہدایہ تک جو سندیں پہونچی ہیں ان میں بعض کا تذکرہ

یہ بیان مصنف، اس کے خصوصیات اور اس کی تصانیف سے متعلق ہے۔

چند اور عنوانات حسب ذیل ہیں۔

(۴) هداية فى تراجم من ذكر فى الجلدين الاولين من الهداية[۵]   ہدایہ کی دو جلدوں میں جن رجال کے نام آئے ان کا تذکرہ

(۵) هداية فى الانساب والقبائل و نحوها والواقعة فى الهداية[۶]   انساب قبائل وغیرہا کا بیان جو ہدایہ میں آئے ہیں۔

(۶) هداية فى شرح اسماء المواضع الواقعة فى الهداية[۷]   ان امکنہ کی شرح جن کے نام ہدایہ میں آئے ہیں۔

مذکورہ عنوانوں کے تحت ان رجال، انساب قبائل اور امکنہ کے حالات لکھے گئے ہیں جن کا ذکر ہدایہ میں آیا ہے۔

50

آخر اور نصف اول کے نصف جو شرح کی ان مبہمات	(۷) هداية فى شرح المبهمات الواقعة فى النصف
ان کا جانا بہت اہم ہے۔ جاتے ہیں پائے میں دونوں	الاول من الهداية والاخير كليهما و علمها من
	المهمات [۸]

مذکورہ عنوان کے تحت ان امور کی تشریح کی گئی ہے جنہیں صاحب ہدایہ نے مبہم چھوڑ دیا۔

ان لغزشوں کا ذکر جو صاحب ہدایہ سے نصف اول	(۸) هداية فى المسامحات التى وقعت من صاحب
میں ہوئی ہیں۔	الهداية فى النصف الاول منها [۹]
ان لغزشوں کا ذکر جو صاحب ہدایہ سے نصف دوم میں ہوئی	(۹) هداية فى ذكر بعض المسامحات التى وقعت
ہیں۔	فى النصف الاخير من الهداية [۱۰]

ان عنوانوں کے تحت ان لغزشوں کی تصحیح کی گئی ہے جو صاحب ہدایہ سے واقع ہوئی ہیں۔

معلم ثانی بونصر فارابی اور ارکان مقدمہ: اگر علمی طریقہ پر یہ معلوم کرنا چاہو کہ کسی کتاب یا کسی علم و فن کے سمجھنے کے لئے کن کن باتوں کا
بہ طور مقدمہ جاننا ضروری ہے تو ان امور پر غور کرنا چاہئے جن کا معلم ثانی بونصر فارابی (المتوفی ۳۳۹ھ) نے اپنی تصنیف ''ما ینبغی ان

تعلیم فلسفہ ارسطو سے پہلے جن اشیاء کا جاننا پہچاننا مقدم ہے ان	تیقدو الفلسفہ'' میں ذکر کیا ہے۔
کے بیان میں، جن پر اللہ پر بھروسہ کیا ہے اور وہ نو امور ہیں	توكلت على الله الاشياء التى يحتاج الى تعلمها و
	معرفتها قبل تعلم الفلسفة التى اخذت عن ارسطو
	وهى تسعة اشياء
اول فلاسفہ کے فرقوں کا نام	الاول منها اسماء الفرق التى كانت فى الفلسفة
دوم ارسطو کی غرض کا جاننا جو کچھ انہوں نے اپنی ہر ایک کتاب	والثانى معرفة غرضه فى كل واحد من كتبه
میں لکھا ہے	
سوم اس علم کی معرفت جس سے تعلم فلسفہ میں سر آغاز	والثالث المعرفة بالعلم الذى ينبغى ان يبدء به فى
ہو سکے۔	تعلم الفلسفة
چہارم اس غرض و غایت کی معرفت جو تعلم فلسفہ میں مقصود	والرابع معرفة الغاية التى تقصد اليها فى تعلم
بالذات ہے۔	الفلسفة

والخامس معرفة السبيل التى يسلكها من اراد الفلسفة

والسادس المعرفة بنوع كلام ارسطو كيف يستعمله فى كل واحد من كتبه .

والسابع معرفة السبب الذى وعا ارسطو الى استعمال الاغماض فى كتبه

والثامن من معرفة الحال التى يجب ان يكون عليها الرجل الذى يوجد عنده علم الفلسفة

والتاسع الاشياء التى يحتاج اليها من اراد تعليم كتب ارسطو.

فاما اسماء الفرق التى كانت فى الفلسفة فمشتقة من سبعة اشياء

احدها من اسم الرجل المعلم للفلسفة

والثانى من اسم البلد الذى كان مبدء ذلك الم

علم

والثالث من اسم الموضع الذى كان تعلم فيه

والرابع م التدبير الذى كان يتدبربه

والخامس من الاراء التى يراها اصحابها فى علم الفلفسفة

والسادس من امراء التى كان يراها اهلها فى الغاية التى يقصد اليها فى تعلم الفلسفة

والسابع من الافعال التى كانت تظهر عنه فى تعلم الفلسفة ۔ا

پنجم اس طریقہ کی معرفت جو فلسفہ کی راہ پر چلنے والوں کے لئے ضروری ہے

ششم ارسطو کے کلام کی نوعیت کا بیان جسے ارسطو اپنی تمام کتابوں میں کئی کئی طریقوں سے لاتا ہے۔

ہفتم اس سبب کا بیان جس نے ارسطو کو اپنی کتابوں میں بیان کو مبہم کر دینے پر آمادہ کیا۔

ہشتم وہ شخص جس کو فلسفہ سے لازمی مناسبت ہو اس کا کیسا حال ہونا چاہئے اس حال کی کیا تشریح ہے۔

نہم ان اشیاء کی معرفت کہ طالبان کتب ارسطو کے لئے ان کا جاننا لازمی ہے۔

جو فرق فلسفہ میں گزرے ہیں وہ دراصل سات چیزوں سے نکلے ہیں۔

اول۔ معلم فلسفہ کا نام

دوم۔ اس معلم کی نشو نما کا شہر

سوم۔ اس مقام کا نام جہاں اس نے تعلیم حاصل کی ہے

چہارم۔ وہ تحصیل فلسفہ میں کیا کیا تدبیریں کرتا تھا

پنجم۔ علماء کی وہ رائیں جو فلسفہ میں پیش نظر ہیں۔

ششم۔ وہ رائیں جو اہل علم تعلیم و تعلم فلسفہ میں مقصود بالذات سمجھتے تھے۔

ہفتم۔ تعلیم و تعلم فلسفہ کے زمانہ میں تعلم سے کیسے افعال ظاہر ہوتے تھے۔

ارسطو کا فلسفہ سمجھنے سے پہلے مندرجہ بالا امور کا جاننا بونصر فارابی کے نزدیک بطور مقدمہ کے ضروری تھا۔ یہی امور مقدمہ اور مقدمہ نگاری کا سنگ بنیاد ہیں۔ اس پر بعد کو محدثین اور مورخین نے عمارتیں قائم کر دیں۔ کسی عالم نے خواہ وہ مستشرق ہی کیوں نہ ہوں یہ حقیقت آج تک بیان نہیں کی۔

مقدمہ نگاری کے اہم خصوصیات: مقدمہ ابن الطقطقی (المتوفیٰ ۷۰۲ھ) نقش اول اور ابن خلدون (المتوفیٰ ۸۰۸ھ) کا مقدمہ نقش ثانی ہے۔ مذکورہ مقدموں اور مقدمہ فتح الباری سب کی بنیاد فارابی کے بیان کردہ امور ہیں اور مقدمہ ہدایہ کی بنیاد مقدمہ فتح الباری ہے ان مآخذوں سے مقدمہ نگاری کے یہ خصوصیات ظاہر ہوتے ہیں۔

(۱) ابن خلدون نے تاریخ لکھنے سے پہلے فن تاریخ کی حقیقت اور فضیلت بیان کی ہے، اس کے بعد اس نے تمدن کے اجزاء سے بحث کی ہے خصوصاً ان امور سے جو تمدن اور تاریخ کو متاثر کرتے ہیں مثلاً ایک جگہ وہ لکھتا ہے:

المقدمہ الرابعۃ فی اثر الھواء فی اخلاق البشر   چوتھا مقدمہ ہوا کے اثر میں جو اخلاق انسانی پر ہوتا ہے۔

دوسرے یہ کہ اس نے تاریخ بیان کرنے سے پہلے علوم وفنون اسلامیہ کی حقیقت بیان کی ہے۔ ظاہر ہے کہ اگر کوئی ایسی کتاب کا مقدمہ لکھنا چاہے جو کسی خاص مذہب سے متعلق ہو تو پہلے اس کو اس مذہب کی حقیقت اور خصوصیات بیان کرنا چاہیئے۔

(۲) فارابی کے نزدیک بہ طور مقدمہ کے یہ جاننا ضروری ہے کہ متعلم فلسفہ کا کیا نام تھا، اس کی نشوونما کون سا شہر تھا۔ اس نے کہاں تعلیم پائی تھی اسی طرح کسی مذہبی کتاب کے مقدمہ میں اس خاص مذہب کے بانی کے حالات اور اس کے وطن کا ذکر کیا جا سکتا ہے۔

(۳) مقدمہ فتح الباری یوں تو شرح بخاری کا مقدمہ ہے لیکن اس کا راست تعلق ''صحیح بخاری'' سے ہے اس سے یہ امور مستنبط ہوتے ہیں۔

(ا) پانچویں فصل میں لغاتِ غریبہ کی شرح کی گئی ہے، اس سے ظاہر ہے کہ کسی کتاب کے مقدمہ میں متن کتاب کے جزئیات کی بھی شرح کی جا سکتی ہے۔

(ب) چھٹی فصل میں اسماء والقاب وغیرہ کی توضیح کی گئی ہے اس سے اس بات کا اظہار ہوتا ہے کہ کسی کتاب میں کسی فرد یا افراد کا ذکر آیا ہو تو مقدمہ میں بطریق تاریخ وتذکرہ ان کا حال لکھا جا سکتا ہے۔

(ج) آٹھویں فصل میں دارقطنی کے اعتراضات کا جواب اور نویں فصل میں طعنِ رجال کو دفع کیا گیا ہے اس سے اس بات کا ثبوت ملتا ہے کہ کسی کتاب کے متن پر اصولی یا فروعی اعتراض ہو تو مقدمہ میں اس کو دفع کرنا چاہیئے۔

(۴) مقدمہ ہدایہ کی چند خاص فصلوں کا ذکر اس سے قبل کیا گیا ہے، حصہ اول کے مقدمہ میں ''شرح المبہمات'' کا ایک عنوان ہے، اس سے ظاہر ہے کہ متن میں کوئی امر مبہم یا مجمل ہو تو مقدمہ میں اس کی توضیح کی جانی چاہیئے۔

اسی طرح ''ہدایہ فی السماحات'' کے عنوان سے ظاہر ہے کہ صاحب متن سے کوئی لغزش ہوئی ہو تو مقدمہ میں اس سے تعرض کیا جائے گا۔ مندرجہ بالا بحث سے مقدمہ نگاری کے متعلق چار اہم امور کا پتہ چلتا ہے۔

(۱) رجال وامکنہ متعلقہ کی تاریخ وتذکرہ

(۲) شرح مبہمات

(۳) تصحیح مساحات

(۴) دفع اعتراضات

مقدمہٴ سراج الابصار کی نوعیت: سراج الابصار کے مقدمہ میں بھی مندرجہ بالاخصوصیات مقدمہ نگاری ملحوظ رہے ہیں اس کی تفصیل ذیل میں دی جاتی ہے۔

(۱) تاریخی عنصر

۱۔ امام علیہ السلام، آپ کے وطن اور آپ کے اصحاب کے حالات۔

۲۔ مہدوی مبلغین اور مہدوی مذہب کی تبلیغ۔

۳۔ مخالفین مہدویہ کے مآخذ۔

(ب) مشملات کتاب۔

(۱) شرح مبہمات۔ سراج الابصار میں تو کوئی امر مبہم نہیں ہے البتہ بعض امور جو مصنف نے مجمل طور پر بیان کئے ہیں ان کی توضیح کی گئی ہے۔ مثلاً صاحب سراج الابصار نے سفیانی کے متعلق یہ لکھا ہے کہ کتب صحیح میں اس کا ذکر ہی نہیں ہے اس سے استدلال کرنا صحیح نہیں۔

مقدمہ میں سفیانی کی روایت کا ماخذ بتا دیا گیا ہے اور اس کے خروج کی روایت کو جملہ موضوعات شیعہ ثابت کیا گیا ہے۔

صاحب سراج الابصار نے یہ بیان فرمایا ہے کہ امام علیہ السلام کے اخلاق وہی تھے جو رسول اللہ کے اخلاق تھے مقدمہ میں اخلاق مہدی کے ذیل میں اس کی تفصیل دی گئی ہے۔

(ج) تصحیح مسامحات۔ شیخ علی متقی مولف رسالۃ الرّد سے جو مسامحات ہوئے ہیں ان سے بھی تعرض کیا گیا ہے اس کے لئے ایک مستقل باب قائم کیا گیا ہے اس کا عنوان ہے مولف رسالۃ الرّد کا عقیدہ اور دیگر علامات مہدی۔

(۵) دفع اعتراضات۔ مولف ہدیہ نے سراج الابصار کے قائم کردہ دلائل سے گھبرا کر جس قدر اعتراضات امام علیہ السلام اور آپ کے اصحاب کرام وغیرہ پر کئے ہیں ان سب کو مقدمہ میں دفع کیا گیا ہے۔ اس کے علاوہ ابن خلدون سے لے کر آج تک مسئلہ مہدیت اور مذہب مہدوی پر جتنے بھی اعتراضات کئے گئے ہیں ان سب کی تردید کی گئی ہے۔

مقدمہ سراج الابصار کی ضخامت: ابن قتیبہ دینوری (المتوفی ۲۷۶ھ)[۱] نے ادب الکاتب لکھی اس کا مقدمہ یعنی مقدمہ طویل ہونے کی بناء پر اس کو خطبہ بلا کتاب کہا گیا ہے جیسا کہ صاحب کشف الظنون نے بیان کیا ہے۔

ادب الکاتب تصنیف ہے ابو محمد عبداللہ بن مسلم المعروف بہ ابن قتیبہ نحوی (المتوفی ۳۰۰ء) کی اس کا خطبہ طویل ہونے کی بناء پر کہا گیا ہے کہ وہ خطبہ ہے بغیر کتاب کے۔	ادب الکاتب لابی محمد عبداللہ بن مسلم المعروف بابن قتیبہ النحوی المتوفی ۲۷۰ سبعین و مائتین قیل ہو خطبۃ بلا کتاب لطول خطبتہ[۲]

مقدمہ کی ضخامت سے وہ لوگ تعرض نہیں کر سکتے جو محدثین اور مستشرقین کے طریق تحقیق سے واقف ہیں اس سے قبل مقدمہ ابن خلدون اور مقدمہ فتح الباری کا حال بیان کیا گیا ہے۔ اور اس کے ساتھ جوامع الحکایات کا بھی ذکر آ گیا ہے حکایتوں کے اس مجموعہ پر جو

مقدمہ شائع ہوا ہے وہ بڑی تقطیع کے چوالیس (۴۴) سطری تین سو سولہ (۳۱۶) صفحوں پر مشتمل ہے اور اس پر پیش لفظ پروفیسر نکلسن Nicholson نے لکھا ہے۔

رسالہ الثورۃ الھند یہ مصنف، مولوی فضل حق خیرآبادی (المتوفی ۱۲۷۸ھ) شائع ہو گیا ہے، یہ ۱۸۵۷ء کی جنگ آزادی سے متعلق ہے، چھوٹی تقطیع کے ایک سو پچیس ۱۲۵ صفحوں پر مشتمل ہے۔ ہر صفحہ پر عربی متن کے مقابل اس کا ترجمہ دیا گیا ہے۔ صرف عربی کے ساڑھے باسٹھ صفحے ہیں۔

عبدالشاہد خان شروانی (اورینٹل اسسٹنٹ لائبریرین مسلم یونیورسٹی علیگڑھ) نے رسالہ الثورۃ الھند یہ پر تین سو انہتر (۳۶۹) صفحات بطور مقدمہ لکھے ہیں، اس میں مولوی فضل حق خیرآبادی کی سوانح حیات، ان کی تصانیف اور ان کے تلامذہ کا سلسلہ تک بیان کیا گیا ہے، تعارف مولوی ابوالکلام آزاد نے لکھا ہے

یہ بھی واضح رہے کہ برنارڈ شا (Bernard Shaw) شہرہ آفاق مصنف کو ۱۹۲۵ء میں ادبیات کے لئے نوبل پرائز (Noble Prize) عطا ہوا تھا، اس نے متعدد ڈرامے تصنیف کئے ہیں اور ان پر خود ہی مقدمے بھی لکھے ہیں۔ اس کے مقدمے عموماً اصل تصنیف سے ضخیم ہوتے ہیں اس کا ڈرامہ موسوم بہ (Androcles & the Lion) اکتالیس (۴۱) صفحے (صفحہ ۱۰۳ تا ۱۴۴) پر مشتمل ہے اور برنارڈ شا نے اس پر ایک سو صفحے (صفحہ ۱ تا ۱۰۱) کا مقدمہ لکھا ہے۔ اور ڈرامہ کے آخر میں پانچ صفحے (صفحہ ۱۴۵ تا ۱۵۰) بطور ضمیمہ مقدمہ لکھے ہیں۔ ۲

مقدمہ کی ضخامت ان ہی لوگوں کی آنکھوں میں کھٹک سکتی ہے جو جاہل ہیں اور علم سے بے بہرہ ہیں۔

☆☆☆

Translation of the above mentioned Urdu Script:

In the name of Allah, the most benevolent and the most merciful.

"Muqaddama-e-Sirajul Absar"

Submission:(By Allamtul Asr, Hzt. Bazmi (Rh)

Syed Yaqoob Bazmi s/o Miyan Syed Mustafa, alais Khoob Seheb Miyan (burried in Chanchlguda,s/o Miyan Syed Yaqoob (Hyderabad), s/o Miyan Syed Noor Mohammad (Hyderabad) ,s/o Miyan Syed Ashraf (Kirgawal, Mysore), s/o Miyan Syed Abdul Lateef (Trichna Palli), s/o Miyan Syed Raje Mohammad (Channapatna,Mysore) s/o Miyan Syed Abdul Lateef (Surat, Gujrat), s/o Miyan Syed Jalal,Shaheed (Burhanpur). s/o Miyan Syed Abdul Lateef (Bijapur), s/o Bandagi Miyan Hazrat Syed Sharief Tashreef-e-Haq (Rz),(Jalgaon Jamood) s/o Bandagi Miyan Hazrat Syed Khundmir(Rz) (Sudrasan, Pattan,Chapaneer-Gujrat,), comes from the lineage of Imam Moosa Kazim(Rz); Khalifa-e-Hazrat Syed Mohmmed Juanpuri, Mahdi-e-Mauood, Alaihis Salato was salaam, (Farah Mubark, Afghanistan).

Its First Edition had 539 pages, including the Arabic Version of the original "Sirjul Absar", was published in 1365 Hijri at Hyderabad. On instructions from my father, I added more relevant material which doubled the size of the book. I have divided this book in four parts and also I have changed the arrangement of the chapters accordingly. On persuasion by my son Syed Mohammed Tashreefullahi, alias Miranji Miyan, I have started its printing and publication accordingly to his wish.

To reduce the voluminousness of the present edition of the book, I kept it on crown size paper. The previous edition was on royal size (paper), for that reason, the text was separated from "Muqaddama". But as far as the discussions are concerned, the text of "Sirajul Absar" and its translation has been provided for the convenience of the readers, to the extent necessity.

(A detailed discussion is submitted hereunder regarding writing of Muqaddama.)

Kinds of "Muqaddmas:

There are three kinds of Muqddamas.

One: which becomes a book in itself. It is not a part of the book. It is an art which is called "Muqaddama" of a book for which it is written. An example of this kind is an old Arabicbook, called "Muqaddasmatul Jermi", existing since long.

Muqaddamatul jermi was written by Umr ibn Saleh bin Ishaqul Al Jermi Al Basri (D.225 H.) It is written regarding grammar. Abul Hasan Mohammed bin Abdullah, known as 'Ibnul Waraqal Nahvi" (D.381 H.) had written its commentary under the title "Hidaya".

المقدمة الجرمی) وهوا عمر ابن صالح بن اسحق الجرمی البصری المتوفی سنة ٢٢٥ خمس و عشرين و مـائتيـن و هى فى النـحو شرحها ابو الحسن محمد بن عبدالله المعروف با بن الوراق النحوى المتوفى سنة ١٣٨١ احدى و ثمانين وثلا ث مائة و سماه بالهدايه

A. Thus it comes to light that such sort of writing was already in vogue during the 3rd. century Hijri. Another famous Muqaddamma was written by Ibn Salah.

"Muqaddama-e-Ibn Salah":

This Muqaddama speaks about the "Faculty of Traditions". Whoever reads it, he takes this book as a Muqaddama. Unless you read it you cannot understand the traditions of the holy Prophet (PBUH). Ibn Salah died somewhere in 643 H. Or 646 H.

B. Second one is that Muqaddama which becomes part of a book. The author includes such items without reading it, the reader cannot understand the text of the book. This type of Muqaddama was started by the Commentators..

"Muqaddama-e-Sahih Bukhri & Muslim":

Al-Muslim (D 261 H.) had written a Muqaddama at the beginning of his book. He had written the principles and conditions under which he had collected or avoided selection of the traditions in his (well known book on traditions) "Muslim". Commentators had agreed this book as a "Muqaddama".

Novavi had written the explanation of "Muslim" that:

"Narrated by Muslim Rh. that he had distributed traditions in three categories."

ذكر مسـلـم رحـمـه الله عـليه فى اول مقدمه صحيحه انه يقسم الاحاديث ثلاثة اقسام الى آخره

Moulvi Waheeduz Zaman had written about "Sahih Muslim" that: After Muqaddama of "Muslim" is completed, then discussion about "Ieman" starts.

"Muqaddama-e-Sunan-e-Abu Dawood":

Abu Dawood (275 H.) had written a letter to the residents of Makkah in which he had elaborated the significance of the "Sunan-e-Abu Dawood". This letter was written as a Muqaddama in the beginning of his "Sunan" and wrote that:

"Abu Dawood named his letter as "Muqaddama" which was written to the Makkans, by stating salutation: "Assalamo Alaikum" then states that he was offering praises to Allah, the Sustainer."

مقـدمـه قـال ابـو داؤد فـى رسـالة الى اهل مكه سـلام رسـالته عليكم فانى احمد اليكم اللّه الذى لا اِله الا هو والى آخره

Afterwards the commentators and Muhaddeseen developed the art of Muqaddama. Some examples are reported here:

"Muqaddama-e-ibnul Taqtaqi":

Mohammed bin Ali Taba Taba known as "Taqtaqi" had written a history under the title " "Kitabul Fakhri" in two volumes. While Volume One is a "Mqaddamah", Volume Two desals with the Historical Period from the "Khilphat-e-Rashida to the end of the period of "Khilaphat-e-Abbasia". This ewas written in 701 Hijri. Ibnul Taqtaqi himself informs that the First Volume deals with problems relating to a kingdom and about such inevitable issues like as to why a king has a peculiar position among his subjects and about those elements which are necessary to be dealt with by the king alone, and those problems which are relating in between the king and his subjects. It also deals with those affairs which are related to the people of a country. I had made it more lucid by including verses of Qur'an, traditions and interesting stories and poetry.

Jarji Zaidan (D.1333 H.) had written about this "Muqaddama" that:

This book contains a lengthy discussion about those issues which relate to a king, and to his subjects. In that sense this book has bcan righty dersignated as a "Philosophy of History, cultuyre and civilization of a country" and their cause and effect. It is just like that of Ibn Khaldun's, with a difference that Ibn Khaldun had discussed these issues in detail.By summing up, Jerji Zaidn says that while "Muqaddam-e-Ibn Taqtaqi" presents First hand Impressions, Ibn Khaldun's presents detaled impressionsd.

"In the beginning of the book the details of the Muqaddama had been written regarding problems relating to the kingdom and the politics of a country. It is something like historical philosophy, or about the culture and civilization as had been written by Ibn Khaldun in detail."

وفى صـدر الـكتـاب الـمقدمة طويلة فى الامور السلطانية والسياسيات الـملكية وهى من قبيل فلسفة التاريخ اوفى اسباب الحضارة نحوما فعل ابن خلدون فى مقدمته مطولًا

Jarji Zaidan has also written about the "Kitabul Fakhri" that:

"Thus "Muqaddama-e-Fakhri" or books like that deal with historical criticism. But Ibn Khaldoon had gone still beyond this scope in his "Muqaddama."

فمقدمة الفخرى هذا من قبيل الانتقاد التاريخى لكن ابن خلدون خطافى مقدمتة خطوه آخرى

From the writings of Jarji, it comes to knowledge that Kitabual Fakhri's Muqaddama which was written by Ibn Taqtaqi had become a pioneer in writing the Muqaddama, while Muqaddama-e-Ibn Khaldoon became its Second impression.

"Muqaddama-e-ibn khaldun":

Ibn Khaldun (D.808 H.) had written about history containing a Muqaddama and three books. This Muqadamma deals with the importance of the knowledge of history thoroughly researching it as an Art. In the first volume culture and its disorders have been discussed. Generally speaking, first volume deals with his Muqaddama . The Beirut edition, contains 552 pages, which is before us. The second volume is regarding information about the Arab countries and the third book is regarding the Burbers of Western Africa.

Ibn Khaldun had discussed in his Muqaddama that:

"Muqaddama presents the significance of knowledge of history and research of different branches of history and it points out those misunderstandings and apprehensions which the historians face and then discusses something about the causes and their effects."

الـمـقـدمة الفضل علم التاريخ وتحقيق مـذاهبـه والـمـاع لـما يعرض للمورخين من المغالطه والاوهام وذكر شئى من اسبابها

He had discussed about the first volume that:

"Temperaments of the mankind, disposition and their attributes which envelop the mankind from the very inception; like Badvi life, Urban life, culture, forced mastery, economic life, industrial development, education and their causes and effects."

الكتاب الاول فى طبيعة العمران فى الخليقة ومـايعـرض فيهـا مـن البـدو والـحضـرو التغلـب والكسب والمعاش والصنائع والعلوم ونحو ها وما لذالک من العلل والاسباب

His "Muqaddama" discusses particularly about three problems: 1. Regarding research pertaining to the Art of History and its prominence. 2. About culture and those problems which effect on its creation and destruction; and 3. A book regarding Islamic arts and sciences and their attributes.

Jarji Zaidan had written about "Muqaddma-e-Ibn Khaldun" that:

"Thus Muqaddama-e-Ibn Khaldun is the treasure of problems relating to a community, and its political , economics and a treasure of literary knowledge."

فمـقـدمة ابـن الـخـلـدون خزانة علوم واجتماعية وسياسية واقتصادية وادبية

Translation of this Muqaddama had been done in Turkish, English, French and German languages. (*I am doubtful whether it is available in Urdu also?*) Thus Ibn Khaldun had discussed those problems in the Muqaddama which help in understanding both second and third books.

Muqaddama-e-Fathul Bari:

Muhaddeseen gave a good regard to this Muqaddama becsause "Muqaddama-e-Fathul Bari" is an explanation of "Bukahri" which contains many volumes. Ibn Hajar Asqalani (D.852 H.) had written Muqaddama about such problems which could not be easily explained, which is known as "Muqaddama-e-Sharh-e-Bukhari." It relates to the original book, therefore it is correct to name it as "Muqaddama-e-Sahih Bukahri." "Muqaddama-e-Fathul Bari" was published in Egypt along with "Fathul Bari". It contains 494 pages of big size.

"Muqaddama-e-Fathul Bari" contains ten volumes which had been divided into three categories. First category contains about Imam Bukhari, his biography, his books and about his friends. The second category furnishes prominence of "Bukhari"(*as a book on traditions collected by Imam Bukhari*).

Third category discusses about its chapters. Some of them are mentioned hereunder:

"Fifth chapter contains an explanation of the vocabulary which is used in "Bukahri" in alphabetical order."

الـفـصـل الـخـامـس فى سياق ما فى الكتاب من الالفاظ الغربية على ترتيب الحروف مشروحا .

Thus the kind of vocabulary used in "Sahih Bukhari" had been explained in "Sharh-e-Muqaddama".

"Sixth chapter deals with names, patronymic names, titles and their genealogy."

الـفـصـل الـسـادس فى بيان المؤلف والمختلف مـن الاسـمـه والكنى والقاب والانساب مما وقع فى صحيح البخارى على ترتيب الحروف .

The above statement denotes about "Sahih Bukhari" in which the names, titles and chronology are mentioned. The facts are mentioned in the above muqaddama.

""Eighth chapter deals with those traditions on which Abul Hasan Daar-e-Qatni and others had criticized. This contains answers to those criticisms."

الـفـصـل الـثـامـن فى سياق الاحاديث التى انتقد عـليه حافظ عصره ابو الحسن الدار قطنى وغيره من الـنـقـاد وايـرادها حديثا حديثا على سياق الكتاب و سياق ما حضر من الجواب عن ذٰلک .

The above statement is regarding the critic of muqaddama-e-Dar-e-qatni, which is regarded traditions of "Bukhari Shareef"

"Ninth chapter pertains to those persons who had criticised, and written in alphabetical order along with respective answers for the criticism."

الـفـصل التاسع فى سياق اسماء من طعن فيه من رجـال هٰذا الـكـتاب مرتبا لهم على حروف المعجم والجواب عن الاعتراضات معها موضعا .

The third category of a muqaddama is that which is written by a literate on other literate's book. Its inception started from the preface of "Shahnama".

"Muqaddama-e-Shahnama":

There are two prefaces of the Shahnama. About the old one Mirza Abdul Wahab Qazvini had opined that it was written in the fourth century whose translation was done by an orientalist Wellen Bourg in 1810 AD and was published in Viena in Austria (Europe.)

Second preface was written under the orders of Mirza Baysinqar (D.837 H.) Bin Shahrukh bin Timur. "Shahnama's one volume was prepared in 829 H.

The first public attempt to correct the "Shahnama: was made under the orders of Mirza Bayasinaqar, grandson of Timur, which was accordingly appended as a note to its preface. The editor in his preface states that Bayasinaqar Khan took great pleasure in reading the Shahnama but found the text being corrupted and filled with errors of every kind. Thus he directed all the copies in his library to be collected and after correction, one alone to be written. This was accordingly done. And the (correct) copy was completed in AH 829 (1425 AD).

Its preface became famous as a Muqaddama.

We had already said that Wellen Bourg had translated the old preface of Shahnama and later on he translated it in French also. After him, in 1837, Julias Mohl had started French Translation again and he too wrote a Muqaddama on it which describes Shahnama's date of writing and its sources.

Turner Macan published "Shahnama" from Calcutta in 1245 AH. There are two different Muqaddamas, one in Persian and the other in English. English Translation does not contain all matters that had been discussed in the Persian translation, since the English Version was written according to the temperament of the English people.

After writing Muqadmma of "Shahnama" the orientalists started writing Muqaddama on many Persian and Arabic books.

"Muqaddama-e-Tareekh-e-Tabri":

There are two Muqaddmas written by the orientalists and were published in Europe, although voluminous, still got fame. One of them was "Muqaddama-e-Tareekh- e-Tabri"which was published in Leiden (London) contains 803 pages along with its glossary and a supplement about Tabri's biography.

Second one was written on the book of "Jawamul Hikayat" written by Aufi, for which professor Nicholson had written a preface.

Aufi's book contains stories which is clear from its name. A Muqaddama was written on 316 pages of big size. It discusses about the writer, the sources of the book, different translations and historical background of the stories.

"Muqaddama-e-Hidaya":

Moulvi Abdul Hai Farangi Mahli had written Muqaddamah on his book "Hidaya" which was written in two parts. He wrote explaining about his book. The following are the topics of the Muqaddama:

1. Description about the writer and his books,
2. The Style of the writer.
3. Description of the sources which reached to the writer.
4. The names which have been mentioned in both parts.
5. Genealogy of those tribes about whom discussion has been made in those books.
6. Explanation of the houses mentioned in the "Hidaya".
7. Explanation of the apprehensions mentioned in both parts.
8. The description of the mistakes occurred in part one of "Hidaya".
9. The description of mistakes occurred in part two of "Hidaya".

Thus the mistakes which occurred in both parts were duly corrected in the Muqaddama.

Mu'allim-e-Sani, Bu Nasar Farabi and pillars of Muqaddama:

If anyone wants to know and understand what elements are necessary for writing a Muqaddama on a book or to know the art of writing a Muqaddama, then he must study this book" Ma Yanbaghi in Tayaqaddmul falsafa" which was written by Muallim-e-Sani Bu Nasr Farabi (D 339 H.) Thus Farabi wrote in its beginning:

"In order to understand Aristotle's Philosophy, I implored the blessings of Allah. They are nine," as follows:

1. Names of the philosophers and their category.

2. To know the intention of Aristotle in his writtings for each of his books.

3. To understand preliminary knowledge regarding philosophy.

4. The knowledge and the purpose and its motive which seems necessary to understand the very intent of philosophy.

5. Knowledge of the lines on which someone wants to tread to understand his philosophy.

6. The styles of Aristotle's writings maintained by him in his different books.

7. Description of the reasons which persuaded Aristotle to create ambiguity in his statements.

8. The status of the person who had an inclination towards philosophy and the level of his status.

9. Knowledge of particular aspects necessary to understand his books by anyone.

Seven points that emerge in catogarization of Philosophy :

1. Name of the teacher of philosophy.

2. The city where the teacher was brought up.

3. Name the place where he obtained his education.

4. The procedure adopted to obtain knowledge of philosophy.

6. Views of learned people about nature of philosophy.

6. Views necessary to understand the intent of philosophy.

7. Seekers' symptoms and impressions noticed while teaching philosophy.

In order to understand Aristotle's philosophy, the above said points are necessary according to Bu Nasr Farabi. These are the basic features for writing the Muqaddama upon which the later Muhaddeseen and historians had constructed their own structure (for writing Muqaddama). No scholar, even an orientalist, had ever explained such points till today.

Distinctive Features of Muqaddama:

"Muqaddama-e-Ibnul Taqtaqi" (D.702) is the first impression and "Muqaddama-e-Ibn Khaldun" (D.808 H.) is the second Impression. Bu Nasr Farabi had mentioned such points necessary for writing a Muqaddama which are the basics for above mentioned Muqaddamas including "Muqaddama-e-Fatha Bari".

1. While writing about history, Ibn Khaldun had described the art of history and its prominence. Then he has discussed about the elements of culture and civilization. Particularly those items which effect history and culture of a country. For example he writes: Fourth Muqaddama about the atmosphere which effects the character of the mankind. Secondly, before describing history he had described the Islamic arts and sciences and their implications. It is a fact that if a man wants to write a Muqaddama on a book which pertains to a particular religion, then he must describe the details and particulars of that religion and about the founder of that

religion.

2. Farabi thinks it necessary to know the name of the teacher of philosophy, the name of the city in which he was brought up and where he was educated. In the same manner in a religious book it is necessary to write about the founder of that religion and his biography and about his country.

3. "Muqaddama-e-Fathul Bari" is the explanation of "Sharh-e-Bukhari"; still it has a direct link to "Sahih Bukhari" as well as on account of which the following points emerge:

A. The fifth chapter deals with the explanation of glossary which brings to light that for a Muqaddama of a book, not only its text is discussed, but its subsidiaries also.

B. The sixth chapter describes the names and titles. This tells that when discussion about a person or persons whose name or names referred in a book, then in its Muqaddama, their biography, history and some other particulars also require to be discussed.

C. The eighth chapter deals with the answers of the criticism of Dar-e-Qatni and the ninth chapter repudiates the criticism on Rijal. That means to say that if there is any remark about the text, that remark must be answered in the "Muqaddama".

4. We have discussed already about some chapters of "Muqaddma-e-Hidaya". In the first chapter there is a content regarding explanation of ambiguities. It tells that if there are such ambiguities in the text then those must be explained in its Muqaddamah.

In the same manner if the author had made mistakes in the book, then in the Muqaddama those mistakes must be answered.

From the above mentioned discussion we get four important points regarding writing the Muqaddama:

History of the persons and their status.

Explanation of ambiguities.

Corrections of mistakes.

Repudiation of criticism.

Nature of (my Book) "Muqaddama-e-Sirajul Absar":

"Muqaddama-e-Sirajul Absar" maintains the above mentioned particulars of writing the Muqaddama. The details are as mentioned below:

A. Historical facts;

1. About Imam Alihis Salaam, his place of birth, and details of his companions

2. Mahdavi Preachers and propagation of the Faith of Mahdavia community.

3. Sources of the opponents.

B. Contents of the book:

1. Explanation of ambiguities. There is no ambiguity in "Sirajul Absar", still in some matters which had been discussed in brief by the author, those matters had been explained. For example: the author had mentioned about Sufiani whose reference is not available in any books of Sihah, therefore the author had avoided any argument.

This Muqaddama describes the source of "Sufiani" and it had been proved that Sufiani is the creation of the Shias.

Author of the Sirajul Absar had stated that Imamana's characters were the same as what have been mentioned for the holy Prophet. In the Muqaddama under the chapter "Characters of Imam Mahdi". They have been discussed in detail.

C. Corrections of the negligence: A separate chapter deals with the beliefs of the author of "AL Rudd" and the signs of Imamana (As) .

D. Repudiation of criticism: Author of Hadia had raised objections on Imamana and his companions. In the Muqaddama these filthy objections were repudiated. Apart from this the opponents of our Faith, from Ibn Khaldun to those who ever had raised silly objections on Mahdiat and Mahdavi Faith have been properly and befittingly refuted.

Voluminouness of "Muqaddama-e-Sirajul Absar":

Ibn Qutaiba Denoori (D276 H.) had written "Aadaabul Kaatib"and Its Khutbah/Muqaddama was very bulky, hence it was called Muqaddama without book as reported by Author of "Saheb-e-Zannoon":

"Aadaabul Kaatib is a book written by Abu Mohammed Abdullah bin Muslim (D39H.) known as Ibn Qatiba Nahvi. Its muqaddama was so bulky that it was named "Muqaddama without book."	ادب الكاتب لا بى محمد عبدالله بن مسلم المعروف بابن قتيبه النحوى المتوفى ٢٧٠ سبعين ومائتين قيل هو خطبة بلا كتاب لطول خطبته

Those who knew the procedure of research adopted by the Muhaddiseen and the orientalists did not object about the bulkiness of Muqaddama. Before this we have already discussed about "Muqaddama-e-Ibn Khaldun" and Muqaddama-e-Fatha Bari and also about "Jaameul Hikaayaat". The Muqaddama written on the stories contains 316 pages of big size.

"Risala-e-Sourathul Hindia" which was written by Moulvi Fazl-e-Haq Khairabadi (D 1278 H.) regarding Independence battle of 1857 AD contains 124 pages. Every page contains Arabic text and its translation. Arabic version itself contains 52 pages.

Abdul Shahid Khan Sherwani (Assistant to the Oriental Librarin, Muslim Aligadh University) had written Muqaddama about 369 pages in the above mentioned book which contains the biography, his other books of Moulvi Fazl-e-Haq Khairabadi and about his education etc. upon which Moulana Abul Kalam Azad had written an Introduction.

Bernard Shaw, the well known author, who got the Noble Prize in 1825 AD on his writings. He wrote many dramas and he himself wrote Muqaddamas on his dramas. His Muqddamas were more voluminous than his original dramas. For example his Drama on "Andraculous and the Lion" contains only 41 pages (104 to 144) and Bernard Shaw had written Muqaddama on 100 pages. Further at the end he wrote five pages as a supplement also.

Thus the voluminousness of the Muqaddama provides more details of knowledge not available in other books, hence should not be objected.

*****

Arrangement of the "Muqaddama-e- Siraj-ul-Absar".

"Muqaddama-e-Sirajul Absar" is divided in four parts, with chapters, accordingly. On the request of his son Syed Muhammad Tashreefullahi, alias Miranji Miyan, its publication was undertaken.

The present "Muqaddama" consists:

Part One:

1. Chapter one   : Imamana's genealogy, and about his early life;

2. Chapter Two   : Migration and Proclamation of his Mahdiath;

3. Chapter Three   : Proofs of Mahdiat;

4. Chapter Four   : Companions of Imamana (As);

5. Chapter Five   : Daira-e-Mahdavia and religious beliefs of Mahdavis;

6. Chapter Six   : Traditions with regard to Imam Mahdi (As) and criticism of Ibn
                       Khaladun and other decliners.

7. Chapter Seven   : Proofs regarding obligations;

Part Two:

Chapter1   : Characters of Imamana (As);

Chapter2   : Imamana's opinion about the Saints ;

Chapter3   : Imamana's opinion about his companions;

Chapter4   : Imaman's opinion about the prophets;

Chapter5   : Imamana's opinion about monotheism and its explanations;

Chapter6   : Imamana's opinion regarding consistency in the Holy Qur'an

Part Three:

Characters: Imamana's companions and successors:

1. Bandagi Miyan Syed Mahmood, Sani-e-Mahd (Rz)

2. Bandagi Miyan Syed Khundmir, Siddiq-e-Vilayeth (Rz)

3. Bandagi Shah Nemat (Rz)

4. Bandagi Shah Nizam (Rz)

5. Bandagi Shah Dilawar (Rz)

6. Miyan Ilahdad Hameed (Rz) and others.

Part Four:

1. Sources of objections by the opponents;

2. Objections on"Sirajul Absar"; their analysis and replies;

3. Demand for correcting the "Sayings (Naqliats)" and its reply;

4. Belief of the Author of "Al Rudd" and the Signs of Mahdi Alaihis Salaam;

5. Lofty Status of Imamana, as Mahdi-e-Akhiruz Zaman (As).

PART ONE

CHAPTER ONE
Genealogy of Imamana (As) and his early life:

Shaik Ali Muttaqi has said twice in his book "AL-RUDD" that:

"(There are persons who) believe in the Mahdiat of one person who died fifty years ago"

يعتقدون فى شخص مات وله نحو خمسين سنة

(سراج الابصار مع مقدمه ـ طبع اول ـ۴)

With reference to Imaamat (leadership) he says:

"The late Syed was not the Mahdi."

فعلم ان السيد الميت ليس بمهدى

(سراج الابصار مع مقدمه ـ طبع اول ـ۲۱۶)

It may be pointed out that Imamana's opponents have accepted his greatness on account of his continuous spreading the message of monotheism during his long twenty three years journey by propagating his mission in India, Pakistan, Afghanistan, Iran, Turkistan, Arabian Countries etc. Still the author of the AL- RUDD denies accepting the facts of his proclamation as the Promised Mahdi. Thus this chapter tells all about Imamana (As) and his greatness. However, Shaik Ali has conceded about Imamana's lineage, but another author (Zaman Khan) in his book "Hadia-e-Mahdavia" has totally denied Imamana's genealogy and he is doubtful that Imamana (As) comes from the Ahle Bait (Rz). Therefore it was necessary to refute those baseless and wrong statements about Imamana (As), because both authors had tried to create rifts among Muslim masses about Imamana (As).

Chapter two:
Migration and Proclamation of Mahdiat

Author of the "Al Rudd" has written that"

"It means to say that the followers of the late Syed are innovators, but it cannot be said or thought that the late Syed was also the innovator. Wallahu Aalam!

فالمقصود من هذا ان بدعة هذه الطائفة المقرين بمهدوية ذلك السيد المرحوم لا تقتضى ان يكن هو مبتدعا لا يظن به هذا والله اعلم .

(سراج الابصار مع مقدمه ـ طبع اول ـ ٢٣٦)

He further maintained that by admitting him as Mahdi by some persons, it did not imply that Imamana himself had declared to be the Mahdi. Therefore this chapter provides details of his a migration. It was necessary to introduce a fresh chapter regarding his migration and proclamation along with the statements of his non mahdavi contemporaries who had admitted about Imam's proclamation of Mahdiat.

CHAPTER THREE
PROOFS OF MAHDIAT

The author of the "Al Rudd" had said that:

"Some persons had accepted him as Mahdi, just on the presumption that Imamana (As) was the descendant of the Prophet (Slm) and he carries the name as Mohammad (Slm)."

بمجرد علمهم انه اولاد الرسول واسمه محمد يعتقدون انه هو المهدى .

(سراج الابصار مع مقدمه ـ طبع اول ـ ١٢٦)

In this chapter all proofs about Mahdiat have been presented and Shaik's contention had been completely refuted. Further, we Mahdavis believe him as Mahdi (As) according to the traditions regarding his characters to which he acted accordingly.

A. Prophecies in Scripts:

The author of the "Al-Rudd" says that:

(1) "Mahdavis always try to manipulate the meanings of any Hadith according to their beliefs and that they also try to interpret even the Qur'an in their favour and beliefs."

(١) واكثر الاحاديث وجلها يا ولون على رائهم كما ياولون القرآن لا ثبات مدعا هم .
(سراج الابصار مع مقدمه ـ طبع اول ـ ١٠)

(٢) لانهم اعتقدوا ما يخالف ظواهر الحديث
(سراج الابصار مع مقدمه ـ طبع اول ـ ٣٠)

(2) Because they believe in such things which are against the meanings of the traditions.

Therefore in order to refute Shaik's wrong contention, we have provided prophecies of the scriptures about the holy Prophet to show how those prophecies are applicable; and why prophesies about Imamana (As) could not be applicable.

B. Traditions of the Prophet (Slm) about Advent of Mahdi (As)

Shaik Ali Muttaqi has written about the Traditions, regarding the advent of Mahdi that:

""These explicit traditions are against the coming of Mahdi."

والاحاديث الصرائح تخالفه
(سراج الابصار مع مقدمه ـ طبع اول ـ ٤)

This chapter proves the correctness of those traditions which point out about the coming of Mahdi in the 10th. Century Hijri, and thus the Shaikh's assertion has been totally rejected.

C. Verses of the Qur'an:

In this chapter those verses have been mentioned which, according to Imamana (As) refer to the person of Mahdi.

This chapter rejects the contention of the Shaik that we Mahdavis accepted him as Mahdi (As) only because "He belongs to the descendents of the holy Prophet (Slm)".

D. Characters of Mahdi: Author of Sirajul Absar has written with reference to the tradition of Hirql that:

"Thus persons of understanding must know that we Mahdavis have accepted the Mahdiat of that Mahdi (As) and his companions who were blessed with those characteristics mentioned in those traditions."

فاعلم ايها البصير ان من نصدقه بالمهدوية كان من شانه واصحابه ما ذكر فى الحديث .
(سراج الابصار مع مقدمه ـ طبع اول ـ ١٩٢)

According to the clarifications given by author of "Sirajul Absar", various topics have been used to prove that Mahdi's characters were the same as that of the Holy Prophet(Slm).

CHAPTER FOUR:

Companions of Mahdi (As)

Shaik Ali Muttaqi has referred in his Al Rudd that:

"Eminent persons did not take oath of allegiance on Mahdi's hand, hence whoever proves his Mahdiat, his contention has been voided."

لم يقع له بيعة اهل الحل والعقد فسقط قول من يثبت امامة .

(سراج الابصار مع مقدمه ـ طبع اول ـ ۲۱۸)

In order to nullify Shaik's above allegation, we have discussed about those companions including kings, ministers and eminent personalities who have accepted his Mahdiath.

CHAPTER FIVE:

Dairh-e-Mahdvia, Mahdavis and their Faith:

Shaik Ali Muttaqi had stated about the Dairahs that:

"For that reason, you know that commoners and Illiterates became devotees of the innovators."

ولهذا ترى الجهال والعوام يعتقدون لهذه الطائفة المبتدعة .

(سراج الابصار مع مقدمه ـ طبع اول ـ ۴۲)

In this Chapter, it has been proved through the writings of eminent Indian historians and personalities who had visited those Dairahs, that Mahdavis had tried to propagate the spirit of the Real Islam of the period of the holy Prophet (Slm) and acted according to the Qur'an and Sunnah for eradication of innovations and bidet which was engulfed over the Muslim Ummah and discussed about the main goal of Mahdavis was to eradicate those evils.

Mahdavi Preachers:

Shaik Ali Muttaqi tells that Mahdavis were not able to present their purpose:

His words are as follows:

"It is a proof of their ignorance, misguidedness and inability to prove their false faith."

وكفىٰ هذا دليلا على جهلهم وضلالتهم وعجزهم عن اثبات مدعاهم الباطل .

(سراج الابصار مع مقدمه ـ طبع اول ـ ۶۴)

In order to refute Shaik's unwarranted remarks against those preachers, it has been tried to demonstrate how those preachers were able to defeat non Mahdavi scholars in their discussions about Mahdiat.

CHAPTER SIXTH:

Propagation of Mahdavi Beliefs:

Shaik Ali Muttaqi had notoriously stated in his Al-Rudd about Mahdavis:

"Thus one group is available in the Indian cities"

ثم طائفة فى بلاد الهند .

(سراج الابصار مع مقدمه ـ طبع اول ـ ۴)

The truth is that during the time of the Shaik, at many places in the Eastern and the Western India, Mahdavis were living everywhere. Although he has referred about India only, whereas Mahdavis were also residing in Pakistan, Afghanistan, Iran, and Turkistan. In order to refute his comments, this chapter tells regarding propagation of our faith, And in it, his comments that Mahdavis were not able to convince their Faith were refuted. Although there was no government patronage for Mahdavis, but through their convincing arguments based on reasons, propagation was going on smoothly. Further, the author of Hadia also had raised objections on historical facts, that has also been refuted in this chapter.

CHAPTER SEVENTH:

Ibn Khaldun wrote a preamble to his book on history. He has questioned on certain Traditions regarding Advent of Mahdi (As). Traditions of the Holy Prophet (Slm) are the best source to prove Mahdiat. Therefore, this chapter presents authenticity of those traditions.

CHAPTER EIGHT:

Recognition of obligations:

Author of "Sirajul Absar" has maintained that real Islamic Law (Shariah) has been proclaimed by Imam Mahdi (As). The wordings of "Sirajul Absar"are mentioned below:

"Real Islamic Law (Shariah) was that which was pronounced by Imam Mahdi (As)."

بل الشرع الحقيقى هو الذى يبينه .
(سراج الابصار مع مقدمه ـ طبع اول ـ ۱۲۲)

Further he states that:

"That Imam Mahdi (As) was the final authority with regard to Shariat-e-Mustafavai (Slm)."

بل وجدناه حاكما فى الشرع الاجتهادى و مبينا له . (سراج الابصار مع مقدمه ـ طبع اول ـ ۱۷۰)

We have substantiated our discussion on the arguments presented by Miyan Aalim Billah (Rh) regarding obligations of Vilayet.

PART TWO:

Chapters: one to six

Miyan Abdul Malik Sujawandi (Rh) has stated that:

"The aspect that makes affirmation of a person is his characters. Since affirmation of the prophets (As) was also accepted on the basis of their characters. Hence character is the real basics for any affirmation."

لان الذى وجب التصديق به فهو ما وجب به
تصديق الانبياء من الاخلاق لانها هى العلة فى
التصديقات والاصل فيها .
(سراج الابصار مع مقدمه ـ طبع اول ـ ۱۶۸)

As a reply to the above contention, Author of Hadia had raised objections on the characters of Imamana (As) in his book's third, seventh and a portion of eight chapters. In order to refute his nefarious objections on the characters of Imamana (As), we have discussed in chapters one to five of this part about different categories. Imamana (As) had stated that "No verse of t he Qur'an has been abolished".

The author of Hadia on page 198 had labled Imamana (As) as rude; and he had maintained that since some verses of Qur'an are abolished, the Qur'an has become inconsistent. Therefore, in Chapter six, as commanded by Imamana (As), we have submitted proofs of the consistency of the Holy Qur'an.

PART THREE:
Chapters one to six

Shaiak Ali Muttaqi has told that authorities did not accept allegiance of Imamana (As). In refutation of his contention, Aalim Billah Miyan Abdul Malik Sujawandi (Rh) has narrated the ranks of those who had accepted Imamana's allegiance:

"How could the rank of the authorities be equal to that of those who were flanked by the angels."

واين اهل الحل والعقد من مرتبتهم هم القوم حفتهم
الملائكة .   (سراج الابصار مع مقدمه ـ طبع اول ـ ۲۳۴)

To refute the statement of Allama Sujawandi (Rh), author of Hadia had written at the end of chapter 2,3, premises 7 & 8 in which he had raised questions regarding characters of Imamana (As) and created many doubts about them.They have been denied in Chapters one to six.

Miyan Abdul Malik Sujawandi (Rh) had narrated about the peculiarity of the worship of his companions, who were the followers of the successors of Imamana (As).

"I had seen my companions who were weeping during worship and used to offer prayers by standing night after night, for which their legs became swollen."

وجدت نا كثيرا من اصحابنا باكين من الم
الفراق متور مى الاقدام من قيام اليالى الى آخره .
(سراج الابصار مع مقدمه ـ طبع اول ـ ۱۷۴)

He has further written:

"They are the followers of the successors of Imam (As), who are expert in healing spiritual diseases. Then what should have been their opinions about Imamana (As)"

فهو لاء تابعون لاصحاب المهدى فاذا كان اصحابه اطباء هذقاء يداوون المرضى بالامراض الروحانية فما ظنک بذاته .

(سراج الابصار مع مقدمه ـ طبع اول ـ م ـ ۱۷۴)

In order to refute that contention, author of Hadia has accused Miyan Abdul Malik Sujawandi (Rh) by alleging that he had distorted. To refute this unwanted objection, reply had been given in chapters 1,2 and 3 of part 3.

Further, we have aptly refuted his remarks and doubts about Bandagi Miyan Syed Khundmir (Rz), Khalifa Giroh (Rz) and Syed Mahmood, Khaatimul Murshid (Rz) son of Bandagi Miyan (Rz), in chapter six.

PART FOUR
CHAPTER ONE
Sources of opponents of Mahdavia:

In this chapter facts about "Al Rudd" and "Hadi-e-Mahdavia" have been narrated, since these two are the main sources of the opponents.

Chapter Two: Deals with the objections on "Sirajul Absar" itself. We have tried to investigate these baseless objections raised by the author of Hadia. Objections raised in "Muqaddama", pertaining to traditions mentioned in "Bukhari" have been also investigated in order to justify our contention.

Chapter Three: Demand for Correction of Naqliat-e-Imamana(As) and Answers:

Author of Hadia had demanded correction of certain Naqals (Sayings). The same has been minutely discussed in this chapter.

Chapter four: Beliefs of author of AL Rudd and Signs of Mahdi:

This chapter deals with the connivance of the author of Al Rudd.

Chapter Five: Al Rudd tells that Mahdi (AS) was not innocent from errors, but was guarded from committing errors. To refute such charges, this chapter mentions Imam Mahdi's attributes.

"Muqadamma-e-Sirajul Absar" is a befitting Reply to those who oppose:

Answers to Hadia have been given to the objections made in Hadia. These answers pertain to which part and which chapter has been mentioned properly. The answers are mentioned as under:

Answer to chapter one of Hadia-e-Mahdavia has been given in many chapters which is regarding Beliefs, but according to the purpose it has three issues:

(1) Attributes of the Imamana (As)

(2) Obligations of mysticism (Vilayet)

(3) Attributes of the companions and their successors.

Chapters 4 and 5 deal with objections regarding Imamana's attributes. Proof of obligation is discussed in part one, chapter eight: Remarks made against the companions have been refuted in

Part two, chapter three.

Chapter two of Hadia is regarding historical facts. They have been discussed in Part one, chapters 2,4, 5 and 6. As well as in Part four, chapter one.

Chapter three refers to three objections raised in Hadia:

    a. Qur'an and appearance of Imam Mahdi (As).

    b. Traditions of the Prophet (Slm) regarding Mahdi (As).

    c. Characters of Imamana (As).

Part Four's, Chapters 4 and 5 deal with detailed discussion regarding the Qur'an and Mahdi.

Part One, Chapter 2,3; of Part Four, Chapters 2 and 4 deal with those Traditions which have been narrated by holy Prophet (Slm) regarding Mahdi (As), which are compatible.

4. Author of Hadia has raised objections about Imamana (As), those have been refuted in chapters 4 to 8, and about objections regarding Sayings of Imamana (AS) have been discussed in Part two, chapter 1 and 6.

5. Hadia's chapter 4 to 7 contain objections on the companions, answers have been given in Part three, chapter 1 to 6

6. Hadia's chapter 8 is mainly a repetition of chapter one, based on objections regarding "Taswiath" which had been extended in chapter 8, and the answer is given in chapter 5 of part four.

The answers to the objections raised by Ibn Khaldun, Sir Syed Ahmed Khan, Margoliath in part one, chapter 7 and that of Mahmood Shirani in part one's chapter one have been given accordingly.

Al Hamdu Lillah, in writing this voluminous book I got help and inspiration from the Almighty alone. This was completed on the Lailatul Qadr, 27th. Ramazan 1382 H/ 22nd. February 1963. Which presents proof and the characters of Imamana Mahdiie-Maoud, Alaihis Salam.

Translator's Note:

The following Persian couplet compiled by Hazrat Bazmi Rh. after he successfully completed this voluminous Encyclopadic type of book, as a thanksgiving presentation to the Almighty is translated in English..

حـــاصـلِ عـمـــر نثـــار رہ یـــارے کـردم

شـــادم از زنـدگی خـویش کہ کـارے کردم

Roman:"   Haasilay umr, nisaray rahay yarey kardam"

      Shaadam uz zindagi-e-kheesh kay karay kardam"

Translation: Whole of my life, I have spent on the path of (my friend), the Almighty Allah,

    I am happy that my life has accomplished my goal!.

PART ONE
CHAPTER ONE
Genealogy And
Early Life of Imamana Mahdi Alaihis Salaam.

Genealogy:

Imamana's name is Syed Mohammed (As) and his patronymic name is Abul Qasim. His father's name is Syed Abdullah, who was awarded the title of Syed Khan (by the king of Sharqi Kingdom). He was born on Monday, the 14th. Jamadiul Awwal, 847 H, in Juanpur, (UP.India) which was the capital of the kingdom of the Sharqia Dynasty. Moulvi Khairuddin, author of "Juanpur Nama" has written that:

S.M. Jafer's Book "Education in Muslim India" (printed in Lahore in 1936, pages 143 and 144) mention about Moulvi Khairuddin Mohammed of Allahabad.

"Almost about the same time Khairuddin Mohammed of Allahabad, author of "Tazkirathul Ulema", (Memoirs of the Renowned Scholars of Juanpur), Ibrat Nama, Gawaliar Nama, Balwanth Nama, and "Juanpur Nama" kept a madressa at his native city till the sale of Kora and Allahabad by the East India Company to Nawab Shujaud-Daula."

On the margin of Page 144 of this book it is mentioned that Sanaullah Khan had translated "Tazkeratul Ulema".

Moulvi Khairuddin Mohammed Saheb had translated into Persian the book "Eqdul Faraez" of Shaik Abdul Qader Imadi, Juanpuri, one of its copies is available in the State Central Library, Hyderabad, India".

.-- -- --------

"Khaja Abdullah, father of Hazrath Syed Mohammad (As), was granted the title of "Syed Khan" by the Kingdom. And that Imamana's mother Aamina Khatun was the sister of Qiwamul Mulk and became known as Agha Malik. Both father and mother came from the lineage of Saadat-e-Bani Fatima (Rz)".

پدرش خواجه عبدالله از جانب سلطنت سید خان خطاب داشت و مادرش آمنه خاتون که خواهر قوام الملك باشد به آغا ملك مخاطب بود ، هر دو مادر و پدر از اجلّه سادات بنی فاطمه بودند

Author of "Juanpur Nama" had written about the mother of Imamana (As) that she was a Hasani Syeda. The wordings of "Juanpur Nama" are as below:

"Father Husaini and mother Hasani" (Father from Imam Husain (Rz) and mother from Imam Hasan (Rz).

But from the version of "Khatim-e-Sulaimani", she was Husaini. This fact has also been written:"Her father's name also was Syed Abdullah, and according to Syed Jalaluddin, she joined upward to the genealogy of Imamana (As). However it is a confirmed fact that she also belonged to the Husaini Lineage; Thus both sources confirm that she was from Bani Fatima (Rz). As per the author of "Shawahedul Vilayet", Bandagi Miyan Syed Burhanuddin (Rz) (Died 1009 H.) confirms the statement of "Juanpur Nama" and states that:

"Her brother Malik Qiwamul Mulk was a mystic and a pious man."

برادران ایشان المسی ملك قوام الملك كه اہل طریقت و اہل باطن بودند (باب سوم)

In Juanpur there is a grave on which Syed Ali Qiwam (died 905 H) has been engraved, it is possible that the word "Qiwam" is the abbreviation of "Qiwamul Mulk".

Author of "Juanpur Nama" has also written that Imamana (AS) came from the lineage of Imam Moosa Kazim (Rz), which was admitted by Ali Sher Khanay in his "Tuhfathul Kiram", who states that "Syedul Aoulia, Syed Mohammad (As), known as Meeran Mahdi (As), son of Mir Abdullah, known as "Syed Khan", had direct link to Imam Moosa Kazim (Rz).

This statement provides four points:

1. Imamana (As) was known as "Syedul Aoulia (As)".

2. He was also known as "Meeran Mahdi (As)",

3. His father's name was Syed Abdullah and the title was "Syed Khan".

4. He came from the lineage of Imam Moosa Kazim (Rz).

"Tuhfathul Kiram" was written in Sindh, states that Ali Sher Khaney (author of Tuhfathul Kiram, was himself a Mahdavi) had joined the service of Ghulam Shah Khan(Kalhora, a Mahdavi Dynasty) to write the biography of the family of Ghulam Shah Khan. That is how "Tuhfathul Kiram" was written in which it is mentioned that Sahebzada Sir Faraz Khan(Kalhora) son of Miyan Ghulam Shah Khan was the ruler of Sindh. (Vol 3, page 226).

"Juanpur Nama" was written in Juanpur as per instructions of a Judge Mr. Abraham Wiland. Both books agree that Imamana's father's name was Syed Abdullah, who was also known as "Syed Khan". This fact was well known all over India at that time.

Hzt. Aalim Billah Miyan Abdul Malik Sujawandi (Rh) had referred his answer to a third question of Miyan Mubarak (Rh) of Nagore. He has referred this Tradition, in his other book "Minhajuth Taqweem" which states that the name of the father of Imamana (As) will be the same as that of the name of the father of the holy Prophet (Slm). From this it is construed that if the name Abdullah had not been famous at that time, Allama Sujawandi (Rh) would not have referred to this Tradition at all.

Yet another author of "Makhzanul Dalaael" also has referred the same Tradition in which the name of the father of Imamana (As) has been quoted, similar to the name of the father of the Holy Prophet (Slm).

It seems that the name "Meeran" was well known all over India, therefore Mohammad

Masoom Bahekri also known as Naami has written in his "History of Sindh" while referring the name of Qazi Qadan (Rz), that:

"He was one among the denoted disciples of Syed Mohammad Juanpuri (As), known as Meeran Mahdi (As)."

در سلك مریدان و معتقدان سید محمد جون پوری
که به میران مهدی مشهور است انتظام داشته

It is also a fact that in the city of Juanpur:

"He, (Imamana As), was known as Meeranji (As) and he was well known as Khaja among the Scholars."

خودش دراین دیار بلقب میران جیو مشتهر باشد و
و بین العلماء شهرت بخواجه هم دارد

In Mahdavi literature too, while referring to Imamana (As), it is often written as "Meeran (As) stated", or "Meeranji stated". The author of "Farhangay Asafia" has clearly written in the chapter of "Aoulia-e-Hind", that "Meeran Syed Mohammad Junapuri (As), was the twelfth descendant of Imam Moosa Kazim (Rz), was the son of Mir Syed Abdullah, alias Budha Saheb of Juanpur who was born to Bibi Aamina in the year 847 H at Juanpur". In Deccan also the word Meeran has been mentioned for Imamana (AS). Thus it is an established fact that even from the books written by Non Mahdavi authors; Hazrath Mahdi Alaihis salaam comes from the lineage of Imam Moosa Kazim (Rz), therefore the author of "Juanpur Nama" has correctly written about him that:

" Descendant of Hazrath Jafer Bin Moosa Kazim ibn Jafer-e Sadeque (Rz), came from that lineage and Hazrat Jafer (Rz) was also known as Nemathullah (Rz)."

از نسل حضرت جعفر بن موسیٰ کاظم ابن جعفر
الصادق رضی الله عنهم و همین جعفر را نعمة الله می
گفتند(باب پنجم)

Hazrath Ameer Syed Mohammad Mahdi-e-Mauood, khathim-e-Vilayeth, ibn Syed Abdullah, bin Syed Osman, bin Syed Khizer, Bin Syed Moosa, bin Syed Qasim, bin Syed Abdullah, bin Syed Yousuf, bin Syed Yahiya, bin Syed Jalaluddin, bin Syed Ismael, bin Syed Nemathullah, bin Imam Moosa Kazim (Rz).

In" Merajul Vilayath" also the same genealogy has been recorded as "Nemathullah bin Syed Ismael, Bin Imam Moosa Kazim (Rz)." In this way we have two sources:

One states that "Nemathulla bin Syed Ismail": The other states "Syed Ismail bin Syed Nematullah" But just with a minor difference, the whole genealogy could not become doubtful. Both "Juanpur Nama" and the Mahdavi literature are firm to believe that Imamana (As) was the descendant of Imam Moosa Kazim (Rz). The author of "Khatim-e-Sulaimani" also has testified in his book's Part Four, chapter One, in which he has referred the genealogy of Imamana (As) and the genealogy of Hazrath Bandagi Miyan Syed Khundmir (Rz), that both have joined at the twelfth generation to Syed Nemathullah bin Syed Ismael, bin Syed Moosa Kazim (Rz).

The source of this genealogy refers to the genealogy of Malik Sharfuddin (Rz) which was written in 1112 H. as recorded in the "Khatim-e-Sulaimani". The author of "Mazahebul Islam" also had based on the genealogy as reported by "Khatim-e-Sulaimani", stating "Syed Jalaluddin bin Amir Syed Nemathullah, bin Amir Syed Ismail, bin Amir Syed Moosa Kazim (Rz). These Sources have been written long before the book "Hadia Mahdavia" was written. This also confirms that Imamana (As) comes from the lineage of Syed Nemathulla bin Syed Ismail, bin Syed Moosa Kazim (Rz).

Thus the precedence or procrastination does not affect the correctness of the genealogy of Imamana (As), particularly when, in his another book "Hadiqatul Haqaeq", the author of "Shawahedul Vilayeth" has written the same genealogy what had been recorded in other books of genealogy.

Another source "Kitab-e-Kanzul Ansaab" is a very classical source in Persian language, which has been translated by Syed Murtuza Ilmul Huda. In its preface it is stated that."

"The author, Abu Mukhanasuf bin Loot bin Yahiya Khazaie named this book as "Kanzul Ansaab"and "Bahrul Masaab". This book was written by Imam Jafer-e-Sadiq (Rz) and a part of which was written by Imam Hasan Askari (Rz). This venerable book was for a long time kept in Baithul Muqaddas. After 653 years from the date of Migration of the holy Prophet (Slm), this book was brought by Syed Abu Taher bin Jafer, bin Imran, bin Moosa, bin Imam Mohammed Taqi, from Baitul Muqaddas to Persia. Then a long time passed that Syed Abu Taher died in Sabzwar city. The same book was written in Arabic which was translated by Syed Murtuza Ilmul Huda in Persian language."

چنین گوید مصنف این کتاب ابو مخنسف بن لوط بن یحییٰ خزاعیٰ علیه الرحمه و این کتاب را کنز الانساب و بحر المصاب نام کرده و کتاب این کتاب حضرت امام جعفر صادق علیه السلام است که بدست مبارک خود نوشته بودند و بعضی بخط امام حسن عسکری علیه السلام بوده و این کتاب شریف مدتی روزگار در مسجد اقصیٰ بماند و از هجرت حضرت رسول الله صلی الله علیه و سلم به ششصدو پنجاه و سه سال رسیده بود که حضرت سید ابو طاهر بن جعفر بن عمران بن موسیٰ بن حضرت امام محمد تقی علیه السلام این کتاب شریف را از مسجد اقصیٰ به ولایت عجم آورد تا مدتی روزگار گذشت که حضرت سید ابو طاهر در شهر سبز وار بجوار رحمت حق پیوست و این کتاب بلفظ عربی بود حضرت سید مرتضیٰ علم الهدیٰ رحمته الله علیه از عربی بفارسی در آورد

This book "Kanzul Ansab" is an historically reliable book in which the genealogy of Hazrat Imam Moosa Kazim (Rz) has been mentioned as:

"It is stated that Imam Ismail bin Moosa kazim (Rz) had eight sons: Mujeeb, Abid, Saabith, Nemat, Asad, Habeeb, Ahmad and Majid."

اما اسماعیل بن حضرت موسیٰ کاظم راهشت فرزند بود بدین اسامی مجیب و عابد ، ثابت ، نعمت و اسد و حبیب و احمد و ماجد

Hence the genealogy given in "Hadiqatul Haqaeq", "Mairajul Vilayet", "Ansaab Nama" and "Khatim-e-Sulaimani" all are in complete agreement with other books on genealogy.

Thus through the book "Kitab-e-Kanzul Ansaab" it is clear that "Nemat (Rz)" was the son of Ismail ibn Moosa Kazim (Rz). Thus this classical Source also testifies what "Hadiqatul

Haqaeq", "Khatim-e-Sulaimani" and other books endorse that "Nemat (Rz)" was the son of Ismael bin Moosa Kazim (Rz). Nemat (Rz) is the short form of "Nematullah (Rz)" which was well known at that period when it was written, also has been testified by "Saheb-e- Kanzul Ansaab" as follows:

"Abdullah bin Moosa Kazim (Rz) had eleven sons, Asaami,Nauzar,Feroz,Mansur, Asweasd,Azizuyllash,Ismail Amanullah, Hibatuullah, Aunallah, Ibrahim."	امام عبدالله بن حضرت امام موسیٰ کاظم را یا زده فرزند بود اسامی، نوذرا فیروز و منصور و اسود و عزیز و ابراهیم و اسماعیل و امان الله و عون الله وعزیز الله و هییت الله (هبت الله)

Author of "Kanzul Ansaab" has also written that :

Imam Ahmad Bin Moosa Kazim (Rz) had six sons: Fatehullah, Noorullah, Ainullah, Roohullah, Najeebullah and Ibaadullah."	اما م احمد بن حضرت امام موسیٰ کاظم راشش فرزند بود بدین اسامی فتح الله ، نور الله و عین الله و عباد الله و روح الله و غیب

Thus it is obvious that the pattern "Nematullah" was well known in that period of pious people.

It is a fact that during the period of Mamoon Rashid, sons and grandsons of Hazrat Syed Moosa Kazim (Rz) had arrived in Khurasan from Baghdad, according to "Kanzul Ansaab".

"When Mamoon Rashid brought Haz. Ali bin Moosa Raza (Rz) from Madinathul Rasool (Slm) to Taaus and made him his Murshid, (priest) Imam Moosa Kazim (Rz) migrated to Khurasan from Baghdad along with his sons and grandsons."	در روایت آورده انـد کـه چـون مامـوں رشید حضرت علی بن موسیٰ رضاء را از مدینه رسول خدا به شهـر طـوس بـرده بـود ، و پیشـوائـی خـود ساخته جمه فرزندان و فرزندزادگان حضرت امام موسیٰ کاظم از بغداد رومی بولایت خراسان نهاد

Thus it may be right to infer that Hazrath Nematullah (Rz) also might have migrated to

Khurasan along with his other relatives. Thus it is a proven fact that Imamana (As) comes from the lineage of Nemathullah bin Ismael bin Syed Moosa Kazim (Rz). And that has been correctly mentioned in Mahdavia literature according to the authentic and classical record of "Kanzul Ansaab" (which was written by Imam Jafer Sadeq (Rz) and Imam Hasan Askari (Rz); which is confirmed as most authentic).

Author of Hadia has referred to another book "Umdatul Matalib" which was written at a very later period than "Kanzul Ansaab" in which it is wrongly stated that Ismail bin Moosa Kazim (Rz) had only one son by name Moosa. Whereas no book mentions the name of Moosa Bin Ismael. "Umdatul Matalib" was written in 802 H, and author of this book died in 828 H. while "Kanzul Ansaab" was written in 653 H. long before 802 H, therefore this book should not be taken as an authentic source of genealogy. Since it denies even the genealogy of Hazrath Abdul Qader Jeelani for the sole reason that his father's name "Mohammad" carried the name of "Jungi Dost"

"It is stated that the name "Jungi Dost" is an Ajami, which should be taken as a title, and not the name."

وهذاالاسم اعنی جنگ دوست اعجمی صریح

In the genealogy of Imamana (As) if Nematulla son of Ismael (Rz) comes or instead Ismael Bin Nematullah (Rz) comes, it does not make the genealogy incorrect. If we study the lineage of the Prophet (Slm) we come across many gaps. It is an established fact that the lineage of the holy Prophet (Slm) correctly links to Adnan, but there are many gaps in between Adnan and Hazrath Ismael (As). It is stated by the author of "Madarijul Nabuwat" that:

"Some have reported 30 gaps and some have reported less than 30 in between Adnan and Hazrath Ismael (As)."

بعضی میان عدنان و اسماعیل سی تن ذکر کرده اند کـه معـروف نیسـت اشـخاص و احوال ایشان و بعضی کم و بعضی بیش

"The Author of "Rouzatul Ahbaab" has mentioned just fourteen successions in between Adnan and Haz.Ismail (As), and some reported forty."

بعضی میان عدنان و اسماعیل چهارده عدّ کرده اند و بعضی زیاده تابه حدی که به چهل عدو رسیده

Could these differences and the said gaps, deny the genealogy of the holy Prophet (Slm) connecting with Hazrat Ismail (As)?

In another objection, author of Hadia has pointed out that there were twelve generations between Imam Moosa Kazim (Rz) and Imamana (As) and that these 12 generations took just 664 years with an average of 56 years, which, according to him seems not possible and had plunged into a long unnecessary discussion which is rejected in limini.

It is a fact that Shaikh Ali Muttaqi, author of "Al Rudd" had accepted that Imamana's lineage links to the Saadath-e-Bani Fatima (Rz), in two places.

First, he discussed about "Mazhab-e-Mahdavia", in which he had stated that:' It is a fact that a group of persons in Indian cities had accepted an exalted person as Mahdi-e-Maouud (As) who was born in Juanpur and whose name is Syed Mohammad of Juanpur (As), son of Syed Khan and who said to have died forty years ago. Here, if Imamana (As) to be the son of Syed khan, becomes a point of objection, then Shaik Ali Muttaqi should not have written the name as "Syed" for Imamana (As). At another instance, although he had denied Imamana's Mahdiath, yet he says: "thus it is a fact that this"Syed" was not the Mahdi (As)". In both of his writings Shaik has admitted that Imamana (As) has come from Saadaath family. Thus we have tried our best to present the satisfactory proof regarding Imamana (As) that he comes from the lineage of Imam Moosa Kazim (Rz). However, author of Hadia should accept the reference of the book he had presented is nothing but a book of narratives only, and it does not come under the category of a genealogical record.

If a person writes about someone who had been the son of so and so, we have to see how righteous was he? And that person should prove his statement that shall be scrutinized on the basis of his characters and if his characters are proved, then whatever he reports shall be taken as authentic otherwise not.

1. The confirmation of the lineage of the Prophet (Slm) is proved by his infallible words and not by the book of the genealogy, because as per the version of the Prophet (Slm) "they often lie in reporting." Same way, we accept what Imamana (As) had said that he came from the lineage of Imam Moosa Kazim (Rz) as reported by "Shawahedul Vilayeth" and other books. Since we have accepted the fact of the lineage of the Prophet (Slm) on Prophet's proclamation, likewise we have to accept the correctness of the lineage of Imamana (As) as well as on his personal assertion.

The undersigned (Hazrat Bazmi) has heard such legends from the scholars of juanpur which according to old ladies until fifty (now 75) years hence used to state "Miranji" for the month of Jamadiul Awwal, in which Imamana (As) was born; since "Bara Wafath" is named for the month of Rabbiul Awwal, the month in which the Holy Prophet (Slm) passed away. So also the month of Rabbius Sani is known as "Dastagir" in which month Hazrath Abdul Qader Jeelani (Rz) was born. Further, it is a fact that the locality where Imamana (As) was born was known as "Miran Pur", which later on became known as "Miyanpura", changed in usage in course of time.

One more proof is produced of a masjid which stands at the banks of the River Gomthi, where it is recorded in the annals of history that Imamana (As) used to offer his prayers often in that masjid and used to stay alone in one of its rooms. It has become such a stop over place that whoever rests there gets satisfaction in meditation only because Imamana (As) used to stay in it.

(Note: In June 2006, a delegation of seven persons from Hyderabad, along with Br. Syed Iqbal Mehdi, Syed Nematullah, Architect, Sadeq Mohd. Khan, Maqsood Ali Khan, and others, had visited Miyanpur locality, now known as "Purana Bazar, in Juanpur in June 2006, to pay homage to the birthplace and the residence of Imamana (As). After thorough search they met one Babu Shah, Mujawer of the Rouza of Maqdoom Shaik Daniyal (Rh).Babu Shah is the owner of a house adjacent to the Rouza, which is located some 1.75 Kilometers from the Khokri Masjid and 1.25 Kilometers from the Havali of Hzt. Syed Osman (Rh), grandfather of Imamana (As) where he was born. After paying homage and offering flowers on all graves, they came back to Babu Shah's residence which, luckily has a separate plot of bout 500 sq. Yds.

After dinner, they sat down with Babu Shah and some other persons of that place. Br. Iqbal made known to them about themselves as Mahdavis, followers of Imamana (As), coming from Hyderabad and they have a firm desire to construct a Saraey with all amenities, having facility to accommodate 20 or more people, and a small masjid, for the convenience to the Zaereen whenever they visit.

Terms were discussed and a "Memorandum of Understanding" with the terms and conditions that all expenses for such construction shall be borne on by Mahdavis, but actual ownership shall rest with Babu Shah and his heirs, after him. Babu Shah agreed to welcome whoever visits Juanpur and allow them to stay free in the aforesaid Saraey, as long as they wish and have their own meals, cooked in the kitchen. He was permitted to use the building for his income purposes by using it as a Community Center and he shall bear maintenance charges and keep it clean as his own property.

On their successful visit, Br. Nematullah prepared a plan for a Jama'at Khana, comprising:

1. Gents Hall (25'x20'), along with a washroom.

2. Ladies Hall (20'x18') along with a washroom.

3. A staircase for going on the terraces.

4. A small kitchen and a store beside the halls.

5. A small room at the entrance as office and for the gaurd.

6. Proper water and electricity shall be provided by Babu Shah.

After finalizing the estimate of Rs.12 lakhs, they started collecting money from many places, including Los Angeles and California.

Construction started under the supervision of Br. Nematullh in January 2007 and completed in 2010, as and when the funds were made available.

A map has been drawn and appended herewith, to locate the places of importance as a guide to the Zaereen, who would be received and properly guided by Babu Shah and his heirs. Zaereen are requested to visit the venerable places often where Imamana (As) was born and bred.

The locality is full with Shia people, still it is amazing that even after 500 years they respect Imamana (As) and his members of the family and keep these places in good condition with care at their own expenses.

A Sign Board has been fixed with the nomenclature "Mahdavia Jama'at Khnana" along with a description of the "Memorandum of Understanding" for guidance to the visitors.

with courtesy from Br.Nematullah.

Imamana's early life

It is reported in the "Tuhfathul Kiram" that:

"Syedul Aoulia (As) was born in the year 847 H. He memorized the entire text of the Holy Qur'an at his age seven, in 854 H. And at his age twelve, in 859 H, he mastered in all branches of knowledge and was proclaimed as Syedul Ulema"(by the scholars of Juanpur of that period).

بسـال هشـت صـدو چهـل و هـفـت تولد کرده و در هـفـت سـالگـی حـفـظ قرآن نمـوده و در دوازده سالگی بـجـمـیـع عـلـوم ماهر شد ـ سید العلماء لقب یافت

However, the author of "Juanpur Nama"wrongly wrote that Imamana (As) was the disciple of Hazrath Shaik Daniyal (Rh). The fact is that Imamana (As) had only attended the Shaikh's School in his childhood . It is also a fact that when Imamana (As) was proclaimed as "Syedul Ulema" the Shaikh himself used to get clarification for some intricate Sharaie problems from Imamana (As). This fact has been reported by Miyan Abdul Rahman (Rh) in his "Moulood" that for certain intricate problems, the Shaikh (Rh) used to approach Imamana (As) for clarification.

Shaikh Abdullah Al Imadi Juanpuri had stated that he had seen a voluminous book in which Imamana (AS) has given answers to the questions raised by Shaik Daniyal (Rh). This book was written by one of the Shaikh's disciples.

While the author of "Tuhfatul Kiram" had reported that:

"Imamana (As) was proclaimed as "Asadul Ulema." (By the Scholars of Juanpur).

همه علماء اتفاق کرده اسد العلماء گفتند

However in the version of Mahdavia literature, the title "Asadul Ulema" is written instead of "Syedul Ulema" which has been testified by the "Moulood" of Miyam Abdul Rahman (Rh) that:

"At that period all scholars unitedly agreed that Hazrat is "Asadul Ulema.""

در آن زمان میان شیخ دانیال حضرت را سید الاولیاء حکم می کردند

Thus the author of "Tuhfatul Kiram" had reported that all scholars of Juanpur had accepted him as 'Asadul Ulema" (lion of the learned) and granted that title also to him. The same author has also reported about Imamana (As) that Shaikh Daniyal (Rh) had proclaimed Imamana as "Syedul Aoulia". This fact also had been testified by Miyan Abdul Rahman (Rh) in his "Moulood".

(Note: After going through History of Sindh,. it came to notice that Ali Sherr Khaney, author of "Tuhfasrtul KIrsam"was a Mahdavi and was serving the Kalhora Dynasty of Sindh which also was the Mahdvi Dynasty, ruled one hundred years from 1701 Ad to 1789 Ad. On instructions from the Mahdavi Rulers,he wrote "Tuhfatul Kiram"

Read also Addendum for further information.) Khundmiri

Author of "Tuhfatul Kiram" had reported about Shaikh Daniyal (Rh) that he was a very pious and noble man who had the opportunity to be in the company of Hazrath Khaja Khizar (As). This fact has been testified by the author of "Khazinatul Asfia" that:

"Shaik Daniyal (Rh) was the Khalifa of Hazrath Syed Raji Hamed Shah and happened to be in the company of Hazrat Khaja Khizar (As)."	شیخ دانیال چشتی قدس سرۂ مرید و خلیفه سید راجی حامد شاه است و صحبت دار خضر علیه السلام بود

Hazrat Shaik Daniyal (Rh) had accepted Imamana (As) as "Syedul Aouliah", and named him the "Promised Mahdi (As)". According to the Mahdavi literature Hazrat Khaja Khizar (As) had handed over the Trust, which was said to have been given by the Holy Prophet (Slm) with instructions to hand over to Imamana (As), which he handed over at the Khokri Masjid and declared Imamana (As) as the "Mahdi-e-Maood (As)" and Hazrat Shaik Daniyal (Rh) also accepted this fact along with Imamana's brother Syed Ahmed.

City of Juanpur Founded:

The city of Juanpur was founded by the order of Sultan Feroz Shah Tughlaq on the banks of the river Gomthi. It is narrated in the first chapter of "Juanpur Nama" that:

"Luckily at the time of returning from the village of Zafarabad, in the year 772 H, at the end of the month of Jamadiul Akhir, the Sultan saw an elevated even land abutting to the banks of the river Gomthi and he selected it to establish a city there. It is stated that during the night he witnessed a dream in which Mohammad Shah Juna had directed him to name the city after his name "Juna Khan."	اتفاقاً چون وقت مراجعت در اواخر ماه جمادی الآخره سنه هفت صدو هفتا دو دو هجری قصبۂ ظفر آباد مخیم سراوق شاهی شد سلطان رابه جانب مغرب برلب دریائی گومتی زمین هموار به نظر آمد و پسند خاطر افتادو خواست که درین مقام شهرے آباد کند ، همان شب سلطان محمد شاه جونارا درخواب دید که شهر را بنام من موسوم ساز

Thus he named the city as "Juanpur." It may be pointed out that Mohammad Shah Juna was none but Mohammad bin Tughlaq, Sultan Feroz Shah's ancestor. The city was established in the village of karara. In "Juanpur Nama" it is further stated that

""In an early morning the Sultan went towards that open elevated land which was located in the village Karara, near the banks of the river Gomthi. There was a big temple known as the temple of	صباح آن که بطرز سیر سوار شد گزارش بر موضع کراره که بر بلندی گریوه گومتی واقع بود ، افتاد، در آنجابت خانه کلان ید که آن رادیول "کراربیر" می گفتند، فرمان داد که این بت خانه را

84

Karabeir. The Sultan decreed to dismantle the temple and to build a fortified fort and to establish a city in the surrounding vicinity of the fort. Eloquent writers who were with him deduced the date of establishment of the city with that name and got favors from Sultan."

شکسته بجائے آں قلعه سنگین طیار و در حوائی آں شهر جون پور آباد سازند سخنواران رکاب سلطانی تاریخ آغاز بنائے این شهر جون پور را از همین لفظ برآوردند بانواع نوازشات سرفرازی یافتند (باب دوم)

The fort which was built after dismantling the Kararabeir temple was given the name of Karara Court. Hence the author of "Juanpur Nama" narrated under the title "Fort of Karara Court" as follows:

He thus named it Juanpur. The chronogram was composed by the words "Shaher-e-juanpur", when if each word's value is added, - the total of each numerical number of each word gets the year of its foundation as 772 H."

"It was the belief of the Hindus that during the period of Raja Ram Chandra of Ayodhia, there had been a devil by name Kararbeir in the village Karara. As the legend goes that the devil was very disobedient and arrogant to Raja Rama Chandra. Hearing the devil's arrogance and disobedience, Raja Ram Chandra came to Karara, killed the devil, threw his head at one place and the body was at another place and went away."

هنود را اعتقاد است که در تیرتیاجك بعهد حکومت راجه رام چند روالی اجودهیا کراربیر دیوے بود در موضع کراره که سر باطاعت احدے فرونمی آورد و مسافران رامی انجانید ، راجه چندرایں خبر شنیده از اجودهیا برآمد و در سواد موضع کراره که اکنوں پرستش گاه کراربیر است آن ظالم را کشت سرش جائے دوست و پایش جائے انداخت و برگشت (باب دوم)

After some time a temple was constructed by the devotees of that Devil on the spot where he was murdered.

Author of "Juanpur Nama" has also mentioned this fact in Chapter two that:

"The followers of the Kararbeir (Devil) had constructed a temple in his name and started worshipping his idol. Some rulers of nearby areas started sending oblations and offerings and further took part in construction of this temple."

تابعانش به مقتل اوبت خانه ساختند و به پرستش او پرداختند و راجه هائے این نواحی نذور و ارمغان می فرستادند و در تعمیر عمارت آں بت خانه تردد ها بکار می بردند(باب دوم)

On the instructions of the Sultan, foundations of the city of Juanpur were laid down. However, the name of the fort was declared as Karara Court and the East-Northern area is still known as Karara locality. Still there is a stone on the West-Southern side of the Fort which is called Kararabeir and Hindus worswhip that stone taking it as the symbol of Kararabeir Devil.

Author of "Juanpur Nama" has also narrated that:

"When the Sultan left to his capital, he started deputing prominent persons of learning and scholars to the city of Juanpur on one hand, and able administrators and civilians on the other hand for city's better administration. He used to remit scholarships to the saints and religious scholars. During his period alone, the city was much populated and its fame reached world wide."

القصـه سلـطـان بعد رسيدن دارالخلافت ارباب دانـش و فطانت و اصحاب علم و معرفت را از ممالك مـحروسه انتخاب كرده بتوطن اين شهر برگماشت و بـه ضبـط و نسـق ايـن شهر امرائ صاحب حشمت و ديانت را ما مورساخت و برائ علماء و مشائخ اين شهر اوراد و ظـائف بسيـار فرستاد تاآن كه شهر جونپور در عهـدوی آن قدر آباد شد كه صيت آن بگوش ساكنان هفت اقليم رسيد(باب اول)

Thus slowly but steadily Juanpur became famous for its learning where hundreds of scholars were busy in imparting education to thousands of students who were coming for learning. And in a short period, even during the period of the Founder, Sulan Feroze Shah, Juanpur's fame reached the four corners of India and even outside India. Its fame attracted persons from all over the world who came to Juanpur and it was then being called "Shiraz-e-Hind", par with that of "Shiraz of Persia.

Importance of Juanpur:

Thus Juanpur gained much importance during the reign of the rulers of Sharqia Dynasty. During the period of Sultan Ibrahim Sharqi (Died 844 H.) Juanpur became known all over the world as a place of peace, prosperity and learning.

1. Mulla Nizamuddin Ahmed Bakhshi wrote in his book "Tabqaat-e-Akbari":

"After the demise of Mubarak Shah, the nobles of the Sharqia Kingdom selected his younger brother and installed him as Sultan Ibrahim on the throne. During whose period there was complete peace and prosperity in the kingdom. Those scholars who were disturbed on account of anarchy and chaos in their places, migrated and settled down in Juanpur and became famous; and on account of their arrival, Juanpur became famous as the "Seat of Learning."

بعـد از فوت مبارك شاه امرائ دولت شرقی برادر كهتـر اور اسلـطـان ابـراهيـم خـطاب داده بر تخت سلـطنت و اورنگ حكومت اجلاس نمودند و طبقات انام اور مهدامن و امان قرار گرفتند علماء و بزرگان كه از آشوب جهـان پريشان خاطر بودند به جون پور كه درآن ايـام دارالامـان بـودسر برآوردنـد و آن دارا لسلطنت از فرقدوم علماء دارلعلم گرديد

2. In his "Memoirs" Farishta, states that:

"Sultan Ibrahim Sharqi was himself a pious, religious and a man of deep understanding. He assembled many learned scholars, intellectuals, grand sufis and saints from all over the World, particularly from Persia, Turan and Arabian countries. In view of anarchy in other places of India, all came to Juanpur and thus Juanpur of the 9th. Century Hijri. was known as "Delhi" the Second."

شـاهـی بـود متـصف بـه عقل و دانش و تدبیر در عـصروے فضلائے ممالك هندوستان و دانشمندان ایران و توران كـه از آشـوب جهـان پـریشان خـاطر بودند دارالامان جون پور آمده در عهد امن و امان غنودند

3.Another Scholar, Shaik Abdul Haq, Muhaddis-e-Dehalvi wrote in his "Zikrul Mulook" about Sultan Ibrahim Sharqi that:

"The sultan was a pious man of admirable characters, having an amiable nature and a staunch supporter of religion. Hence he gathered around him religious minded people. He had given a high position to Qazi Shahabuddin as the"Qaziul Quzzath" who died in Juanpur in the year 844 H."

وے مرد نيك ذكريم و خوش طبع و ظريف و صالح و عـادل و مـحب و معتقد علماء و مشائخ بود ، قاضی شهاب الدین در عهدوے معتبر و مقدم بودو درسنه اربع و اربعین و ثمانمایته هم درجون پور وفات یافت

4.Mir Ghulam Ali Azad has written in his book "Ma'asarul Kiram" that:

"Emperor Shah Jehan had acknowledged Juanpur as Shiraz of his kingdom which until 1130 H. maintained its position where Religious Teachings by the renowned Scholars became famous all over the world."

صـاحب قـران ثانی شاه جهان انارا الله برهانه می گـفت" پورب شیراز ملك ماست" و تاحدود ۱۱۳۰ه ثـلثیـن و مـایتـه و الف هـنگامه علم و علما درایں گل زمین گرمی داشت

In this writing "Poorb"(East) was called as "Shiraz-e-Hind". That means the city in the East, known for its "Learning and Architecture" became famous all around the Muslim world was none but Juanpur. Another scholar wrote in" Mir'athil Aalam"that:

"During the period of Sultan Ibrahim, Juanpur had become a city of peace and prosperity where learned scholars and religious authorities, assembled and resided there and from where every now and then books, magazines and weeklies were being published and circulated around the Muslim World."

صاحب مرأة العالم نے جون پور کو "دارالخیور"

نمائس ہفتم در ذکر شرقیاں دارالخیور جون پور

Juanpur became famous for learning.

Author of "Mirathul Aalam" had declared Juanpur as "Darul Khuyur." (House of Virtues)

Within the vicinity of Awadh in India, where the Sultans of the Eastern Dynasty made the city a hub of learning in religion, arts and sciences, and where dignified scholars and sufis were busy with teaching and imparting education in all worldly and religious subjects to hundreds of students who were coming from all over India and as well from other parts of the world. Naturally these scholars got their remarkable position in the eyes of the rulers and among the masses as well.

5. Shah Valiullah, another Muhaddis-e-Dehalvi (died 1176 H) had written a poetry in Arabic with reference to Juanpur and mailed it to Shaik Abdul Qader Juanpuri whose English translation is as under:

"The pleasant and heart touching winds of Juanpur, inspire the whole of the universe and the mankind."

منهما تعطرت الدنیا وما فیهم من جو نفورا

ذاهبت ریاح رضی

This particular piece of poetic exaltation by a scholar of high caliber, like Shah Vliullah, points out that Juanpur was the hub of learning from where literature spread all over the world. One of the books written by Mulla Mahmood of Juanpur is known as "Shams-e-Bazigha" on philosophy which was included in the University curriculum not only in India, but in Persia and some Arabic countries also.

Mulla Mahmood's another book "Fawaed-e-Qazi Azad" is written on Rhetoric-Eloquence- it nullified the Persian dominance over the Arabic literature which is remarkable. Author of "Juanpur Nama" has commented that:

"Mullah Mahmood has written an illustrious commentary on "Fawaed of Qazi Azad", known as "Faraed" which eradicated the unwanted Persian dominance over Arabic literature. What Sikaki and Taftazani tried to influence the Arabic Eloquence, in the same manner, this book also has rightly tried to eliminate the Persian influence and brought the Arabic literature on the right path."

فوائد قاضی عضدرا که متنی است متین درعلوم ادبیه عربیه به کمال جزالت شرح داده و بنام فرائد موسوم کرده عجمیت را که بر عربیت استیلا یافته ازیں کتـاب دورتـوان کـردتـاوجدان صحیح که از زمـان سکـاکی و تفتازانی ذوق عجم دریافته باز به منهاج مستقیم گرایدـ

Another writer Shaik Abdul Rasheed (Died 1083 H) wrote "Rashidia" a book on Dialectics which got fame worldwide.

Qaziul Quzzat of Juanpur, Malikul Ulema Shahbuddin had written a commentary on "Kafia" which became famous during his lifetime. Author of "Jaunpur Nama" in chapter five has written about him that Qazi Shahbuddin:

" He wrote commentary on "Kafia" which got fame in a short period all over the world of learning. Mulla Abdul Rahman Jami has also written a commentary on Qazi, which contains a charming taste of logic and philosophy, and provides sweetness in the literature."

شرح مستـوعـب بر کافیه ابن حاجب شاهد فضل اوسـت کـه مـطـرح علمائے عرب و عجم بوده است ، فوائد ضیائیه رادیده باشی که مولانا عبدالرحمن جامی مـدون فرمـوده هـمیں شرح قاضی است که چاشنی مـنـطـق و فـلـسـفـه جـابجا برآں افزوده ، ذوق ادب را شیریں کام نموده است ، غیر ازیں هیچ فرقی نداردـ

The same had been appreciated by the author of "Juanpur Nama", who states that the commentary on "Kafia" of Ibn Haajib acquired fame all over the world on account of its logical and philosophical approach..

The chief Qazi of Juanpur, Qazi Shahabuddin, died in the year 844 H, just three years before the birth of Imamana (As). It indicates the environment which was prevailing at a time when Imamana (As) appeared on the horizon of Juanpur.

The author of "Juanpur Nama" had reported that when Humayun went to Iran, Shah Tahmasp of Iran particularly inquired about Juanpur. Such inquiry asserts how famous had become Juanpur that the Shah of Iran inquired about it.

6. Author of "Juanpur Nama", in its preamble has mentioned Mulla Isfehani's book, "Sairul Mulook" that:

"On the outskirts of Allahabad, there is a city which was founded in 772 H. by Sulatan Feroz Shah, known as Juanpur, which became the capital of Sharqi Kingdom. Hundreds of Masajids and schools spread all over the city. Many scholars and saints came and settled down here. Rulers had granted scholarships, grants and jagirs to them in order to inculcate education without fear of poverty. When Humayun went to Iran, Emperor Tahmasp particularly inquired about Juanpur. He expressed deep sorrow on the ruins of Shiraz, and praised Juanpur which stole the fame of Shiraz of Persia."

از مضافات اله آباد شهریست که سلطان فیروز دهلوی آن را در سنه هفت صد و هفتاد و دو هجری بنا نهاده و به جون پور موسوم ساخته در عهد سلاطین شرقیه دارالسلطنت شده صدها مساجد و مدارس در شهر و حوالی آن معمور شدند، علماء و فقراء از اقالیم دور و دراز در آن بلده رسیده، سلاطین و حکام برائے هر یکی وظائف والتمغا و جاگیر بخشیده، شهنشاه ایران شاه طهاسپ از امیر همایوں اور نختیں ملاقات از فضلائے جون پور پرسید و بادراک کثرت و انبوه علماء در آن دیار بردیرانی شهر شیراز آه حسرت کشید۔

Emperor Tuhmasp's inquiry about Juanpur is an indication that Juanpur became so famous even in Iran and likewise its fame had reached all around the Muslim world for its learning, art and architecture.

7. Author of "Juanpur Nama", while referring to "Zubdatul Tawareekh", had elaborately written in its preamble that:

"Juanpur had been one of the marvelous cities of India which was nourished by all Sultans of Eastern Dynasty, who in order to keep the city attractive, left no stone unturned for its upbringing. Those Sultans were themselves very much fascinated with the learning and took deep personal interest and they invited many acclaimed scholars and religious masters to come over to Juanpur just for the sublime cause to inculcate learning in all dimensions. They invested hundreds

شهر جون پور از عجائب بلاد هندوستان است سلاطین شرقیه پیوسته مصروف آبادی آن بودند و زبدۀ فضلائے اطراف را بصرف مبالغ به کمال خواهش به جون پور می فرستادند۔ ارباب کمال هر فرقه را از ممالک محروسه چیده و پسندیده باقامت ایں شهر ماموری نمودند۔ در عهدسلطان حسین شرقی وسعت ایں بلده در طول و عرض از دوازده کروه گزشته ونود و شش محله از اصناف خلائق آباد شده، ارباب علوم و اصحاب فنون جوق جوق از ممالک دور دراز آمدند، و مشائخاں و درویشاں گروه گروه از هفت اقلیم دریں شهر جلوه افروم شدند،

and thousands towards scholarships, grants, monetary assistance for the noble cause of imparting learning in all spheres and in all branches of arts, sciences and religion. They allotted Jagirs and grants to the scholars so that they should engage their time and energy for the cause of education without fear of poverty. The city had extended to more than 25 square miles containing 96 localities where scholars of every walk of life were busy in their avocation with full zeal and enthusiasm. That is why ambassadors from all over the world used to bring gifts to the Sultans as a mark of respect and appreciation because of their personal endeavour to bring the City at a formidable standing which attracted hundreds of scholars and thousands of students to get a proper education in all branches of learning."

خوبان هر قوم و نیگان هر گروه درای خطه آباد شدند ، دور ماندگانِ هر ملك و مستمندان هر كشوردرین شهر به مطلبِ دلی رسیدند صهیت فضل و کمالِ کاملان ایں شهر باعثِ رشك و حسد سلاطین توران و ایران شده و علم و عمل عالمان ایں بلده موجب حیرت و تعجب خوافین روم و شام گرویده ، ایلچیان بادشاه هر اقلیم که باتحفه و هدایا بحضور سلاطین شرقیه و سلاطین بابریه می رسیدند ، حسب الحکم سلاطین نتائج طبع فضلائ ایں بلده رابه طرز ارمضان می بردند۔

From this, two issues emerge for consideration:

1. famous scholars from all over the Muslim world had settled down in Juanpur.

2. The written books of these scholars were used to be sent to the Muslim countries which brought more fame to Juanpur for its famous literature.

8. The Imperial Gazetteer of India in its 4th. volume dated 1908 states that:

"Juanpur remained the seat of governor till the re-organization of the empire by Akber, who raised Allahbad to the position of provincial capital; from that period, Juanpur declined in political importance, though it retained some of its former reputation as a center of Mohammedan learning, which had gained the title of "Shiraz-e-Hind."

9. Narendra Nath has thus written: "During (Sultan) Ibrahim's reign (1402-1440 AD) the court of Juanpur far out shown that of Delhi and was the resort of all the learned men of the East."

10. In a book "Indian Education in ancient and later times", an educationist Mr. F. A. Kaey writes about Juanpur that "The city in India which was most famous as a Mohammedan place of learning was none but Juanpur. It was compared to Shiraz of Persia and thus was called it "Shiraz of India."

11. Syed Sulaiman Nadvi in his book,"Muqaddama-e-Hayath-e-Shibli" has written that the

center of learning was transferred from Lahore, Multan and Delhi towards the East; that is to Juanpur. He had elaborately written further that "Khaja Jehan died in the year 802 H. and his son Mubarak Shah took the reign of the kingdom which became an independent kingdom of the East. Mubarak Shah too died just after two years in 804 H. Ibrahim Shah took the reign of the government. He was very wise and became famous for his administration. During his lengthy forty year period Juanpur attracted scholars and religious preachers from Multan, Delhi, Lahore and many other places who migrated and settled down here under the benign stewardship of Ibrahim Shah who was himself a scholar."

That golden period belongs to Sultan Ibrahim Sharqi and his son Sultan Mahmood Sharqi. The development of Zafarabad and Juanpur enlightened so much that scholars, artisans and architects from all over the world flocked together in Juanpur.

Juanpur and Indian Scholars:

It may be pointed out that many of the Indian scholars had religious relations with Mullah Nizamuddin Suhalvi (D.1161) which had been stated by Mir Ghulam Ali Azad Bilgrami in his book "Mua'asirul Kiram" about Mulla Nizamuddin that :

"Presently, many scholars of various parts of India have learning relations with Mullah Nizamuddin and they boast for the relations and whoever relates his connection to him becomes famous. It is also seen that many, although got their education from elsewhere, still they tried to get certification from this Moulvi."

امروز علمائے اکثر قطر هندوستان نسبت تلمذ به مولوی دارند و کلاہ گوشه تفاخری شکننده کسے که سلسله تلمذ باومی وساند بین الفضلاء علم امتیاز می افرازد و مردم بسیار را دیده شد که تحصیل جا هائے دیگر کردند برائے اعتبار فاتحه فراغ از مولوی گرفتند

As a matter of fact Mullah Nizamuddin was the pupil of Shaik Ghulam Nakshbandi Lukhnavi (D.1126) about whom much had been written in "Mua'asirul Kiram" by stating that: "Lastly (Nizamuddin) met with Janab Shaik Ghulam Nakshbandi Lukhnavi and completed his education under him and got certificate from him."

Shaik Ghulam Nakshbandi was just known as Lukhnavi, on account of his residence, but really he belonged to Juanpur. "Mua'asirul kiram" reports about Shaik Ghulam Nakshbandi that "His forefathers lived in Khosi, near Juanpur and became famous as great scholars of Juanpur."

Author of "Juanpur Nama" wrote about Ghulam Nakshbandi that "His family lived in Khosi, in the outskirts of Juanpur. They were famous for their religious knowledge. But Shaik Ghulam surpassed them all in learning and piety. He was well versed with the faculty of the commentary of the holy Qur'an. He lived in Lucknow and died also there. (he is known as Lukhnavi, since he migrated to Luknow from Khosi, although he was actually brought and bred in Khosi, near Juanpur.)"

12. "Muqaddamah-e-Hayath-e-Shibli" confirms that after Tamer Lane's attack and destruction of Delhi and Punjab, scholars migrated towards East where fortunately a new

independent state was in the offing, and that was the time that Shaik Nizamuddin and Qazi Shahabuddin decided to migrate and settled down in Juanpur where the rulers welcomed them with respect and honour and provided them all amenities to stay without fear of poverty.

Juanpur's excellence:

As regards Juanpur's excellence in learning, it is enough to narrate what Qazi Shahabuddin, who was the Qaziul Quzzat of the kingdom of Salateen-e-Sharqia, had written on Sultan Ibrahim Sharqi which is more than a testimony and a certificate for the Sultan's deep interest in enhancing learning in his kingdom. He states that:

"The Sultan had administered justice at a high level. He was a pious man of amenable characters who always struggled to uphold Islamic Sharia in all his personal and political administration. He was himself a very learned man who took personal interest in discussions relating to religion, philosophy and logic. These discussions usually took place at the dinner table in which eminent scholars, Qazis and men of high academic caliber used to be invited by the Sultan and he himself used to start discussion by introducing an important topic for discussion. This healthy atmosphere provided many scholars to prove their

mantle at the court of the Sultan who happily used to award them jagirs and grants to spend their full time for the betterment of education system in and around the kingdom."

بر گزیده حضرت اله سلطان المعظم ابوالمجاهد
ابراهیم عادل شه ایدالله سلطنته و ابد مملکته
ایزدش یار و بخت یاور باد
دین و شرعش همیشه رهبر باد
هرچه خواهد زجمله هر دو جهان
بی توقف همه میسر باد
شرع را شعار خود ساخته دور کافة
امور بعلم و علماء پر داخته ، کارو نواختن ارباب
علم و تقویٰ وانشراح اوبه مصاحبت اصحاب درس و
فتویٰ در عهد همایون اور علم و هنر رواج یافته ، و
در وقت میمون اور شرع و دین رونق و ابتهاج گرفته
، و ذهن ثاقب اوبانواع علوم مائل و فکر صائب
اوبانواع شمائل شامل
برهر هنر که روی بیاورد مالک است
در هر فنی که رائے گمار دازآن اوست
و مجلس مائده خاص را که انوذج الجنان و محتوی بر
نعمت بی پایان است مقام فائده عام ، گردانید و مائده
که قوة ابدان است بافائده که قوت ارواح است جمع
کرده ، در مباحث و قایق اصناف علوم می باشد و در
تحقیق انواع فنون رهنمائی می نماید، خصوصاً علم
اصول فقه که صنعت رجال علم الجتهاد است به طبع
فیاض اومالوف تراست و ذکائی کامل او و در لطائف
این فن مشغول تر

From this testimony we come to conclusion that:

The Sultan was himself a learned man and an authority on Islamic Jurisprudence; and he took much interest to be among the learned people always; and also that Sultan's interest in the "After Dinner Talk" (An English System) was just to enrich his understanding about philosophy and religion.

All these facts prove that Sultan Ibrahim wanted that scholars of high intellectual caliber should assemble in his kingdom to make the kingdom a heaven for learning. In this manner he became known as "Mamoonur Rasheed" of India and this fame brought as many intellectuals as possible in Juanpur to make it "Shiraz-e-Hind" or to say "Delhi the Second".

Even today there are certain families in Juanpur who had migrated from Baghdad, Qurtaba, and far off places, which is a proof that the Sultan had invited them to make his kingdom a hub of education and learning.

This fact has also been reported by the author of "Akhbarul Asrar" who says that:

"At the Bismillah Ceremony of Imamana (As) more than twelve hundred scholars had assembled to witness the ceremony, which was organized by Shaik Daniyal (Rh) in which a sumptuous dinner was served to all."

براۓ مـكـتـب آنـحـضـرت بـسـيـار ضـيـافـت و تـكـلـف نـمـودنـد دوازده صـد عـلـمـاۓ آں زمـاں در شـهـر جـونـپـور بـودنـد و هـمـه اكـابـران آں شـهـر را طـلـبـیـده سـتـوده خـصـال مـخـدوم شـیـخ دانـیـال را آورده مـجـلـس بـه آرائـش بـهـشـت نـمـوده (باب اول فصل اول)

By telling all these facts, any body can infer how beautiful and provoking environment had been in and around Juanpur, when Imamana (As) opened his eyes in that heaven of learning known as Shiraz-e-Hind.

Sultan Ibrahim Sharqi died in 844 H. and Imamana (As) was born in 847 H. just three years after Sultan's death. Imamana (As) was born in Juanpur when Juanpur was known as a hub of Islamic Learnings around the Muslim world.

History tells us that Prophet Ibrahim (As) was born in a place which was known for its high culture and education. In the same manner, Prophets Moosa (As) and Esa (As) were also born in cities which were known as cradles of civilization. And our Holy Prophet (Slm) was born In Makkah which was known as "Ummal Quraa" whose Arabic literature, oratory and poetry were well known. There should not be any wonder if Imamana (As) was born at a place which was also well known for its learning and Islamic jurisprudence.

Battle with Rai Dalpat (of Gaud):

Not only learned scholars, but the Sultan Husain Sharqi, himself was very much captivated and became a devotee of Imamana Alaihis salaam. Imamana's sermons were based on the teachings of the Qur'an and complete adherence to the traditions of the Holy Prophet (Slm). Imamana (As) had promulgated the tradition of Jihad in which he defeated the army of Rai Dalpat and slaughtered him in the battlefield along with the army of Sultan Husain Sharqi. If the fact of the battle against Rai Dalpat had not been recorded in any history book, it does not mean that this battle did not take place at all. The fact is that historical record of Bengal is very limited and dubious. This fact has been correctly reported by a famous historian, known as

Farishta in his Volume Two, chapter Seven that:

"Historical record of Eastern or Western India was mostly blank. For that reason I based my information on the writings of my teacher, Mulla Ahmed Tatvi's "Tareekh-e-Alphi" only, and did not accept hearsay legends; for which I may be excused and should not be blamed, because I had tried my best to get authentic record and whatever I got, I honestly tried to produce it before you."

پوشیده نماند که بسیارے از متون کتب تواریخ از شرح و بسط قضایائ سلاطین پوربی و شرقی خالی است بنا بر آں مدار نقل بر کتاب الفی که تالیف استادی مولانا احمد تتوی است بردایات دیگر نه پرداختم اگر دریں باب اختلافے بنظر مطالعه کنندگان در آید به عفو مقرون سازنده مواخذ نگر دانند که بقدر طاقت بشرے کوشیدم و انچه علم ناقص محیط آں بود درج کردم

Farishta's narration tells that he was not sure about the legends of Bengal. However two historical books were written at the same time: One being "Riazus Salateen" by Ghulam Husain Zaidpuri" on the request by George Adni in the year 1202 H. and the other being "Juanpur Nama" by Moulvi Khairuddin Mohammed of Allahbad who wrote on the advice of a Juanpur Judge Mr. Abraham Viland in the year 1216 H. While "Riazus Salateen" is the history of Bengal, and "Juanpur Nama" is the "History of Sultan Husain Sharqi" and about the Salateen-e-Sharqia, but both present different versions.

1. Successar of Sultan Naseeb shah and Difference of Openion of Historians:

"Riyazus Salateen" states about Sultan Feroze Shah that:

"When Sultan Nusrat Shah died, his son Feroz Shah on the advice of the nobles, proclaimed himself as king and ruled for three years but just after three years Sultan Mahmood Bengali (one of the eighteen sons of Sultan Alauddin Husain Shah to whom Nusrat Shah had favoured and treated him like a noble) murdered Feroz Shah and captured the capital and became ruler of the kingdom as heir of his father."

چوں سلطان نصرت شاه شربت ناگوار اجل چشید پسرش فیروز شاه یه تجویز امرا به تخت سلطنت فرماندهی جلوس نمود ـ هنوز سه سال سلطنت کرده بود که سلطان محمود بنگالی که یکی از هجده پسر سلطان علاء الدین حسین شاه و نصرت شاه اورا با مارت سربلندی داده بود و تازندگی نصرت شاه سلوک امرایانه می داشت ـ درایں وقت قابو یافته فیروز شاه راجه قتل آورده بر سریر سلطنت بورثه پدر خود جلوس نمود

It may be pointed out that Nusrat Shah was also known as Naseeb Shah. Author of "Riazus Salateen" states that "His elder son Nusrat Shah known as Naseeb Shah was enthroned."

On the other hand the "Juanpur Nama" mentions about the heirs of Sultan Husain Sharqi. It states that:

"When Sultan Husain was defeated by Sultan Sikendar Lodhi, he was wandering here and there and after a long time he approached his son Sultan Jalaluddin, who had married the daughter of Sultan Naseeb Shah, died heirless, therefore his son in law, Sultan Jalaluddin took control of the kingdom. Thus it is clear from this version that as there was no son to Naseeb Shah, Sultan Jalauddin, son of Sultan Husain Sharqi became king."

چوں سلطان حسین از سلطان سکندر شکست خورده بطرف بنگاله رفت ـ مدتی ازیں طرف به آں طرف گذشت آخر نزد سلطان جلال الدین پسر خود که بادختر نصیب شاه گور که از کشوو بنگاله است کد خدا بود رفت و مدت العمر همان جابسر کرد، چوں سلطان نصیب شاه بجز آں دختر فرزندی نداشت ـ بعد وفات نصیب شاه سلطان جلال الدین بخاری اونشت

Thus it is clear from this that Sultan Naseeb Shah had no son. Therefore his son in law, Jalaluddin was enthroned in his place as the king who was the son of Sultan Husain Sharqi. But according to "Riazus Salateen", after the Sultan Naseeb Shah, his son Sultan Feroz Shah sat on the throne and after Feroz Shah, Sultan Mahmood, son of Sultan Alauddin Hasan Shah took his place. In such contradictory statements how could it be said that no battle took place between Sultan Husain and Rai Dalpat. Therefore in such categorical differences about the historical record of Bengal, it should not be inferred that there had been no battle against Rai Dalpat of Gaud. However Mahdavia literature of that period has ample and authentic record about that battle in which Imamana (As) personally took part and when Dalpat himself encountered Imamana (As), Imamana (As) had killed Rai Dalpat and whose nephew was brought by Sultan Husain after the battle as a captive, who became servant of Imamana (As) and later on converted to Islam and offered allegiance to Imamana (As) and became known as Shah Dilawer (Rz), the fifth Caliph of Imamana (As).

Raja Kauns Captured Gaud:

It is possible that one among a few Rajas might have defeated the Sultan and captured Gaud from him. It is also reported in the "Riyazus Salateen" that a powerful landlord by name Kauns had killed Sulatn Shamsuddin of Gaud and captured Gaud. This fact also had been testified by Farishta that Raja Kauns had ruled for seven years.

"About Raja Kauns there are two different versions, while Farishta states that:

"Raja Kauns was not a Muslim, however he had friendly terms with Muslims, therefore some Muslims treated him as a Muslim and when he died they wanted to bury him under the rituals of Islam."

راجه کانس هر چند مسلمان نبود امابا مسلمانان آمیزش و محبت بسیار داشت بنوعی که بعضی از مسلمانان گواهی بر اسلام او داده می خواستند که بطریق اسلام اور انجاك سپارند

But to its contrary, "Riyazus Salateen" reports against Raja Kauns that he was a bitter enemy of Muslim scholars and killed them and tried his best to eradicate Islam from his dominion.

Such is the difference in the historical record pertaining to Bengal. Therefore it cannot be inferred that Rai Dalpat was not the ruler of Gaud during the time of Sultan Husain Sharqi and that no battle took place between them. It may be possible that Rai Dalpat also might have been one of the landlords like Raja Kauns, or even Rai Dalpat might have been one of the members of the family of Raja Kauns who ruled Gaud.

Landlords of Juanpur:

It was a period when landlords also used to maintain huge army. This fact has been narrated by an eminent historian Abdullah in his "History of Dawoodi" with reference to Sultan Sikander Lodhi, who writes that the landlords of Juanpur headed by a Hindu by name Joka, gathered a huge army of about 100,000 troops and fought against Mubarak Khan Suhani.

It all boils down to say that Imamana (As) introduced Jihad as Sunnah and as reported in "Moulood" by Miyan Abdul Rahman (Rh) that Sultan Husain Sharqi never went to any battle without Imamana (As). Thus it may be inferred that Imamana (As) certainly had taken part in many battles along with Sultan Husain Sharqi. Therefore it proves that when Sultan waged a Jihad against Rai Dalpat of Gaud in Oraisa on suggestion by Imamana (As) who himself took part in it. It is also a fact that Imamana (As) went into trance in the year 875 H. soon after Imamana (As) killed Rai Dalpat in that Jihad which took place in that year. This fact had been testified not only by Farishta, but by "Khatim-e-Sulaimani" that the battle took place against Rai Dalpat in the year 875 H. when Imamana had attained the age of 28 years and after that battle only he went into trance/ecstasy in the year 875 H. for twelve years which ended in 887 H.

Imamana' Period of Trance

It is reported in Imamana's biographies that he did not take regular meals during this twelve year period of trance. This fact had been questioned by the author of Hadia that it was not humanly possible that a man could survive without food for twelve years?

In reference to this we quote the verses of Holy Qur'an in which Prophet Ibrahim (As) states:

"Thus, those idols are my enemy. But my Rabbul Aalameen is my friend who created me and who guided me. He is the One who provides meals and water to me and when I am sick, he alone cures me and who would alone kill me and give life back to me."

فَاِنَّهُمْ عَدُوٌّ لِّىْ اِلَّا رَبَّ الْعٰلَمِيْنَ . الَّذِىْ خَلَقَنِىْ فَهُوَ يَهْدِيْنِ . وَالَّذِىْ هُوَ يُطْعِمُنِىْ وَ يَسْقِيْنِ . وَ اِذَا مَرِضْتُ فَهُوَ يَشْفِيْنِ . وَالَّذِىْ يُمِيْتُنِىْ ثُمَّ يُحْيِيْنِ

Author of "Tafseer-e-Husaini" had commented about these verses that the reference of Meals is an absolute thing in its nature containing every nutrition that is required for a man's survival.

In one of the traditions, it is reported that the holy Prophet (Slm) often informed that:

"Used to live in the audience of Allah whole night who provides me meals and water."

ابيت عذر بى يطعمنى و نفقين مى توان برد

Another tradition as reported by Imam Ahmed Hunbal (Rh) which states that:

"Certainly I am served with meals and water."

انى اطعم و اسقى

Some people say that here food and water is meant for vitality and strength which obtained from food. Thus our Prophet (Slm) said that My Lord grants me the strength and stamina in such a manner that it becomes easy for me to obey and Pray Him without feeling any weakness even without food etc.

"Tirmizi" and "Maja" also reported that:

"Do not feed your sick or cause them to drink, since Allah feeds and makes them drink."

لا تكرهوا مرضاكم على الطعام فان الله تعالى يطعمهم و يسقيهم

A. The references made here regarding meals and water, do not belong to real meal and water. But according to the commentators they refer to vitality and vigour. Sheik Abdul Haq, Muhaddiss-e-Dahalvi states in his book "Sharh-e-Safarus Saadath" about this Tradition that:

"Some said, food and water which provide vital for survival, thus Allah provides that much which is required for a man for his survival, thus Allah alone helps me for prayers and I never feel weakness."

بعضى گفته اند كه مراد به طعام و شراب اينجا قوت است كه لازم اوست ، پس گويا فرمود مرا پروردگار من قوت آكل و شارب مى بخشد و افاضه مى كند چيزے كه قائم مقام شراب و طعام ميگردد دو بدان قوت برطاعت و عبادت مى يابم بے ضعف دفتور

Further it is stated that here eating and drinking is meant for complete satisfaction, which even without meals the holy Prophet (Slm) got and never felt any trouble without them. Further it is narrated that it relates to spiritual food.

Ibn Qeem has written "Kitab-e-Huda" and Ibn Hajib wrote "Lathaaef" , both say that:

"Food and water should not be construed as material things, but they refer to satisfaction and vigour and actually they refer to spiritual food which are beneficial and manifestations of the Almighty which fell on the heart of the Prophet (Slm) which relieved the Prophet (Slm) from hunger and thirst and made him contented from those desires."

از ابن قيم در كتاب هدىٰ و از ابن حاجب در لطائف نقل كرده اند آنكه مراد طعام و شراب محسوس نيست نه لازم دے از قوت و شبع بلكه مراد غذاے روحانى بود كه از معارف و لذات مناجات و فيضان لطائف الهى كه بر دل شريف وے صلى الله عليه و سلم وارد مى گشت وانچه توابع آن است از احوال شريفه از نعيم روح و شادى نفس و روح دل و روشنائى چشم كه بآں چندان قوت و قدرت و مسرت حاصل آيد كه بدن از غذائے جسمانى مستغنى شود

In this connection Shaik Abdul Haq had maintained that:
"A time comes when even after a lapse of considerable time, man does not require food, rather he forgets food. This is the real love of Allah which provides actual contentment."

مدت مديد بگذرد كه احتياج بغذا نيفتد بلكه يادازان نيايدوايں در محبت هائے مجازى و مسرت هائے صورى تجربه است چه جائے محبت حقيقى و مسرت معنوى

Thus, it is evident that when real love overpowers an individual, he can survive for many years without meals.

So far we have discussed about the constituents of this problem which have links to language, literature and the traditions, now we shall discuss how science treats it.

Shaikhur Raees states that:

"If you hear that a certain mystic or a devout had forsaken food since a long time, take it as true. This matter relates to physics. From a physical point of view, an available physical vitality which pertains in us, discontinues to release real matter, but instead releases imperfect material for digestion, thus real substance is saved since they are not being dissolved and they remain. These are such materials which less likely to dissolve but provide contentment. At this stage, one needs no food for a long time and when it happens the condition becomes the same and if the tenth portion of that period requires no meals, it is possible that the man may die, even though in such condition his life is safe."

Imam Fakhruddin Razi has commented that:

"What ever the Shaikh has stated, he had given an example of a thing which is not comprehensible, and must not be discussed. Any person when suffering from any disease for a long time, does not take meals during this period, and remains alive. When this fact is understandable, then there is no reason to disbelieve other situation. Since there is no difference between these two."

Tusi has commented further that:
"Avoidance of bare sustenance may be the result of unnatural causes, which include diseases, either bodily or psychological, for example apprehension causes to avoid even bare sustenance. This is all to convince that even without food for a long time, a man can survive. It is a different issue that there may be different causes as to why a man avoids food for a long time."

اذا بلغك ان عارفا امسك عن القوت المرزؤله مدة غير معتارة فاسمح بالتصديق و اعتبر ذلك من مذاهب الطبيعة المشهورة تنبيه يذكر ان القوى الطبيعية التى فينا اذا اشتغلت عن تحريك المواد المحمودة بهضم المواد الردية انحفظت المواد الحمودة قليلة التحليل غنية عن البدل فربما انقطع عن صاحبها الغذاء مدة طويلة لو انقطع مثله فى غير حالته بل عشر مدته هلك و هو مع ذلك محفوظ الحيٰوة

الغرض من هذا لفضل ذكر مثال لهٰذا المسئلة دفعا للاستبعاد فان الانسان قديقى فى المرض الحار مدة مديدة من غير تناول الغذاء و اذا عقل ذلك هناك فليعقل مثله فى هذه المسئللة لايقال بينهما فرق

الامساك عن القوت قد يعرض بسبب عوارض غريبة اما بدنية كالا مراض الحارة و اما نفسانية كالخوف و اعتبار ذلك يدل على انه الا مساك عن القوت معه العوارض الغريبة ليس ممتنع بل هو موجود قلنا الغرض من ايراد هذه الصورة ليس الابيان انتقاض الحكم بامتناع الامساك عن القوت فى مدة طويلة على الاطلاق و هو حاصل و اختلاف سبب الامساك ليس بقادح فيه

Shaikhur Raees, Imam Fakhruddin Raazi and Nasir Tusi also have their firm belief that in certain conditions even without taking food or water a man can survive for a long period.

Here are some instances reported by Aienul Quzzat Hamdani in his "Zubdatul Haqaeq" who writes that:

1. Shaik Abu Omar Alwan did not take food for thirteen years. Thus he had commented that: "When a man gets food from paradise, there remains no need of worldly food for him."

2. Abdul Wahab Shirani writes in his "Al Yawaquthu wal Jawaher" that:

"Sheik Abu Taher had reported about a person who did not take food for 23 years. During this period he was busy in prayers, day in and day out, and he did not feel any weakness. When you come to know about such instances then it is certain that Tasbeeh and Glorification of Allah can give one the strength like that of Jesus Christ.'

قال الشيخ ابو طاهر و قدشاهدنا رجلا السمه خليفة الخراط كان مقيما بأ بهرمن بلاد المشرق مكث لا يطعم طعاما سنذ ثلاث و عشرين سنة و كان يعبد الله ليلا و نهارا من غير ضعف فاذا علمت ذلك فلا يبعدان يكون قوت عيسى عليه السلام التسبيح والتهليل

3. Author of "Akhbarul Akhiaar" has reported in his book about the commitment made by Hazrat Sheik Abdul Qader Jeelani (Rh) that:

"I had sworn to Allah that until Allah does not feed me, I would not eat; with such commitment a long period elapsed and I did not break the promise."

باخدا عهدمى بستم كه نخورم تانخورانند و مدت هائى مديدمى گزشت و عهد نمى شكستم

4. The continuous remembrance of Allah, becomes food for the staunch believers of Allah who submerge in acute love of Allah. In this connection a tradition has been reported by Nayeem Bin Hammad in his "Kitabul Fitan" that:

"Mohammed Bin Fuzael heard from Abu Sufian and Abu Sufian heard from Hasan (Rz), who stated that the Prophet (Slm) informed that on that day (Day of Judgment) the food of the faithful would be his continuous remembrance of Allah, praise of Allah and exaltation of Allah."

قال محمد بن فضيل عن ابى سفيان عن الحسن قال قال رسول الله صلى الله عليه و سلم طعام المومنين يومئذ التسبيح والتحميد والتهليل والتقديس و التكبير

From the above instances it can be proved that in certain conditions a man can survive a long period even without taking food and water, and what Sheik Abu Taher had told was his observation and not a hearsay gossip. This fact has been accepted by the scholars of Arab and Ajam; otherwise Abdul Wahab Shirani and Sheik Abdul Haq Muhaddis-e-Dahlavi would not have mentioned those facts, if there was any doubt about them. These facts are recognized by the scholars of the Ummah.

Thus it is certain that even without meals for a long time man's survival is possible. Therefore in the presence of so many examples, objections of Hadia's author do not stand to save his ignorance in any manner, and as a matter of fact Imamana's trance belongs to a period which occurred before Imamana's proclamation of his Mahdiat and it is for his information that we do not take even this episode as a proof for his Mahdiat. Since nobody questions about the event of the "opening of the chest of the holy Prophet (Slm)" since it should not be taken as a proof of his Nabuwwat. (Soora-e-Alam Nashrah - 94)

So far we had presented what had been reported in "Moulood". Now let us present some more instances from "Hashia Sharief", which states:

"Imamana (As) had gone into trance for twelve years. He was not conscious of anything of this world. But he used to become conscious for prayers, and after prayers, again used to go into trance. Bibi Alahdadi (Rz) used to help him for the changing of clothes or to feed him occasionally, and when he asked for water for ablution, she used to bring water; thus in this situation 12 years passed."

حضرت میراں علیه السلام را ابتداء حال دوازده سال جذبه بود کلی خبر این عالم نبود مگر وقت نماز هشیار شدے چون نماز کردندے بازمست شدے بی بی الهدتی زوجه حضرت میراں علیه السلام آں وقت خدمت کردند جامه پوشانیدند ، اند کے طعام خورانید ندوقت نماز میراں آب برائے وضو طلب کردند آں وقت آب آورده پیش کردندے همچنیں دواز ده سال شد

From the above, it is clear that whenever Imamana (As) used to wake up from his trance for prayers, Bibi Alahdadi (As) used to feed him sometimes during the twelve year period. Thus it is proved that the contention of the author of Hadia is awfully baseless.

The battle against Dalpat Rai took place in 875 H, then Imamana (As) went into trance for twelve years and when he came out from his trance completely in 887 H. Imamana (As) left Juanpur, as has been stated in Miyan Abdul Rahman's "Moulood" that:

"On receiving Commands from Allah

"Oh. Syed Mohammed migrate for our cause, and proceed to Hajj, where your proclamation would appear."

بعده ، فرمان حق تعالیٰ رسید که اے سید محمد برائے ما هجرت کن و به حج بیت الحرام بروهمان جاد عوت توروی خواهد داد

Sultan Husain Sharqi Went to Bengal:

Professor Mahmood Shirani's contention that after the defeat at the hands of Sultan Bahlol Lodhi, Sultan Husain went to Bengal does not seem to be correct, as per Farishta's contention:

""The Sultan found an appropriate time and returned to Juanpur along with his army, when the nobles of Bahlol Lodhi left Juanpur to Majholi to meet Qutub Khan."

سلطان حسین فرصت دیده با جمعیت تمام به جونپور آمد و امرائے سلطان بهلول جونپور را گذاشته پیش قطب خان به مجهولی رفتند

However, the second time also the Sultan was defeated by Bahlool Lodhi and at that time also the Sultan did not go to Bengal. As per "Tabaqaat-e-Akberi":

""Sultan Husain stayed in a portion of his Kingdom whose revenue was about five crores and became satisfied since Bahlol Lodhi also did not object for his stay."

سلطان حسین بـه یك قطعه ولایت خود کـه محصول آن پنج کـردربـود ـ قـانـع شده اوقات میگذرانید و سلطان بهلول طریق مروت مسلوك داشته متعرض اونمی شد

It may be pointed out that what Mahamood Shirani has written about Sultan Husain, it happened only when he was defeated by Sikander Lodhi, who captured Juanpur. On that defeat Sultan Shaik Husain, becoming frustrated, arrived to his son Alauddin who was the ruler of Bengala.

""When Sikander defeated the Sultan in 905 H. and after the defeat the Sulatan went to (his son) Sultan Alauddin, the ruler of Bengal, who provided refuge to his father."

لیکن دریس کرت سلطان سکندر جون پور ا از تصرف او بیرون کشید و سلطان حسین پریشان و بد حال پناه به سلطان علاء الدین حاکم بنگاله برد

This episode pertains to the period of Sikender Lodhi in the year 905 H.and not b

elonging to the period of Bahlol Lodhi, as reported by Shirani. Thus, the period when Imamana(As) had migrated from Juanpur in 887 H. Sultn Husain was the Ruler of Juanpur. In support of this fact H.R.Nevil's writing is submitted who reported that Sulatan Husain Sharqi's Coins ran on without a break till 889 H., while Imamana(As) left Juanpur for ever in 887 H.

CHAPTER TWO

Migration And Proclamation of Mahdiat

Importance of Migration:

The first significance of migration was that Imamana (As) performed migration only on firm commands of Allah.

1. According to "Hashia-e-Insaf Nama", Imamana (As) had migrated only on the commands of Allah:

"It is narrated that where ever he had gone, he went on the Commands of Allah. His followers used to join him leaving their cooking etc; and those who were busy in the bazar used to rush and join him leaving everything."

نقل است حضرت میران علیه السلام هر جاکه روانه شدند بامر الله روانه شده اند بعضی نان پخت یا نه پخت همچنان گرفته رفتندے بعضی درباز از رفته بودند همچنان دویدندے

2. Second significace was that whenever his expulsion orders arrived from the authorities, Imamana (As) left everything in the house and started soon as mentioned in "Hashi-e-Insaf Nama":

""When authorities issued orders for his expulsion, he immediately left that place without taking any provision from the house, never cared for those provisions saying it belongs to Allah."

نقل است حضرت میراں را هر وقت مخالفان بیرون کردند هرچه درخانه بود همه گذاشتند هیچ التفات نه کردند و فرمودند این همه برائے الله است

Third significance was that Imamana (As) never stayed at any place for more than 18 months, according to "Shawahedul Vilayet":

"It is narrated that except Chapaneer, Bidar, Ahmadabad, Peeran Patan and Farah, Imamana (As) never stayed at any place for more than 18 months."

نقل است که حضرت امام علیه السلام بجز این چهار مقام چاپانیر و احمد آباد و پیران پٹن و بڑلی هیچ جا هژده ماه اقامت نه کردند (باب نیز دہم)

Fourth significance was that people accompanied him leaving everything as reported in "Moulood" of Miyna Abdul Rahman (Rh):

"At every place people used to accept his hand for allegiance and after becoming his disciple used to join him in his migration, leaving everything with a hope of the vision of Allah."

فی کل نزول کثیر الناس بحضور پر نور حضرت امیر آمده مریدمی شدند و تارک حطام دنیا و طالب لقائے مولیٰ شده همراه آنحضرت روان می شدند

Fifth significancee was that at the time of departure to Khurasan, as reported by Professor Mahmood Shirani, there were 900 persons with him, 360 were along with families. In another report it is also said that there were 2200 disciples, out of them 900 were along with family and the rest were singles.

Sixth significance was that the place he went, he used to give his sermon on Qur'an in the language of that place, as reported in "Shawahedul Vilayet":

"Imamana (As) used to give his sermons in the colloquial language of that city or country."

در هر شهر که رفتی و در هر ولایت که قدم سعادت فرمودے بزبان آن ولایت بیان قرآن کردے

The following is the list of places where he stayed during his migration:

1. Danapur: This city lies towards East of Juanpur, 170 miles away. Now it has a Railway station.

2. Kalpi: It lies towards West of Danapur, 370 miles away, just 45 miles South-West of Kanpur.

3. Chanderi: 160 miles from Malwa, towards South West of Kalpi.

4. Chapaneer: 360 miles from Chanderi, towards South-West. He stayed here for 18 months.

5. Mandu: he came in the year 892 H, which lies to the East of Chapaneer about 100 miles . which was the capital of Malwa. In "Shawahedul Vilayet" and in "Matleul Vilayet" it is written that he went first to Mandu and then to Chapaneer.

6. Burhanpur: This is 260 miles from Mandu, where he stayed just one night.

7. Dowlatabad: it lies towards West, some 180 miles. He stayed there for one week only.

8. Ahmadnagar: it lies 90 miles from Dowlatabad towards South-West. He arrived in the year 899 H. when construction of the city walls was under progress.

9. Bidar: 240 miles towards South-West of Ahmadnager. He stayed there for 18 months during the reign of Qasim Bureed Shah.

10. Gulbarga: 70 miles, south-west of Bidar. He went to Mausoleum of Sheik Sirajuddin (Rz) where he retired for a week to offer undisturbed prayers. (Aitakaf) (He also visited the Mausoleum of Hazrat Khaja Gasoodraz (Rz.)

11. Bijapur: It lies 100 miles towards South-West of Bidar and stayed there for some days..

12. Cheetapur: Lies East of village Rai Bagh, from where he went via Kokan to Dabhol Bandar which lies towards North-West of Bijapur, some 200 miles away. From here in the year of 900-901 H. he went to Hajj via Jeddah along with 360 disciples. He stayed in Aden for three days. At Yalmalam he wore Ehram and then went to Jedda, stayed at Jedda for a few days and went to Makkah and stayed here for some months. There seems a difference in the period of his stay in Makkah. Some say he stayed for three months, some say seven months and some say nine months. Here he proclaimed his Mahdiat for the first time in 901 H., in between Rukun and Maqam-e-Ibrahim.

13. Dev Bander: He returned from Makkah and came to Dev Bander and went to Ahmadabad, and some say, he landed at Khambaeth and went to Ahmadabad which was the capital of Gujrat. He stayed here for 18 months. He proclaimed his Mahdiat for the second time in 903 H.

14. Santhej: Lies North-West of Ahmedabad, just nine miles away.

15. Pattan: He stayed here 18 months and some say 15 months.

16. Badhli: It lies towards West of Patan some 6 miles, where he stayed for 14 months and proclaimed his Mahdiath for the third time in 905 H.

17. Jalore: Some 140 miles from Pattan, he reached here via Tirad and Sanchor, towards East.

18. Nagore: It lies East of Jalore some 170 miles.

19. Jaisalmir: it lies 190 miles West of tNagore.

20. Nagar Thatta: it was the capital of Sindh, 490 miles from Jaisalmir. (Now in Pakistan)

21. Kaha: This place is very near (just 12 miles) to Thatta where he stayed for some months and offered "Dugana-e-Lailathul Qadr" on the commands of Allah for the first time.

22: Qandhar: This city is 600 miles from Thatta, towards North-West. It is surrounded by hills and mountains; he stayed here for two weeks.

23. Farah Mubarak: It is 180 miles, a city North-West of Qandhar. He stayed here for two years and five months, as per "Moulood" of Miyan Abdul Rahman (Rh):

"After he entered Farah, he stayed for
two years and five months."

بعد از داخل شدن در فراه دو سال و پنج ماه حیات
آنحضرت ماند

At first Imamana's stay was outside the city of Farah, as per "Moulood":

" His stay was in a garden, outside the
city of Farah."

امامقام آں سر در در فراه بیرون شہر در باغ بود

Author of Hadia has written that Imamana (As) stayed here for nine months.

"While he was in old Farah, he stayed in
the Sarai of Sikanderji Malik Kewan."

الـغرض چونکه امام علیه السلام در فراه کهنه قدم
سعـادت فـرمـودند در سرائی ملک سکندر جی ملوک
کیوان فرود آمدند (باب بست ودوم)

From the old Farah he went to the city of Farrah where he stayed for nine months.

"After arrival of Bandagi Miran Syed
Mahmood (Rz) and Bandagi Miyan
Syed Khundmir (Rz), he lived for six
months. Before their arrival Imamana
(AS) had already moved to Farrah and
lived there for three months. Thus in the
city of Farrah he lived for nine months."

الـغرض بعـد از آمـدن بنـدگی میران سید محمود
بنـدگی میران سید خوندمیر رضی الله عنهما حضرت
ولایـت پنـاه راشش ماه حیات شده است وسه ماه قبله
هـذا ور فـراه الـمفرح المقام حضرت امام علیه السلام
آمـده بـودنـد منـجمـله نه ماه حیات شاهنشه در این
جاشده است (باب بسیت وپنجم)

Thus Imamana (As) stayed two years in old Farah and five months in new Farah. And on Monday, 19th Zee Quaeda, 910 H. he passed away. Farah is 180 miles from Qandhar. Once it was the city of Iran, now it is in Afghanistan. Afghanistan at that time was not existing at all.

Invitation of Mahdiat:

It is evident from the world's history that no prophet had ever covered so long a distance as Huzoor (As) did to invite people towards Allah. At his age of 12, he was awarded the title of "Asadul Ulema" and thereafter he started his sublime sermons where ever he went.

(Note: The distance covered by Imamana (As) from Juanpur to Makkah, back from Makka to Ahmadabad, then proceeding from Jaisalmir to Thatta and to Farah approximately comes to more than 7,000 miles on land apart from sea journey to Makkah and back another 6,000. Thus Imamana (As) travelled more than 13,000 miles for the cause

of Allah. As far our knowledge goes none had travelled such a long journey for the cause of Allah. It is astonishing that at that time except horse, ox-cart and by walk, no modern kinds of conveyance were available, apart from the dangers of burglars and wayfarers were always lingering. Still it is important to state that nothing untold miseriers clamped over him. It was nothing but miracle that he never stopped his mission with the Help and assitance of the Almighty. There is no record to point out that he ever suffered from any disease or fatigue. He, by the grace of Allah Subhn O Tallh, was healthy and smart enough to face the visctitudes of the continuous journey for the cuase of Allah, the Almighty.)

Long back, Sheik Daniyal (Rz) and the religious scholars of Juanpur had given their verdict that Huzoor (A) is "Syedul Aouliah" and from then onwards he was well known for his "Sainthood". After a considerable period, Sultan Husain Sharqi, who too was like a Saint and an upright Ruler, became Imamana's devotee.

The details of the period, after he was designated as "Asadul Ulema" to his taking part along with Sultan Husain Sharqi in the battle against Rai Dalpat is not available, yet it is proved that the people were getting beneficence from him, which fact had been written by Miyan Abdul Rahman (Rh) about his early period.

It is a fact that Imamana's whole life was spent in the propagation of "Mazhab-e-Ma Kitabullah, WA Itteba-e-Mohammed Rasoolullah (Slm)". (*My religion is based on the Holy Quran, and I am the follower of Mohammed Rasoolullah (Slm)"*. Complete 23 years were spent for the propagation of this Message. As had been narrated in "Shawahedul Vilayet", Imamana (As) asserted that "For 18 years, I was getting un-emphasized commands from the Almighty "You are Mahdi, so proclaim it". But this servant assimilated it. Now from five years, it is emphatically commanded with Reproof:

"Oh. Syed, you are the Promised Mahdi, so express it and disclose it." Thus Imamana (As), thereafter proclaimed his Mahdiat with full force. This Proclamation is called "Emphasized Proclamation" (Ghair Muqqaiyed-Un-fettered) announcing, "whoever denies my Mahdiat, he would be accounted for on the Day of Judgement". The author of Hadia had written that Imamana's "Delayed Proclamation" was an act of disobedience (God Forbid) that Imamana (As) had taken so many years to pronounce that "his denial makes one Infidel".

It may be pointed out that even the Holy Prophet (Slm) did not declare his Prophethood for more than three years openly. And when Allah's command came emphatically, then only the Holy Prophet (Slm) openly declared his prophethood and invited the Qureish to stop worshipping the unholy Idols and accept Allah as the Sole Sustainer, and Creator of the universe. This fact had been mentioned in the "Madarijul Nabuwwat" which states that:

"For three years the mission was kept secret and when a particular verse was Revealed "Fasda' Bima Tu' Mar A'riz 'anil Mushrikeen", then only the holy Prophet (Slm) declared what was ordered to him by Allah, he was also ordered to keep himself away from the polytheists."

تا سه سال حال بریں منوال بود و مامور بود آنحضرت صلی الله علیه و سلم باخفاء این امر و صبر بر آن ، پس آنحضرت بخفیه دعوت می کرد قافازل شد آیه کریمه فاصدع بماتؤمر و اعرض عن المشکرین یعنی اظهار کن آنچه امر کرده شدی بدان ، آشکارا کن دعوت را و بگردان روے خودرا از مشرکان

When emphasized Orders came to the Holy Prophet (Slm), then only he declared boldly about his Mission. In the same way, until Imamana (As) was not ordered to proclaim his Mahdiat openly, he did not declare his Mahdiat. In this way he followed the holy prophet (Slm) who also did not declare openly till the command came from Allah through the verse abovesaid. And when an outright command came to proclaim openly in 905 H. at Badhli, Imamana (As) declared boldly. Another absurd objection was raised by the author of Hadia that "on continuous insistence from his followers, Imamana (As) agreed to declare his Mahdiat."

"On the continuous insistence from his Companions to openly declare his Mahdiat, Imamana (AS) passified them by telling "stick to your duties, when Allah's command come, I shall certainly declare."

یاران تکرار بر تکر مار کردند حضرت میران همیں جواب دادند که شمادر کارخود باشید هر وقتی که حق تعالیٰ می خواهد آشکارا می کند

This is an absurd remark of Zaman Khan, since no where this sort of advice from his companions was recorded in any of the Mahdavi literature. But it is narrated that when his companions got inspiration that Imamana (As) was the Promised Mahdi (As), "Then, they (companions) requested continuously to declare his Mahdiat, on which Imamana (As) "reprimanded them to be busy with their work and asserted that whenever Allah wills, I shall certainly disclose."

From this assertive remark that the fact of the proclamation was subject to Allah's command; and of course not at all on the advice of his followers, then how could the author of Hadia foolishly remark that on the advice of his followers Imamana (As) did proclaim?

The author of Hadia's remark that on the advice of the followers Imamana (As) proclaimed himself to be the Mahdi is so ridiculous, as if to say that the verse of prohibition of wine was revealed on the advice of Hazrat Omar's request. Yes, it is correct that Hazrat Omer (Rz) prayed to Allah to grant an order for the prohibition of wine. Thereafter it is said that the Prohibitory Verse was revealed and the wine was prohibited.

It may be pointed out that not only this prohibition order was decreed, there are twenty instances of Hazrat Omer's suggestions on different occasions and there came the Revelations. Such instances are pointed out in "Tanqul khulfa" and the same have been narrated in "Ash'athul Lama'at" that:

"Told Ibn Murudia Mujahid that soon after Hazrat Omer (Rz) suggested something, and the verses of the Qur'an came as per his suggestions."

روایت آورده است ابن مرودیه از مجاهد گفته می بود عمر که رای می زدپس نازل می شد به آن قران

Should these Revelations or those verses of the Qur'an not bde taken as the words of Allah? but were based (Naoozo Billah) on suggestions by Haz. Omer (Rz)? It is utterly wrong to say that what ever Hazrat Omer (Rz) suggested, Allah might have revealed on the Holy Prophet (Slm) accordingly. Is it not just a false allegation on the Holy Prophet (Slm)? Who was called "Sadeq"/ Trustworthy even by his opponents!

It is a fact that Imamana (As) had proclaimed his Mahdiat in Makkah, in between the Rukn and Muqaam, and the oath of allegiance was taken at that time. It was in accordance with the Tradition. Nayeem Bin Hammad had reported what Hazrat Abu Huraira (Rz) had heard the Prophet (Slm) was saying that:

"Oath of allegiance would be taken in between Rukn and Muqaam by Mahdi (As). He would neither awake the sleeping one, nor he would cause massacre or blood letting, at the time of taking oath of allegiance."

قال علیه السلام المهدی بین الرکن والمقام ولا یوقظ نائما ولا یهریق دما

Yet another Tradition has been reported by Nayeem Bin Hammad referring to Hazrat Qatada (Rz) that:

"On arrival of Mahdi (As) from Madinah to Makkah, people after meeting him, took oath of allegiance on the hand of Mahdi (As), although he would not like such allegiance."

یخرج المهدی من المدینة الی مکة فیستخرجه الناس من بینهم فیبایعونه بین الرکن والمقام و هوکاره

It may be pointed out that in Arabic, "Madinah" means " city". Here the use of the word of Madinah should not be construed to the real "Madinatun Nabi". At many occasions in Qur'an this word has been used, viz;

"A group of women of the city (Madinah) were told that the wife of the ruler of Egypt had been trying to woo her young servant towards herself." (12:22)

و قال نسوة فی المدینة امرات العزیزتراودفتها نفسه

Here Madinah means Egypt.

Hazrat Abdullah bin Yasir has reported in "Abu Dawood" who heard the holy Prophet (Slm) saying that:

"Abdullah bin Busair heard the Prophet (Slm) saying that "the period of six years would pass in between the great battle and the subduing of Madinah; and in the seventh year the Antichrist would emerge."

عن عبدالله بن بُسر ان رسول الله صلى الله عليه و سلم قال بين الملحمة وفتح المدينة ست سنين و يخرج الدجال فى السابعة رواه ابو داود و قال هذا الاصح

Here also Madinah means city of Qustuntunia. But the real "Madinathu Nabi" shall be safe. Imam Bukhari (Rz) referred Abi Bakr (Rz) as saying that:

"There would never be any terrifying pomp and glory of Dajjal (Anti Christ) in Madinah, since it would have seven gates and at every gate two angels would be posted there for the protection of the city."

عن النبى صلى الله عليه و سلم لا يدخل المدينة رعب المسيح الدجال لهايوميئذ سبعة ابواب على كل باب ملكان

The literates in Arabic have clarified about Madinah which would be a selected place on which the fort would be constructed. In "Ashathul Lamaat", Sheik Abdul Haq has stated about Madinah, that:

"As per classification (of Madinah), the village comes first, then comes town and then the city."

ترتيب اسماء براين طريق است كه قريه است و بالاتر ازوے بلدو بالاتر از بلد مدينه و فوق همه جامع تراز همه مصر و بعضى بلده و مدينه را دريك مرتبه نهاده اند

Emergence of Mahdi from Yeman has no proof:

In this referred Tradition it has been reported that Mahdi (As) would emerge from Madina (city). It nullifies such saying which tells that Mahdi (As) would emerge from a village Kurah.

Abu Bakr Miqri has reported that Imam Mahdi (As) would emerge from a village named Kurah. Author of "Muajjim-e-Baldan" stated that :

"Abdullah Bin Omro Bin al Aass has said that the holy Prophet (Slm) had mentioned that Mahdi (As) would come from a **village of Yeman named Kurah.**"

روى عن عبدالله بن عمربن العاص قال قال رسول الله صلى الله و سلم يخرج المهدى سن قرية باليمن يقال لها كرعة

Author of Hadia has tried to change the word Kurah to Karimath, and he has tried foolishly to bring Yeman in India. The author of "Safer-e-Saadath" has mentioned:

"Baithul Muqaddas, Asqalan, Quzween, Andalus and Damascus (probable cities where the emergence of Mahdi (As) was speculated) but no tradition had pointed out any particular city among the above mentioned cities."

در بـاب فـضـائل بیت المقدس عسقلان ، قزوین و
اندلس و دمشق حدیثی صحیح نه شده

*(Note: While Sultan Feroz Shah Tughlagh was passing from the village, Kararah, abetting to the River Gomti, there was a temple of Krarabeir, which was dismantled by order of the Sultan and foundation of Juanpur was laid down. Then, according to the tradition, the name of the city was said to be "Kurrah", or actually it was Kararah where the city of Juanpur was founded by the Delhi Sultan.. Thus the prophecy regarding the **appearance of Mahdi from the city of Kurah or Karara, later on named Juanpur, is true.)***

The prominence of Juannpur during Ninth and Tenth Century Hijri had been well established and had been discussed in earlier paragraphs. On that score the word Madinah fits to Juanpur in all respects. However, in some books relating to jurisprudence, whenever the word Madinah or Misr has been used, certainly it does not point out to "Madinathun Nabi" at all. If "Madinah" was the city for emergence of Mahdi (As) then the Prophet (Slm) would have used the word TABA (Madinatun Nbi). "Muslim" has reported that Jaber bin Samrah had heard what Prophet (Slm) was telling that:

"The Prophet told that Allah has named Taba for Madinah."

قـال سـمـعـت رسـول الله صلی الله علیه و سلم
یقول ان الله تعالیٰ سمی المدینة طابة

Book"Ashia-e-Paighamber" narrates that "Allah told me to rise and assemble and inform whatever you see". Thus he rose and saw that one rider was on a donkey and another on a camel, who were telling that Babel and its sculptures have been capitulated. Hazrat Sheik Abdul Haq had narrated with reference to Qateeba that the rider over the camel means the Holy Prophet (Slm). It may be pointed out that camel is in use for the purpose of riding in places like Arabia, Iraq, Syria, Egypt, Tunis and Morocco etc., where sand is in abundance. However, Arabia has been particularized because the Holy Prophet (Slm) was born in Makkah. In the same sense, if Juanpur is taken as Madinah, why should any doubt arise? There exists only one tradition, which tells that allegiance on the hand of Mahdi (As) would be taken by the people in between the Rukn and Muqaam. Even if the tradition reported by Nayeeem Bin Hammad is taken for granted then also it fits for the Imamana (As) since it had been reported that allegiance had been taken in between Rukn and Muqaam, on the hands of Imamana (As) when he pronounced his Mahdiat in Makkah in 901 H. for the first time, on the commands of Allah.

The author of "Hadia-e-Mahdavia" asserts in his book that "had Imamana (As) pronounced his Mahdiat in Makkah, the scholars and authorities would have killed Imamana (As), is simply baseless and prejudiced. It may be pointed out that when the Holy Prophet (Slm) vehemently rejected the Idols of Makkah and forcefully declared his Prophethood, none could dare to kill him (since Makkah was declared Haram, by Quresh, a place where there should be no battle) Therefore at the same score, since Imamana (AS) was the Khalifatullah how could anybody empower him? Sheik Abdul Haq has narrated in "Zaadul Muttaqeen" that Sheik Ali Muttaqi once had proclaimed that he was Mahdi, but later on after some days he repented.

"It is stated by Abdul Haq Muhadis-e-Dehelvi: "On one morning, sheik Ali Muttaqi in the presence of a crowd declared: "I am the promised Mahdi, I am the promised Mahdi". It made the crowd to astonish about him that: whether he was mentally upset?"

در حرم شریف در آمدند روز جمعه بود و خلایق بسیار حاضر در حضور همه فریاد آوردند انا المهدی الموعود انا المهدی همه حیران بماند ند که این چه حالت است ۔

It is a fact that Sheik Ali Muttaqi was an arch rival of Imamana (As). He himself proclaimed about his Mahdiat in Makkah but nobody resisted his claim or killed him. Therefore, when Imamana (As) declared his Mahdiat in between Rukn and Muqaam, how could anybody object? When it is a fact that Imamana (As) stayed in Makkah for a long period and had spent the whole of his life in the propagation of Islam. Mullah Abdul Qader Badayuni has particularly written in his "Najathur Rashid" that:

"When Mir Syed Mahdi (Hazrath Mahdi (As) has pronounced his Mahdiat during his stay in Makkah, orders for his expulsion were issued."

تا به مکه مشرفه شده .... می گویند که میر مذکور این دعویٰ را در آنجا کرده حکم باخراج او نموده اند

It is a fact that Mahdiat was pronounced in Makkah, for the first time, as per the traditions, but there is no book which informs any such expulsion orders except as reported by Badayuni.

The author of "Shawahedul Vilayet" in Part twelve reports that:

" Imam Alaihis Salaam on the command of the Almighty proclaimed his Mahdiat in between Rukn and Muqaam in these words: "Whoever follows me is a Momin and the faithful". Bandagi Miyan Shah Nizam (Rz) and Qazi Alauddin (Rz) the companions of Imamana (As), exclaimed "Aamanna wa Saddaqanna" on that proclamation, then they took allegiance on Imamana's (As) hands. Then Imamana (As) started his sermon and after the sermon, some Arabs also had taken oath of allegiance on his hands. When asked why he had not allowed others for allegiance, he said Allah informed him that two witnesses were enough."

امام عليه السلام بامر ملك العلام در محضرهٔ خاص و عام ميان ركن و مقام دعویٰ مهديت بدين عبارت فرمودند كه من اتبعنى فهو مومن ، در آن وقت بندگى ميان شاه نظام و قاضى علاء الدين كه هر دو صحابه كرام اند و صدقنا گفته دست بيعت كردند و بعضى ياران درائ آن بعضى مرد مان نيز توجه آوردند كه دست بيعت بآنحضرت كنند ، حضرت ميران بر حكم آيات قرآن نصيحت آغاز كردند بعد از فارغ شدن از نصيحت بعضى اعراب هم آمده دست بيعت كردند بعضى ياران پرسيدند كه ميرانجى بديگر ياران چرا بيعت نفرمودند گفتند كه مرا امر بارى تعالیٰ رسيد كه ائ سيد محمود و گواه برائ ثبوت دعویٰ بس اند

This fact has also been reported in the "Hashia Sharif" that:

"Immana (As) went to Makkah and sitting on a pulpit he pronounced that "Whoever follows him is the Momin."

حضرت ميران به كعتبه الله رفته بودند بالائ منبر نشسته دعوت كردند من اتبعنى فهومومن

Traditions prove that Imamana (As) had pronounced in between the Rukn and Muqaam, by sitting on the pulpit. But nowhere it is mentioned that the pulpit was placed in between the Rukn and Muqaam.

One more objection has been raised by the author of Hadia that the witnesses of his own companions were not enough proof for Imamana's Mahdiath and also that this witness does not commensurate with Fiqha. The author must know that those who are the companions, they alone are the substantial proof, and not those who reject the claim. Allah witnesses that the Prophet (Slm) was true (Al-e-Imran). And further Allah states

"It is He (Allah) who has named you Muslim both before the revelation and in the (Qur'an) that messenger may be a witness over you and you will be witness over mankind." (22:78)

هوسمكم المسلمين من قبل و فى هذا ليكون الرسول شهيد اعليكم و تكونوا شهداء على الناس (ج-ع۱۸)

Invitation for Witness::

Allah States in Almaida:

"They say Our Lord we believe, so write us down among the witnesses. (5:84)

يقولون ربنا آمنا فاكتبنا مع الشاهدين

(المائده - ع ١١٤)

Thus those who have faith in the Prophet (Slm) they alone are the witnesses of the Prophet (Slm).

The author of "Tafseer-e-Husaini" writes about witnesses that

"You are witnesses that the prophets have invited people towards Faith."

باشيد شما گواهان به مردمان برسانيدن انبياء دعوت حق رابديشان

Thus the companions of Imamana (As) are the true witnesses of the fact that Imamana (As), as per the traditions, pronounced his Mahdiat in between the Rukn and Muqaam. The author of Hadia has also objected that there were only two witnesses, while the Holy Prophet (Slm) has produced only one witness that too invisible.

"It is stated that the Prophet (Slm) went to the house of Zainab (Rz) who was not wearing any veil. She asked, how was it possible without a witness and the Sermon? The Holy Prophet (Slm) said Allah arranges matrimony and Gabriel (As) is the witness." Then he arranged the valima next day."

مروى است كه رسول الله صلى الله عليه و سلم بخانهٔ زينب رفت درحاليكه دى سر برهنه بود گفت يا رسول الله بى خطبه و بى گواه حضرت فرمود الله المزوج و جبرئيل الشاهد پس طعام وليمه ترتيب نمود

It may be pointed out that for the marriage two witnesess are compulsory. In "Ashathul Lama'at" it is mentioned that:

"It is written that without two witnesses marriage is null and void. It is a compulsory Sharaie order about the witnesses, which has been accepted by the Ummah and by the companions and successors of the Prophet (Slm)."

نكاح بى شهود باطل است و همين است مذهب ائمه و همين است منقول از صحابه و تابعين

Could anybody dare to question about the (invisible) witness for the marriage of Bibi Zainab? In this connection, "Muslim" has reported about Anas (Rz) who heard the Prophet (Slm) saying that:

"It is an admitted fact that there was a Prophet and for whom there was a single man who stood witness for him."

و ان من لانبياء نبيا ما صدقه من امة الارجل واحد

Thus it may be inferred that the witness of a single man is enough. But in the case of Imamana (As) there were two companions and some Arabs who had also witnessed. Even if only one companion had witnessed, it is enough for his claim on the basis of his righteousness. To this fact, the author of Hadia says that it was a quack (page 26).

Whereas, it is a fact that before Hazrat Omer (Rz) had accepted Islam, the Prophet (Slm) was offering prayers secretly.

Imam bin Hanbal (Rz) and "Tirmizi" had reported that:

"It is narrated by Ibn-e-Abbas (Rz) that: Rasoolullah (Slm) supplicated thus: "O' Almighty Allah, grant esteem and power to Islam through either Abu Jahal bin Hishaam or Omer bin al Khattab." Hence the same day, Haz Omer (Rz) came to the holy Prophet (Slm), and accepted Islam and Prayers began being offered openly from that day onwards."

عـن ابـن عبـاس عـن النبی صلی الله علیه و آله و سـلم قـال الـلهم اعزالاسلام بابی جهل بن عشام او بعمر بن الخطاب قاصبح عمر فغد اعلی النبی صلی الـلـه عـلیه و سلم قاسلم ثم صلی فی المسجد ظاهر ارواه احمد و الترمذی

As reported in "Ashathul Lama'at" that:

"Before Omer's conversion, none used to offer prayers openly and the Prophet (slm) himself was secretly offering prayers."

پس نمـاز گزارد آنحضرت در مسجد آشکارا و پیـش از اسلام وے هیچ کس نماز آشکار نمی توانست گزارد و آنحـضرت صلی الله علیه و سلم مختفی بود در دار ارقم

Only after Omer's conversion, the Prophet (Slm) offered his prayers openly in the Masjid. Is there any objection for those prayers being offered secretly before Omer's conversion? In such a scenario, could any person raise any objection for Imamana's proclamation of his Mahdiat in between Rukn and Muqaam to which his two companions had taken allegiance on his hand and thereafter other Arabs also followed them to offer their allegiance.

Witness of His contemporaries:

It was 900 H. when Imamana (As) was in Bidar, his contemporary Abul Fatha Shah Mohammed Multani (Died 935 H) to whom Imamana (As) wanted to meet. But Sheik Multani sent his four sons viz; Sheik Ibrahim, Sheik Ismail, Sheik Ishaq and Sheik Badruddin to meet Imamana (As).

"After the meeting (with Imamana As) they came back and asked their father whether the Imamana (As) was the true Mahdi (As)?"

حضرت بـندگی مخدوم شیخ بدر الدین می فرمانید که چـون از ایشـان بـاز گشتیم بخدمت حضرت والدی آمـدم و پرسـیدم کـه یا سیدی ایشان که خود را مهدی میگویا نند مهدی معهود ایشان باشند(صفحه ۹۸)

The details of their meeting are written in "Ma'adanul Jawaher" by Sheik Multani. We are not discussing whether Sheik Multani accepted Imamana (As) as the true Mahdi (As), or not, but the point of interest is to mention that even five years before Imamana's proclamation in Makkah, the fact of his being the Promised Mahdi (As) was under discussion in Bidar. "Ma'adunal Jawaher" was written by Sheik Shah Mohammed Multani, which was printed in Maktba-e-Deccan by Syed Shah Malik Mahmood Qadri in 1304 H. It was translated in Urdu under the name "Makhzanul Karamat". This particular point may be found on page 34.

Witness by Indian Historians:

Many historians have accepted that Imamana (As) has pronounced to be the Mahdi-e-Maood (AS).

1. Mulla Abdul Qader Badayuni has written about Imamana (As) in his "Muntakhab-ut-Tawareekh" that:

"Imamana Syed Mohammed Juanpuri (As) was a great mystic and a saint who has claimed himself to be the true Mahdi (As)."	میـر سید محمد جونپوری قدس الله سره، العزیز از اعاظم اولیائ کبار دعویٔ مهدیت از و سربرزده بود

2. Abul Fazal has written in his "Aieen-e-Akbari", that:

"Syed Mohammed Juanpuri (As) was the son of Syed Budh Owaisi who had bountiful beneficence. He was perfect in worldly life as well as spiritual knowledge. He proclaimed his Mahdiath and many became his devotees."	سید محمد جونپوری پورسید بده اویسی از فراوان روحـانیـه فیض بر گرفته در صوری و معنوی علم چیره دست از شوریدگی دعوی مهدیت کردو بسیارے مردم برو گرویدند

Abul Fazal wrote that Imamana (As) was the son of Syed Budh Owaisi. In that period the word Budh was being used to honour a man of repute. It has been proved that Imamana (As) was going to be designated as the Mahdi (As), hence Allah selected the most noble family of Saadaath who were staunch followers of the Holy Prophet (Slm). For that reason only Imamana's father was acclaimed as a dignified Syed and among the general public he was known as Syed Budh, the great Syed. Author of the "Farhang-e-Asafia" has mentioned Imamana's father's name as Syed Abdullah, alias Budha Saheb. In Jaipur there is a Mahdavi Daira which is still known even today as Budh Daira. (Bada Dairah)

(Note: It was prophesied by the holy Prophet (Slam) that Imam Mahdi's father's name would be "Abdullah" as the holy Prophet's father's name was "Abdullah," and mother's name would be "Aamina" as was his mother's name "Aamina". Thus matrimony of these personalities was arranged by the Almighty alone. Since Hazrat"Abdullah and Bibi Aamina (of Makkah), became parents of the holy Prophet (Slm) in Makkah, and also, as per the Prophecy of the holy Prophet (Slm), the sacred matrimony of Hazrat Abdullah and Bibi Aamina (of Juanpur) was arranged by the Almighty, who became parents of Imam Mahdi (As)..

Imamana's ancestor's chain of Mystic Order:

3. Although Abul Fazal has written Imamana's father's chain of the mystic order to be from that of Owaisi, but actually he was linked to Chishti Order. Farishta has written in his History that:

"Be it known that Mahdavis are Hanafi. A prominent man among them by the name Syed Mohammed (As), who in the year 960 declared himself to be the Mahdi (As), and of course some signs, attributed to the person of Mahdi (As), were found on him corrrectly, therefore people accepted him as the true Mahdi (As)."

باید دانست که مهدوی را اعتقاد آنست که شخصی حنفی مذهب سید محمد نام در هندوستان ور اواخر سنه ستین و تسعمایته دعوی کرد که من مهدی موعود بلسان شرع ام چون بعضی آثار و علامات که در مهدی آخر الزمان علیه السلام قرار داده اند دروے بود تصدیق قول او نمودند وآن اظهر من الشمس است

Although Farishta belongs to nearly to the same century, still he wrote the year 960 H. as the year of declaration of Mahdiat by Imamana (As), which is wrong, since Imamana (As) already passed away in the year 910 H. However from his writings two things have been confirmed.

One, Imamana's declaration of Mahdiat was recognized by him and others.

Two, the attributed signs pertaining to the person of Mahdi (As) were recognized by one and all to be perfectly correct to be present on the person of Imamana (As).

4. Author of "Mir'ath-e-Sikandari" writes: It is an established fact that:

"Syed Mohammed Juanpuri (As) who pronounced himself to be the Promised Mahdi (As), came to Ahmadabad in the last days of Sultan Mahmood."

مخفی نماند که در اواخر ایام عمر سلطان محمود، سید محمد جونپوری که دعوی مهدیت میکر داز جون پور به شهر احمد آباد آمده

5. Author of "Mir'ath-e-Ahmadi" has written with reference to Sultan Mahmood Begdah and about Imamana's proclamation of Mahdiat in these words:

"At the same period, Syed Mohammed Juanpuri (As) who proclaimed himself to be the Mahdi (As), came to Ahmadabad and stayed in the masjid of Taj Khan bin Salar, situated near the gates of Jamalpura and invited people towards his Mahdiat."

هم در آن آوان سید محمد جون پوری که دعوی مهدیت کرده بود و ارد احمد آباد گشت و در مسجد تاج خان بن سالار که قریب دروازه جمال پور است فردو آمد و مردم را دعوت نمود

Witness from Arabic History:

6. Abdullah Mohammed Bin Omar Makki has written in his "Zaferalwala", (Arabic) History of Gujrat that:

""Then Syed (Imamana Mahdi Alaihis Salaam) came from Ahmadabad to Naherwala Patan and then went to Badhli, a village, some 3 Farlang (6 miles) from Pattan and stayed there and declared his Mahdiat. A great number of people accepted him as Mahdi-e-Maoud (As) and followed him while many prominent people adopted that faith."

ثم ان السيد خرج (من) احمد آباد الى نهر واله بتن واقام على ثلاثة فراسخ منها بقرية بقال لها برلى و بها ادعى انه المهدى الموعود و تبعه جم غفير من العوام ثم تسلسل الى الخواص

7. Apart from these historians, Shah Abdul Aziz has subscribed in his

"Tuhfa-e-Asna-e-Ashria" that:

"Syed Mohammed Juanpuri (As) openly declared his Mahdiat. Many Afghans of Deccan and Rajputana became Mahdavi and followed him, and none could dare to kill him."

مير سيد محمد جونپورى در هندوستان ببانگ بلند ادعائ مهديت نمود و جماعه ، كثير از افاغنه ، دكن در راجپوتانه خود را مهدويه لقب كرده اتباع او كردند و هيچ كس اور اقتل و سياست نكرو

The word "Openly", determines that Imamana's proclamation of Mahdiat was in sound health and vigour and never in a condition of trance or intoxication, who announced his Mahdiat publicly and openly, wothout having any fear of being killed or harassed.

8. Author of "Nuzhatul Khawathir" narrates that:

"Then went towards Badhli which is 3 miles from Pattan, and for the fourth time, declared his Mahdiath that he was the true Mahdi (As)."

ثم الى قرية برلى على ثلاثة اميال من فتن وادعى فيها مرة رابعة انه مهدى

Explanation about His Assertions (Claim of Mahdiat):

Hazrat Bandagi Miyan Syed Khundmir (Rz), Imamana's prominent Khalifa has written "Aqueeda-e-Sharifa" which contains a complete record of Imamana's Sayings:

"Whoever wants to scrutinize our truthfulness, he should examine our actions and sayings whether they commensurate with the Qur'an and the following of the Holy Prophet (Slm) and understand."

اگر كسى خواهد كه صدق مارا معلوم كند بايد كه از كلام خدا و از اتباع رسول اور احوال و اعمال مابجويد و فهم كند

"Aqueeda-e-Shariefa" is an authentic book which has been recognized by all companions (Rz) of Imamana (As). Miyan Syed Husain has commented about the "Aqueeda-e-Shareefa" in these words:

"Whatever commands and orders of Imamana (As) have been recorded in the "Aqueeda-e-Shareefa" have the sanctity of all Companions of Imamana (As) and none of them has been contradicted by anyone."

الـغـرض بر صحت احكام محكمات كه در عقيده بنـدگيـميـان وارد اند اتفاق همه مهاجران شده است و هيچ يكى از اينها اختلاف نه كرده اند

According to the "Insaf Nama's Chapter five, the Ulema said that:
"We follow the Hanifa Rituals mostly" Imamana (As) declared."

ما مقيد به مذهب ابوحنيفه هستيم

"But we are not bound to any one religion (four schools). Our religion is based on the Holy Qur'an and we follow Mohammed Rasoolullalh (Slm)."

مـا يـه هيـچ مـذهب مقيد نيم مذهب ما كتاب الله واتباع رسول الله صلعم

Imamana (As) has explained about his mission that:
"I have presented the Holy Qur'an and I invite people towards Monotheist system of worship of the Almighty, since I had been deputed by Allah for that Mission particularly."

مـن كتـاب الله پيش كرده ام و خلق را سوے تـوحيد و عبادت دعوت ميكنم و من مامور براے ايں كارم از حضرت بارى تعالى
(انصاف نامه باب پنجم)

"If any person relates any sayings of mine, it should be examined whether it commensurate with the Holy Qur'an, and if it does, then it should be taken as my Saying, otherwise if it does not agree, then it must be believed that it was not mine. Or it may be taken as if the reporter did not understand what we said or it may be that, at the time of our Saying, the reporter's mind was not attentive."

اگر كسى از بنده نقل كند بايد به آں نقل را به بينـد اگر بـا كلام خدائے تعالى موافق باشد از بنده است و اگر بـا كـلام خـدائے موافق نيست آں نقل از بنده نيست يا آنكه سخن مارافهم نكرده است يا نقل كـننده را در وقت شفيدن دل حاضر نبودو بدان سبب سهو شده باشده (مقدمه انصاف نامه)

That is what the Holy Prophet also said:
"To examine my Traditions, if it is agreeable to The Holy Qur'an, then take it to be mine as I had myself stated."

اعـرضـوا حـديثى عـلـى كتـاب الله فان وافقه فهومنى و انا قلته

Thus if any tradition or saying of Imamana (As) does not agree to the holy Qur'an, should be rejected and should not relate either to the Holy Prophet (Slm) or to Imamana (As). Imamana's letters are the best explanation of his Mission which were written to the kings of his period. Miyan Abdul Rahman (Rh) has elaborately written about the Badhli's Proclamation:

"Miran wrote that "I am in my full senses and neither in ecstasy nor suffering from any ailment, have perfect understanding, Allah Jalle Shanhahu feeds me, I am not suffering from poverty. Having been endowed with family, never alone, and now as ordained by Allah I proclaim my Mahdiat and for witness thereof I present the holy Qur'an and the traditions of Mohammed Rasoolullah (Slm). Hereby you are commanded to investigate thoroughly my claim of Mahdiat; otherwise you will be put to test and cursed. If you accept me as true Mahdi (As), follow me otherwise explain to me my fault, and kill me if I am on the wrong path. If you do not do this, I shall propagate the same Mission of mine where ever I go, and as the worldly scholars say about me that I might be misguiding the Ummah."

حضرت میران کتابت نوشتند واضح باد که مرا صحواست زحمت نیست ، بنده را عقل تمام است و هیچ فوت نشده و خداوند تعالیٰ روزی میر ساند تمام فقر هم نیست ، بنده اهل و عیال میدارد مفرد هم نیست مع ذلك بفرمان خدائے تعالیٰ دعویٰ مهدیت اظهار کردیم و بر آن شاهد كلام الله و اتباع محمد رسول الله آوردیم تاشما رابایدکه تفحص کنید و گرنه بهر دو جهان حاکمان سیاه روئ گردند چراکه اگر بنده برحق باشد روے به اطاعت آرید ، اگرچه بر حق نباشد تفهیم کنید و اگر تفهیم نه شوم بقتل رسانید تا معلوم باد هر جا که خواهم رفت بر حقیقت خود دعوت خواهم کردو خلق را راه نمایم و به مدعائ علمائے ظاهر گمراه خواهم ساخت

In chapter Eight of "Shawahedul Vilayet", occurances in Sindh have been narrated, particularly about Mulla Sadruddin who said that:

"Miranji (As) whatever Khundkar says may be correct; but I feel apprehension that if I accept your Mahdiat and in fact you are not the Promised Mahdi ((As), then what should be my fate and how can I accept you? Miranji (As) replied: "You have fear of Allah of accepting a false Mahdi (As). Don't I have that much fear also to proclaim myself Mahdi (As) falsly, without the command of Allah, how cruel is he who mischievously relates himself to Allah?"

میرانجی انچه خوندکار میفر مایند همه حق است فاما در باب تصدیق کردن امر مهدیت ترس خدامی آید مبادا خدام مهدی نبا شد چگونه قبول کنیم حضرت میران در جواب شان فرمودند که چنانچه شمارا ترس خدای تعالیٰ در باب قبول کردن دروغ مهدی می آید پس مقدار شمارس خدا نیست که من از خدا مهدی نباشم و دروغ خودرا مهدی میگویانم بعده امام اولوالالباب این آیت در این باب خواندند که **فمن اظلم ممن افتری علی الله کذبا الی آخرها**

Basic Principles of the Mission:

Bandagi Miyan Valiji bin Miyan Yousuf (Rh) has carefully collected those principles ordained by Immmana (As) as narrated by Imamana's companions in his book "Insaf Nama", a very authentic source of those principles and had carefully recorded them category wise. The following are some of the chapters relating to those categories:

1. Chapter 5. (In Persian): "Her ke hayath-e-duniya ra talabad wo kafer asth": (Whoever demands Dunuiya, he is an Infidel) This Saying nullifies yearnings towards worldly life. This saying is based on the verse:

"Then, for such who had transgressed and had preferred the life of this world, the abode will be hell fire." (79:36,37,38)

فاما من طغیٰ و آثر الحیوة الدنیا فان الجحیم هی الماویٰ (نازعات)

2. Chapter 6: "Dur Rah-e-Khuda, there are four curtains (Hijabs):

1. World, 2. Khalq, 3. Satan, and 4. Passions". " These are four barriers." As regards the world and Khalq we can try to avoid, but we cannot avoid Satan and the Passions. We must pray to Allah to help us in desisting from the wrong doings of these two.

3. In Chapter 7. those naqliat have been dealt with which the emphasis is made for migration.

4. Chapter 9. tells "Tyyuein is Laeen," Any fixed amount if given regularly to a Godly man "is a curse" therefore adopt Tawakkul. It has bearing on Ushr and Sawiath, which will be explained under Chapter Daira-e-Mahdavia.

5. Chapter 11. deals with Remembrance of Allah.

6. Chapter: 12. Vision of Allah;

7. Chapter 13. deals with Amar Bil Ma'roof, wa Nahi anil Munkir" Enjoin what is right and abhor what is evil.

8. Chapter 14. Importance of Action with firm faith.

9. Chapter 15. teaches cooperation and forbearance; which are interconnected for betterment of the society, while differences and enmity destroys peace in the society.

Imamana (As) had continuously preached the masses towards monotheistic beliefs and advised them to offer prayers properly by understanding what is being recited and to offer thankfulness to Allah.

The discussion between Hirqul, the Roman Emperor and Abu Sufian:

Hirqul: "What are his orders to you by the Holy Prophet (Slm)?"

بما یا مرکم

Abu Sufuian: "He orders us for offering prayers, paying Poor Tax to the relatives, help the relatives and to adopt Chastity."

قلنا یا مرنا بالصلوة والزکوة والصلة والعفاف

Hirqul: "If whatever you say is correct, then he is the true Messenger of Allah."

ان یک ماتقول حقافانه نبی

When Hirqul's declaration is taken as a proof of Holy Prophet's truth worthiness, why should not we assert Immaman's Mahdiat being true on the basis of his teachings which commensurate to the Holy Qur'an and traditions of the Holy Prophet (Slm)?

Chapter Three
Proofs Regarding Mahdiat

For the proof of Nabuwwat three facts have been mentioned. 1. Prophecies of the Scriptures, 2. Miracles, and 3. Characters. Thus proofs of the Mahdiath also are based on three items:

1.Traditions of the Holy Prophet (Slm) 2. Miracles and 3. Characters. First of all we shall start with proofs regarding the Holy Prophet (Slm).

1. Prophecies in the Scriptures: Allah says that:

"I will depute a Nabi, one among their brothers, and put my words unto his mouth, and whatever I order him to do, he will do the same."

اقیـم لهـم نبیـا من وسط اخوتهم مثلک و اجعل کلامی فی فمه فیکلهم بکل ما اوصیه به

In this prophecy Allah addresses Hazrat Musa (As), that one among the brothers, just like Musa (As), he would send one prophet. Hazrat Musa (As) came from Bani Ishaq (As), whoever his brother shall be, he too shall be from Bani Ishaq (As) only. But the Holy Prophet (Slm) belongs to Bani Ismail (As). Therefore this prophecy relates to the Holy Prophet (Slm) being correct in all respects, because Bani Ismail (As) are brothers of Bani Ishaq (As). Here the word brother is absolute. The Jews regard Bani Ismail (As) as brothers of Bani Israel (As). (Kitabul Muqaddas Asha 18, Verse 18.)

The author of "Lisanul Muslimeen" comments on the above prophecy that:

"Had the purpose related to Bani Israel (As), then it must have been interpreted that I am going to appoint one Prophet among you and not among your brothers."

اگـر مـقصود بنی اسرائیل بودباید تعبیر بکند که از میان شما پیغمبر مبعوث می کنم نه از میان برادران

2. Thus, he said that:

"Thus he said "The Cherisher came from Sina; and for them enlightened from Sa'eer, and glittered from Mount Faaraan, And arrived along with ten thousand angels who had held in his right hand a fiery jurisprudence for them."

فقـال جـاء الـرب مـن سیـنا و اشـرق لهم من سعیروتلأ لا من جبل فاران و اتی من ربوات القدس و عن یمینه نار شریعة لهم

In this prophecy, the words coming from Sina, mentions to Hazrat Musa's (As) who arrived from the Mount Sina. The word Sayeer refers to Prophet Jesus (As) and the word Faaraan determines to the holy Prophet Mohammed (Slm). Jews and Christians believe that Faaraan locates in Syria, but Faaraan is a Hebrew word. There are so many mountains in Makkah, in one of them the Holy Prophet (Slm) used to meditate, which is known as "Hira Cave" on a mountain which is now named as the "Jabal-e-Noor". Sheik Abdul Haq Muhaddis-e-Dehlvi had referred to a Saying of Ibn Qatiba that glittering of Allah from Sina, Sayeer and Faaraan denotes to Revealing of the Scriptures from those mountains. As regards ten thousand angels, they mean sacred people. Since the appearance of the Prophet (Slm) had been taken as appearance of Allah, ten thousand angels may be taken as his companions. This prophecy perfectly relates to the Holy Prophet (Slm), because when he went to conquer Makkah, he went from Madinah along with ten thousand companions. As regards Fiery Jurisprudence is concerned, that jurisprudence is to burn and eradicate infidelity. (Kitabul Muqaddas, Asha 23, Verse 2).

3. "Allah asked me to appoint guards, so that whatever they see, should inform. He saw the riders, coming in two, two, in rows riding on the donkeys as well as on the camels. He listened very attentively then yelled loudly like a tiger and told that he stood in his place all day and night and saw riders who were coming in rows of two, and told that Babel had fallen and all the sculptures were destroyed. (Kitabul Muqaddas"- Asha 21, Verses 6,7,8,9)

لانه هكذا قال لى السيد اذهب اقم الحارس ليخبر بما يرى فراى ركابا ازواج فرسان ركاب حمير ركاب جمال فاصغى اصغا شديد اثم صرخ كاسد ايها السيد انا قائم على الموصد دائما فى النهار و انا واقف على المحرس كل الليالى وهوذ اركاب من الرجال ازواج من الفرسان فاجاب و قال سقطت سقطت بابل وجميع تماثيل الهتها المنحونة كسرها الى الارض

But the author of "Madarijun Nabuwwat" states that:

"In the Book Ashia, the Prophet (As) said that Allah directed me to rise and inform whatever you see, thus I rose and saw two riders who were coming one on a donkey, and the other on a camel, who were telling each other that Babel had fallen and the sculptures too were destroyed."

در كتاب اشعيا آمده كه گفت مراپروردگار تعالى برخيزو جمع كن و خبر ده بانچه مى بينى پس برخاستم و ديدم دو سواران را كه پيش مى آيند يكى برحمار و ديگرے برجمل مى گويد يكى مرديگرے را افتاد بابل و بتان وے كه تارشيده شده اند

There is a fundamental difference in the translations done by the Christians and that was done by the Muslims. While Christian's translation refers to plural, that donkey riders and camel riders are coming, but the Muslim translation refers to two riders, one on donkey and the other on camel. It seems the text was not understood clearly by both of them. Correct translation has been done in Arabic: Rikab Hameer, Rikab Jamal; while, as per Urdu translation: riders on donkeys and riders on camels; the same is referred in English as: A chariot of asses and a chariot of Camels. That is : one chariot of donkeys and other of camels.

However, what Ashiah had seen on a donkey, it refers to Propohet Jesus (As) and the man on the camel refers to Holy Prophet Mohammed (Slm). It is what Shaik Abdul Haq had presented the elucidation of Ibn-e-Qatiba. Moulvi Inayath Rasool Chiriyakovi has written in his book "Bushra" referring to the Hebrew Passage: Our Allah directed us to go and report what we see. Then I saw riders; a pair of two, one on a donkey and the other on a camel. This also mentions two riders. The rider on the camel denotes to the holy prophet Mohammed (Slm), since camels are the main source of riding and transportation in Arabia.

Prophecy in Torah.
In the above mentioned prophecy the word Babel has come. This should not be read as UBL

means camel. In "Madarijul Nabuwa" Uftad-e-Babel" (Babel has been captured) is mentioned and the English translation of Torah" Babylon fallen" (Babel was captured) is mentioned. Both translations agree on Babel, the name of a city.

Thus Babel was not captured during the life of the holy prophet, but Makkah was captured. The sculptures of Babel were not destroyed, but the 360 idols of Makkah were destroyed which were on the floor of the Kabathullah. However, Babel and its sculptures were destroyed by the successors of the holy Prophet (Slm). Thus this prophecy correctly applies to the Holy Prophet Mohammed (Slm) in words and spirit..

4. Daniyal Asha 2, verse 44

"During the period of these rulers, Allah shall establish a kingdom which would never be destroyed or shall be captured by another nation. It will crush and destroy all other kingdoms and shall remain until the Doomsday."

وفى ايام هؤلاء الملوك يقيم اله السموات مملكة لن تنقرض ابدا و ملكها لايترك لشعب آخر و تسحق و تفنى كل هذه الممالك و هى تثبت الى الابد

This prophecy also relates to the Holy Prophet (Slm) to an extent. But the kingdom which would destroy all other kingdoms, is a vague reference, since that sort of kingdom was never established either by the Prophet (Slm) or by his successors. Here nominal dominance was meant, not otherwise.

5.Safar Habqooq Asha 3, verse 3,4

"Allah came from Yathman and Quddoos came from Faaraan. Both of you ask him. Its grandeur covered the entire horizon; and all over the land his praise is being glorified. Its glitter has been just like luminosity. His hand will create sparkles. His omnipotence was hidden. The epidemic will go forward before him and from his foot stream will emerge. He stood and thus trembled the Earth. His daring sight shook the nations. Old Mountains were crushed like carded wool. Antiquity has been perished and the ways of eternity were for Him."

الله جاء من يتمان والقدوس من جبل فاران سلاه جلاله غطى السموات والارض امتلأت من تسبيحه و كان لمعان كالنور . له من يده شعاع و هناك استتار قدرته قد امه ذهب الوباء و عند رجليه خرجت التحمى وقف و قاس الارض نظر فزحف الامم و دكت الجبال الدهرية و خسفت آكام القدم مسالك الازل له

Here Faaraan also refers to the Holy Prophet (Slm) and all further assertions are compatible to the occurrences at the time of the Holy Prophet (Slm):

A. Glorification to cover the entire world, seemingly, may not be seen, and may not be proven.

B. Sparkles denote to Shariath which had already been discussed.

C. Other nations did not tremble during the Prophet's period, but it happened during the time of his successors, hence this prophecy fits to the holy Prophet (Slm).

D. Trembling of mountains (big empires) did occur after his birth, and small and big kingdoms were certainly destroyed, some during his life time, and others after him. This also fits to him.

6. Bible Luqa. Chapter 24, Verse 49:

"And now I shall depute that promised one by my Father, thus you stay in the city of Jerusalem till you get your power and strength from Almighty Allah."

وها انا ارسل اليكم موعد ابى فاقيموا فى مدينة اور شليم الى ان تليسوا قوة من الاعلى

For this prophecy, the Christians argue that the advent of the Prophet (Slm) would take place in Baith-ul-Muqaddas, but it is not correct, because it is not mentioned so.

It is said only to stay in Jerusalem. Hence it means that the religion of the Prophet (Slm) would itself reach Jerusalem.

It is an historicl prtoof that, Hazrat Omer (Rz) conquered Baithul Muqaddas and got the keys of Jerusalem from the christian priest.

7. Bible Yuhunnah, Chapter 14, Verse 30:

"I would not talk much to you, since the leader of this world is coming and I do not have that what he possesses."

لا اتكلم ايضا معكم كثيرا لان رئيس هذا العالم ياتى و ليس له فى شئى

This prophecy also refers to The Holy Prophet (PBUH), in which his attributes have been exemplified as a leader of the world as we call him "Sarver-e-Aalam".

8. Bible Yuhanna , Chapter 12, verse 31:

"Now it is ordered to the world, that the leader of this world will be sent."

آلا ن دينـوثة هـذا العـالـم آلان يطـرح رئيس هذاالعالم خارجا

The word "Al Aan" denominates to shortly afterwards. The advent of Huzoor (Pbuh) took place a few centuries after Haz Isa (As). Holy Prophet was born in Arabia in the year 571 AD. Hence this also fits on him.

9. Bible Yuhunna, Chapter 15, verse 26:

"And when the consoler would be sent to you on behalf of my father, and the Spirit of Allah which would be infused in him, he would stand witness for me."

ومتى جـاء الـمـعزى الذى سارسله انا اليكم من الاب روح الحق من عند الاب ينثبق فهويشهدلى

This too fits on the Holy Prophet (Slm); since he witnessed Hzt. Jesus (As) as the Prophet of Allah.

10. Bible Yuhunna , chapter 16, verse12 to 14:

"There are so many problems for you, but you cannot bear them. But when Ruhul Ameen (Slm) would come, he would explain to you the right path. He would not tell from his own self, but he would reveal only which was revealed to him and would inform you about the future."

ان لی امور کثیرة ایضالا قول لکم و لکن لا تستطیعون ان تحتملوا الآن و امامتی جاء ذالک روح الحق فهو یرشدکم الی جمیع الحق لانه لا یتکلم من نفسه بل کل مایسمع یتکلم به و یخبرکم بامور آتیة

This prophecy fits on him completely. The words" Ma Yantiqu Anil Hawa", refers to: "He tells only what was revealed to him and would guide towards the straight path only". It determines completion of the Deen. He would inform you about the future. It points out about those prophecies which cover the prophecies regarding the Advent of the Mahdi (As). It should not be construed that we can not argue from the prophecies mentioned in the abrogated Scriptures. Since Allah tells:

""If you do not know, ask from those who had scriptures". (Nahal)

فسئلوا اهل الذکر ان کنتم لا تعلمون (نحل)

Had they been abrogated and prohibited, why should Allah indicated towards the Scriptures of Christianity and Jews?. This all speak that we have to interpret those prophecies of the Scriptures, sometimes metaphysically and sometimes rhetorically.

Traditions relating to Advent of Mahdi (As):

Those traditions in respect of Immana Mahdi (As) are trustworthy, in the same manner as that of the prophecies regarding the holy Prophet (Slm) which have been testified by the guardians of the Traditions. Now we go to those traditions which have been recorded in the "Sihah Sittah" which perfectly fit to the person of Imamana (As) and in which the Word Mahdi (As) had occurred:

It is narrated by Umme Salma (Rz), who heard the Holy Prophet (Slm) saying that:

"Mahdi (AS) would be from my progeny (of Bani Fatima (Rz)."

عن ام سلمة قالت سمعت رسول الله صلی الله علیه و سلم بقول المهدی من عترتی من ولد فاطمة (ابو داؤد)

This tradition correctly fits to Imamana (As), since Imamana (As) comes from Bani Fatima (Rz). "Juanpur Nama" and "Tuhfatul Kiram" have reported that Imamana (As) came from Imam Moosa Kazim (Rz). "Juanpur Nama" also reported that mother of Imamana (As) was Hasani Syed. Even Sheik Ali Muttaqi, arch rival of Imamana (As), too had accepted Imamana (As) in his "Al Rudd" that Imamana (As) came from the lineage of Bibi Fatima (Rz). Many historians belonging to that period have written "Syed" for Imamana (As), the word "Syed" is used for the "Saadaat" lineage of Bibi Fatima (Rz) alone.

As Abul Fazal in his "Aaien-e-Akberi", and Mulla Abdul Qader Badayuni in his "Muntakhaabatut Tawareekh" and"Najatur Rashid", and Nizamuddin's "Tabkhaat-e-Akberi" all had accepted this fact while writings with reference to "Daira-e-Mahdavia" and about

"Ulema-e-Herat". Sheik Badruddin, son of Multani Pasha (died 935 H) had reported from his father in "Ma'adenul Jawaher" when Imamana (As) had arrived in Bidar. He had mentioned the words "Syed" and Mahdi (As) in his book saying that: Syed Mohammed Juanpuri (As) proclaimed himself to be the Mahdi (As) even in the year 900 H."

(2) Hazrat Anas Bin Malik (Rz) narrated that he heard the Holy Prophet (Slm) saying that:

"We, the descendents of Abdul Mutallib are the leaders in Paradise. Hamza, Ali, Hasan, Husain, Mahdi and myself."

عن انس بن مالک قال سمعت رسول الله صلی الله علیه و سلم یقول نحن ولد عبدالمطلب سادۃ اهل الجنۃ انا و حمزہ و علی و جعفر والحسن والحسین والمهدی (ابن ماجہ)

While the first tradition confirms that Mahdi (As) belongs to Bani Fatima (Rz), this tradition further confirms that Imamana (As) belongs to Bani Abdul Mutallib, (Bani Hashim.)

(3) Sayeed Bin al Musayib (Rz) narrated that when they were in the house of Umme Salma (Rz) and were discussing about Mahdi (As), Umme Salma (Rz) said that she heard the Prophet (Slm) telling :

"Mahdi (As) comes from the progeny of Bibi Fatima (Rz)."

عن سعید بن المسیب قال کناعندام سلمۃ فتذاکرنا المهدی فقالت سمعت رسول الله صلی الله علیه و سلم یقول المهدی من ولد فاطمۃ (ابن ماجہ)

(4)"Hazrat Ali (Rz) narrated what the Prophet (Slm) was saying that: "Mahdi (As) belongs to the Ahl-e-Baith (Rz). And that Allah will bestow on him the required capability within one night, (means in a short period)."

عن علی قال قال رسول الله صلی الله علیه و سلم المهدی منا اهل البیت یصلحه الله فی لیلۃ (ابن ماجہ)

Thus, It was already stated that Mahdi (As) comes from the Ahl-e-Baith (Rz). The words "Yeslahullah" refer to Mahdi (As) who shall have direct communications from Allah. Author of Hadia declines to link this tradition to Mahdi (As) in his book chapter 3, Evidence 8, on the basis of Mahdavi literature which confirms him to have been born as a mystic. It may be pointed out that "LAILATH" (Only one night) means a very short period.

It is not correct to say that the ability, which became visible then, was not present in him earlier; i.e., even before the proclamation of Mahdiat also he had the splendour of guiding people towards righteousness. Almighty Allah made him Mahdi (As) in order to complete the Mission started by the holy Prophet and thus Mahdi (As) completed the Deen as prophesied by the holy Prophet. Mahdi's excellent characters and the Signs of Allah which were manifested on the person of Imamana (As) are the undeniable facts, which none can deny.. Some scholars have explained about this tradition that "Almighty Allah would make Imamana (AS) able for His Caliphate (Khilafat) within no time".

Author of Hadia states incorrectly that Mahdi (As) might not have possessed required characters before he was granted Mahdiat. It is wrong, since it is an historical and undeniable fact that at his age 12, he was declared "Asadul Ulema" by the prominent scholars of Juanpur, and it is also a confirmed fact that at his age 21, he was declared as "Syedul Ouliah" by the eminent scholars, including his childhood teacher Haz.Shaik Daniyal(Rh) of Junpur. Thus, no body can dare to deny that even before his commissioning as the Promised Mahdi(As), he had that much capacity and capability to convince a large number of audience about his Mahdiat. Further to this, the holy Prophet (Slm) had already informed that Mahdi's (As) characters shall be resembling to his own characters. It means to say that what characters the Prophet (Slm) had even before his prophethood, same were the characters of Imamana (As) perfectly resembling to that of the Holy Prophet (Slm). Otherwise the prophecy "Yeshabahu Fil Khulqi" (Resembling to my characters) could not stand as an evidence.

5. Hazrat Abdullah bin Haris bin Juzail Zubaidi (Rz) narrated to have heard the Prophet (Slm) saying that:

"People would rise from the East to assist and help Mahdi (As) for his dominance."	عـن عبـدالله بن الحـارث بن جزء الزيدى قال قال رسـول اللـه صـلى اللـه علـيه وسلم يخرج ناس من المشرق فيوطئون المهدى يعنى سلطانه (ابن ماجه)

It has already been stated referring to his migration that where ever he went and propagated religious fundamentals, he was accepted by one and all and many followed him in his journey for their own betterment and also for enhancement of his Mission. This is a fact that after leaving Juanpur to Bidar and therefrom to Deccan, Hijaz, Gujrat, Sindh, Qandhar, Khurasan and Farah, all these places are situated to the East of Madinah. Persons of every region, and of every category and understanding had accepted his Mahdiat. The details of which shall be discussed under the title "kings, nobles, scholars, pious peoples and propagation of Mahdiat." Further we have narrated Abdullah Bin Omerul Makkki's assertion that when Imamana (As) proclaimed his Mahdiat at Badhli a large gathering accepted him to be the Promised Mahdi (As) and afterwards prominent persons continued Imamana's Mission as an exalted and sublime Mission.

Mulla Abdul Qader Badayuni in his "Najatur Rashid " has stated that:

"Imamana (As) arrived in Farah from Hijaz via Gujrat; when Mir Zunnoon was the ruler of Qandhar. There happened to be a tumultuous uproar about his Mahdiat and hundreds and thousands, accompanied him both ordinary people and the elite as well."	زمـانے کہ حکـومت قندھار تعلق بذوالنون بیگ داشت اواز زمـین حجـاز بـه قـصبۂ فراه رسید غلغلۂ عظـیـم در آن ولایت افتـاد و خلایق لایعدو لا یحصیٰ بدوجمع آمده

As regards "Tumaltuous Uproar", Abdullah bin Mohammed bin Omerul Mukki had narrated in his "History of Gujrat" that:

"Several times Sultan Mahmood (Gujrati) desired to meet Imamana (As), but his court nobles restrained the Sultan not to meet him on account of the apprehension that Imamana (As) had certain magnetic "God-Given" powers which attract toward him and keep one away from the worldly affairs; therefore courtiers did not allow the king to meet Imamana (As)."

وغيرمرة احب السلطان محمود ان يراه فالتمس اركان ملكه ان لا يفعل و صرفوه عنه لانه كان له قبول يجذب زائره و يحمله على التجرد من الدنيا

What more proof could be presented about Imamana's spiritual dominance that even rulers yearned to join him, leaving all worldly affairs behind them. These findings are not from any Mahdavi writer but these are the observations of non Mahdavi scholars about Imamana (As) of that period.

6. Hazrart Abu Sayeed Khudri (Rh) narrated that he heard the Prophet (Slm) saying that:

A. "Mahdi (As) is from my genealogy, having a shining forehead, elevated nose, who would fill the earth with Justice and would be the master for seven years."

عن ابى سعيد الخدرى قال قال رسول الله صلى الله عليه و سلم المهدى منى اجلى الجبهة اقنى الانف يملاء الارض قسطا وعدلا كما ملئت ظلما وجورا ويملك سبع سنين (ابوداؤد)

This Tradition has the following points for consideration:

a) "Mahdi (As) is from me", the above three traditions vouchsafe the genealogy of the Imamana (As).

b) Shining forehead and elevated nose. As stated by Miyan Abdul Rahman (Rh) in his "Moulood" that:

B. "When Hazrat Sheik Daniyal (Rz) asked about the features of the new born, Hazrat Abdullah reported "a shining forehead, with wheatish colour and an elevated nose and compressed eyebrows."

باز شيخ عليه الرحمه پرسيد ند که اصول آن طفل بچه نوع است سيد عبدالله فرمودند لون او گندم گون روشن پيشانى بلند بينى و متوسط ابرو يعنى پيوسته

C. Will fill the earth with justice.

Here "Al-arz" does not mean the whole of the earth. Even if that contention is admitted then we have to verify what explanation would be given when a like situation had been prophesied about the Holy Prophet (Slm) that:

"His (Holy Prophet's) grandeur would cover the entire horizon and the entire earth would be filled with his praise."

جلاله غطى السموات والارض امتلاءت من
تسبيحه (كتاب حبقوق باب ۳ آیت ۳)

(Kitab Habqooq, Chapter 3, Verse 3)

For example, during the life of the Holy Prophet (Slm), when the entire earth could not be filled with his grandeurs, then there is no reason to suggest as to why the earth was not filled with Justice during Imamana's time?.

It is a fact that Allah Himself confirmed that:

"That revelation which is revealed to you by your Allah, is the truth, but many do not believe it."(! 3:2)

والذى انزل اليك من ربك الحق ولكن اكثر
الناس لايومنون (الرعد ع۱)

And it is a fact that during the lifetime of the Prophet (Slm), whole of the world did not accept him as the Prophet (Slm); then how was it possible that during the period of Imamana (As) whole of the world would accept him as the true Mahdi (As)? And it is also a fact that believers are always in the minority, as mentioned in the Holy Qur'an.

In order to substantiate our suggestion, we refer one more instance referred by Hazrat Ibn Abbas (Rz) who happened to praise Hazrat Omer's good governance before the later's demise by telling:

"I swear to Allah, that during your reign the earth is filled with justice."

والله لقد ملأت امارتک الارض عدلا

The fact is that during the period of the Hazrat Omer (Rz) whole of the world was never filled with justice.

Author of "Makhzanul Dalael" has stated that, although, the Prophet (Slm) was designated by the Almighty to be the "Rahmatul Lil Aalameen" (Mercy to All) but the Prophet's mercy was only for those who were his followers. So also, in the verse "Qaalu Awalum Nunhaka unal Aalameen". They said: "Did we not forbid you not to protect any of the Aalameen (Strangers from us)

Author of "Tafseer-e-Husaini" had taken the word "Aaalimeen" for Strangers.

"Yamla ul Arz" refers to that place where people were living and who had accepted Imamana (As) as Mahdi. Regarding "Yamla ul Arz," Haz. Aalim Billah (Rh) had discussed in detail in "Sirajul Absar." (Refer "Sirajul Absar", pages 16 to 26)

Narrating these instances the author of "Makhzanul Dalael" had stated that: Mahdi (As) shall be the master for his affairs for a period of seven years. Affairs means Imamath, commands, invitation to the mystic way of life.

The prophecy in the Torah regarding the Holy Prophet (Slm) also refers " Wa Malika ash Shaam"saying that the holy Prophet (Slm) would reign over Syria."

In this connection, author of "Ash'athul Lam'aath" interprets that:

"Reigning" means Deen-e-Islam and
Nabuwwwath."

مراد بباد شاهى دين و نبوت است

Thus, the interpretation by the author of "Makhzanul Dala'el" regarding "Yamlak Amarul Imama" that "the reign of the whole world was entrusted to the Holy Prophet (Slm)." As mentioned in "Bible: Chapter 14, Verse 30" meaning "The emperor of this world is coming". Here kingdom is used in general meanings, without any condition that the whole of the world would come under his Reign. Then how can Imamana (As) be questioned that he did not fill the earth with justice? It may be pointed out that the Arabs do not take the meanings of the word "Malik", what the Persians (Ajamis) call one as a "Ruler". As regards seven years, it may be described that in 903 H. Imamana (As) pronounced his Mahdiat, while he was staying in the Masjid of Taj Khan Salar, in Ahmadabad. Thus from that year, he lived till 910 H. therefore seven years had been mentioned which fits on him.

"Abu Sayeed Khudri (Rz) narrated that he heard the Prophet (Slm) saying about Mahdi (As), that he would be born in the Ummah and shall live either seven years or nine years. That Mahdi (As) would grant divine blessings which nobody so far had given. Ummah would be bestowed with plenty of food, but nobody would hoard it for the next day. There would be so much of stock that whoever requested Mahdi (As) to give; Mahdi (As) would give without any limit."

عن ابى سعيد الخدرى ان النبى عليه السلام قال يكون فى امتى المهدى ان قصر فسبع والا فتسح فتنعم فيه امتى نعمة لم ينعموا مثلها قط توتى اكلها ولا تدخر منه شيئاً والمال يومئذ كدوس فيقوم الرجل فيقول يا مهدى اعطنى فيقول خذ (ابن ماجه)

From this tradition following points come to light:

A. Mahdi (As) comes from Ahl-e-Bait (Rz). This fits to Imamana (As) since he comes from the descendants of Imam Moosa Kazim (Rz).

B. Mahdi (As) would be either living for at least seven or nine years. This also fits with him. Imamana (As) had proclaimed his Mahdiat in the year 903 H. at the Masjid-e-Taj Khan Salar, in Ahmadabad. Thus he lived for seven years (He passed away in 910 H.) As per Mullah Abdul Qader Badayuni "Imamana (As) declared his Mahdiat in 901 H. in Makkah. Thus he lived nine years after his first proclamation of Mahdiat".

C. The Ummah would get an abundance of bounty, which had no parallel in the past. What sort of bounty is that? Bounty is described as a provision for living, which would not be hoarded for the next day. As mentioned in "Tirmizi" the holy Prophet (Slm) never hoarded anything for the next day. Abu Zarr Ghifari (Rz) too favoured the same method. A tradition states that the Ummah would never hoard items of food. This suggests the Ummah gets the bounty of religion and not the food. The same was stated by Imamana (As) that "Momin

Zakheera Namikunad" Meaning, Momin does not hoard. Thus this portion of the above tradition fits on him.

D. "Walmalu yaumaizin Kudoos" Author of Hadia had written for this tradition in chapter 3, Argument 14 that the meaning of the word "Kudoos" is an harvest. Therefore we have translated "hoardings." In Arabic, the plural of 'Kuds' is 'Ikdas' and not 'kudoos' as translated by the author of Hadia. Even if we take as he had stated then also it fits to Imamana (As) because this prophecy also had been accomplished by him. A tradition states that wealth would be in plenty. but it does not say whether Mahdi (As) would keep that wealth under his control? Further it is not mentioned who would demand what? If we take wealth, it also fits to Imamana (As), because When Imamana (As) was staying in Mandu, Sulatan Ghiasuddin Khilji donated sixty Qintars of gold. As mentioned in "Moulood" of Miyan Abdul Rahman (Rh) "The Sultan sent sixty Qintars gold and a precious Tasbeeh (bead for counting) to Imamana (As) whose value was one Million Mahmoodi(Gold Currency) of that period."The Author of "Shawahedul Vilayet" states that: This pious king was in Mandu where Imamana (As) was staying in the vicinity of the fort. Therefore that place where Imamana (As) was staying, was visible to the king. He sent a lot of bounty in many carts which covered the area from the Fort to the place Imamana (AS) was staying". This proves that wealth was in plenty.

(Note : Following paragraphs pertain to the wealth of the Sultan, description of Qintar, about Mehar etc. which are omitted for the purpose of brevity and also are irrelevent.)

Descend of bounty and blessings:

Haakim (Rz) Narrates that the sky would not hold a single drop, but would pour whatever is in it and the land would not keep any thing unto it, but spread it out. But so much of rain is not a blessing but instead it causes havoc and destruction on the land, leave aside heavy production, it will cause typhoon and arson and loss of harvest.

Such a tradition does not have any place in the "Sihah Sitta" and the name of Mahdi (As) also is not mentioned in it. Even if we accept it, we may infer that during the period of Imamana (As) such descension of bounty and blessings was a fact. This sort of statement is familiar. Allah states that:

"The land which is chaste, produces much and that which is not chaste, produces less and worse."

والبلد الطيب يخرج نباته باذن ربه والذى خبث لا يخرج(الاعراف)

For this verse "Saheb-e-Madaarik" had commented that:

This is an example of a Momin who is affected by the sermon. On the other hand, there is a person to whom the sermon does not affect, is an infidel.

وهذا مثل لمن ينجع فيه الوعظ وهو المومن ولمن لا يوثر فيه شىء من ذٰلک وهو الكافر .

Another commentary for this verse is mentioned in "Saheb-e-Mawaheb-e-Alaih:, that:

"Allah Taallah compares a Momin to a chaste land and infidel to a wasteland."

تشبیہ کردہ است دل مومن را بہ زمینے پاکیزہ و دل کافر را بہ زمینے شورہ زار ۔

Thus from the above verse chaste land means heart of a momin and wasteland means heart of an infidel. Therefore how can it be objectionable to take the heavy rains for blessings and heavy production as excessive beneficence from Allah, especially when Allah says that excessive food causes disobedience on the part of His slaves. And Allah further says that "And if Allah were to enlarge the provision for His slaves, they would surely rebel on the earth (Soora-e-Shura-Ruku 3)

"Abu Sayeed Khadri (Rz) narrated that he heard Prophet (Slm) was saying that:

"We are afraid about the person who would come after the holy Prophet (Slm)? Then the Prophet (Slm) informed that Mahdi (As) is from my progeny who would come and live for five or seven or nine years. Someone will come and ask Mahdi (As) to give; Mahdi (As) would give with his both hands, to which he would take in his clothes to the extent the cloth may contain."

عن ابی سعید الخدری قال خشینا ان یکون بعد نبینا حدث فسالنا النبئ قال ان فی امتی المھدی یخرج یعیش خمسا او سبعا او تسعا (زید الشاک) قال قلنا و ماذالک قال سنین قال فیجی الرجل الیہ فیقول یا مھدی اعطنی اعطنی قال فیحثی لہ فی ثوبہ ما استطاع ان یحملہ ھذالحدیث حسن (ترذی)

These traditions have six important points to note:

A. Mahdi would be born in the Ummah, and thus it fits to Imamana (As),

B. Mahdi will, either live for five, seven or nine years. This also fits on him. It had already been explained that, for the first time, as reported by Mulla Abdul Qader Badayuni, when he was in Makkah he declared himself to be the "Promised Mahdi (As)" in between Rukn and Muqaam in 901 H. He passed away in 910 H. Thus he lived nine years from his first declaration. Further, for the second time he declared his Mahdiat when he was in Ahmadabad and was staying in the Masjid of Taj Khan Salar in the year 903 H. where he declared for the second time and he lived seven years after the second declaration. Third time Imamana (As) had emphatically declared to be the "Promised Mahdi (As) at Badhli in 905 H. Thus the prophecy of all five, seven and nine years fits on Imamana (As).

C. Mahdi (As) would hand over such thing which would not have been given by any one so far. This also fits to him. During this period there would be plenty of food stuff that nobody would like to hoard for the next day. This was also the habit of the Holy Prophet (As) who never hoarded anything for the next day. That was what Abu Zar Ghifari (Rz) desired to make every Momin's way of life. One of the Sayings of the Imamana (As) particularly about the hoarding confirms that" Momin Zakheera Nami Kunad" (Faithful never hoards any thing).

D. As per tradition there would be abundant stock, but it does not say where this stock would be available. It was already stated in previous paragraphs that when Imamana (As) was in Mandu, Sultan Ghiasuddin Khilji donated sixty qintars (gold currency) and a precious Tasbeeh (Beads). It is said that the Tasbeeh it self was very costly and precious whose value could not be determined. When Imamana (As) disrtibuted everything, except that Tasbeeh, one Duffzan (musician), demanded that Tasbeeh. The Imamana (As) threw it with a stick to the Daffzan. His way of throwing away the tasbeeh tells that he did not have any love even for a precious thing and even he did not like to touch that precious Tasbeeh with his hands at all.

(Note: it points out how he was against the reckoning of the sacred names of Allah on the beads.)

E. It is stated that Mahdi (As) would distribute wealth with his both hands and the receiver would get it in his clothes, to the extent the cloth could contain. It is a fact. Miyan Waliji bin Miyan Yousuf (Rz) has reported in his "Hujathul Munsifeen" that when Imamana (As) was in Mandu, he handed over gold straws with his both hands. In conformity of this tradition of Imamana (As) even today Mahdavi Murshids/priests give Nareeza (cooked beans) at the Bahr-e-Aam ceremonies with their both hands and the receiver gets it in a cloth.

F. There is no sanctity for a tradition in which it is said that during the period of Mahdi (As) the planet earth would emit treasures. However, there exists a tradition which tells that at the time of the appearance of Antichrist, Earth would emit its treasures.

Author of Hadia has taken "Qanateer-e-Zarr", as gold coins., which is wrong; because the word "zarr" denotes to gold as well as to currency; and that currency may be in gold or silver or of any metal. According to "Farhang-e-Nizam" Zarr refers to currency either of gold, silver or of any metal.

According to Farishta, Sultan Ghiasuddin Khilji had sent some elephants loaded with full of currency, Arabic horses and an eulogy (from the king of Persia) as a gift to Imamana (As). Here also Zarr does not mean gold but to currency only; since he mentions the word "Mehar-e-Tilaa", we have to take as gold currency only. Thus the translation of Zarr, by the author of Hadia is wrong. However, if Zarr represents gold, then there should be no objection. Since one Qintar is equal to two hundred Dinars. However, if Sultan Ghiasuddin had sent sixty Qintar gold loaded on elephants with Zarr; there should be no reason for any objection.

Author of "Muwaheb-e-Aliah" mentions about the verse of the chaste land as stated by Allah to the heart of a Momin and waste land refers to the heart of an infidel. Thus excessive rain brings excessive production of food stuff. Thus there should be no objection if the excessive rain means bestowing of excessive Beneficence and excessive production means excessive Blessings. Particularly when Allah reprimands that excessive supply should not become the cause of stubbornness among the people.

Author of Hadia had an apprehension that during the period of Imamana (As) Allah would bestow abundance of food grains which would cause tyranny and rebellion among the Ummah. This apprehension is baseless.

Hzt. Thuban (Rz) narrated that he heard the prophet saying that:

"Near the treasure three persons will fight. All would be the sons of a Khalifa, but no one could get the treasure. Then black flags would emerge from the East and there would be a ruthless slaughter which would have no parallel. Then the Holy Prophet (Slm) said something which was not heard and could not be remembered.After a pause, further told that when you see him, go to him, even if you have to crawl on the snows, and take oath of allegiance on his hands, since he is the Khalifathullah."

عـن ثوبان قال قال رسول الله صلعم يقتل عند كـنـزكـم ثـلاثة كـلهـم ابـن خليفه ثم لا يصير الى واحـد مـنهـم ثـم تـطـلـع الـرايـات الـسـود مـن قبل الـمـشـرق فيقتلـونكـم قتلا لم يقتله قوم ثم ذكرشيئا لا احـفـظـه فقال اذا راتيموه فبا يعوه ولوحبوا على الثلج فانه خليفة الله المهدى (ابن ماجه)

This tradition has the following points:

It is mentioned that three sons of Khalifa would fight to get the treasure, means "Khilafat" and none would get it, (It is a fact that three sons of Hazrat Ali Karramallahu Wahjhu fought for the Khilafath. (1) Imam Hasan (Rz), had although become Caliph for a few months, but he was made to relinquish it on account of coercion by Amir Muaviya.

(2) Although Imam Husain (Rz) never aspired for Khilafat, still he never accepted the Khilafat of Yazid. Yazid had the apprehension that Ummah would not accept him as the Caliph, if Imam Husain, the grandson of the holy Prophet was alive in Madinah, therefore Yazid planned the Battle of Karbala against Imam Husain (Rz) in which Imam Husain (Rz) was martyred.

(3) On behalf of the third son Mohammad bin Hanifa (Rz), one of his relatives, Mukhtar fought against Abdullah Bin Zubair, the then Khalifa, he too was martyred in a battle.

Thus all three sons of Hazrat Ali (Rz) fought for the Treasure (Khilafat); and none could get that as mentioned in the tradition.

A. In this tradition the word "Kanz" had been used. Author of "Muntahi-ul-Arab" had described it as "a place, or a thing in which property is stocked". It may be taken as a box or even a Baithul Maal. This tradition mentions that the Prophet (Slm) was given two Makhzans; one red and the other white. Sheik Abdul Haq, Muhaddis-e-Dehalvi, had stated about that tradition that it refers to two countries. One is Syria whose population has red skin and the other Persia, whose population has white skin. Thus this tradition refers to the peoples of two regions one is Arab and the other being Ajam, who had assembled under the prophet's flag.

The word "Kanz" also refers to Paradise. And if we infer, "Baitul Maal" also may be taken as Kanz; then there should be no objection; because it is connected to the Khilafat only.

B. It was said that black flags would emerge from the East. This prophecy is for the Khilafat-e-Banu Abbas (Rz). A movement started in Khurasan, for installation of Banu Abbas (Rz) against the khilafat of Banu Ummiya which became successful and Banu Abbas (Rz) got the Khilafat by subjugating the Ummayeds. Khurasan lies to the East of Damascus, capital of the Ummayeds, therefore emergence of blak flags from the East was a correct statement as Banu Abbas' favourite colour is Black. And it was also true that the Banu Abbas (Rz) slaughtered the Ummayeds ruthlessly.

C. The narrator had said that something was said, which was not heard properly hence could not be remembered. Thus this tradition does not determine the period of emergence of Mahdi (As), but the author of Hadia says that soon after the emergence of black flags Mahdi's emergence was necessary. His contention is wrong. Since the Word "Summa" has been used between the words "emergence of black flags and appearance of Mahdi (As)". It is clear that the appearance of Mahdi (As) is not necessary to accompany with the emergence of black flags, but the word "Summa" determines its time for an indefinite time in future.

In the Bible it was prophesied that:

"Now the leader of the world would be sent who would be the last of the prophets."

الا يطرح رئيس هذاالعالم خارجاً

Prophet Eisa (As) has referred the word "Al Aan" means "now." If the word "now" took about 571 years for the birth of the holy Prophet Mohammed (Slm) from the demise of Hzt. Esa (As), then the word "Summa" should denote to a "longer period" for appearance of Imam Mahdi (As). Thus it took 847 years from the demise of the holy prophet (Slm); and about 200 years from the emergence of the Black flags; since Imamana (As) was born in the East in the year 847 H. Thus it is not necessary to relate the appearance of Mahdi (As) soon after the emergence of the black flags, and it is also true that it was not mentioned in any tradition that Mahdi (As) would appear along with the black flags which would appear from the East. From this tradition we have to infer that since the movement to install Banu Abbas (Rz) on the Khilafat was started in Khurasan, and Khurasan lies to the East of Damascus, the capital of the Ummayeds, therefore the question of the appearance of Mahdi (As) soon after the emergence of the Black Flags does not arise. Hence this tradition fits on Imamana (As) completely. Further, as per Imam Ahmad's saying:

"Thuban (Rz) heard the Prophet (Slm) telling that when you look black Flags which would emerge from Khurasan, then approach; Since Mahdi Khalifatullah (As) is there."

قال قال رسول الله صلى الله عليه و سلم اذا رايتم الرايات اسود قدجاءت من قبل خراسان فاتوها فان فيها خليفة الله المهدى

The author of the Hadia (page 57) while commenting on this tradition "Ar Rayatus saud" he had taken the word "HA" as a pronoun which, as an antecedent to the words "Ar Rayatus Saud", but actually it refers to Khurasan, since in Arabic "HA" is used for a village or a city or even to a country".

In order to point out towards a thing which had already happened, Allah tells in this way:

"Alam Tara Kaifa Fa'ala Rabbuka Bi As-habil Feel" Did you not see how your Sustainer dealt with the As-habul Feel? (Abraha king of Yemen brought a contingent of elephants to destroy Kabatullah). The As-habul Feel episode belongs to a period before the birth of the holy Prophet (Slm). Therefore the words "Alam Tara" denote whether you (Allah addresses the holy prophet) did not hear or know?"

The Author of "Madarik" had commented about "Alam Tara" that" Did you hear in this regard in continuity?"

The Author of "Mawahib-e-Ladunnia" writes about it that" Did you not know how your Sustainer had dealt with"? Thus the above said tradition"Iza Rayatumur Rayatus Soud" tells "when you hear that the black flags have come from Khurasan then go towards Khurasan, because Mahdi (As) would emerge from Khurasan."

From another tradition it is clear that there is no connection between Mahdi (As) and the black flags.

"Kanzul Ummal" refers the sayings of Ibn Abbas (Rz) and Abu Huraira (Rz) that:

"When black flags appear before you, then proceed in reverence towards Persians, since they would establish your government."

اذا اقبلت الرايات السودفا كرموا الفرس فان دولتكم منهم

It is clear that it refers to the Persians and not to Mahdi (As). Abdul Haq, Muhaddis-e-Dehalvi with reference to the miracles of the holy Prophet (Slm) has written that:

"The Prophet (Slm) informed about the emergence of Banu Abbas (Rz) along with the black flags."

خبرداد بخروج بنى عباس به علم هائے سياه

This also confirms that emergence of the black flags relates to the appearance of the Banu Abbas (Rz) and not at all to the appearance of Mahdi (As). Thus the tradition reported by Imam Ahmad (Rz) does not say that Mahdi (As) would appear along with the black flags and according to "Kanzul Umaal" the black flags relate to Persians and not to Imam Mahdi (As). In another tradition it refers to Palestine;" Black Flags would emerge from Khurasan and no force would stop them until they reach Ailiya (Palestine) and a flag would be hoisted there. Ailiya is a city in Baithul Muqaddas, as per historical record, Banu Abbas (Rz) fought a battle at the river Zaab and captured even Palestine. Thus it is confirmed that the black flags refer to the Persians and of course not to Imam Mahdi (As).

Abu Yala Moosli's Narration:

As per Abdullah Bin Masood's narration Imam Mahdi (As) was not referred in that tradition. Thus as Imam Ahmed Bin Hanbal (Rz) has said the black flags refer to Khurasan is correct. Sayouti in his journal "Al Arfil Wardi Fi Akhbaril Mahdi (As)" states that:

"One nation would come from the East, along with black flags." ياتى قوم من قبل المشرق معهم رايات سود

With reference to this Hafiz Imamuddin Ibn Kaseer (Rz) said:

"This expression refers to the Khilafath of Bani Abbas (Rz), It is also evident that Mahdi (As) would appear only after the end of the Khilafath-e-Abbasia." قال الحافظ عماد الدين ابن كثير فى هذا السياق اشارة الى ملك بنى عباس و فيه دلالة على ان المهدى يكون بعد دولة بنى عباس

This also proves that black flags have no connection to Imam Mahdi (As), but they relate to Bani Abbas (Rz) and after completion of the Abbasia Califate only, the question of the advent of Imam Mahdi (As) arises.

It took almost two hundred years from the fall of the Khilafat-e-Bani Abbas (Rz) that Imam Mahdi (As) appeared in the East. As regards Imam Mahdi's appearance in Khurasan is concerned, this also fits on Imamana (As) because at his last leg, Imamana (As) came in Khurasan from Qandhar and stayed there for two years and five months where his demise took place. The tradition of "Sihah Sittah" emphasizes about coming of Imamana (As) in Khurasan, but it does not mention any particular city of Khurasan.

2. Author of Hadia has referred to another tradition which relates to Hazrat Ali (Rz) who had narrated that:

"Pity on Taliqan, there are neither any treasure of gold nor silver, but there are such venerable people who would be able to recognize Allah in a befitting manner and they are Mahdi's Companions."

This has been reported by Abu Ghanam (Rz) in "Kitabul Fitan"which has been described that it does not belong to "Siha Sittah". Thus we come to conclusion as follows:

It is said that this tradition does not belong to "Siha Sittha", as mentioned by the author of "Kanzul Ummal."

It does not inform whether Imam Mahdi (As) would born in Taleqan or would be commissioned among them.

It refers to those companions of Imam (As) who were from Taleqan;

It is not clear that all the companions would belong to Taleqan;

There is no proof that Taleqanis would become companions of Imam Mahdi (As) but it confirms that those companions may be living in Taleqan or it means to say that some persons of Farah would migrate to Taleqan and reside there.

As regards Taleqan, there are two cities by the name Taleqan. One lies in between Abhar and Quzveen, (in Central Asia) and the other is in Khurasan. One tradition refers to the fact that Imam Mahdi (As) shall appear in Khurasan. Then according to the Saying the city of Taleqan which is in Khurasan may be that city which situates in between Muroorood and Balkh, some three manzils from Muroorood. In this regard author of "Muajjimal Baldan" states:

"One of them is in Khurasan, between Muroorood and Balkh at a distance of three Marahel."

احـد همـا بخراسان بين مروالرود وبلخ و بينهـا و
بين مروالرود ثلاث مراحل

It also confirms that the city of Taleqan situates in between Muroorood and Balkh, at 3 miles. It is a fact that the companions of Imamana (As) were not only from Khurasan, but also from Turkistan, and even from Baghdad. The following narration confirms that even people from Baghdad were the disciple of Imamana (As):

"On one day Miyan Abdullah "Baghdadi" told"

روزے میـان عبـداللـه بـغـدادی عرض کردند الیٰ
آخره

It may be possible that there may be people from Taleqan who accepted Imamana (As) as the true Mahdi. There should be no doubt that during the Tatar's tribulations or Tamore's disturbances many Taleqanis might have migrated towards Herat and Farah. If the name of Taleqan does not appear in any writing, then how can anyone deny that Taleqanis were not the followers of Imammana (As). Even if someone denies that no Taleqanis were the followers of Imamana (As) it does not negate Imamana's Mahdiat.

In "Ka'ab-e-Ahbar", some signs of the holy Prophet (Slm) have been narrated in Torah as under:

"His birth place shall be Makkah and he would migrate to Taibba, and his kingdom would be in Syria."

مولده بمكة و هجرته بطیبة و ملکه بالشام

Two of these signs fit on to the Holy Prophet (Slm), except the kingdom of Syria. It is correct that he was born in Makkah, and then migrated to Madinah (Taiba), but he was not the king of Syria. On the other hand he refused to be known or even to be called a king as reported in "Madarijun Nabuwwat" which narrates that:

1."Thus a man threw his balance (in his shop) and stood to Kiss the hands of the Prophet (Slm), but the Prophet (Slm) pulled his hands and told that this is the practice of the people of Ajam (non-Arabs) who used to honor their nobles.""I am not a king, but I am a man one among you."

پس آن‌مرد میزان از دست بینداخت و برخاست تا بوسه زند دست مبارک آنحضرت را پس آنحضرت دست بکشید فرمود یه این کار اعاجم است که بامملوک و روسا خود می کنند و من ملک نیستم مردی ام یکی از شماست۔

"A man came to the Prophet (Slm), he was actually trembling. The Prophet (Slm) consoled him and asked him to perform his work with no fear and not to tremble, because he was not the king. He told that he was the son of a Qureshi woman who used to eat dry minced meat."

درآمد بر آنحضرت مردی پس لرزیدن گرفت از هیت وی صلی الله علیه و سلم فرمود آسان کن برخود کار وملرزمن بادشاه نیم من پسرزنے ام از قریش که میخورد قدیدرا

"2. Thus, if the Prophet (Slm) was not the king (as per the prophecy) of Syria, can anybody deny his prophethood? In this connection Sheik Abdul Haq has rightly commented that here King refers not to the worldly kingship, but to the kingship of the Religion of Islam and Nabuwwat. Another point is that a portion of this prophecy may not fit for him, because during his lifetime, Syria did not come under the fold of Islam. From this prophecy we may infer that Islam, somehow, shall flourish in Syria also at any time, even after him.

The same is true for Imamana (As) that his Mission would reach to the remotest part of Khurasan, known as Taleqan. Further the word "Ansar" may not be taken in a technical term but as a literal meaning. For example, Allah says "Nahnu Ansarullah" (We are Allah's helpers). In the "Tafseer-e-Husaini" it is mentioned as "We are helpers for the Religion of Allah." Here Helpers of Allah means, Helpers for the cause of furtherance of the Religion of Allah. In the same sense, "Ansaaril Mahdi" means, Helpers for the cause of furtherance of the Mission of Mahdi (As). This prophecy became truly visible during the period of Miyan Shah Burhan (Rz), when he performed his journey from Kabul to Balkh and from Balkh to Herat for the propagation of Deen-e-Mahdi (AS). He has narrated in his "Hadiqathul Haqaeq" that:

I went from Kabul to the capital of Turkistan, Balkh, and from Balkh to Marujaq and from Marujaq to Herat. I preached the teachings of Imamana (As) in "Andkhud" as well, from where I wrote a letter to my friend stating:"I reached Andkhud after six days and stayed about 18 days. Whatever I knew about the Mahdiat, I tried to preach and convinced them to the best of my ability as guided by our Imamana (As). I had distributed at least more than one hundred pamphlets which were with me. Believe me, many of the scholars who understood my preachings, accepted and became Mahdavi. Some of them kept quite, and did not reply. To my understanding they were very receptive and far better than Indians and Khurasanians."

از کابل به شهر دارالسلطنت ترکستان یعنی بلخ و از بلخ به مارو جاق و از مارو جاق به شهر هریو .... آمدیم

بعد از پنج یا شش روز به شهر اندخود رسیدیم دراینجا دوراه می شود یکی به مشهد میرود ویکی به هرات .... دراینجا کم وزیادهژده روز اقامت کرده شد انچه حسب المدعا سوال وجواب دراثبات مهدیت به قدر حوصله خود معلوم بود و بعون الله و حسن توفیق بصدقهٔ حضرت مهدی علیه السلام و صدیقین وی اظهار کردیم ، باوجود کم و زیاد صدرسالهٔ حجت برابر فقیر بود درآنجا گذراند حق آگاهٔ است که بسیار منصفان از علماء وغیره بلا تعصب و عناد تفهیم شده تصدیق کردند و اکثر واغلب ساکت ماندند و بعضی کسان مخالفت کردند جواب دادن نتوانستند معلوم باد که درباب تصدیق امام علی التحقیق از یک راه از اهل هند و خراسان منصف و نرم یافتم

Author of " Mujam-ul-Baldan" has written about Andkhud that "It is a city in between Muroorood and Balkh, abetting the corner of a desert. Miyan Shah Burhan (Rz) had travelled from Andkhud to Farah and Herat via Chachaktu and wrote to his friend that:

"After all I travelled from Andkhud to Chachaktu and Marujaq and from Marujaq to Herat and from Herat to Farah; it took one month to reach and had the privilege of offering my humble respects to the shrine of Imamana (As)."

آخر الامر از شهر اند خوبه چچکتو (چاچکتو) و به مارو جاق ازمارو جاق تا به هرات و از هرات تابه فراه که از بلغ تاهرات یکماه راه است ، بشرف زیارت روضه مبارک بیت العتیق امام المشارق والمغارب علی التحقیق مشرف شدیم

The city of Andkhud lies one hundred miles, North-West of Taleqan and Chachaktu lies near the ruins of Taleqan. Mr. J.Le. Strange writes about these cities, that:

" About three marches (Manzils) distance from Mary-Ar-Rud towards Balkh was the city of Taleqan, the name of which no longer found on the map, but the ruins and mounds of bricks near Chachaktu probably mark its site, which probably determine the whereabouts of Taleqan. Shortly after this time, Yakut wrote that: "In the year 617 H/1220 AD, Taleqan was stormed and destroyed after a seven month siege by Chenghez Khan and whole population was massacred and its castles were raised to the ground."

Thus, from the above recorded fact, it is established that Miyan Shah Burhan (Rz) had actually visited those remote places and propagated Deen-e-Haqqa.

As far as the Sayings of Imamana (As) that during the period of Mahdi (As) "there would be no Helpers (Ansars) to me". Here the literal meaning of the Ansars, (Helpers) is being negatived. Because during the migration of Imamana (As), his stay at one place was not for more than 18 months, hence there was no particular group to provide help to him. However, as a matter of fact migration continued and Bandgi Miyan Syed Khundmir (Rz) was declared as "Sultanun Naseer" and this Glad Tidings had been mentioned in "Shawahedul Vilayet". This is not to compare with those Ansars who helped the Prophet (Slm) and his companions who migrated from Makkah to Madinah, that this particular sort of help was not available for the reason that Imamana's short stay at any place. It happened because during his lengthy 23 year period of contuinuous journey he did not stay at any place for more than 18 months and he spent his entire lifespan for propagation of Islam and Shariath-e-Mustafavi (Slm). Imamana (As) did not permanently stay at any place, but the act of migration was continuing till he finally migrated and settled down at Farah as the last abode, which became his last Resting Place. It means to say that after completion of the migration, at a particular place there had been no special group as Ansars for him, because there was a continuation of migration. In the absence of any such group of Ansars, the Title "Sultanun Naseer" awarded by Imamana (As) to Bandagi Miyan Syed Khundmir (Rz) was nothing but a Glad Tiding for Bandagi Miyan (Rz).

This glad tiding said to have been bestowed, as per "Shawahedul Vlayeth" that:

"Imamana (As) informed Bandagi Miyan Syed Khundmir (Rz): "You are "Sultanun Naseer", Naasir-e-Vilatet-e-Mustafa Sallalahu Alaihi wa sallam. (Your help is for furtherance of the cause of Vilayeth-e-Mustafavi (Slm)."

نقل است کــه حضــرت میــراں عـلیـه السلام فرمودنـد کـه بـرادرم سیـد خـوندمیر سلطانا نصیر ناصـر ولایت مصطفی صلی الله علیه و سلم هستند (باب هفدہم)

As per the "Naqliath-e-Syed Aalam", Imamana (As) has given many glad tidings to Bandagi Miyan (Rz), the second among them is "Naasir-e-Deen "It is a fact that Imamana (As) emphatically stated that "Mahdi (As) has Muhajereen only and no Ansaars". And further Imamana (As) told that "his Muhajereen are not wealthy enough, still they have gained that much abundance of "mystic knowledge" which they could eloquently propagate the Deen-e-Haqqa to the satisfaction of the seekers.

"La Mahdi illa Esa", had been confirmed a weak tradition." Means "there is no Mahdi except Esa." thus it is confirmed to be a weak tradition. Haafiz Ibn Taimya also has referred this Tradition as being "Weak."

نقل (ہم

Abdul Haq, Muhaddis-e-Dehalvi refers about a Tradition in "Lama'ath" that:

"In another tradition the words "La Mahdi Illa Esa" (Without Mahdi (As) there will be no Esa (As), but this tradition is said to be weak according to the traditionalists."

قـدوددنـی حـدیـث لا مـهـدی الا عیسٰی و هو حدیث ضعیف باتفاق المحدثین

In "Lam'ath" it has been mentioned that: "There would be no perfect guided man, except Esa Ibn Maryam (As)."

لا مهدی کـامـل معـصـوم الا عیسٰی بن مریم (باب اثرات الساعة الفصل الثالث)

"One Tradition speaks about "La Mahdi (As) illa Esa (As)" and that has been confirmed as a weak tradition by the traditionalists."

قـدودنـی حـدیـث لا مـهـدی الا عیسٰی و هو حـدیـث ضعیف باتفاق المحدثین (لمعات قلمی نصف ثانی ورق ۴۶۸ حدیث عربی ۱۱۳۰۲ اسٹیٹ سنٹرل لائبریری)

It means to say that when Hazrat Esa (As) would emerge before the Doomsday, there would be none who would claim himself to have been guided by Allah and none would claim himself to be an innocent, except Esa (As). This Tradition negates the idea of those who think that Mahdi (AS) and Esa (As) would emerge at one and the same time. And through this it is inferred that when Esa (As) would descend the same time, but in view of he traditions the question of emrgence of Mahdi (As) along with Eisa Ibn Mariyam does not arise.

Some Traditions do not describe about Mahdi (As), but they simply mention about the person who would be from the Ahl-e-Baith (Rz). The author of the "Sihah" has included, as per his own guess, under the chapter of Mahdi (As). For example, "Tirmizi" states that:

"Hazrat Abdullah (Rz) had heard the Prophet (Slm) saying that the world would never finish till it had the owner of the Arabs, the man who comes from Ahl-e-Bait (Rz) carrying my name."

"عن عبدالله و قـال قـال رسول الله صلی الله علیـه و سـلـم لا تـذهب الدنیا حتی یملک العرب رجل من اهل بیتی یواطی اسمه اسمی"

Previous to this we have already discussed about the Tradition No.6 which refers "Yamlak Sub'a Sanain." We have explained about the meaning of "Malik". We have also pointed out that in Arab countries, the word "Malik" does not carry the same sense as being carried in Ajam (Non-Arabs lands) who designate the word as "Shah (Emperor) to their king." Another point is that the word "Al Arab" has been used here, which means "Arab Nation", but does not indicate Arabian Peninsula.

A. Umme Shariek (Rz) says that:

"The Holy Prophet (Slm) told that people would flee when they see the Antichrist, till they reach the mountains. Then Umme Shariek (Rz) asked the Prophet (Slm), "How many Arabs would be available there? He told that they would be in minority."

عن ام شریک قالت قال رسول الله صلی الله علیه و آله و سلم لیفرون الناس من الدجال حتی یلحقوا بالجبال قالت ام شریک یا رسول الله فاین العرب یومئذ قال هم قلیل رواه مسلم (شعتہ اللمعات طبع نولکشور جلد رابع صفحہ ۳۳۴)

It means to say that the word "Al Arab" denotes to the Nation of Arab only. The Prophet (Slm) said that at that period the Arabs would be in the minority. It does not refer either to any Arabian city or Arabian Peninsula. Since wherever the word "Arabian land" has been used it refers to Arzul Arab or Jazeerathul Arab.

For example:

1. Thus, even in Arabian lands there would arise pastures and canals.

2. From the Jazeeratul Arab all mushrikeen and infidels would be expelled.

3. From the Jazeeratul Arab all Jews and the Christians would be expelled.

4. In one tradition the word "Hijaz" has been reported. "The Day of Judgment would not arrive till the land of "Hijaz" would not emit fire.

Sheik Ali, Author of "Kanzul Ummal" under the chapter Jazeeratul Arab, has mentioned five Traditions; "Jazeeratul Arab" has been used in four and in one it refers "Arzul Arab".

Thus, in the above tradition:

A. Al Arab does not mean Arzul Arab or Jazeeratul Arab.

B. Prophet Musa (As) exclaimed "La Yamlik" as mentioned in the following:

"My Lord I am not the owner, but of my own person and of my brother." (5:R4)."

قال رب انی لا املک الانفسی واخی (المائدہ رکوع ۴)

This verse denotes that "Yamlik" applies to a man also. Thus the word "Yamlik" in that tradition, also applies to Al Arab.

C. It is given to understand that a person would emerge from Ahl-e-Bait (Rz); who would be the owner of Arabs, but he may not be the Mahdi (As).

D. This tradition tells about the person of Ahl-e-Bait (Rz), but there is no reference that he would fill the land with justice. It is also possible that someone who may become leader of the Arabs, but he might not fill the land with justice. Then on what basis this tradition shall apply to Imamana (As)? It is also reported that, the person would carry the name of Mohammad, but it does not say whether that man's father's name also shall be Abdullah?, which is the name of the Prophet's father.

E. While discussing about the Tradition No.7, we have pointed out that during the period of Mahdi (As), the Ummah would get Beneficence of Allah. It means that the advent of Mahdi

(As) is for the Ummah and not for any region.

F. The prophecy No.7 of the scripture, refers to the holy Prophet (Slm) as the "Rayees-e-Aalam", "Emperor of the World", but as a matter of fact, at the time of the Prophet's demise he was the Rayees or king of just one lakh twenty four thousand Arabs. The prophecy No.3 refers about ten thousand angels, for that we have taken ten thousand companions (who accompanied the Prophet (Slm) and arrived in Makkah to conquer it. Thus, there should be no objection if according to the referred saying, if we apply this tradition to Mahdi (As) then the word "Al Arab" shall be taken as the "Nation of Arab". For example the Mughals have lived in India since many centuries, still they are called Mughals. And in the same sense the Turks who live in Qustuntunia for the last many centuries, are still called Turks. Therefore those Saadath and Shuyukhs who are the descendants of the Arabs, why should they not be called Arabs? Sindh had been the center for Arabs for centuries, therefore not only the public but the elites also had affirmed the Mahdiat of Imamana (AS).

Author of "Khatim-e-Sulaimani" has confirmed:

"The kings of Sindh are Abbasaids who are Mahdavis."	تخت نشینان ملك سنده عباسی اندومهدوی (گلشن دوام دهم چمن چهارم)

The details shall be discussed in the chapter "Religious doctrine of Mahdiat."

During the period of the descendants of the companions of Mahdi (As), propagation of the Deen-e-Mahdi (As) had reached upto Malabar. Even today Mahdavis reside in Palghat and Southern Malabar. The Malabarians are the descendents of Arabs which is a well known fact. This point will be further discussed in future.

"Ainul Quzzat Hamdani has elaborately written in his "Zubdathul Haqaeq" that:

"Whoever adopted Islam, is an Arab."	من اسلم فهو عربی (مرقاة شرح مشكوة طبع مصر)

When the word Arab applies to every Muslim, then why should not we accept Arab Nation as the Arab race?

Mulla Ali Qari has gone further to state that whoever becomes Muslim, he is an Arab. Thus, when every Muslim becomes an Arab, then why should not the Arab generation be accepted as the Arab Nation?

G. Miyan Shah Burhan (Rz) in Chapter 12 of the "Shawahedul Vilayat" states that:

"When Imamana (As) was staying in Makkah, many Arabs had accepted his Mahdiat and became his devotees."	حاصل الامر چند روز حضرت خاتم الولایت در شهر مكه مبارك اقامت كردند در آنجا بسیار اهل عرب منقاد شده سربر آستانه شریف نهادند

The tradition of "Ibn Maja" tells that Mahdi (As) is the Khalifathullah. Hence whoever is the Khalifatullah of the Almighty, he need not be pronounced as the king of any place. Hazrat Adam (As) was the Caliph of Allah, yet he was not the king of any place.

Hazrat Abdullah's second tradition has been narrated in "Tirmizi" that:

"He heard the Prophet (Slm) saying that one person of my Ahl-e-Bait (Rz) would be the guardian of the Ummah whose name would be on mine."

عـن عبـدالله عن النبي صلى الله عليه و سلم قال يلى رجل من اهل بيتى يواطى اسمه اسمى

In this tradition "Yali" is used which means (vaali hoga) that is to say he would be the guardian of the Ummah. Here the word Al Arab was not used. Thus this saying would clash with the first one and the connection of Mahdi (As) to the "Yamlikul Arab" would be eliminated. Thus it must be maintained that the person coming from the Ahl-e-bait (Rz) will be the guardian of the Ummah and certainly he would not be the king.

Meaning of "Yali Rajul":

Allah States in Qur'an"

"Zakaria (As) requested Allah: "Bestow upon me my heir."

فرزندے کے متولى امور دين باشيد(مواهب عليه)

Author of "Muaheb-e-Aliah" writes under this verse that Zakaria (As) requested for a son who would become the Trustee of Deen-e-Haqqa.

Author of "Madarik" had written about "Valia" that:

"A son who becomes Trustee under Your (Allah's) commands after me."

ابنا يلى امرك بعدى (تفسير مدارک)

Thus, in view of that tradition under discussion, as regards "Yala Rajula min Ahl-e-Baiti" confirms that whoever would come from the Ahl-e-Bait (Rz), he would be the guardian of the Ummah and thus he would be the "Trustee of the Deen-e-Haqqa".

2. Abu Dawood (Rz) refers to one another tradition that:

"Reported by Ibn Ishaq (Rz), while referring to Hazrat Ali (Rz) who by pointing out towards his son, Hasan (Rz), confirmed that the holy Prophet (Slm) named him "SYED", whose offspring's name would be on the name of the Prophet (Slm), he would be like the Prophet (Slm), and his characters and appearance also would be resembling to that of the Prophet's. And further said that he would fill the Earth with justice."

عن ابن اسحق قال قال على و نظر الى ابنه الحسـن قـال ان ابـنى هذا سيد كمـا سمـاه رسـول اللـه و يـخرج مـن صلبه رجل يسمى بـاسـم نبيكـم يشبهه فى الخلق ولا يشبهه فى الخـلـق ثـم ذكر قصة يملا الارض قسطا ولم يذكر القصة (اشعة اللمعات جلدرابع صفحا ۳۲۱)

This tradition has been included by Abu Dawood (Rz) in the chapter of "Mahdi (As)". We have already discussed that those traditions in which the word Mahdi (As) is not mentioned may not necessarily have the attributes of Imam Mahdi (AS). Thus such traditions should not be attached to the person of Imam Mahdi (As).

If it is said that except Imam Mahdi (As) none would be resembling to the characters of the holy Prophet (Slm) in the Ummah and if resemblance in all respects had not been visualized, then it would not have been particularly mentioned because partial resemblance may occur in some persons also. And if this tradition is referred to Imam Mahdi (As), thus it also fits on Imamana (As) perfectly.

A. Mahdi (As) is the descendant of Imam Hasan (Rz) as well:

While referring to the genealogy of Imamana (As), we have discussed with reference to "Juanpur Nama" that Imamana's mother comes from the progeny of Imam Hasan (Rz), "Tuhfathul Kiram" and "Juanpur Nama" both testify that Imamana (As) comes from the line of Imam Moosa Kazim (Rz) and Imam Moosa Kazim (Rz) comes from the line of Imam Mohammad Baqer (Rz) and Imam Mohammad Baqer's mother was the daughter of Imam Hasan (Rz). This fact also had been confirmed by Mulla Abdul Rahman Jami (Rh) in his "Shawahedul Nabuvwat" that his patronymic name was Abu Jafer (Rz) and his name was (Imam) Baqer (Rz) and whose venerable mother Bibi Fatima (Rz) was the daughter of Imam Hasan (Rz) Ibn Hazrat Ali (Rz). Thus the line of Imam Moosa Kazim (Rz) (directly reaches to Imam Hasan (Rz) also from the mother's side.)

B. Imamana's name Mohammad (As), being Prophet's name is also attested by so many books of history.

C. Characters also resemble to that of the Holy Prophet's which had been accepted in History.

It was already discussed that the characters of Imamana (As) had perfect resemblancee to that of the Holy Prophet (Slm).

Mulla Abdul Qader Badayuni had referred what the scholars of Herat had said about Imamana (As) which had been recorded in his " Najatur Rashid" that:

"This person (Imamana (As) is one of the signs of Allah and the knowledge we have so far, has no value before Imamana (As)."	این مرد آیتے است از آیات خدا و علمے کہ ماسالها خوانده ایم اینجا قدر و قیمتے ندارد (نجات الرشید قلمی تصوف فارسی نمبر ۱۵۲۴)

Moulvi Khairuddin, in part five of his book, "Juanpur Nama", chapter 7, under the title: Khaja Syed Mohammad (As) writes that:

"Imamana (As) is one of the signs of Allah and one of the Miracles of the Holy Prophet (Slm)."	آیتے است از آیات الهی و معجزۀ از معجزات رسالت پناهی

D. "La Yashbahu Fil Khulqi:"

In this connection Sheik Abdul Haq , Muhaddis-e-Dehalvi writes that:

"May not have an obvious facial resemblance in all respects, however Imam Mahdi (As) shall have a certain resemblance with the Holy Prophet (Slm) which are testified by the traditions."

مشابهت ندارد آنحضرت را در صورت ظاهر یعنی در همه چیز و همه وجوه والا در احادیث مشابهت به صورت نیز به بعضی جهات ثابت شده است (اشعة اللمعات جلد رابع صفحه ۳۲۱)

Here, what Sheik Abdul Haq had stated about "La Yashbahu", whose translation is "May not resemble"; but it means that "may not completely resemble" in all respects.

But the reality is that in "La Yashbahu" the word "La" had come to emphasize and for research as it was used in "La Manaka in La Tasjudu". The author of "Kasshaf" had written about this verse that:

"When the word "La" is used before any verb, it means to "emphasize" that verb."

The author of "Madarik" had commented that "La Uqsimu bi Yaumil Qiamah" that: It means "I swear" as reported by Ibn Abbas (Rz).

Author of "Muahibe Alaiha" had said about "La Uqsimu" that: "No doubt I swear."

These all instances point out that the word "La" is used to emphasize. Thus the meanings of "La Yashbaho Fil Khalqi" shall mean "Absolutely shall have obvious facial resemblance."

Thus, Shaik Abdul Haq had accepted that according to the traditions as regards facial resemblance, Imamana (As) may have resemblance to some extent to that of the holy Prophet (Slm). So in spite of taking "La" as negative, it is correct to say that "La" has been used to emphasize it.

Holy Prophet (Slm) himself had asserted that he had the resmblence to his fore-father Hazrat Ibrahim Alaihis Salam.This tradition states that he saw Hazrat Ibrahim (As) (in a dream), and asserted that among the progeny of Hazrat Ibrahim (As), in which the holy Prophet (Slm) was the most resembling person among his successors. And it is also a confirmed fact that both Imam Hasan (Rz) and Imam Husain (Rz) had a perfect resemblance to the Holy Prophet (Slm). Thus accordingly, the Prophet (Slm) might have predicted about his descendant Imamana (As) who came from the Ahl-e-Bait might have perfect resemblance to the Holyu Prophet(Slm)

Hazrat Anas (Rz) reported that:

"No-one had a resemblance to the Holy Prophet (Slm) except Imam Hasan (Rz), and the same opinion was asserted about Imam Husain (Rz) who too had much resemblance to the holy Prophet (Slm)."

قال لم يكن احد اشبه بالنبی صلی الله علیه و آله و سلم من الحسن بن علی قال فی الحسین ایضاً کان اشبهم برسول الله صلی الله علیه و سلم (اشعة اللمعات جلد رابع صفحه ۷۸۸)

Thus " La Yashbahu Fil Khalqi" means that Imam Mahdi (As) shall have explicit features of the Prophet (Slm) as he (Slm) resembled to that of his forefather Hazrat Ibrahim (AS).

In both "Moulood" and "Shawahedul Vilayet" the description of the features of Imamana (As) has been recorded, which certify to have complete resemblance to that of the Holy

Prophet's.

However, the author of Hadia has pointed out about two features which do not resemble:

1. One of them is taken from "Hujjathul Musnnafeen"; in which it is stated that: "Reported by Akhi that he heard from Syed Ameen (Rh) who had heard from his uncle that:

"When Imamana(As) arrived in Baroda, Gujrat, I visited Imamana(As). Whenever Imamana(As) was standing, I saw that Imamana's hands were reaching to his knees. The same was the features of the Holy Prophet(Slm)."	روایت است از سیداخی اور روایت کرده از سید امین و اوروایت کرده از او در خویش اودرگفته که امام مهدی چول قصبه بروده رسیدند بنده صحبت کرد هر وقت که امام را ایستاده دید دست امام تازانوی امام رسیدے و در کتب در حلیه رسول هم صفت دست هائے رسول هم چنین نبشته شده است

The author of Hadia states that it was nowhere written that the hands of the holy Prophet (Slm) reached his knees, while Imamana's hands were reaching to his knees.

Had the fault finder been a scholar, then he must have conversant with Muslim Jurisprudence. Moreover he was not perfect in persian language too. What he had pointed out about the words "Ta Zanuey" and without understanding the meaning of "Ta" he objected about Imamana's hands reaching to his knees and stated that "it was not the case with the Holy Prophet (Slm)."

What has been written in the "Hujjathul Musannafeen" is that " Ta ba Zanu Raseeday" means that the hands were reaching upto the knees. It has two meanings. One is that, hands were so long that they reached to the Knees. The second is that they reached near the knees. The same has been noticed in the case of the holy Prophet (Slm). We have now to see about the hands of the Prophet (Slm)."Tirmizi" reports that they were"Tawelluz Zindain" means "Taweeluz Zaraeen", that is to say that from the elbow to the tip of the middle finger. That points out that holy prophet's hands were long enough from the elbow to the tip of the middle finger. Thus it may be possible that his hands may reach up to the knees, not connecting or adjoining to the knees."Hujjathul Musannafeen" points out that prophet's hands were reaching to the knees. It does not say that hands joined to the knees. Hence" Ta Ba Zanu" means not necessarily touching to the knees. That is what "Hujjathul Mussannafeen" informs. It only refers to the longevity of the hands and not at all about touching to the knees. The same is reported in the "Moulood" that Imamana's hands were long enough to reach near the knees. On this basis author's objection is totally rejected.

2. Another objection about the resemblance:

The author of Hadia has raised another objection about Imamana (As) that at the time of his demise, the hair of Imamana's beard was half gray and half black, whereas only twenty hair, at the most, were gray of Rasoolullah (Slm) at the time of his demise. He had argued this point by saying that after the demise of Imam (As), Miran Syed Mahmood's (son of Imamana (As) hair became "Do Moya" i-e; half black and half gray. The author had raised objection as the following :

That Miran Syed Mahmood's black hair which were in abundance, "Bisiyar", became half white and half black "Does the word "abundance" is used as an adjective?. It means to say that Miran Syed Mahmood's hair of the beard was half black and half white. Imam's beard also was thick and in abudance with black hair; and so also the holy Prophet (Slm) had many hair in his beard. Thus it is not proved that Miran Syed Mahmood (Rz) had gray hair in his beard before the demise of Imamana (As) as has been written in"Tazkertus Saleheen" that "the beard of Miran Syed Mahmood's hair was black." From this, it becomes clear that the beard of Miran Syed Mahmood(Rz) was totally black and not bi-coloured", as the author had objected. Thus the beard of Miran Syed Mahmood (Rz) became bi-coloured after the holy burial of Imamana (As) and thus Miran Syed Mahmood (Rz) got the resemblance of Imamana (As), and from this event it is proved that Imamana's beard was also bi-coloured. But it does not mean to become "bi-colour" (do moya) half gray and half black. Sheik Abdul Haq, Muhddise Dehlvi has used the word "do moya" for the beard of the holy Prophet (Slm), though they were said to be only twenty or even less gray hair was present. Abdul Haq's statement is as follows:

"Indeed the front part of head and beard were both "do moya" (bi coloured) to the extent just twenty hair, the words "do moya" were used which is totally wrong to say that Imamana's beard was half gray and half black. So far nobody had included the colour of the hair as one of the features of either of the holy Prophet (Slm) or of Imamana (As). The fault finder's objection is just an absurd one, non-sensical and totally foolish which is untenable and rejected in limini.

As regards emergence of a person from the Ahl-e-Bait (Rz), Abdullah Ibn Masood (Rz) has narrated in "Abu Dawood" that he heard the Prophet (Slm) telling:

"If a single day is remaining for the Dooms Day, then Allah shall enlarge that day so much that a person would emerge from his Ahl-e-Bait (Rz), whose name would be of mine and his father's name also would be of my father's name and who would fill the earth with justice and order."	قال لو لم يبق من الدنيا الايوم لطول الله ذلك اليوم حتى يبعث الله فيه رجلا منى او من اهل بيتى يـواطى اسـمـه اسـمـى و اسـم ابيه اسم ابى يملاء الارض قسطا وعـدلا كمـا مـلئت ظلما وجورا (اشعة اللمعات جلد چهارم صفحه ۳۱۷)

This tradition points out some issues for consideration:

A. From the Ahl-e-Bait (Rz) a person would emerge. It fits to Imamana (As) since he comes from the line of Imam Moosa Kazim (Rz) which is a recognized fact even by the Non- Mahdavi Writers.

B. His Name should be the name of the Prophet (Slm). This also fits for Imamana (As) since Imamana's name is Mohammad (Slm) which is recognized by all history books.

C. His father's name would be that of the Holy Prophet's father's name, it is also proved since Imamana's father's name was Syed Abdullah. "Syed Khan" was his title granted by the Sultan.

D. To fill the Earth with justice and order.

Here, the author of Hadia has objected about the title, "Syed Khan", of the father of Imamana (As). What has been narrated in the "Insaf Nama" we shall try to investigate about that allegation:

A."When Imamana (As) was in Badhli, commands of the Almighty came to Imamana (As), which were in the form of an admonition,"Are you afraid of the people and do not want to pronounce your Mahdiat openly?" After this stern command only, Imamana (As) declared his Mahdiat emphatically.Then the Mullahs from Naherwala came to Imamana (As) and asked how could you declare yourself as Mahdi?

Imamana (As) answered them: "It is not I that claiming to be Mahdi (As) to myself, but it is Allah who ordered me to declare". Mullah told that "Mohammad Ibn Abdullah (As)" (and not Mohammad bin Syed Khan) should be the Mahdi (As), whereas your father was Syed Khan.

Imamana (As) inquired "whether Allah is not empowered to grant Mahdiat to the son of the said so called "Syed Khan"?

Mullah Moinuddin Patni sent two scholars with four questions;

(۱) چون میران در قصبه بڑلی آمدند فرمان شد که چرا اظهار نمی کنی مهدیت خود بلکه بطریق عتاب فرمان شد که از خلق می ترسی بعده بندگی میران مهدویت خود اظهار کردند ، بعد ازان ملایان از شهر نهروالـه پیـش میران آمدند و عرض کردند که خودرا مهدی میگویانید بندگی میران فرمودند که بنده نمـی گویـد خدائے تعالیٰ گوید ملایان می گفتند که امـام مهدی محمد بن عبدالله باشد و نام پدر شما سید خان است بعده بندگی میران جواب دادند که خدائے تعالیٰ قادر نیست که پسر سید خان را مهدی کند

B." The second question was: "What is the name of your father?" Imamana (As) told :"Syed Khan". Then Scholars told "As per traditions, father's name of Mahdi (As) should be "Syed Abdullah" as that of the name of the Prophet's father's name.

"Imamana (As) retarded: " Go and declare war against Allah as to why He had made Syed Khan's son, the Mahdi (As)."

دوم آنکـه سـوال کـردنـد کـه اسم پدر شمـا چیست میـران فرمودند که اسم پدر بنده سید خان است پس مـلـایان گـفتند که اسم نبی محمد بن عبدالـلـه بـاشـد و اسم مهدی هم محمد بن عبدالله بـاشـد ، فـرمودند که بـاخدا جنگ کنید که پسر سید خان را چرا مهدی کردی

C. It is reported that the scholars had questioned Imamana (As): "Mahdi (As) should be Mohammad Bin Abdullah, but your father's name was Syed Khan?" Imamana (As) replied."Ask Allah as to why he had made Mahdi to the son of Syed Khan"?

(ج) نقـل است مـلـایان پیـش میران گفتند که مهدی محمد بن عبدالله باشد ، نام پدر شما سید خان است بـعده حضرت میران فرمودند که خدائ تعالیٰ رابگوئید که پسر سید خان راچرا مهدی کردی

2. It is reported that the scholars submitted to Imamana (As): "As per the traditions, Mahdi's name shall be Mohammad (Slm), same as the name of the holy Prophet (Slm) and your father's name should be Abdullah as that of the name of the Prophet's father. But your father's name is "Syed Khan."On that Imamana (As) said that the father of holy Prophet (Slm) was an infidel, how could an infidel be Abdullah (The servant of Allah). But Prophet Mohammad's name is really "Mohammad Abdullah (Slm)" and not Mohammad Bin Abdullah (Slm); and as such Mahdi (As) also is "Mohammad Abdullah (As)", it is just a clerical mistake, that the writer has mistakenly written"Mohammad Bin Abdullah (Slm)."

نقـل است که ملایان حدیث رسول الله صلـی الـلـه عـلـیه و سلم پیش میران عرض کردند که یواطی اسمه اسمی و اسم ابیه اسم ابی و نام پدر شما سید خان است ، حضرت میران فرمودند که پدرِ رسول الله مردے کافر بـود آن عبدالله چگونه باشد بلکه محمد رسول الـله هم محمد عبدالله باشد و مهدی هـم مـحـمـد عبدالله و لفظ ابن سهو کاتب است که محمد بن عبدالله نبشته است

These questions and answers were reported in "Insaf Nama" in its Chapter One.The Author of Hadia described these answers were crooked and unfair. As a matter of fact such eloquent answers nobody could offer. These eloquent answers could only be understood by those who had studied the traditions in respect of Mahdi (As) and who could distinguish the signs of

Mahdiat and conditions of Mahdiat and also that under what circumstances such answers were given, we have to clarify and understand some relevant matters in this regard:

1. Father's name of Imamana (As) actually was Syed Abdullah as had been mentioned in "Juanpur Nama" and "Tuhfathul Kiram" and Syed Khan was the Title . This is also mentioned in "Shawahedul Vilayeth", which states that:

"Miran's father's name was Syed Abdullah Alias Syed Khan. But in order to counter the argument of the fault finder, Imamana (As) replied in the same manner as it was questioned.."

نــام پدر حضــرت مهدی مـوعود میـراں سید عبدالله عرف سید خاں بود اما از جهت الزام مدعی در ہماں سوال سائل جواب فرمودند (باب ہیجدہم).

As regards the biography, Miyan Abdul Rahman's "Moulood" is the oldest one which was written before 908 H. in which name of Imamana's father has been written as Syed Abdullah which is a clear proof. If at that time this tradition had no bearing to Imamana (As), then the author of the "Moulood" would not have recorded it at all.

2. Non Mahdavi scholars were very well conversant about Imamana (As) as the descendant of the holy Prophet (Slm). Had they any doubt, then they would not have presented this tradition in which the father's names of both the Prophet (Slm) and that of the Imamana (As) should be "Abdullah." Instead they would have reported that tradition which refers "Ahl-e -Bait (Rz)" only.

"Mahdi (As) is from the Ahl-e-Bait (Rz)." According to Ibn Maja (Rz)."

المهدی من اہل البیت (ابن ماجہ)

Above mentioned questions of the scholars do not repudiate Imamana's authenticity of the Promised Mahdi (As). It is a fact that his father's title was Syed Khan; still scholars had tried to object his Mahdiat on that single baseless point.

3. Since scholars were adamant on the issue of Syed Khan, Imamana (As) too seemingly mentioned the title of "Syed Khan" and arguably convinced them by telling "yes, my father's name is Syed Khan also".

Traditions written in the "Sihah", under the chapter Mahdi (As) point out that Mahdi's father's name should have been Abdullah. Abu Dawood's tradition, already referred above which states the words "Rajula Minni aou min Ahl-e-Baiti (Rz)." Meaning," He will be from my Ahl-e-Bait (Rz)".

Author of Hadia had referred a tradition which is reported in chapter 3, Argument 2 also, does not mention "Mahdi(As)" The tradition is as follows :

"The Prophet said: "world would not end, until Allah will Send a person, carrying my name and his father's name will be my father's name who would fill the earth with justice and tranquility against tyranny." Reported by Ibn Sheeba (Rz) and Tabrani (Rz), Abu Nayeem (Rz) and Hakim Bin Masood (Rz)."

قـال رسـول الـله صلی الله علیه و سلم لا تذهب الدنیا حتیٰ یبعث الله رجلا من اهل بیتی یواطی اسمه اسـمـی واسـم ابیـه اسـم ابی فیملاء الارض قسطا وعـدلا کـمـا مـلـئت ظلمـا وجورا رواه ابن ابی شیبه والطبـرانی فی الافراد و ابو نعیم والحاکم عن ابن مسعود (هدیه مهدویه) (طبع کانپور صفحه ۵۴)

Imam Mahdi's name was not specifically mentioned in it.

The scholars were basing their allegation on that particular point and they were thinking that this point was strong enough to nullify Imamana's Mahdiat. Imamana's answers were in conformity to the one put before him. Befitting answers could be given only by a well versed scholar of traditions and by a very learned philosopher only.

First answer was whether the Almighty has no power to grant Mahdiat to a son of Syed Khan?

The second and third points were to suggest to them to wage a war against Allah as to why He had granted Mahdiat to a son of Syed Khan? These answers point out that Imamana's such answers were not given by himself, but were given on the Commands of Allah. Therefore, these answers point out that Imamana's proclamation was based on firm commands of Allah and not on his personal desire and the referred signs could not go against him. Author of Hadia feels that Imamana (As) did not give convincing answers to the questions. As a matter of fact, the Imam's replies were quiet in accordance to Qur'anic argument, and according to the traditions. In such circumstances we have to refer to Allah's way of dealing with such circumstances. Allah Asserts that:

"The infidels say as to why no sign had been revealed by Allah? Tell them, "verily Allah misleads whom He wills and guides those who turn to him in repentance."

و یـقـول الـذین کفرو الولا انزل علیه آیة من ربـه قل ان الـله یـضل من یشاء و یهدی الیه من اناب (الرعد ۴)

In this verse, Allah did not mention what signs He had sent to the Prophet (Slm), but His answer was that: "whomsoever he wants He misleads him." This answer is well suited since the infidels knew the signs which had been revealed to the Prophet (Slm), still the infidels wanted some more, hence it was the befitting reply. Another instance is given about the holy Prophet (Slm), who, in such circumstance had dealt with:

Hazrat Anas (Rz) reported that a person asked the Prophet (Slm): "when would come the Doomday?" Answer was given: "Pity on you, what provision have you made for that day?" Is that answer was not correct? The question was for something and the answer was something other.

Sheik Abdul Haq Muhaddis, has written regarding this tradition that:

Clearly, that question was not appealing to the Prophet (Slm), he suspected it to be either it was a taunt one or out of fear.

Thus, if the questioner was posing any taunt, then answer given by the Prophet (Slm) was according to his dignity and cannot be said to be degrading his position as the Prophet (Slm). Can anyone raise any objection on the reply given by Huzoor Rasoolallah (Slm), by saying that the question was something about and the answer was given about something ?

4. So also, the answer given by Imamana (As) was meaningful and decisive, since the Non Mahdavi Scholars were presenting a sign which was against Imamana (As) and they wanted to negate the assertion of Imamana (As). The question was : "Mahdi's father's name as per traditions should be Syed Abdullah, whereas, you are telling Syed Khan was your father, therefore your Mahdiat is not correct. Imamana's answer puts forward the stipulation of his Mahdiat, which proves that no sign can defeat the already accepted claim.

Scholars were insisting that Mahdi's father's name was Syed khan, whereas the name should be Syed Abdullah. On such insistence, Imamana (As) did not deny his father's title being Syed Khan. Then he said that Prophet's father was an infidel, this is correct according to the tradition, as "Muslim" reported that:

"Haz. Anas (Rz) reported in "Muslim" : One person came to the Prophet (Slm) and asked:"where was his father?" the answer was given to him that "Your father is in the Hell." The man went away. But Huzoor (Slm) called him back again and said:"my father and your father both are in the Hell."

عـن انـس ان رجلا قال يا رسول الله اين قال فى النار فلما قفى الرجل دعاه فقال ان ابى و اباك فى النار (صحیح مسلم طبع مصر ۱۳۹ الجزءالاول صفحہ ۷۶)

This reply was given just to console the questioner that "my father and your father both are in the Hell" was based on holy Prophet's courtesy and grace, as it gives solace to the questioner, if he was told that some one else also was suffering the same calamity, he became contented.

"Prophet's reply that his father and questioner's father, both are in the hell speaks politeness towards the questioner who became satisfied with the answer that both his and Prophet's father were equally suffering in the hell."

وقولـه صلى الله عليه و سلم ان ابى و اباك فى النار هومن حسن العشرة تسلية بالاشتراك فى المصيبة (منهاج شرح مسلم برحاشيةارشادالسارى طبع مصر الجزءالثانى صفحہ ۲۰۰)

Imamana (As) also said that the name of Abdullah does not apply to the Prophet's father because the Prophet (Slm) himself was Abdullah, since Abdullah means "perfect servant, devotee of Allah". It gives the meaning that even if the father of the Prophet (Slm) was called Abdullah, he was not at all a perfect devotee or a servant of Allah. And it is a fact that the

Prophet (Slm) also was named as Abdullah by the Almighty as well:

"And when Abdullah (Mohammad Slm) stands for offering prayer, people surround him." (72:20)

وانـه لـمـا قـام عبـدالله يدعوه كا دوا يكون عليه لبدا (الجن ع۱)

Author of "Muwaaheb-e-Ludannia" reports about Naqqaash (Rz) who reported that what the Prophet (Slm) was saying:

"There are seven names of mine in the Qur'an: Mohammad, Ahmed, Yaseen, Tahaa, Al Muzammil, Al Mudassir, Abdullah."

روى النقاش عنه عليه الصلوة والسلام لى فى القرآن سبعة اسماء محمد واحمد و يٰسن و طه والمزمل والمدثر و عبدالله (مواهب مدينة طبع المطبقه الشرقية مصر، الجزء الاول صفحه ۱۸۲)

Thus, whereever the name Abdullah (Slm) has come in the Qur'an, it refers to the Holy Prophet (Slm), because he was the perfect servant of Allah. Therefore the answer given by Imamana (As) was correct as confirmed by the Holy Qur'an and also by the Holy Prophet himself.

Naming prophet as Abdullah (Slm) had some bearing because it is one of the conditions of the Nabuvwath, and the Prophet (Slm) himself said he is just nothing but a servant (Abdullah) of Allah, and then he became Messenger of Allah. On that Novavi had commented about this tradition, that this sort of reply was given to console the questioner; that my father and his father both are in the Hell. This answer shows holy Prophet's courtesy and gracefulness to console and satisfy that the Prophet's father too was in the Hell along with the questioner's father, this sort of answer gave the questioner complete satisfaction.

In continuation of the answer, Imamana (As) presented himself as Abdulalh (As). Since it was necessary to become the perfect servant for getting the position of the "Promised Mahdi (As)." Here also "Khulq-e-Azeem" is the criterian for becoming Abdullah (As). The tradition confirms that Imam Mahdi (As) shall possess the same sublime characters as that of the Holy Prophet (Slm). Thus, in what sense the Prophet (Slm) is Abdullah (As), Imam Mahdi (As) also should have the same attributes to become Abdullah (As).

Even Imamana's opponents have accepted the sublimity of his characters and awarded him the title of "Syedul Aoulia" even before he proclaimed himself to be the Promised Mahdi (As). Therefore, the wrong assumption of his adversaries that Imamana's father's name was Syed Khan, instead of Syed Abdullah, can never negate his assertion as the Promised Mahdi (As).

It is a fact that even the bitterest enemy like Abu Jahal had accepted the Prophet (Slm) as Trustworthy, on the same score Imamana's claim of toeing the footsteps of the holy Prophet (Slm) had been broadly accepted by his opponents as well. At many occasions Imamana (As) informed the gatherings that:

"I am Abdullah and the follower of Mohammad Rasoolullah (Slm)."

انی عبدالله تابع محمد رسول الله
(عقیده شریفه)

The writer of "Shawahedul Vilayet" states:

"The tenth name of Imamana (As) was recorded as "Abdullah (As)."

اسم دهم آنکه حضرت عبدالله کما وردفی
المنقول (باب ۲۹)

Imamana's statement that instead of "Mohammad Abdullah", by a clerical mistake it was written wrongly as "Mohammad Bin Abdullah". Thus this interpretation of Imamana (As) should be taken as correct according to the Qur'an and the traditions.

Allah has named the Prophet (Slm) as "Abdullah (Slm)" and not as "Mohammad Bin Abdullah (Slm)." And the Prophet (Slm) himself asked others to call him "Abdullah" first and then "Rasoolullah." Hazrat Omer (Rz) reported what the Prophet (Slm) told:

"I am nothing but the servant of Allah."

فانما انا عبده فقولوا عبدالله و رسوله (اشعة
اللمعت جلدرابع صفحه ۹۳)

This was the Prophet's favourite name, as mentioned by the author of "Madarik" that:

"Allah did rarely call the Prophet (Slm) 'Rasool' or 'Nabi', because 'Abdullah' was one of his favourite names."

لم یقل نبی الله او رسول الله لانه من احب
الاسماء الی النبی صلی الله علیه و سلم (تفسیر

مدارک الجزء الرابع صفحه ۲۲۶)

Allah has called him Abdullah (Slm) and not Mohammad Bin Abdullah (Slm), therefore the Prophet (Slm) asked others to call him "Abdullah" first and then "Rasoolullah (Slm)." Since this name was his favourite name. The author of" Madarik" further reported that: "Allah did not call him "Nabiallah or Rasoolullah", because the name " Abdullah" was most desirable to the Almighty.

The author of "Muaheb-e-Alliah"reports that the most desired name of the Prophet (Slm) was Abdullah. It is because Allah's choiced name was Abdullah. As per "Safarus Saadath":

"The Prophet (Slm) used to say that out of the most favourite names, Allah had called the Prophet "Abdullah or Abdul Rahman."

و میگفت دوست ترین نام ها بخدائی تعالی عبدالله
و عبدالرحمن است (سفرالسعادت، طبع لکهنو صفحه ۳۸۴)

Now it is left to the better judgment of the Ahl-e-Eiman (Momins) to ascertain whether was it not a clerical mistake to write prophet's name as "Mohammad Bin Abdullah", instead of "Mohammad Abdullah (Slm)"? Particularly when the Holy Prophet (Slm) disliked calling 'Akrmah' the son of Abu Jahal as "Akramah Ibn Abu Jahal" by the Ansar-e-Madinah. And it is also a fact that whenever the holy Prophet (Slm) had represented himself as a person commissioned by Allah, he had written "Mohammad Abdullah" (Slm). This is an unanimously accepted fact by both "Muslim" and "Bukhari" that he wrote "Mohammad Abdullah (Slm)" and certainly not "Mohammad Bin Abdullah". It is a different issue that at the time of "Treaty of Hudaibia": the infidels of Makkah insisted upon him to get the name written as "Mohammad Ibn Abdullah" and not "Mohammad Rasoolullah (Slm)". In view of these basic facts, Imamana's contention about inscribing the name of the holy Prophet (Slm) as "Mohammad Ibn Abdullah " was a clerical mistake, becomes hundred percent correct because this name (Abdullah) was his most choiced one. It does not mean that whatever Imamana (AS) has asserted, as if he had denied Prophet's ancestry.

The opposing scholars were insisting that how could a son of Syed Khan be accepted as the Promised Mahdi (As), when according to the traditions, the son of Abdullah alone had the authority to proclaim himself as the Promised Mahdi (As). In reply to this wrong contention, Imamana (As) said that his being as the promised Mahdi (As) depends upon his being the perfect servant (Abd-e-Kaamil) of Allah, just as the Prophethood of Rasoolallah (Slm) depended upon his being the perfect servant of Allah that is (Abd-e-Kaamil). And it was already clarified by Imamana (As) that even if it is taken for granted that Imamana's father's name Syed Khan was not the title, but the actual name, then too nobody could deny his Mahdiat. The reply given was just in accordance to the Holy Qur'an and according to the traditions, which cannot and should not be said to be a crooked one. On the other hand it tells upon lack of understanding of the author of Hadia himself.

However, all particular points reported in the tradition as was written in "Abu Dawood", completely fit and rightly adjust to the person of Imamana (As).

Appearance of a person from behind a Canal:

In one of the traditions, without mentioning the name of Mahdi (As) or Ahl-e- Bait (Rz), appearance of a particular person has been reported and that tradition has been included in the traditions relating to Mahdi (As) and the same has been reported by "Abu Dawood" which states as below:

عـن علی رضی الله عنه قال قال رسول الله صلی الـله علـیـه و آلـه و سلم یخرج رجل من وراء النهر یـقـال لـه الـحـارث حراث علی مقدمه رجل یقال له منصور یوطن او یمکن لآل محمد کما مکنت قریش لـرسـول اللـه و جـب عـلـی کل مومن نصره اوقال اجابته (اشعة اللمعات)

"Hazrat Ali (Rz) reported having heard the holy Prophet (Slm) saying that there would appear a man from behind the canal and he would be called Haris, thus he would be Harras. Even before his appearance, another man by name Mansur, would help descendants of the Prophet (Slm) as the Qureysh helped the apostle of Allah. It is, therefore, an obligation on every Momin to help that man and to accept his Call."

In this tradition, the appearance of a man has been informed, but neither his relation to

Ahl-e-Bait (Rz) has been described nor about any description of Mahdi (As) has been pointed out. However if we link the said man appearing from behind the canal to Mahdi (As), then some of the particulars mentioned above correctly adjust to Imamana (As).

Tradition refers to "Min Wara-un Nahar". We like to point out here that the area of the city of Turan is called "Ma Wara-un Nahar" in Arabic, and not "Min Wara-un Nahar." The geography of the Khilafath-e-Mashriqi mentions that:

River Oxus (in Arabic "Jaihoon") separates Persian and Turkish nations residing in Persia and Turan and the portion of the land which falls beyond the North of this river was called "Ma Wara-un Nahar" by Arabs. But the tradition refers "Min Wara-un Nahar" which means "from behind the canal". Tradition informs that a man would appear from behind the Canal.

In "Juanpur Nama" it has been mentioned that:

"In between Juanpur and Zafarabad a river by name Gomthi runs. Thus at the North of Gomthi situates Juanpur and to the South of Gomthi lies Zafarabad.

میاں اس در مصر جامع رود گومتی رواں است که بریک سوئے کنارہ اش ظفر آباد است به سوئے دیگر جون پور (باب پنجم)

Imamana (As) had started his migration from Juanpur, that is from North of Gomthi river; that is "From beyond the canal (here Gomthi may be taken as Canal) certainly it deterrmines the appearance of a man to appear "from behind the canal", and accordingly it correctly fits to Imamana (As). Whoever comes from the rear side of the Canal would be called Haris (tiger). This also fits to Imamana (As). Miyan Abdul Rahman 's "Moulood" refers that:

"All the scholars unanimously declared Imamana as "Asadul Ulema", (Tiger of Scholars)."

همه علماء اتفاق کردہ اسد العلماء گفته

Thus Imamana (As) according to this tradition had been designated a Asad (lion or tiger). The tradition refers that person as Haris (tiger). The author of "Muntahiul Arab" describes about Haris that it means" to probe and teach Qur'an" and there is a tradition which directs to investigate and ponder on the subjects of Qur'an and discuss about the "Mutashabihat and Muhakkamath" and the commands.

Authors of "Lisanul Arab" and "Tajul Uroos" have discussed about the word "Haris":

"Search and educate Qur'an". Tradition tells to search in the Qur'an, means ponder over the Qur'an and discuss over its knowledge and commands."

کاویدن و درس کردن قرآن و منه الحدیث احرثواهذ القرآن ای فتشوہ ثوروہ (منتہی الارب طبع لاہور)

That had been referred to a tradition:"Ahrasoo Haazal Qur'an". "Ahrasoo" means to investigate and discuss about the knowledge and the commands mentioned in the Qur'an. Thus the word "Harras" denotes to a person who uncovers the secrets of the Qur'an. This also perfectly fits to Imamana (As), because the Qur'an was bestowed to him as a miracle and he was made the embodiment of "Summa Inna Alaina Biyana". (Thus it is our responsibility to interpret it).

With reference to "Ala Muqaddamath", the author of "Ash'athul Lam'aath" has described it to be mentioned as "Paish uz way" meaning , before his appearance, one person by name Mansur, will emerge. Author of " Miqat" describes "Mansur" as a noun or an attribute. The manner in which Mansur emerged, it tells his attribute. This also adjusts to Imamana (As), since, even before the migration took place, Sultan Husain Sharqi became victorious (Mansur) over Rai Dalpat, with the Blessings of Imamana (As) "(Laqad Nasarakumullah) verily Allah made you victorious." Thus with this victory, the Ummah became victorious over the infidels. The word "Mansur" denotes Nusrath, the victory of the Ummah over infidelity.

Every Muslim is obliged to help assist the Haris (tiger) and also to accept his Call. These all fit to the personality of Imamana (As).

Effects of Solar or Lunar Eclipse;

What Mohammad Bin Ali (Rz) has said about the Saying in the "Dar-e-Qatni" that:

Omro bin Shumar told that he heard Jaaber was telling to Mohammad Bin Ali (Rz) that there are two signs for the Mahdi (As), and those signs had never occurred since the inception of the Earth and Heavens, Those signs are:

1. On the very first day of Ramazan there would be a Lunar Eclipse, and

2. In the middle of Ramazan (15th of Ramazan) there would be the Solar Eclipse. These signs had never occurred since the creation of the earth and the skies."

حدثنا ابو سعيد الاصطخرى ثنا محمد بن عبدالله بن نوفل ثنا عبيد بن يعيش ثنا يونس بن كبير عن عمر وين شمر عن جابر عن محمد بن على قال ان المهدينا آيتين لم تكونا منذ خلق السموات والارض تنكسف القرمر الاول ليلة من رمضان تنكسف الشمس فى النصف مه و لم تكونا منذ خلق الله السموات والارض (سنن الدار القطنى مع التعليق المغنى)

Its first answer is that this tradition is not from the "Sihah" and whatever is said in it is not necessary to have any bearing on the person of Mahdi (As). Second answer is that the two persons who narrated to Mohammad bin Ali (Rz) are not reliable persons and about whom Shamsul Haq Azeemabadi has referred about those persons in his "Al Tauleequl Mughni" that:

"Whatever they said to Shumar, is weak and unreliable."	قول عمر و بن شمر عن جابر كلا هما ضعيفان لا يحتج بهما (التعليق المغني على سنن الدار القطني)

Therefore whatever was said to Mohammad Bin Ali (Rz) is doubtful. Even otherwise what Mohammad bin Ali (Rz) said becomes invalid as per the traditions of the Prophet (Slm) reported by Hazrata Bibi Ayesha (Rz) in "Sahih Muslim

"Thus the Holy Prophet (Slm) informed the audience that the eclipses of the Sun or Moon are two signs of the Almighty and they have nothing to do with any person's life or death."	فخطب الناس فحمد الله و اثنىٰ عليه ثم قال ان الشمس والقمر آيتان من آيات الله لا يخسفان لموت احد ولا لحيوته (اشعة اللمعات)

The tradition narrated by Abdulla Bin Abbas (Rz) in "Sahih" also contains that the Saying of Holy prophet (Slm) that the Solar or Lunar Eclipses are two signs of the Almighty and they do not appear at the time of a person's birth or death. Then how would there be any eclipse for Mahdi (As)?

Therefore to assert that the eclipse would become the sign of some one's birth or death is to negate the undeniable words of the Holy Prophet (Slm).

Nayeem Bin Hammad (Rz) had stated in "Kitabul Fitan" that:

"A tradition was reported by Haakam Bin Nafey (Rz) who heard from Jarrah (Rz) it is from the "Artat" that it is reported that Mahdi (As) would live for forty years and then would die at his bed. Then a person would emerge from Qahtan having his ears pierced, who would be having characters of Mahdi (As) and who would live for 20 years. Then he would be martyred. Then one person from the Ahl-e-Bait (Rz) would emerge who would have good characters and who would attack the city of Madinah. He would be the last from the progeny of the Prophet (Slm); then the Anti Christ would emerge and soon after Eisa Ibn Maryiam (As) would descend."	حدثنا الحكم بن نافع عن جراح عن ارطاة قال بلغني ان المهدى يعيش اربعين عاما ثم يموت على فراشه ثم يخرج رجل من قحطان مثقوب الاذنين على سيرة المهدى بقاءه عشرين سنة ثم يموت قتيلا بالسلاح ثم يخرج رجل من اهل بيت النبى عليه السلام مهدى حسن السيرة يغزو مدينة قيصر و هو آخر امير من امة محمد صلى الله عليه و سلم ثم يخرج فى زمانه الدجال و ينزل فى زمانه عيسىٰ ابن مريم (كتاب الفتن حديث عربى قلمى نمبر ۱۳۷۴، اسٹیٹ سنٹرل لائبریری) الجزء الخامس شمارہ حدیث ۱۱۷۶

This tradition has been recorded by Seyuthi in "Al Arfil Vardi"; and Sheik Ali Muttaqi also recorded in"" Risala-e-Burhan" and Mullah Ali Qari had also recorded in the "Risalathul Mahdi (As)." This tradition adjusts to Imamana (As) to some extent only. The details are as mentioned below:

1. Mahdi Would Live For Forty Years:

It does not necessarily limit the age. It does mean to say that Mahdi (As) would not die in his bloom age, but would passaway only after crossing or reaching forty years. In Arabic the word "Summa" had come in between "Arbaien Aama" and Yamooth". Here "Summa" defines both for the near and far periods. Here period of forty year indicates to an age in which a man becomes much matured. This is substantiated by the Wordings of the Almighty Allah who said:

"Thus he reached his maturity and attained the year of forty". (46:16 Part)	حتىٰ اذا بلغ اشده و بلغ اربعین سنة (احقاف رکوع (۲

According to this verse, the words "Arbaeen Aama" denotes complete maturity, that means to say that Mahdi (As) would reach his maturity and then would passaway, and not at his bloom age.

" Kanzul Ummal 's "Second Narration" also testifies that Mahdi (As) would be commissioned at the age of forty.

A further narration by Qatada is reported to have been told that Mahdi (As) would be of the age of forty. The author of "Tafseer-e-Madarik" has written a reference from the chapter "Al Qasais" of the holy Prophets, states that:

"No apostle was commissioned, but after the age of forty."	یروی انه لم یبعث نبی الاعلی راس اربعین سنة

Imamana (As) too was commissioned only after becoming matured, at the age of forty when he had proclaimed his Mahdiath on the commands of the Almighty, and then only he left Juanpur for migration (after his age forty.)"

2. Mahdi would pass away at his Bed:

It is reported in the "Hashia Sharief" that:

"At the time of Mahdi's passing away, there was only a palm leaf mat on the ground, and not even a cot."	نقل است حضرت میران علیه السلام راوصال شد بوریا برزمین گسترانیده بود چهار پائی نبود (صفحہ نمبر ۱۳۵)

Therefore it adjusts to him that he passed away on a mat made as a bed for him.

3. After Mahdi, Man Emerges From Qahtan:

And who would be martyred after 20 years after the demise of Imamana (As) (as prophesied).

This refers to Hazrat Bandagi Miyan Syed Khundmir (Rz) who was martyred after 20 years from the date of demise of Imamana (As). Regarding this martyrdom, the author of "Nuzhathul Khawathir" has written:

"Thus, Ainul Mulk, commander of Naherwala, went with his army; fought against them and martyred them on the battlefield, the one who was martyred was called by his followers as Siddiq-e-Vilayeth (Bandagi Miyan Syed Khundmir Rz)."

فسـار اليـه عيـن الـملک بعساکره و کان والیا علـى نهـروالـه فقاتله و قتله فى المعرکة و کان لقبه فى اهـل مـذهبـه صـدیق الولایه (نزهتة الخواطرطبع حیدرآباد،الجزءالرابع صفحه ۱۰۶)

Bandagi Miyan Syed Khundmir (Rz.) was a Moosawi Syed, coming from Adnan. Both Qahtan and Adnan are the sons of Hazrath Ismail (AS). The word Qahtan points out that, that man also should be one of the sons of Prophet Ismail (AS). Nadeem bin Hammad (Rz) has reported to Ka'ab that:

"After the demise of Huzoor Mahdi (As), a man of Ahl-e-Bait (Rz) would be the guardian."

یـمـوت المهدى ثم یلى بعده رجل من اهل بیت النبى

Qahtan has links with Yemen and Yemen's tribes are from the sons of Prophet Ismail (As). Imam Bukhari (Rz) has written a separate chapter regarding the tribes of Yemen. Such example could not be objected. For instance the prophecy about Nabi Aakhiruzzama (Slm) was that he would be from the brothers of Banu Ishaq (As). Whereas the holy Prophet (Slm) is from Banu Ismail (As). The authenticity of this prophecy cannot be denied as Banu Ishaq and Bani Ismail are both the descendants of Hazrat Ibrahim (AS). Even otherwise all tribes of Yemen are from the lineage of Qahtan. The proof of this is that in one of the traditions, the Prophet (Slm) had referred the words "Al Yemeni al Qahtani". The holy Prophet (Slm) has given a glad tidings about the Yamenis, by saying "faith and wisdom are the domain of Yamenis." Thus the Yemenis who are actually the Qahtanis had been certified by the Holy Prophet (Slm) as the true believers. Imamana (As) had given his glad tidings for Hazrat Bandagi Miyan Syed Khundmir (Rz) to be a perfect Muslim, and as per the glad tidings of the Prophet (Slm) "Qahtanis are true believers, then there is no reason to deny as to why Bandagi Miyan (Rz) should not be referred as Qahtani.

However there are two different versions. One is that the person who would emerge after Mahdi (As) would be an Adnani; and the other states that he would be a Qahtani.

In view of these facts it can be determined that the man who would be martyred was an Adnani, but on account of his beliefs he was a Qahtani. The fact is that as Hazrat Ishaq (As) and Hazrat Ismail (As) are both the sons of Prophet Ibrahim (As), in the same way both Qahtan and Adnan are the sons of Hazrat Ismail (As).

5. That Qahtani recognized from pierced ears:

It means that; the man (mentioned in the tradition) with "pierced ears" denote that he would become a staunch follower of Imam Mahdi (As). Thus it adjusts to Hazrat Bandagi Miyan Syed Khundmir (Rz).

6. He had characters of Mahdi (As). This too adjusts to the person of Hazrat Bandagi Miyan (Rz), since Imamana (As) had given him the glad tidings that "you have been bestowed with the ability to spiritually have a "Sair"/immersed into my person:

"Thumko meri zat mein Sair hai". You
are immersed in my person." شمارا در ذات بنده سیر است (اشعته اللمعات جلد رابع صفحه ۴۱۷)

The other issues narrated in the "Artat" have no bearing to the period of Imamana (As), since it actually pertains to the period of the Prophet Esa (As), when the emergence of Anti Christ "Dajjal" is expected.

7. As regards the news of Mahdi (As) that he would also appear at the time of prophet Esa (As), is being said just in a literal sense, and of course he would not be the real Mahdi, since this Mahdi does not carry 'AL', therefore, here Mahdi means a person who is guided one in a general sense. It may also be pointed out that the Real Mahdi (As) would emerge before the appearance of Qahtani and not after Qahtani.

8. In the tradition it is mentioned that Mahdi (As) shall be from the Ahl-e-Bait (RZ) and shall attack the city of Qaiber. But as per the authentic traditions, (a commander) of Banu Ishaq would conquor Qustuntunia.

The tradition referred to in the "Artat" is perfectly adjusting both to Imamana (As) and to Bandagi Miyan (Rz). From this tradition it can be inferred that the periods of Prophet Esa (As) and that of Imamana (As) would be quite different and far apart. Therefore this tradition has the sanctity to be a real tradition.

It all boils down to say that as the prophecies of the Scriptures adjust to the Holy Prophet (Slm), in the same manner, prophecies of the Holy Prophet (Slm) perfectly true for Imamana (As) and therefore correctly adjust to the person of Imamana (As), particularly those traditions which are mentioned in "Sihah".

The Signs Of Allah:

Miracles testify Nabuvwat but there seems some resemblance between miracle and magic. For example; the scepter of prophet Moses (As) became a python (in the court of Pharaoh), so also the ropes of the magicians too became snakes. Both inanimate things became animate. However, we can only differentiate on account of the person's character (who uses that particular thing). Since the Prophet is the Preacher of virtue and the magicians are the instigators of evil; this difference can be visualized easily.

Another thing is that miracles are not the domain of the Prophets. But the duty of the Prophet is propagation of Allah's Mission only and Allah the Almighty, whenever, feels necessary to assist the Prophet (As), He helps through some miracles, but unfortunately whoever denies the character of the Prophet (As), asserts miracle as an act of magic.

The third issue is that the Holy Qur'an never made miracle as a test of the Nabuvwat, but it has presented the character of the Prophet (Slm) alone as the test of his Nabuvwat.

Verse: "Had they not recognized their
Prophets (As)."(23:7)

ام لـم يعـرفوا رسولهم (المومنون ركوع ٣، رساله
اثبات المهدی جواهر التصديق کے نام سے شائع ہوگیا ہے)

"Had they not recognized their prophets (As)"? It means "they had recognized them". The commentators of this verse have all agreed that this verse refers to the infidels who had recognized the Holy Prophet (Slm) through his sublime characters. Whenever Allah desired to support His Holy Prophet (Slm), He administered Miracles and those miracles were seen as presented by the Prophet (Slm) only. In the same manner, Allah had supported Imamana (As) through His miracles which have also been recorded in the books like "Hujjathul Musannafeen" of Miyan Vali JI ibn Miyan Yousuf (Rz), "Moulood" of Miyan Abdul Rahman (Rh), "Kitab-e-Mu'jazath-e-Mahdi (As)", in which more than 100 miracles of Imamana (As) have been written. And also other books like "Matle-ul-Vilayet", "Jannathul Vilayet", "Shawahedul Vilayet" Etc. mention some such miracles which assure prominance of Imamana (As).

The author of "Isbath-e-Mahdi (As)" states that the "Kitab-e-Mu'jazath-e-Mahdi (As)" is full with hundreds of Miracles attributed to Imamana (As).

Miyan Abdul Rahman (Rz) was one among the migrants; and Miyan Valiji (Rz) is the son of the companion of Imamana (As). Both have recorded what have been reported by the companions of Imamana (As). If their recorded facts are not taken as authentic even though they have reached us from a direct single source, then what would be the credence of those traditions which have come to us from many remote and that too, not from direct sources, but indirect sources (that even after a long period of even more than one hundred years). If such authentic record about Imamana (As) is doubted, then what would be the fate of those recorded facts of so many prophets (As) whose traditions have come to us through so many channels of a very remote period whose narrators were their followers of those Prophets only. Hazrat Syed Esa Alias Aalam Miyan (Rh), had referred to a book, "Mukhbarul Aouliya" authored by Shaik Rasheedudin, a non Mahdavi, in which miracles of Imamana (As) have been recorded which is available in the Library of Mahmood Miyan, who is well known among the priests of Ahmadabad.

Syed Abu Zafar Nadvi, Retired Professor of Ahmadabad college, Gujrat, has written at page 128 of "Tareekh-e-Aouliya-e-Gujrat" about this book "Mukhbarul Aouliya" that this original book was written by Sheik Rasheduddin Chishti who was the contemporary of the author of "Mir'ath-e-Ahmadi". The original book is in a decayed condition and still available in the library of the Royal Asiatic Society, Bombay. Another original book is also available with Sheik Naseeruddin Miyan Saheb, son of Shaik Fareeduddin, son of Sheik Mahmood Saheb Chishti. Had that been got printed it would have been a source of authentic knowledge to so many scholars to know about the miracles of Imamana (As).

Mahmood Miyan who had been referred by Aalam Miyan Saheb, was the grandfather of Naseeruddin known as Shaik Mahmood Chishti. It is a point to be noted that even in the books of Non Mahdavi scholars the references of Imamana's Miracles have been mentioned. It is better to mention first what had been recorded from the Non Mahdavi sources; then we shall mention such recorded facts from our sources to justify the correctness of both recorded facts. Thus it is better to mention first what Abdullah Bin Omar Makki had reported in his "Zafar Wala" with reference to Imamana (As); that:

"Once, a person who was very much infatuated with a lady, went in the night to her house, and suddenly came out from her house in a furious mood with a sword in his hand and went towards his house. It was almost getting morning that he happened to pass towards a river, where Imamana (As) was present. In a ferocious mood he asked Imamana (As) as to why he was here. The Imamana (As) coolly answered him: "The person who had become displeased with his beloved one, would surely accept my Vilayet and join with my companions". Hearing this the man became unconscious for some time. When he came to his senses he repented and became a celibate thereafter. From here Imamana (As) went to Pattan Naherwala."

واتفق لمن كان عزام بامراة قد زارها ليلا انه خرج مغضبا و قائم السيف بيده الى صوب منزله و قد طلع الفجر فتوجه الى النهر فاذا بالسيد و اصحابه على الماء فقال للسيد ماحاجتك عندالماء و ما مهرتك فاجابه من خرج مغاضبا لمحبوبه يقطع بولايتى ويدخل فى اصحابى فاعتراه غشى فلما افاق تاب و تجردثم ان السيد خرج من احمد آباد الى نهر واله بتن (ظفرالواله بمظفر واله طبع ليدن جلداول صفحه ٣٦)

In "Shawahedul Vilayaet" it is reported in Chapter 13 about the same person who was the nephew of Sultan Mahmood Begdah. This event is thus narrated in it:

"On a certain night, the nephew of Sultan Mahnmood Begdha went out with some of his notorious friends with a fornication intention and came to one of his beloved's houses. Unfortunately he became furious and having a sword in his hand came out in an intoxicated condition and went towards his house. It was getting morning, when he reached near the river Sabermati, he found Imamana (As) and his companions standing there (for the purpose of making ablution for the morning prayers). He questioned Imamana (As) as to why he was there? Imamana (As) very politely replied thus "The reason who became saddened by the behavior of his dearest friend, he would surely get guidance from us and amicably settles the matter. Hearing this befitting reply, he yelled loudly and became unconscious. When came out to his senses, he repented and changed himself as a celibate and became Imamana's disciple."

نقـل اسـت کـه خـواهـر زاده سلطان محمود بیکـره شبـی بـاچنـد اوباشان به قصد زنـا در خانه مـحبوبۀ خود آمده بودو اتفاق صحبت خوب برنیا مـده رنجیده شد آخر شب از آنجامست شمشیر دردسـت گـرفتـه روبه سوی خانه خود نهادو چون صبـح صادق مید مید دید که در کنار آبجوی (که آن) را سابهر متی خطاب است حضرت امام اولو الالبـاب بـا اصحاب خویش ایستاده پرسیـد۔ شما چـه کـاره ایـد اینجا چه کار میکنید حضرت امام علیـه السـلام فـرمـودنـد هر که از دست رنجیده بـر آیـد از دلالت مایه صلح درمی آید و از استماع مـقوله بـا انتفـاع آن مردرا حالتـی روی داده که نعره بزدو تامدتی بیهوش افتاد و بعد ز افاقت بتوفیق توبه رفیـق شـد۔ خـرقـه تجریـد وکلاه فقر پوشیده در صحبت آنحضرت مشرف گشت

In this manner, Allah, in order to change the thinkings of someone, bifurcates the moon in two pieces and sometimes the Scepter becomes a Python. These are Allah's signs or Miracles.

Author of "Nuzhathul Khawathir" while referring to Ibnul Mubarak writes:

"So many miracles were attributed to him and so many persons in the congregation came to him and accepted his Mahdiath."

صـدرمـنه الخوارق الکثیرة فهجم علیه الناس و صدقوه فی ادعائه
(نزهتة الخواطر الجزء الرابع صفحه ۳۶۴)

When proofs of Imamana's miracles are recorded even by Non Mahdavi scholars, then why should not we believe what had been written in our books? A few of them are reported here:

1. "Imamana's mother, Bibi Aamina (Rz), was a very pious and virtuous lady, saw a dream one midnight that the Sun descended from the sky and vanished in her clothings. She narrated her dream to her brother, Malik Qiyamul Mulk, a mystic and a God fearing man. He told her that she would give birth to the Promised Mahdi, since the same sort of dream was seen by Bibi Aamina (Rz), mother of the holy Prophet (Slm) before Holy Prophet's birth (Source- Shaswahedul Vilayeth)."

(۱) مادر آنحضرت سیده عابده صالحه کامله شب خیز بودند که در شبی ثلث اللیل معامله دیدند که آفتاب پرتاب از آسمان در گریبان مبارک آمده غائب شد ملک قیام الملك که صاحب حالات و کرامات اهل طریقت بودند تعبیرش فرمودند که ازین معامله شما معلوم می شود که در شکم شما خاتم ولایت محمد یعنی ظهور مهدی خواهد شد۔ چراکه والده حضرت رسالت پناه بوقت ماندن حمل مبارک آنحضرت همین معامله دیده بودند آخر الامر چنانچه همچنان درباب خاتم النبی و خاتم الولی صلی الله علیه و سلم شد (شواهدالولایت باب ۳۲)

2. It is reported in the "Moulood" by Miyan Abdul Rahman (Rz) that on the day Imamana (As) was born, the idols and deities were seen laid upside down on the ground.

Further it is mentioned in " Shawhedul Vilyet" that:

"One day Hazrat Shah Nizam (Rz), inquired Imamana (As), as to what Imamana (As) has to say about the tradition regarding one of the signs of Imam Mahdi (As), who would make the dry leaves green. At that time Imamana (As) was holding a stick, known as Miswak, (used as tooth brush), to which he grounded in the earth. The stick became green, and leaves started sprouting. He took it out from the ground and told "Miyan Nizam this job even a magician can perform". The meaning of the tradition was that during the period of Mahdi (As), depressed and dejected hearts would become lively and jubilant. (From Mahdi's Teachings)."

نقل است که یک روز صحابه کرام بندگی میان شاه نظام سوال کردند که میرانجی علما می گویند که علامت مهدی است که درختان خشک را سبز گرداند آنحضرت در آن وقت در دست مبارک مسواک داشتند در زمین نشاند ند فی الحال سبز و برگ دارشد باز هم مسواک از زمین کند یدند فرمودند که میان نظام این کاربازیگران است مراد حدیث آن است که در زمانه آن ذات در زمانه مهدی موعود درخت مرده دل زنده شود (باب سی ودوم)

3. The same thing has also been reported in " Hashia Sharief" stating that during the period of Mahdi (As) dried down hearts would become green. Author of Hadia states that this episode pertains to the period when Imamana (As) did not proclaim his Mahdiat. But actually it pertains to the period after his declaration as mentioned in the " Math-Leul-Vilayeth" that:

"One day, In Jalore, Imamana was cleaning his teeth with a stick (Miswak) while Hazrat Shah Nizam (As) was with him who narrated the tradition that Mahdi (As) would bring the dried leaves to life"

نقل است کہ در مقام جالور روزے بندگی میاں
نظام آنحضرت را مسواک کنانیدہ بودند در آں حال
عرض نمودند کہ در حدیث نبوی دیدیم کہ مہدی
موعود درخت ہائے خشك را تر و تازہ سازو الی
آخرہ (مطلع ولایت صفحہ ۶۳)

The tradition, referred by Shah Nizam (Rz) states that:

"Nayeem Bin Hammad (Rz) heard Hazrat Ali Ibn Abu Talib (Rz) as saying that "if Mahdi (As) points out to any bird, the bird would fall before him and if he grounds any branch of a tree, it would become green and leaves would sprout from it."

اخرج نعیم بن حماد عن امیر المومنین علیابن
ابی طالب رضی اللہ عنہ قال یؤم المہدی الی الطیر
فیسقط علی یدیہ ویغرس قضیبا فی بقعۃ من الارض
فیخضرو یورق (عقدالدرالباب السادس حدیث عربی قلمی
نمبر ۴۷۴)

This tradition is not from "Sihah", however, whatever is said in it, why should not fit onto Imam Mahdi (As). Such traditions which point out about the signs pertaining to Imam Mahdi (As), are self explanatory as they proved to be the attributes of Imamana (As). When the interpretation of the reported tradition becomes a reality as proved, then this tradition should be recognized as if it is from "Sihah Sitta".

The author of Hadia requires proof of that event which is meaningless, since those dignified persons have witnessed what they saw and reported accordingly in their books. Accordingly there should be no reason to demand proof of the miracles belonging to the Holy Prophet (Slm).

As far the meanings of tradition, both real and metaphorical meanings have been mentioned by imamana (As). The stick of the Miswak became green is apparent and the hearts becoming lively is clearly manifested. It was the result of mystic teachings which will be discussed in a separate chapter.

The author of Hadia points out the difference in the meaning of some words of the tradition "Yaghras and Buq'ath Minal Arz" as said by Imamana (As). Thus the word "Yaghras" denotes as mentioned in "Kanzul Ummal" that:

"Allah shall put plants in the Deen and will make them to devote themselves to prayers till the Day of Judgment."

لایزال اللہ یغرس فی ہذا الدین غرسا
یستعملھم بطاعتہ الی یوم القیامہ (کنزل العمال الجزء
السادس صفحہ ۳۳۸)

The same tradition is also mentioned in Ibn Maja and Ahmed Bin Hanbal reported as below:

"Allah shall plant trees always and make them pray Him and cause them to pray to Him."

قال لا یزال اللہ یغرس فی ہذا الدین غرسا
یستعملھم فی طاعتہ (الرحمتہ المہداۃ المعروف بہ تکملہ
مشکوۃ طع مطبع فاروقی۱۳۰۱ھ صفحہ

The author of Hadia, while referring to this tradition mentioned by Nayeem bin Hammad

(Rz), writes that "Hearts are kept in the chest and not under the ground". Thus he is wrongly objecting on these traditions by saying that trees are planted in the ground not on the religious plank.

We would like to submit another verse of the Qur'an in which it is written:

"Thus, Allah accepted Mariyam (Rz) (for her good behavior) and planted unto her, a lofty plantation."(3:38 Part)

فتقبلها ربها بقبول حسن و انبتها نباتا حسنا (آل عمران ركوع ۴)

The interpretation of this verse is that Bibi Mariyam (Rz) would be nourished with utmost care by the Almighty.

Had the author of Hadia any objection here also that trees are planted in the ground and not on the human beings?

The point of consideration is that if Mahdi (As) makes the stick green and overlooks greening the hearts, his endeavor would become futile. Thus the meaning of the tradition what Imamana (As) has told should not create any objection in the light of how the commentators of the traditions have explained. It is further explained from the following example what the holy Prophet (Slm) reported about Prophet Esa (As):

"Esa (As) will break the Cross and slaughter the pigs."

فيكسر الصليب و يقتل الخنزير (اشعة اللمعات جلد رابع صفحه ۳۵۲)

If all the crosses available on the Earth are broken and all the pigs are slaughtered, this act would not stand as a proof of his Nabuvwath. Therefore we have to read what Taibi had written in the commentary of "Mishkath"which asserts:

"By breaking the Cross, prophet Esa (As) would negate the beliefs of the Christianity, and by slaughtering all the pigs means he would eradicate evil from the Earth."

يريد بقوله يكسر الصليب ابطال النصرانية والحكم بشرع الاسلام و معنى قتل الخنزير تحريم اقتنائة و اكله و اباحة قتله (الكاشف باب نزول عيسى احديث عربي قلمى نمبر ۸۲ ورق ۳۵۰)

Allama Badruddin Aini (Rz) had commented on this issue that through this tradition it comes to light that it is an order for relinquishing the rituals of the Christianity.

In the same manner it has been reported under the chapter of Mahdi (As) that: just on the indication of Mahdi (As), birds will fall before him. It means to say that he would be granted such power of captivation that even the birds would fall before him. So also the fact of turning the dry stick into green, means that he would make the dead-hearts lively by the teachings of "Ihsaan". Under the context of the tradition, Mahdi (As) shall plant the trees on the religious plank.

Further to this Al Ruviani and Abu Nayeem have mentioned in the chapter of Mahdi (As) thus:

"The inhabitants of Earth and sky would resign to the Khilafat of Imamana (As).

يرضى بخلافته اهل الارض واهل السماء والطير في الجو (فتاوى الحديث طبع مصر صفحه ٢١٩)

With this example we only have to ascertain what power of captivation shall Mahdi (As) be bestowed with; otherwise birds become also submissive to the one who provides them with feed.

4. Miracle No.23rd. is that Imamana had told:

"This servant's (Imamana's) single glance is better than thousand year's worship" Thus his glance and his "left over food" had the same healing effect as the glance and the"leftover food" of the Prophet (Slm) possessed. The fact is that whoever met Imamana (As) whether man or woman, learned or illiterate, boy or an elder person, the very moment his longing for the world vanished from his heart and instead he would get intuition for the remembrance of Allah; which was not possible even for years of worship."

(٤) معجزه بست و سوم آنكه حضرت فرمودند كه يك نظر بنده بهتر از عبادت هزار سال است بنا بر جمله تاثير او چه در نظر و چه در پس خورده آن سرور همچو خاتم پيغمبر بود عليه السلام هر كه بدو رسيدى محبت دنيا فى الحال از دل او رفتى و ذكر ذات حق و فكر حق در دل او قرار و آرام گرفتى آنچه به رياضت و خلوت به سالها در يك ساعت شدى نه يك كس را بلكه هر كس راهر كه بدو پيوست واصل حق گشت از مرد و زن بالغ و صبى و امى و عالم حر و مملوك كمترين خارق مهدى موعود اين بود كه گفته شد (شواهدالولايت باب ٣٢)

The same thing has been reported by Mulla Abdul Qader Badayuni in his "Najathur Rasheed" about Imamana (As) that:

A: "Whoever came to meet him, often it happened that either he would relinquish his relations with his family and join Imamana's circle, or, for the least he would repent for his past and absorbed himself in continuous remembrance of Allah. His power of captivation was so strong in the hearts of those who happened to be the ruthless killers and from whose swords drop of blood trickled, when they attended to his sermons, they left everything of the past, repented and joined his circle and some of them became qualified mystics.

B: It is narrated in "Shawahedul Vilayeth" that he was so sure of his Mahdiath that he challenged to rip open his shroud at the time of his burial, and asserted "if his body was found in the shroud, take me as an imposter, and if my body was not there, then believe me to be the Promised Mahdi (As) and none else". When Imamana (As) passed away his grave was prepared and his body was laid down to rest in the grave. Then Imamman's son, Miran Syed Mahmood (Rz) reminded whoever was present at the time of burial:

"What Imamana (As) had told and thus according to Imamana's bequeath, Bandagi Miyan (Rz) ripped open the shroud, Imamana's body was not found in the shroud, as prophesied by Imamana (As). This prophecy was a challenge and came true. Had that prophecy not been fulfilled why should his companions stay there for more than a year and spread his Mission near and far in other countries as well? It is mentioned as an "Hujjath-e-Mahdi". That challenge was not an ordinary thing. Thus it is proved that Imamana (As) was firm on his assertion till his last breath. It all boils down to say that this extraordinary miracle testified Imamana's Mahdiat in word and spirit."

A: هركس به صحبت شريف اوپيوست اكثر اي بود كه از اهل و عيال گسته و از دنيا برآمده در آن حلقه داخل مى شد والا كمترين پايه آن توبه از معاصى و مناهى بود و اشتغال بذكر الهى تصرف مير مذكور در قلوب عبادالله بمثابه بود كه بعضى از قطاع الطريق شمشير خون چكان آمده ملازمت كرده و چون بيان قرآن شنيده اند صحبت او اختيار نموده به ولايت رسيده اند (نجات الرشيد قلمى صفحه ٨٥ تصوف فارسى نمبر ١٥٦٤ اسٹيٹ سنٹرل لائبريرى)

B: (٥) نقل است حضرت حبيب ذوالجلال از وصال فرموده اند كه اگر كسى رادرياب مهدويت اين بنده شك باشد در قبر بنده به بينيد اگر مارا در قبر يا بد مهدى بناشم و اگر نيابيد مهدى موعود باشم ، چونكه وصال آنحضرت شده است و درجائى كه قبر مبارك مستعد كرده اند در آن وقت بندگى ميان سيد محمود رضى الله عنه فرموده مهدى ياد دهانيده اند كه حضرت ميران عليه السلام اين چنين فرموده اند ...... آخر الامر چون ذات پيغمبر صفات در قبر مبارك آورده اند آنحضرت رادر قبر مبارك نيافتند (شواهد الولايت باب ٢٨)

Characters of Mahdi (As):

It had already been discussed that the Qur'an never presented any miracle as a proof of the Holy Prophet's Nabuvwath. However, it is an another issue that whenever Allah desired He presented miracles in support of the Prophet (Slm). And it never happened that at every demand of the infidels of Makkah, any miracles was presented.

It is a fact that the infidels demanded from the Prophet (Slm) to spread water canals for them, or bring the date palm groves and vineyards with canals of water running through the groves, or to destroy the skies and throw upon the infidels or even to make their houses wrought with gold or even to help them to ascend the skies. Upon such demands see what answer was given?:

"Glorified be my Lord alone, all that evil they associate with Him! Am I anything but a man sent as a Messenger?"

قل سبحان ربى هل كنت الا بشرا رسولا (سوره بنى اسرائيل)

When the infidels told why any treasure was not granted to the Prophet (Slm), or that's why no angel was sent to assist the Prophet (Slm). It was answered:

"But you (Prophet) are a warner. And Allah is all powerful over everything."

انما انت نذير والله على كل شئى وكيل (سوره هود)

"And nothing stops Us from sending the proofs, but that the people of old denied them."

(ج) و ما منعنا ان نرسل بالآيات الا ان كذب بها الاولون (سورہ بنی اسرائیل)

It is a fact that, on demand by infidels no miracle was presented. This is also a fact that miracles were never presented as the proof of the Nabuvwath of the holy Prophet (Slm). But according to the prophecies of the scriptures, the infidels would recourse to the reality, they may demand for appearance of Ten thousand angels at Faaraan, or the Holy Prophet (Slm) emerge from Jerosalem or the holy Prophet (Slm) should have been belonged to Banu Ishaq (As) (and not to Bani Ismail (As). As regards an absolute proof, it was the Prophet's characters alone presented as the proof of his Nabuvwat and in this connection, Prophet's early life in Makkah before prophethood was presented as the proof, for example:

"Verily, before that, I lived with you for a long period, could you not understand still?"(the difference before and now).

فقد لبثت فيكم عمر امن قبله افلا تعقلون (سورہ يونس)

Apart from this, "Bukhari" refers to the Saying of Haz. Abdullah Ibn Abbas (Rz) which also has been mentioned in "Mishkath" about the signs of the prophethood in which emperor Hirql inquired about prophet's progeny, about his followers and about his education etc., but he never asked about any miracle. It is a fact that we present his characters as a proof alone which are sufficient to prove his Nabuvwat. Even if there had been no references in the Scriptures, or there would have been no reference of any of the signs or miracles, his characters were sufficient enough to prove his Nabuvwath. In the same manner, had there been no prophecies about Imamana (As) or had there been no signs attributed to him, his characters and his convincing knowledge are sufficient to prove his Mahdiat. In his "Kanzul Ummal", Sheik Ali, Imamana's arch rival, has referred Imamana (As) as "a venerable personality (Shariful Azeem)". It shows that even Imamana's opponents also had accepted the nobility of his characters. Therefore, as far as characters are concerned, one should be content with Sheik's comments about Imamana's venerable characters. Here it is necessary to submit some more such comments of other impartial commentators, as to what they say about Imamana (As):

ATTRIBUTES OF IMAMANA'S (AS) VILAYET (Sainthood):

1. Mullah Abdul Qader Badayuni writes in his "Najatul Rasheed" about Imamana (As):

"Mir Syed Mohammad Juanpuri's sainthood was awe-inspiring. His majestic excellence could not be doubted."

در ولایت و جلال و بزرگی و کمال میر سخن نیست (نجات الرشید قلمی صفحہ ۱۹ تصوف فارسی نمبر ۱۵۶۴ اسٹیٹ سنٹرل لائبریری حیدرآباد دکن)

Author of "Muntakhabut Tawareekh" writes:

"Mir Syed Mohammad Juanpuri (As), Qudsullahul Azeez's holiness is unquestionable, he came from a sect of holy men and who had proclaimed his Mahdiat."

میر سید محمد جونپوری قدس الله سره، العزیز از اعاظم اولیائی کبار دعوت مهدیت از و سر برزده بود (منتخب التواریخ طبع کلکته جلداول صفحه ۳۱۸)

The words "Qudsullahul Azeez" used by Mulla Abul Qader Badayuni have the sanctity in "Muheetul Muheet" which tells that:

"Allah had cleansed him and showered on him His blessings and attributed him with the quality of Quddoos."

قدس الله تعالیٰ طهره و بارک علیه قدس الرجل الله نزهه و وصفه بکونه قد و سا (محیط الحیط طبع بیروت حصہ دوم صفحہ ۱۷۳)

Badayuni also had declared him a Vali and a Saint. The meaning of Vali has been explained in "Kasshaf-e-Istelahathul Funoon" that:

"Wali is that man whose affairs are guarded by Allah. Allah Himself states that He is the Guardian of pious people. Thus Vali comes under direct control of Allah, who never lets him to recourse towards his sensual appetites for a single moment."

آن کسی است که حق تعالیٰ متولی امورا و باشد کما قال تعالیٰ وهویتولی الصالحین پس اووا نگذارد حق تعالیٰ به سوے نفس اویک لحظه (کشاف اصطلاحات الفنون طبع کلکته جلد ثانی صفحه ۱۵۲۸)

Mulla Abdul Qader Badayuni has referred a saying of Ulema-e-Herat about Imamana (As) that:

"Ulemae Herat sent their feelings to Shiekhul Islam by telling that: "He is one of the signs, among the signs of Allah, and whatever knowledge we got during so many years of worship, has no value before him."

بہ شیخ الاسلام گفته فرستادند کہ این مرد آیتی است از آیات خدا و علمے کہ ماسالها خوانده ایم اینجا هیچ قدرے و قیمت ندارد (نجات الرشید قلمی صفحہ نمبر ۸۸)

2. Abul Kalam Azad had stated about Miyan Hatim Sumbhali, that he was one of the learned men of his time and became known as the teacher of teachers. That venerable Sumbhali also had accepted Imamana's greatness. "He praises Imamana (As) that there should be no doubt about Mir Syed Mohammad Juanpuri's excellence and perfection in the matters of religion."

3. Ali Sher Khaney writes about Imamana (As) in his "Tuhfatul Kiram" that "Syedul Aouliya, Syed Mohammad (As)", is rightly called as "Miran Mahdi (As)". This proves Imamana's Vilayeth, because he was awarded the title "Syedul Aouliya (As)". He further says, "Many pious men had become his disciples and achieved the greatness in Imamana's company. If the disciples become exalted on account of Imamana's beneficence, then what degree of exaltation you would suggest to that emancipator, (Imamana As). "Thufatul Kiram" also refers

about Darya Khan who was the governor of Thatta, (capital of Sindh) who had earned the beneficence from Imamana (As). Darya Khan states that:

"He attained beneficence in the company of the Saaheb-e-Zamaan. i.e; ("Imamana As)"

بهـره و افى از رضائى خاطر آن صاحب زمان يافته

(تحفة الكرام جلد سوم صفحہ ۵۴)

4. Moulvi Khairuddin Mohammad Sahib has written under the chapter "Khaja Syed Mohammad (As)" in his "Juanpur Nama" that:

"Khaja Syed Mohammad (As) was one of the signs of Allah; and one of the miracles of the Holy Prophet (Slm)."

آیتے بود از آیـات الٰهـی و معـجزے از معجزات رسالت پناهی

5. Moulana Abul Kalam Azad has narrated in his "Tazkera" that Moulana Jamaluddin (Rh) Dahalvi had written a book on the Proofs of Imamana's Vilayat. Moulvi Jamaluddin (Rh) had narrated with utmost authenticity and with positive arguments about the Vilayat of Imamana (As) in his book. It may be said that Moulana Jamaluddin (Rh) was the pupil of Hafiz Asqalani (Rh) with two links. (Tazkera Pages 11 and 12).

6. Hazrat Shah Valiullah Muhaddis-e-Dehalvi (Rh) also regarded Imamana (As) as "immersed unto the Divinity". What Shah Valiullah has said about Imamana (As), Shah Abdul Aziz, his son, has copied it in his letter, which states that" Syed Mohammad (As) was a mystic and immersed in the ultimate Divinity."

7. Professor Mahmood Shirani has written about Imamana (As) that there is no doubt about his most elevated dignity. His opponents too accept his venerability. His name was echoing equally among both his friends and foes during the Tenth Century. He was a perfect and learned man of scholastic supremacy. His ability in both worldly and intrinsic knowledge was exemplary. During his lifetime his followers were innumerable. Under his influential circle there were not only common men, but elites, learned, scholars, nobles, even kings and dignified persons too were in his company. His perfection in knowledge was superb. He had been bestowed with such charming effect in his tongue that whoever hears him once was mesmerized. His eyes were given such a magnetic power that even the staunch enemies became appeased and modified themselves. No one could stand before him for any dialectic discussion. Even the powerful enemies had accepted their defeat before him.

The infidels of Makkah used to call the Prophet (Slm) the trustworthy (Ameen), even before his prophethood and it became one of the proofs of his Nabuvwat. Then in the case of Imam Mahdi (As) when his staunch opponents used to call him "Magnificent Saint" and Sheik Ali Muttaqi, Imamana's arch rival even called him "noblest of nobles", why could not we present these attributes as super qualities of Imamana (As)?

Public Recognition of his Beneficence:

A. Abdullah Omer Makkki has written in his "Tareekh-e-Zaferwala" about Imamana (As) that:

"He had such a magnetic power that whoever once met him (Imamana As), had been incited the will to relinquish his worldly life."

كان له قبول يجذب زائره و يحمله على التجرد
من الدنيا (ظفر الواله جلد اول صفحه ۳۶)

"Tuhfatul Kiram" has mentioned one instance regarding Mulla Sadruddin who had such a magnetic power that thousands of his disciples became highly accomplished through him. In the beginning he was opposing the Imamana's Mahdiat, but when he once met, he surrendered to him. Whatever has been written in "Tuhfatul Kiram", it has been testified by "Hujjatul Musannifeen." It states about Mulla Sadruddin (Rh) that:

"After all he visited Imamana (As), and when he saw the splendour of his face, fell onto his feet and exclaimed: "now I had become the Muslim."

بعده آن شيخ آمده بديدن تجلى روى مبارك برپائے مبارك افتاده و گفت كه اكنون مسلمان شديم الى آخره

Splendour of his Facial Complexion:

It is reported in Chapter 19 of "Shawahedul Vilayet" that on instructions of Imamana (As) a cow was slaughtered in Jaisalmir, where slaughtering of cows was legally forbidden. When the Raja heard the news of the slaughter of a cow, he became mad and went to meet Imamana (As). It was a time when Imamana (As) was delivering a sermon and after hearing that sermon about the holy Qur'an, the Raja became subdued and fell at his feet and surrendered. The wordings of "Shawahedul Vilayet" are:

"Thus, the great infidel, Raja met Imamana (As), heard the sermon of the holy Qur'an; fell on the feet and surrendered, telling "when the creator of the cow had slaughtered, with whom should we fight.""

القصه آن كافر بزرگ با حضرت ملاقات كرده و بيان شنيد ـ سر خود برپائے مبارك ميران نهاده منقاد گشته مى گفت آخريد گار گاؤ را كشته است مايه كه جنگ كنيم

This episode tells about the splendour of his facial complexions which was also existing on the faces of the Prophets (As) to attract them towards the "Deen-e-Haqqa".

There is a Saying that an infidel, in Makkah, after looking at the face of the Prophet (Slm), exclaimed "how could it be a face of a liar?" This episode is sometimes presented as a proof of the prophethood, then why should not the exclamation of the Raja that "the creator of the cow had slaughtered the cow", be taken as the proof of Imamana's Mahdiat?

Khaja Mohammad Ibadulla Akhter Amratsari has written under the title" Syed Mohammad Juanpuri (As)" that:

"Whenever he rose to the podium for the sermon, thousands of people had witnessed a sublime divinely splendour on his face which denoted his selflessness and attracted the audience impressively."

جب وہ کھڑے ہوکر ہزارہا لوگوں کے درمیان خطبہ پڑھتے ، ایک فوق العادت جلال ان کے چہرے پر ظاہر ہوتا جوان کے بے لوث ضمیر کا عکس تھا اس لئے سامعین کے دلوں پر ایک گہرا نقش چھوڑ جاتا۔

Beneficence of his Company:

Author of "Sirajul Absar" has narrated at page No. 185 that:

"Many arrogant tyrants who used to torture people, when they happened to get access to his company for a day or two, they used to be so impressed with the venerability of his company that they used to repent for their past life. They decided to distribute their entire wealth for the benefit of the poor and needy ones and assumed the way of contentment and piety as preached by Imamana (As). Those who were highway robbers, burglers and house breakers, when they got the chance to attend his circle for a day or two, they became subdued, repented and enunciated their bad habits and joined the company of this Godly man and began remembrance of Allah in the manner he taught."

فكم من ظـالـم صـاحـب الجـاه
والـتـكـبـر يـا كـل دمـاء الـنـاس لـمـا
استصـحـبـه يـومـا او يومين رجع عن
ذلك كـله و بذل امواله فى سبيل الله
و آثر الـفـقـر والقناعة و كم من سارق
قـاطـع الطريق و ثاقب الجدر لما آنس
معه يوما اويومين رجع عن ذالك كله
و اختـار الـذكـر و الفكر و استغرق فى
الاشتغال مع الله (صفحه ۱۸۵)

Author of "Muwahib-e-Ludannia" has written that the companions of the holy Prophet (Slm) also attained tenderness of heart, abstinence and inclination towards the Hereafter by the beneficence of the venerable company of Rasoolallah (Slm).

"The author of "Muwahib-e-Ladunnia" has written thus:

"Those meetings were the cause of repentance, abstinence and inclination towards life after death. Abu Huraira (Rz) reported in "Tirmizi" and Ibn Ahmed Hayyan (Rz), inquired from the Holy Prophet (Slm): "When we are in your company, our hearts become tender and we become detached from this world and become much inclined towards the Hereafter. But when we are out of your sublime company we have again immersed ourselves in the worldly affairs and show love to our kith and kins. And thus we feel ourselves the changed personalities. After hearing him Holy Prophet (Slm) informed that "if, even after you had gone out of my company, had you the same obsession when you were in my company, then angels would come to meet you at your houses."

فلـذلك كانت تلك المجالس تو
جب لا صحـابه رقة القلب والذهد فى
الـدنيا والرغبة فى الآخرة كما ذكره ابو
هـريره فيما رواه احمد والترمذى و ابن
حبان فى صحيحه قال قلنا يا رسول الله
مالنا اذا كنا عندك رقت قلوبنا وزهدنا
فى الدنيا من اهل الآخرة فاذاخرجنا من
عـندك عافسنا اهلنا و شممنا اولادنا
وانكرنـا انفسنا فقال صلى الله عليه و
سـلـم لوانكم اذا خرجتم من عندى كنتم
عـلـى حـالـكم ذلك لزارتكم الملائكة
فى بيوتكم الحديث (المواهب الدنية طبع مصر
جزءاول صفحه ۲۹۹)

The author of "Shawahedul Vilayet" has written the same feelings about the company of Imamana (As):

"Who ever met Imamana (As), he would renounce the worldly affairs and became immersed in the remembrance of Allah. The attainment which a man can't get into many years of worship, he would get within no time in the company of Imamana (As)."

هركه بدورسيدى سيدى محبت دنيا فى الحال ازول اوبه رفتى و ذكر ذات حق و فكر حق در دل اوقار گرفتى آنچـه بـه ريـاضت و خلوت بسالها نشدى دريك ساعت شدى (شواهدالولايت باب ٣٢)

The author of "Insaf Nama" has written in chapter 8 of his book: that "Imamana (As) assserted that" a glance of this servant is better than one thousand years of approved worship."

The author of Hadia has written in his Chapter 1, about this Saying of Imamana (As), and had tauntingly interpreted that:

"Equals to twelve Shab-e-Qadr's worship"; whereas "Insaf Nama" never mentioned that one glance of Imamana (As) is better than twelve Shab-e-Qadr's worship. Here one thousand years may be taken as a very, very long period and whereas Shab-e-Qadr's worship is equal to "Alf Shahr" (one thousand months) as had been said by Allah, which is equal to be round about 84 years or so, may be taken as a man's long life. Amazingly the author of Hadia is badly suffering from Shab-e-Qdr Phobia, *(Pity on him that he even taunts on Allah who had provided a Soora in appreciation of the worship of that powerful night grants eaquality to the worship of a thousand months' worship. How dejected is he who looses this beneficence from Allah)*

Such sort of utterances are often heard. In a chapter regarding Hazrat Ali (Rz) it is mentioned in "Kanzul Ummal", Page 152 that:

"If you put both earth and skies on one side of the balance, and on the other Hazrat Ali's faith, still Hazrat Ali's side of the balance will be heavier."

لـولا ان السمٰوات والارض موضوعتان فى كفة وايمـان عـلـى فى كفة لرجح ايمان على (الديلمى عن ابن عم) (كنز العمال الجزء السادس صفحه ١٥٢)

In view of this narration can it be said that all the Prophets, Messengers of Allah and if even the holy Prophet (Slm) all included are put on the other side of the balance, Hazrat Ali's side of the balance shall be heavier? And whether the faith of Haz. Ali (Rz) may be stronger than of those personalities?. Actually it means to say that Haz. Ali's faith was strong enough. However, author's reference to Shab-e-Qadr, carries no subsisting meaning, since he or his friends do not regard much about the Shab-e-Qadr, then why this phobia about Shab-e-Qadr?

However, interpretation of the assertions of Imamana (As) is that if one who had been in the company of Imamana (As) for even a short period, he would attain that much excellence which would be more commendable to that man's worship who was not in the company of Imamana (As). Beside this, Haakim (Rh) and Tibrani (Rh) narrated from Ibn-e-Masood and Imran bin Haseen (Rh) that "just a glimpse of Hazrat Ali's face becomes a worship". This worship means which is approved by Allah. When a single glimpse of Hazrat Ali (Rz), the companion of the Prophet (Slm), gets the degree of approved worship, then why should not the glance of

Imamana (As) get the same degree of approved worship? After all, Imamana (As) was designated as Khalifatullah by the Holy Prophet (Slm).

Efficacy of Narrations:

"Mulla Abdul Qader states in his "Najatur Rasheed" about Imamana (As) that "The personality of Imamana (As) was so impressive and effective that even the highwaymen, stubborn, tyrants, cruel and hard hearted persons, holding blood rinsing swords in hand, if happened to hear the narration of the Qur'an by Imamana (As), they were so impressed that they relinquished everything and joined his circle and attained a high degree of mysticism and they became so eminent that many pious persons emerged as saints under their influence."

تصرف میر مذکور در قلوب عباداللہ بمشابۂ بود کہ بعضی قطاع الطریق مشہور (یا) شمشیر خول چکاں آمدہ ملازمت کردہ چوں بیان قرآن شنیدہ اند صحبت اواختیار کردہ بدرجۂ ولایت رسیدہ اند و چندا زاہل اللہ از دامن ایشان برخاستہ (نجات الرشید قلمی صفحہ ۸۵)

The resemblance in the writing of "Najatur Rasheed" and "Sirajul Absar" is that both have mentioned the words of "Highway men too attained an exalted degree of sainthood"; for example, Bandgi Miyan Shah Nemat (Rz), before becoming one of the companions of Imamana (As), was a robber. After meeting Imamana (As), he attained such an exalted degree of mysticism that Qazi Muntakhabuddin (Rh), author of "Maghzanul Dalael" became his disciple.

"Shawahedul Vilayet" states with what deep interest the people used to hear Imamana's sermons is that:

"If there was no room in the Mosque, people would stand in the courtyard of the Mosque, and if that space would also fill, then people used to climb on the walls or on trees, somehow, they used to hear his sermons with deep interest."

چوں گرد اگرد آنحضرت جائے نماندے مردماں در صحن مسجد ایستادندے و چوں در صحن مسجد ہم جائے نماندے برسر دیوارہا و درخت ہا ایستادہ شدہ اسماع بیان پر انتفاع آنحضرت میکردندے (باب۱۳)

Imamana's method of teaching was just like that of the Holy Prophet (Slm) which has been mentioned in the Holy Qur'an:

"Verses of the Qur'an are recited for them to Cleanse them, to teach wisdom through the revealed knowledge, although before that they were in sheer negligence."

یتلو علیھم آیاتہ و یزکیھم و یعلمھم الکتاب والحکمۃ و ان کانوا من قبل لفی ضلال مبین (الجمعۃ)

These verses point out that teaching which was being disseminated by Imamana (As) in furtherance of religion of Islam of the period of the holy Prophet (Slm) through wisdom and to bring them out of the ignorance and from all sorts of darknesses. Mulla Abdul Qader Badayuni described this feature by saying: "Famous robbers under Imamana's guidance attained mysticism and became renowned persons of repute. These verses are the proof of Holy Prophet's Nabuwwat, so also they became proof for Imamana (As) as well. Abul Kalam Azad opined about Imamana's sermons in his "Tazkera" that: "the gravity and depth of his selfless love, chaste and forceful thrusting power of his deliberations were so heart touching, impressive and effective that within a short spell of time thousands joined his circle with devotion and among them were many kings, scholars and prominent personalities who with utmost respect became his disciples." About Imamana's companions, Abul Kalam Azad says that "their way of life, manners and behaviour were so superb, amorous and lively that reminded the superb peculiarities of the companions of the holy Prophet (Slm)." Khaja Mohammed Ibadullah Amritsari writes that "what a magnetic power he (Imamana As) had that whoever heard his name moved towards him with respect and once attended his sermons were enourmously became captivated by him. His sermons were so touching and filled with virtuous blessings that the audience became mesmerized profusely and some of them were overpowered by ecstasy."

Asceticism:

Prophet's asceticism has been described in "Tirmizi" in one of its chapters that: the holy Prophet (Slm) did never hoard for the next day. Imamana (As) declared "Momin does not hoard." Not only Imamana (As), but all his companions and the followers strictly followed this dictum. During the period of Mulla Abdul Qader Badayuni the same system was in vogue. On seeing this system, he wrote:

"Many persons were seen keeping empty their household utensils with cereals and flour and even with water. They had so unflinching faith on the Sustainer that they did not keep any provision with a motto to earn and spend on a daily basis."	بسیارے راچنان دیده شد از لوازم خانه و ظروف و آلات طبخ لاحتیاز نمك و آرد و آب هم خالی ساخته سرنگـون می ماندند وهیچ چیزے از اسباب معیشت بـاخـود از غـایـت اعتـمـاد بـر رزاقی حـق تعالیٰ نمی گذاشتند روز نو روزی نو دستور العمل ایشان بود

What ever Mulla Abdul Qader Badayuni has written about "Tawakkul", the "Trust in God" was his personal observation and not at all a hearsay gossip. As regards Prophet's asceticism, it is said that at the time of his demise he had one armour which was mortgaged with a jew. Likewise when Imamana (As) passed away he had clothes which he was wearing and a few swords which were distributed to companions. The chapter 28 of "Shawahedul Vilyet" vouchsafe that:

"After his demise, Imamana's clothes and swords were distributed among companions, who were not his heirs, since he, before his demise, Imamana (As) read a Tradition which tells:

"After his demise, he had some clothes, which he was wearing and some swords. Those items were distributed among the companions, since Imamana (As) narrated the tradition: We are neither the heir of any one, nor anyone is our heir."

بعد از رحلت آنحضرت جامه مبارك آن ذات
پیغمبر صفات و چند شمشیر ها که بدست اصحاب
بطریق بارگیر بود همه بفقرا بخش کرده وادند و بوار
ثان ندادند زیرا که آنحضرت لانرث ولا نورث
فرموده اند

Imamana (As) passed away on a palm leaf mat. Professor Mahmood Shirani writes about Imamana (As) in a befitting manner that:

"There is no doubt about his being a perfect Reformer. His mission was to strengthen the cause of Islam and upholding the Divine law as presented by the Holy Prophet (Slm). He never yearned for a worldly kingdom. Had he desired to have one, there would have been no difficulty for him to establish his own kingdom; and in that scenario, in the annals of Indian History, there would have been two kingdoms of the Saadaath, instead of one. He was a staunch follower of the holy Prophet (Slm), therefore he was a selfless preacher who propagated the Islamic jurisprudence to its entirety. He was the true emblem of the tradition "Khulquhu Khulqi", means "his characters would be of mine". The holy Prophet (Slm) had prophesied about him like that.

Author of "Muwaheb-e-Ludunnnia" states that:

"Allah gave option to the holy Prophet (Slm) either to choose prophethood cum kingship or prophethood cum servitude. The Prophet (Slm) selected the second one."

خیره ربه تعالیٰ بین ان یکون نبیا ملکا او نبیا
عبدافاختار الثانی (المواهب الدنیه، جزواول صفحه ۲۹۳)

It may be pointed out that asceticism of the prophets (As) is the touchstone for their trustworthiness.

It is a fact that even the great scholars are badly tempted by "Wealth", and for that reason they become weak enough in the matters of monetary benefits and become easy prey to it and commit unholy practices and avoid teachings about the Real Faith. For example, during the period of Akber,' Deen-e-Ilahi' was introduced, the scholarly, so called, sacred big guns of Akber's time accepted it for their worldly benefits. But when we study the periods of both the holy Prophet (Slm) and that of Imamana (As), we find even very famous nobles have relinquished their families, their brotherhood and kicked wealth for ever and joined into the sacred circle of Mahdiat. If we do not accept the miraculous effectiveness of the preachings of those God-Sent personalities as a criterion, then how could it be possible to prove their saintliness. Apart from it in Mahdavi dairas there were "No Heart-Won people". "Heart-Won" people were those who were "Weak in faith" to whom the holy Prophet (Slm) tried to help them with worldly material; so that they become staunch followers of Islam and become perfect Muslims in the future.

☆☆☆

A Comparative Study of Characters and Attributes
Of the Holy Prophet (Slm) and Immana (As)

1.Generosity:

Author of "Madarijun Nabuvwat" has, under the chapter " Generosity" written that how generously the holy Prophet (Slm) distributed to such "Heart-Won" people out of the Hunain Booty, that:

"The generosity of the Prophet (Slm) was most visible at Hunain. To every Bedoun he granted 100 camels, and 1000 goats to each. Most of the Hunain Booty was distributed among the "Heart-won" people, who were still weak in their faith. His purpose was to help them with worldly material so that they become perfect Muslims."

ظهور اثر جودو فتح باب کرم آنحضرت صلی الله علیه و سلم در روز حنین زیاده از حد حصر و قیاس بود بهر کدام از اعراب صد صد شتر و هزار هزار گوسفند داد ، بیشتر عطائے اودراین روز برائے مولفه القلوب بود که ضعیف الایمان بودند خواست که بمدد دنیا دین ایشان را ثابت دارد (مدارج النبوۃ جلداول صفحہ ۴۹، طبع نولکشور ۱۹۱۴ء)

It should not be deduced from these statements that we are comparing (Naoozoo Billah) the excellence of the companions of Imamana (As), it is not at all to find fault of the companions of the holy Prophet (Slm). With that spirit we want to emphasize on the opponents of our faith that why everyone from any category and mentality whether nobles, illiterates, soldiers or even commanders, had joined the daira only after kicking the worldly life. It may be pointed out that during the migration to Khurasan, the companions used to eat the leaves of the trees for the purpose of continuity of their companionship with Imamana (As).The author of "Shawahedul Vilayet" has reported on this issue thus:

"Bandagi Miyan Yousuf (Rz), a staunch follower of Imamana (As), was suffering from acute hardships of hunger and thirst, he had only one piece of cloth to cover his body; and a rope to coil his head to save his head from the sun rays and was chewing leaves of the trees to kill his hunger; and his feet too were wounded and he was suffering from stomach ailments, still he questioned Imamana (As) by sitting before him as to "when those days of acute sufferings would come, during the period of Imamana (As) on the Muslims"? Imamana (As) informed him that, "these are the same days; but on account of your forbearance, you do not recognize them."

بندگی میاں یوسف کبار مهاجر حضور حضرت امام الابرار در این فقر و اضطرار مشقت مسافرت بسیار نشسته بودند باوجود یکه در ستر عورت یك فوطه داشته و سر را رسنی بسته و قوت برگ درختان بود هر درختی که در راه مقابل آمده بدو دست رسید برگ هائے آں گرفته چیزے خوردند و پاے را زخمی رسیده بود و شکم را جلندر که از زحمت بزرگ میشود و مع ذلك آنحضرت را پرسیدند که میرانجی آں وقت کجا است که در زمان ظهور ختم ولایت محمدیاں را بسیار مشقت می شود ـ حضرت میراں فرمودند که میاں یوسف آں وقت همین است لیکن قابلیت شما بزرگ است بدان واسطه شمارا معلوم نمی شود

By eating leaves Prophet's companions too got mouth wounds, still they did not leave the venerable company of the Prophet (Slm). Ibn Maja (Rz) refers under a chapter relating to the economic status of the companions; by furnishing what Abu Bakr bin Abi Sheeba (Rz) had revealed:

"Ibn Ghazwan (Rz) addressed a sermon on the podium that he was the seventh man among the companions of the holy Prophet (Slm), that we did not have food for a week; consequently we had to eat tree leaves, and on account of that we had eaten tree leaves and got mouth wounds."

قال خطب بنا ابن غزوان على المنبر فقال لقد رایتنی سابع سبعة مع رسول الله صلى الله عليه و سلم مالنا طعام ناكله الاورق الشجر حتى قرحت اشد اقنا (سنن ابن ماجه، طبع لاهور، جلد ثالث صفحه ۳۷)

Thus generosity and munificence are the domain of kings and landlords, but those who give away everything having no fear of lack of sources is the domain of the God sent sacred ones. Under the chapter, Generosity of the holy Prophet (Slm); as reported by Moosa Ibn Anas (Rz); telling that:

"Thus, a man came to the holy Prophet (Slm) to whom the Prophet (Slm) gave away so many goats which covered a space between two hillocks. That man went to his people and advised them to convert to Islam and approach the holy Prophet (Slm) who gives away having the least concern of poverty."

فجـاء ه رجل فاعطاه غنما بين جبلين فرجع الى قومه فقال يا قوم اسلموا فان محمد يعطى عطا من لا يخاف الفقر

Author of " Muwaheb-e-Ludunnia" states:

"It is reported in "Maghazi wal Aqeeda" that the holy Prophet (Slm) had given Safwan, on that day, so many camels and goats which would fill a valley on which he proclaimed that such sort of generosity is the domain of the holy Prophet (Slm) alone and none else."

و فى المغازى الواقدى ان النبى صلى الله عليه و سلـم اعطى صفوان يومئذوا ديا مملوا ابلا و نعما . فقال صفوان اشهدما طابت بهذا الانفـس نبى (المواهب الدنيہ، جزاول صفحہ ۳۰۹)

It was the day of Hunain. From this sort of generosity two points come out for discussion: One: The granter had full faith on his Sustainer; and was not afraid for his future needs.

Two: He has least ambitions for the worldly wealth. When this sort of generosity becomes a proof for prophets' Nabuwwat, why should not the same sort of generosity become proof for Mahdiat?

We have already discussed about the booty of Sultan Ghiasuddin, Mandu's Ruler, who donated a big treasure to Imamana (As) and Imamana (As) distributed entire treasure to his followers, except a Rosary, worth one crore Mahmoodi (gold coin of that age). Soon after a Duff Nawaz (Musician) came and requested Imamana (As) for something. Imamana (As) saw that Rosary, he took it with a stick and threw it over to him. On that occasion, Miyan Salamullah (Rz) was there and informed Imamana (As) that the Rosary was very precious. Imamana (As) replied "Qul Mata'ud Duniya Qaleel" {Tell them that worldly wealth has no value (to me)}". If a precious and costly thing is given to a king or a minister, it gives some satisfaction to the donor. But by giving that to an ordinary person, indicates, that the thing had no value for Imamana (As). He was always in migration from one place to another; that too in a difficult and unhealthy journey. Naturally he would require some such resources to meet the expenses for his travelling. Thus, inspite of his own necessities, his giving away all the wealth even a costly Rosary is the evidence of his asceticism first and then generosity which was just like the generosity of the holy Prophet (Slm). Keeping all these eventualities, any person may suggest that Imamana (As) might have not given away everything which he got from the king of Mandu. Imamana's generosity was selfless and no purpose was attached to it. He had full faith on his Sustainer who would provide him from invisible sources to meet his needs in every eventuality.

2. Bravery:

An example of the bravery of the holy Prophet (Slm) was seen at the battle of Hunain. At that battle the infidels attacked with a barrage of arrows on Muslim army which was badly shaken and many of them fled away from the battle field. But the holy Prophet (Slm) was firm at his place and never wavered. He was riding on a mule whose stirrup was held by Abu Sufian (Rz). The author of "Muwaheb-e-Ludunnia" wrote about that:

"Reported in "Bukahri", that a man from the tribe of Quise inquired why you people had fled away from the battle of Hunain, when the holy Prophet (Slm) never moved from his place?"	و فى البخارى من حديث البراء و ساله رجل من قيس أفرر تم عن رسول الله صلى الله عليه و سلم يوم حنين فقال لكن رسول الله صلى الله عليه و سلم لم يفر الى آخره (المواهب الدنيه، طبع مصر جزء اول صفحه ۲۰۳)

The same bravery Imamana (As) inherited. Sultan Husain Sharqi's army could not stand before Rai Dalpat's army. Sultan suggested Imamana (As) to withdraw from the battlefield. But Imamana (As) along with his group of 1500 people was firm at his place. One of the Raja's elephant was carrying a huge iron chain in its trunk and it was let loose which was just to attack Imamana (As). But Imamana (As) aimed it with an arrow which made the elephant to turn back and rushed against its own army and caused to shatter Raja's army. Taking a position, Raja himself confronted Imamana (As) and struck with his sword which wounded Imamana's horse's neck. Imamana (As) retaliated that attack and struck on Rai Dalpat's right shoulder with his sword which split apart all the way through Raja's left shoulder unto his heart which popped out from the confines of his chest. This event has been rightly described in "Moulood" of Miyan Abdul Rahman (Rz):

"Sultan's army was defeated, but Imamana (As) was firm at his place along with 313 (some say 1500) companions."	لشکر اسلام منهزم شد مگر حضرت میراںؑ باسه صد و سیزده تن بجائے خود مستقیم بودند (صفحه ۲۵)

The bravery of the Prophet (Slm) presented as a proof of his Apostleship, author of "Sharh-e-Aqaed" states that when he used to forward himself in the battleground, even the known champions withheld their onslaught. The same bravery is demonstrated by Imamana (As) in the battlefield against Raja Dalpat.

3. Patience:

When torture was inflicted on the holy Prophet (Slm) he bore it with acute patience. It is reported in the "Madarijul Nabuwat" that:

"The holy Prophet (Slm) prayed for the wretched people when they poured guts of the camel upon him."	همچنین دعا کرد آنحضرت بر آں جماعت اشقیا که اندا ختند شکنبۀ شتر بریشت وے (مدارج النبوۃ جلد اول صفحه ۷۳، طبع نولکشور)

"Bukhari" narrates Hazrat Anas (Rz) was saying that he was going along with the Prophet (Slm) who was covering his body with a sheet whose border was rough. A Beduon came before the Prophet (Slm) and pulled the sheet with force which caused a deep scratch on the Prophet's neck. Still that man demanded from the Prophet (Slm) "to give something from that which you have". The holy Prophet (Slm) gave him something, without grumbling on him

رواه البخاري من حديث انس بلفظ كنت امشي مع النبي صلى الله عليه و سلم و عليه برد نجراني غليظ الحاشية فادر كه اعرابي فجبذ بردائه جبذة شديدة قال انس فنظرت الى صفحة عاتقه و قد اثرت حاشية البرد من شدة جبذته ثم قال يا محمد مرلي من مال الله الذي عندك قالتفت اليه فضحك ثم امرله بعطا (المواهب الدنية، طبع مصر، جزء اول صفحه ٢٩١)

The Prophet (Slm) was strong enough to repulse that man's wrong doing, but he bore for the cause of the propagation of Islam. Through this, he taught Muslims that for the cause of Islam one should bear such hardships with utmost patience.

While describing about Imamana's episode of Qandhar, author of "Matle-UL-Vilayet" has stated that:

"Shah Beg's (governor of Qandhar) soldiers came to Imamana (As) and informed him that Shah Beg had asked them to bring him with them. Imamana (As) told them he would go. But they did not listen and held his belt and pulled him. Imamana (As) stood up and went barefooted. Somebody called to bring shoes, on which Imamana (As) uttered he would go barefooted even one thousand miles for the cause of Islam."

مرد بان از جانب شه بيگ آمده بيگ گفتند كه شه بيگ طلبيده است حضرت فرمودند ما مى آئيم باز مرد مان بسيار بجد شده آمدند و گوشهٔ كمر بند بدست گرفتند و گفتند برخيز يد ميرزا طلبيده است امى آئيم مى آئيم چه ، زود بيائيد در آن زمان حضرت بامرالله برخاستند و چند قدم پا برهنه رفتند كسى از نقيبان گفت كه نعلين مير بياريد حضرت فرمودند چه عيب است هزار ميل راه برائ خدا تعالىٰ بنده پا برهنه بياد

Hundreds of brave and devoted companions were with Huzoor Mahdi (As) but he did not demand any help from someone. So also, Huzoor Rasoolullah (Slm) granted the wealth to that person, who pulled his coverlet so harshly which caused the holy Prophet (Slm) rashes on his neck. In the same way, Imamana (As) said the man, who pulled his belt, this servant of Allah would walk bare footed even thousand miles for the sake of Allah. This tolerance was just a Jehad with nafs.

4.Surrendering to Allah's Will:

When Imamana (AS) was staying in Mandu, he arranged a grand feast with an aim to celebrate Urs ceremony of the Prophet (Slm) for feeding the poor and indigent. Meanwhile, he asked his son Miran Syed Mahmood (Rz) to take care of the cooking, and he went for a nap. Unluckily, Hazrat Syed Mahmood (Rz) was holding his younger brother Ajmal aged 6 or 18 months old in his arms. Suddenly the minor child gushed forth from the arms and dropped onto the flames and succumbed to death. On this tragic event, Hazrat Syed Mahmood (Rz) felt very much and went to his room and closed the doors. This tragic event had been narrated in "Moulood", thus:

"Miran Syed Mahmood (Rz) felt very much and closed the doors of his room. When Imamana (As) heard about this tragic event, he went to Miran Syed Mahmood (Rz) and consoled him not to feel very much stating that had Miran Ajmal alive, he would have attained Miran Syed Mahmood's position."

میـران سیـد مـحمـود ازیـں واقعـه جانکاه بسیار غـمـنـاك و انـدوهگین شد و حجره بر خوو بسته بحال زاری نشستنـد ـ حـضـرت میـراں خبر یافته به طرف حـجره میاں سید محمودؒ و رواں شده پیش خود طلب فـرمـودنـد فرمودند که چرا غمگین و ولگیر گشتید ، اگرچه سید اجمل زنده بماندے بمقام شمار سیدے

The author of Hadia has commented on this incident sarcastically, whereas, it is mentioned in "Sihah" that whoever dies accidentally with burns in a fire, is a martyr. Thus Imamana (As) conceded to this tragic event bravely and consoled even Miran Mahmood (Rz) and thus resigned to the Will of Allah.

5. Affection:

The author of "Madarejul Nabuwat" writes: " Prophet (Slm) tried to point out vices and evils of the society, and then advised with love and affection for their betterment." Here the affectionate means one who fears about the welfare of others and is considerate to save someone from troubles. Therefore the Prophet (Slm) would never neglect about his followers who would be avoiding righteous deeds, which would cause them tobe punished in the Hereafter. Allah addresses the Holy Prophet (Slm) that: "you are covetous and sympathetic for your followers." It means Holy Prophet (Slm) was very serious to see his followers to be busy in religious duties for their betterment. Once holy Prophet (Slm) had suggested that "your brother is he who admonishes you; not one who keeps you in the dark (about an evil)." In that sense affectionate is one who admonishes regarding evils. This quality was one of the attributes of Imamana (As) as well. The author of "Insaf Nama" writes:

"Scholars pointed out to Imamana (As) that he scarcely states about optimism and compulsions; instead he always refers about fear, wrath and calamity. Such statements make one desperate. Imamana (As) referred to a saying of the Holy Prophet (Slm) who said: "Your brother is he who admonishes you; not one who keeps you in dark" (about an evil)."

بـعد از آں سوال کردند که شما آیت رحمت درجـا کمتر بیان میکنید و آیت خوف و قهر بیشتر بیـان میکنید بنده نا امید می شود فرمودند که نبی عـلیه السلام فـرموده است اخوك من حذرك لا من غرك (باب پنجم)

"Miyan Sheik Mohammed Kabeer (Rz), Muhajir-e-Mahdi (As) states that, once he was beating the millet. Imamana (As) happened to come to him and asked him what was he doing. He informed that he was beating the Millet. Imamana (As) suggested." If you give someone handful of millet, he would perform the job and you can be busy in remembering the Almighty."

(ب) نقل است از میان شیخ محمد کبیر که مهاجر مهدی بودندیک روز ایں بنده باجری میکوفت حضرت میراں برسر ایں بنده آمدند و فرمودند که چه کار میکنید کفتم میرانجی باجری کوفته میگنم فرمودند اگر (از) یك مشت دانه دادن ایں کارمی شود وقت راضائع نباید کردیك مشت بدهید و خود به یاد خدائی تعالیٰ باشید (باب یازدہم)

"Miyan Bhai (Rz) states that at a place where two followers were busy in discussing; Imamana (As) went to them and asked what they were doing? They said that they were discussing on some religious issue. Imamana (As) informed them that you cannot reach Allah without his remembrance."

(ج) نقل است از میان بھائی که حضرت میراں دوسہ بار آمدند و دیدند که برادران دو کس یك جانشستہ اند فرمودند که شماچہ نشستہ اید برادران عرض کردند که میرانجی چیزے حکایت دینی میکنیم حضرت میراں فرمودند که اے بھایاں خدائی رانخواہید یافت جز ذکر (انصاف نامہ باب یازدہم)

From these, we may deduce that Imamana (As) was following the holy Prophet (Slm) in pursuing his followers that they should not go astray from the right path.

6.Tolerance:

The author of "Muwaheb-e-Ludunnia" reports about Zaid Bin Sa'ana (Rz), who was a Jew, but, after examining the attributes and behaviour of the holy Prophet (Slm), converted to Islam; and he informed Hazrat Omer (Rz) what he thought about the Prophet?

"Thus Omer (Rz), when I focused on the prophet's face, I found all signs of Nabuvwat, but the point which I examined was his tolerance, which is more superb than ignorance; and intensity of ignorance increases his ability to tolerate which motivated me to accept Allah as my only Sustainer, Islam as my religion and Mohammed (Slm) is my Apostle."

فقلت یا عمر کل علامات النبوۃ قد عرفتها فی وجه رسول الله صلعم حین نظرت الیه الا اثنتین لم اخبر هما لیسبق حلمه جهله ولا تزیده شدۃ الجهل الا حلما فقد خبرتهما فاشهدک انی قدرضیت بالله ربا و بالا سلام دینا و محمد نبیا (المواهب الدنیہ، طبع مصر، جزءاول صفحہ ۲۹۱)

When Tolerance could be one of the proofs of Nabuvwath, then why should it not be the proof for Mahdiat too?

The author of "Insaf Nama" reports in his chapter 11 that:

"One Khurasni with an aim to examine tolerance of Imamana, came to him keeping a bottle of wine in his sleeves. The Imamana's companions asked permission to break the wine bottle. Imamana (AS) told them that his intoxication of wine will vanish within minutes. Many came before me and left their frenzy behaviour. The people who are intoxicated with worldly love, when come to this servant, leave their worldly craze."

نقـل اسـت کـه یـك خراسانی بـرائـے آزمودنِ علم حضـرت میـران عـلیـه السلام آونـد شراب در آستین خـود آورد و بـعضـے کسان عرض کردنـد اگر رضـاے خـونـدكار بـاشد ایـن بشكنیم بعده میـران فرمودنـد شمـا ایـن چنیـن فهم کردیـد ایـن مستی شراب بعد از دو سـاعـت دور خواهـد شد پیش ایـن بنده مستان دنیـا می آینـد(گزاشتہ میرونـد)

The companions of Imamana (As) wanted to break the wine bottle, but Imamana (As) had stricken his heart so that he should relinquish addiction to wine forever.

7.Forgiveness:

The author of "Muwaheb-e-Ludunnia" has referred about the forgiveness of the holy Prophet (Slm):

"Out of many examples of forgiveness of the holy Prophet (Slm) just two, which are very peculiar, are reported: One: Labid Bin Aasim, a jew who had administered magic on the personality of the holy Prophet (Slm); and Two: A Jewish woman who offered poisoned meat to him." He politely forgave both of them."

و مـن ذلک انـه عـلیـه السلام لم یواخذ لبیدِ بن الاعـصـم اذا سـحـره و عفا عن الیهودیه التی سمت فی الشاة (المواهب الدنیہ جزءاول صفحہ ۲۹۳)

When Imamana (As) was in Farah, the Qazi of Farah ordered his soldiers to snatch belongings and put them behind the bars. After snatching the belongings, they lef, postponing to put them behind the bars for the next day. The same night the commander in chief, Sarwer Khan saw the holy Prophet (Slm) in his dream who was saying: "In your dominion, my son is getting troubles". The same moment he got stomach pain. In the morning he called for reports from the police chief of the town; who informed about the episode of snatching the belongings of Imamana (As). Sarwer Khan went to Imamana (As) and asked for his left over water (Paskhurda), after drinking he was relieved from the pain. Then he repented for whatever had happened. He wanted to return back the things but Imamana (As) replied that:

"We do not possess anything except Allah which could never be snatched away from us."

پیش مـا بجز خدا هیچ نیست کہ آن تلف شود و آن هرگز تلف نہ شود (حجۃ المصطفین)

In this regard there is a tradition which states as mentioned in "Tuhfaie Asna-e-Ashria"

"Everything which comes to their hand, they take it as lent by Allah to them."

هـر چیز را که دردست ایشان افتد عارتیه خدامی دانند (صفحه ۴۴۴)

Although Sarwer Khan commander of the Army became Imamana's disciple and Imamana (As) could take revenge through the commander against the Qazi who ordered to snatch away everything belonging to Imamana (As), but he forgave the Qazi.

8.Trust in Allah:

Jaber bin Abdullah (Rz) has reported in "Muslim" about the Prophet's trust in Allah:

"Jaber Bin Abdullah (Rz) reported that while they were at war, roaming in a valley of Najad, full with thick thorny plants, where we saw the holy Prophet (Slm), after hanging his sword on a tree, was sleeping. When he awoke, he reported them that when he woke up he saw a man dragging his sword, came towards him and asked "Who would save you." Prophet simply replied "The Almighty". Hearing this he sheathed the sword and repented, finally converted to Islam (then the holy Prophet (Slm) pointed to that man who was sitting nearby). The Prophet (Slm) thus forgave him."

قال غزونا مع رسول الله صلى الله عليه و سلم غزوة قبل نجد فادر كنا رسول الله صلعم فى واد كثير العضاة فنزل رسول الله صلعم تحت شجرة فعلق سيفه بغصن من اغصانها قال و تفرق الناس فى الوادى يستظلون بالشجر قال فقال رسول الله ان رجلا اتانى وانا نائم فاخذ السيف فاستيقظت وهو قائم على راسى فلم اشعر الا والسيف صلتا فى يده فقال لى من يمنعك منى قال قلت الله ثم قال فى الثانية من يمنعك منى قلت الله فشام السيف فها هوذا جالس ثم لم يعرض له رسول الله صلى الله و عليه و سلم

A similar episode happened in Farah. Mir Zannoon (governor of Farah) came to Imamana (As) and said that it was reported that sword would not affect on the true Mahdi (As). Imamana (As) calmly informed him that the sword should cut, water should drown and the fire should burn. That means that these three things would never overpower a true Mahdi (As). Telling this, Imamana (As) handed over his sword to Mir Zannoon and asked him to try and kill him. Miyan Abdul Rahman (Rz) has reported this event in his "Moulood" thus:

"Imamana (As) offered his sword to him. Mir Zannoon grabbed the sword and struck on Imamana (As). His hand became numb. Then he took the sword in his other hand and struck with force on Imamana (As), again his other hand too became stiff and could not kill Imamana (As)."

شمشير خود پیش اوبداشتند میر ذوالنون شمشیر برداشته برخاست و دست بالا کردد ستش سیخ شد پس بدست دیگر گرفت و برداشت آن نیز سیخ شد

Then Mir Zannonn fell down unconsciously. Imamana (As) woke him up and asked him to try again and again. Mir Zannoon tried for three times and failed. He surrendered to Imamana (As) and became his staunch follower. This episode informs us what Trust in Allah he had that he handed over the sword to strike on him.

9.Social Etiquette:

The author of "Madarijul Nabuwwat" has reported that:

"Reported by Tabri (Rz), that the holy Prophet (Slm) asked the companions to slaughter a goat. A companion told it is his duty to slaughter, another one told that he would skin out the goat, third one told that he would cook it, then the holy Prophet (Slm) told that he would collect wood for cooking."

طبری ذکر کرده است که آنحضرت صلی الله
علیه و سلم در سفر بود و امر کرد اصحاب را با
صلاح گوسفندی پس برخاست مردے از اصحاب و
گفت برمن است ذبح آن و دیگرے گفت برمن است
سلخ و دیگرے برخاست که برمن است طبخ پس
آنحضرت گفت برمن است هیمه گرد آوردن
(مدارج النبوۃ جلد اول صفحه ۳۲۲)

This tells prophet's courtesy and social behavior and cooperation. It also tells that he never pretended himself to be higher among others. A similar episode has been recorded in "Shawahedul Vilayet" about Immaana (As) that:

"One day Imamana (As) went to bathe himself in the river Sabermati, where he saw another man was sitting for the same purpose. Imamana (As) asked that man to rub his back. When he did, Imamana (As) told him that he would rub that man's back. When he put a hand on that man's back, the man went into ecstasy and he witnessed the invisible world."

نقل است که روزے حضرت امام برائے غسل در
جوی احمد آباد سابهرمتی می رفتند یك شخص
اجنبی غیر آشنا دیدند که درجوی بود اور افر مودند
بیابنشین پشت ما بمال آن کس آمده پشت مبارك
بمالید ـ انگه حضرت میراؑن فرمودند که تو بنشین
ماهم پشت تو بمالیم چونکه دست مبارك برپشت
اوانداخت همان وقت جذبه حق در ربودو پرده از
پیش او برخاست عالم مغایبات معائنه شد

This episode tells Imamana's courtesy and etiquette. He did not take himself higher than others. Kings and nobles became impressed by this sort of ettiquette. He did not mind to rub the back of an unknown man, only because that man had rubbed Imamana's back.

10.Humility:

The holy Prophet (Slm) had two distinuished positions. 1. He was the most exalted Prophet (Slm) among all prophets. Accordingly, he emphasized that he was head of the mankind. 2. He is the descendant of Hazrat Ibrahim (As). Hence he named Prophet Ibrahim (As) the best of Creation. The scholars of the tradition have written about this tradition that: "this saying of the holy Prophet (Slm) is based on his humility which was embedded in his veins from his ancestor, Prophet Ibrahim (As)".

Miyan Abdul Rahman (Rz) reports in his "Moulood" about Imamana (As) that:

"Imamana` (Slm) said, whatever Allah had bestowed to Mohammed (Slm), the same He had given to me, and whatever He gave to me, He had not given anyone before Mohammad (Slm), nor He would give after me."

حضرت میران علیه السلام فرموده اند که هرچه خدائ تعالیٰ به محمد داد به من داد و هرچه به من داد به محمدؐ داد نه قبل محمدؐ کسی راداده بودنه پس بنده کسی راداده شود (صفحه نمبر ۸)

Inspite of this Bandagi Shah Burhan (Rz) reports that:

"Imamana (As) said that he is struggling hard to qualify himself to get blessings from the holy Prophet (Slm)."

نقل است که حضرت امامؐ فرمودند که بسیار مشقت کرده می شود که لائق صدقۀ رسول الله صلی الله علیه و سلم شویم (دفتر دوم رکن ششم باب اول)

Imamana (As) also had two distinguished positions. a) Imam Mahdi (As) is the Khalifatullah and had the same characters as that of Rasoolullah (Slm); that is why he said "Whatever was given to Rasoolullah (Slm) by Allah, the same was also given to Imamana (As) by Allah. b) The second aspect is that he is the descendant of the Holy Prophet (Slm). Still, he asserted that he was struggling hard to get the benevolence from Huzoor Rasoolullah (Slm).

The author of Hadia remarks that, by this way, Imamana (As) was struggling hard to become equal to the Prophet (Slm). That remark, made by him was nothing but out of his crookedness. However, it is proved that Nabuvwat and Vilayet require hard labour only. A tradition runs like this:

"Oh! Ayesha! Prominent prophets (As) and my brothers who preceded me were exalted by Allah, I fear if I become lazy, then I may be degraded."

یا عائشه اولوالعزم از پیغمبران و برادران من پیش از من رفتند و از حق تعالیٰ کرامت ها یافتند بترسم که اگر من تنعم کنم درجۀ من از ایشان کمتر باشد (کیمیائے سعادت رکن سوم اصل سوم اصل دوم، طبع نولکشور ۱۲۵۱ھ صفحہ ۱۲۷)

It tells that the Holy Prophet (Slm) tried hard to become equal to other Prophets (As) by struggling hard. Thus to argue that the holy Prophet (Slm) struggled hard just to get Apostlehood is wrong.

Imamana (As) also wished to become equal by labouring hard is correct because he was khalifatullah and was having the same attributes what the holy Prophet (Slm) was carrying. He desired to get the blessings from the holy Prophet (Slm) on account of his being related to the Ahle Bait (Rz); where the holy Prophet (Slm) was like a father to him. It may be pointed out that both of them were trying to act as per commands of Allah: Allah ordained: "When you are free from propagation of Islam, then be busy for worship." Fa Iza Farghtha Fansub, Wa Ila Rabbika Farghab" (Alam Nashrah).

11. Humour:

It is a fact that the humour of the holy Prophet (Slm) was always based on truth only.

"Abu Dawood" and "Tirmizi" have reported from Anas (Rz) about Prophet's humour:

"Once a man asked for a conveyance from the holy prophet (Slm). In reply to his request, Huzoor (Slm) said to him "I will make you sit on an offspring of a she camel". That man questioned: "What would I do with an offspring"? On that Huzoor (Slm) said that "every camel is the offspring of a she camel only! Is it not?"

ان رجلا استحمل رسول الله صلی الله علیه و سلم فقال انی حاملک علی ولد ناقة فقال ما اصنع بولد الناقة فقال رسول الله صلی الله علیه و سلم و هل تلد الابل الا النوق (اشعة اللمعات جلد چهارم صفحہ ۸۸)

Mulla Moinuddin patni used to give some questions to his pupils, who used to attend the sermons of Imamana (As) and used to get answers from those sermons. One day, Imamana (As) was passing in front of the house of that Patni. Companions informed Imamana (As) about Patni's house. Imamana (AS) sent words that he would like to meet him."

"Moinuddin Patni first climbed upon a wall of his house and sent words that "Mulla had gone out riding on a conveyance". Imamana (As) told that "he was riding on such a conveyance which would never take him to his destination."

بر دیوار سوار شده گویانید که ملا همیں زمان سوار شده اند ، درون خانه نیستند ۔ فرمودند برچوں مرکب سوار شده اند که هر گز به منزل نه خواهد رسید (مولوی میاں عبدالرحمٰن)

12.Instruction for Peace:

Imamana (As) never wished to propagate Deen-e-Mehdi (As) with the power of a sword or pressure for acceptance of his Mahdiat. Mir Zannoon, the governor of Farah after becoming his disciple informed:

"I am the follower of Imamana (As) and also his servant and helper. Whenever necessary I shall use my sword and slaughter whoever opposes Imamana (As). Imamana (As) reprimanded by saying: "use the sword on your baser self (Nafs) so that It should not mislead you. Mahdi (As) and his companions are helped by Allah alone."

مصدق ایں مهدی و نوکر و ناصر مهدی و غلام مهدی ام هر جا که تیغ زدنی باشد تیغ بزنم و مخالفان مهدی را بکشم حضرت فرمودند تیغ بر نفس خود بزن که در گمراهی نیفگند ناصر مهدی و کسان مهدی خدای است (مولود میاں عبدالرحمٰن)

Thus Mahdiat flourished through sermons of the holy Qur'an and not with the sword.

13.Renounce your baser self:

What he told to Mir Zannoon, the same he instructed to his followers to use the sword on the baser self (Nafs). The same is reported in "Hashia Sharief":

"Companions asked Imamana (As) "could we curse Yazeed"? Imamana (As) told them "to curse your baser self, since it disgraces you. Baser self creates hardships to you."

حضرت میران را برادران عرض کردند بر یزید لعنت فرستادن چوں است میراں فرمودند برنفس خود لعنت بفرستید که نفس شمارا خوار میکند و هریکی را نفس و شواراست (صفحه ۱۳۵، ۱۳۶)

14.Following Shariat in its Entirety:

Imamana's whole life was spent by following the Sharait to its entirety. Even during the period of trance, before he migrated from Juanpur, he never missed any obligation of the Shariath. "Moulood" of Miyan Abdul Rahman (Rz) testifies that:

A. "That period of trance was so severe that he had lost control of his worldly dealings and like that seven years passed; however he did not miss any prayer or fasting."

در آں وقت آنحضرت راچناں حال غالب آمد که ازیں عالم هیچ آگاهی نماند چنانچه تامدت هفت سال همیں حال بود مگر نماز و روزه فرض ادا کردیـ

"Matleul Vilayet" chapter 3, states:

."He neither missed any obligation nor neglected a single Sharaie mandate.

گاهی انچه فرائض حق تعالیٰ است فوت نشده دیك ذره خلاف شرع صدور نیافته

B. Imamana (As) travelled thousands of miles and underwent many hardships, but he never accepted more than three days' feast from any person, by following the custom of the Prophet, (As) who set the example not to accept more than three days' feast from any person. Author of "Matleul Vilayet" states that Mir Zannoon had tried to offer hospitality with utmost respect, but Imamana (As) never accepted his feast for more than three days.

"Imamana (As) did not accept any one's hospitality for more than three days, toeing in line to the holy Prophet (Slm) who too never accepted feast for more than three days."

آنحضرت بعد از سه روز قبول نکردند وقتیکه کوشش بیغایت کردـ فرمودند که سنت مصطفی صلی الله علیه و سلم مهمان داری بیش از سه روز قبول نه کردند

15.Plenty of Worship:

The holy Prophet (Slm) used to stand for prayers in the night till his feet become swollen. This has been reported in many traditions. It is further reported that he used to pray the whole night in a standing position. Yet another report says that he used to recite one verse repeatedly after Isha prayers whole night which caused his feet to swell. The same was the practice of Imamana (As) and his followers. The author of "Sirajul Absar" writes about some of his friends who were descendants of the followers of the Imamana (As):

193

"I have seen many of my friends who were weeping out of agony and pain. Their feet became swollen and their eyes also were swollen and became reddish for the reason of praying all night standing and weeping. A few of them are such who had sleepless nights and were weeping as well. Some of them were seen laying down restlessly groaning, lamenting and wailing."

لقد وجدت اما كثيرا من اصحابنا باكين من الم الفراق متورمى الاقدام من قيام الليالى منتفخى العيون من البكاء سهر هاوكم منهم صارخ مرتفع الاجفان و كم منهم متاوه قائم على الاقدام وكم منهم متضرع ساقط على الجنوب و كم منهم صائح مستلق على الظهور فهولاء تابعون لاصحاب المهدى (سراج الابصار صفحه ۱۷۴)

It shows the gravity of their worship which rendered their feet and eyes to swell and become reddish which reminds how our holy Prophet (Slm) used to worship and got his feet swollen. These facts have been truly testified by Sheik Wahab, a pupil of Sheik Ali Muttaqi, arch rival of Imamana (As). Sheik Abdul Haq Muhddiss-e-Dehalvi, had reported what Sheik Abdul Wahab had stated about a Mahdavi relative of Sheik Ali Mutaqi, the same author of "Al Rudd" that:

"Sheik Abdul Wahab stated that when he went to the relative of Sheik Ali, who came out weeping and lamenting from his privacy. We handed over to him the amount sent by Sheik Ali and brought to his notice what was told by Sheik Ali. After listening, he kept quiet."

ميفرمودند نزد آن مرد رفتيم از خلوت برآمد گريه كنان داه زنان مبلغ رابوے رسانيديم و اين حرف كه شيخ فرموده بودند نيز گفتيم خاموش ماند

Sheik Abdul Wahab states that "His lamenting and groaning was very impressive". This statement testifies the statement of the author of "Sirajul Absar" It may be pointed out that this is a statement of a Non Mahdavi writer. Author of "Juanpur Nama" has written about Khaja Syed Mohammad (Imamana As):

"I have seen many followers of this faith in a condition of severely lamenting, groaning and weeping. They have been busy always with the Qur'an, pondering over the universe and attributes and signs of the Almighty."

جمعى را كه براى عقيده بودند بادل هاى بريان و چشمان گريان يافتم كه جزبه قرآن كارے ندارند و بغير تدبر و تفكر شعارے ندارند

16.Emphasis on Practice:

The holy Prophet (Slm) advised his daughter, Fatima (Rz), "to practice and forget that she is the daughter of a Nabi (Slm)". The same spirit lies in the statement of Imamana (As)."

"Allah would never ask whether someone is the son of Ahmed or Mohammed (Slm), but He would ask for sincere practice and love of Allah."

حضرت ميران فرمودند كه خدائى تعالى همچنان نخواهد پرسيد كه پسر احمد است يا محمد حق تعالى عمل با محبت خواهد پرسيد (انصاف نامه)

Imamana (As) had always emphasized on practice. Ther Author of "Shawahedul Vilayet" had furnished an example in this regard of Malik Barkhurdar (Rz), who wanted to have shoes of Imamana (As) to wear for salvation: the narration is as follows:

"Oh, Malik Barkhurdar what is in this slipper? Malik did not answer, showing respect. Then Imamana (As) said that "its upper portion is the skin of a goat. The bottom is cow's skin. You had been with me for so many years, did you get only that Mahdi (As) provides deliverance through skins of a goat and of a cow? Thus, if you wear even my skin and do not practice what I preach and suggest between prayers of Asr and Maghrib, believe me, my Allah will take out my skin from you and clothe me and punish you."

اے ملك بـرخـوردار ایں كـفـش چه چیز است ، ایشان از روئے ادب خـامـوش بودند باز فرمودند كه بالا پوست گوسفند وزیر پوست گاؤ پس چندیں مدت كه صحبت بنده مانده اید چنیں حاصل كردید كه مهدی از پوست گـوسـفـند و پوست گاؤ نجات می دهند ـ خیر جی اگر بنده مـحـبـت كـرده پوسـت خـود بپو شاند انچه بنده درمیان عـصـر و مـغـرب میگویدنه كنید خدای من قادر است پوست بنده به بنده بپو شاند شما را عذاب كند

17. Preference to Divine Law "Shariat":

Regarding preference to divine law, an incident is mentioned in "Hashia Sharief":

"One of the followers came late and joined the prayers when already two prostrations were over of a prayer. Imam saluted towards the right and the newcomer stood up with-out waiting for the left side's salutation by the Imam. Others objected and reported to Imamana (As), who called that man and asked: "why did you not wait for the left side's salutation? He told: "I got intuition (Kashf) that Imam (As) did not have compensatory prostration, that is why I stood". Imamana (As) reprimanded him by saying 'It would have been better that you did not have intuition; and you would not have avoided the Divine Law."

The same incident is narrated in "Shawahedul Vilayet" in other words:

"This is not intuition which negates the Divine law. Let your intuition go to hell, you have violated the Divine law. You have to repeat the prayer."

فرمودند آں را كشف نمی توان گفت كه رعایت شرع محمدی از و قائم نه شود باز فرمودند كه معلومات شما در تنور افتاده باد كه خلاف شرع محمدی كردید نماز را باز اعادت كنید (باب بسیت و چهارم)

Imamana (As) always preached the sanctity of the Islamic jurisprudence, then how could there be any lapse with regard to Sharaie curriculam?

In respect of characters of the holy Prophet (Slm), let there be no record available in any books of tradition or in his biographies, still Abu Jehal's admission of Prophet's trustworthiness is enough to prove sublimity of his characters. Author of "Madarijul Nabuwwat" narrates that:

"Akhnus bin Shareeq met Abu Jehal during Badr battle and asked him to tell, (when no person was there to hear their discussion), whether Mohammed (Slm) is a trustworthy person or not? Abu Jehal first swear on trustworthiness and truthfulness then told that Mohammed (Slm) is trustworthy and he is true, who never told any lie."

آورده اند که اخنس بن شریق ملاقات کرد ابوجهل را روز بدر گفت یا ابا الحکم نیست اینجا جز من و تو که بشنود سخن مارا خبر ده مرا از محمد که وی صادق است یا کاذب پس گفت آن ملعون والله بدرستی و راستی که محمد صادق است و هرگز دروغ نه گفته است (مدارج النبوة جلد اول صفحه ٥٥)

Whatever we have written regarding Imamana's characters is very short. It requires a particular book. Even if such material is not available, Sheik Ali Mutaqi's one sentence is enough: who said:

" La Yazne Bi hi Haza", there should be no suspicion about his characters.

Abdul Qader Badayuni has written in his "Najatur Rasheed" that:

"I happened to be with them (companions of Imamana As). I found their pleasing manners and commendable attributes which did not change even in poverty or hunger. It is a fact that they did not educate themselves to become scholars, but their command of the intricacies of the Qur'an was superb and unmatchable. Facts and inner meanings of the holy Qur'an and mystic realities of the Hereafter I had heard from them are so voluminous that if they are compiled in a book, it would become another "Tazkira-e-Aouliya."

جمعی را ازین سلسله ملازمت کرده ام و اخلاق رضیه و اوصاف مرضیه ایشان را در فقر و فنا به مرتبهٔ عالی دیده و بیان قرآن و اشارات و دقایق حقایق و لطائف معارف بی کسب علوم رسمی چنان شنیده ام که اگر خواهند مجملی از آنها در قید کتابت آرند ـ تذکرة الاولیائی دیگر باید نوشت (نجات الرشید قلمی ، تصوف فارسی نمبر ٥٦٤ ،اسٹیٹ سنٹرل لائبریری ،حیدرآباد)

When the memoirs of the companions, their descendents and sons of the descendants could become another book of "Tazkiratul Aouliya", then why should not the statements of Imamana (As) and the Holy Prophet (Slm) get the same status. When the Holy Prophet (Slm) had told about Imamana's characters "Yeshbahu Fil Khulqi," thus it is a known fact that Imamana's characters had a complete resemblancece to that of the holy Prophet (Slm). While Allah had referred characters of the holy Prophet (Slm), by telling: "Wa Innaka la 'alla Khulukhin Azeem.", "No doubt you possess sublime characters". Thus the verse and the tradition prove Imamana's attributes to be the same as that of the holy Prophet (Slm) also. Prophet (Slm) said about Imamana (As) that Mahdi (As) would have my attributes, what more can be said about Imamana's characters.

18.Revival of the Divine Law:

The holy Prophet (Slm) declared about Imamana (As) that "Yukhfi Asri Wala Yukhti"

"Mahdi shall follow my foot prints and will never err". That means to say: Imamana (As) shall present the same Islam of the previous golden period in which, Imamana (As) would also demolish the unhealthy rituals, bid'ats, innovations and evils from the Muslim Ummah. Thus Imamana (As) had revived the Divine Law of the holy Prophet (Slm) by eradicating innovations, rites and rituals. In this connection we refer to chapter one of "Insaf Nama" which states that:

"Imamana (As) declared that he was sent by the Almighty at a time when the purpose and the meaning of the religion had been wiped out by means of rituals, innovations, Bid'ats and rites. Advent of Mahdi (As) is for nothing but to eradicate all these innovations, rites rituals and to revive the religion of the holy Prophet (Slm) to its entirety."

حضرت میرانؑ فرمودند که مهدی را خدائے تعالیٰ انگه فرستاد که معنی دین از جهان رفته بود معنی دین از سه چیز رفته بود ـ رسم و عادت و بدعت وقتی مهدی در ظهور آید رسم عادت و بدعت را دور کند و دین محمد را نصرت کند الیٰ آخره

It is mentioned in "Insaf Nama" thus: Huzoor Imamana (As) declared that his beneficence cannot be attained by those who will be busy with innovations, customs and rituals.

The Ninth Century presented no such Islamic country which was not enveloped in rituals, innovations, rites and shism. Unfortunately, the same innovations, the rituals became the very part of Deen-e-Islam. It was a period when Imamana (As) presented those supreme ideals of the previous Islam pertaining to the Golden period of Islam which flourished during the lifetime of the Holy Prophet (Slm) and during the Khulufai Rashedeen's 30 year period. Moulana Abul Kalam Azad had depicted the conditions of the Ninth Century Islam in his "Tazkera" thus:

"The period of the Ninth Century which passed away before Akber was known for chaos, atrocities and anarchy. Day in and day out new kingdoms emerged as mushroom and disappeared soon under their own burden. There was no central authority to administer the Divine Law and take responsibility to maintain peace and order in the country. Religious minded scholars were few, while worldly scholars were spread all over the country. Fraud, cheating and deceit were the order of the day. The innovations and bid'ats had enveloped the entire atmosphere which were spread by the illiterate scholars who were dominating the helpless Ummah (Tazkera page 27).

What effect Imamana's teachings caused, shall be discussed under the chapter pertaining to the "Characters of Imamana (As)", but before that we shall see what Moulana Abul Kalam Azad describes about Imamana (As).

"Looking this sorry state of affairs, 'Syed-e-Mousoof' (As) raised his voice for the revival of the Divine Law of Shariat and called the Ummah on the holy Qur'an's dictate" (Amar Bilmaroof-e-wa Nahi Anil Munkar" "enjoin what is good and forbid what is bad"). Hence he emphatically declared that there is no need for aimless struggle or telling the beads hours together, but it is time to help-assist the Ummah to come towards the right path and he inculcated the spirit to establish Shariat at every level by jeopardizing even his life. Chastity of love and cleanliness of his heart and soul had made his sermons so effective that in a very short spell of time thousands of people came under his Godly circle and several kings had become his devotees".

About Imamana's followers, he further writes: "Their behaviour and manners were so lovely and charming that they reminded the attributes of the companions of the holy Prophet (Slm) for whom devotion and love of Allah was the supreme purpose of their life. They were so immersed in love of Allah and the Hereafter that they relinquished their blood relations, love of land and nation had no place to them, comparing to the virtues of love and affection with the Almighty and the holy Prophet (Slm). It was a group of devoted people who had sacrificed the transitory love of blood relations, land and nation for the sake of love for the Almighty and the Faith. Abandoning every thing they became friends and comfort for each other on the sublime path of rightuousness. Their sublime goal was the service of humanity by propagating the superb commands of Shariat, the Divine Law". ("Tazkira" pp-26,27,28)

"Shawahedul Vilayet", chapter 24 refers to someone who described the qualities of Sultan Ba Yazeed before Imamana (As) in this way:

"Sultan Ba Yazeed (Rh) was passing through a lane in which there was a wine shop. A musician was playing a tambourine, suddenly the sultan lost his control and fell on that tambourine which was broke down. The musician stroke on the sultan's head and abused him for breaking his instrument. Still Khaja behaved to the musician with politeness and got his instrument repaired and gave back to him and paid some money also to him." Hearing this all, Imamana (As) said: "Khaja Ba Yazeed (Rh) had many qualities and he was a perfect Muslim. But the thing you told is against the Qur'an and Shariath-e-Mustafavi (Slm). Allah has directed to help virtue and forbearance and avoid helping tyranny and sin."

سلطان بایزید را روزے بکوچہ میخانہ گزرافتاد و قوال طنبورہ می نواخت خواجہ استماع نمود ہوش از دست دادہ برطنبورہ افتادند طنبورہ او شکستہ شد او بہ خشم آمدہ برسر خواجہ زد و گفت کہ چہ درویشی است کہ ساز مرا شکست خواجہ اور ابسیار ملائمت نمود و طنبورہ اور ادرست کنانیدہ دہانیدہ اند و چیزے مبلغ نیز مرحمت فرمودند

کمالیت خواجہ بایزید رحمتہ اللہ علیہ مناقب بسیار اند و ایشان کامل انداما ایں کہ تو گفتی نقیض متابعت شریعت رسول اللہ صلعم و خلاف قرآن است کما قال اللہ تعالیٰ تعاونوا علی البرو التقوی ولا تعاونوا علی الاثم والعدوان

"Abu Huraira (Rz) reported that the holy Prophet (Slm) referred to a battle which would be fought in India. Abu Huraira (Rz) yearned for that battle and said: "If I were to be alive, then, I would take part with all my resources. If I am killed in it, I would become the most distinguished martyr, and if returned alive, I am that Abu Huraira who would be free from the fire of the hell."

عـن ابـى هريره قال و عدنا رسول الله غزوة الهند فان ادركتهـا انـفـق فيهـا نـفـسى و مالى فان اقتل كنت من افضل الشهدا و ان ارجع فانا ابوا الهريرة المحرر

Sultan Ba Yazid's action had been an example of Islamic training; but Imamana's assertion about Ba Yazid (Rh) is the example of Mahdavia training. As Imamana had eradicated rituals, rites and Bid'ats from the Ummah, the holy Prophet (Slm) also had propagated about Jehad. It was earlier stated that Imamana (As) had completely followed the Holy Prophet (Slm) in all his actions and deeds and had also taken part personally in the Jehad against an infidel Rai Dalpat (and many more along with Sultan Husain Sharqi); and it relates to a period when he had not openly declared his Mahdiat. But it is a fact that according to the prophecy of Imamana (As), the prophesied group (Bandagi Miyan (Rz) had taken part in a battle, the same was also a prophecy of the Holy Prophet (Slm).

Abu Huraira (Rz) became Muslim in 7th.H. and took part in all battles along with the holy Prophet (Slm) till the conquest of Makkah. Still his desire to take part in that Indian battle which had been prophesied by the holy Prophet (slm) that it would be waged by someone who should be designated by Allah. But who should be that designated person; could be described from the tradition of Nisaai (Rh) reported by Soban (Rz):

"Soban was the servant of the holy Prophet (Slm) who reported Prophet (Slm) was saying that there will be two groups in the Ummah, who would be saved from the fire of the hell; one would be that who would wage a war in India, and the other would be with Prophet Jesus (As)."

عـن ثـوبانؒ مولى رسول الله صلعم قال قال رسول الله صلعم عصابتان من امتى احرز هما الله من النار عصابة تـغزوالهند و عصابة تكون مع عيسى ابن مريم عليهما السلام

With this tradition it comes to notice that there would be two groups, and both would be saved from the chastisement of the Hellfire. The Prophet (Slm) also pointed out that there would be two, who would save the Ummah from extinction. These two had been pointed out in another tradition, which says: "How my Ummah would be extinct, when I am in its beginning, Prophet Esa (As) would be at the end, and in the middle there would be Mahdi (AS) from my Ahl-e-Bait." Thus these two personalities, Imamana (As) and Jesus Christ (As), along with the holy Prophet (Slm) shall save the Ummah. As regards the two groups that would be waging war against the infidels are those, one belongs to Mahdi (As) and the other belongs to Esa (As). The group of Imamana (As), as prophesied would wage a war in India under the leadership of Bandagi Miyan Syed Khundmir (Rz), on behalf of Imamana (As) as Badl-e-Zat-e-Mahdi (As).

19. Completion of Deen:

The Holy Prophet (Slm) had said about Mahdi (As) that "Mahdi (As) would establish Deen at the end of the period", as the Holy Prophet (Slm) did it at its beginning. (vide "Sirajul Absar" page 212). Then in yet another tradition, the Prophet (Slm) said that "Mahdi (As) would complete the Deen". (vide "Sirajul Absar" Page 206). Now we have to clarify about Deen. "Muslim" has referred Hazrat Omer (Rz) as saying that:

"Reported by Hzt. Omer (Rz) that when we were sitting in the Masjid along with the Holy Prophet (Slm) a person, clad in white robes, and whose hair were black, came to Masjid, having no fatigue on his face, as if coming from a far off place. None of us knew him. Thus he narrated that:

"One day when we were sitting along with the Holy Prophet (Slm) a man, fully robed in white clothes, with black hair came. He had no symptoms as if he is coming from a far off place. None of us knew him. He came and sat down close enough to the Holy Prophet (Slm), knees to knees.

قال بينما نحن عند رسول الله ذات يوم اذطلع علينا رجل شديد بياض الثياب شديد سواد الشعر لايرى عليه اثر السفر و لا يعرفه منا احدحتى جلس الى النبى صلى الله عليه وسلم فاسند ركبتيه الى ركبتيه و وضع كفيه على فخذيه و قال يا محمد اخبرنى عن الا سلام قال ان تشهد ان لا اله الا الله و ان محمد ارسول الله

He put his hands on prophet's thighs. Then he addressed the Prophet (Slm): "Mohammed (Slm) tell me about Islam": Prophet (Slm) answered: "You must assert that there is no god, but Allah, Mohammed is His servant and Messenger; perform five times Prayers, pay Zakat, observe 30 days fasting during Ramazan, and perform Hajj once in a life time, if able to bear to and fro charges".

The stranger said, "you are right". We were astonished that he himself questions and certifies also. Then he asked "tell me about Iman, Faith". Prophet (Slm) told:

"Have firm belief in Allah, His Angels, His Scriptures, His Messengers, and on the day of judgment and have faith in the destiny, whether good or bad" the stranger certified this answer also.

Then he asked to describe "Ihsan"; Prophet (Slm) answered: "Worship Allah, as if you are seeing Allah, but if you could not witness Him, then you must at least think that Allah is witnessing you".

The Stranger certified this also and went away. Hazrat Omer (Rz) stayed there for some time. The holy Prophet (Slm) asked Omer (Rz), "did you know who was that stranger"? Omer (Rz) told, "Allah and Allh's Messenger (Slm) knew better". The Prophet (Slm) told that "he was Gabriel (As) who came here to teach you, your Deen."

و تقيم الصلوٰة و توتى الزكوٰة و تصوم رمضان و تحج البيت ان استعطت اليه سبيلا قال صدقت فعجبنا يسئلة و يصدقة قال فاخبرنى عن الايمان قال ان تومن باالله و ملائكته و كتبه و رسله واليوم الآخر و تومن بالقدر خيره و شره قال صدقت قال فاخبرنى عن الاحسان قال ان تعبدالله كانك تراه فان لم تكن تراه فانه يراك قال صدقت .... ثم انطلق فلبثت مليا ثم قال لى يا عمرا تدرى من السائل قلت الله و رسوله اعلم قال هذا جبرئيل اتاكم يعلمكم دينكم (اشعته اللمعات جلد اول صفحه ۳۸، ۴۵)

This tradition is called "Hadees-e-Gabriel" (Tradition of Gabriel (As), which teaches us that there are three pillars of Deen; "Islam, Faith and Ihsan". Some say first comes faith, then Islam and lastly Ihsan. It seems correct, since in the beginning Faith was sufficient, then stress was made for Islam. Obligations and responsibilities were clearly defined in due course of time which became the Rules and Regulations of Shariat, then at the third stage came Ihsan which means, "to create apreciability and firm concentration in our actions particularly when we are offering prayers and remembering the Almighty with devotion". Author of "Mirqaat" wrote about the words: "Kannaka Tarah" means: "to worship Allah having firm faith that you are seeing Allah, or atleast you must keep in mind that Allah is seeing you". Here "Kanaka Tarah" places you as a devotee. From this it is inferred that "Vision of Allah" is possible, and if it is attained it is known as "Ihsan which creates gracefulness in the actions that is called accomplishment of the purpose of our life."

According to the holy Prophet (Slm), there are two meanings of Ihsan. One is that: "Vision of Allah is possible" and the second is that: "Ultimate aim of the Worship is "Vision of Allah." and that is what Ihsan is about.

You try to help a man to avoid polytheism and bring him near to Allah; this is called inviting towards faith, Iman. You try to keep a man abstain from sins and the prohibited things and initiate in him the spirit to offer prayers and observe fast. This is an invitation to Islam. These two invitations are common to all, with no exception. But the third one is a specific one and has the quality of exception. Every one offers prayers, but could that be equal to that one in which an arrow has to be taken out from the body of a companion (Rz) and the companion (Rz) does not feel any pain at all. Generally, in such cases the surgeon uses anesthesia, but here the case is different. The devoted companion (Rz) says "you can take it out when I am offering prayers. Then only you may take that arrow out". Here the surgery was done, the arrow was taken out and bandage was administered, but his concentration and absorption with Allah was not disturbed and when he completes his prayer he sees everything was over peacefully without hurting and troubling him. This is the result of the teaching of Ihsan. This is a fact which occurred to Hazrat Ali (Rz). The holy Prophet (Slm) did teach this to a few only who had attained complement in Deen to its entirety and who had immersed themselves into the Divine Entity, but not to all, since every Budwee or a common man could not understand and practice it. Author of "Maghzanul Dalael" has described Iman and Islam as under:

"The holy Prophet (Slm) had taught about Faith and Islam openly, because people were easily attracted to these teachings which belong to Shariat. As regards Ihsan, the prophet taught only to those who had attained completion in the faith and were true lovers of Allah and were immersed in Allah's nearness."

كـان رسـول اللـه صـلعم يعلم الامة الايمان والاسلام جهرا لان طبـاع النـاس كلهـم مستعد النيل هذا الا مـرفهـذاالامـر مـن ظـاهر الشرعية و اما الاحسان فلم يـعلـمـه الامـن راى طبعه محظوظا بنور الايمان بنعت المحبة والشوق الى الله تعالىٰ الى آخره

From the above, it is clear that during the period of the holy Prophet (Slm) the teaching of Faith and Islam was open, but that of Ihsan was limited to a few only that is why it was not popularized. Some traditions also inform the aspects of Ihsan which were taught to some companions only, but not to all, since all could not digest it. Abu Huraira (Rz) said that:

"I got from the holy Prophet (Slm) two utensils. I disclosed one, and if I disclose the other, my throat would be cut."

قال حفظت من رسول الله صلى الله عليه و سلم و عائين فاما اجـدهما فبثثتة و اما الآخر لو بثثتة لقطع هذا البلعوم (طبقات ابن سعد، جزء رابع قسم ثانى صفه ٥٧، وصحيح بخارى كتاب العلم باب حفظ العلم)

What Abu Huraira (Rz) could not speak about the second utensil, that is what Ihsan is. Some have commented about this tradition and said that the second utensil denotes to the teaching of the Divine Secrets. Just as during the period of the holy Prophet (Slm) teachings of Faith and Islam were open and apparent; during the period of Imamana (As) the teaching of Ihsan was open and apparent. The Author of "Maghzanul Dalael" has written that Imamana (As) was commissioned to teach Ihsan openly.

It may be pointed out that the holy Prophet (Slm) was first asked by Allah to keep his clothes clean, then he was ordained to come out of the filth, then after a long time he was ordained to purify the masses and teach Qur'an and its attributes. But Imamana (As) was from the very beginning ordained to purify the mind and heart of the peoples. It does not mean that Imamana (As) was, God forbid, superior to the holy Prophet (Slm). The teachings of Ihsan brought the teachings of Faith and Islam to a higher degree as well. In this connection Sheik Abdul Haq, Muhaddis-e-Dahlavi states that:

"The essence of Ihsan is that it creates concentration, presence of mind and heart and attachment to the Divinity during the prayers and that is what is needed and which becomes an emblem of the high degree of Faith and sincerity towards Islam."

حـاصـل آں اخـلاص و حـضور و خشوع است در عبـادت و آن بـه حـقيـقـت شرط کمـال بلکـه نشان صحـت اسـلام و ايـمـان است (اشعته اللمعات جلد اول صفحه ٤١)

It is a fact that during the period of Imamana (As), invitation to Ihsan was common, therefore Mahdavia society was bestowed with teachings of Ihsan commonly and openly. In this connection Mulla Abdul Qader Badayuni refers to Bandagi Malik Ilahdad (Rz):

"Fani Fillah, Baqi Billah Sheik Burhanuddin (Rh) of Kalpi resided in the company of Sheik Ilahdad (Rz) of Village Bari, just for three days and attained nearness to Allah."

الشيخ الفانی والباقی به برهان الدين مشهور ساکن کـالپی سـه روزه در صحبت شيخ الهداد ساکن قصبه بـاری رسيـد واز مـقـربـان درگاه کبریا گشته (نجات الرشيد قلمی صفحه ٨٥ نمبر ٥٧٦٤ اسٹيٹ سنٹرل لائبریری حيدرآباد)

It is an open fact that Sheik Burhanuddin (Rh) was not alien to the teachings of Faith and Islam. Thus, just a three days' teaching by Bandagi Ilahdad (Rz) made him closer to the Creator. This tells the depth of the teachings of Imamana (As) regarding Ihsan. This is a testimony provided by a non Mahdavi writer. When this can be accepted, then why should not those referred by Mahdavi writers be accepted?

In this connection Bandagi Shah Burhan (Rz) had reported about Bandagi Syed Shahabul Haq (Rz) that:

"Bandagi Malik Peer Mohammed (Rz) asked Bandgi Miyan Syed Shahabuddin Shahabul Haq (Rz) that why you take much time for Tahreem which causes delay for the prayers. He answered: " I could not do it without visualizing the vision of Almighty Allah, when I immersed in the Divinity, then only I could do the rest, that is why the delay."

بنـدگی ملک پير محمد پرسيدند .... ذات شريف شمـادر تـحـريـم بستـن تـاخير می نمايد سبب چيست فـرمـودنـد بهائی پير محمد آں نماز نماز نيست که بجز ديـدن حـق تـحـريـم بستـه شود بنده را چوں حضوريت روزی می شـود تـحـريـم می بند دبنا بر تاخير می شود (دفتر دوم رکن نهم باب پنجم)

Bandagi Miyan Syed Shahabuddin (Rz) was the elder son of Hazrat Bandagi Miyan Syed Khundmir (Rz) who taught the gravity of the worship among Mahdavis. A tradition says where "Yaqoma Bid deen" comes: It means Mahdi (As) shall establish Deen. It tantamount to tell that during the period of Imamana (As) Faith and Islam shall be revived. And where "Yakhtamullah bid deen" comes: it means that Allah shall complete the Deen through Mahdi (As). This tantamount to say that teachings of Ihsan shall be open to all and the purpose of Allah shall be completed in all respects.

When Imam Mahdi (As) completes the purpose of Deen it asserts that the holy Prophet (Slm) had actually completed the Deen. A tradition says that ﴾يقيم امر هذه الامة كما فتح هذا الامرينا﴿
﴾ارجوان يختم الله بنا﴿

Yaqueema Amr-e-haza al-umatha Kama fatha hazal amraina arju in Yakhtamallhi yana' (Sirajul Absar page 208) it means that Mahdi (As) will establish the order for the Ummah as was established by the holy Prophet (Slm). Prophet (Slm) who asserted that "I am hopeful that Allah shall complete the Deen through us only". That means to say the Deen shall be completed by the descendant of the Ahl-e-Bait (Rz) only, that is by Imamana (As) who comes from the Ahl-e-Bait (Rz). As for as the verse "Akmaltu Lakum Deenakum" is concerned it is a revealed fact that Deen had been completed as had been declared, still the holy Prophet (Slm) would not have said that Allah shall complete the Deen through Mahdi (As).

(Note: It is a fact that untill the Fifth pillar of Islam, the Hajj, is performed, the Deen was incomplete. And when the Holy Prophet(Slm) performed the Hajj and instructed how to perform it, and when to perform it, then only the Fifth pillar of Islam was taught by the Holy Prophet(Slm) and the Deen was complete. On that completion, this verse "Wa atmum to lakum Deenkum" was revealed to inform that now the Deen is complete.

The decliners state that, in view of that verse, there is no need of any Mahdi to complete the Deen. But they forgot why the Hoply Prophet(Slm) informed that the "Deen was established by him, now it would be completed by Imam Mahdi". Here we have to refer the verse "Summa Inna Alaina Bayanahu (75.19)" meaning, Imam Mahdi(As) shall interpret the Holy Qur'an, in the sense that, since the Holy Prophet(Slm) had openly taught the two constituents of Deen, "Islam and Ieman", leaving third one "Ehsaan" to be taught openly by Imamana(As). Therefore, Imamana(As) from the very beginning openly clarified the meanings of Ehsaan, as taught by Gabreil(As). Thus, unless the teaching of Ehsaan is complete, still the Deen is incomplete. Thus, Imamana(As) openly declared that "his Mission is to guide the way through which one can have the vision of Allah". and that is the sole purpose of the creation of JIn O Ins, to worship Allah and have the dersire to "Witness the sublime Vision of Allah", through the teachings of Imamana (As). And when it is accomplished, then only the Deen is complete. That is why the Holy Prophet prophesied that "As the Deen was established through us, it will be completed by Imam Mahdi, who is from us). Khundmiri

20.Completion of Divine Blessings:

Completion of the Blessings on the holy Prophet (Slm) is not an impediment for the completion of the Divine Blessings on Prophet Ibrahim (As) and other prophets. Hence Prophet Yaqoob (As) gave the glad tidings to Prophet Yusuf (As), which is mentioned in the holy Qur'an that:

"And your Sustainer would complete His Blessings on you and on the descendants of Yaqoob (As) as he had completed his Blessings on your grand father and great grand father, Ibrahim (As) and Ishaq (As)."

ويتم نعمته عليک و علىٰ اٰل يعقوب كما اتمها على ابويک من قبل ابراهيم و اسحٰق (يوسف ع ا)

In this manner completion of Divine Blessings had been on the holy prophets (As). Thus Allah says, addressing the holy Prophet (Slm) that: "We have completed upon you Our Divine Blessings."

"And had completed His Blessings on you."

ويتم نعمته عليک (الفتح ع ا)

☆☆☆

CHAPTER FOUR

Companions of Imamana
Scholars, Kings, Nobles and Ministers

The author of "Shawahedul Vilayet," in chapter 21 has reported that Imamana's migration has three peculiarities: one being: he did not stay at any place for more than 18 months; second being: the moment Allah's command came, whether it was day or night, summer or winter, he started his journey, with great piety and meager provisions; and third being: in pursuance of love of the Almighty he was very strict even used to scold (on the leniency in performing obligations). Even with such hardships, some of them who had accepted him as Mahdi-e-Maoud (As) had accompanied him for the journey. The author of "Tuhfathul Kiram" has written that:

"A world had accepted him as
"Mahdi-e-Maoud (As)"

عالمے وے را مهدی موعود خوانده" (تحفت الکرام طبع

بمبئی ، جلد دوم صفحه ۲۲

Companions of Imamana:

Following is a short summary of the companions whom Imamana (As) had given glad tidings. They include scholars, saints, nobles.

1. Bandagi Miran Syed Mahmood (Rz): He was the son of Imamana (As) born in 867/868 Hijri. After the demise of Imamana (As), he stayed at Farah for one year, then arrived at Radhanpur (Gujrat), and settled down at Bhelote. On account of his sermons, multitudes of people accepted Mahdavi Faith. When opponents felt inability to stop propagation and to stop people from becoming Mahdavi, they started instigating Sultan Muzaffer of Gujrat to arrest and put him behind the bars. He was arrested in 919 or 920 H. But Sultan's two aunts who had accepted Mahdavi Faith, influenced the king for his release and he was released after forty days. But as his legs were chained, they became ulcerated which resulted in his demise in 920 Hijri. His mausoleum is in Bhelote.

(Which was rejuvenated recently by Mahdavis where all facilities to the pilgrims like separate rest houses for ladies and gents and bathrooms, masjid, a house for mujawer are constructed with facilities of water etc. Now it is safe for the pilgrims to stay with comfort for a longer period. Bhelote is very near to Palanpur. Conveyance facilities are available.)

2. Bandagi Miyan Syed Khundmir (Rz.): He was born in 886 H. He is Kazami Syed. His forefathers migrated from Samerkhand and Bukhara and settled down in Baariwal and Biyana. His father Syed Moosa was an officer with a cavalry of 500 horses. His maternal grand father's brother, Mubarezul Mulk, was the commissioner of Pattan. Bandagi Miyan (Rz), offered his allegiance to Imamana (As). Mubarezul Mulk detained him in his mansion. After six months Bandagi Miyan (Rz), somehow escaped and met with Imamana (As) at Badhli. He went along with Imamana (As) up to Nasarpur (Sindh) and returned to Gujrat. Then he went again to Khurasan along with Sani-e-Mahdi (Rz) and came back to Gujrat after the demise of Imamana (As) and started propagation of the Mahdavi Faith. Thousands became Mahdavi and joined Mahdavia dairahs. After the death of Sultan Mahmood, his son Muzaffer Shah was enthroned and since the king was inexperienced the worldly scholars took undue advantage and did whatever they wanted to harass Mahdavis. Thus they, however,obtained a Fatwa for killing Mahdavis and proclaimed that:

"Whoever kills a Mahdavi he would be rewarded as if he had killed one hundred burglars of Dantiwada and will get the reward as if he had performed seven Hajj."

On that score, Mahdavis were martyred. Bandagi Miyan (Rz) too caused the killings of those mischief mongers, viz; Mullah Hameed and others. In order to eradicate the Mahdavia Faith from the root, the worldly scholars poisoned the ears of the Sultan and alarmed the Sultan that if action was not taken now, he would lose his kingdom. The sultan's large army attacked his dairah on the 12th. Shawwal 930 H. under the command of Ainal', as prophesied by Imamana (As), the king's army was miserably defeated by a small group of Bandagi Miyan (Rz), on the first day battle and when defeated the army fled away about one and half mile, while returning they martyred 40 companions who were directed by Bandagi Miyan (Rz) not to move beyond a line for the purpose of safety of ladies and children of the dairah. Then again the army gathered their forces, and attacked on 14th. Shawwal 930 H. and martyred Bandagi Miyan (Rz) and his 62 companions. According to the prophecy of Imamana (As), he lived twenty years after the demise of Imamana (As) and was buried at three places. He was expelled twenty times from his Dairah in twenty years. He had written several pamphlets: viz;

List of pamphlets of Bandagi Miyan (Rz):

"Aqeedai-e-Shariefa", "Maqsad-e-Awwal","Maqsad-e-Sani", "Maktoob-e-Multani", "Risala-e-Bazul Aayaat", "Risala-e-Khatim-e-Vilaayat". They are very popular, Shah Burhan (Rh) has thus written about them that:

"Above referred pamphlets are filled with veracity and saintliness and available not only in India but in Khurasan also."

آن هـمـه رسـاله هائی مذکور از دلائل حق پر نورچه در هـنـدوستان و چه در خراسان در همه جا حاضرات(دفتر اول رکن پنجم باب اول)

"Maqsad-e-Awwal" is also known as "Risala-e-Kalan", about which Miyan Shah Abdul Rahman (Rh) has written in his "Daftar-e-Awwal", Chapter five that:

"Some Indian Rulers, Humayun Shah and Khusro Shah, when visited Gujrat, happened to read it, praised and asked to get it written with gold water."

"بـعـضـی پـادشاهان هند خصوصاً همایون پادشاه قطب شـاه چـونکه رساله پر ظهور نور رب غفور دیدند بسیار به پسندید ندو به آب طلا نویسا نیدند"

List of Books written on martyrdom of Bandagi Miyan (Rz):

On Bandagi Miyan's martyrdom many books have been written, some of them are:

1. "Risala-e-Chund Sharief": written by Ali Miyan (Rh) in Burj Bhasha in poetry during the

period of Bandagi Miyan Shah Dilawer (Rz) (died 944 H.) just after fourteen years from the martyrdom, thus it is the oldest source.

2. "Maqtal": written by Miyan Mohmmad Jamal (Rh), a narrative poetry in Persian language, describing the facts of martyrdom, written in 1090 H.

3. "Prem Sangram" in Burj Bhasha, written by Bandagi Malik Yousuf (Rh), a noble attached to the court of Abul Hasan Tanashah, king of Golconda.

4. "Tej Nama": Written by Miyan Syed Husain (Rh), disciple of Bandagi Miyan Syed Raju Shaheed (Rh), In Hindi language in 1068 H, including the facts of the martyrdom of Bandagi Miyan Syed Raju (Rh), Shaheed also.

5. "Masnavi-e-Israr-e-Haq", written by Miyan Abdul Momin (Rh) in 1093 H. It contains some facts about Imamana (As) also.

There are so many narratives in which biography of Bandagi Miyan (Rz) has been written, in detail, but most explicit biography was written by Miyan Shah Burhan (Rh) in two volumes in Persian language, when he was in Farah, Khurasan, in 1060 H. But amazingly, "History of Gujrat" is blank about this tragic episode. The author of "Mir'ath-e-Sikandari" had correctly opined as to why the correct record is not available in the history of Gujrat:

"It is fact that "Tareekh-e-Muzaffer Shahi" was written during the period of Muzaffer Shah; "Tareekh-e-Ahmed Shahi" was written during the reign of Ahmed Shah and "Tareekh-e-Mahmood Shahi" was written during the life of Mahmood Shah. "Muzaffer Shahi" and "Bahadur Shahi" histories were written during the period of Sultan Muzaffer's and Sultan Bahadur. Thus it is evident that whoever was the author had expected rewards, from those Rulers, therefore in order to place himself in the good books of those Rulers and to gain monetary help, they purposely avoided to record the Battle in which a large army was defeated by a few God Loving Mahdavis on the 1st. day battle?."

مخفی نه ماند که مظفر شاهی در وقت سلطنت و بادشاهی مظفر شاه تالیف یافته و احمد شاهی در زمان حیات احمد شاهی و محمود شاهی در آورن بقائی سلطان مظفر مظفر شاهی و بهادر شاهی در وقت وجود سلطان مظفر و سلطان بهادر ظاهر است که مولفین هر کدام چشم صله و پاس خاطر آنحضرت میداشته اند ازیں جهت تواریخ مذکوره اشتمال بر تمام حقایق احوال ندارند غیر از قصه که مشتمل برمدح باشد در آن تواریخ تحریر نیافته (مراة سکندری طبع بمبئی صفحه ۳)

In these circumstances, any author could not dare to write that on the first day Muzaffer's large army was defeated by a small group of Bandagi Miyan (Rz). In the same sense, if the Holy Wars fought by the Holy Prophet (Slm) were not mentioned in the history books of Christians and Jews, should anybody deny those wars?

However a bold historian by name Shaik Zainuddin of the period of Nizam Shah (King of Ahmed Nagar) wrote in his "Kashful Israr" that:

"And after the demise of Imamana (As), Syed Saadat (Rz), one of his companions, Bandagi Miyan Syed Khundmir (Rz), was living in Gujrat. The Sultan when heard about his preachings of Mahdavi Faith openly as against the Decree of the wordly scholars, sent a large army of about 16,000 troops coupled with a cluster of elephants. When the news reached to Bandagi Miyan (Rz), he prepared himself along with his (100) companions for the battle. When carnage started, Allah helped Bandagi Miyan (Rz) to defeat the Sultan's army which fled away on the first day. Thus whatever we have revealed is correct. If anybody has any doubt, should inquire from those who knew it. This is really similar to the one which occurred at the battle of Badr, the Holy Prophet (Slm), who with the help of Allah, defeated a large army of infidels with a small group of just 313 companions."

اما بعد موته فان صاحبا من اصحابه المسمى سيد السادات السيد خوندمير الذى هو تابع المهدى كان فى بلاد كجرات وسمع سلطانها مثل ذلك فارسل سرية عليه و كانت مثل ستة عشر الف فارس و فيها جماعة من الفيل فلما سمع السيد المذكور بذالك استعدهو ايضا مع اصحابه فقاتلو افهزم الله سرية السلطان فهربوا فافهم ما اوردنا من القصة و ان شككت فيها فتفحص عندمن يعلم تلك كما ان الله ارى الكفار جيش النبى مثل جيش الكفار فى وقعة بدر حتى انهز موار (الفصل الثانى)

In this passage the reference given to a Sultan who was none but Sultan Muzaffer of Gujrat.

(Note: Yet a detailed biography under the title "Siddiq-e-Vilyat" was written by Mashaeq Syed Ismail, alias Moosa Miyan (Rh), now un available, requires re-print, provided Manzoor Miyan, his heir, perrmits for re-printing.") Khundmiri.

"3. Bandagi Miyan Shah Nemat (Rz): His grandfather Shaik Baday, known as Malik Baday was a confident noble of Sultan Mahmood Beghda of Gujrat. He belonged to the clan of Haz. Abu Bakr Siddiq. After the demise of his father, he became less important officially and monetarily. Consequently, on account of govt.'s negligence, he revolted against the kingdom. Once he killed seven nobles of Gujrat with the help of a gang of 25 to 30 criminals. He started plundering in and around Ahmadabad. Even he killed the son of the Shahi servant Abdullah, Habshi. The Sultan arranged a five hundred force to capture him, but he was at large. However, a turning point came in his life and luckily he met Imamana (As) at Santheige where after hearing Imamana's sermon, he offered his allegiance to Imamana (As). When Imamana (As) heard his past history, he advised him, to approach each of those who were hurt by him, when he gets their pardon, Imamana (As) asked him to "meet me again". On that advice, he went to Habshi Abdullah's house first and offered his sword to him and asked him to take revenge of his son. When the Habshi investigated as to why he had so easily offering himself for the revenge, he found out that Shah Nemat is now a changed person, thus the Habshi pardoned him. In this way he got pardons from all who were affected by his atrocities. Then again he presented himself before Imamana (As) who permitted him to join his company. After the demise of Imamana (As), he came to Gujrat from Farah. He established his Dairahs at Pattan, Jalore, Ahmadabad, Ahmadnagar, Khandes and finally at Logadh, near Pune. When he was in his dairah near the fort of Logadh, he was martyred along with his 17, or 21 companions at his age 61. The reason for this carnage was said to be the Tasbeeh :

"La Ilaaha Illallahu ,

"Mohammedur Rasoolullah."

"Allahu Ilahuna, Mohammed Nabiuna".

"Al Qur'an wal Mahdi Imamana, Amanna wa Saddaqna."

لااله الاالله محمد رسول الله ،

الله الهنا محمد نبينا ،

القرآن والمهدى امامنا آمنا و صدقنا

Which was a routine feature after Isha prayer, not only by Hazrat Shah Nemat (Rz), but all Mahdavis loudly pronounce it. These holy words could not be digested by the officer who was appointed at the fort and became the cause of Shah Nemat's expulsion and finally at his martyrdom. The miscreants used to poison the ears of the superiors that these words (Tasbeeh) "caused the break of their Nikah". (How surprising!)

The author of "Shawahedul Vilayet" in Chapter 33 writes that:

"These words are not absurd. They wake people up in the name of Allah, Mohammed (Slm) and Mahdi (As) and it is arranged in a rhythmic sound."

"سخـن لغونگویند و بنام خدا و رسول صلى الله عليه و سـلـم و مهدىؑ هشيار كنند بدين ترتيب تسبيح قرارداده اند "

Bandagi Shah Nemat (Rz) had many companions, namely: Vali Mohammed (Rh), Qazi Abdullah (Rh), Qazi Muntakhabuddin Bidri (Rh), Kabeer Mohammed Sujawandi (Rh), Abdul Momin Sujawandi (Rh), Syed Badey (Rh) etc.

4. Bandagi Miyan Shah Nizam (Rz): He was born in the Jaais Kingdom of his own dynasty in the vicinity of Lucknow, UP of India. He comes from the lineage of Shaik Fareed Shakergunj (Rz). He relinquished affairs of the kingdom in favour of his brother. He went to Hajj and after sightseeing in Syria, Iraq and upto "Koh-e-Qaaf" returned to India and visited Chapaneer and offered his allegiance to Imamana (As) at the age of 27. He was born in 873 H. and died in 940 H. He was buried in Anondra, of Ahmadabad District, Gujrat. He had seven companions, including Miyan Abdul Rahman (Rh), his son, author of " Moulood" and Miyan

Abdul Fatah (Rh) who are very famous as staunch Mahdavi.

(Note: Anondra shrine of Shah Nizam (Rz) had been in a dilapidated condition since long. Mahdavis of Palanpur and elsewhere collected funds and refurbished the shrine and repaired the graves and a tomb was constructed in the year 2007 AD. Still amenities like Masjid, Saraey to stay, latrine and water facility are missing. If further funds are arranged for providing these amenities, it would help the Zaaereen to perform their Ziarat and help them to have a short stay. Funds may be mailed to Br.Salamullsah T.Syed, Mutavalli, of Palanpur, for further construction.)

5. Bandagi Miyan Shah Dilaware (Rz): He was the nephew of Raja Dalpat, of Gaud. He had been in the company of Imamana (As) from his childhood as the personal servant. When became major, converted to Islam and became Mahdavi on the hands of Imamana (As) and attained that much exaltation to make him a venerable personality of that period, under whose guidance, a caliber like the author of "Sirajul Absar" Aalim Billah Abdul Malik Sujawandi (Rh), became Mahdavi on his hand and became his disciple. He died in 944 H. and was buried in Borekheda, Khandes (Maharashtra).

(Note: the shrine was recently repaired, but lacks amenities. A Hindu family is taking care of the shrine. Haz. Shah Dilawer's Beneficence attracts more Hindus than Muslims. Hence it is apprehended that if the situation is left to remain like that, the Hindus may convert the shrine as their temple (God Forbid). Therefore it is high time that Mahdavis who live in the vicinity of the shrine should take care of the shrine by appointing a Mahdavi Mujawer who will look after the shrine personally and keep it save without any hindrance from the Hindus any more.   Khundmiri)

6. Bandagi Malik Ilahdad, Khalifa-e-Giroh (Rz): Bandagi Malik Ilahdad is well-known as Khalifa-e-Giroh (Rz), an eminent companion of Imamana (As). He was a very learned scholar who had written the DOTLESS commentary of the holy Qur'an. It is not an easy job. It was a God-Given miraculous achievement for him.

In the beginning he was one of the nobles of Sultan Ghiasuddin Khilji. His "dotless Devan" is famous which points out his dominant mastery over literature. He had written many books which became famous for his mastery in literature, particularly on "Proof of Mahdiat". His pupil Mehri, was another literary scholar, whose writings are famous as literary masterpieces. Author of "Sirajul Absar"has written about (Hazrat Bazmi's great great grandfather) Hazrat Syed Ashraf son of Hazrat Syed Abdul Lateef (Rh) that he had memorised a large portion of "Devan-e-Mehri". Author of "Nuzhatul Khawathir" had mentioned Miyan Ilahdad's " Risala-e-Bar-e-Amanat" and "Risala-e-Isbat-e-Mahdi" which are his masterpieces.

After some years, he was welcomed by Sultan Mahmood Beghda of Gujrat and got a formidable position in that court. He had the inclination towards mysticism from the very beginning and was in search of a Spiritual Guide who could pacify his passions to have the

Vision of Allah. Luckily when Imamana (As) came to Pattan, he happened to meet Imamana (As) and at the very first sight he became his devotee and lived with Imamana (As) till Imamana's demise in Farah Mubarak.

After the demise of Imamana (As) when Miran Syed Mahmood, Sani-e-Mahdi (Rz), returned from Farah after one year and established his Dairah at Behlote, Malik Ilahdad (Rz) became his disciple and lived there for a long time, then Hzt. Sani-e-Mehdi (Rz) permitted him to establish his own dairah. But instead establishing his own dairah, he went to Bandagi Shah Nizam (Rz) and became his disciple and after three years he left Shah Nizam (Rz) and joined the dairah of Hazrat Bandagi Miyan (Rz) and became his disciple and lived there even after the martyrdom of Hzt. Banadagi Miyan (Rz) and safe-guarded the diarah as well as brought and bred the teen aged children of Hzrt. Bandgi Miyan (Rz).

He accompanied Bandagi Miyan(Rz) in the First Day Battle and was wounded and became Ghazi. Since he was severely wounded, Bandagi Miyan did not allow him to join in the Second day battle, by instructing him to handle the responsibility of the Dairah and womenfolk and propagate and inculcate the Teachings of Imamana (As), and particularly take care of his young children by carefully maintaining, educating and training them on the directions given by Imamana (As) and take them as his own sons so that they become the harbingers of Mahdiat.

He is called the "Khalifa-e-Giroh, because he became disciple of Imamana (As), and after Imamana(As), he became disciples of all Caliphs of Imamana (As). He trained with utmost selfless sincerity and affection to all the sons of Hzt. Bandagi Miyan and made them perfect on the basics of the Imamana's Mission and permitted Hzt. Syed Shahabuddin Shahabul Haq (Rz) to take charge of his own dairah and continue independently the Mission of Imamana (As).

Then he went to Shah Nemat and became his disciple after some years he visited Shah Nizam at Anondra and became his disciple too. Lastly he established his own dairah in Kapadwanch, a village near Bharounch, Gujrat. It is said that while he was in Dongarpur, King Humayun happened to meet him along with his brothers to whom Khalifa-e-Giroh (Rz) gifted "Maktoob-e-Multani" of Hazt. Bandagi Miyan (Rz). Humayun after reading with atmost respect, ordered to get it copied with Gold-Waters and to keep it in his library.

After fifteen years from martyrdom of Bandagi Miyan (Rz), since Khalifa-e-Giroh became Ghazi in the first day battle, as per Bandagi Miyan's prophecy, the wound started bleeding, which he got on his head, thus he passed away on 14th. Ramazan 945 H. and was buried in his dairah by his son Malik Peer Mohammed (Rz).

(Note: Very recently, Mahdavis of Hyderabad constructed the Shrine of Hz. Khalifa-e-Giroh (Rz) which was in a dilapidated condition. The present shrine is built at a very high level altitude to save it from the raging waters of the nearby river. A Masjid and a Saraey with all amenities have been provided for the pilgrims under the supervision of Janab Syed Ibrahim Saheb of Musheerabad.)

7. Bandagi Malik Burhanuddin(Rz) was a pious and a learned personality of Ahmadabad.

He held an official position in the king's court, . After hearing a sermon of Imamana (AS), he offered his allegiance to Imamana (As). He was the son in law of Imamana (As) also. He died in 915 H. He was buried in Achter Mutera locality, some three miles from North-East of Ahmadabad.

8. Bandagi Malik Gauher (Rz): He was the treasurer of the king of Bengal. After some years he migrated to Gujrat, where he became a minister in the kingdom of Sultan of Gujrat. Then he was employed in the kingdom of Sultan Ghiasuddin of Mandu and within a short spell of time he became minister and after taking permission from the Sultan went to Hajj. One day by chance he happened to meet Imamana (As) and under the influence of Imamana (As), relinquished worldly affairs and accompanied Imamana (As). He died in Thatta, Sindh, in 914 H.

9. Bandagi Malik Ji, governor of Nagore (Rz): He was a Mughal by birth. Malik Ji (Rz) was himself a learned man. when Imamana (As) was in Nagore, he went to Imamana (As) along with some other scholars to discuss about Imamana's claim of Mahdiat. Imamana (As) called him "Prince of Lahoot" on hearing these words, he became unconscious and when he came to his senses, became Imamana's disciple. After relinquishing the worldly affairs, he accompanied Imamana (As) along with members of his family. During the period of Burhan Nizamul Mulk he came to Deccan. His dairah was in Chichond of Ahmadnager, where he was buried.

10. Bandagi Shah Abdul Majeed Noori (Rz.): He comes from the lineage of Shaik Fareed Shakergunj (Rz). He was a priest in Delhi. Nobles and administrators were his disciples. He was a very pious and God-fearing man. Till the time Imamana (As) was in Ahmadabad he was reluctant to offer his allegiance; and when Imamana (As) migrated from Ahmadabad, he came to him and became his disciple. His sons also became Imamana's disciples. His dairah was in Miyanpur, Ahmadabad and was martyred during the period of Muzaffer Shah.

11. Bandagi Malik Ma'roof (Rz): He was the cousin of Hazrat Bandagi Miyan Syed Khundmir (Rz); holding an official position and was a noble at the court of the king. After hearing sermons of Imamana (As) in Pattan, Gujrat, he offered his allegiance to Imamana (As). After becoming Imamana's devotee he did not go to his house. His brother Malik Burhanuddin (Rz) too offered his allegiance to Imamana (As). And just after six months he passed away. His mother wrote to him to meet her. He replied as his brother Burhanuddin (Rz) has died for her, Ma'roof (Rz) also had died.

12. Bandagi Miyan Yousuf (Rz.): He was one of the scholars and nobles of Ahmadabad. He offered his allegiance to Imamana (As) at Ahmadabad. He felt acute troubles during the journey of Khurasan and never became perturbed. He was buried near the Chandola tank In the vicinity of Ahmadabad.

13. Bandgi Miyan Shah Ameen Mohammed (Rz): He is the brother of Shah Abdul Majeed Noori (Rz). He too offered his allegiance to Imamana (As) along with his brother in Gujrat. After the demise of Imamana (As) he travelled to many countries and propagated Mahdavi Faith. His sermons attracted many persons who became Mahdavi. He died in 935 H.

and was buried in Daulatabad, Maharashtra.

(Note: It is said that he witnessed a Dream, regrding Tasbeeh-"La KIlaha Ilul Lah". He reported to Imamana(As), who directed all his followers to announce it after every Ish prayer and at Religious Functions. Mahdavis adopted this Tasbeeh as a "Declaration of Faith".)

Other Pious people. (From Sindh-Pakistan)

Author of "Tuhfatul Kiram" has written about Imamana (As) that:

"Many pious persons became his disciple and attained a position for which they desired for."

بسا اهل الله به نسبت مریدیش رسیدند انچه رسیدند"
(تحفته الکرام جلد دوم صفحه ٢٦)

1. Pir Aasaat(Rz): "Tuhfatul Kiram" mentions about Pir Asaat (Rz) that: "Brother of Maqdoom Arabi, of Hala Kandi, Sindh, was a staunch devotee and was completely absorbed in Divinity, who by chance met Imamana (As) and became his disciple. One of his descendants , Mohammed Husain (Rh), another pious man, resides , where Peer Asaat (Rz) was buried".

(١) پیر آسات: پیر آسات سالك مجذوب واصل محبوب برادر مخدوم عربی هاله کندیست بخدمت سید میران محمد مهدی جونپوری شرف ارادت حاصل کرده گروه اهل الله ایشان را اقدام اکثر مشائخ شمردند، مدفنش معروف از اولادش محمد حسین نام فقیری صاحب حال گذشته (تحفته الکرام جلد سوم صفحه ٢٤٩)

The same author reports that his descendants still live in Thatta.

2. Shaikh Jhanda Patni (Rz): Author of "Tuhfatul Kiram" states that:

"Shaik Jhanda Patni (Rz) was one of those pious and saintly people who happened to have the beneficence from Imamana's miraculous glance, he obtained capacity to absortb into the Divinity. It is said that when Imamana (As) came to Thatta, one Jam Nizamuddin,on the ill advice of some miscreants, mistreated Imamana (As), and with a vicious intension of drowning, Imamana (As) he caused Imamana(AS) to sit in

a boat. When the boat was stuck up in the mud, the boatsmen left it and ran away. Then Shaik Jhanda Patni came to Imamana's rescue through inspiration and got from Imamana (As) what he could get."

(٢) شیخ جهنده پاتنی (پتنی) : شیخ جهنده پاتنی از فیض یابان نظر کرامت سید میران محمد مهدی جونپوری است گویند که چون سید مذکور و اردتته گردید نظام الدین باشاره علمائ ظاهر سلوك معتقدانه بعمل نیا ورده و باراده دیگر در کشی راکب نمود وقتی که ملا حان کشتی رادر خلاب زده رفتند ای را توفیق ازل قائدآن گردیده که آمده ایشان را سالم از آن مهلکه عبورداده یافت انچه یافت

"Author of "Sair-e-Masood" has written about the details of Imamana's stay at Thatta and that episode of the boat. He states that: the companions of Sheik Jhanda fixed the baadban (thick cloth curtains to get directions) for the boat and left it with Sheik Jhanda Patni and the boat reached where Imamana (As) was stuck up in the mud. Thus Sheik Jhanda was able t o rescue Imamana(As) from the mud.

بالجمله درگاهش عجب جائی با فیض واقع بزرگانی که بزیارت سائر مکلی میر سند انتها یا ابتدا بادمی نمانیدد زیارتش را خاتمه یا مقدمه فتوح میدانند (تحفت الکرام جلد سوم صفحه ١٨٤)

Further Author of "Tuhfatul Kiram" states that:

"Really the shrine of Sheik Jhanda Patni (Rz) is so venerable and bountiful that whoever visits Thatta, prefers to pay respects at the Mukalli shrine and get benefitted spiritually.

Mukalli is such a bountiful place where many pious and saints have been buried. Once a saint under the influence of ecstasy exclaimed: "Haza Mukkat Li" (This is Makkah to me) which in due course of time was being pronounced " Mukalli". In Vellor, Sindh.

Now Sajjada Shah Ihsanullah Abbasi lives here and is known as "Pir Jhanda", probably he may be the descendant of Sheik Jhanda Patni (Rz). Reason for calling him Pir Jhanda (Rz) was that, after the Fall of Baghdad, his grandfather migrated to this place holding the flag of the holy Prophet (Slm). This family has been bestowed with both religious beneficence and worldly dignity and grandeur. Thus he was named Pir Jhanda (Rz) (Flag holding pir).

3. Miyan Abu Bakar(Rz): He was a very pious and a Godly man; became one of the disciples of Imamana(Rz). He was buried in Bhakkar.This place became famous after his name and thus became a venerable place for seekers of Divinity."

(٣)میان ابو بکر : میان ابو بکر درویشی صاحب کمال از مریدان و فیض یابان سید میران محمد جونپوری است مدفنش بربکر موسوم به اسمش مشهور و (از) زیارات معروف اهل حضوراست (تحفته الکرام جلد سوم صفحه ٢٥١)

4."Shaik Daniyal" (Rz): Mir Mohammed Yousuf, son of Mir Mohammed Jadum was the disciple of Syed Mubarak Shah, who was drawing inspiration from Sheik Daniyal (Rz).And Sheik Daniyal (Rz) was an ardent disciple of Imamana (As). "

(٤)شیخ دانیال : میر محمد یوسف ولد میر محمد جادم فیض یافته جناب سید مبارک شاه است وے تربیت پذیرفتهٔ نظر لطف شیخ دانیال اجل مریدان سید محمد جونپوری (تحفته الکرام جلد سوم صفحه ٢٠٣)

It may be pointed out here that, this Sheik Danyal (Rz) is different from the one, Hazrat Shaikh Daniyal Khizri (Rz), of Juanpur, who was Imamana's teacher in his childhood and afterwards when Hazrat Khaja Khizer (As) pronounced Imamana (As) to be the Mahdi-e-Maood (As), he had taken oath of allegiance on the hand of Imamana (As) and became known as the most gracious disciple of Imamana (As).

5. Qazi Sheik Mohammed Oucha (Rz): "Tuhfatul Kiram" narrates about him that:

"He belongs to the line of Imam Jafer-e-Sadeq (As). Oucha is a town in Multan. He was one of the renowned scholars of his period. It was a period of Jam Nizamuddin as the ruler of Sindh. When Imamana (As) arrived in Thatta, some of the miscreants labeled Imamana (As) as an infidel. But it was Sheik Ahmed (Rz) who was himself

(۵) قاضی شیخ محمد اچه : قاضی شیخ محمد اچه منسوب به آل جعفر از مشاهیر علمائ زمانه است نخست از هرات باه رسیده و در عهد جام نظام الدین چون سید میران محمد مهدی و اردته گردیده علمائ آن زمان براو نسبت تکفیر بستند نامبرده که بمعنی رهی داشت و مقامات اهل حال را مطلع بود ۔ حجت اهل

a pious and saintly man and knew the reality of Imamana's Mahdiat, bitterly criticized the miscreants who named Imamana (As) as an infidel. On account of his selfless service to Imamana (As), Imamana (As) invoked Blessings for his progeny, who even after so much of the turmoil and disturbances, did never suffer troubles at the hands of the miscreants. In view of some disturbances in Multan, he migrated to Bhakkar and settled down there. Still on account of his fame as a pious and God fearing man, he became well known as Oucha (Rz)."

ظاهر را در تکفیر آن ولی اکمل بوجه الیق رو نموده ، سید میران بحالش متوجه گردیده و دعائے پایش بزرگی و دوام آثار سترگی باولادش کرده ازآن است که خاندان آن بزرگ باوجود حوادث شتی هرگز انقلاب زده نمی شود بالجمله قاضی معزالیه بعد فترت اچه و ملتان به بهکر متوطن گردیده بنا بر کثرت شهرت منسوب باچه مانده (تحفته الکرام جلد سوم صفحه ۲۱۶)

Another writer Mohammed Ma'soom, alias Nami, had also written about Sheik Ahmed Oucha (Rz):

"Qazi Sheik Mohammed Oucha (Rz) was a renowned scholar of his period, well versed with religious learning and was also known as a learned teacher for Arabic Language."

قاضی شیخ محمد اچه از مشاهیر علمائ زمانه بود ...... در علوم دینی ماهر بود ۔ عربیت را نیز خوب میدانست (تاریخ سنده قلمی ورق ۹۶ نمبر ۱۳۷۳، تاریخ فارسی اسطیت سنٹرل لائبریری، آندهراپردیش)

6. Sheik Sadruddin (Rz): Author of "Tuhfatul Kiram" has written him about that:

"He was one of those scholars who understood the spirit of the traditions and for a long time upheld its superiority over all branches of knowledge and who had excellence in furtherance of mysticism and understood the meanings of "Akramakum Indallahi Atkhakum".

(٦) شیخ صدر الدین : طبقه علمائے کرام که بمنطوقه علمائے امتی کانبیا بنی اسرائیل علم تفوق بر عرصه ایجاد برافروخته اندو طبقۀ صلحائ اهل تقوئ که بمصداق آیه **ان اکرمکم عند الله اتقکم** بر جمیع قبائل و شعوب قدم پیشی دارند

Further it is stated that:

"He was the contemporary of Jam Nizamuddin. Sheik Sadruddin (Rz) himself was so perfect in comprehensive knowledge that thousands of his disciples attained their perfection in religious understanding under his guidance and was known as "Afzalul Ulema." In the beginning he opposed Imamana (As), but once he met Imamana (As), he became one of the ardent disciples of Imamana (As)."

شیـخ صدر الدین اجل علماء و افضل اتقیاء معاصر جام نـظـام الدین است درجامعیت علوم بدان غایت بود که هـزار شـاگـرد بـه مـرتبۀ کمال رسانیده نخست بورود میران سید محمد مهدی جونپوری ادعای خصمی پیش کـرده آخـربدیدنش داخل زمره مریدین راسخ گردیده (تحفته الکرام جلد سوم صفحه ۲۱۷ ، ۲۱۸)

7. Qazi Qadan (Rz):"Tuhfatul Kiram" narrates about him that:

"Qazi Abu Sayeed (Rz), son of Qazi Zainuddin Bhakkri was one of the eminent personalities of this place (Bhakkar). After his demise his son Qazi Qadan (Rz) took the mantle of his father and attained perfection in all branches of learning. He memorized the Qur'an in his childhood and was well versed in recitation also. He was an authority in Islamic jurisprudence, commentary, traditions, mysticism and literature. In search of reality he ventured many places to the best of his ability. He performed Hajj and finally became the disciple of Imamana (As)."

(۷) قـاضی ابو سعید ولد قاضی زین الدین بهکری بـوفور فضیلـت و حضور قریحت در ممتاز ان روز گـار و نـامـدار ان ان دیار زیسـت کـرده بعد فـوت وی پسـرش قـاضی قـاضن سـرآمد وقت بـرآمـده بـانواع فضائل آراسته بود ، حفظ قرآن و علم قرأت نیکو داشت در فقه و تفسیر و حدیث و تـصوف و عـزیـمت و انشا کافی زیسته در وادی سـلوك ریـاضـات بسیار کشیده بزیارت حرمین رسیـده سیر و سفر بسیار کرده آخر ها در سلك مریـدان سیـد مـحـمـد جـونپوری منسلك گردید (تحفته الکرام جلد سوم صفحه ۲۱۷، ۲۱۸)

Another Historian Mohammed Ma'soom Nami wrote about Qazi Qadan (Rz) which certifies what the author of "Tuhfatul Kiram" has written about him correctly that:

"Forefathers of Qazi Qadan (Rz) Ibn Qazi Abu Sayeed son of Zainuddin Bhakkri used to live in the cities of Thatta and Seestan. His great grandfather Qazi Abul Khair was a well learned scholar and a mystic who had settled in Bhakkar. Qazi Qadan (Rz) was a man of asceticism and abstinence. He had the company of God-fearing personalities. Inspiration and manifestation were his domain. Had been always busy in remembrance and worship of Allah. He had perfected in the commentary of the Qur'an and of traditions. He was well versed with minute details of the obligations. He was perfect in all branches of learning. He had memorized Qur'an and was well versed in recitation and phonetics. He was perfect in commentary, traditions, mysticism and Islamic jurisprudence. In literature too he was an expert writer. In search of reality he had taken much trouble. He became the disciple of Syed Mohammed Juanpuri (As) who was well known as Meeran Mahdi (As)".

قاضی قاضن بن قاضی ابو سعید بن زین الدین بھکری اجداد ایشان در بلده تهته و سوستان سکونت داشتند وجدایشان در بلده تهته و سوستان سکونت داشتند و جدایشان قاضی ابو الخیر که صاحب حالت و فضیلت بود رحل اقامت در بکر انداخته و قاضی قاضن بزهد و تقوی آراسته بود به صحبت بزرگان بسیار رسیده و از اهل مکاشفه بود همیشه به ظائف و عبادات اوقات شریف خود را مصروف می نمود و در علم تفسیر و حدیث دخل وافر داشت و از چند جا علم تحصیل نموده بود و در جزئیات فرائض بسیار دخل داشت اکثر اوقات به ادائے طاعات و عبادات مصروف میداشت نسب اواز جانب پدر بایں طریق قاضی قاضن بن قاضی ابو سعید بن قاضی زین الدین قاضی بانواع فضائل علمی آراسته بود ـقرآن مجید و فرقان حمید یادداشت و قرأت و تجوید نیکو میدانسته و در علم حدیث و تفسیر و اصول فقه و تصوف دخل و افرداشت و در انشاء مستثنیٰ عصر بود و سیاق میدانست و در وادئ سلوک ریاضت بسیار کرده و در سلك مریدان و معتقدان سید محمد جونپوری که به میران مهدی مشهور است انتظام داشته (تاریخ سندھ قلمی ورق نمبر ۹۸ ، ۹۹، فن تاریخ فارسی نمبر ۱۳۷۳ اسٹیٹ سنٹرل لائبریری آندھراپردیش)

Mohammed Ma'soom Nami had written in the preamble of his book " Khuldullahu Mulkahu" for emperor Akber. It denotes that the book was written during the period of Akber. On pages 326 to 329 of " Ma'sirul Umara" Qazi Qadan's particulars have been written that he died in 1019 Hijri. Apart from it Shamsul Ulema Mohammed Zakaullah also has written his particulars in his "Tareekh-e-Hind" under the chapter "Sindh" which has references from both M'asoom's "History of Sindh" and also about "Tuhfatul Kiram".

(Note: Very recently Janab Namdar Khan Saheb of Karachi, Pakistan, had written a comprehensive article on Hzt. Qazi Qadan (Rh) which is available on "khalifatullah.com".)

8. Mohammed Taj (Rz): Author of "Mir'at-e-Sikandari" has written about Mohammed Taj (Rz)who was a perfect scholar of his period. Scholars of Ahmadabad had written a fatwa against Imamana's contention of "Vision of Allah", to which Mohammed Taj (Rz) refused to attest his signature on that wrong fatwa. "Mir'at-e-Sikandari" narrates thus :

"Every scholar had signed the fatwa except Moulana Mohammed Taj (Rz) who was a very learned man and the teacher of the scholars of that city. He questioned: "whether you had learned only to issue Decree for killing the Syed (As)"? After this episode the Syed, (Imamana (As) went from Ahmadabad to Pattan. He stayed at Badhli, some six miles from Pattan where he declared his Mahdiat."

همه فتویٰ نو شتند الا مولانا محمد تاج که علمائِ عصر بود او ستاد او ستادان شهر به علما گفت که شما علم را برائے همین آموختہ اید که بر قتل سید فتوی دہید بعد از وقوع این واقعہ سید از احمد آباد انتقال نموده به طرف پٹن روانہ شدند و بسہ کروہی پٹن موضع بڑلی نام آنجا اقامت نمود و دعوت مہدویت کرد (مرآة سکندری طبع بمبئی صفحہٗ ۱۳۸)

Mohammed Taj (Rz) had been an eminent scholar who avoided to support the worldly scholars. It is a fact which is proved by the non Mahdavi writers who confirmed about Moulana Mohammed Taj's brother Moulana Yousuf Suheet (Rz) who had accepted Imamana's Mahdiat at Pattan, After that Mohammed Taj (Rz) also offered his allegiance to Imamana (As) and accompanied him and migrated to Sindh from Rajasthan.

The details of all companions shall be discussed in part four of this book.

*   ******

Companions of Prophet Isa (As).

Those who have accepted Hazrat Isa (AS) was a group of persons called Hawaris. Thus Allah states: that:

"When Isa (As) asked (his companions) whether they want to help me? His companions answered that they are helpers (to You) for (the Religion of) Allah."

قال من انصاری الی الله قال الحواریون نحن انصار الله (آل عمران)

Who were those helpers? The details are available in " Muwaheb-e-Aliah":

A."When Isa (As) started inviting towards religion, the Jews decided to kill him. At that moment Isa (As) ran away from Syria to Egypt. He saw fishermen were busy in fishing on the banks of the river Neil. Isa (As) asked them to come to him for hunting (killing those men who were trying to kill him).

B. Those were fishermen, washermen and dyers."

الف : چون عیسیٰ آغاز دعوت کرد جہودان بہ قصدوی بر خاستند عیسیٰ فرار نمود از ولایت شام بجانب مصر و بر لب دریائے نیل ـ جماعتی صیادان دید کہ ماہی می گرفتند عیسیٰ بایشان گفت ...... بیائید تامرو مان راصید کنیم ـب ـ گفتند حواریان یعنی این جماعت صیادان و گویند گاز ران و رنگریزان بودند

It is a fact that barbers and shoe makers were the companions of Hazrat Noah (As), and the companions of Isa (AS) were fishermen, dyers and washer men. When barbers, shoemakers, fishermen and dyers could provide proof of the prophet hood of Hazrat Noah (As) and Hazrat Isa (As), then why should the witnesses of above mentioned scholars and nobles in the preceding chapters be doubted to have accepted Imamana (As) as the Promised Mahdi (As)? Apart from them, scholars of Herat too had accepted Imamana's Mahdiat. Their details are given hereunder:

Scholars of Herat:

Mulla Abdul Qader Badayuni has written about Imamana(As) in his "Najatur Rashid" that:

زمانی که حکومت قندهار تعلق بذوالنون بیگ داشت اواز زمین حجازیه قصبۀ فراه رسید غلغلۀ عظیم در آن ولایت افتاده و خلایق لا یعدولا یحصیٰ بدو جمع آمده و شیخ الاسلام هروی مشهور از جمله تلامذه خوود و شاگرد رشید را انتخاب نموده برائے تحقیق حال اوازهری فرستاده او شبهۀ چند کرده تا حال آن نمایند از آنجمله آنکه ازین مذاهب اربعه مشهوره کدام مذهب دارید ـ دوم آنکه شنیده شد که دعوی رویت الله در دار دنیا میکنید سوم میگویند که خود را مهدی میگیرید و آن هر دو کس در وقتی که میر بیان آیه کریمه یا ایها الناس اعبدو اربکم الآیة میفرمود بملازمت رسیده اند و چندیں شبهـات کـه تـرتیب داده بودند در ضمن تفسیر آن آیت مرتفع شده به مثابة که آن همه به تحیر قـدرت بـر سـوال نـداشتند و هیچ احتیاج باستفسار نماند و این معنی را حمل برخارق میکردند و میر اشارت فرمود که بـمـوجب مـا عـلی الرسول الابلا غ انچه شیخ الاسلام پیغام داده است چرانمی گذارید ایشان ادای رسالت کردند ـ جـواب از سـوال اول چنین داد که من حیث الاطلاق مذهب خداوند تعالیٰ و من حیث التقلید مذهب رسول الله صلعم دارم و چنـانـچـه پیغـمبر عـلیه السلام مبعوث برائے نفی اصنام بود من مبعوث برائے نفی اجسام رافع اختلافم و اگر اصحاب مذاهب در این زمان می بودند در حقایق الٰهی و معارف یقیی غیر از متابعت من نمی گزیدند واز دوم آنکه بـرویـت قلبی که عبارت از مشاهده است همه کس قائل است و همچنین امکان رویت بصر نیز ماندو وقوع در دنیا نـمـی بینیـد کـه پیغـمبر علیه السلام را خود رویت بصری واقع در همین دار ابتلا شد اگر کسی که ذات اودر ذات رسـول صلعم و صفات او در صفات صلعم فانی شده باشد و محو مطلق گشته به طفیل متابعت آن سرور ازآن دولت بهـره مـنـد گـردانند چه عجب ، فلان بزرگ در فلاں کتاب آورده که "رایت ربی" و دیگراں نیز درجاهائی متعدد چنیں میگـویند کـه "رایت الله " عجب است که اینهارا مسلم میدارید و انکار نمی آرید غاتیش تاویل این اقوال خـواهیـد کـرد و مارا تاویل چه ضرور است در ظهور موداے این عبارت چه قصور است تاصرف معنی از ظاهر نموده بتـاویل قائل شوم بلکه چنین میگوئیم که هر جا در قرآن مجید ایها الذین آمنوا واقع شد قابل این خطاب همان کس تـوانـد بـود که اورا رویت الله به بصر یا بصیرت یا در منام حاصل شده باشد اگر ازیں هاهیچ کدام صورت نه بند دلا اقـل در طـلب رویت در رویا و مشاهده بیقرار گرد و تا اطلاق لفظ مومن بروے صادق آید و هر که ازیں مراتب اربعه هیچ کدام ندارد نزد من مومن کامل نیست اما از سوم آنکه اگر باذن الله باشد چه مانع و آن هر دو آن روش و طرح جـذب و تـصرف دیده گفتگوے علمی را فراموش ساخته داخل اصحاب شدندو به شیخ الاسلام گفته فرستادند که این مرد آیتی است از آیات خدا و علمی که ماسالها خوانده ایم اینجا هیچ قدرو قیمتی ندارد و شیخ الاسلام را ترغیب ملازمت او کردند (نجات الرشید قلمی صفحه ۸۷ ، ۸۹)

"When Zunnoon Baig was the ruler of Qandhar, Imamana (As) reached Farah, via Gujrat and Qandhar, there was an uproar about his coming in Farah and multitudes accompanied Imamana (As). The Shaikhul Islam of Herat sent his two students-scholars for investigation (of the particulars about Imamana (As) to Farah).

The Sheik had selected a set of questions, those are :

1. Which one of the four renowned Imams of fiqha that Imamana (As) follows ?

2. It is heard that you challenge to cause Vision of Allah in this mortal world.

3. People say that you had proclaimed yourself to be the Mahdi (As).

When Imamana (As) was busy in his sermon on " ايهـــا الـنـــاس اعبـدوا ربـكـم الـلــه
"Aiyuhannasu' Budoo' Rabbukumullah)"Oh! People pray to your God;" at that time those scholars arrived. Whatever answers were required for those questions, they were all well replied in that sermon by Imamana (As). Most important was the situation that they did not have the strength to speak out those questions to Imamana (As) and they did not feel any reason to put forward those questions at all, since they were replied in the sermon. This fact was to them a miracle of Imamana (As). However, when Imamana (As) asked them to put forward what was asked for by the Shaikhul Islam: When the questions were repeated by the scholars. For the first question, Imamana's answer was as under:

1. Our religion is based on Allah's command and as far as following is concerned, we follow Rasoolullah (Slm). Rasoolullah (Slm) was commissioned to negate the polytheism, I am commissioned to negate the "Self" and also to eradicate differences in religious matters. Those who had prescribed the rituals, had they been born in my period, they would prefer to follow me in search of the intricacies of the Reality.

2. The answer for the second question was that: All agree that observance of the Divinity by heart is possible. Therefore the observance through eyes in this mortal world is also possible. Do you deny that Rasoolullah (Slm) witnessed the Vision of Allah during his lifetime, particularly at the Mairaj?. Therefore if any person submerges his "Self" and his own attributes into the personality and the sublime attributes of Rasoolullah (Slm), with his kind benevolence the Vision of Allah is possible for anyone during his own lifetime. Some persons in some books had referred that" Ra-aithu Rabbi" "I had witnessed my Allah", and many more had said like that. It is surprising that you accept their words, and do not deny those who uttered those words, instead you may even try to interpret them wrongly, but what is the necessity for any interpretation for us? Why should you avoid the real meanings and try to interpret the real sense of those Sayings? Actually our comments for "ايهـــا الـذيـن آمـنـوا" (Aiyyu hallazeena Aamanoo") is that these Qur'anic versions are addressed only to those who had witnessed the vision of Allah by inspiration or in their dreams, and if both of them were not possible then at least you must be restless and have faith to have the vision in a dream or in contemplation. Then only you are the perfect Momin . And out of these four situations, if a person had attained none of them, then "he is not a perfect Momin."

3. The answer for the third question was: "If I declare myself to be Mahdi (As) on the commands of Allah, who could stop me?" Hearing all this, the scholars were so

impressed that they became disciple of Imamana (As) and sent word to the Shaikhul Islam that " This man is one of the signs of Allah and that the knowledge that we have got during so many years, is worthless to him". And they insisted on the Shaikh to join the company of Imamana (As)."

Note: References of the Scholars had been given by Abdul Qader Badayuni in his"Najatur Rashid" *along with the short notes about those scholars. There are two copies of "Najatur Rasheed" in the State Library, Andhra Pradesh. (Refer volume 4, page 188, Tasawuf-Persian No. 1564 (Qalmi) total 314 pages, written in 1115 H. at Shahjahanbad. We have referred pages 84 to 91 which contains details about Imamana (As).*

What Mulla Abdul Qader has written, Mahdavia literature differs in certain matters.

1. Mulla Badayuni had referred that two scholars were sent to Imamana (As) by Shaikhul Islam, while our books refer to four scholars and their names are: 1. Mulla Ali Fiyyaz, 2.Mulla Mohammed Sherwani, 3. Mullah Darwesh Mohammed Herati, and 4. Mullah Abdul Samad Hamdani or Haji Mohammed Khurasani, or Mulla Ali Sherwani or Mulla Ali Gul or Mulla Maqdoom, (Fourth Scholar may be one of them.)

2. Second is that Badayuni had referred three questions, while our literature states, four questions. Fourth question was regarding commentary of the Qur'an. Third point is regarding a verse of Holy Qur'an "Laqad Zaraaen La Jahannamma Kaseeram minal jinn o ins".

Fourth point of difference is that as regards Vision of Allah, Badayuni referred the Sayings of "Rayath-e-Rabbi" or "Ruyat-e-Allah", but our books mention something else. What Bandagi Miyan Abdul Rahman (Rz) has mentioned in " Moulood" has been mentioned in "Matleul Vilayet" also that Imamana (As) had referred those verses which point out about the Vision of Allah . Those verses are:

"Thus whoever wishes to meet Allah, must practice virtuous deeds." (18:110)

إنّ فمـن كـان يـرجـو الـقـاء ربـه فليعمل عملا صالحا (الكهف)

"The man who is blind here, would be blind in the Hereafter also." (17:72)

(ب) من كان فى هذه اعمىٰ فهوفى الآخرة اعمىٰ (بنى اسرائيل)

"Verily: they are doubtful about their meeting with Allah, Beware He surrounds everything." (41:54)

(ج) الا انهم فى مرية مـن لـقاء ربهم الا انه بكل شى محيط (حم السجدة)

"No one could comprehend Him but He surrounds your visions." (6:103)

(د) لا تدركه الابصار و هويدرك الابصار (الانعام)

"He (Moses. As) called Allah: let me see you; Allah said: you cannot see me." (7:143)

(ه) قال رب ارنى انظر اليك اليك قال لن ترانى (الاعراف)

It may be pointed out that those verses which negate the "Vision of Allah" should not be argued as such on their literal meanings alone, because "La Tudrikuhul Absar" negates the perception and not the sighting (observation). (Here we have to investigate and research the meanings of "Perception" and " Observation (Sighting)".

Ibn Hazam (Rz) had refuted the contention of the dissenters in these words:

"The verse "La Tudrikuhul Absar" is not a proof for the dissenters (To negate the sighting), because Allah had negatived perception. Perception means more than sighting or viewing as mentioned in our dictionaries. But it means consciousness which is different from sighting or viewing. Thus perception or denominating Allah in any form or guessing Him in a physical form is not possible either here or Hereafter."

هذا لا حجة لهم لان الله تعالىٰ انما نفى الادراك والا دراك عندنا فى اللغة معنى زائد على النظر و الروية و هو معنى الاحاطة ليس هذا المعنى فى النظر والروية فالا دراك منفى عن الله تعالىٰ على كل حال فى الدنيا والآخرة (الفصل فى الملل والا هواء والنحل ، طبع مصر ، الجزء الثالث صفحه ٢ ، ٣)

Qur'an certifies that perception is different from sight.:

"Thus when both groups started looking at each other, then companions of Moosa (As) told that they were surrounded. Moosa (As) nullified it persistently and told : "My Lord is with me and He shall show me the right path." (26:61)

فلماء تراء الجمعٰن قال اصحاب موسىٰ انا لمدركون قال كلا ان معى ربى سيهدين (الشعراء ركوع ٤)

This verse refers to " Tara'al Jum'aan" which determines the possibility of sighting and the word "Lamudrekoon" in the Qur'anic version "Inna lamudrekoon Qaala Kalla", denotes for perception which is being negatived. In the same manner from " La Tudrikul Absar" perception is negatived, not the sighting." Allah's firm reply" Lun Tarani" never shall you see me". From this, how can you prove that "Allah could never be sighted"?. Imam Fakhruddin Razi (As) has commented on this verse that:

When Allah said to Prophet Moses (As) "Lan Tarani" ("You cannot see Me" and he did not say " La ar'ie" (I could not be seen). Thus we assume that Allah's Entity is sightable.

Despite this all, Allah had substantiated that his Vision is only possible if the mountain stands firm at its place, which is clear from this verse" Fanas takher makana tarani" (thus if the mountain remains at its place, then only you could see Me)."If the mountain remains at its place, then only it is possible to see me", thus if anything is based on a possibility, then it becomes possibile to have the Vision of Allah. Imam Fakhruddin Razi (As) had commented on this verse, further:

"It is proved that Allah had conditioned his Vision on permissible matter or command. And the matter depends upon permissibility, then it becomes possible. Thus Allah's Vision as a whole is possible."

"فـلـمـا قـال لـن تـرانـی و لـم یـقل لا اری علمنا ان هـذایـدل عـلـی انـه تـعـالیٰ فی ذاتـه جائز الرویة" (تـفسیـر کبیـر طبـع دارالـطبـاعـتـه عامره استانبول الجزء الرابع صفحه ۴۲۱)

Author of "Tafseer-e-Husaini" has commented on this verse That:

"Moosa's request for seeing (Allah) proves its possibility. Because if it was not possible, then a Prophet would never have asked for, because Prophets never ask for anything which is not possible."

"بـدانـکه طلب موسیٰؑ روایت رادلیل جواز رویت است چـرا کـه اگـر رویـت مـحـال بودی موسیٰؑ ایـن سوال نه کـردی چه طلب مستحیل از انبیا روانیست"

Sheik Abdul Haq, Muhaddis-e-Dehlavi has written that:

"Sheik Muhiuddin Novavi (As) had said that eminent scholars had preferred and asserted that Rasoolullah (Slm) had sighted the Vision of Allah with his own eyes."

"شیخ مـحی الـدین نـووی گـفتـه راجح و مختار نزد عـلـمائـ کبـاراست کـه آنحضرت دید پروردگار خود را بچشم سر (اشعته اللمعات، طبع نولکشور ۱۳۵۵ء جلد رابع صفحه ۴۳۱)

"Rasoolullah's assertion "Un Ta'budullaha ka-annaka Tarahu" : "Worship Allah as if you are seeing Allah" points out that during worship Allah's Vision is possible.Otherwise he (Slm) would not have told like that which is not possible.

Proofs regarding "Sighting the vision of Allah" had not been mentioned by Badayuni. Miyan Abdul Rahman's "Moulood" is the oldest source regarding biography of Imamana (As) in which it has been reported that:

Imamana (As)inquired from the scholars:"How many witnesses does a qazi require? The scholars replied "Two". Then Imamana (As) informed the scholars that Hazrat Ibrahim (As) and Rasoolullah (Slm) are present here, confirm the matter from them. Such assertion none could assert except a commissioned one. Had the scholars any doubt about the presence of two Prophets as the witnesses, they could demand their presence, but they were satisfied that whatever Imamana (As) was telling was a fact, therefore they kept quiet.

Prophets Ibrahim and Rasoolullah as Witness:

224

"Then asked: "Do you (Imamana) assert 'Sighting of Vision of Allah' and invite people towards it?" Imamana (As) presented those verses of the Holy Qur'an which point out regarding the Vision. Imamana (As) did prove sighting from those verses. Then Imamana (As) asked "how many witnesses a qazi demands according to Shariat"? The answer came: "Two witnesses". Then Imamana (As) Informed (Scholars of Herat) that "Ibrahim Alaihis Salaam and Rasool-e-Maqbool are standing as witnesses. Ask them. I am also a witness". At the same moment, under the influence of ecstasy, Mulla Ali Fiyyaz testified and said: "Wallah! One witness is enough for me". Other three scholars also said: "Aamanna WA Saddaqanna" and remained in the service of Imamana (As) and sent Mulla Abdul Samad Hamdani to Mirza Sultan Husain to inform him what had transpired between them and Imamana (As)."

باز پرسیدند که دعویٰ روایت میکنید و خلق را هم بررویت میخوانید آنحضرت آیت هائے قرآن که بر جواز رویت آمده اند به قواعد علم بدو تطبیق داده بزبان اوشان دیدن خدای در دنیا ثابت کردند باز فرمودند در شرح قاضی بچند گواه راضی می باشد گفتند بدو گواه فرمودند اینك محمد رسول الله صلعم و اینك ابراهیم خلیل الله ایستاده اند به پرسید و یکی بنده نیز شاهد است فی الحال مولانا علی جاذب شده تصدیق کردند و گفتند والله مارا همین یك گواه بسنده است دیگر هر سه کس نیز آمنا و صدقنا آغاز کردند اماسه علما را به صحبت ملازم شاند و مولانا عبدالصمد را پیش سلطان فرستادند (صفحه ۱۳۲)

It is also mentioned in "Matleul Vilayet" in which the reference of "Rasoolulalh (Slm) is here" was given, but not of prophet Ibrahim. However in "Shawahedul Vilayet" both names have been referred.

The author of Hadia had remarked that "Shawahedul Vilayet" had tried to fill up the gap by inserting the name of Prophet Ibrahim (As), which was omitted in "Matleul Vilayet". Whereas both books testify each other about what Imamana(As) had referred..

It is a fact that "Moulood" is the oldest one comparing to"Matleul Vilayet" and "Shawahedul Vilayet" and which testifies about both prophets, Hazrat Ibrahim (AS) and Rasoolullah (Slm). Thus the author's contention is based on nothing but maliciousness.

This particular Saying has three parts: In the first part, Imamana (AS) had proved that "Vision of Allah is possible" in this world and he based his contention on the verses of the Qur'an. The second part deals with the Signs of Allah as mentioned in the Holy Qur'an. Third part deals with the acceptance of Imamana's Mahdiat by the Scholars of Herat and who informed the facts of their discussions with Imamana (AS) to Mirza Sultan Husain.

As regards second part, the author of Hadia has written that Imamana (AS) had simply pointed out on the air. There were none to see nor any one heard any voice. The manner in which the author is pointing out is nothing but atheism and pointing out his inability to conceive the mysticism. Since according to a tradition, the Satan could not personify Rasoolullah (Slm). Imamana's assertion that Rasoolullah (Slm) is here was a fact, because it was asserted by a Khalifatullah (As).

Opponents of Imamana (As) had testified that Imamana (As) was one of the eminent mystics. How could it be said that the person who had been accepted to be one among the eminent mystics, without contemplating Rasoolullah (SLM) would point out in the air? Particularly when the scholars had faith in Imamana's contemplation.

Like the author of Hadia, an enemy of the holy prophet (Slm) also can say that the revelations were nothing but rumors. This can be refuted on the basis of the characters of She prophets (As).

Huzoor Rasoolullah (Slm) had contemplated prophet Younus (AS), (probably in the Meraj) and he had heard him saying "Labbaik" These narrations have been mentioned in the "Kanzal Ammaal":

"So to say, I was looking towards Younus (As)who was riding on a She Camel whose nukail is made up of date palm's rope and his robe is of costly woolen cloth. He is telling me "Labbaik, Allahumma Labbaik." Thus I was looking at Younus bin Mati (As) who was wearing two silkish robes and telling "Allahumma Lab baik". Mountains were answering to him. Allah too is saying "Labbaika oh! Younus (As), I am with you."

(ا) كانى انظر الىٰ يونس على تاقة خطامهاليف و عليه جبة من صوف و هو يقول لبيک اللهم لبيک (عن ابن عباس) (كنزل العمال جلد ششم صفحه ۱۳۰)(ب) كانى انظر الىٰ يونس بن متى عليه عباء تان قطو انيتان يلبى تجيبه الجبال و الله عزو جل فيقول له لبيک يا يونس هذا انا معک (عن ابن عباس) (كنزل العمال جلد ششم صفحه ۱۳۰)

If any one had demanded, Rasoolullah (Slm) would have made him observe Hz. Younus (As) and also to make him listen the voice of Younus (As).

"Muslim" has narrated with reference to Ibn Abbas (Rz) that Rasoolullah (Slm) had also seen Moosa (As). The tradition says:

"Rasoolullah (Slm) was saying that he was looking towards Moosa (As) and said about his complexion and about his hair. (Ashatul Lam'aat Vol.4,P.457)

قال كانى انظر الىٰ موسىٰ فذكر من لونه و شعره شئيا (اشعته اللمعات جلد رابع صفحه ۴۵۷)

"Sarwer-e-Anbiah, Rasoolullah (Slm) said that he was looking at Moosa (As) who had come to Hajj along with his 70,000 Israelites."

سرور انبياء صلوة الله عليه و سلم فرمود موسىٰ رامى بينم كه باهفتا و هزار نفر بنى اسرائيل به حج مى آيد (اشعته اللمعات جلد اول صفحه ۱۱۱)

These traditions report that Rasoolullah (Slm) had seen Prophets Younus and Moosa (As), along with 70,000 Israelites; then why should Imamana's pointing out about Ibrahim (AS) and Rasoolullah (Slm) be questioned, since Imamana (AS) was the Khalifatullah?

It may be pointed out that answers given by Imamana (AS) have two aspects: One being, according to the custom of the scholars it was argued through the Qur'an; second as the person designated by Allah, he presented the Signs of Almighty Allah. Thus, it points out about the reality of the righteous path, which is the same what had been of the holy Prophet (Slm) and Hzt. Ibrahim (AS). Thus, incidentally, points out the reality of his program to be in accordance with Rasoolullah's and Prophet Ibrahim's.

If the scholars of Herat demanded, Allah would show His signs through Imamana (As). And Imamana (As) would have made them to contemplate Rasoolullah (Slm) and Ibrahim Alai His Salaam and caused to answer to those scholars; as Rasoolullah (Slm) had seen Gabriel (As) and he caused to be seen or in the manner he showed the splitting of the moon. Apart from these all, Hazrat Zainab (Rz) questioned Rasoolullah (Slm) "how can you come to me without Nikah"?, Upon her explicit question, Rasoolullah (Slm) answered:

اللّٰه المزوج و جبرئيل الشاهد (مدارج النبوة
جلد دوم صفحه ۲۷۸)

"Allah arranged matrimony under the witness of Gabriel"

We ask, whether the author of Hadia and his followers had guts to question as to no witness was seen and neither was there the actual performer of the Nikah. Whoever questions on this; he would become an infidel and atheist as well only. The fact is that, if any person had questioned, then Rasoolullah (Slm) would have made him observe the facts what he had asserted.

Significance of Questions of the scholars of Herat:

Mulla Abdul Qader Badayuni never felt any doubt for the questions and answers of the scholars of Herat, but the author of the Hadia found two doubts; one being why the scholars had taken two months for framing four questions?

It was no where mentioned whether they had served all 24 hours in framing the questions , or they might have discussed occasionally and arrived at the conclusion?

On the other hand, opponents had studied "Sirajul Absar" for four years. And it had come to the knowledge that a team of opposing scholars was busy in the compilation of "Hadia-e-Mahdavia" by Zaman Khan. After four years of minute consideration, the opponents had pointed out just three objections. Then, why should there be any objection as to why the scholars of Herat had taken two months to prepare four questions in respect to an important issue of Mahdiat? Another objection was that these questions and answers were very simple and easy, but it was never asserted as the proofs of Mahdiat. The delicacy of the questions of the scholars of Herat could be understood by a person who is well versed with psychology.

The fact is that there had been serious discussion between scholars of Herat and Imamana (As) at Farah for more than one year. The signs pertaining to Mahdiat had already come into verification. There is much difference in the books of "Sihah" and "Non Sihah" regarding the signs. Imamana's characters had been accepted to be that of the Holy Prophet (Slm) and became famous worldwide. Several scholars of Farah had accepted his Mahdiath. Imamana's miraculous glance had such a captivating power that it attracted thousands on account of his sermons which had such a mesmerizing effect that whoever listened, he has enamored towards him. These are the clear facts that even the opponents had accepted his excellence and eminence.

Under these circumstances, the scholars of Herat just wanted to know the fact that Imamana's proclamation of his Mahdiat was made actually on the commands of Allah or not? To treat this discussions as a dialectic discussions is nothing but ignorance of the decliner.

According to "Matleul Vilayet", the first question was that:

"Mulla Ali Faiyaz asked Imamana (As) that you declare Mahdi (As) by yourself, if so, then on what grounds?"

(۱) ملا علی فیاض نقل است که سوال اغاز کرد و گفت شنیده می شود که شما خود را مهدی موعود میگوئید از کجا میگوئید

"Az kuja me goed" (From what source you say). This question is an absolute one, which demands many answers. For instance: "I carry all signs of Mahdi (As), but these signs are not themselves the perfect proof for Mahdiat until Allah did not declare me as the Mahdi (As). Therefore Imamana (As) answered:

"I am not saying that I am the Mahdi (As), but Allah informed me that Syed Mohammed (As) you are the promised Mahdi (As)".

بنده نمی گوید فرمان خدای تعالیٰ می شود که اے سید محمد تو مهدی موعود آخر الزمان هستی

Imamana (As) answered that "I am not declaring myself Mahdi (As), but Allah declares about me that "you are Mahdi-e-Akhiruzzaman (As)." When Imamana (As) told that "I had declared my Mahdiat on the commands of Allah, then incidentally confirms those obvious signs attached to the person of Mahdi (As), since Allah would never command a person as Mahdi (As) who did not carry those signs.

"The second question was that which religion you follow?"

(۲) سوال دوم پرسیدند که شما کدام مذهب دارید بر کدام مذهب هستید

This question also has a psychological blend. If a person was not commanded by Allah would have told one of the names of the four Imams of Jurisprudence whom he would be following. For example, Hanafi will tell Imam Abu Hanifa (Rz); a Shafai will tell Imam Mohammed bin Idrees Shafai (Rz). But Imaman's answer was:

"We adopt the religion of Rasoolullah (Slm) and are not bound to any other school of religion."

فرمودند که ما مذهب مصطفی داریم ، ما به هیچ مذهب مقید نه ایم

Imamana (As) told that his religion was of the Rasoolullah's religion and his Shariat is Shariat-e-Mustafavi (Slm). Therefore he was not bound to any one of the famous four schools of religions. The scholars of Herat wanted to know to which school Imamana (As) follows?

"Third question was: Which commentary you follow?"

(۳) سوال سوم پرسیدند که شما به کدام تفسیر بیان می کنید

This question relates to any particular commentary of the Holy Qur'an. Any scholar could say that he had studied all reliable and credible commentaries and may state about which he is most fascinated. With that question, the scholars of Herat wanted to know whether he himself believes to be the Mahdi (As) or not. And if he affirms to be the Mahdi (As), then he would not bind himself to any commentary of others.

"Imamana (As) answered that he narrates the objectives of Allah; which ever commentary is in accordance with his narrations is worthwhile."

فرمود که مراد الله بیان می کنم و هر تفسیری و جزآن که بابیان این بنده موافق باشد آن صحیح است

From this answer the scholars were satisfied to hear that Imamana (As) narrates meanings and objectives of the Qur'an and that he was not bound to any commentators, because Mahdi (As) is the Khalifathullah (As); then how could he bound himself to any particular commentator or any Imam?

Apart from this, Imamana's contention was based on: "Mazhab-e-Ma Kitabullah WA Ittebaye Mohammed Rasoolullah (Slm)" and for 23 years he spread this message only. His every action and narration was based on Qur'an and Traditions. Therefore if any commentator had written anything against the Qur'an and tradition, that would be null and void, according to him, since he is Khalifatullah (As), the sole authority to narrate, and had the repelling force to stop annihilation of the Ummah.

"Fourth question: you claim to have a Vision of Allah and you invite others on this issue?."

(٤) شما دعوی رویت الله میکنید و همه خلق را برآن دعوت می نمائید

Answer for this question is available in so many verses of the Qur'an which are self explanatory for the Vision of Allah in this mortal world. Any eminent scholar could offer this explanation.

"Imamana's answer was challenging one that if you desire to ask about "the Vision of Allah" ask Hazrat Ibrahim (As) and Rasoolullah (Slm) who are present here. Thus Imamana (As) was presenting a "sign". This could be done by none else other than one who had been appointed by Allah. Had the scholars of Herat demanded to see in person; then Allah would have accomplished their desire through Imamana (As). Hence the questions of Scholars of Herat were not about the specific signs of Mahdiat but they wanted to know whether Imamana (As) considers himself to be "the Mahdi (As)" on the command of Allah? Because whatever the signs and attributes were existing in the person designated by Allah to be Khalifatullah (As) were indeed existing on the person of Imamana (As). Thus the answers given by Imamana (As) were convincing in all respects to the satisfaction of the scholars of Herat. Thusd, invitation to accept him as Mahdi (As) was virtually under the commands of Allah;

1. Mahdi (As) is not the disciple of any jurist;
2. Mahdi (As) was not the follower of the jurists.
3. His narration of the Qur'an is not bound to any commentator;

4. There was a possibility of manifestation of the signs of Allah through him. These answers gave full satisfaction to the scholars of Herat, that Imamana (As) has proclaimed himself to be the Promised Mahdi (As) on the commands of Allah. Answers given by Imamana (As) about the ranks of Mahdi (As) were so appropriate about the person of Mahdi (As), that satisfied the questioners to the best of their understanding.

We have already discussed about the answers given were to substantiate the ranks of Mahdi (As). What ever points have been discussed, answers were given completely in accordance with the Qur'an and traditions; otherwise they would become against the claim of Mahdiat.

Apart from this, the author of "Matleul Vilayet" had not categorized this discussion as a proof of Mahdiat, but presented as an informative event only; since every point of discussion of a trustworthy person should be taken as a proof of his trustworthiness.

Abdullah Bin Salaam (Rz) had put three questions to the Holy Prophet (Slm) telling that these are such questions which could be answered by a prophet only and none other. It is reported in "Bukhari", that:

" Abdullah bin Salaam (Rz) heard from Anas (Rz) about the coming of a prophet, at that time he was gathering fruits. He went to the holy Prophet (Slm) and told him that he would put three questions to him to answer, which nobody could give except an apostle of Allah.

1. What is the first sign of the Day of Judgment?

2. What is the first diet of the residents of the Paradise?

3. What is that element which makes a son or daughter resembling to his parents?

The Holy Prophet (Slm) told him that Gabriel (As) has just now informed him about these questions. Rasoolullah (Slm) answered that "the first sign of the Day of Judgment would be a fire which would gather persons from the East to the West".

"The first diet of the residents of the Paradise shall be a portion of the liver of the fish"

The answer to the third is that "When the sperm of a man overpowers the woman's ovum, then the child will resemble the father and when the woman's ovum overpowers man's sperm, child resembles the mother". Abdullah Bin Salaam (Rz) exclaimed that there is no god, but Allah and you are the apostle of Allah."

Three questions were answered by the holy prophet as under:

1. Sign of the Day of Judgment is a fire which would drive people from the East to the West.

2. The first diet of the residents of the Paradise shall be a portion of the lung of the fish.

3. For the resemblance of a child, he said that if the sperm of a woman dominates man's sperm, the child would resemble to the mother and if the man's sperm dominates the woman's sperm child would resemble the father.

Now the question arises whether the author of Hadia would be satisfied with those answers which the holy Prophet (Slm) had given and whether these answers prove Mohammed (Slm) to be the Apostle of Allah? Since he may doubt that those answers might have been obtained from the Jews who used to come to Makkah for business or obtained from the infidels who used to go to the Jewish countries for business. Apart from this, what is the criterion to judge the sanctity of those answers? However, we accept the sanctity of those answers, because the questioner became satisfied. More importantly the answers were given by the Apostle (Slm) of Allah. Thus in the same manner why not the answers of Imamana (As) be taken as correct since the scholars of Herat became satisfied and offered their allegiance to Imamana (As).

And more importantly, those answers were given by a Khalifatullah (As).

There may be differences in reporting in the "Najaatur Rasheed" and other Mahdavia books, but it is a fact that the scholars of Herat became satisfied with those answers and accepted Imamana's Mahdiat, and they became Mahdavi and joined the circle of Imamana (As). Mulla Abdul Qader Badayuni and Moulana Abul Kalam Azad have referred "Najatur Rasheed" and certified that "Najatur Rasheed" was written as a detail history of the Mahdavis, which is authentic. Apart from this "Tazkeratul Waaseleen" also provide details of Mahdavis with reference to the discussion about Hazrat Sheik Dawood (Rz).

Kings who accepted Imamana (As) as True Mahdi:

Now we shall discuss about those kings who had accepted Mahdiat of Imamana (As):

1.Sultan Husain Sharqi: While discussing about the battle of Rai Dalpat, we have given details of Sultan Husain Sharqi who was a staunch devotee of Imamana (As).

2.Sultan Ghiasuddin Khilji: Farishta had written that the Sultan's period of governance was 33 years. According to "Tabkhat-e-Akbari" his period has been shown as 32 years and 70 days. He died in 906 H. Professor Mahmood Shirani has determind the year of his inauguration of the enthroning ceremony to be the year 858 Hijri.

While Oriental College Magazine writes that Sultan Ghiasuddin and Sultan Nasiruddin were not the correct names, instead they were Ghias Shah and Nasir Shah, whereas Farishta and Author of "Tabkhat-e-Akbari" had written in many places as being Sultan Ghiasuddin and Sultan Nasiruddin. Farishta has written that:

"Sultan Ghiasuddin made his elder son Abdul Qader his heir by giving him the title of Sultan Nasiruddin and abdicated in favor of his son, by handing over administration to the confident and trustworthy nobles, by saying that he had served 34 years, now is the time of his retirement. In the year 894 H. Imamana (As) had arrived at Mandu, but Sultan Ghiasuddin was so helpless on account of his son, Sultan Nasiruddin that he could not meet Imamana (As). Although Sultan Ghiasuddin was the king, but his son Nasiruddin was controlling the reign of administration, that is why Sultan could not meet Imamana (As) but sent words by a confident person that he desired to offer homage, but unable to visit Imamana (As). On this, Imamana (As) sent Miyan Syed Salamullah (Rz) and Miyan Abu Bakar (Rz) who were received by the Sultan with utmost respects and offered his oath of allegiance to Imamana (As) through them and asked them to convey to Imamana (As) his three wishes:

1. To die with humility 2. Prefer martyrdom over natural death and 3. To die in faith.

Imamana (As) prayed for him, accordingly and informed him that his three wishes would be fulfilled positively. He sent an elephant loaded with gold coins to Imamana (As), which had already been mentioned previously.

One of his court nobles was Miyan Ilahdad Hameed (Rz) who became Mahdavi at the hand of Imamana (As) and accompanied Imamana (As). He was a very talented person and a scholar who wrote a "Dewan" without dots, "Risala-e- Bar-e-Amanat", "Rislai-e-Suboot-e-Mahdi" and "Marsia-e- Mahdi-e-Maauood".

Translator's note: Much has been written about conspiracies of the court against king Ghiasuddin. His wife Rani Khurshid wanted her son to be declared Heir Apparent. These historical facts have been omitted from translation since they had nothing to do with our Faith or about Imamana (As). That portion only had been translated which pertains to our faith, for the purpose of brevity.

3.Sultan Mahmood Beghda:

At the time when Imamana (As) was in Chapaneer, Sultan Mahmood was also in Chapaneer. After hearing thefame of Imamana's sermons, the Sultan sent his two nobles, Saleem Khan and Farhadul Mulk to Imamana (As), who after meeting Imamana (As) became disciples. Sultan desired to meet Imamana (As), but nobles of the court did not allow the Sultan to meet with an apprehension that lest the Sultan should become a disciple, the kingdom would perish. However Sultan's two sisters, Raji Seun and Raji Murari had already offered their allegiance to Imamana (As). Author of "Mir'at-e-Sikandari" writes: that:

"Sultan Mahmood Begdha attempted to meet Imamana (As), but the nobles obstructed on the premise that after hearing Imamana (As), Sultan might relinquish the kingdom itself."

سلطان نیز قصد ملاقات سید نموده وزراء مانع آمدند مبادا سخنان سید سلطان را از جابه برد و مهمات مملکت تعطل پیدا کند (مرآه سکندری طبع بمبئی صفحه ۱۳۷)

Same version is written by Abdullah Mohammed Bin Omar Makki, that:

"Many a times the Sultan tried to meet Imamana (As), but his ministers advised him not to meet since Imamana (As) had such a forceful captivating power which attracted anyone who met him once, which meeting might motivate the king to renounce the worldly life."

وغیر مرة احب السلطان ان یراه فالتمس ارکان ملکه ان لا یفعل و صرفوه عنه و ذلك لانه کان له قبول یجذب زائره و یحمله علی التجرد من الدنیا (ظفر الواله بمظفر و آله جلد اول صفحه ۳٦)

Author of "Nuzhatul Khawathir" writes that:

"Mahmood Shah Kabeer attempted to attend Imamana's sermons, but nobles felt that Sultan would become captivated by Imamana (As), hence, they objected."

فعزم محمود شاه الكبيران يحضر مجلسه فلما رای العلماء میله الیه منعوه عن ذلك القصد (الجزرا الرابع صفحه ٣٢٢)

Anyhow it is a fact that Sultan Mahmood Beghda had become a devotee of the Imamana (As). Abul Fazal had written under the chapter : Syed Mohammed Juanpuri (As)" that:

"The fountain head of Mahdiat had started from Juanpur and came to Gujrat, then Sultan Mahmood was the first to become his devotee."

"سرچشمهٔ مهدویه او از جونپور به گجرات شد و سلطان محمود کلاں به نیایش برخاست" (آئین اکبری ،طبع کلکته، جلد دوم صفحه ٢٢١)

Mulla Abdul Qader Badayuni writes that the Sultan met Imamana (As) and became his devotee:

"Sultan Muzaffer Gujrati's father Sultan Mahmood Begdha who was a commentator, a muhaddis, met with Imamana (As) and lived in his company. But when the scholars instigated him to leave the company of Imamana (As), he preferred to go to Hajj."

و سلطان محمود بیگڑه پدر سلطان مظفر گجراتی که بادشاه مفسر عالم عادل بوده اورا دیده و صحبت داشته و تبحریض علما رضا باقامت اودر آن دیار نداده رخصت مکه معظمه فرموده (نجات الرشید قلمی صفحه ٨٥، ٨٦)

Abul Kalam Azad has written in "Tazkera" that " At the very sight of Imamana (As) he (the Sultan) became his devotee." (Page 30)

4.Ahmed Nizam Shah of Ahmed Nagar:

When Imamana (As) came to Ahmed Nager, the city wall was under construction in 899 H. However, Ahmed Nizam Shah heard Imamana's sermons and became his devotee. Imamana (As) gave him his Chewed betel leaf (Puskhurda/ left over) which caused him to have a male baby. He ruled 19 years and died in 915 H. Khaja Ibadullah Akhter Amratsari has written that when Imamana (As) came to Ahmed Nagar he was profusely welcomed and Ahmed Nizam Shah had become his devotee.

5.Burhan Nizam Shah:

After Ahmed Nizam Shah's death his son Burhan Nizam Shah also adopted his father's religion. Author of "Muntakhabul Bab" writes:

At that time "Mahdavi Faith" was so popular that comparing to other faiths, it did not have any vice, therefore Burhan Nizam Shah got engaged his daughter to one of the priests of his Faith who was one of the best scholars of that time."

چون در آن ایام مذهب مهدویه به مرتبهٔ رواج پذیرفته بود که مقابل مذاهب دیگر قبح آن در نظرها نمی نمود برهان شاه دختر خودرا به یکی از مشائخ و پیشوائے آن قوم که به حسب ظاهر در جمال و کمال و وفور مال از مشاهیر بود نسبت نمود (منتخب الباب ، طبع کلکته، حصه سوم صفحه ١٦٢)

This priest was none but Miran Syed Miranji (Rh), son of Miyan Syed Hameeed (Rz), grandson of Imamana (As). Author of "Shawahedul Vilayet" in chapter 34 writes that:

"Deccan's king, whose name is Malik Nizam called the Mahdavi priest, Miran Syed Miranji (Rh) and arranged his daughter's wedding with him in which many of the Mahdavi companions were invited whom he treated well with much respect and love."

ميـان سيـدميرانجي را بادشاه دكن اسمه ملك نظام غـفـر الـلـه ذنـوبـه طـلبيـده دختر خود براي خدمت ايشان داده اكثر صحابه آنحضرت امام عليه السلام راطـلبيـده مـحبـت و خـدامـت (فدايت) بسيار پيش آورد چنانچه معروف و مشهور است

It is said that Shah Tahwer Ismail influenced him to adopt Shia Faith, but in his last days he again reverted to his Mahdavi Faith before Miran Syed Miranji (Rh) and Miyan Pir Mohammed (Rh) and after that in their presence took his last breath. Malik Pir Mohammed (Rh) is the son of Malik Ilahdad Khalifa-e-Giroh (Rz). One Shaik Zainuddin's brother's name was also Pir Mohammed (Rh), but it is not known whose son he was. Author of "Asami Musaddaqueen" states that:

"Shaik Zainuddin (Rh) also known as Nahnnay Miyan (brother of Pir Mohammed) was one of the ministers of Nizam Shah, who had written a detailed journal regarding proof of the Mahdiat of Imamana (As).

شيـخ زيـن الـديـن المعروف به نهني ميان برادر ملك پير محمد مملكت مدار نظام شاه بودند و عالم بودند رساله مطول در ثبوت مهديت مهدى عليه السلام نوشته اند

The fact of Burhan Nizam Shah's again reverting to Mahdavi Faith, was not made public, however Miyan Syed Burhanuddin (Rh), prayed for Burhan Shah's salvation in his "Shawahedul Vilayet". It is a fact that Burhan Nizam Shah the Second, was a Mahdavi, following his father Ahmed Nizam Shah. Burhan Nizam Shah had died in 961 H. just after five years from the death of Shah Tawaher Ismail who died in 956 H. Farishta had written that Burhan Nizam's son Ismail Nizam Shah also was a Mahadavi.

Farishta had written that:

"Within a short spell of time, Mahdavis from all over India flocked together around Nizam Shah and became his well wishers".

”در انـدك زمـان از اطـراف و جـوانب هندوستـان طـائفه مهدويه مجتمع گشته فدوى اسمعيل نظام شاه شـدنـد“ (تـاريـخ فرشته ، طبع نولكشور ۱۳۰۱ء جلد دوم صفحه ۱۵۰)

6.Mirza Sultan Husain, Ruler of Khurasan:

When Imamana (AS) arrived in Farah, hundreds of people accompanied him. Badayuni has written that countless people accompanied him. These words are clear to denote that countless people had become his devotees. As per Badayuni, at this occasion Shaikhul Islam Harvi sent his student-scholars for investigation. It means to say that Imamana's news regarding arrival and staying at Farah had reached Herat also. From Mahdavia literature we came to know that Mir Zannoon after becoming Imamana's disciple wrote in detail to the Sultan the facts that Imamana (As) has proclaimed himself to be the Promised Mahdi (As) which fact had been accepted by thousands of his devotees.

Ninth Century had been a very hectic century in which Herat became a hub for scholars who were busy in investigating the burning issue of Mahdiat. Those scholars who were deputed for investigating the mission of Imamana(As) were known to Mirza Sultan Husain since those scholars were sent along with four hundred horsemen. As per Badayuni, those scholars after becoming satisfied with the answers given by Imamana (As), became his disciples and wrote to the Shaikhul Islam that "Imamana (As) was one of the signs of Allah and the teachings what we got during so many years from you had no value to Imamana (As). Therefore they had accepted him as the true Mahdi (As)". Thus they pursued the Shaikhul Islam also to pay a visit to Imamana (As) and become his disciple. The name of the Shaikhul Islam was Mulla Shah Baig. When this message was received through one or two of the scholars, Mirza Sultan Husain and Mulla Shah Baig have accepted Imamana (As) as the true Mahdi (As) in absentia and after some time started to meet Imamana (As) in person, but unfortunately the Sultan died for whom Imamana (As) offered the Funeral Prayer for him in Absentia at Farah.

Difference of date of Sultan's demise:

Old Mahdavia literature confirms that Mirza Sultan Husain, king of Khurasan whose capital was Herat died during the lifetime of Imamana (As). Imamana (As) lived in Farah for two years and five months. After one year from the date when he arrived in Farah, Mir Zunnoon sent a letter to the Sultan for investigation of Imamana's claim of Mahdiat. Accordingly scholars were sent and they converted to the Mahdavi Faith after being convinced by Imamana's deliberations. Then Shah Baig persuaded the Sultan to meet Imamana (As). Residents of Farah had taken one year to investigate, and then they informed Shah Baig. Mirza Sultan Husain died in 910 H. according to Miyan Abdul Rahman's "Moulood", the most authentic historical record tells that the Sultan died during the lifetime of Imamana (As). Thus it is confirmed that both Imamana (As) and the Sultan died in the same year, but the sultan died prior to Imamana's demise and not afterwards.

However there are differences regarding the date of demise of the Sultan in Mahdavi and non Mahdavi reporters; because these are two different sources. Still it is a fact that even two people of the same group furnish different dates which creates minute differences. Psychologically speaking, such instances and episodes become most rememberable which have public importance. In this connection Just take the case of the date of demise of the holy Prophet (Slm) which is the saddest and touchy event for the Ummah. How awful it is that such an important date had been reported differently. Generally, the 12th Rabiul Awwal is taken as the authentic date of the demise; and its correctness is an approved fact, since this month still has been designated as " Bara Wafat", vouchsafing the date of twelfth Rabbiul Awwal as the date of his demise, but unfortunately the Muhaddisseen had preferred some other date. Surprisingly, the Shia people had reported the month of Safar as the month of the Prophet's demise.

Holy Prophet's Age?:

1. From one source it is said that the Holy Prophet's age was 60. Urwa Ibn Zubir (Rz) had

reported that he was bestowed with the prophethood at his age 40 and passed away at his age 60.

2. Another source states that he lived 65 years as narrated by Ibn Abbas (Rz): "He passed away at the age 65".

3. The third source admits his age was 63, when he passed away. Sayeed Ibn Musayib (Rz) states that the holy Prophet (Slm) received his first Revelation at his age 43. He lived ten years in Makkah and lived in Madinah ten years and died at his age 63. (It seems he had not calculated those three years in which he was offering prayers secretly in Makkah).

The first source states that he was commissioned as the Last Prophet at his age 40, and the other source states that his age was 43 when he proclaimed himself as the Messenger of Allah.

One source states that he lived in Makkah for ten years while Ibn Abbas (Rz) reported that he lived for 13 years in Makkah.

The Karbala Episode:

This episode is a well known fact in the Ummah, but still there are differences in the date of its occurrence. Badruddowla had written in his "Dastan-e-Ghum" that:

"It is a well known fact that it happened on Friday, the 10th day of Muharram 61 H. and was accepted by all scholars . But some state that it occurred in the month of Safar. Hissham Bin Kalabi (Rz) states that Martyrdom occurred in the year 62 H., one says the year was 63 H. and some say it was 60 H."

قـول مشهور وصحیح آن است که شهادت آن امام روز جمعه دهم محرم سال شصت ویك هجری است واقدی وغیره ائمه فن نیز بهمین جزم کرده اند بعضی گویند که درمـاه صـفـر واقع گشت ، هشـام بـن کلبی گوید که شهـادتـش در سال شصت و دو واقع شده گویند شصت و سه بقولے شصت

Thus the year of the Martyrdom may be one among these years: 60, 61, 62, 63. But preference is given to 61 H. As regards the month, some said it to be Safar and another said Muharram, but the latter one is correct.

Mistakes of Indian Histories:

Some matters which do not relate to "Tareekh-e-Mahdavia", Indian Historians had wrongly referred in their books, which are clarified here:

A."Tareekh-e-Farishta" had mentioned the date of Proclamation of Imamana (As) was 960 H. And those who have referred and translated it, without investigating from Mahdavia sources, committed the same mistake and reported wrongly the same year of demise as 960 H.

1. "Be it known that Mahdavis had faith in a person by name Syed Mohammed (As), a Hanafi, who had proclaimed himself to be the Promised Mahdi (As) in the year 960 H. In India, just on the basis of those signs which are attributed to the person of the True Mahdi (As) according to the Traditions, and the same were found on him. Therefore he was accepted as the Promised Mahdi (As), which is a well known fact." (Vide Farishta, Vol. 2, page 150, printed Noel Kishore.)

باید دانست که مهدوی را اعتقاد آن است که شخصی حنفی مذهب سید محمد نام در هندوستان در اواخر سنه ۹٦۰ء ستین و تسعتماتیه دعویٰ کرد که من مهدی موعود و به لسان شرع ام دچوں بعضی آثار علامات که در مهدی آخر الزمان علیه السلام قرار داد اندو دروی بود تصدیق قول او نمودند وآں اظهر من الشمس است (تاریخ فرشته جلد دوم صفحه ۱۵۰ طبع نولکشور

2. "Mahdavis have faith in a person by name Syed Mohammed (As), a Hanafi, who proclaimed himself to be the True Mahdi (As) in India in 960 H.. And it is a fact." (vide Farishta, Vol 2. Page 294, printed in Bombay 1832.AD)

(۲)مهدویه را اعتقاد آن است که شخصی حنفی مذهب سید محمد نام در هندوستان در اواخر سنه ستین تسع مائة دعویٰ کرد که من مهدی موعود به لسان شرع ام الیٰ آخر (تاریخ فرشته جلد دوم صفحه ۲۹٤ طبع بمبئی ۱۸۳۲ء

3. "Mahdavis have faith in a person by name Syed Mohammed (As), a Hanafi, who declared himself to be the Promised Mahdi (As) in the year 960 H. and that is a fact." (Vide Frishta , hand written, referring to Ismail bin Burhan Nizam Shah, Persian No. 998, State Central Library, Hyderabad.)

(۳) مهدویه را اعتقاد آن است اے شخصی حنفی مذهب سید محمد نام در هندوستان در اواخر ستین تستعماتیه دعویٰ کرد که من بلسان شرع ام الیٰ ام آخره (تاریخ فرشته قلمی ذکر اسمعیل بن برهان نظام شاه تاریخ فارسی نمبر ۹۹۸اسٹیٹ سنٹرل لائبریری آندهرا پردیش -

From the above volumes of "Tareekh-e-Farishta", the date of the declaration had been mentioned as 960 H. But the fact is that both Mahdavia or non Mahdavia literature agree to a date of demise of Imamana (As) to be 910 H., But the irony of the fact is that none had tried to rectify the mistake what Faishta had committed.

The reason of such glaring mistake might have been on two grounds:

1. Farishta himself might have committed the mistake and the translators had carried the same mistake without scrutinizing, may be un-knowingly. Farishta was in Ahmad Nagar which became a hub for Mahdavis. While referring to Ismail Shah he states that: "The writer came from Bijapur to Ahmad Nagar on 19th. Safar 998 H." Thus he had complete knowledge about Mahdavis, because he was arrested by Mahdavis for he had become abnormal. This episode, he had mentioned as under:

"The writer got some bruises and became weak, therefore could not accompany the shah and lived in that village where Mahdavis arrested him, but later on they released."

اس مولف کـه در آں معرکه چند زخم برداشته از کثرت ضعف همراهی رکاب شهریار نه نموده در آں قصبه مانده بود گرفتار مهدویه گشته به لطائف الحیل از دست ایشاں خلاصی یافت رسیده بود بلائے ولے بخیر گذشت

Surprisingly, as an historian, was not his responsibility to check, investigate and record the correct dates of Imamana's declaration and demise from Mahdavis who, according to him only, had gathered in thousands from all over India in Ahmed Nagar.?

2."Mu'asirul Omara" states that: The author, Shah Nawaz Khan, also had written the same wrong date as being the date of declaration being 960 H., even after, as he said that, he had met with Mahdavis of that period, still did not care to correct from the Mahdavi literature the said wrong date. (Vide "Mua'sirul Omara", printed in Calcutta in 1888 H., Vol one, pages 124, 125.)

1. He had mentioned the date 960 H. as the date of declaration of Imamana (As) as the Promised Mahdi (As), when Imamana (As) had already passed away 50 years ago, that is in 910.H.

2. He also had wrongly written that Imamana (As) had travelled from Iran to Hijaz (for Hajj). The fact is that Imamana (As) had travelled to Hijaz from India (Dabhol Bander) and returned to India (Ahmadabad) and after visiting many cities in India, proceeded to Sindh from India and went to Qandhar and Khurasan.

3. He also had wrongly declared that Imamana (As) had pronounced himself to be the Mahdi only and not as the Promised Mahdi (As).

The oldest Mahdavi source is that of Bandagi Miyan (Rz) who wrote "Aqeeda-e-Shariefa", before his Martyrdom in 930 H. In which it was particularly mentioned that when the tradition "Yamlaul Arz" was presented to Imamana (As):

"Imamana (As) had emphatically told that all had accepted him (as the Promised Mahdi (As) and followed him accordingly."

همه مومنا ن ایمان آوردند واطاعت کردند

It is clear that even the non Mahdavi too knew this fact of his declaration as the Promised Mahdi (As).

4. How far the author's contention is correct that Mahdavia faith is against the beliefs of the four "Schools of Thought" presented by four Imams? Since Mahdavia Faith is basically based on the holy Qur'an and the Traditions of the holy Prophet (Slm) only. As regards (their objections regarding Faraez-e-Vilayet), it is a fact that they are all based completely on the relevant verses of the holy Qur'an.

5. He had also mistakenly written that only the commoners and illiterates had accepted him as the Promised Mahdi (As). This is a white lie. In this connection we would like to refer "Tuhfatul Kiraam" in which it is stated that (Mahdavis) had inculcated their teachings in such a

manner that thousands of their followers attained that much prominence that it attracted even Allama Sadruddin (Rz), a well known scholar, who too had offered his allegiance to Imamana (As). Very recently, Omer Bin Mohmmed Dad Potha (A well known scholar of South Africa, and a renowned preacher of Islam, like Dr. Naik of India) had commented on the History of Sindh, written by Syed Ma'soom Bhakri (printed in Bombay, pages 200, 201) who had compared Qazi Qadan's mystical knowledge and Qur'anic understanding with that of Shah Nawaz Khan by stating that Shah Nawaz Khan could not stand before Qazi Qadan's prominence.

C. "Mir'ath-e-Sikandari" is a History of Gujrat comprising historical events up to 1000 Hijri. In the preamble he had accepted that many facts written by other writers unfortunately failed to furnish real facts. Thus whatever he had written, it may be taken as correct to the best of his knowledge. Still while referring the date of demise of Imamana he too had mistaken by writing 917 H. These are the old writers. Now we furnish the glaring mistakes written even recently in 1922 AD .

D. Abdul Haq, author of "Tafseer-e-Haqqani" had written while referring about the Tenets of Islam that during the "period of Akber the Great", Imamana (As) had declared himself to be the Promised Mahdi (As), whose followers are still residing in the Deccan. Whereas it is an historical fact that Imamana (As) passed awayin 910 H., long before Akber took the reigns of his kingdom in 963 H.

How far an orator knows the historical facts can be well explained by the above mentioned passage. The fact is that Imamana (As) had migrated during the period of Sultan Sikander Lodhi from Juanpur about the year 887 H., which had been accepted by Mullah Abdul Quader Badayuni. After the demise of Sultan Sikander Lodhi, his son Sultan Ibrahim Lodhi was enthroned. Then the period of Baber emerges, followed by Humayun, who was defeated by Sher Shah Soori , and then the period of Saleem Shah Soori started, then comes the period of Sultan Sikander Shah Soori. Then Humayun returns from Iran and defeats Sikander Shah. After Humayun, Akber the great becomes the Moghal emperor in the year 963 H. while Imamana's demise took place in the year 910 H. On such flagrant mistakes, should historical facts furnished by Mahdvia writers be corrected on wrong statements of the non Mahdavi writers? It is utterly a wrong suggestion, by the non Mahdavi writers of the Muslim period of India, to correct. They had flagrantly and wrongly quoted even the historical facts of Mahdvis that too about the correct date of the demise of Imamana (As). Now we like to verify Dr. Abdul Haq's knowledge about the traditions of Mahdi (As).

He says that whatever the signs had been referred as the attributes of Mahdi (As), none was applicable to the person of Imamana (As). In this connection he refers to a very wrong, unbelievable and erroneous tradition which states that:

One among many signs of Mahdi (As), is that Mahdi (As) shall stammer, and unless his sentence is complete he would strike on his knees (to complete the sentence). Thus according to the author of "Tafseer-e-Haqqani", the sign of stammering was not found in Imamana (As), hence he did not recognize Imamana (As) as the true Mahdi (AS). Is it not ridiculous?

Surprisingly, such a sign of stammering was not reported by any of the Muhaddiseen nor it is found in "Sihah" Then it is nothing but bias and illiteracy on the part of the author who had referred to such an unbelievable sign. Such a ridiculous, unreported and unbelievable foolish sign should not and could not become a prerequisite condition for a sublime post like that of Mahdiat.

E. Abul Hasan Ali Nadvi had maintained that Shaik Alaai (Rh) was the founder of the Mahdavia Faith. He wrote: " Some four hundred years ahead, during the period of the Sultan Saleem Shah, Sheik Alaai, "Founder of the Mahdavia Faith", had a dielectic dialogue with the scholars of that period, when none of the so called, eminent scholars of his court, could stand before Sheik Alaai in the discussion, finally the king sent him to one prominent Bihari Scholar and asked him to decide about the facts of Mahdiat of Sheik Alaai (Rh). This narration is utterly wrong since many non Mahdavi scholars had accepted Imamana (As) as the "Founder of Mahdavia Faith" who passed away in 910 H. Whereas Sheik Alaai (Rh) was the Khalifa of Abdullah Khan Niazi (Rz) and that Shaik Alaai (Rh) died in the year 957 H. who had never seen Imamana (As) at all, but he was a staunch devotee who propagated the Mahdavi Faith without any fear of his even death.

E. Syed Manaazirul Hasan Geelani also made Sheik Alaai (Rh) the caliph of Imamana (As). He wrote that Sheik Alaai (Rh) was the caliph of Imamana (As). On the insistence of Maqdoomul Mulk Sultanpuri, Saleem Shah ordered flagging Sheik Alaai (Rh) who was very weak and died just after the brutal third flagging. But as a matter of fact, according to "Muntakhabatut Tawareekh" and "Tabqaat-e-Akberi," Sheik Alaai (Rh) was the caliph of Miyan Abdullah Khan Niyazi (Rz). Manaazirul Hasan had not cared to mention that Sheik Alaai (Rh) was suffering from the plague and had a wound on his tongue on account of which he could not bear even the third brutal flogging, consequently died. Instead, he had simply mentioned that he was very weak. He had mistaken by saying that he was the caliph of Imamana (As), which is utterly wrong, since he was the caliph of Abdullah Khan Niyazi (Rz), a "Tabe-Tabie" (son of a companion of Imamana (As).

The facts reported in the Mahdavia books cannot be corrected on account of the wrong statements made by the non Mahdavi writers like "Tareekh-e-Farishta", or "Mir'atul Sikandari", or even written by prominent Islamic Scholars like Abul Hasnat Nadvi or by Manaazirul Hasan Gilani etc;.

Imamana's Date of Demise as per encyclopedia:

The date of demise of Imamana (AS) also has been recorded in the "Encyclopedia of Religion and Ethics" as 911 H. and it is stated that Farah was a part of Baluchistan. It reads thus:

"He died in 911 (1505) at Farah in Boluchistan, where his tomb became a place of pilgrimage." ("Encyclopedia of Religion & Faith" Vol.8.)

It is a fact that the date of Imamana's demise is 19th. Zee-Qaida, 910 H. and Farah is located geographically in Afghanistan. Thus it was not at all the city of Baluchistan. Should we negate our record just on the basis of wrong entries made even in encyclopedia?

As far as the date of demise of Sultan Husain is concerned, we must prefer Mahdavia record, because he had accepted Imamana (As) as the Promised Mahdi (As) which had been recorded in the oldest book of Miyan Abdul Rahman's "Moulood" and that the Sultan died during the lifetime of Imamana (As) and it is a historical fact that Sultan Husain died while he was on the way to Farah to meet Imamana (As). It is a fact that. on inspiration that the Sultan had died during the journey to Farah, imamana(As) offered Sultan's Funeral prayer in absentia, then what more authentic record is required?

Even after the demise of Imamana (As) in 910 H. his companions were residing in Farah for more than a year. Therefore we have to accept what the companions have said, and also reported by the Scholars of Herat which should be taken as correct, since it is based on facts. However there are two non-Mahdavia sources about Sultan Husain. One is "Baber Nama" and the other is "Rouzatus Safa" apart from Mahdavia record..

"Baber Nama":

The oldest and the confirmed Turkish context was printed in 1905 under the Gibb Memorial Series and one of its copies is available in the Salar Jung Museum, Hyderabad. On the 2nd. and 3rd. Lines on the back side of page 163, it is written that "at the end of the year in the month of Zil Hajjah or Zee Qaida, Sultan Husain died when Baber attacked Shabani Khan. *(And it is a fact that Imamana (As) died in the month of Zee Qaeda of 910 H.0 and surely not in Zil Hajjah)* The Turkish context does not mention the year of his death. On page 156, dates must have been mentioned, but the year is not written. Likewise page 183 is also empty. Thus the Turkish context and the Persian translation both do not refer the year of his demise. But according to Mahdavia literature, date of the demise of the Sultan has been written as being Zee Qaeda of 910 H, which is also the date of demise of Imamana (As). Thus it can be inferred that with just some difference of days, both have died, since Imamana (As) according to his inspiration, had offered Sultan's funeral prayer in absentia in Farah. Thus it is certain that the sultan died even before Imamana (As) with some difference of days in the month of Zee-Qaeda of 910.H

"Rouzatus Safa":

In "Rouzatus Safa" the date of demise of Sultan Husain had been mentioned as 911 H. But while comparing to the Mahdavia sources, this also becomes unreliable like Farishta and "Mirat-e-Sikandari". Nobody rectified the actual date mentioned by the author. Thus Mahdavia record cannot be corrected on the basis of the Non Mahdavia unscrutinized record. It is just like that while Muslims confirm Faraan to be in Makkah, the Jews and the Christians say that it is in Syria.

Thus Mahmood Shirani's version that Mirza Sultan Husain, ruler of Khurasan, died in 912 H. is not correct according to either from the Mahdavia or from the non Mahdavia sources.

(Note:7.Hzt.Adam Shsah Klhora (Rz) From the recent research of the History of Sindh, it came to notice that Miyan Adam Shah Kalhora was the founder of Mahdavia dynasty of Kalhora, which ruled Sindh for a century. Adam Shah(Rh) became Mahdavi on the hand of one of the descendants of Imamana(As, may be on the hands of Hzt.Abdulalh Khan Niyazi (Rh).

He adopted Sawieth as the principles of his states's economy and foubnded "Miyanwali Movement" which brought Green Revolution on the **Dictates of Imamana(As)** *that the Tiller is the owner of the land.*

Some seven Kalhora Ruler administered Sindh and brought pece and prosperity to Sindh.The canal system of the Sindh River was their innovation to bring thousand and lakhs acres of land undrer cultivation on "joint Cultivtion under the system", where the cultivators shared equally, that is how Green Revolution was witnessed in Sindh. The details of this dynasty have been provided in the Addendum for the benefit of the readers.)

Nobles And Ministers who became Devotees:

1. Zubdatul Mulk, Osman Khan was the ruler of Jalore. Zubdatul Mulk was his official title. His forefathers were the rulers of Bihar, but subsequently settled down in Gujrat. When Imamana (As) went to Jalore in 906 H. Osman Khan (Rz) happened to hear Imamana's sermons and had accepted him as Mahdi (As). His entire rayaat, (population) along with his army, all became Mahdavi enblock. Apart from this, 900 scholars too became Mahdavi. Ruler of Palanpur, Nawab Taal-e-Mohmmed Khan Bahadur, is the last Ruler of Palanpur, who is the descendant of Osman Khan (Rz), Zubdatul Mulk, is still a Mahdavi who lives in Bombay.

(Note: In 1963/64 Anjuman-e-Mahdavia, Chanchalguda had celebrated an all India Mahdavia Conference at Chapaneer. This Translator as the Joint Sercretary of the Anjuman, and of the Conference, invited Nawab Tale Mohammed Khan to attend the Conference in which he had whole-heartedly graced his presence in the said Conference and addressed the gathering of about five thousand Mahdavis in 1963/64 AD.)

2. Darya Khan (Rh)

Author of "Tuhftul Kiram" states that Darya Khan's name was Qaboola. Really he was a Syed, but unfortunately he was imprisoned, now he became a free man. Once, Jam Nizamuddin went for a game. It was a very hot day, he asked for water from Qaboola, who brought water and put over it sweet-scented grass. He drank water slowly due to the grass. When asked as to why he put grass in the water?, Qaboola told that since it was a hot day and being thirsty, water should not be drunk in haste, therefore he put grass in it, so that you should drink slowly. Jam Nizamuddin appreciated his wisdom and granted him the title "Darya Khan (Rh)" and brought along with him. Author of "Tuhfatul Kiram" writes about him that:

"Jam Nizamuddin granted him the title of "Darya Khan (Rh)" who on account of his abilities obtained high position and became Madarul Muham, surpassing all other dignitaries of the court of Jam Nizamuddin. When Imamana (As) arrived in Thatta, although Jam Nizamuddin did not show due respect to Imamana (As), still Daraya Khan (Rh) became a staunch devotee of Imamana (As) and attained whatever he could get from Imamana."

دریــا خــانــش خــوانــدو بمعائنه جوهر ذاتی تربیت یافته به مـرتـبـه بـلـنـد تـصـاعـد نموده ، بردلشاد وزیر و سائر امر اتفوق یافته مدار المهام و امیر الامرا گردید ، مبارک خان خـطـابـش شـد چـون میر سید محمد جونپوری واروتته گـردیـد بـآنکه جام تبحریك علما معتقدانه پیش آمدوی نـکـرده متبصمیم ارادت آن بزرگوار کمر بست و بهرهٔ وافی ازرضائے خـاطـر آن صـاحب زمان یافته (تحفته الکرام ، طبع بمبئی جلد سوم صفحه ٥٤)

3. Shah Baig (Rh):

He was the son of Mir Zannoon (Rh). Mirza Sultan Husain made him governor of Qandhar. When Imamana (AS) arrived at Qandhar, scholars advised Shah Baig to call Imamana (As) at Jama Masjid and investigate about his claim of Mahdiat. Officials mistreated Imamana (As) and his companions. Imamana (As), however, came to the Jama-e-Masjid and sat in the first row facing Qibla. Shah Baig came in an intoxicated condition. The companions asked Imamana (As) to speak politely. Imamana (As) retorted "people who are intoxicated with worldly love, wake up before this servant". Scholars started abusing and rebuking and situation reached to the extent of an entanglement, and then Shah Baig asked scholars to hear what Imamana (As) has to say. Imamana (As) started sermon of the verse "Afa Mun Kana Ala Baiyyina". At first Shah Baig became mesmorized and when sermon of three verses was over, he became restless and offered his apology to Imamana (As). But until the sermon was completed, Imamana (As) did not give any attention towards Shah Baig. After completion, Shah Baig fell down at Imamana's feet. Imamana (As) lifted his head and pardoned him. Then Shah Baig accepted Mahdiat and became convinced about Imamana's claim of Mahdiat. Farishta says that Shah Baig was excelled in learning who wrote commentary on Kafia. Shah Baig's son, Mirza Shah Hasan, also was a Mahdavi, who used to appoint Mahdavi Qazis, prominent among them were Sheik Mohammed Oucha (Rz) and Qazi Qadan (Rh). Mohammed Ma'soom Nami has written about Qazi Oucha (Rz) that:

"Qazi Sheik Mohammed Oucha (Rz) was a learned man of his period. On account of bloody disturbances in Multan, he settled down in Bhakkar. After some time Mirza Shah Hasan appointed him Qazi of Thatta."

قاضی شیخ محمد اوچه از مشاهیر علمائے زمان بود بعد از فترات اوچـه و مـلتان به بكر توطن نمود بعد چندگاه مـرزا شـاه حـسـن ایشـان را بتقلید قضائے بلده تته تکلیف نمودند (تاریخ سندھ قلمی ورق ٩٩ ، تاریخ فارسی نمبر ٣٧٣ اسٹیٹ سنٹرل لائبریری حیدرآباد)

Author of "Tuhfatul Kiram" had also written about Oucha That:

"When Qazi Shakrullah Shirazi desired to relinquish his post of Qazi of Thatta, he recommended Sheik Mohammed Oucha's name for that position. Forefathers of both Qazis had cordial relations with each other in the past; therefore both came to know each other very well. On account of nobility and Imamana's blessings the post of Qazi had become hereditary in Oucha's family."

وقتی کـه قـاضـی شـکـر الله شیرازی استعفائے خدمت قـضـائـی تـتـه چـنـانچـه سبق یافت درخواست میر زا شاه حسن حسب تجویز قاضی میر مذکور که در وطن قدیم هـرات بـهـم از اسـلاف رابطه ، خاصی داشتند بربنائے آن واسطـه ایـس جـانیز قرب مفاخر (ظاهر) و پیوند صورت یـاب گـرویـده وی را طـلبیـده بـآں مـنصب جلیل القدر مـختـص فرمود و بـه بـرکت قدیم نجاتبش و دعائے میراں سیـد مـحـمد مهدی جونپوری آں منصب تبوارث وقف اولادش هست (تحفته الکرام جلد سوم صفحه ۲۱۶)

Thus Qazi Shakrullah too was a Mahdavi that is why he recommended the name of Qazi Oucha for that honorable post. "Tuhfatul Kiram" was written in 1181 H., till that year the post of Qazi was being retained by Oucha (Rz) family and it is also a fact that Oucha was the Qazi till the Mahdavi population was residing at Thatta. In the same manner Mirza Shah Husain had appointed Qazi Qadan (Rz) as the Qazi of Bhakkar. Mohammed Ma'soom Nami has written about Qazi Qadan that:

"After the demise of Shah Baig, Mirza Shah Husain had appointed Qazi Qadan (Rz) as Qazi for Bhakkar and for its vicinity. Whatever cases came to him he used utmost consciousness and honesty in settling the cases. He retired only after he became very old and after him his brother Qazi Nasrullah was appointed to that post."

بعد فوت شاه بیگ ازیں مرحله فانی منظور نظر عاطفت اثـر میرزا شاه حسیـن گشتـه بـلوازم قضاے بلده فاخره بـکـرونـواحی آں قیام مـی نـمـود قـضایاے شرعیـه کـه بـخدمت اومرافعه کردند کمال احتیاط و دینداری ظاهر سـاختـه در کبـرسـن ازآں امر خطیر استعفا نموده و آں مـنصب بـه بـرادرش قاضی نصر الله قرار یافت (تاریخ سندھ قلمی ورق ۹۸، ۹۹)

By appointment of Mahdavi Qazis, it may be deduced that not only the elites, but general population also were predominantly Mahdavi, since Mirza Shah Hasan also was a Mahdavi as his father Mirza Shah Baig.

4. Mir Zanoon (Rz), Ruler of Farah:

He was the commander in Chief of Mirza Sultan Husain's army of Herat and teacher of his son Badiuzzama. Farah was given under his administrative control where hundreds of Mahdavis were living with Imamana (As). Shaikhul Islam sent four scholars to investigate the Claim of Mahdiat by Imamana (As), which fact was already mentioned earlier. It is a fact that the scholars of Farah became Mahdavi after being convinced with the deliberations of Imamana (As). This fact was also recorded by Badayuni that those scholars sent by Shaikhul Islam too had accepted Imamana (AS) as Mahdi-e-Akhiruzzaman (As) and resided along with Imamana (As) at Farah. Other historians also had written that his grandson had appointed Mahdavis to the venerable post of Qazi. Even today nobles and elites, like Nawab of Palanpur and Radhanpur, are still Mahdavis. Thus, there should be no doubt to accept what had been written in Mahdavi literature. It is a fact that Mir Zannoon (Rz), with pomp and glory, came to hear Imamana's sermon with opposing intent, and when he was trying to reach Imamana (As), Imamana (As) asked him by name to sit down where he was, and became surprised to know that Imamana (As) addressed him by name and sat obediently. After hearing the sermon, he became Mahdavi. The episode of striking the sword on the person of Imamana (As) had already been reported earlier, wherein his hands became numb and stiff and the sword did not work. Imamana (As) told Mir Zannoon (Rz) that the sword had to cut, fire to burn and water to drown, but they could not affect on the person of the True Mahdi (As) (under the commands of Allah).

5 & 6:Fahaadul Mulk And Saleem Khan:

When Imamana (As) came to Chapaneer, Sultan Mahmood Begdha sent his two confident nobles, Farhadul Mulk and Saleem Khan, to Imamana (As) for discussion and for collecting facts about Imamana (As). When they came to the Ek-Minara masjid, where Imamana (As) was delivering his sermon, they saw hundreds were there to hear him and none paid any attention to their arrival. They felt it very much. Still after hearing the sermon they accepted him as Mahdi (As) and they informed Sultan Mahmood about what they saw and how they accepted him as the True Mahdi (As). On that Sultan too became Mahdavi. As per Mulla Abdul Qader Badayuni's version, the Sultan had really met Imamana (As) and offered allegiance to Imamana (As) personally.

7. Mubarizul Mulk (Rz):

He was the son of Malik Yaqoob who was the son in law of Malik Sulaiman Baadiwal, and the Commissioner of Patan, Gujrat. Two thousand troops were under his command. During his life time Malik Sulaiman had transferred his Jagir in favor of his Son In law. His mausoleum is still standing at the Northern side of Patan, near Pati Pall Gate abetting to the river. The entire family of Malik Sulaiman (Rz) accepted Imamana (As) as Mahdi-e-Mauood (AS), the fact of which is recorded in chapter 40 of "Shawahedul Vilayet".

It had already been pointed out that countless people had accepted Imamana (As) as the true Mahdi (As) and this fact had been further certified by Badayuni that: "when he arrived at Farah a sea of people accompanied him. Among this multitude there were nobles, scholars, Sufis, elites, ministers, administrators whose names could not be recorded in our books for lack of information"; however, author of "Shawahedul Vilayet" had written few names of renowned companions and their successors and stated that:

"May it be known to all that these names are just a fraction of one out of a thousand; if all names are recorded it will become a voluminous book."	بدانيد و آگاه باشيد كه اين اسامى نوشته شد از هزار يكى و از بسيار اند كے نوشته شد و اگر سربسر نوشته شود كتاب مطلول مى شود

The names mentioned above are a very few which denote that men of every rank and file and every walk of life had accepted Imamana (As) as Mahdi-e-Mauood (As), whether they were kings, administrators, nobles, ministers, scholars, elites, Sufis, commoners, and even soldiers.

When an infidel affirms "Wajhu Laisa Bi wajhe Kazib", "this face could not be of a liar" is presented as a proof of the prophethood of the holy Prophet (Slm), then why wee shouldf not present so many people of every walk of life who had accepted Imamana (As) as the true Mahdi-e-Mauood (As) from the depth of their heart and soul and with utmost devotion and love, as the concrete proof for Imamana's Mahdiat? Particularly there had been no pressure, coercion , fear of sword or offer of greed or monetary temptations!!!

CHAPTER-FIVE
Daira-e-Mahdavia, Mahdavis, Mahdavi Faith and Mahdavi Preachers

Dairah-e-Mahdavia and "Tabqaat-e-Akberi":

Nizamuddin Ahmad Bakhshi has written in his book "Tabqaat-e-Akbari" about Abdullah Khan Niyazi (Rz) and Sheik Alaai (Rz) that:

شیـخ عبـداللـه نیازی افغان که از مریدان نامدار شیخ سلیم چشتی بود از مکه معاودت نمود و روش مهدویه که بـعقیـده ایشـان سیـد محمد جونپوری مهدی موعود است اختیار کرده در بیانه رحل اقامت انداخت شیخ علائی را وضع خوش آمد فریفتهٔ صحبت او گشت و طریقه آبا و اجداد را ترک داده خلائق را بروش مهدویه دعوت می نمود ، رسـم ایـس طائفـه در بیرون شهر (در)همسائیگی شیخ عبدالله توطن باجمعی کثیر از احباب و اصحاب خـود کـه بـوی گرویده بود بطریق تجرد بسرمی بود و هر روز در وقت نماز تفسیر قرآن مجید به نوعی می گفت که هـر کـس کـه در مجلس او حاضر می بود اصلاً پئ کار خود نمی رفت و ترک اهل و عیال کرده داخل دائره مهدی می گشت و یا از معاصی تائب شده به مجاز سید محمد مریدی میکرد و اگر کشت یاز راعت و تجارت میکرده وه یك در راه خـدا صرف می نمـود ـ پـس همـچنان شده که پدر از پسر وزن از شوهر مفارقت گزیده راه فقر و فنا پیش گـرفتـنـد و درنـذ ورو فتـوح که بادمی آمد خورد و کلان علیٰ السویه شریك بود و اگر چیزے بهم نمی رسید تادو سه روز بـه فاقه می گزرانید و اظهار نمی نمودند و به پاس انفاس اوقات خود مصروف میدا شتند و شمشیر و سپر و سائر اسـلحه همه وقت همراه داشته در شهر و بازار هر جا نا مشروع میدیدند اولاً برفق و مدارا منع نموده اگر پیش نمی رفت قهـراً و جبـراً نا مشروع آن را تـغیـیـر میداد و از حکام شهر هر که موافق اومی بود در امداد اومی کو شید و هر که منکر بود قدرت مقاومت نداشت (طبقات اکبری ،طبع نولکشور ۱۲۹۲ء صفحه ۲۳۷)

"Sheik Abdullah Niyazi (Rz): An Afghan Pathan who was one of the khalifas of Sheik Saleem Chishti, returned from Makkah and settled down at Biyana having accepted Mahdavia Faith. According to this faith Syed Mohammed Juanpuri (As) is the Promised Mahdi (As). Another elite Sheik Alaai (Rh) became fascinated with Abdullah Khan's way of worship and was so attractive that he joined his company. He left his forefather's way of life and accepted Mahdavia faith and started propagation of this faith. Following the way of life of Mahdavis, he started living in the outskirts of the city in the vicinity of the Daira of Shaikh Abdullah Khan Niyazi (Rz) along with his several friends and companions who had become his devotees adopting celibacy and solitude. Every day after prayers he used to deliver the commentary on the holy Qur'an in such an impressive and effective manner that whoever attended these deliberations would forget his business and abandoned his family and friends and joined into his Dairah. He used to politely request the new comers to repent from the past sins, he used to make disciples in the name of Syed Mohammed (As). Those who were agriculturists or business men, they used to pay "Ushr" ten percent of their income for the cause of Allah. Thus fathers left their sons, husbands left their wives and joined the Daira adopting the life of poverty, hunger and self denial. Whatever gifts and offerings were amassed in the Daira, were used to be distributed equally among themselves. If they could not get anythin, they used to starve and fast for days together and never beg and always were busy in remembrance of Allah. They used to keep their swords and ammunitions always along with them when they go outside the Diara. If they happened to see anything against Sharia, they used to stop it in a polite manner first. Then if they do not comply they used force. If officials who were in favour of them used to extend their help, and those who were against them, had no strength to stop them."

Mahdavi Daira and "Muntakhabatut Tawareekh':

In the same manner Mulla Abdul Qader Badayuni had written about Shaikh Alaai in his "Muntakhabatut Tawareekh" that:

شیخ علائی چوں روش اورادید بسیار خوش کردو باصحاب خویش گفت که دین و ایمان این است که میاں عبدالله نیازی دار دو روشے که ما گرفتار آنیم جز بت پرستی و زنارداری نیست

رباعی

تا یك سر موے از تو هستی باقی است

اندیشه كار بت پرستی باقی است

گفتی بت و زنار شکستم رستم

این بت که زپندار پرستی باقی است

و طریقهٔ آبا و اجداد خود را ترك داده و كان مشیخت و مقتدائی رابرهم زده و پا برسر پندار و غرور نهاده دریِ استرضائِ اقربائِ خویش گشت و بطریق فروتنی و خواری کفش پیش پاے جماعه، که ایشان را سابق آزرده بودمی نهاد و مد و معاش و لنگر و خانقاه گزاشته و وادی ترك و تجرید پیش گرفته آنچه اسباب دنیوی تا کتب هم که داشت همه

رابرفقرا ایثار کرد و با حیلهٔ خویش گفت که مرادرد طلب حق گریبان گیر گشته اگر بر فقر و فاقه صبر می توانی کرد همراه من باش بسم الله و گر نه حصه خود ازای اموال برآور و زمام اختیار بردست خود بگیر و برو

مـصـرع ، داری سرمـا و گـر نـه دورا زبـرمـا

اوخـود بـرایـن شیـوه اشـد رضـا داشـت

بیت

کـار دیـس بـعـضـی زنان شایـد بـه از مـردان کنند

در دلیـری شیـر مـاده بهـتـر از شیـر نـراسـت

و در جـوار میـان عبدالله آمده از و بطریق پاس انفاس تلقین ذکر بروشی که میان این طائفه مقرر اسـت گـرفـت مـعـانـی قرآن و نکـات و دقـایـق آن بآسانی براو مکشوف گشت و جمیع کثیر از احباب و اصحاب که باوی جهت اتحاد و اعتقاد داشتند بعضی مجرد و بعضی متاهل صحبت اور ابجان اختیار کرده راه سلوك را بقدم توکل سپرده سـی صـد خانه دار مردم بی کسب و تجارت و زراعت و حرفت دیگر بسرمی بروندو هرگاه چیزی از غیب می رسیـد ـ قسـمـت به رؤس افراد بطریق سویت و عدالت میکردند و فحوائی کریمه " رجال لا تلهیهم تجارة ولا بیع عن ذكر الله " راشـعـار خـود سـاخـته اگر از گرسنگی می مردندهم می مردندند دم نمی زدند اگر کسی ترك عزیمت بموجب قرار داد ایشان داد و کسبی میکردو البته وه یك در راه خـدای تعالیٰ صرف می نمود و دو وقت بعد از نماز فجر و نماز دیگر صغار و کبار درآن دائره جمع آمده بیان قرآن می شنید تدو شیخ علائی را نفس گیرائی موثر چنان بود که در وقت تفسیر قرآن مجید از و هـر کسی کـه مـی شنیـد اکثر خود دست از کاروبار دنیوی باز داشته آن صحبت اختیار میکردند و ترك خانمان و عیـال و اطفـال نموده و برشدت فقر و فاقه و مجاهده صبر کرده دیگر پیرامون کسب و کار خود نمی گشتند و اگر آن هـمـت نمی بود لا اقل توبه از معاصی و ملاهی و مناهی خود هیچ جانه رفته بود بسیارے را خود چنان دیده شد که شب از لـوازم خـانـه و ظـروف و آلات طنج را حتی از نمك و اردو آب هم خالی ساخته سرنگون می ماندندو هیچ چیزے از اسباب معیشت باخود از غایت اعتماد بر رزاقی حق تعالیٰ نمی گذاشتند و روز نوروزی نو دستور العمل ایشان بود و شۀ از احـوال ایـن طـائـفـه در کتـاب نـجـات الـرشید ایراد یافته آنجا باید دید و باوجود این اسلحه و آلات حرب برای دفع مخالفان همیشه باخود میداشتند تا اگر کسی بر حقیقت معامله ایشان اطلاع نمید اشت کسی خیال میکرد که ایشان اغنیا اند یـحسبهم الـجـاهـل اغنیـاء مـن التعفف و هر جا در شهر و بازار نا مشروعی و منهی میدید ند جبراً و قهراً رفته احتساب میکـردند و مـلاحـظـه از حاکم نمید اشتند و اغلب اوقات غالب بودند و از حکام شهر هر که موافق مذهب و مشرب ایشـان بـود در امـدادمی کـو شیـدند دهر منکر بود تاب مقاومت نداشت در امدادمی کو شیدند دهر منکر بود تاب مقاومت نداشت و کار بجای کشید که پدر از پسر و

بـرادر و شوهـر از زن مفارقت گزیده در دائرۀ مهدویه در آمده راه فقر و فنا پیش می گرفتند (منتخب التواریخ طبع کلکته جلد اول صفحه ۳۹۶ تا ۳۹۸)

When **Shaikh Alaai (Rz)** noticed his (Abdullah Khan Niyazi's) way of living, became very much fascinated and told his companions that: "Religion and faith is that which Abdullah Khan Niyazi (Rz) is performing, and the way we are performing is nothing but idolatry". He relinquished his forefather's way of life; abandoning the pride and vanity and kicking haughtiness and boasting, started heartening his relatives and very submissively and humbly served with devotion to whom he had previously treated badly, thus, he left every means of earning and adopted the life of solitude. Whatever he had, even books, he distributed among poor and said to his wife "craving for Truth is so captivating that: If you agree to bear the hardships of poverty and hunger, you are welcome, otherwise take whatever you require from me and go free from all entanglements". But his wife, too, was very appreciative of that sort of life. She agreed to go hand in hand with him for the cause of Allah and religion. They came under the guidance of Miyan Abdullah Khan Niyazi (Rz) and got necessary instructions for remembrance of Allah as practiced by Mahdavis. This opened the way for understanding the intricacies and secrets of the Holy Qur'an. A vast number of his relatives and friends who had faith in him and who were ready to cooperate, assembled around him. Some were singles and some had families. All with love and affection cultivated cordial relationship purely on firm trust on Allah. Three hundred families without any source of fixed income either through business or employment or cultivation were living together. Whatever they received from invisible sources they used to distribute equally among themselves. Even in acute hunger they would never demand or beg. If any Mahdavi earned livelihood, then he would donate ten percent for the cause of Allah. Every one after the prayer of Fajr or after prayer of Asr, joined to hear the commentary of the Qur'an by Hzt.Shaik Alaaii(Rh).. The efficacy of the sermons of Shaikh Alaai (Rz) was so impressive and heart touching that if anyone who happened to hear once, would leave his business, family and every source of income and joined the Daira, agreeing to bear hardships, let what may come. Some were there who instead of joining the Daira life, used to repent their past sins and started living the life of austerity. Most of the people used to empty their utensils even with water during the night with the firm belief and trust in Allah, the Sole Sustainer and the Provider. They never used to hoard anything.

"Their motto was to earn daily, spend daily. I have written their life pattern in "Najatur Rasheed" also, which may be referred for further details. They used to be ready with ammunition to defend themselves from the opponents. If they come across any action or thing against Shariat, in the city or bazaar, they used to stop it even by force.(These happened rarely.)

(Note: We may take the above extra ordinary erfforts were just for eradicating the innovations, bid'ats as an exemption, since Imamana and his five caliphs never permitted any coercive method or forrce with regard to implementation of Mahdavi Doctrine. Khundmiri).

They had least fear from the officials and often they prevailed. If any official was of their creed, would help in their zeal to uphold Shariat, and if the official was of another creed, he would not confront them. The matter had gone so far that father and son, husband and wife, brother and brother became alien and joined the Diara with full trust in Allah and were ready to bear every eventuality."

Mahdavi Dairahs And "Ma'asira-e-Raheemi":

Mullah Abdul Baqi Nihavandi had written about Daira-e-Mahdavia in his "Mua'sar-e-Raheemi" that:

از قضایائ غریبه که در زمانه سلیم خان دست داد واقعه شیخ علائی است و تفصیل آن برسبیل اجمال آن که پدر شیخ علائی شیخ حسن نام داشت و بخدمت شیخ سلیم در قصبۀ بیانه برجادۀ شیخی ارشاد طالبان می نمود ، چون او در گذشت شیخ قائم مقام او شد و بار شاد طالبان قیام نمود اتفاقاً شیخ عبدالله نیازی افغان که از مریدان شیخ سلیم چشتی بود از مکه معاودت نمود ، روش مهدویه که بعقیدۀ ایشان سید محمد جونپوری مهدی موعود است اختیار کرده در بیانه رحل اقامت انداخت ، چون شیخ علائی را اوضع و خوش آمد فریفته او شد و ترک روش آبا و اجداد او نموده بروش مهدویه دعوت می نمود و برسم این طائفه در بیرون شهر در پهلوی شیخ عبدالله توطن اختیار نمود و باجمعی از مریدان در آنجا به طریق توکل بسر می بردوهر روز دو مرتبه تفسیر قرآن میگفت و بنوعی از روی اثر می گفت که هر کس می شنید داخل مهدویه می شد و بسیار این چنین شد که از سخنان اوپسر از پدروزن از شوهر برآمده با ایشان محشور شدند و راه فقر و فنا پیش گرفتند و در نذر و تحف که باومی آمد خرد و کلان در تقسیم علی السویه بودند و اگر چیزی نمی رسید سه روم فاقه می گذرانید ندو اظهار نمی نمودند و پاس انفاس اوقات مصروف می داشتند و اسلحه از همه چیز باخودمی داشتند و در شهر و بازار هرنا مشروع می دیدند اول رفق و مدارامی نمودند و اگر پیش نمی رفت قهراً و جبراً تغیر آن نا مشروع میدادند و از حکام شهر هر که موافق ایشان می بود در امداد اومی کو شیدند و هر که منکر بود قدرت مقاومت نداشت (مآثر رحیمی ،طبع کلکته ، جلد اول صفحه ٦٣٧ ، ٦٣٨)

It is stated that during the period of Saleem Shah Soori, a rare thing happened relating to Shaikh Alaai (Rz). In short, the details are that Sheik Alaai's father was Sheik Hasan who, under the patronage of Sheik Saleem Chishti was employed as a Shaik. He used to guide the seekers. After his demise Sheik Alaai (Rz) succeeded his father and started guiding his disciples. By chance, Sheik Abdullah Khan Niyazi (Rz), an Afghan, who was a disciple of Sheik Saleem Chishti came back from Makkah and adopted Mahdavi Faith by accepting Syed Mohammed Juanpuri (As) was the real Mahdi-e-Mauood (As), and settled down in Biyana. Sheik Alaai (Rz) was very much fascinated by this faith and the way of worship. Thus, he left his forefather's way of life and adopted this faith and started properly propagating it. He adopted the same system of life that the Mahdavis were following, and established his own Dairah in the outskirt of the city near the Dairah of Shaik Abdullah Khan Niyazi (Rz) and lived there along with his followers with austerity and trust in Allah. He used to deliver sermons twice a day on Qur'an. His sermons were so impressive and captivating that if a person heard it once, he would become Mahdavi. That was not enough, son left father, husband left his wife and joined the Daira of Sheik Alaai (Rz) and accepted to bear hunger and poverty under Mahdavi way of living. Whatever gifts or grants were received in the dairah, used to be distributed equally among the residents of the dairah. And if nothing was received, they used to bear it for days and spent their whole time in perpetual remembrance of Allah. They had such an un-flinching faith and trust in Allah that they never hoarded for the next day and used to empty their utensils even with water during the night. They used to keep their ammunitions always with them. If they happened to see any act against Shariat, they used to reprimand first, with kindness and softness, if not abided, they used to stop it by force. Officials who knew would help them, and if an opponent, he would never question for their strict actions."

These are a few facts of the Daira-e-Mahdavia which was established by Sheik Alaai (Rz) in Biyana. Author of "Tabkhat-e-Akberi" states that there were 600 to 700 families in that Dairah. These are the facts of a "Tab'-e-Taba'ie" (successor of the companion), since Shaik Abdullah Khan Niyazi (Rz) was the disciple of a companion of Imamana(As). According to the Author of "Khatim-e-Sulaimani, " Sheik Abdullah Khan Niyazi (Rz) had accepted Mahdavia faith in Gujrat or in Deccan from either through any of the companions of Imamana (As) or the successors of the companions. Some say he was benefitted by Shah Nemat (Rz) or by Miyan Khund Sheik Muhajir (Rz).

The distinctive features of Dairah-e-Mahdavia have been well mentioned in the books, "Mua'sir-e-Raheemi","Tabqat-e-Akberi" and "Muntakhabat-e-Tawareekh" etc.; written by non Mahdavi writers. From them we came to know the routine which was in vogue in the dairahs of Mahadvis. They are:

1. Congregational Prayers were made obligatory in the Dairah; Everyone whether elder or younger, used to be present for prayers in time.

2. Commentary of the Qur'an used to ber delivered twice, in which every one used to attend without fail, one after the prayer of Fajr, the other after the prayer of Asr. These commentaries were so impressive and captivating that initiated the listener to leave his worldly affairs.

3. They were very particular in propagating the true and practical purpose of "Amar Bil Maroof WA nahi Anil Munkar", meaning, "Enjoin virtue and abhor evil". They were themselves very strict about it and used for emphasise on others with kindness and softness first, otherwise with pressure and if necessary with the help of the sword, having no fear of government officials.

4. Trust in Allah was their motto.

5. They got inspiration when they start the commentary of the Holy Qur'an and those deliberations were very impressive and heart touching.

6. Whatever money received in the Dairah, they used to distribute equally among all residents. Thus it reminds the tradition "Yaqsimul Maal Sihahan" (Distribute Equally).

7. Businessmen and agriculturists used to pay ten percent of their income for the cause of Allah which was in conformity with the Holy Qur'an and traditions.

Description of Ushr.

"Oh ye who believe; Give of the good things, which you have honorably earned with skills and from the fruits of the Earth, which We have produced" (2:267).

يـا ايها الذين آمنوا انفقوا من طيبات ما كسبتم و مما اخرجنا لكم من الارض (البقرة ركوع ٣٧)

From this verse we may not be able to decide how much to spend from what we earn with our labour and how much to spend from the produce of the Earth? Anyhow, Sheik Abdul Haq, Muhaddis-e-Dahlavi, had stated that Imam Abu Hanifa (Rz) had deduced from this tradition in the following manner: "Ma Akhrajatal Arz fafihil usher" meaning, "Take ten percent from the produce of the Earth". The words "Ma Akhrajna " coordinates to "Ma Kasabtum". Whether it be a produce from the earth, or an income from service, on both the same formula is applied, therefore, ten percent of either produce of earth or of personal earnings, each of the category is required to give away ten percent of the earnings. The verse and the tradition both confirm this about paying ten percent. Therefore it is imperative to take out ten percent not only from the produce from Earth, but also from that which a man earns through his service. "Hashia-e-Insaf Nama" informs:

"Hazrat Miran Alaihis Salaam said whatever Allah gives you, give ten percent of it, whether much or less."

نقل است حضرت میران علیه السلام فرمودند هرچه خدا تعالیٰ شمار ابد هد عشر بد هید اگر اند کے باشد یا بسیار الیٰ آخره (صفحه ۱۹۴)

Apart from this, Hazrat Ali (Rz) stated:
"One person came to the holy Prophet (Slm) and informed that he had 100 Ooqiah (Currency) out of which he handed over ten (in charity). Another man told that he had 100 Dinars and he had given 10 out of it. Another man said he had 10 Dinars , he had given one out of it. The holy Prophet (Slm) praised them all and said "all of you are equal in the Blessings of Allah because you have paid ten percent (Ushr) from your earnings. Then the Prophet (Slm) recited" "Yanfiqoo was'atha Min Sa'atha" Spend as per your ability."

عن علی قال جاء الرجل الی رسول الله فقال کانت لی مایة اوقیة تصدقت منها بعشرة اواق و قال آخر یا رسول الله کانت لی مایة دینار فتصدقت منها بعشرة دنانیر و قال آخر یا رسول الله کانت لی عشره دنا نیر فتصدقت منها بدینار فقال کلکم قد احسن و انتم فی الاجر سواء تصدق کل رجل منکم بعشر ماله ثم قرء رسول الله صلعم لینفق ذوسعة من سعته (کنزل العمال طبع حیدرآباد، جلد سوم، صفحه ۳۱۰)

Both the Verse and the Tradition direct for paying ten percent which is called "Ushr". It may not be doubted from the verse, "Yanfiqoo Min Taiyyibat" which refers to Zakat, because other verse tells that whatever you have to spend, spend for your parents and for your relatives because Zakat is not meant for them. Therefore "Zakat" and "Infaq" are two different categories. It is a fact that during the Islamic Rule, Muslims were not levied with Khiraj, but only with Ushr which was being collected. In case of other than produce of land, a cloth merchant used to give cloth, and the herd of cattle used to give cattle. Thus it is clear that Ushr is not Zakat for Mahdavis, because Ushr is over and above Zakat. Another tradition tells that your asset is bound to pay zakat plus ten percent over and above Zakat.

(Note: unfortunately, Mahdavis do not want to hear about Ushr any more and if anyone speaks about it, he is ridiculed and asked to keep quiet, since some of them even avoid paying Zakat every year, leave aside Ushr. On the other hand, we have examples of other sects like Agha Khani and disciples of Syedana Burhanuddin have adopted collection of

Ushr systematically which has become a healthy and the wealthy economic source for the betterment of their society, like distribution of monthly income to the needy ones, to the destitute, to the divorcees. And also they help for mass marriages of the poor un-married girls. Sometimes they help monetarily for those who have some special skills to establish their own enterprises, or for intelligent students for furtherance of their educational ambitions. If we adopt according to the injunctions of the holy Qur'an, traditions and directions of Imamana (As) our society too will become prosperous like the other sects. I humbly pray Allah to inspire among us the zeal and enthusiasm to donate Ushr for the betterment of our poorest members, students, the destitute and the real needy ones. There is no Dairah system nowadays, hence the localities where we live should organize ourselves to collect funds systematically and have enumeration of the needy ones and distribute accordingly. For your information I am practically adhering to the dictates as mentioned above. A humble request by this translator is to all Mahdavis to adopt Hzt. Omer's method or Hzt. Abu Zarr Ghifari's method which is described on the following pages for guidance).

Daira-e-Mahdavia & Socialism:

The founder of Socialism was Karl Marx was born in Germany in 1818. When he was expelled from France, went to England in 1845 till his death in 1883. His communist ideology was practically established in Russia in 1917 AD. It has three defects.

1. Religion has no place in it.

2. In order to invoke equal distribution much of the bloodbath was the result, on account of which it had utterly failed.

3. In administrative set up, the president is above every one.

As against it, in Dairas of Mahdavia:

1. Religion has a dominant force which presented the early period of Islam.

2. For equal distribution there was no bloodshed. Daira was composed of every type of people and of every walk of life. All actions were in full conformity with the dictates of the Holy Qur'an.

3. Whatever was distributed it was an equal distribution. The leader of the Daira had no preference over other residents.

Margoleouth a famous Orientalist of England, read a thesis on "Mahdavis and Mahdiat" on 8th.December, 1915 AD. This thesis was already published in which he had written about Imamana (As) and Mahdavis, mostly based on the writings of Mullah Abdul Qader Badayuni's "Muntakhabatut Tawareekh" and particularly with reference to Miyan Sheik Alaai (Rz), stating that: "According to the contemporary historians, he started a sort of communistic society, bestowing all his worldly possessions, and even distributed his books among the poor" (On Mahdi and Mahdism: by D. S. Margoleouth). He was of the opinion that Dairas-e-Mahdavia were based on communism. The real fact is that Banu Hashim, the very forefathers of the holy prophet (Slm) were the founders of the equal distribution system. Author of "Al Aqdul Fareed" had stated that: Ibn Abbas (Rz) had addressed Ibn Muaviya and his companions by saying that:

"We swear to Allah that whatever you give to the world, we give more than that for Hereafter. And whatever you give for evil, we give moré than for virtue. Whatever you spend for your passions, we spend more than that for righteousness and distribute equally and do justice for all.".

و نـحـن واللّـه اعـطـى لـلآخـره منكم للدنيا واعـطـى فـى الـحق منكم فى الباطل و اعطى على التـقـوى مـنـكـم عـلـى الهـوى والقسم بـالسوية والعدل فى الرعية الى آخره (العقد ،الفريد ،طبع مصر، ١٢٩٣ء،الجزءالثانى صفحه ١٠٨)

The holy Prophet (Slm) also prophesied about Mahdi (As) that he would distribute equally. Thus Dairah Mahdavia performed in total conformity with this tradition.

Margoleouth had wrongly stated that Miyan Abdullah Khan Niyazi (Rz) was the pupil of Imamana (As). His assertion that there was little difference in the way of life of Ibn Timiya (Rz. died 524 H.) and after him whoever claimed Mahdiat in Islam. This is wrong, because according to Ibn Timiya (Rz) Ibn Tumurt had done good deeds as well as bad deeds. In yet another book it is written that Ibn Tumurt was an embodiment of both evil and virtue.

On the other hand Mullah Abdul Quader Badayuni, in spite of not being a Mahdavi, had written about Imamana (As) after one hundred years from the demise of Imamana (As), he had never mentioned anything bad about Imamana (As).

Distribution of Wealth And The Holy Prophet (Slm):

Sheik Abdul Haq has written about distribution of wealth during the period of the holy Prophet (Slm) in his "Madarejun Nabuwat" that:

"In brief, whatever the holy Prophet (Slm) used to get, he distributed everything without any fear of poverty and without feeling any anxiety about the future.'

بـالجمله هر چه بدست آمدے بدادے و چناں بدادے كـه از فـقـر و نيستى نه ترسيدے ونه انديشيدے (مدارج النبوة ،طبع نولكشور ١٩١٤ء، جلد اول صفحه ٤٩)

The following are some instances:

"Hazrat Anas (Rz) had stated that the holy Prophet (Slm) never hoarded anything even for the next day."

(١) عـن انـس قـال كـان الـنبى صلى الله عليه و سلم لايدّخرشئا لغد (ترمذى باب الزهد)

2."Reported in "Tirmizi" that 90,000 Dirham were brought before the holy Prophet (Slm) and were kept on a mat, he distributed them all without refusing any person till every thing was gone."

(٢) تـرمذى روايت كرده است كه آورده شد نزد آنحضرت نـود هزار درم پس نهاده شد بر حصيرے پس قسمت كرد همه راورد نكر هيچ سائلے را تا فارغ شد از آن (مدارج النبوة ،طبع نولكشور ١٩١٤ء، جلد اول صفحه ٤٨)

3."Reported in "Sahih Bukhari" by Anas (Rz) that: Bulk of wealth came from Bahrain. The holy Prophet (Slm) asked to keep it on the mat of the Masjid. When he completed his prayers, he came to the place where amount was kept and sat down. He distributed everything and when he stood up there was not a single Dirham left undistributed."

(٣) در صـحـیـح بـخـاری از حدیث انس آمده که آورده شـد نزد آنحضرت مالے از بحرین فرمود بریزید آں را در مسـجـد پـس بیـرون آمـد بـه سوے مسجد و نگاه کرد جـانب آں و چوں برگشت از نماز آمد و نبشست بر آں مـال و نـدید هیچ کس را مگر آں که داد بوے از آں مال .... پس برخاست آنحضرت و باقی نه ماند یك درم (مـدارج الـنـبـوۃ ،طبع نولكشور ١٩١٤ء، جلد اول صفحه ٤٩)

Booty from Bahrain:

Ibn Abi Sheeba (Rz) tells that about one hundred thousand Dirham had come which were sent by Ali Bin Al Hazrami (Rz) towards revenues for the first time from Bahrain which was brought before the holy Prophet (Slm) and was distributed equally among the present.

Distribution during the period of Khulfa-e-Rashedeen (Rz):

Whatever the system of distribution was in vogue during the period of the holy prophet (Slm) was continued during the period of Hzt.Abu Bakr(Rz) , and whatever wealth was received was distributed among all by Hazrat Abu Bakr (Rz) and it was continued also during the early period of Hazrat Omer (Rz) as well. But later on Hazrat Omer (Rz) established Baitul Maal, with an aim to distribute to the needy ones alone. This was objected by many companions of the Prophet (Slm) since they considered Baitul Mall was a symbol of hoarding money. But Hazrat Omer (Rz) wanted to systematize distribution of wealth to the needy ones first. For that purpose he collected data of those who were poor enough and deserved systematic distribution so that none should be left unattended and those who had enough money should not get anything from the Baitul Maal.

Abu Zarr Gifari's Faith:

Sheik Abdul Haq states that:

"Abu Zarr (Rz) was one of the eminent companions of the holy Prophet (slm). Hoarding of wealth was forbidden according to him, even after paying zakat."

ابـو ذر از زهـاد صحـابـه و کبرائ ایشـاں بود بـمـذهـب وے ادخار حرام است اگرچه بعد از ادائ زكـوٰۃ باشد (مدارج النبوۃ ،طبع نولكشور ١٩١٤ء، جلد اول صفحه ٤٨)

This tells that Abu Zarr Ghifari (Rz) was against hoarding and declared it unlawful. The divorced wife of Abdul Rahman bin Aouf (Rz) was given 80,000 Dirham. When Abu Zarr (Rz) heard it he named Bin Aouf as a Kafir, although according to "Tuhfa-e-Asna-e-Ashria", he knew what glad tidings had been given by the holy Prophet (Slm) to Bin Aouf (Rz). Author of "Keemia-e-Sa'adat" has stated that a group of companions did not feel good with Abdul Rahman bin Aouf (Rz), because he left a plentiful inheritance. Some of the companions even feared that his act of hoarding would drag him towards the Hell.

It is said that on account of Abu Zarr's strictness, Hazrat Muaviya did not let Abu Zarr (Rz) to stay in Syria. Similarly Hazrat Abu Zarr (Rz) could not stay in Madinah also during the period of Hazrat Osman-e-Ghani (Rz). Author of "Tabri" thus stated that:

"Thus stood up Abu Zarr (Rz) in Syria and started telling to take care of the poor. Some were reprimanded for hoarding silver and gold and who did not spend for the cause of Allah. He reprimanded those who hoard would be stamped with fire on their forehead, on the back and on both sides of their faces. It was the firm belief of Abu Zarr (Rz) which was supported by many who justified that the wealth of the rich should be distributed to the poor. The matter became very troublesome for the rich who went to Hazrat Muavyia and complained. Muavyia in turn wrote to Hazrat Osman (Rz) that Abu Zarr (Rz) had created disorder in the country."

قام ابو ذر بالشام و جعل يقول يا معشر الاغنيا واسوا الفقراء بشر الذين يكنزون الذهب والفضة ولا ينفقونها فى سبيل الله بمكا و من نارتكوى بها جباهم و جنوبهم و ظهورهم فما زال حتى ولع الفقراء بمثل ذلك و اوجبوه على الا غنيا حتى شكا الا غنياما يلقون من الناس فكتب معاويه الى عثمان ان ابا ذر قد اعضل به و قد كان من امره ذيت و ذيت الى آخره (تاريخ طبرى جلد پنجم صفحه ۲۸۵۹)

At this juncture, on orders of Hazrat Osman (Rz), Hazrat Muavyia asked Abu Zarr (Rz) to go to Madinah. In Madinah too, Abu Zarr (Rz) expressed the same opinion. Hazrat Osman (Rz) replied" La Abarahum al zahad; "I do not insist the rich to adopt asceticism". Hearing this from the Khalifatul Muslimeen, Abu Zarr (Rz) did not like to stay in Madinah and asked Hazrat Osman (Rz) to allow him to leave Madinah since this place was not for him. Then he left for Zubdah which was four Manzil from Madinah.

Shah Abdul Aziz had written in "Tuhfa-e-Asna-e-Ashria" that:

"During the period of Hazrat Osman (Rz) bountiful stock of wealth arrived in the kingdom and the Muhajereen became millionaires. Abu Zarr (Rz) started lamenting on them. First he spoke to Hazrat Muavyia and reminded him about a p a r t i c u l a r   v e r s e !

در عهد عثمان دولت و ثروت و اموال عظيمه بدست اهل اسلام آمد و هرهمه از مهاجرين صاحب لكوك شدند ابو ذر زبان طعن در حق جميع مالداران دراز نمود اول با معاويه گفتگو كردو و اين آية را متمسك

"Whoever hoards silver and gold in the treasury, and do not spend for the cause of Allah, reprimand them of the pitiable fire of the hell." Then said that it is an obligation to spend the whole wealth. Although Hazrat Muavyia and other companions tried to convince Abu Zarr (Rz) that "Infeqaq" means Zakat (Which is wrong) only and not the entire wealth. They even referred to two verses which described how the legacy was to be distributed among the heirs of the deceased. But Abu Zarr (Rz) never went against his doctrine."

ساخت "والـذيـن يكـنزون الذهب والفضة ولا يـنـفـقـونها فى سبيل الله فبشرهم بعذاب اليم" و كسانيكه گنج مى كنند زرو نقره را و خرج نمى كـنـند آن را در راه خدا پس بشارت ده ايشان را بعذاب درد دهنده و انفاق كل مال را فرض قرار داد هـر چند معاويةؓ و اصحاب ديگر اور افهمانيد نـد كـه مـرا و انفاق قدر زكوة است نه كل مال و شـاهـد بـرايـس اراده آيـت ميراث و فرائض است زيـراكـه اگر انفاق كل مال واجب مى بود تقسيم متـروكـه و جهى نـداست اصرار بر معتقد خود نـمـوده (تحفته اثنا عشريه مطبوعه ثمر هند باب دهم صفحه ۵۰۸، ۵۰۹)

It may be made clear that there is no difference between "Infaqaq"and "legacy". Shah Abdul Aziz's statement informs that Muhajereen became millionaires. Abu Zarr's doctrine was that there should be no capitalism in Islam. Zakat itself could not stop capitalism. He wanted that the treasures full with silver and gold should be distributed to all Muslims. According to him if it was distributed, naturally, their heirs would get their legacy, but not the treasures of silver and gold, which should not become legacy to them. Abu Zarr (Rz) wanted that these hoardings should be legally stopped. Here "Kanz", means treasure, which is being prohibited and not the legacy. When asked by companions how much wealth is permissible? The holy Prophet said: Lisan Zakir WA Qalb Shaker", means, *(that much, to which, your conscience is satisfied, then offer gratitude to Allah). (Ash'atul Lum'aat")*:

1. "It is said that when Hazrat Osman (Rz) had paid Marwan bin Hakam (Rz) whatever was due to him, about 3 lakh Dirham. Haris bin Hakam (Rz) and Zaid Bin Sabit Ansari (Rz) were paid one lakh each. On that Abu Zarr (Rz) reprimanded them that the burning fire of the Hell was their fate and recited the verse" Al Lazeena Yaknuzoonal Zahba Wal Fazztil Ayata"; those who hoard silver and gold would get hell firteas their reward". Thus Marwan Bin "Hakam (Rz) wrote to Hazrat Osman (Rz), who sent Natil, his servant, to prevent Abu Zarr (Rz) from his deliberations. On that Abu Zarr (Rz) told whether Osman (Rz) wanted me not to recite the verses of the holy Qur'an and not to say about those who were not following the dictates of Allah? I am ready to displease Osman (Rz) and to be resigned to the will of Allah, and not otherwise."

(١) قالوا الما اعطا عثمان مروان بن الحكم ما اعطاه اعطى الحارث بن الحكم بن ابى العاص ثلاثة ماية الف درهم و اعطى زيد بن ثابت الانصارى ماية الف درهم جعل ابو ذر يقول بشر الكانزين بعذاب اليم و يتلو قول الله عزو جل الذين يكنزون الذهب والفضة الآية فرفع ذلك مروان بن الحكم الى عثمان فارسل الى ابى ذر ناتلا مولاه ان انته عما يبلغنى عنك فقال أينهانى من قرأة كتاب الله و عيب من ترك امر الله فوالله لَأن أرضى الله بسخط عثمان احب الى وخير لى من ان اسخط الله برضاه (انساب الاشرف بلاذرى، مطبوعه عبرانيه، بيت المقدس ١٩٣٦ء جز خامس صفحه ٥٢)

2. "Hazrat Muavyia constructed, Khizra a Palace for himself in Damascus. Abu Zarr (Rz) asked Muavyia that if that palace was constructed from the money of Allah (Government money), then it is an embezzlement, and if it is yours, then it is an extravagance. Muavyia kept quiet. Abu Zarr (Rz) told that I am seeing such things are being introduced which are neither in Qur'an nor existing in traditions; therefore they are against the Qur'an and against Rasoolullah's Traditions. I see that truth is purposely being suppressed and the false is being flourished."

(٢) و بنى معاوية الخضراء بدمشق فقال يا معاوية ان كانت هذه الدار من مال الله فهى الخيانة ، ان كانت من مالك فهذا الاسراف فسكت معاوية و كان ابوذر يقول والله لقد حدثت اعمال ما اعرفها والله ماهى فى كتاب الله ولا سنة نبيه والله انى لأرى حقايطفا و باطلا يحيى و صاد قايكذب واثرة بغير تقى و صالحا مستاثراعليه(انساب الاشرف جز خامس صفحه ٥٢)

It is a fact that Abu Zarr (Rz) never allowed capitalism, according to him, it causes the wrath of Allah. Even the Prophet (Slm) praised Abu Zarr (Rz) as the most truthful person.

In view of the traditions and strict strictures from Hzt.Abu Zarr, there was no hoarding in Mahdavia Dairas. The sublime dictates of Imamana (As) "Momin Zakheera nami Kunad" means "Momin does not hoard" confirming the Doctrine of Abu Zarr(Rz).

"Hazrat Abu Huraira (Rz) narrates: Prophet Mohammad (Slm) came to Hazrat Bilal (Rz) who was holding a bag. He (Slm) asked Bilal (Rz) as to what was in the bag? Bilal (Rz) replied he was keeping dates in it for tomorrow. Prophet (Slm) reprimonded: "do you not fear from that fire which would be coming from the bag on the Day of Judgement to burn you? Oh! Bilal (Rz), spend and have trust in Allah, and never fear about poverty (that would envelop you). The Sustainer would keep you out of poverty."

عـن ابـى هـريره ان النبى صلى الله عليه و سلم دخل علـى بـلال و عـنده هرة من تمر فقال ما هذا يا بلال قـال شـے ادّخرته لغد فقال اما تخشى ان ترى له غذا بـخارا فـى نـار جهـنم يـوم الـقيـمة انفق يا بلال ولا تـخشـى مـن ذى الـعرش اقلالا (اشعته اللمعات جلد ثانى صفحه ٣٨)

Does Imamana's phrase "Momin does not hoard" not commensurate to the above traditions?

Scholars of non Mahdavi Faith adopt such methods which are against the above said dictates of both the Holy Qur'an and the traditions. Author of "Tabkhaat-e-Akberi" wrote about Mulla Abdullah Sultanpuri, and about Maqdoomul Mulk that:

"Maqdoomul Mulk died in Ahmadabad in 990 H. Akber appointed Fateh Ali to investigate the left over wealth of Maqdoomuil Mulk. Fatyeh Ali found many treasures and hoardings kept underground in the shape of graves which when opened, he found boxes filled with bricks of gold. These treasures were confiscated and deposited into the government treasury."

مـخـدوم الـمـلك در احمد آباد در گذشت در نهصد و نود قاضى على را از فتحپور به جهت تحقيق اموال اونا مزد شده به لاهور آمده چندان خزائن و دفائن اوپديد گشت كه قفل آن را به كليد وهم نتوان كشاد، از آن جمله چند صـندوق خشـت طلا از گورخانه مخدوم الملك كو به بهـانـه امـوات دفن كرده بود ظاهر شد و آنچه پيش مردم ماندعدد آن را اجز آفريدگار عزشانه ديگر كس نداند و همـه خشـت هابا كتب وے كه نيز حكم خشت داشت داخل خزانه عامره گرديد (منتخب التواريخ طبع كلكته جلد دوم صفحه ٣١١)

According to one tradition, whoever commits 40 days for Allah (In remembrance of Allah) his heart and tongue would be filled with springs of wisdom (vide page 60 "Sirajul Absar") For Mahdavis, it was not a matter of 40 days, remembrance is an obligation for the whole of the life. That is why justice loving historians, like. "Tabkhat-e-Akberi", "Muntakhabatut Tawareekh", "Najatur Rasheed", "Juanpur Nama", "Tuhfatul Kiram" have written in favour of Mahdavis, since Mahdavis' asceticism was an accepted attribute of Mahdavis. They knew that it was easier to become a Muslim than to become a Mahdavi.

Alamgir And Mahdavi Faith:

Aurangzeb Alamgir established his headquarters at Ahmed Nagar in 1094 H. He was informed that Mahdavis live in majority in Ahmed Nagar. Alamgir sent Qazi Abu Sayeed to the village Chichond of Ahmad Nager to bring Mahdavi scholars: viz; Miyan Sheik Ibrahim, Sheik Azam, Sheik Abul Qasim etc., for discussion about Mahdavi Faith. The details of this discussion had been written by Sheik Abul Qasim and at the end what Qazi Abu Sayeed had told to Alamgir about Mahdavis, had also been written in his own words:

"Alamgir asked (Abu Sayeed, the Qazi) whether he had understood about Mahdavia Faith and did you investigate about their Faith? Qazi replied: Mahadavis believe in the Oneness of Allah and propagate Shariat-e-Mustafavi (Slm). They are friendly with four companions of the Prophet (Slm). They take all four schools of faith as true. They are Ahl-e-Sunnata wal Jama'at and proclaim that Imam Mahdi (As) had come and gone." Alamgir asked: Whether any thing according to Shariat incumbent upon them? Qazi said: any penalty, ordering murder, imprisonment

"ابادشاه فرمودند عقیدۀ مهدویان واقف شدید و مذهب ایشان تحقیق کردید ، قاضی گفت ایشان بریگانگی خدائے تعالیٰ و برتبلیغ رسالت قائل اند و چهار یاران را دوست میدارند و چار مذهب برحق میدارند و اهل سنت جماعت هستند و امام مهدی آخر الزمان را آمد و گزشت میگویند ، بادشاه پرسید که برایشان چیزے از شرع می آید قاضی گفت که برایشان نه حدے و نه قتلے و از حبس و اخراج به حکم شرع هیچ لازم نیاید۔ بادشاه گفت ما خوب می دانیم که ایشان متشرع و عالم و عامل اند و سوال و جواب بدلیل آیات و احادیث واقوال بزرگان دین می سازند و کلمه گوے پیغمبر ما اند و خلاف شرع روانه ارند و برموافقت حکم خدا و رسول عمل می کنند و اعتقاد اهل سنت و جماعت

or expulsion, according to the Shariat, could not be decreed against them. Alamgir said: "We know very well that they are the followers of Shariat and true scholars. Their answers are based on Qur'an, traditions and sayings of ulema, They are believers of our Prophet (Slm). They would never tolerate anything against Shariat and their faith is of the Sunnat Wal Jama'at. As regards faith on Mahdi (As) and their firm belief that Mahdi (As) had come and gone does not fringe any Sharie jurisprudence. Hence let them go". Qazi came to his place and called us from Shah Sharief Majzoob's mausoleum where we were staying, and informed us about the discussion what had transpired between Alamgir and him. Finally Alamgir had given permission through the Qazi that they may go unhindered. Thus, we came back to Chichond."

میدارند و اینکه مهدی را آمد و گزشت میگویند ازیں سخن هیچ حکم شرع شریف برایشان لازم نیاید اوشان را رخصت کنید چوں قاضی بجای خود آمد مایان را از درگاه شاه شریف مجذوب طلب داشته حقیقت مجلس بادشاه ظاهر کرد گفت که پیش پادشاه رخصت ایشان حاصل شده است باید که بر مکان خود بروند پس به کساں از قاضی ابو سعید رخصت گرفته از روضه شاه شریف به موضع چچوند رسیدیم (مباحثه عالمگیری صفحه ۹)

Progress in age develops mental capacity and seriousness in a man. When Alamgir (as a young officer) was appointed as the Commissioner of Ahmadabad, on the decree given by the opponents of Mahdavis, the prince (Aurangzeb) ordered martyrdom of Syed Raju (Rz) and others in 1056 H. Author of "Mir'at-e-Ahmadi" had written that:

"Older people state that when Alamgir was an Heir Apparent, working as Commissioner of Ahmadabad, Syed Raju (Rz) who is well known as Syed Raju Shaheed, was ordered by the prince for his martyrdom" (of Syed Raju), here prince means Alamgir.

"از نقل کهن سالان ولیعهده مسموع شد که قتل سید راجو که اکنوں راجو شهید مشهور و معروف است ـ در ایام صوبه داری بامر بادشاه زاده به عمل آمد" (مراة احمدی ، طبع مطبع فتح الکریم بمبئی، جلد اول صفحه ۲۳۲)

(Note:"Mubahisa-e-Alamgiri"are reported in the Addendum for information of the readers, Along with Mabahesa-e-Khamsa, between Haz. Sheik Mustafa Gujrati (Rh) and the scholars of Akber's court.)

Farhang-e-Asafia And Mahdavia Faith:

Syed Ahmed Dehalvi, author of "Farhang-e-Asafia", under chapter "Aoulia-e-Hind" had written about Miran Syed Mohammed Juanpuri (As) and has discussed about the faith of Mahdavis that; "Faith of Mahdavia is based on the following points.:

1. To confirm to be a Mahdavi;
2. To repent (for past unjust actions, if committed) from one's depth of heart;
3. To perform work without any show;
4. Perpetual Remembrance of Allah is a must;
5. Worship of Allah;
6. Never to beg;
7. Relinquishing worldly desires;
8. To distribute whatever is surplus;
9. No hoarding for future.

Mahdavia Faith and Syed Abu Zafer Nadvi:

Syed Abu Zafer Nadvi, retired professor of Maha Vidialiya (College) Gujrat has written "Tareekh-e-Aoulia-e-Gujrat" which is translated in"Mir'at-e-Ahmadi" had said that:

"This author had met them(Mahdavis) many a time in Ahmadabad, Palanpur, Mysore, Channapatna etc.; and found them very peace loving and resolute persons, very strict in their faith. They are convinced about "Vision of Allah", possible during one's lifetime. To them 27th. Ramazan is the Shab-e-Qadr. After Isha, they offer Two Rak'aths more, behind their Murshid, as Dugana-e-Lailatul Qadr as a Thanksgiving to Almighty for starting His Revelation of Qur'an in that night on the holy Prophet (Slm) and lastly they proclaim Tasbeeh loudly in the congregation:

La Ilaha Ilallah   Mohammedur Rasoolullalh;

Allahu Ilahuna   Mohammed Nabiunah;

Al Qur'an wal Mahdi Imamana Aamanna Saddaqna".

All other acts are according to the Ahl-e-Sunnat. There are some differences in minor problems. Renunciation of worldly affairs; patience; trust in Allah; are the best principles of their life. I have read their books………. The force of their writings is manifested in practicing traditions (Sunnat-e-Mustafavi (Slm) and firm faith in mysticism which teaches Ihsan……….. This is not true to say that they do not invoke Blessings from Allah after prayers. They prefer to go in prostration and invoke Blessings after ablution, they offer Two Rak'ats as "Tahyyetul Wazoo". Their going in prostration and invoking Blessings secretly from Allah seems to any on-looker as if Mahdavis just had gone in prostration and not invoking for Blessings, which is not correct."

Mahdavi And Mahdavia Faith:

Mahdavia faith is that what had been dictated by Imamana (As):

"Mazhab-e-Maa Kitabullah wa Itteba-e-Mohammed Rasoolullah (Slm)". The secret of its expression lies in Narration of the holy Qur'an. The manner in which the Qur'an was revealed to the Holy Prophet (Slm) as a Revelation, in the same manner the efficacy and ability to narrate and comment the Qur'an was bestowed to Imamana (As) which is also may be taken as a Revelation. Imamana (As) has presented it as a Revelation before every person. Thus Allah had granted victory to Imamana (As) over others through his sublime Preachings based on the holy Qur'an and the Traditions. If any person had attended his sermons with an aim to discuss some pertinent issues raised in his mind; he would get his issues solved through that sermon even without questioning. That was a miracle of his sermons. Had any person come to him, with an evil intention to hurt Imamana (As), it had been noticed that, after hearing his sermon the evil minded person became captivated and finally became Imamana's devotee. The center of the faith's propagation was Daira. **Through these Dairas, Islam in its original form was being presented. The proof of it is that those Scholars, who had even visited the eminent preachers of Makkah and Madinah, Iraq and Khurasan etc.; when they approached Imamana (As) in India, they had preferred to accept Mahdavia Faith. This is the solid proof** that the Deen was being presented in its original form and spirit, which was nowhere available. Not only the principles of "Iman and Islam" were being inculcated, the intricacies and the divine teachings of "Ihsan" (according to the tradition of Gabriel (As) was also being engrained in the hearts and minds of the masses; leave aside the literate and elites.

Previously we have discussed about Qazi Qadan (Rz), as an example, who had after visiting holy places of Makkah and Madinah, even, he himself, being perfect in art and literature and even knew the secrets of Deen, still he got satisfaction in the dairas only. This fact can be ascertained from the details of Hazrat Shah Nizam (Rz). Like him, Sheik Abdullah Khan Niyazi (Rz) who was the disciple of Sheik Saleem Chishti, after returning from Makkah and Madinah, adopted Mahdavia faith which fact had already been mentioned in "Tabkhat-e-Akberi" written by Nizamuddin Ahmed Bakhshi (a Non Mahdavi Scholar).

Mulla Abdul Qader Badayuni had reported in "Najatur Rasheed" the impressions of the scholars of Herat about Imamana (As) that:" This man (Imamana (As) is one of the signs of Allah". While the author of "Juanpur Nama" had said about Imamana (As) that:" Khaja Syed Mohammed (As) (Mahdi-e-Maouood (As) is one of the signs of Allah and one of the miracles of the holy Prophet (Slm)."

Mahdavi Predecessors:

Abdul Qader Badayuni's "Najatur Rasheed" speaks about Imamana (As), his companions (Rz) and the successors (Rh) of the companions (Rz) that:

"During the period of Sultan Sikander Afghani, having complete trust in Allah, along with a multitude of seekers of Allah,Mir Syed Mohammed Juanpuri (As), Qudasallhu Rooha, went to Hajj. Who ever met him, joined his company by relinquishing relations with his wife and children. Someone had joined after repenting his past mistakes and then he

became able in his company to be absorbed himself in perpetual remembrance of Allah. The efficacy of his sermons was so impressive and heart-touching that even burglars who were holding swords in their hands, after hearing his Narration of Qur'an; became his disciples and attained the position of mystics, and even under their guidance many became pious people. The mystic Burhanuddin (Rh) of Kalpi, who happened to stay just for three days with Sheik Ilahdad (Rz) in the village Barriwall, had attained complete annihilation unto Allah. The same Miyan Ilahdad (Rz) was one of the burglars (No, this was Shah Nemat and not Miyan Ilahdad) who became a disciple of Miyan Shah Dilawer (Rz) and became a perfect saint and finally he became the medium for those who desired to enter the kingdom of the Heaven".

میر سید محمد جونپوری قدس الله روحه ...... در عهد سلطان سکندر افغان بقدم توکل و تجرید باجمعی از متوکلان و طالبان عاز حج اسلام شده و هر کس به صحبت شریف او پیوست اکثر این بود که از اهل و عیال گسته و از دنیا برآمده درآن حلقه داخل می شد والا کمترین پایهٔ آن توبه از معاصی و مناهی بود و اشتغال بذکر الهی و تصرف میر مذکور در قلوب عباد الله بمثابهٔ بود که بعضی از اقطاع الطریق مشهور شمشیر خون چکان آمده ملازمت کرده و چون بیان قرآن مجید شنیده اند صحبت او اختیار کرده بدرجهٔ ولایت رسیده اند و چند از اهل الله از دامن ایشان برخاسته چنانچه الشیخ الفانی والباقی به برهان الدین مشهور ساکن کالپی سه روزه در صحبت شیخ الهداد ساکن قصبهٔ باری رسید و از مقربان درگاه کبریا گشته همچنین شیخ الهداد از طالبان میان دلاور بوده که در ابتدائی حال چون فضیل عیاض قطع طریق می نمود و بردست میر مشار" الیه تائب شده از اکمل اولیاء گشته و چندین از "کاملان مکمل" دواصلان موصل در صحبت او تربیت یافته اند (نجات الرشید صفحه ۸۵ نمبر ۱۵۶٤،تصوف فارسی ،اسٹیٹ سنٹرل لائبریری ،حیدرآباد)

In this statement the reference to Burglary had wrongly been attached to Bandagi Ilahdad (Rz). As a matter of fact it was Shah Nemat (Rz) who was a burglar before he met Imamana (As). After meeting Imamana (As), Shah Nemat (Rz) became so perfect in mysticism that under his guidance a caliber like Qazi Muntakhabuddin (Rh), Author of "Maghzanul Dalael" got exaltation and perfection.

According to Mahdavia literature, Bandagi Malik Ilahdad (Rz) was one of the nobles of the court of Sultan Mahmood Begdha. When Imamana (As) came to Patan, Malik Ilahdad became his disiciple. After the demise of Bandagi Miran Syed Mahmood, Sani-e-Mahdi (Rz), he got the company of the Shah Nizam (Rz), first and then of Bandagi Miyan Syed Khundmir (Rz). In this way he got beneficence not only from Imamana (As), but also from all the five prominent companions of Imamana (s), therefore he had been given the title of "Khalifa-e-Giroh-e-Mahdavia" The last two lines of " Najatur Rasheed" refer to the sons of the companions of Imamana (As).

Mulla Abdul Qader Badayuni was born in 947 and died in 1004 H. Therefore his contemporaries are successors or sons of the successors of the companions of Imamana (As) about whom "Najatur Rasheed" states:

"I had lived with many persons of this Faith. I found their admirable manners and attributes even in poverty, had been exemplary. Although they were not educated well, still whatever they narrated the intricacies and truths and inner meanings of the of Qur'an and about mysticism were so perfect that nobody could object. Thus if we venture to write about them, it would become another "Tazkiratul Aouliya".

جمعی را از یں سلسله ملازمت کرده ام و اخلاق رضیه و اوصاف مرضیه ایشان رادر فقر و فنا به مرتبه عالی دیده بیان قرآن و اشارات آں و دقایق حقایق و لطائف معارف بے کسب علوم رسمی چنان شنیده ام که اگر خواهند مجملی از آنها در قید کتابت آرند تذکرة الاولیائی دیگر باید نوشت (نجات الرشید صفحه ۹۰)

What Mulla Abdul Qader had written, the same had been reported by " Juanpur Nama" in its chapter 5, under the caption: Khaja Syed Mohammed (As): that:

****

"Khaja Syed Mohammed (As) had been one of the signs of Allah and one of the miracles of the holy Prophet (Slm). Whoever was benefitted under his guidance he became busy in uplifting the purpose of "Amr Bil Ma'roof-WA-Nahi Unil Munker". (Enjoin virtue and abhor evil). Always ready for Jihad in the cause of Allah and was prepared to help-assist in furtherance of the cause of religion.

What ever they received they used to distribute equally among themselves, and never hoard for the next day. Their emblem was sword in the hand and Qur'an on the head. They followed Imam Azam for minor issues and were very harsh in the matters of Shariat. They never accepted guess or analogy. They never required any one as regards guidance for truth except the Mission of Syed Moahammed (As). To them, Mahdi (As) was Syed Mohammed (As) alone."

He wrote about Imamana (As) further that:

"The truth is that, the meaning of guidance, fits on him that he is the best one to guide the Ummah, whether they are elite or commoners."

آپتی بود از آیات الهی و معجزے از معجزات رسالت پناهی مستفید انش همه بامر بالمعروف و نهی عن المنکر علانیه مشغول ، در جهاد فی سبیل الله جانباز و در نصرت شرع سرفروش ، هرچه دست داد با همه علی السویه قسمت کردند و ذخیره برائے فردانگاه نداشتند ، تیغ در دست و قرآن بر سر بودن خاصهٔ ایشان است ، در فروغ تقلید امام اعظم کنند امادر اتباع حدیث تشدد دارند و در این باب قیاس را مسلم نمی شمارند جزبه هدایت حق کارند و جز خواجه سید محمد دیگرے را مهدی نمی پندارند (جونپور نامه باب پنجم)

والحق ازروے هدایت ایں خطاب شایان اوست که خودش مامور به هدایت عام و ارشاد کافهٔ انام بود

Mir Mohammed Husain Azad had written about the predecessors of Mahdavia that they had surpassed in asceticism and righteousness. (Darbar-e-Akberi, Lahore, page 813, 1898) And Moulana Azad had presented some precepts of Imamana (As) and his companions in these words:

"Therefore many saints and scholars had a favourable opinion about them or for the least, they used to keep quiet or restrained to opine about them. Hazrat Sheik Dawood Jahniwal (Rh) and Moulana Jamaluddin's opinion had been reported earlier (Moulana Jamaluddin (Rh) had already written by confirming Imamana's Mahdiat).When the fatwa proclaiming infidelity of Imamana (As) was presented to Sheik Wajihuddin Gujrati (Rh), the senior scholar of that period for signature, he refused to sign and told that "the group which had relinquished the worldly affairs and had devoted life for the preservation of truth, I cannot write against them". Sheik Ali who was the arch rival of Imamana (As), even after criticizing Imamana's followers to have been indulged in exaggeration and departure (from the right path), still he had a strong opinion about Imamana (As) by saying that:"Kaf-e-Lisan-e-Oola asth." Another Sheik Budha Danapuri, known as the "teacher of teachers" and Syed Rafiuddin (Rh) Muhaddis and a pupil of Hafiz Asqalani (Rh) had a good opinion about Mahdavis as reported by Abdul Qader Badayuni that:

"They had a good opinion about the Mahdavis."   ”با مهدويه حسن ظن داشتند“

What Shah Valiullah (Rh) had written about Imamana (As), his son, Shah Abdul Aziz, had endorsed his father's opinion by saying "Syed Mohammed (As) was truly a learned man who was immersed in the Divinity. ("Tazkera", page 40, published in Al Balagh Press, Calcutta).

Moulana Azad had written about the companions of Mahdavis that:

"Their behavior and manners were so lovely and captivating that reminded the godly attributes of the companions of the holy Prophet (Slm). A highly devoted group of persons joined together with a common goal of love of the Almighty, had relinquished blood relations and mortal attachment to the land and country. They sacrificed everything for the cause of Allah and they became friendly and sympathizers to each other. Be he a poor or peer, a high or a low, every one of them had coloured themselves in a single colour of Allah. They were always seen being absorbed in the Divinity. Their main aim was to serve and guide the human beings in establishing the high objects of the Divine Law and Shariat-e-Mustafavi (Slm)." ("Tazkera" Pages 27 ,28)

Further in another chapter "characteristics of the Mahdavis" he had described as under:

"After the demise of the celebrated Syed (As) this group flourished in which renowned scholars and pious people joined to them. Among them were Abdullah Khan Niyazi (Rh) and Sheik Alaai (Rh) who lived in Biayana and attracted thousands by their captivating power and infused in them the sublime knowledge of the Divinity through humility, sincerity and selflessness. If the particulars written by a non-partial and trustworthy historians are genuine, then those people were no human beings, but they were angels from the heaven, who were deputed by Allah, in the shape of men to cleanse the Earth. Whenever good fortune and prosperity is destined for the world by Allah, He takes work from the mortal men, what the angels of heaven are supposed to do. It is out of question that the angels of heaven had any time habituated among the humans.

"Allah never changes His routine   ولن تجد لسنة اللّٰه تبديلا
actions".

Moulana Azad had further wrote that Mullah Abdul Qader Badayuni In his "Muntakhatut Tawareekh"and in "Najatur Rasheed"; and Nizamuddin Hiravi in "Tabkhaat" had written in detail their particulars. But more details are available in "Tazkeratul Waseleen" in the Chapter relating to Hazrat Sheik Dawood (Rh). When you read them, your heart is thrilled with absorption and fascination and you become obsessed so much that you would like to leave everything and go on reading and reading the details of these pure and pious people. Centuries have passed, still such is the efficacy in their characters, God Knows what strength of affection would have resulted from the virtuous company of those pretty pure complexions of those pious and saintly persons." (Tazkera)

Middle Order Mahdavis:

Author of "Juanpur Nama" had written under chapter 5 'Khaja Syed Mohammed (As)" and about his (author's) contemporaries.

"I had seen many persons of this faith who were found weeping and wailing. They had no work except recitation of the holy Qur'an and they were absolutely absorbed in pondering over holy Qur'an and their inquisitiveness to understand intricacies of the Divinity. "Enjoin virtue and abhor evil" was the cherished goal of their life. Always equipped with sword and dagger in hand and the Qur'an on the head. We pray for those who are busy in upholding the religion of the holy Prophet (Slm)."

جمعی را که براین عقیده بودند بادلهاے بریان و چشمان گریاں یافتم که جزبه قرآن کارے ندارند و بغیر تدبر و تفکر شعارے ندارند و تیرۂ ایشان امر معروف است و نهی منکر و زینت ایشان تیغ است و خنجر اللهم انصر من نصر دین محمد صلی الله علیه و سلم

And Their Followers:

Moulvi Sanaullah Amratsari while discussing about the Qadiani's Journal "Review of Religions" of Shawwal 1341 H. and the journal of Ahl-e-Hadees dated 14th.Zeeqaeda 1341 H. in which some discussion about Mahdavis had been referred by saying that:

"We have differences with these two groups (Mahdavis and Qadianis). But we cannot avoid saying what is right and therefore shall like just to speak the truth that Mahdavia group's leaning, had been, from the very beginning, towards asceticism and avoidance of sensualism;

still these virtues persist in them. As against them, Qadianis are embedded with the spirit of dialectics and contention, leaving aside asceticism and piety."

Distinctive features of Mahdavis:

Moulana Abul Kalam Azad had written in "Tazkera" that:

"It was a period in which the worldly scholars and the priests were just looking for their earthly passions, possessions and were interested in controlling the masses through innovations and Bidaat. Guidance, admonition, pursuing the very meanings of "Enjoin virtue and Abhor evil" had lost their spirit. On the other hand Syed Mohammed Juanpuri (As) and his followers had founded their invitation on those sublime principles for revival of Islamic jurisprudence to its entirety. That was the call of that period, thus they invested their energies for the furtherance of this sublime principle. The very first condition was to eradicate evil at any cost where ever they found it and propagate the sublime principles of the Divine Law. As against this zeal, the worldly scholars were on the wrong path. Therefore what Mahdavis were preaching became their identity. The work which had been abandoned by others, if that work is carried away by a single group of peoples, it becomes their specialty." ("Tazkera" and "Albalagh" Press pages 270,271)."

That is why to help-assist Mahdavis in the cause of Islam was considered to be a piety. The same fact Moulana Azad had further mentioned in "Tazkera" that:

"History is full with the facts that faith and practice, nobility and sanctity are found in both Hazrat Sheik Jamaluddin (Rh) and Sheik Dawood (Rh). Even without these qualities, their opposition to Maqdoomul Mulk and their support to Sheik Niyazi (Rz) and Sheik Alaai (Rh) and writing a book praising Syed Mohammed Juanpuri (As) was enough for us to declare frankly that this act was one of the best attributes to claim superiority over all other attributes." ("Tazkera" pages 85,86, Al-Balagh Press, Calcutta).

Dairah-e-Mahdavia and propagation of Quran and traditions:

Akber Shah Khan Najeebabadi had recognised the work of propagation of the holy Qur'an and the Traditions by Imamana (As) in these words:

"Witnessing the flood of ignorance, acute illiteracy, idolatry, Bida't which had enveloped the entire society, Syed Mohammed Juanpuri (As) started his sublime Mission by upholding the dictates of the holy Qur'an and the Traditions of the holy Prophet (Slm). The sanctity of his efforts was even recognized by his opponents that not only Imamana (As) had personally devoted his energies in furtherance of the mandates of the Qur'an and superiority of the Divine Law; but also his companions were sincerely indulged in propagating the inner meanings of the Qur'an and the Traditions to the best of their ability and they had no other work except furtherance of that sublime mandate. He further states that Imamana (As) started his Mission from Juanpur to Rajputana, Gujrat, Deccan and even he went to Sindh and sincerely propagated the Holy Qur'an and the Traditions and influenced highly acclaimed nobles, kings and commanders and made them strict followers of the Qur'an and Traditions everywhere."

Even after the demise of Imamana (As), in what way the propagation of the Faith was carried out by his companions had been clearly mentioned by Akber Shah Khan Najeebabadi who had described and accepted their way of propagation in these words:

"Finally, after witnessing the uncontrollable ocean of innovations and Bid'ats, Hazrat Syed Mohammed of Juanpur (As) started the propagation of the Qur'an and the traditions. This fact had also been certified even by his opponents that not only himself but his group were strictly following the dictates of the Qur'an and the traditions and they never indulged in any other matter".

Akber Shah Khan further narrates about Imamana's companions that: Sheik Khizer Nagori (Rz), Syed Mahmood (Rz) Ibn Syed Mohammed (As), Bandagi Miyan Syed Khundmir (Rz), Sheik Abdulla Khan Niyazi (Rz), and many others had continued the propagation of the Qur'an and traditions. The most zealous among them was Sheik Alaai (Rh) who spent his whole life with utmost fervor and enthusiasm in spreading the mission of Imamana (As). When Saleem Shah Ibn Sher Shah Soori demanded Fatwa against Sheik Alaai (As), the most unscrupulous, irreligious and most corrupted persons under the influence of worldly benefits issued fatwa for his martyrdom, but those who were pious and literate and men of godly nature rejected that fatwa. Anyhow the majority of those referred above had wrongly influenced the Sultan against Sheik Alaai's death and that was done ultimately and Sheik Alaai (Rh) was no more."

Thus from the above, it became known that Mahdavis had always preferred to spread the message of Qur'an and the Divine Law with their charming and captivating manners only.

Harmony between practice and knowledge:

Moulvi Abdul Ghafoor, professor of a Muslim University, had written a thesis on "Educational Movement in India". It refers to "the movement of Arabic Schools" and under it he has referred to Daira-e-Mahdavia:"

"Even before Akber, the worldly scholars had established their special position. Nothing to do with the official position of any prime minister or ministers, they were busy in amassing wealth in the shape of gold bricks. Contrary to the above said scholars, Mahdavi scholars were simple men whose social maneuvering were exemplary and who were busy in helping destitute by bringing water for them, or those who became helpers to the travelers by holding their baggage, and those who were brave enough to pronounce the word of Allah even in the courts of the tyrant kings by wearing coffins always over them. There is a vast list of those personalities from Hazrat Mujaddad-e-Sani to Syed Ahmed Barailvi and Shah Ismail Shaheed who lived in this mortal world just to elucidate their mission in order to make the purpose of life better and better. Among them were Syed Mohammed Juanpuri (As) and Moulana Vilayet Ali who with their knowledge and practice and their lively sermons created the harmony between these faculties and they became venerable personalities in the field of spreading the Divine Law."

An important point to note in his thesis is that in the beginning, he has referred about the non

Mahdavi scholars and about those who were busy in amassing wealth in the shape of gold bricks, then he referred to the Daira-e-Mahdvia who were living in them, and who used to help destitute by bringing water to them. This refers to the Daira of Miyan Sheik Niyazi (Rz) at Biyana (Bharatpur). And the reference of coming to the court of the then Sultan, wearing coffins, tells about Miyan Sheik Alaai (Rh) who went to the court of Saleem Shah and Miyan Sheik Mustafa Gujrati (Rh) who went to the court of Akber for dialectic discussions with non Mahdavi scholars in respect of Mahdavi Faith. Then he had referred Sheik Ahmed Sar-e-Hindi and Syed Ahmed Barailvi, both Non Mahdavi scholars. These were the middle order scholars, but in the beginning, he had referred to Imamana (As) and his Mission; in which he had elaborated two distinguished features. One being "harmony between knowledge and practice"; the other being "harmony between character and deliberations". Here knowledge means Islam and Deen and where knowledge and practice had become harmonious. That was the sign of Mahdiat and the same is the Islam of the pioneering period. Thus the beginning of the "harmony between knowledge and practice" was actually initiated by Imamana (As) in India. Then the thesis refers to those scholars who are not from the Daira. It is clear from it, that those non Mahdavi scholars had been profusely benefitted from the Mahdavia Movement only. The manner in which the thesis writer had shown respect for the names of Non Mahdavi scholars, the same respect was not shown to Imamana (As). It shows his deep bias and prejudice with Mahdavis. Apart from this he had praised the philosophy behind "harmony between knowledge and practice" which was the backbone and the specialty of the Daira which impressed his mind and he could not hide this in his thesis.

'It is a point of interest that Mujaddad-e-Sani (Died 1034 H) belonged to Sar-e-Hind. And it may be noted that Sar-e-Hind of Tenth century Hijri was the center of Mahdavia Movement. Hence, there should be no doubt that his movement must have been affected by the Mahdavia Movement only.'

Daira-e-Mahdavia and Aaliat (Adopt most preferable):

Author of "Insaf Nama" had reported that:

"It is narrated that people asked Imamana (As) whether"Rukhsat (To Dismiss or to leave) is permissible? Imamana (As) answered :"Aaliat only represents Deen. If any one fails to adopt Aaliat, he comes at Rukhsat. But if he falls from Rukhsat, where he would go?"

نقل است که بعضی کسان پیش حضرت میران عرض کردند که رخصت هم دین است ، بعده میران فرمودند که دین عزیمت است اگر از عزیمت بازماند تا در رخصت ماندو اگر از رخصت بیفتد تادر کجا ماند (باب پنجم)

This Saying of Imamana (As) was recorded in the "Insaf Nama" the original written copy is available in State Central Library, Hyderabad. Thus from this it is clear that Imamana (As) had preferred "Aaliat" which is the root of Islamic jurisprudence and that was mostly preached in Daira-e-Mahdavia.

Distinct Mahdavi Preachers:

It is a known fact that the center of propagation of Mahdavi Faith was Daira. The cause of the success of the preachers was:

1. Their asceticism and piety was an admitted fact; the bitterest of their enemies had accepted this fact. This fact had been also accepted even by Sheik Ali in his "Risalatur Rudd" he sarcastically states that people were "duped" (Instead of telling attracted, he had used "Duped") by their "asceticism and piety". ("Sirajul Absar" pages 42,43)

2. Their commentary and narration of the holy Qur'an was very impressive and captivating. Which had been recognized even by the opponents;

3. There was much disparity about the signs of Mahdi (As), therefore even strong scholars could not prove that Imamana (As) and his followers were innovators.

4. Tenth Century Hijri was full with the air for the advent of the "Promised Mahdi (As)";

5, Even opponents had recognized Imamana's excellence. Worldly scholars having failed to dissuade people from joining the Dairas, they attempted to influence administration by saying that such and such commander, along with his troops had accepted Mahdavi Faith. The worldly scholars had an utterly wrong apprehension that the kingdom would be lost to the Mahdavis, thus they tried to create many obstacles for the preachers. It is a fact that not only all the companions were preachers, but also every Mahdavi became a preacher. Here some examples are presented regarding those preachers whose names have been mentioned in the Non Mahdavia literature also.

1.Miyan Sheik Alaai (Rh):

Mulla Abdul Qader Badayuni had recorded the facts as to how Maqdoomul Mulk had poisoned the ears of Saleem Shah against Sheik Alaai (Rh):

"Maqdoomul Mulk poisoned the ears of Saleem Shah, stating wrongly that this innovator proclaims himself to be the Mahdi (As) and that Mahdi (As) would become king of the world. Therefore, not only his expulsion, but he deserves death."	مــخــدوم الـملك خاطر نشان سلیم شاه ساخته بود که مبتـدع دعـوی مهدویت می کند و مهدی خود بادشاه روئی زمین خـواهـد بـود چون سرخروج دارد واجب الـقتل است (منتخب التواریخ ،طبع کلکته ، جلد اوّل صفحه ۵۱)

Death was proposed because Maqdoomul Mulk and the scholars of Delhi and Agra, joined together were unable to defeat Sheik Alaai (Rh) in the dialectic discussions. This situation had been elaborately discussed by Badayuni:

"With the power of being moderate and cleanliness of mind and heart, Sheik Alaai (Rh) was able to overpower his opponents in religious discussions."	"بـقوت حدت طبع و صفائی باطن به هر کدام ایشان در بحث غالب آمد"

The same fact had been recognized by the author of "Tabkhaat-e-Akberi":

"On being called by Saleem Khan (Saleem Shah) Sheik Alaai (Rh) visited the court of Saleem Shah and avoided to maintain Shahi protocol, instead offered an Islamic way of salutation which was responded by Saleem Shah with disagreeableness and which hurt the courtiers also. Saleem Shah appointed Mir Syed Rafiuddin, Mullah Jalal Danishmand, Mullah Abul Fatah Thaniseri and other competent scholars to investigate and settle the claim of Sheik Alaai (Rh). Sheik Alaai (Rh) overpowered all the scholars with the force of his tone and cleanliness of his mind and heart. Whenever he narrated the Holy Qur'an, Saleem Shah became captivated and was deeply impressed. Saleem Shah even offered him the post of Muhtasib, if he leaves the claim (of being the Mahdi as propagated wrongly against him by the opponents that he calls himself as Mahdi). Saleem Shah informed Sheik Alaaie "So far you had been issuing decrees without my permission, now if appointed, you would be able to have my permission for issuing decrees, to which offer he refused point blank."

Author of "Mu'asir-e-Rahimi" has also written that:

"Those who were overpowered by Sheik Alaaie (Rh) were Rafiuddin, Mulla Jalal and Mulla Abul Fatah. On hearing the commentaries of the Holy Qur'an, Saleem Shah became very much impressed."

Badayuni had further written that:

"At the beginning of the session, Sheik Alaai (Rh), according to his custom, narrated commentaries of the verses of Qur'an, referring to the contempt of the world, events of the Day of Judgment, insulting the worldly scholars in such an impressive and eloquent tone that Saleem

بموجب طلب سليم خان او حاضر آمد برسميات و آداب ملوك مقيد نشد سلام مشروع به سليم خان گفت واو عليك السلام بكره گفت ، اين معنى به مقربان او دشوار آمد .... سليم خان مير سيد رفيع الدين وملا جلال بيهم دانشمنده ملا ابو الفتح تهانيسرى و ديگر علمائى آن وقت را احضار فرموده تشخيص اين قضيه حواله ايشان نمود در اين مجالس بحث شيخ علائى بهر كدام ايشان بقوت طبع غالب و گاه گاهى كه تفسير و بيان قرآن ميكرد در سليم خان اثر كرده باوى ميگفت يا شيخ ازين دعوئ باز آئى كه تامن درقلمرو خود محتسب گردانم تاايى زمان بى حكم من امرمى كردى حالا باذن من ميكرده باش علائى اين معنى قبول نه كرد

"رفيع الدين و ملا جلال و ملا ابو الفتح تانيسرى راحاضر ساخته اين قضيه حواله بايشان نمود ، در مجلس شيخ علائى برهمه ايشان غالب مى آمدوگاه گاهى كه تفسير و بيان قرآن مى كرد ـ در سليم خان اثر كرده بود"

پيش از انعقاد مجلس بحث علائى بموجب عادت معهود خويش چند آيت قرآنى را تفسير كرده و چنان وعظى نافع به عبارتى بليغ مشتمل برذكر مذمت دنيا و احوال قيامت و اهانت علمائى زمان و سائر خطابيات گفت كه سليم شاه و ديگر امرائى حضار مجلس بآن قسادت قلب بسيار موثر افتاد و آب در چشم كرده

Shah and his hard hearted courtiers became so impressed that they could not stop tears and became puzzled. Saleem Shah went to his private lounge and arranged feast for the Sheik (Rh) and his companions. Sheik (Rh) did not eat anything and told others if they desired they may have meals. He did not offer any respect to Saleem Shah when he came back. When Saleem Shah asked as to why he had not eaten the meals, he replied it was for those who had become extravagant."

حیران ماندند و سلیم شاه از مجلس برخاسته و خود مقید شده از اندرون محلسر اطعام برائ شیخ و همر هانش فرستاد و شیخ نه خود از آن طعام تناول نمود و نه هنگام آمدن سلیم شاه تعظیم اوبجا آدرد و به یاران خود همین قدر گفت هر کر که اخوش آید بخورد و چون از و پرسیدند که سبب امتناع از طعام خوردن چه بود جواب داد که طعام تو حق مسلمانان است که بخلاف شرع زیاده از خود متصرف شده (منتخب التواریخ طبع کلکته ،جلد اول صفحه ٤٠٠)

Author of "Tareekh-e-Dawoodi" writes about Sheik Alaai (Rh):
"Islam Shah (Saleem Shah) gathered all scholars and asked them to investigate and settle the dispute".

اسلام شاه به حضار جمیع دانش مندان حکم فرموده تشخیص این قضیه حواله ایشان نمود شیخ علائی در مجلس بحث برهر کدام اشان به قوت طبع غالب می شد (تاریخ داودی)

Author of "Mu'asirul Umra" writes about Sheik Alaai (Rh) that:
"Mulla Abdullah blamed him (Sheik Alaai Rh) of bid'at and decreed the expulsion and poisoned the ears of Saleem Shah to call him from Biayana for dialectic discussion, in which Sheik Alaai (Rh) became successful."

ملا عبدالله اور ابه ابتداع و خروج مهتم ساخته سلیم شاه رابر آن داشت که از بیانه طلبیده با علماء مذاکره فرمود فرمود شیخ علائی غالب آمد (مآثر الامرا، طبع کلکته ، جلد سوم صفحه٢٥٤)

Author of "Nuzhatul Khawatir" writes that:
Saleem Shah arranged a debate between Shaik Alaaii and the Scholars, to investigate the matter of Advent of Mahdi.When the debate started, Sheik Alaai (Rh) made them to surrender and thus scholars became puzzled and surrendered."

وامرالعلماء ان یباحثوه فی مسئلة خروج المهدی فباحثوه فاقحمهم واتی بما تحیربه الناس (الجزء الرابع صفحه ٢٢٨)

When Saleem Shah became convinced that the scholars of Delhi and Agra were unable to discuss with Sheik Alaai (Rh), he decided to send Sheik Alaai (Rh) to Sheik Budh of Bihar. When he reached Bihar, They were both busy in discussing about the Traditions.

"Since there were many differences to fix up signs for Mahdi (As), Sheik Budh decided not to invoke the decree of infidelity or sinfulness on Sheik Alaai (Rh)"

اختلاف بسیار در باب تعین علامات مهدی واقع است بنا بر آن حکم به کفر و فسق شیخ علائی نمی توان کرد (منتخب التواریخ ، طبع کلکته ، جلد اول صفحه ٤٠٧)

But, pity on him, that on the advice of his sons, Sheik Budh did not write the same verdict to Saleem Shah with the apprehension that if that was written, Maqdoomul Mulk may call him to Delhi or Agra. Therefore the sons of Sheik Budh wrote wrongly on behalf of their father that Maqdoomul Mulk was an acclaimed scholar whose Fatwa stands against Sheik Alaai (Rh). Badayuni had thus written about this episode in detail.

Sheik Alaai (Rh) had spread Imamana's mission at Hindia of Malwa, Khawaspur of Jodhpur, Bihar, Delhi, Agra and Punjab (the details of which will be presented under the chapter" Propagation"), but the irony of the fact is that in place of arguments, whips and floggings were the answer; about which Mulla Abdul Qader Badayuni had pointed out that:

"Sheik Alaai (Rh) was like Mansur of his period, BaYazeed, Ainul Quzzat and Shibli of his period, who was ordered whipping by Islam Khan Soori as recommended by Maqdoomul Mulk in the year 957 H. But his soul came out from the confines of the mortal body just in three whippings and ultimately merged to the Eternity. "Wasqahum Rabbuhum Sharaaba" and "Zakerullah" were the two appropriate compositions of his chronograph which correctly calculate the date of his martyrdom. The details of this warrior had been provided in "Muntakhaba-tut-tawareekh" which is the summary of Mirza Nizamuddin's "Tareekh-e-Nizami".

از آن جمله منصور وقت و بایزید عصر و عین القضاة روزگار و شبلی زمانه شیخ علائی بیانه بود که اسلام خان افغان سور به سعی مخدوم الملك سلطان پوری درسنه نهصد و پنجاه و هفت اوراتازیانه چند فرمود و جان پاك اوبه سه تازیانه از قالب خاكی بجانب عالم علوی و روضهٔ رضوان ابدی خرامیده وسقاهم ربهم شرابایك تاریخ اووذاکر الله تاریخ و دیگر اویافته شده بود مجملی از احوال او و در منتخب التواریخ خلاصه تاریخ نظامی تالیف میر زاے مرحومی مغفوری نظام الدین احمد که باعث و بانی این اوراق بود ثبت یافته رحمه الله رحمته واسعة و این قصه طویل الذیل است و فرصت اطناب نیست (نجات الرشید قلمی صفحه ٩١)

How ruthless flogging was administered, Farishta had properly written:

"That was a period when an epidemic of plague had spread. Sheik Alaai (Rh) also unfortunately was affected. The wound was deep in his mouth also. Apart from this he had suffered much from lengthy travels and harassment."

درآن اثنا شیخ را مرض طاعون که در آن وقت شائع بود عارض شده در حلق اوجرا حتی افتاد که مقدریك انگشت فتیله می رفت و رنج سفر علاوه آن گشته (تاریخ فرشته جلد اوّل صفحه ٢٣٣)

Moulana Abul Kalam Azad deplored by saying: "Alas, even death could not satisfy the tyrants. The body of a person who was always absorbed into Divinity, and of a pious man was treated in such a barbarous way which cannot be compared even to the dead infidels of the battles of Badr and Uhad. Badayuni states that the body was trampled and tread by attaching it to the feet of an elephant and when the body became disjointed, the parts were exhibited in the army camp and was ordered not to be buried and arranged a guard to avoid gathering of persons. ("Tazkera" page 61)."

"Swiftly during the night of this cruel event, a storm clamped the body parts with heaps of flowers which covered the body profusely and made a grave for him." (Written by a non Mahdavi Historian)

"شبا شب چندان خرمن گلها بر قالب شیخ ریخته شد
که در آن پنهان گشت حکم قبر پیدا کرده بود "
(منتخب التواریخ طبع کلکته جلد اول صفحه ۲۰۸)

If the scholars of Saleem Shah period could not stand before Sheik Alaai (Rh), a known Tab-e-Tabaie, then imagine how could those scholars face the companions of Imamana (As) or even Imamana (As) himself?

All the preachers were of the same caliber, some of them had been reported and many were omitted and not reported.

Sheik Ali Muttaqi was an arch rival of Imamana (As). Under the pressure of hostility, and having a personal grudge against Imamana (As) he went to Gujrat, then to Makkah and Madinah and back again to Gujrat, just because he could not obtain any effective fatwa against Imamana (As), however with much pursuance he obtained a fatwa from the scholars of Makkah and sent to India. When such fatwahs also did not create any result, he returned to Gujrat and poisoned the ears of the king of Gujrat for mass killings of Mahdavis. The King of Gujrat, who was a youngster, unfortunately issued orders for mass killings of Mahdavis. However, even with these pressures, the enthusiasm of Mahdavis did not vanish. Sheik Ali's pupil, Mulla Sheik Mohammed bin Taherul Fitni had the same envious feelings towards Mahdavis. But the aimless struggle of these two arch rivals against Mahdavis utterly failed in limini. Mir Gulam Ali Azad had written about Sheik Mohammed bin Taherul Fitni in his "Mu'asirul Kiram" that:

"Sheik Mohammed Bin Taher Fitni, like his teacher, resolved to defeat Mahdavi Bohras, who belonged to his community, who were following Syed Mohammed Juanpuri (As). He took an oath that until and unless he erased the stain of innovation from the foreheads of Mahdavi Bohras he would not wear his turban (and threw his turban on the ground with frustration).

واو در شکست بواهیر مهدویه که هم قوم او بودند و
اقتدائی سید محمد جونپوری میکردند مثل استاد خود
کمر بربست و عهد کرد که تاداغ از پیشانی این طائفه
نه شوید دستار را بر سر نه بندد (مآثر الکرام (طبع آگره)
دفتر اول صفحه ۱۹۵)

The way he threw away his turban tells that he had become much powerless and all his efforts were futile in comparison to Miyan Sheik Mustafa Gujrati (Rh). Professor Mahmood Shirani had written in his "Masnawi-e-Faiz-e-Aam" about Miyan Sheik Mustafa Gujrati (Rh) that: "All scholars gathered in front of the king (Akber), and one among them was the said arch rival of Miyan Sheik Mustafa Gujrati (Rh), who threw his turban before the king and said: "Mustafa Mahdavi (Rh) made our turban cast off." The king consoled him and gave his belt to coil on his head as a turban and told that he would manage the affairs according to his desire.

"King (Akber) had coiled his belt like a turban with his own hands on Patni's head and told that "we had heard the reason for throwing your turban. The way, in which you want to adhere to Divine Law, we would take care of."

بادشاه دستار بدست خود بر سر شیخ پیچید و فرمود باعث ترک دستار به سمع رسیده نصرت دین متین بروفق اراده شما بر ذمه معدلت من است (مآثر الکرام، طبع آگره، دفتر اول صفحه ۱۹۵)

2. Miyan Sheik Mustafa Gujrati (Rh):

Mir Gulam Ali Azad wrote that the same year, Gujrat was given under the rule of Khan-e-Azam Mirza Koka who terrorized and made Mahdavis to suffer heavily under his period.

"That year Khan-e-Azam Mirza Koka was made the governor of Gujrat and with his help many innovations were uplifted. Azad had wrongly used the word "Innovations" for propagation of Mahdiat, which is nothing but Islam. However he had accepted that Mahdavis were subjected to cruelty by Khan-e-Azam Mirza, the ruthless ruler of Gujrat in 980 H.

Abdullah Mohammed Bin Omer Makki had written in his "Zaferwala" that under the orders of Khan-e-Azam, Sanjar khan had invited Miyan Abdul Rasheed (Rz), father of Miayn Sheik Mustafa Gujrati (Rh), and his companions for a dinner and after the dinner he mercilessly and dubiously arranged to kill all invitees. "Zaferwala" states that:

"Thus Sanjar Khan met with him (Miyan Abdul Rasheed (Rz) and invited for the dinner, which was the last meal for him. And when he came along with his companions, then he questioned about Mahdavia Faith and about Imamana (As). Miyan Abdul Rasheed (Rz) taking Sanjer Khan into his confidence, that he would not hurt them, stated the facts about Imamana (As) and Mahdiat. Listening this Sanjer Khan kept quiet till they finished their dinner. And at the end got them slaughtered except his son Mustafa (Rh)" (a young boy who witnessed his father being slaughtered ruthlessly).

فتلقاه سنجر خان و هیّأله ضیافة و کانت آخرزاده من دنیاه فانه لما اجتمع به ساله عن المذهب و من صاحب المذهب فلما ابرز ضمیره آمنا من جانبه سکت عنه الی ان افرغ من اکله ثم قتله بسائر اصحابه ماسوئ ولده مصطفیٰ (ظفر الواله جلد اول صفحه ۳٦)

According to the "Risala-e-Asaami Musadaqueen":

"Miyan Abdul Rasheed (Rz) was a famous scholar and a perfect reformer of his time. He wrote a paper on the proofs of Mahdi (As). He had gathered a few Naqliyat (Sayings) of Imamana (As) also. He and his companions were martyred ruthlessly by the tyrants."

میان عبدالرشید عالم عالم عامل صالح کامل از مشاهیر علمائے عصر خویش بودند بر ثبوت مہدویت رسالہ نوشتہ اند بعضی منقولات حضرت امام علیہ السلام نیز (جمع) کردہ اند ...... از دست ظالمان باچند مردمان دیگر شربت شہادت چشیدند

"Miyan Sheikh Mustafa Gujrati (Rh) had written a poem about the martyrdom of his father and about the Mahdavi preachings of that period which is in Persian language which narrates that:

Ah! I had seen such a ruthless slaughter before my eyes, which whenever, I think over, it brings tears to me.

How cunningly he became polite when invited for the dinner.

And how sweet were his words to hear about our faith from the mouth of my father.

After the dinner how ruthless was Sanjar who arranged for the carnage."

نہ دیدہ کس بد نیساں دل ستانی
کہ ہر لحظہ نماید نوشانی
گہے چوں میرزاد رگفت ودربیچ
گہی درخشم چوں خان کلانی
گہے بدخوی چوں قلمچی محمد
گہی شیریں زباں چوں شیر خانی
گہے چوں خواجہ سنجر برسر قتل
گہی مرغوب شکل میزبانی

The fourth couplet of the above poem refers how dubiously Sanjar Khan arranged for the dinner for his father Miyan Abdul Rasheed (Rz) and how brutally murdered him and his companions.

Professor Shirani had commented on this poem that through this poem Miyan Sheikh Mustafa Gujrati (Rh) accepts those turmoil and hardships as a gift from the Almighty at the hands of his opponents..

Mulla Abdul Qader Badayuni had written about Sheik Mustafa Gujrati (Rh) in his "Muntakhabut Tawareekh":

"Miyan She ik Mustafa Gujrati (Rh) comes from the Bohra sect which is engaged in business in Gujrat. After the meeting, one of the companions of Imamana (As), adopted Mahdavia Faith till his death. When Akber came to Ajmer after conquering Patna, he ordered Asif Khan, the second Mir Bakhshi, to bring Miyan Mustafa Gujrati (Rh), who brought Miyan Sheik Mustafa Gujrati (Rh) along with him to Ajmer and presented before Akber. One night Akber called all scholars to his drawing room and asked them to discuss about Mahdiat. Miyan Sheik Mustafa Gujrati (Rh) was vocal in his deliberations, and the debate took a long time. However one Haji Ibrahim Sar-e-Hindi, on account of his bad temper, tried to dictate which hurt Miyan Mustafa (Rh) badly." ("Oriental College Magazine", November 1940, p. 62)

میاں مـصـطـفیٰ گجراتی اصل اوطائفه بوهره است که در گـجرات به سود و سودا مشغول اندبه یکی از یاران بیـواسطـه میـر سیـد مـحمد جونپوری قدس الله سره، پیـوستـه طریـقـه فقر و فنا پیش گرفته تاآخر عمر دران استـقـامت ور زید چون خلیفته الزمانی بعد از تسخیر ولایـت بنك پـطنـه مـراجـعـت نموده باجمیر رسیدند آصف خـان ثانی میر بخشی اور ابه حسب از گجرات همراه آورده شبے در صحن دیوان خانه علما را طلبیده از شیـخ مـصـطفیٰ تـحـقیق مسئله مهدیت نمودند او مـجیب بود مـنـاظـره بـامتـداو کشید حاجی ابراهیم سرهنـدی در بـحـث بـمـوجب شیمه ، سیّه خویـش تـحـکمـات میکـرد شیـخ را آزار داد (اورینٹل کالج میگزین ، نومبر ۱۹٤۰ء صفحه ٦۲)

This is the same Miyan Mustafa (Rh) from whose preachings Sheik Mohammed bin Taherul Fitni became so helpless that angrily threw his own turban on the ground, grumbling that he would not wear it until the so called stain is washed out from the foreheads of those Bohras who had converted to Mahdism. Miyan Mustafa (Rh) was also from the Bohra clan known as Patni. His father Miyan Abdul Rasheed (Rz) was martyred along with his ten companions in presence of his son, by Sanjer Khan for his preachings regarding Mahdavia Movement. His son even saw his father's slaughtering with his own eyes, still he never wavered.

Mulla Abdul Qader Badayuni's statement that Ibrahim Sar-e-Hindi was dictating his terms to Miyan Mustafa Gujrati (Rh) shows his weakness to argue with Miyan Mustafa Gujrati (Rh). Badayuni had just recorded his eyewitness report of one night's debate in which Miyan Mustafa (Rh) was alone against a hoard of scholars. It is stated that Miyan Mustafa (Rh) was being rudely treated during and after the debate. This fact had been stated by Professor Mahmood Shirani:

"Both Miyan Mustafa (Rh) and Miyan Ji Mubarak (Rh) were so torturously straightened in an iron cage that caused their body joints to break, still they did not give up their belief.

Mahdavia books point out that before and after the debate, at Fatehpur Saikri, Akber's capital, Miyan Mustafa (Rh) was used to be imprisoned in a thorny narrow iron cage.

"Khatim-e-Sulaimani's Part 9, Chapter 4 reports that Miyan Mustafa (Rh) had answered the Questionnaire of Miyan Sheik Mubarak. Akber had brought Miyan Mustafa (Rh) to his Capital,

Fathepur, just for dialectic discussion on Mahdiat, and he was asked to stay in Khaja Abdus Samad's house for some days. Bandagi Miyan Shah Burhan (Rh) had written about him:

"The king (Akber) called Miyan Mustafa (Rh) son of Miyan Abdul Rasheed (Rz). Details of his dialectic debates with scholars of Akber's Court, had been narrated and recorded separately. His deliberations in Four Debates, 70 letters and "Risalae-Nasikh-o-Mansookh" are unmatchable which became famous during his lifetime." ("Dafter-Duvwam", Rukn 11, Bob 6)

میان شیخ مصطفی بن عبدالرشید را طلبیده باایشان قصه ها و مناظره ها و مجالس ها گذشت که بیان مجلس میان مشار "الیه جداگانه نوشته شده است که چهار عدد مجلس و هفتاد مکتوبات و رساله ناسخ و منسوخ و مثل ذلک ، کلام شیخ اشهر المشهور است (دفتر دوم رکن ۱۱ باب ٦)

It all boils down to say that Miyan Mustafa (Rh) had to attend many sessions of debates in Gujrat, Ajmer and Fathepur Saikri, in a gathering of so many opposing scholars, among them he showed his caliber and eloquence in arguments. His arguments were so impressive and challenging that Ibrahim Sar-e-Hindi, after becoming humiliated, started to show frustration and high-handedness. Details of Miyan Mustafa's death had been written by Professor Mahmood Shirani in these words: "After some days Miyan Mustafa (Rh) took permission from Akber and left Fathepur to reach Biayana. There were many wounds on his body due to the above said torture. He had become very weak too. He was laid down on a couch and was taken away on the 4th. Zee Qaeda to Biayana which was 30 miles away. He reached Biayana afternoon on 19th, Zee Qaeda, the day of the Urs Ceremony of Imamana (As). The same day he passed away at his age 52 in 984 H. After his demise his relatives reached from Fathepur.

3.Miyan sheik Mubarak Nagori (Rh):

His forefathers were from Yemen. He was born in Nagore in 911 H. He was educated in Ahmadabad by Khateeb Abul Fazal Gazrooni. He settled down in Agra in 950 H. and was busy in the teaching profession for about 50 years in Agra. His excellence and perfection in knowledge was so exemplary that the genius like Abul Fazal and Faizi (author of the Commentary on Qur'an without dots) sat respectfully before him and attained whatever they could get from their father and became famous as un-matched scholars of that time. Badayuni had mentioned about his commentary of Qur'an under the title " Mumba-e-Nafaesul O'yoon" which was written in four volumes just like "Tafseer-e-Kabeer". He was a known Mahdavi among all non Mahdavis. Mulla Abdul Qader Badayuni had written further that:

"Abdul Nabi, Maqdoomul Mulk and other scholars jointly stated that Sheik Mubarak Mahdavi is an innovator."

عبدالنبی و مخدوم الملک و سائر علماء متفق اللفظ والمعنی شده بعرض رسانیدند که شیخ مبارک مهدوی نیز اهل بدعت است (منتخب التواریخ جلد دوم صفحه ۱۹۸)

Badayuni had recognized him as Mahdavi in his "Najatur Rasheed." Sheik Mubarak's chronogram" Maaza Mahdi" 910 H. is the best argument to recognize him as a Mahdavi. 910 is the year of the demise of Imamana (As). As a Mahdavi he told the befitting date of 910 H. By saying"Maaza Mahdi" means "Mahdi went." (It commensurate Our faith " Imam Mahdi (As) came and gone"). The very wording of Sheik Mubarak's questionnaire to Miyan Alim Billah (Rh), author of "Sirajul Absar" tells his compassionate obedience to Imamana (As): He wrote:

"Request is being made by this unfortunate, compassionate man to clear some doubts, for the sake of justice, which have nothing to do with any ulterior motives or any ill feelings."

معروض آنکه شبهٔ چند به این نامراد درد مند از رهگذر انصاف نه از ممر تعصب و اعتساف عارض می شوند رفع آنها ملتمس گردد

Miyan Aalim Billah (Rh) had answered this letter of Sheik Mubarak (Rh) in the Arabic which is recorded in "Minhajut Taqweem".

Sheik Mubarak (Rh) honored Mahmood Khan Mahdavi by the title "Saifullah". Mir Mohammed Husain Azad had written in reference to Mulla Abdul Qader Badayuni that Mahmood Khan was his friend during the period of Saleem Shah; who was so much impressed by Sheik Alaai (Rh) that wherever Alaai's name was heard he would rush to meet him keeping sword in his hand. Therefore Sheik Mubarak (Rh) gave the title of "Saifullah" ("Darbar-e-Akberi", page 812, printed in 1898). Alim Billah (Rh) had written a letter to Sheik Mubarak (Rh) in Arabic :

"Pious brother, an un-matched scholar, resident of Agra who is unique and incomparable, filled with religious knowledge and philosophy, had written a letter (Allah made him Mubarak auspicious as his name) on some of the pertinent points regarding Imamana (As)."

لما جاء منشور من الاخ الصالح العالم التحرير المتورع الساكن فی بلدة اکره الذی هوفریدد هره و وحید عصره المتحلی بالمنقول والمعقول جعله الله کاسمه مبارکا مشتملا اسولة فی مشکلات فی کیفیة المهدی الموعود الیٰ آخره (منهاج التقویم صفحه ۳)

In his letter Miyan Aalim Billah (Rh) had recognized Sheik Mubarak (Rh) as his"Religious brother"and had addressed him as "pious and abstinent"; which denotes that Sheik Mubarak (Rh) was a Mahdavi. Author of "Khatim-e-Sulaimani" had also written about Sheik Mubarak (Rh) that:

"During the religious debates which took place in the presence of Saleem Shah, Sheik Mubarak (Rh) used to help Miyan Sheik Alaai (Rh), and consequently had suffered many hardships and troubles, just because he assisted Miyan Alaai (Rh) as a perfect Mahdavi"

"بامیان شیخ علائی که به حضور سلیم شاه بحث دین باعلماء شده معاونت نموده اند و تعب ها وشدائد کشیده ..... خالص مهدوی و صاحب کمال بودند " (گلشن هشتم چمن چهارم)

From this it becomes clear that Sheik Mubarak (Rh) was a Mahadvi, that is why he, having without any fear, helped Sheik Alaai (Rh) in the court of Saleem Shah. Badayuni had written thus:

"Sheik Mubarak (Rh) helped Sheik Alaai (Rh), in the debates; hence it became known to all that Sheik Mubarak (Rh) was also a Mahdavi".

"چوں در آن مجلس شیخ مبارک ممد او بود نیز بمهدوی شهرت گرفت" (منتخب التواریخ طبع کلکته جلد اول صفحه ٤٠٢)

It may be pointed out that Maqdoomul Mulk and Abdul Nabi were blood thirsty enemies of Sheik Alaai (Rh). In that dangerous situation who would dare to endanger his own life and it was but natural that a Mahdavi only could help Sheik Alaai (Rh). Still Sheik Mubarak (Rh) bravely helped Hzt. Sheik Alaai (Rh) openly in the court of Saleem Shah Soori. Abul Kalam Azad has written about Maqdoomul Mulk that "if any man spoke against him, it was as if to invite death and destruction of his own". ("Tazkera" page 86) Even in those circumstances, Sheik Mubarak (Rh) had gone against Maqdoomul Mulk and supported Sheik Alaai (Rh) in that important issue of Imamana's Mahdiat.

During the initial period of Akber's reign, Mulla Maqdoomul Mulk and Abdul Nabi had much influence on him , but Sheik Mubarak's wisdom and shrewd tactics declined their evil influence. Sheik Mubarak (Rh) had made up his mind to obliterate their evil-motivated influence, which was full of bias and prejudices. Miyan Mubarak's aim was that there should be no hindrance for preachings of the Mahdavi Faith. He never wanted to see anything coming against his Faith. This was such an atmosphere that helped Akber to take undue advantage from it. Moulvi Shibli had written about Faizi that: Through these tactics, the power of the biased scholars had withered away, and Akber got the chance to establish a vast empire with full liberty under whose patronage Hindus, Muslims, Jews and Christians had the liberty in performing their respective religious activities.

Sir Syed Ahmed Khan too had recognized Sheik Mubarak (Rh) as being a Mahdavi in his Thesis on "Mahdi-e-Akhiruz Zaman" by saying: "Thus a Mahdavia Sect was established whose faith is that Mahdi (As) had come and gone. Sheik Mubarak (Rh), father of Abul Fazal also belonged to that Sect".

Akber Shah Khan Najeebaabadi had written in his "Qowl-e-Haq" that Sheik Khizer Nagori (Rz) was also a devotee of Imamana (As). He came from northern Afghanistan and reached Farah before 910 H, via Qandhar. Imamana's devotees were Sheik Khizer Nagori (Rz), Syed Mahmood (Rz) son of Syed Mohammed (As), Bandagi Miyan Syed Khundmir and Abdullah Khan Niyazi (Rz) who were busy in preaching and propagating Mahdavia literature. (Pages 117, 118). From this we come to know that Sheik Khizer Nagori (Rz), father of Sheik Mubarak (Rh), was also a Mahdavi.

Out of three sons of Sheik Mubarak only Faizi was a staunch follower of Mahdiat. During the journey to Bijapur, Faizi had the chance to meet the author of "Matleul Vilayet" where he inquired about the life details of Imamana (As).

Reasons of writing 'Matleul Vilayet' are that:

"Burhan Nizam Shah was an experienced and clever king. He asked us (the Author) to inform the details of the life and demise of Imamana (As). Like that Sheik Faizi too inquired the same about Imamana (As)."

بـرهـان نـظـام شـاه مردے جهاں دیدہ و طرار بود وقتیکہ بامـلاقـات کـردہ قصۂ حضرت میراں؏ از مولود و مبعث تـارحـلـت از مـاپرسیدہ استماع نمودہ و شیخ فیضی کہ عـلامـہ زمـان و ماہر مذاهب و ادیان بودہ اوہم ملاقات از ما کردہ همچنیں التماس داشتہ

The printing year of "Matleul Vilayet" was 1016 H. Faizi's couplet points out that he was a Mahdavi.

"The couplet is in Persian whose translation is: Faizi will not die till he gets guidance from the one who was the last of the Imams."

فیضی نہ شود خاتمۂ ما بہ هدایت تاختم اما مان هدار انشنا سیم

Thus Sheik Mubarak (Rh) had pragmatically defeated the unwanted influence of the biased scholars which helped Mahdavi Faith to flourish without hindrance during and even after the period of Akber.

CHAPTER V1

Dissemination and Propagation of Mahdavia Faith

Mahdavi Faith And Moderation:

It had already been discussed that the holy Prophet (Slm) had determined three pillars of the religion:

1. Faith, 2. Islam and 3. Ihsan. Some sects based their preachings to two only; Faith and Islam, particularly giving much care to rituals, rites and innovations. Thus they neglected Ihsan. The teachings of Faith and Islam without Ihsan is lifeless. Some others left the word "Ihsan" which occurred in the tradition (of Gabriel) which commensurate to the word "Mysticism:" and thus they became so obsessed that Islam's importance was completely ignored. However, someone exaggerated to the point of extremity and some minimized it. The moderation means to practice all the tenets of Faith: Iman, Islam and Ihsan since they have their own values in a religious way of life.

The meaning of Ihsan according to the holy Prophet (Slm): "Worship Allah, as if you are seeing Him; if you do not see Him, consider that He is looking at you." It will be discussed in the chapter "Convictions and Obligations" with reference to Qur'an: "any one who does not desire "Vision of Allah", according to the Qur'an he is punishable with fire of the Hell. Therefore sighting the vision of Allah is obligatory. Thus, as regards Mahdavia Faith is concerned it emphasizes on all three pillars which are the constituents of Deen. This is called

"Moderation". Before the advent of Mahdi (AS), Ummah did not know the meanings of Moderation. That was the sole reason that even without government's patronage Mahdavi Faith attained much fame and consequently kings, elites, eminent scholars, ministers, commanders, soldiers and persons from all walks of life enjoined Mahdiat.

Abdullah Mohammed bin Omer Makki in his History of Gujrat "Zaferwala" had elaborately discussed about the dissemination and propagation of the Mahdavia Faith:

"Mahdavis were spread in every nook and corner of India and they attracted multitudes of people towards their faith. They were though un-lettered, but their well mannered description of their faith overpowered even the wise men. And when their faith got acknowledged by one and all, then nobles and the armed forces accepted it, then they prepared themselves for successfully spreading the message of their faith."

ولم تخل جهة فى الهند منهم و استما لوا الكثير من اهلها ولم اقل تبعهم جها لهابل جاز تلبيسهم حتى على عقالها ولما فشاء مذهبهم قال به الامراء العسكر قويت شوكتهم و تجردوا النصرة مذهبهم (ظفر الوالہ بمظفر والہ جلداول صفحہ ۳۵)

Thus during the life time of Imamana (As) multitudes had become his followers. And this saintly line was adopted by eminent people also.

Selflessness of Mahdavis had been described as below:

"Every Mahdavi was struggling for the success of his faith. Martyrdom for them was the cause of nearness to Allah. He used to push himself in any military engagement without fear, They seemed to be like Ismaili devotees."

و كان الواحد منهم فى كفرة مذهبهم يقوم مقام الجمع ويرى بذل نفسه قربة يتخلل المهلكة ولا يبالى وكانوا كالا سما عيلية الفداوية (ظفر الوالہ جلد اول صفحہ ۳۵)

Ibn Omer Makki's reference of "Ismaili Assassins (devotees)" is not correct. Because those Ismaili devotees wanted to exterminate Islam. And, on the other hand, Mahdavis desired to spread Islam of the Holy Prophet's period. Secondly, these Ismaili devotees with ulterior motives assassinated elites of Islam as if they were Thugs. As against their ulterior motives, Mahdavis always defended Islam. When the scholars utterly failed to stop preaching the Faith through arguments; they resorted to getting Fatwas for killing Mahdavis, under the wrong presumption as if they were fulfilling some obligation and thus they started martyring Mahdavis at any cost. Thus Mahdavis too became convinced to nip the bud before it shoots. Sheik Ali Muttaqi and Abdullah Bin Omer Makki had both written that Mahdavis used to kill scholars. And Abdul Qader al Idroos had named Mahdavi as "Terrible slaughterers." In his book "Al Noorul Safer". The fact is that those scholars (who were killed by Mahdavis) were the same who got the Decree from authorities that the killing of Mahdavis was an obligation. In this connection they based their judgment on the fatwa said to have been given by Imam

Ghazali (Rh):

"Imam Ghazali (Rh) had decreed against some (Notorious) sect that if any one man of that sect is killed, the killer would be rewarded as if he had killed one hundred robbers."

وقد قال الغزالى رحمه الله تعالىٰ فى نحو هؤلاء الفرقة ان قتل الواحد منهم افضل من قتل ماية كافر (الفتاوى الحدثيه مطبوعه صفحه ۲۷)

Sheik Ali had even written in his "Risala-e-Rudd" that "to declare Jihad against Mahdavis is better than declaring against the infidels". ("Sirajul Absar" page 40). Thus in these circumstances, actions of Mahdavis may be taken as "Defensive and surely not Offensive".

Omar Bin Makki's writings bring out three points for discussion:

1. Mahdavi faith had reached every nook and corner of India.

2. Every Mahdavi had the capacity to confront an entire group of killers. It may be pointed out that these wordings are from an Arab and not from any Indian scholar ort historian.

3. Those who had embraced Mahdiat were nobles, soldiers, un-lettered ones as well as highly literates also.

This verdict is given by an alien which certifies that intellectuals and the nobles had accepted the Faith.

Author of "Tuhfatul Kiram" had said that many Godly people had joined this Faith. He wrote about Imamana (As) that many of the Godly men when they became Imamana's devotees they attained that much ability which they were yearning for. Moulana Abul Kalam Azad too had written in his "Tazkera" that : "After the demise of Imamana (As), this Sect spread everywhere in India and the renowned Godly men joined this Sect and accepted its Faith".

Khaja Mohammed Ibadullah Amratsari had written that: "Mahdavia Sect had a formidable force for a long time in India. From that sect, such known people had emerged whose names are recorded in History". The following pages will provide those places where Mahdavia faith had spread and its dissemination was in progress.

Spread of Mahdavi Faith:

Bengal to Turkistan:

Miyan Mustafa Gujrati's details of his discussion have been elaborately mentioned by Mulla Abdul Qader Badayuni and Professor Mahmood Shirani, It was also clearly mentioned that on orders of Akber, Asif Khan, the second Mir Bakhshi had brought Miyan Mustafa (Rh) from Ajmer, then he was shifted to Fatehpur where the debate ran for one and half years.

As per " Risala-e-Asaami-e-Musaddaqeen":

"Reported that for 18 months the debate ran in which all the scholars took part on one side and on the other hand just Sheik Mustafa Gujrati (Rh) was alone, regarding the subject matter relating to Imamana (As), in which Sheik Mustafa Gujrati (Rh) alone prevailed against all scholars."

"آخر الامر در بحث مهديت امام عليه السلام نصره الله تعالیٰ علی جميع علماء عساكر بادشاه جلال الدين كما هو مشهور كه تاهژده ماه مباحثه شد"

The details of just five debates had been recorded by Miyan Mustafa (RH) which are available.

(NOTE: *(These five sessions have been recorded by Hz. Mustafa Gujrti (Rh) in Arabic, later on were translated in Urdu, the same have been translated by Faqir Syed Ziaullah of Channapatna, from Urdu into English and had been recorded in "Khalifatullahilmehdi.info", which is reprinted in Addendum with courtesy from the Team of "Khalifatullahilmahdi.info*

1. Goud - Portion of Bengal:

It appears that Mahdavi Faith had reached Goud. It is a fact that Sultan Husain Sharqi and his descendants were the devotees of Imamana (As). Previous to this it was reported that Sultan Husain Sharqi had moved to Bengal. Thus it is confirmed that residents of Goud were the devotees of Imamana (As).

2. Bihar:

At the orders of Saleem Khan, Sheik Alaai (Rh) was sent to Sheik Budh, Tabeeb of Bihar. Thus, it may be deduced that propagation of Mahdavia faith had reached Bihar as well.

3. Juanpur:

A. A book known as "Rashidia" is noted for dialectic discussions. The author of this book is Devan Rasheed Mustafa who was the contemporary of Shah Jehan. He has written one couplet regarding Imamana (As):

B. Author of "Juanpur Nama" had mentioned in Chapter Five" Khaja Syed Mohammed (As)" in which he had written about Mahdavis that: "I had visited these people who were found weeping and wailing. But it was not clear that in which place he had seen those people. However, Juanpur was not alien to Mahdavis. Author of "Juanpur Nama" had copied the "Aqaaed Nama" of Syed Miran Jeo Bin Miyan Syed Salamullah (Rz)" in its original form. "Juanpur Nama" was written in Juanpur in whose preamble the reference of that "Risala" had been discussed. The "Risala" which was copied in its original form in "Juanpur Nama" was written by Hazrat Syed Miranji (Rz) also known as Saidoo Miyan Saheb, Murshaduz Zaman (Rz). He died in 1117 Hijri and was buried in Jalgaon Jamood, a town of Berar, in Maharashtra. Thus it might have been written in Jalgaon or in Hyderabad; which was one hundred years prior to the writing of "Juanpur Nama" which contains seven pages.

"Author of "Khatim-e-Sulaimani": had written that: "In Juanpur, around the Masjid-e-Khokri some three hundred Mahdavi families were living."

در بـلـدهٔ پـر نور جون پور حوالی مسجد کهوکری خانه هـائی مهـدویـان قـدرسی صد بودند (گلشن دواز دهم چمن چهارم)

Mahdavia faith was widely known till the beginning of the fourteenth century Hijri. Sheik Mazher Husain Juanpuri (died 1311H) had written a couplet which was read by Sheik Abdullah Imadi Juanpuri before this author (Hazrat Buzmi)"

"When the period of Mahdi started, Muslims became perfect Muslims."

چون دور مهدی آغاز کردند
مسلمان را مسلمان باز کردند

4. Allahabad:

Author of "Mu'asirul Umra" had written about Abul Fatah Deccani that Miyan Syed Abul Fatah (Rh), son of Miyan Syed Ilahdad (Rz) was appointed by Khan Khanan as commissioner of Ilahabad and granted him the Jagir of Manakpur. The facts are thus written:

"When Syed Abul Fatah (Rh) arrived to Khan Khanan, he was granted five thousand Mansab and then he was further granted Manakpur as his Jagir and also was appointed as the commissioner of Allahabad, where he became famous for his bravery."

خـان خـانـان مقدم اور اگرامی داشته منصب پنج هزاری تـجویز فرموده صاحب طبل و نقاره گردانیدپس از آن به تـیـولـداری مـانک پور و صوبه داری اله آباد مامور گشته در آن دیارنامـی به شجاعت و مردانگی برآورده (مآثر الامرا، طبع کلکته، جلد اول صفحه ۱۲٤)

Thus as per "Mu'asirul Omara" Syed Abul Fatah Khan (Rh) was a Mahdavi who died in 1023 H. in Thana Kothalmir. The author had also written about some details of Mahdavi faith, but wrongly written 960 H. as the year of the proclamation of Mahdiat by Imamana (As). He had also stated that the writer had met with one of the devotees of Imamana (As).

Author of "Shawahedul Vilayet" had mentioned about Miyan Abul Fatah Khan (Rh) in chapter 34 that:

"Miyan Abul Fatah (Rh) was a Punj Hazari noble. He was very generous, therefore known as "Hatim-e-Zaman". Most of his Army was Imamana's devotees."

مـیـان ابوالفتح ه (از) امـراء پنج هزاری حـاتم زمـان در سـخـاوت شـده بـودنـد و اکثر واغـلب لشکر ایشان مصدقان حضرت امام آخر زمان بودند

Author of "Shawahedul Vilayet" had written that he was the descendant of Miyan Abu Bakar Muhajir, son in law of Imamana (As). The "Tuzak-e-Jehangiri" wrote about Abul Fatah (Rh) that:

"Abul Fatah Deccani (Rh) was one of the reliable nobles of Adil Khan who had taken allegiance two years ago and joined the companionship and was awarded the robe of honour and the sword."

ابو الفتح خاں دکنی که از امرائے معتبر عادل خاں بود
قبل ازیں بدو سال دولت خواهی اختیار نموده خود را
داخل اولیائی دولت قاهره ساخته دردهم امرداد به
ملازمت آمد و منظور عنایت و تربیت گشته به شمشیر
و خلعت سرافرازی یافت و بعد از چند روز اسپ خاصه
نیز بدو مرحمت نمودم (توزک جهانگیری قلمی)

In "Tuzak-e-Jehangiri" the facts of his becoming Jagirdar and governor have been mentioned as under:

"Abul Fatah Khan Deccani (Rh) was the Jagirdar of Manakpur and its surrounding areas. He was permitted to attend the duties of his Jagir and as well as his duty was to safeguard the kingdom."

ابوالفتح خاں دکنی در سرکار مانک پور و آں حدود
جاگیر یافته بود مرخص گشت که هم سر انجام جاگیر
خود و بحفظ و حراست آں ملک قیام نماید (توزک
جهانگیری)

According to "Tazkeratus Saleheen", Miyan Abdul Fatah (Rh) was the son of Miyan Ilahdad (Rz), bin Miyan Abdul Fatah bin Miyan Abu Baker.

5. Jaais-Lukhnow:

Malik Mohammed Jaaisi was the famous Hindi poet, about whom it is reported in "Khazinathul Asfia" that:

"Malik Mohammed Jaaisi, known as "Muhaqqiq-e-Hindi" was the devotee and Khalifa of Hazrat Sheik Ilahdad (Rz) who was the Caliph of Syed Mohammed Mahdi (As). He had been heavily praised in Mahdavi literature."

ملک محمد جائیسی ......لقب او محقق هندی است
مرید و خلیفۀ شیخ الهٰداد خلیفه ، محمد مهدی است
انچه از کلام وے مفهوم میگردد و همیں است در کتب
خود مدح بسیار کرده (خزنیته الاصفیاء طبع مطبع
نولکشور جلد اول صفحه ٤٧٣)

From "Khazinatul Asafia" it had become clear that Malik Mohammed Jaaisi was a Mahdavi. But in another book "Malik Mohammed Jaaisi", written by Syed Kalab-e-Mustafa, published by Anjuman-e-Taraqi-e-Urdu (Hind) in 1941, pp. 29-31, his Mahdavi Faith was not mentioned. Malik Jaaisi had written "Padmawat" in which he had mentioned his Priest's name as "Ilahdad (Rz)" and "Syed Mohammed (As)" as his benefactor, Mahdi Alaihis Salaam. Miyan Ilahdad (Rz) is the same "Khalifa-e-Giroh", about whom Mulla Abdul Qader Badayuni had mentioned in "Najatur Rasheed" that when Sheik Burhanuddin of Kalpi had resided in Bandagi Ilahdad's company for three days he became trusted friend of Allah. This "Khazinatul Asfia" also informs about Malik Mohammed Jaaisi that:

"According to the author of "Shijrai-e-Chishtia" Malik Mohammed Jaaisi became disciple of Ilahdad (Rz) at his old age and within a short period he became a perfect Godly man."

صاحب شجرۂ چشتیہ میگوید کہ وے بہ آخر عمر ارادت بخدمت الہ داد آورد دور اندک زماں از کاملین وقت شد (خزینتہ الاصفیاء ،طبع نولکشور جلد اول صفحہ ٤٨٣)

Jaaisi's poetry had been acclaimed as a treasure of mystical exaltation, which was the result of the teachings of the Mahdavia faith. He had written many books, famous among them are: Padmawat, Chinawat, Chitrawat, Khurwa Nama, Murari Nama, Mehra Nama, Etc.

It is also mentioned in "Khazinatul Asafia" that he was presented before King Akber. Jaaisi was hunchbacked, on which Akber after seeing laughed at him. Jaaisi forthrightly told Akber, Whether he was laughing at the utensil or at the potter? Akber praised Jaaisi for his intelligent rebuke.

He was a wonderful poet of Hindi. What was the position of Moulana Rome in Persia and Turan, the same position Jaaisi had enjoyed in India. Professor Asmatullah Javeed had recognized him as belonging to Mahdavia Sect.

6. Amethi:

Malik Mohammed Jaaisi died in Amethi. It proves that in his last days his family moved from Jaaisi to Amethi. Gori Sri Saran Wastu had written the famous book " Hindi Kay Naqsh-e-Awaleen" (First Impressions in Hindi Literature") in which he had mentioned about Jaaisi that the Raja of Amethi had best regards to him, therefore the Raja invited him to his kingdom and awarded many gifts and a place for his residence, where he died whose grave still exists in Amethi and is much respected by many.

7. Muradabad:

One edition of "Sirajul Absar" was written in Muradabad, in 1119 H. which is under our review (Author Bazmi (Rh). In the last passage the name of the Caligrapher is written as : Faqir Haqeer Syed Khizar son of Syed Rustum son of Syed Miyanji Mahdavi, Bukhari, resident of Muradabad" the words Faqeer Haqeer denominate that the said Syad Zada was one among the spiritual guides of that period, which points out to the fact that there should have been a Mahdavia Dairah in Muradabad as well. The Calligrapher had copied "Sirajul Absar" which indicates his literary capability and proficiency in Arabic.

"Risala Hashda Aayaat" also is before us which was also written by Miyan Abdul Ghafoor Sujawandi (Rh), The last passage states :" Kaatib Faqeer Haqeer Az'af Ibadullah Syed Khizar son of Syed Rustum Ibn Syed Miyanji Mahdavi, resident of Muradabad, adjacent to Haveili of Nawab Taher Khan, grandson of Rustam Khan Daccani and adjacent to Haveli of Sheik Mohammed Mufti, dated 26th. Shaban 1128 H". These passages inform that Murdabad had been a hub of Mahdavis where Nawab Rustum Khan Deccani's Mansion was located. Rustum Khan was the son of Syed Ilyas Sharza Khan Bijapuri, as mentioned in "Mu'asirul Umara's Volume 2, pages 502-504. And Taher Khan was the grandson of Nawab Rustum Khan Deccani.

Nawab Rustum Khan Deccani's Mansion was situated at the banks of River Ram Ganga at Muradabad, where a Govt. school had been built now. It is a known fact that the Mansions of Nawab Rustum Khan were constructed underneath the ground. It is mentioned that when Rustum Khan Deccani was made Commissioner of Muradadbad, his Mahdavi relatives and servants also migrated to Muradabad along with their families and a big locality was established for Mahdvis.

8. Sumbhal:

Author of "Tareekh-e-Sulaimani" had written about the Miran Saheb Miyan son of Syed Karimullah that:

"Miran Saheb Miyan was the king's servant with 500 cavalry holding the post as Ziladar of Sumbhal, Muradabad. Sumbhal was his Jagir and he died there."

میـران صـاحـب میـان نوکر بادشاه دهلی بودند باپانصد سـوار ضـلـع دار سـمّـل مـراد آبـاد یعنی بلاد مذکور در جـاگیـر و تـصرف شان بود و هم در آن ملك کار آمدند (تاریـخ سلیـمـانـی قلمی ، ریاض اول ، چمن چهارم گلشن پنجم)

This passage shows that Delhi's kings used to award responsible positions and jagirs to Mahdavis as well.

9. Badayun:

Badayun had never been an alien place to Mahdavis. Mulla Abdul Qader had written his "Najatur Rasheed" at Badayun only in which particulars about Mahdavis had been recorded in detail. Mir Mohammed Husain Azad had certified that Badayuni had gone to his native place and written"Najatur Rasheed" in 999 H. which had become its Chronograph,which was written five years before his death. Akber Shah Khan Najeebabadi had also written that Mullah Sheik Abdul Qader Badayuni personally knew Sheik Alaai (Rh). The Badayuni's father was the devotee of Syed Mohammed (As) and Sheik Alaai (Rh). "Qoul-e-Haque" written by Najeebabadi mentions that there were Mahdavis in Badayun too.

10. Agra:

a. Miyan Sheik Mubarak Nagori (Rh) was an Arabic scholar who has lived in Agra since 950 H. till his demise. He was also a Mahdavi whose particulars had been mentioned in the chapter "Preachers of Mahdavia". On account of Mahdavia preachings many relatives of Saleem Shah Soori had become Mahdavis in Agra.

b. According to Farishta, Mulla Abdullah Sultanpuri had informed Saleem Shah that: all troops of his army had accepted Mahdavi Faith and some of his relatives too had become Mahdavis in secrecy."

"تـمـام لشـکر تو باو گرویده اند چنانچه خویشان تو نیز در خـفیـه بـمذهب اودر آمده اند" (تاریخ فرشته ، طبع نولکشور ۱۳۰۱ء جلد اول صفحه ۲۳۲)

c. Mulla Abdul Qader Badayuni has stated that he had met with Sheik Abul Fatah Gujrati

(Rh) along with Abdullah Qandhari in Agra in the locality of Sheik Bahauddin, where the tradition was recited by Abul Fatah Gujrati (Rh) which says that:

"They would be such people who would be always remembering Allah whom the angels would be surrounded. They would be content and Allah would remember them. After reciting this tradition, Abul Fatah (Rh) instructed Badayuni to remember always the names of Allah the Almighty"

قـوم يذكرون الله حفتهم الملائكة وعليهم السكينة و ذكر هم الله فى من عنده

Badayuni was very much impressed with religious instructions given by Abul Fatah (Rh) and thus stated:

"For a long time what ever voice and the call struck to my ears, was that of Abul Fatah (Rh) who told me to recite and remember the names of Allah."

وچندگاه چنىن بود که هر صداوندائى که سمع مراقراع مى کرد ذکر پنداشتم

This is all the effect of Mahdavi teachings by Miyan Abul Fatah (Rh). If such effect Badayuni had felt then what effect others might have not received?. Badayuni had also stated about Abul Fatha (Rh) that:

"Abul Fatah (Rh) was the son in Law of Imamana Syed Mohammed Juanpuri (As), but never met Imamana (As). Because this relationship was accomplished only after Mir's demise. Miyan Abul Fatah was a man of honour of high position having the quality of formidable excellence. He had firm belief and deep devotion to the Mahdavi Faith."

دامـاد حضـرت سيـد مـحـمـد جونپورى قدس الله سره الـعـزيز امـا ميـر راندىده و اىن نسبت بعد از رحلت مير واقع شـده بسيـار صـاحب جلال و کمال بوده و بروش سـلسـلـه مهـدوىـه ثابت قدم و با استقلال بود (منتخب التواريخ، طبع کلکته، جلد سوم صفحه ١٧)

It is said that had Maqdoomul Mulk not poisoned wrongly the ears of Saleem Shah about Sheik Alaai (Rh) that he himself had proclaimed as being the Mahdi (As), Saleem Shah would have accepted Mahdiat. The fact is that Sheik Alaai (Rh) was just a staunch preacher of that faith and a perfect devotee of Abdullah Khan Niyazi (Rh). That is what Badayuni came to understand:

"Saleem Shah became fascinated by Sheik Alaai's narration of Qur'an and said that Alaai (Rh) was correctly commenting on the Qur'an. Saleem Shah proposed to him to withdraw his claim of being the Mahdi by secretly renouncing in my ears so as I could appoint you as "Muhtasib" of the kingdom."

"It is stated in "Khatim-e-Sulaimani" that the descendants of Sheik Muhibbullah resided in the locality of Kacchi Pull of Agra, where more than two hundred Mahdavi families lived."

سلیم شاه فریفتۀ بیان و کلام او شده گفت که تفسیر معانی قرآن می کرده باشی و پیغام به شیخ داد که ازین دعویٔ که مهدی موعودی باز آئی و آهسته در گوش من ازیں سخن انکار کن که من ترابر قلمرو خویش محتسب الٰهی میگردانم (منتخب التواریخ، طبع کلکته، جلد سوم صفحه ۴۰۸)

در شهر آگره در کچی پل اولاد میان شیخ محب الله مهاجر است خانه هائے مصدقان زیاده از دو صد بودند (گلشن دواز دهم چمن چهارم)

11.Biyana:

Miyan Sheik Abdullah Khan Niyazi (Rz had established his Daiarah at Biayana about which author of "Muntakhabut Tawareekh" had stated that:

"When Sheik Saleem reached after performing Hajj via land route, Sheik Abdullah Niyazi Afghan (Rz) requested king's permission for going to Makkah for performing Hajj. Permission was granted along with a scroll of papers in which references of some Godly men's details had been written with whom Sheik Saleem had met in Makkah and elsewhere. Accordingly Abdullah Khan Niyazi (Rz) while visiting so many cities met those Godly men also. After returning he happened to meet the companions of Imamana (AS) who had accepted Imamana (As) as the True Mahdi (As) in Gujrat and Deccan. After meeting with them he adopted the same Faith and for some time he stayed in Biyana during the period of Saleem Shah. As had already been stated he lived a life in seclusion in Biyana and became anonymous without any fixed earnings and led a life of poverty and hunger."

چوں شیخ سلیم مرتبہ اول کہ از حج کہ براہ خشکی رفتہ بود ـ تشریف آوردو رخصت مکہ معظمہ طلبیدہ شیخ طومارے مشتمل برذکر مشائخ و اھل اللہ کہ از ولایت عرب و عجم و ھند دیدہ بود نوشتہ داد و در اکثر بلاد سیر کردہ این طبقات مشائخ رادریافت و صحبت یاران میر سید محمد جونپوری قدس اللہ روحہ کہ دعوی مھدیت کردہ بود بہ گجرات و دکن پیوستہ آخر ھمان طریقہ اختیار کردہ چند گاھی در بیانہ در عھد سلیم شاہ بطریقی کہ سابقاً مذکور گشت درزاویہ خمول و گمنامی بہ بے تعینی و بے تکلفی صرف نمودہ (منتخب التواریخ ، طبع کلکتہ ،جلد سوم صفحہ ٤٥)

Mulla Abdul Qader Badayuni had stated about Sheik Alaai (Rh) who had established his Dairah in Biyana; which became a hub of Mahdavi Faith where hundreds of Mahdavis were residing leaving their kith and kins:"

"Brother and brother, husband and wife had relinquished their relationship with each other and started living in the Diarah by adopting the life of poverty and hunger."

برادر از برادر و شوھر از زن مفارقت گزیدہ دائرہ مھدویہ درآمدہ راہ فقر و فنا پیش می گرفتند (منتخب التواریخ ، طبع کلکتہ ،جلد سوم صفحہ ٣٩٨)

According to "Tabkhat-e-Akberi", some officials of Biyana had also adopted Mahdavi Faith. It is further stated that those officials who had a soft corner with Mahdavi Faith used to help them. The same version Mulla Abdul Qader Badayuni had stated that those officials who had adopted that Faith used to help them.

12.Bisawer:

It was a place where Badayuni met with Sheik Alaai (Rh) and stated that:

"When Sheik Alaai (Rh) came from Biyana to Bisawer, my father took me to him when I was a minor, whose features stuck in my memory as a dream forever."

زمانی که از بیانه به قصبه بساور آمد جامع این اوراق را پدر مرحوم بملازمت اوبرده از بس خورد سالی صورت اومانند خوابی و خیالی در متخیله من مانده (منتخب التواریخ، طبع کلکته، جلد سوم صفحه ۳۹۹)

This tells that Miyan Sheik Alaai (Rh) was residing in Bisawer also. It is a proof that Mahdavia faith had already been propagated in that place as well.

13. Delhi:

A. According to Badayuni, Sheik Alaai (Rh) had accepted Mahdavi Faith at the hands of Miyan Sheik Abdullah Khan Niyazi (Rz) and started living with him in his Dairah; but according to "Tareekh-e-Sulaimani" it is stated in Part 8, Chapter 3, that when Bandagi Miyan Lad Shah (Rz), a companion of Imamana (AS) came to Delhi, Miyan Sheik Alaai (Rh) became his first disciple and started living with him till Bandagi Miyan Lad Shah (Rz) left Delhi to Gujrat, then he met Abdullah Khan Niyazi (Rz) and entered into his Dairah. It is also said that Sheik Alaai (Rh) accepted the faith only after being convinced regarding the Mahdavia Faith. Thus "Sulaimani's statement confirms that:

"When Sheik Alaai (Rh) put his questions and reservations about the Faith, he got befitting and extempore answers and after satisfaction and being convinced that the denial of Imamana (As) is infidelity, then only he accepted Mahdavia Faith."

پس شیخ انچه سوالها و اشکالها پیش آوردند از آنحضرت جواب برجسته و با صواب و ذهن نشین یافتند و بالکل یقین عالی درست شده در انکار موجب کفر دانسته فی الفور تصدیق نموده (گلشن هشتم چمن سوم)

It is understood that Sheik Alaai (Rh) had started preaching in Delhi first, that is why Sheik Alauddin Dehlavi had prepared a questionnaire, whose replies were given in Arabic by Sheik Alaai (Rh), which is well known to the Ummah.

B. Moulana Abul Kalam Azad had written in "Tazkera" that Allama Jamaluddin Dehlavi (Rz) had written a book on the proof of Mahdiat of Imam Mahdi Alai Hissalaam in the following words:

"Moulana Jamaluddin (Rz), had written a book, when he was in Delh, submitting incontrovertible arguments and conclusive proofs about the sanctity of Mahdiat of Imamana (As) (page 13). It is mentioned that Moulana Jamaluddin (Rz) was the pupil of Hafiz Asqalani (Rz) through two sources. He was living in Delhi and was known as the perfect teacher for religious and philosophical teachings. Particularly he had no parallel to him in the field of religious teachings. Apart from teaching he had adopted the path of righteousness and mysticism for which many people used to visit him to get blessings from him. ("Tazkera" Page 11,12).

C. Shah Burhan (Rh) had written a letter from Farah to one of his contemporaries who was residing in Tigria (Jaipur). This is also a proof that Mahdavis were living in the vicinity of Delhi. The letter reads:

"From Samana, I had reached Lahore in Jamadiul Awwal and it was my firm desire to offer my life in Imamana's name and to write a letter to the king at Lahore regarding the troubles faced by Mahdavis by the opponents. But my desire could not be fulfilled and we lived for just fifteen days in Lahore and left."

از سامانه به لاهور بتاریخ جمادی الاولیٰ رسیدیم و در آنجا خواسته بدیم که جان خود بنام حضرت مهدیؑ کنیم که یك کتابت بادشاه لاهور رابنویسم بسبب آن که مصدقان آنحضرت را درد هلیو منکران آزار رسانیده بودند لیکن خواست فقیر با تقدیر موافق نیامد ، پانزده روز در لاهور مانده بودیم

Bandagi Miyan Shah Burhan (Rh) had reached Farah in 1052 H. Thus this letter might have been written either the same year or earlier. Thus it is a proof that at that time Mahdavis were living in Delhi.

14.Sar-e-Hind- Punjab:

"Some Mahdavia books mention that Miyan Abdullah Khan Niyazi (Rz) had established his Dairah first at Sar-e-Hind; where it is said that more than 1800 people were receiving Sawiat (equal distribution of wealth) in that dairah. Author of "Nazhatul Khawatir" states that Sheik Abdullah Khan Niazi (Ez) of Sar-e-Hind was a great preacher of Mahdavia Faith."

الشیخ الکبیر عبدالله النیازی المهدوی .... السرهندی احد دعاة مذهب المهدویه کان من مشاهیر اهل الهند (نزهته الخواطر الجزء رابع صفحه ۲۱۲)

Thus, it can be inferred that "Sar-e-Hind" movement was the result of Mahdavia Teachings.

15.Bunn (Punjab):

It is stated that Miyan Sheik Alaai (Rh) was martyred in Bunn, a place in Punjab. According to "Tabkhaat-e-Akberi" when Saleem Shah was traveling in Bunn, Punjab, some persons came to him and handed over a sealed letter. After reading that letter of Miyan Alaai (Rh), he called Miyan Alaai (Rh) and asked him to tell in his ears secretly that he had renounced Mahdavia Faith. Miyan did not reply and kept quiet. Then he said to Maqdoomul Mulk that you know better what to do about him. "On this he ordered to flag Miyan Alaai (Rh). Miyan Alaai (Rh) was so ill and weak that just on the third strike the innocent passed away." (Page 789 Darbar-e-Akberi, Lahore)

Mulla Abdul Qader had written that:

"After that, his body was tied down to the leg of an elephant and it was drawn in the camp and was ordered not to bury his body and appointed guard on it".

بعـد ازان جثـهٔ نـازك اورا بـه پائـے پیل بسته پارهٔ در اردو گردانیـد نـد و حکـم فرمودند تا قالب اورادفن نسازند و موکـلان گمـاشتـنـد ((منتخب التواریخ ، طبع کلکته ، جلد سوم صفحه ٤٠٨))

Appointment of the guards was ordered with an apprehension that Mahdavis should not come and bury him. It is a clear proof that at that time many Mahdavis were living there who might take the body of Shaik Alaaii(Rh) and bury at a safer place. That is why gaurd was appointed to sdfe gaurd the body.

16.Lahore:

One of the sincere friends of Bandagi Miyan Shah Burhanuddin (Rh) was living in the vicinity of Lahore. He wrote to his friend that "If you wish to send a letter to me, send it through my brother, Abdul Mohammed, who would direct it to me to Farah.

17.Jah'ni: (Lahore)

Sheik Dawood (Rh) was the resident of Jahni, so he became famous as Jahniwal. Abul Kalam Azad had mentioned about him in "Tazkera." in these words. "But the interpretation of "Tazkiratul Waseleen" tells that he was suspected to be a Mahdavi and Maqdoomul Mulk had regarded it as mischief making on account of his opposition" Further he writes: "In case of Sheik Abdullah Khan Niyazi (Rz) and Sheik Alaai (Rh) his opinion was against Maqdoomul Mulk and other ulemas. Sheik Dawood (Rh) was of the opinion that "the treatment with these venerable personalities was nothing but cruelty and tyranny against innocent Muslims". It is also proved by a hint given in "Akhbarul Akhiar" which certify the opinion of Sheik Dawood (Rh).

Moulana Abul Kalam Azad had mentioned regarding "Tazkeratul Waseleen" that some scholars, particularly Sheikhul Islam Moulana Abdullah Sultan Puri had a grudge against Sheik Dawood (Rh). Reason of such a grudge was said to have been is the fact that Sheik Dawood (Rh) was convinced that Imamana Syed Mohammed Juanpuri (AS) was one among the acclaimed venerable mystics who held a high position in the Ummah.

18.Shergadh:

Author of "Bahr-e-Zakkhaar " wrote that Sheik Dawood Jahniwal (Rh) died in 972 H. and his shrine is in Shergadh, in the vicinity of Punjab, which is a venerable place for one and all as a pilgrim center. His way of life had been so simple that whatever was given to him as gifts or oblations, he used to distribute for the cause of Allah. He kept with him just a mat and a small earthen pot for his use. (Was it not the way of living of Mahdavis of that period?) Can we not assume that Sheik Dawood (Rh) had not declared to be a Mahdvi on the apprehension of Maqdoomul Mulk's atrocities?

19.Saamana:

Bandagi Miyan Shah Burhan (Rh) had written in chapter 40 of "Shawahedul Vilayet" about one of the successors of Muhajereen, Miyan Alauddin (Rh) who had established his Dairah in

Saamana. It is stated that Sheik Budh was living in the company of Bandagi Miyan Lad Shah (Rz) whose Dairah was in Saamana. Many nobles and commoners were his devotees. Particularly Bairam Khan, Punj Hazari, was the most devoted noble who was also living in Saamana.

20.Narnole:

Bandagi Miyan Shah Burhan (Rh) had preached in Narnole, Saamana and Lahore. He wrote that he had started his journey from Gujrat to Marwad, to Dhondaru to Narnole and to Saamana and then reached Lahore. A copy of a Pamphlet "Dalael-e-Mahdiat" which was copied in 1121 H. is with us (with Hzt. Bazmi Rh). Through this we ascertain that Mahdavis were living in Narnole in the vicinity of Ajmer during the 12th. Century Hijri.

21.Multan:

A. Author of "Intekhabul Mu'aleed" in Chapter 11, wrote about Bandagi Miyan Syed Khundmir (Rz) that :

"Thus Bandagi Miyan Syed Khundmir (Rz), after returning from Hajj sent a letter, (Maktoob-e-Multani), to the scholars of Multan (Now in Pakistan), through Miyan Haji (Rh), his Khalifa. Miyan Haji (Rh) resided their and preached for some years in Multan. Eighteen scholars after studying the contents of the letter accepted Mahdavi Faith on Miyan Haji's hand and many more joined the Faith. Martyrdom of Bandagi Miyan (Rz) took place in 930 H. Thus the said letter was written even before 930 H."

پس بندگی میاں بعد از آمدن حج میاں حاجی را خلیفه خود کرده کتابت نوشته داده به ملتان فرستادند میان مذکور چند سال در ملتان خلق را ارشاد کردند ، هژده علماء بعد از مطالعه کتابت بندگی میان روی بتصدیق آوردند و از دست میان حاجی تصدیق مهدی کرده تلقین شدند و دیگر بسیار کسان از فیض میان حاجی مستفیض شدند

B. Bandagi Miyan Burhan (Rh) had written in chapter 40 of "Shawahedul Vilayat" that Miyan Shah Jalaluddin Khuka (Rh) was one of the descendants of a Muhajir of Imamana (As). Miyan Sheik Mustafa Gujrati (Rh) had written a letter to Miyan Sheik Multani (Rh); which points out that Mahdavis were living in Multan for a long time.

22.Dhamtod:

"Khatim-e-Sulaimani" mentions that:

"The Godly preacher Miyan Murad (Rh) and his brother Miyan Dhanka (Rh) lived in Dhamtod, after paying donations to king Jehangir, they occupied this place, this fact is also mentioned in "Jehangir Nama"."Times Gazeteer" published in London in 1899 AD had mentioned about Dhamtod which is a valley in Punjab's Hazara District where Abotabad was founded. Syed Gulam Husain Sheikh Kazimi had written that: At the beginning Dhamtode was the capital and later on it became famous as Hazara. In 1857 AD/1273 H. it was selected as an Army cantonment, because its location was central. Major James Abbot also had approved for its moderate temperature. Later on this place was named as Abotabad on the name of Major Abot.

(Note: Now it is a military headquarters of the Pakistan Army. It is stated that Osama Bin Laden, an Arab by birth, known as an Al-Qaeda Leader, the most wanted person by USA for his entanglement in September Eleven (9/11) debacle, that destroyed America's two tallest buildings by two planes driven by two Saudis in which more than 3000 people died and a property loss of thousands of Billions Dollars, was hiding in a building compound at Abotabad for the last six or seven years. On a tip, one Dr. Afridi covertly planned fake medical program and took the DNA of the inhabitants of the persons living in that compound and confirmed to CIA that Asama Bin Laden was living here in hiding. On that information, the Us Marines, without permission from the Government of Pakistan, raided that compound during the midnight of May 2, 2012 and killed Asama Bin Laden and took away his body and it is said that his dead body was thrown by them in the ocean.(But it is doubtful) On that treacherous act, Dr. Afridi was convicted for 33 years imprisonment by Government of Pakistan. Thus this issue had flared up so much that relations between USA and Pakistan have become very precarious.)

23.Dera Ismail Khan:

Really it was a Dairah in the past, known as Dairah-e-Ismail Khan, founded by a Mahdavi General by name Ismail Khan, keeps its name still and is a well known place in Northern Pakistan."Khatim-e-Sulaimani" states that:

"Dhondar's Afghan, in order to purchase Turk Horses went via Dairah-e-Ismail Khan and Shikarpur, and further went to Khurasan."

فغانان ڈھونڈار برائے اشترائے ختلی ترکی از دائرہ اسماعیل خان و شکار پور بیشتر شدہ بخراسان رسیدہ بودند (خاتم سلیمانی گلشن دواندھم چمن چھارم)

The word Dairah denotes that this Dairah was a center for Mahdavis, is still known as "Dairah-e-Ismail Khan" situated in the North-Western Province (Sarhad) of Pakistan. Like that other Dairah was established by another Mahdavi General; at Ghaziabad, known as **24.Dera-e-Ghazi Khan, where many Madavis were residing.**

(It may be pointed out that there are more than ten such Dairahs, still availble in Punjab, Sindh and Baluchistan, established by Mahdavis. The list is available in the Addendum. Khundmiri)

25.Kabul:

In Chapter 35 of "Shawahedul Vilayet" it was written about Miyan Abdul Ghani who was residing in Kabul. Bandagi Miyan Shah Burhan (Rh) had also visited Kabul. Author of "Tareekh-e-Mahdavian" states that Syed Abdul Wahab Sujawandi had been the Qila Dar of

Kabul.

26.Badakhshan:

Miyan Mustafa Gujrati (Rh) had written the first session of the Debate in which he had mentioned an opponent's remark that: " your "mischief" (Mahdiat) had even reached in Badakhshan. That means the Mahdavia Faith had already flourished in Badakhshan.

Turkistan, Persia upto Raskumari (India)

27.Ghor:Bandagi Miyan Shah Burhan (Rh) had written a letter to his friend: that:

"Between Kabul and Balakh there remains Ghor city. On account of lack of conveyance, I had to stop for some days. The Public Preacher met and extended his helping hand to me. When the description of the Mahdiat of Imamana (As) was furnished, some of the reliable people by name Mohammed Husain Chughtai and Miyan Sulaiman Hindi who were both intelligent persons accepted Mahdiat."

يك شهرے است غور نـام درميان كابل و بلخ در آنجا رسيـديـم از جهـت مـعـذورى مركب ها چهار پنج روز مـانـديـم خـطـيب غـورى ملاقات كرده محبت بسيار اظهار نـمـوده بـعـد از اظهار معاملت مهديت حضرت عليـه الـسـلام يك شـخـص معتبر محمد حسين چغتہ و ميان سليمان هندى بافهم و ادراك تصديق كردند

This letter shows that Mahdavis were living in Ghor and Bandagi Shah Burhan's preaching brought others under the fold of Mahdiat.

27.Balakh: (Turkistan)

Bandagi Miyan Shah Burhan (Rh) happened to visit Balakh and propagated Mahdavia Faith in Balakh and Maroojaaq.

28.Maroojaaq:

"Came to Balakh, the capital of Turkistan, then went to Maroojaaq and finally from Maroojaaq to Herat:" (Shawahedul Vilayet)

از كـابـل بـه شهر دارالسلطنت تركستان يعنى بلخ و از بـلـخ بـهـمـار و جاق و ازمارو جاق به شهر هريو .... آمديم (دفتر دوم ركن دواز دهم باب هفدهم)

29.Undkhud:

Bandagi Miyan Burhan (Rh) had written a letter, stating that:

"Reached after five days to Undkhud city, from here there are two routes, one goes to Mashhad and the other to Herat, where I stayed for 18 days. During the stay we preached according to our skill and to the extent we understood the Faith by the Grace of Allah, as taught by Imamana (As) and his companions and tried to explain the Faith and distributed about one hundred pamphlets regarding proof of Mahdiat. Many scholars who were men of justice and did not have any bias or prejudice, accepted and became Mahdavi, but those who kept quiet and opposed, did not reply properly. With regard to preaching of the Faith, I did my best. Comparatively I found them polite and peace loving people better than Indians and Khurasanis."

بعد از پنج یا شش روز به شهر اندخو (اندخود) رسیدیم دراینجا دوراه می شود یکی به مشهدمی رود ویکی به هرات در اینجا کم و زیاد هژده روز اقامت کرده شد ، انچه حسب المدعا سوال و جواب دراثبات مهدیت بقدر حوصلهٔ خود معلوم بود بعون الله و حسن توفیق بصدقه حضرت مهدی علیه السلام و صدیقین وی اظهار کردیم باوجود کم زیاده صدرساله حجت برابر فقیر بود در آنجا گذراندیم حق آگاه است که بسیار منصفان از علما وغیره بلا تعصب و عناد تفهیم شده تصدیق کردند و اکثر واغلب ساکت ماندند و بعضی کسان مخالفت کردند ، جواب دادن نتوانستند معلوم باد که درباب تصدیق امام علی التحقیق ازیک راه از اهل هندو خراسان منصف و نرم یافتم

This proves that in Undkhud many persons, elite and scholars became Mahdavi on account of the preachings by Shah Burhan (Rh).

30. Herat:

It was already stated that Mulla Ali Fayyaz went from Farah to Herat and upon his testimony Mulla Shah Baig, Sheikhul Islam and Mirza Sultan Husain, King of Khursan, converted to Mahadism. It is a fact that Mahdavis were living in Herat, Farah and Qandhar. Bandagi Miyan Shah Burhan (Rh) had gone to Balakh and Maroojaaq, then he arrived in Herat, and stated in chapter 2 that:

"From Maroojaaq came to Herat which was the capital of Khurasan and from there went to Farah and performed Ziarat of Imamana (As) between Maghrib and Isha prayers on the 7th. Ramazan.1052, H."

ازماروجاق به شهر هریو واز شهر هر یو که دارالسلطنت خراسنت است بولایت فراه دریک هزار و پنجاه و دو سال ماه رمضان بوقت میان نماز شام و خفتن بشرف زیارت ...... ولایت پناه حضرت امام محمد المهدی مشرف شدیم (دفتر دوم رکن ۱۲ باب ۱۷)

31. Farah Mubarak:

A. While discussing about scholars of Herat, it was already stated that when Imamana (As) arrived at Farah, hundreds of people followed him. Imamana (As) stayed for two years and five months in Farah.

B. After the demise of Imamana (As), Bandagi Miyan Syed Mahmood (Rz) and many companions resided at Farah for one year. During this period also many people converted to Mahdiat. Bandagi Miyan Shah Burhan (Rh) had mentioned in "Shawahedul Vilayet" in chapter 40 that in Farah scholars like Mir Syed Ismail bin Amir, Syed Khaleelullah, Amir Syed Ahmed, Amir Syed Abdullah. Amir Syed Ismail and Bandagi Miyan Syed Qutubuddin were very famous scholars of Farah who had written their particulars to Bandagi Miyan Shah Dilwer (Rz) and became Mahdavi.

C. According to Bandagi Miyan Shah Burhan (Rh), even after the demise of Imamana (As) many officials of Farah had become devotees of Imamana (As). In chapter 38 of "Shawahedul Vilayet", written in the year 981 H. during the period of Bandagi Miyan Syed Shahabul Haq (Rz), Shah Qasim Iraqi, ruler of Farah had started construction of the Dome of the Imamana's Shrine. Then after him Yagan Sultan, another ruler of Farah completed that Dome. His elder brother Sheik Birji had accepted Mahdavi Faith at the hand of Miyan Mohammed Pushtavi, the Khalifa of Mohammed Zikria and wrote a book "Mir'atul Ushshaq". "Shawahedul Vilayet" reported that: The Book contains 5000 couplets in praise of Imamana (As) profusely.

D. Hz. Bandagi Miyan Shah Burhan (Rh) had written in the beginning of "Shawahedul Vilayet" that Qazi Abul Qasim and Qazi Badruddin Farahi requested him to write the biography of Imamana (As). Thus on that instance the writing of "Shawahedul Vilayet" was started by him. The words "Marhoom wa Maghfoor" are written along with the name "Qazi Abul Qasim" which informs that by the time the book was completed, Qazi Abul Qasim had already passed away. Hence it is obvious that during the period in which the book was written, there were many scholars, qazis and elites who were Mahdavi and living in Farah Mubarak. From the above mentioned passages it is proved that propagation of Mahdiat not only reached Herat, but to many places in Khurasan.

E. Many Pamphlets of proofs regarding Imamana's Mahdiat were written by prominent scholars of Farah; This is indicated in chapter 22 of "Shawahedul Vilayat" that:

"Be it known that Sheik Sadruddin Khurasani, one of the eminent scholars had accepted Imamana's Mahdiat and Mulla Haji Mohammed who was a perfect religious scholar had written some pamphlets in favour of the Mahdiat of Imamana (As); one among them is famous here as a proof of Mahdi (As)."

واضح باد که (از) علمائے عامل و فقہائے کامل شیخ صدر الدین خراسانی تصدیق امام ربانی کردہ اند و نیز ملا حاجی محمد دھی کہ کامل بودند درباب اثبات مہدیت چند رسالہ ہاتصنیف فرمودند کہ یکی از آں رسالہ درباب حجت امام الابرارھم درایں دیار مشہور است

F. Miyan Shah Burhan (Rh) in his "Shawahedul Vilayet" had mentioned some eyewitness particulars about some Shia officers and scholars who became impressed by Imamana (As), thus state that :

"A large number of Asna-e-Ashri nobles and officers had respect for the Shrine of Imamana (As). Those who had constructed Gumbad-e-Ali, House Sarposh, big Saraey, Saqaya, Big Door etc. in Iran; now they feel that they should also take care of this Shrine (Imamana's) with due respect. Such are the eye witnesses, if we go into the detail, it would take much time to write; hence decided to end here.

اكثر امراء و ملوك اثنا عشر معتقد اين آستانه شدند و كارهائ بزرگ چو گنبد على منظر و حوض سرپوش و خانقاه بزرگ و سقايه و در مسجد كلاں بنا كردند و بنده و غلام اين جانب ميگويانيد ند و انچه معامله به حضور اين فقير حقير سگ آستانۀ حضرت اميرديده شده است اگر تفصيل كنم عبارت دراز مى شود مختصر كرديم

During the period of Shah Burhan (Rh) there remained relics of the houses of the companions at Farah, about which "Shawahedul Vilayet" informs in Chapter 25 that:

"There are relics and traces of the houses of the companions. And particularly the ruins of the house of Bibi Malkan had been visited with respect."

اكنوں در اين زمان نشان خانه هائ مهاجران و حجره هائ ايشاں عليهم الرضوان در اينجا ظاهرات و نشان خانه هائ بى بى ملكان رضى الله عنها معروف و باهراست

Farah

فراه

(Note: a brief about Farah Mubarak: The resting place of Imamana (As).

Imamana (As), after migrating at his age 40, on the Command of Allah, from his birth place Juanpur, and after crossing over more than 13000 miles from Juanpur through Dabhol to Makkah, back to Ahmednagar to Badhli to Jaisalmir to Baluchistan to Thatta to Qandhar, finally to Farah (Khurasaanm) and resided here, for two years and five months, and passed away in the Morning of Monday, 19th.Zee Qaeda 910/ 1505 AD and was buried by some 313 bereaved disciples.

City Farah is the capital of the Province Farah of Afghanistan. Early legend goes as back as 330 BC, when Alexander the Great stayed here to amass his forces before attacking India, via Qandhar.

Farah (Pashto/Persian) is one of the thirty-four provinces of Afghanistan, located in the western part of the country abetting to Iran. It is a spacious and sparsely populated province, divided into eleven districts and contains hundreds of villages. It has a population of about 110,925,(As in 2010 AD) which is a multi-ethnic and mostly a rural tribal society. The Farah Airport is located near the city of Farah, which serves mostly for military purposes.

Geographically the province is approximately 18,000 square miles (47,000 km), making it

comparatively of the size of Telangana, The province is bounded on the north by Herat, on the northeast by Ghor, the southeast by Helmand, the south by Nimroz, and on the west by Iran. It is the fourth largest province in Afghanistan. The province is home to a great many ruined castles including the " Shrine of Mahdi-e-Mauood" just south of Farah City.

The Shrine and the Tomb were built by the Persian Architects, who had constructed the Holy Shrines of Najaf-e- Shrief and of Imam Moosa Kazim (Rz) in Iran. They did it, for they too had great respect for Imamana (AS). It is inscribed on the Epitaph:

*"**Hazrat Syed Mohammed of Juanpur, Mahdi-e-Akhiruz Zaman- born 847 H. Died 910***

As far as, our knowledge with reference to Farah Mubarak,we have read the impressions of Nawab Bhadur Yar Jung who had visited the holy shrine of Imamana (As) in the 1930s, which are recorded in his Travelogue, then we have heard about Dr. Syed Ali's visitation, who brought pictures of the Shrine. We too had tried to visit in 1976 and wrote to the Afghan Embassy in New Delhi, who turned down our Visa application for the security reasons. Still there might have been many persons who might have visited, but most important was that of Peer-o-Murshid Hazrat Mohammed Miyan Saheb Akailvi (Rh), who visited along with his relatives. His program was to stay for a week . But suddenly he was forced to leave the Shrine just after three days. He felt someone pusing him to leave early. Thus, he along with his relatives, left for Kabul Airport and reached just in time to catch the last flight to New Delhi at 11.30 and boarded the plane, and when they reached New Delhi, they came to know the tragedy of invasion by Soviet Forces at 12.00 in 1979 who took over the control of the Kabul Airport to bring their forces to Afghanistan.. Had Hazrat Mohammed Miyan Saheb Qibla not acted swiftly on the directions of the invisible hands who were pushing him to leave early, it is horrible to imagine their fate.

After that there was a long period of lull, in which none was allowed to visit the Holy Shrine. But fortunately, to my knowledge, the late Syed Yaqoob Roshan Yadullahi was the first to get visas to visit Farah Mubarak along with a delegation in the early years of the present Century. Then many delegations had the opportunity to visit. Among them was the visit of Mashaeq Syed Abid Khundmiri, who along with some 11 persons visited from Dubai. They stayed there for a week and during their stay, they refurbished the entire Shrine along with the Holy Grave, with the active involvement of local persons, who have great respect to the Shrine. It is said that more than Rs.156, 000, they spent for that work and came back.

Brother Faqeer Syed Nemathullah, architect also had visited along with Najaf Miyan of Naya Dairah and has elaborately written the details of expenses about obtaining a Visa, boarding Flight from New Delhi to Kabul, then to Herat, and then to Farah Mubarak, by Bus. If anyone is interested he may contact him who lives in Chanchalguda, Hyderabad.) Faqeer Syed Shrief Khundmiri.

32.Khurasan: Preachings:

"There are hundreds of persons who had accepted this Faith, if their names are recorded, a voluminous book would emerge. Still there may be some whose names are not available; for example; When Miyan Syed Abdul Lateef, disciple of Miyan Darvesh Hervi Muhajir (Rh) went towards Ajam (Iran), many became converted and accepted Mahdavia Faith. And Bandagi Miyan Ahmed (Rh), disciple of Miyan Abdul Ghani (Rz) Muhajir-e-Mahdi and his successor Mulla Ruknuddin Qandhari (Rh) and Bandagi Miyan Mohammed Husain (Rz) and his disciple Sheik Burj Ali Baig (Rh), a very learned man of his time who wrote more than twenty two volumes known as "Kaamiluz Zaman". Such are the names which were never heard in India. Thus, we came to know that many elites and literates accepted Imamana (As) and started preaching in Qandhar and Khurasan." (Shawahedul Vilayet")

اے عزیز باتمیز آنها که علماء بالله ورثه الانبیاء تارك الدنیا و ریابودند بعد از ...... حق بحکم دلائل حق را قبول کردند که عدد ندارد و اگر نام هائے ایشان نوشته شودیك کتاب مطول گر دو هزار درهزار هم هستند که نام ایشان رانمی دانند مثلاً میان عبداللطیف میان درویش هروی مهاجر حضرت مهدیؑ چون به طرف عجم رفتند از تاثیر فیض ایشان بسیاران مستفید شدند و به شرف تصدیق مهدی مشرف گشتنده به لقب شیخ العجم مشهور است نیز بندگی میان احمد خلیفۀ میان عبدالغنی که مهاجر مهدیؑ بودند و نیز تابع شان ملا رکن الدین قندهاری و نیز بندگی میان محمد حسین مرشد بندگی میان پشتوی و مرید شان شیخ برجعلی بیگ که عالم عامل و کامل بودند و اکثر بست و دو جلد تصنیف کرد و به مثل شان علمائے کامل الزمان مصدق خلیفته الرحمن که در ملك خراسان شدندو در ولایت هندوستان نام و نشانِ ایشان نه شنیده شد

Miyan Darvesh Harvi (Rz) was the Muhajir whose disciple Miyan Abdul Lateef (Rh) known as Sheikhul Ajam had been a formidable preacher of the Mahdavia Faith in Ajam. Shah Burj Ali Baig (Rh) was the contemporary of Shah Burhan (Rh), who had written "Mir'atul Usshaqe"; a narrative poetry about Imamana (As). Burj Ali (Rh) was the disciple of Bandagi Miyan Mohammed Pushtavi (Rz) and had written some poems about his Murshad and about Imamana (As). Those poems are masterpieces.

Bandagi Shah Burhan (Rh) had visited Farah for three times for offering respects on the shrine of Imamana (As). When he visited third time, then settled down there. He had invited one of his friends to visit Farah.

33.Qandhar:

A. Miyan Shah Burhan (Rh) in chapter 40 of "Shawahedul Vilayet" had stated about many successors of the companions of Imamana (As), like, Miyan Haji Mohammed (Rz) Muhajir, Miyan Syed Baday (Rz), Miyan Ahmed (Rz), Miyan Ahmadi Miyan (Rz), Miyan Jamal Mohammed (Rz), Miyan Mohammed Pushtu (Rz) and many more. Particularly Miyan Syed

Baday (Rh) was the disciple of Bandagi Miyan Shah Nemat (Rz) who was living in Qandhar. Apart from these preachers who had invested their time and energy for the furtherance of the Message of Imamana (As), Shah Burhan (Rh) himself had done a lot by staying permanently and visiting hundred many cities and traveling the areas mentioned above just for the sake of furtherance of the message of Imamana (As) which has been elaborated in Second Volume that:

"From Farah, a city of Khurasan, went towards India, then reached Fort Buss. After staying here for some days, went again to Qandhar where stayed for a few months where we had discussed about the proof of Imamana (As) and his Message. But none had power to answer and to speak against us."	از فراه کـه خـلاصـه ولایت خراسـان است بطرف هنـدوستـان روانـه شـدیـم ثـم مـن بعد ذلك بقلعه بس رسیدیم و چند روز در آنجا اقامت کرده بطرف قندهار روانـه شدیم و چند ماه در قندهار مقام کردیم و در آنجا گفتگو در بـاب ثبـوت مهدیـت حضرت امام محمد مهدی علیه السلام وقوع یافت فاماهیچ کس طاقت رو جواب نداشته اند

B. Miyan Syed Miran (Rh) had written a letter from Qandhar in which it was mentioned that from Qandhar to Farah hundreds of Mahdavi were living. The wording of his letter says: "From Qandhar to Farah many persons live who were the disciples of Imamana (As)."

34.Kashikor of Iran:

From a Pamphelete in Persian under the name "Zikr-e-Shuda-e-Jakigor" printed in Karachi in June 1937, by Pir Buksh Qamber, Shadad Zai (Kalachi), which is in front of us (Hazrat Buzmi), From this, it comes to light that Mahdavis were also living in Kashikor a region of Iran, In that book it had been stated that:

"Whatever I had written about Zikri Mahdavis and their way of worship and living, I had not added a single word of my own. For the last six months having leisure time I visited Palanpur, Keech, Makran, Sindh, Lasbela and Kashikor of Iran and after investigating and finding facts about the Mahdavis of these places I had written this pamphlet."	چیز هائے که دریں کتاب راجع به طریق و ترتیب ذکر یا عبادت مهدویان نوشته ام من از طرف خود نه حرفی زیاده کرده ام و نه کم ششماه گذشته به وقت فرصت از مهدویان ریاست پالن پور و کیج مکران و کشیکور ایران و سندھ و سبیله تحقیق و تدقیق نموده این مختصر را نوشتم (ذکر وحدت ،طبع کراچی، صفحه ۲۳)

Pir Baksh had written in that pamphlet that Qazi Abdullah Bin Mohammed Serbaz had caused the murder of Zikri Sheikhan of Kashikor in 1355 H. (1935 AD):

"Zikri Sheikhan of Kashikore, was martyred just for having Mahdavi Faith on Sunday, the 6th. Rabiul Awwal 1355 H. by Mullah Abdullah Bin Mohammed Qazi Sarbaz and his disciples of Qallat."	ذکری شیخان کشیکور سرباز محض عقائد مذهبی صبح یکشنبه ششم ربیع الاول ۱۳۵۵ه از دست ملا عبدالله بن محمد قاضی سرباز و مقتد یانش کشته و شهید شدند (ذکر وحدت ،طبع کراچی، صفحه ۱)

After the martyrdom of Zikri Sheikhan, Alhaj Noor Mohmmed Bin Malik Mohammed

Kohmestigi wanted to submit a petition to Raza Shah Pehalvi in Tehran against Abdullah Bin Mohammed Sarbaz, and for that purpose he started his journey but he died when he arrived in Karachi. It is reported that:

"Alhaj Moulvi Noor Mohammed Bin Malik Mohammed Kohmestigi, also known as Noori Qazi , in order to submit a petition at Tehran to Raza Shah Pahalvi of Iran, against Abdullah Bin Mohammed Sarbaz for his atrocities and murdering Zikri Sheikhan of Kishikoor, started along with Shukr Bin Shai Gulabi, but unfortunately died after reaching Karachi."

نوری تخلص مرحوم الحاج مولوی نور محمد بن ملك محمد کو همسیتگی سر بازی است که راجع به سفاکی و غارتگری قاضی عبدالله بن محمد سر بازی نسبت به ذکری شیخان کشیکور برخلاف قاضی مذکور و احتجاجاً ترك وطن گفته بعزم سفر طهران بشرف حضور شاه پهلوی جهت تظلم همراه" شی شکر بن مقتول شی گلابی" به کراچی آمدند ولے مع الاسف چند روز پس ازورود شان دراینجا جان شیرین به جان آفرین سپرده به رحمت ایزدی پیوست (رساله ذکر وحدت)

Moulvi Noor Mohammed Noori was a Persian poet and had compiled his poetical Divan, known as "Gulshan-e-Makran". He had also composed a poem on the martyrdom of Zikri Sheikhan, in which he had addressed Shah Raza Shah Pahlavi to do justice on the innocent's martyrdom by the cruel Abdullah Sarbaz.

35.Kashaan of Iran:

Bandagi Shah Burhan (Rh) had written a letter to Qazi Abul Qasim Farahi, which denotes that Mahdavis were also living in Kashaan (Iran). It states that:

"This faqeer had investigated that the late Qazi Badruddin was the disciple of Syed Ayub (Rh) who was a staunch devotee of Imamana (As). If any person had a doubt about my assertion, then one fact is enough to certify my claim that he had left his "Will to bring his body for funeral from Kashaan to Farah." It is a fact that in Khurasan none is supreme to Hazrat Imam Moosa Kazim (Rz), but Qazi Badruddin did not like to be buried there, he preferred to be buried at Farah, since Imamana (As), to him, was second to the Holy Prophet (Slm). Since his belief was correct, he wrote the Will for his burial thinking that his burial in Farah would become the source for his salvation."

ایں فقیر حقیر تحقیق کرده است که مرحومی مغفوری قاضی بدر الدین غفر الله له مرید بدست سید ایوب رحمته الله علیه شده بودند و میر مذکور معتقد خاص باعتقاد حق و خاتم ولایت صدق بودند و اگر کسے فرضا و محال ایں سخن را درست ندارد تا اور ابردلیل صدق اعتقاد قاضی بدر الدین غفر الله له همیں حجت بس بود که جنازهٔ خود را از کاشان تادر اینجا آوردن وصیت نمود زیراکه ظاهر الاظهر است که هیچ کس درایں ولایت خراسان فاضل از حضرت امام موسیٰ علیه الرضوان نیست که در آن خود را داشتن وصیت نه کردند مگر حضرت خاتم الولایت که نظیر خاتم نبوت است علیهما السلام چونکه اوشان را ایں اعتقاد درست بود تاچنیں وصیت که موجب رحمت و مغفرت است فرمود (مجموعه مکاتیب و رسائل قلمی)

It is clear that Qazi Badruddin was the disciple of Miyan Syed Ayub (Rh). Qazi Badruuddin wrote his Will to bring his corpse from Kashaan to Farah, since he was a Mahdavi. Thus from this, it comes to light that in Kashaan many Mahdavis were living.

36.Baluchistan:

Mulla Abdul Qader Badayuni had written in "Najatur Rasheed" that:

"After the demise of Imamana (As), one of his disciples Sheik Mohammed Farahi whose lineage and connection was well known, overpowered the Baluchis and dominated over them."

يكى از اصحاب مير كه شيخ محمد فراهى نام داشت و نسبت او و پدر او معلوم است بعد از فوت مير در طائفه بلوچان بر بعضى اقطاعات استيلا پيدا كرده (نجات الرشيد قلمى صفحه ٨٩، تصوف فارسى نمبر ٥٦٤، اسٹيٹ سنٹرل لائبريرى)

"According to "Khatim-e-Sulaimani" Baluchistan was half of Khurasan, and its capital was Asfehan. Previous to these two portions of Baluchistan were under the control of Persia and the other third portion was under Mahdavi Baluchis, whose capital was Keech, in Pakistan."

موازى سه دانگ ملك خراسان است و تخت گاهش اصفهان است و قبل ازين دو دانگ در ضبط ايران بود يك دانگ در تصرف مهدويان كه از قوم بلوچ اند بود و تخت گاه بلوچان مذكور بلدهٔ كيچ است (خاتم سليمانى گلشن دواز دهم چمن چهارم)

According to "Khatim-e-Sulaimani":

"Miyan Noor Mohammed(Kalhora)was a very noble man who on the basis of his mystic abilities attained an exalted position and became known as a sacred man of miraculous powers and had arranged under his control more than one lakh troops. He was bestowed with sons and daughters, among them Khudadad and Mohammed Murad(Both from Kalhora dynadsty) ruled Sindh and became famous."

ميان نور محمد بسا بزرگ و جامع كمالات مسند نشين شدند و چند كرامات از ذات ايشان در خلق اشتهار داشت و جمعيت يك لك سوار بلكه بيشتر بهم رسانيد و ايشان را چند پسران و دختران شدنديك خدا داد دوم مراد (خاتم سليمانى گلشن دواز دهم چمن چهارم)

This proves Baluchistan was a cradle of Mahdavis, where Noor Mohammed Baluchi (Kalhora) was maintaining an army of one lakh troops who were Mahdavis apart from other Baluchis.

(Note:A brief report on Zikri Mahdavis of Baluchistan is available in the Addendum No.9 for information of the readers by calling suggestions how to bring them in the main stream.)

37. Isfahan:

"Muneer Bin Noor Mohammed, Mahdavi, was the leader of more than 80,000 families living in another sub-division of Baluchistan. He used to live in India for some time and in Isfahan for some time He controlled more than one lakh troops."

دیگر پرگنه است سردار آنجا منیر .... بن نور محمد .... مهدوی هشتاد هزار خانه هارا سردار است گاهی به ضلع هندوستان و گاهی به ضلع اصفهان می ماند و قدر یك لك سوار جمعیت دارد (خاتم سلیمانی گلشن دواز دهم چمن چهارم)

Thus Isfahan too was the hub of Mahdavis. Before Partition entire Baluchistan was under British India. After Partition, half Baluchistan had gone to Persia and the other half is under Pakistan. This indicates that lakhs of Mahdavis are still residing in Isfahan of Iran and Baluchistan in Pakistan.

38.Ferat:

According to "Khatim-e-Sulaimani" there were five thousand Mahdavi troops living in Ferat.

39.Keech and 40. Makran:

The king of Makran was also a Mahdavi. His grandfather was the disciple of Imamana (As), according to "Khatim-e-Sulaimani."

"City of Keech was the capital of Baluchis and their country is Makran. The king Sultan Ahmed Mahdavi bin Sultan Zaher, bin Sultan Pir Dil Khan, bin Sultan Fatah Khan, bin Sultan Mir Mandu, Bin Sultan Mir Kamal Shah Danishmand (Rz) who had taken oath of allegiance on the hand of Imamana (As) and became Mahdavi."

تخت گاه بلوچان مذکور بلده کیچ است و ملکش مکران و قبل ازین شاه آنجا سلطان احمد مهدوی بن سلطان زاهر بن سلطان پیردل خان بن سلطان فتح خان بن سلطان میر مندوبن سلطان میر کمال شاه دانشمند که بذات حضرت میران آورده و تصدیق نموده است (گلشن دواز دهم چمن چهارم)

According to "Khatim-e-Sulaimani" Hyderbad (Sindh) and Muradabad of Pakistan were habituated by Mahdavis:

King"Mohammed Murad of Kalhora dynasty had migrated to Muradabad adjacent to Kaha (Pakistan) and populated that city while Shah Gulam Shah Kalhora had populated Hyderabad (Sindh). Believe it that, till the period of Mohammed Murad all of Abbasis and Baluchis were Mahdavi. Both Mohammed Murad and Ghulam Shah, Kalhora, were the contemporaries of Nader Shah who invaded India in 1149 H.

As per "Khatim-e-Sulaimani" the Sultan of Keech and Makran was a Mahdavi. Mir Mahrab was one of the nobles also was a Mahdavi. Mir Mahrab was very proficient in Arabic, Persian, Turkish and Pushtu.When Afghans of Dhondar, Jaipur, went via Dairah Ismail Khan and Shikarpur to Khurasan for purchasing Khatli Horses, they happened to meet with Mir Mahrab who after knowing about Palanpur; came to Palanpur via Sindh and met with many elites of Palanpur, like, Miyan Syed Taher, Miyan Syed Tayyab, Miyan Syed Shakerullah, Miyan Syed

Karimullah. He also met with Miyan Malik Sharfuddin, the grandfather of the Author of "Khatim-e-Sulaimani". He was given "Mu'aleed" for reading and when "Sirajul Absar" was given to him he copied it in the year 1124 H. These legends are heard even these days in Palanpur and elsewhere in its vicinity.

41. Qallat:

According to "Khatim-e-Sulaimani" the leader of Qallat Mir Chaaker Bin Mir Khurd was a Mahdavi. Professor A.S. Ansari had stated in his Thesis which was published in Islamic Studies that: "The Zikris, a sub Sect of the Mahdavis are still found in large numbers in the former Baluchistan and Qallat Regions."

42. Lasbela:

Lasbela is situated in the South-East portion of Baluchistan, where there are several Zikri Mahdavis.

43. Sindh:

A. Author of "Insaf Nama" had reported in chapter 11, that Bandagi Miyan Shah Nemat (Rz) had established his Dairah in Sindh. According to "Khatim-e-Sulaimani", Adam Shah Kalhora (Rz) along with Miyan Ilyas (Rz) and his cousin had taken oath of allegiance on the hand of Imamana (As). It says:

"The rulers of Sindh are Abbasi and they are Mahdavi by faith whose title was "Kalhora" At first Miyan Ilyas (Rz) Kalhora, his uncle's son and Miyan Adam Shah (Rz) whose details of birth are not known, these two and his servant Miyan Ilyas Langdaja (Rz), all three had taken oath of allegiance on the hand of Imamana (As) and had gone with Imamana (As) to Farah. After Imamana's demise they came back to Sindh and established themselves in Sindh."

تخت نشینان ملک سندھ عباسی اندو مهدوی و کلوهره خطاب است اول میان الیاس کلوهره پسرعم او ومیان آدم شاه و بیشتر کرسی و مولد و منشاء شان مسموع نشد و ایں هر سه در خدمت گزار شان میان الیاس لنگر اجای هر سه در بلدة ٹهٹه بذات مبارک حضرت میرانؑ مشرف به تصدیق شده و در هجرت همراه جناب ولایت مآب بودند و در فراه نیز حاضر بودند و بعد از وصال حضرت میران علیه السلام ایں هر سه در ملک سندھ آمده ساکن شدند (گلشن دواز دهم چمن چهارم)

(Note: Kalhora Dynasty of Sindh, Pakistan, was the only Mahdavia Dynasty who ruled Sindh for more than one hundred years, whose founder was Miyan Adam Shah Kalhora, a faqeer Manish, pious man, who, on the dictates of Imamana (AS) proclaimed "Land belongs to Allah, and the tiller is the temporary owner of land". Thus this proclamation brought "Green Revolution" and a new "Miyanwali Movement" came into being in and around Sindh and in the Punjab, which gave a new meaning to the Economic Prosperity under the "Sawi'ath" System, where tillers enjoyed equality in earnings as well as social status. "Miyanwali" is still a well known constituency of Srikai Speaking population of Pakistan, whose MNA is the famous cricketer-turned Politician Mr. Imran Khan, whose

Tahreek-e-Pakistan Party became a prominent Political Party of Pakistan.

The Only Mahdvia Kalhora Dynasty has been elaborately discussed as item 10 in the Addendum for information of the Readers.   Khundmiri)

This proves that the rulers of Sindh were Abbasi and religiously they were Mahdavi.

Author of "Nuzhatul Khawatir" had written about Imamana (As):

"Thus he went towards cities of Sindh and people entered into his Deen in large numbers.	فـرحـل ابـی بـلاد السند و دخل الناس فی دینه افواجاً (الجز ، الرابع صفحه ٣٢٣)

44.Lukki of Sindh:

A.Syed Sadruddin Mohammed Wani (Rz), was the Muhajir-e-Mahdi (Rz) whose mausoleum is in Lukki where his descendants live in the Lukki city of Sindh.	اولاد سیـد صدر الدین محمد وانی مهاجر مهدی موعود و روضـه سیـد صدر الدین محمد نیز در شهر لکی است (خاتم سلیمانی گلشن دواز دهم چمن چهارم)

Times Gazettier" writes about Lukki that: Lukki is a village of Sindh in India, Bombay, (before the Partition) is located near Karachi, abutting to the West Bank of the River Indus (Sindh)."

45.Thatta, 46. Bhakker, 47. Mukalli:

A. It had already been stated that Sindh became a hub of Mahdavis. In Thatta and Bhakker, Qazi Qadan (Rh), Mahdavi, was appointed as Qazi and in Mukalli Peer Aasaat (Rh), another Mahdavi was working as Qazi.

B. According to "Shawahedul Vilayet" Miyan Abdullah Bhakkri (Rh) and Miyan Zakriah Bhakkri (Rh) had full dominance over the residents who were Mahdavi.

C. Miyan Sheik Mustafa Gujrati (Rh) had written letter No. 10 to Miyan Abdullah Bhakkri (Rh) with these words" to the "Mine of knowledge" of the divine and the leader of the Mahdavia Sect."

D. Author of "Mu'asirul Omara" wrote about Khuda Yar Khan (Rh), Mir Zaban-e-Sindh that after the capture of the fort of Qallat, Khuda Yar Khan was given the title of "Sabit Jung" whose forefathers were leading the life of piety and poverty following the perfect way of life under the leadership of Imamana Mahdi-e-Mauood (As)." Further it states that:

"After this victory (at Qallat) he was granted "Sabit Jung" title and punj hazari mansab along with "Naubat o Nakhara" and also was granted Thatta and Bhakkar under his administration and thus the entire Tarkhanian territory came under his control."	بعـد ازیـن فتح از پیشگاه خلافت بخاطب خدا یار خان بهادر ثابت جنگ و منصب پنج هزاری باصل و اضافه و عـطیه نوبت و خلعت فاخره پیرایه امتیاز پوشیده در سنه هـزار ویـک صـد و چهل ونه هجری حکومت صوبه تهڅه و سـرکـار بهـکـر نیز بوے مـقـرر شد و جمیع مملکت ترخانیان مع شئی زوائد در قبضه، اقتدار اودر آمد

The details of Khuda Yar Khan (Rh) and his family had been recorded in "Mua'sirul Omara" Volume One, on pages 825-829, it is particularly mentioned that when Nader Shah of Iran wanted to invade India through the territory of Sindh, he was repulsed by Khuda Yar Khan (Rh), therefore Nader Shah had adopted Kabul as en route to attack India.

F. Author of "Tuhfatul Kiram"had written about Adam Shah (Rz) (Sindhi) that he had established the path of righteousness under the guidance of Imamana (As), the ultimate Guide. It is also mentioned that Nawab Khan-e-Khanan had come to Adam Shah (Rz) for grant of Blessings and offered his humble tributes to him.

Sindh is still a center for Mahdavis.

(Note: Mashaeq Haz. Syed Murtuza Saheb of Gujrat (Rh), was the first Mahdavi Murshid to migrate to Karachi, from Hyderabad, even before Pakistan became a reality, he settled down in Sindh and established his Dairah at Shadadpur. After his demise, his second son Syed Shahabuddin Yadullahi became the Murshid. Shahabuddin Saheb had taken much pains to find out about the Zikri Mahdvis. He lived with them and learned their way of life and slowly infused among them the real tenets of Mahdism. But it takes a long time to bring them into the mainstream. Once he had come to Hyderabad, I had the opportunity to meet him and obtained first hand information about the Zikri Mahdavis. Accordingly a brief summary is provided in this book for information of the readers, as an Addendum. After the demise of Shahbuddin Saheb, his sons are taking care of the Daira, where Dugana and other prayers are performed regularly in congregation.)

48.Moorbi: (Khatiawar)

Miyan Abdul Rasheed (Rz), father of Miyan Mustafa Gujrati (Rh) is buried here, details of his martyrdom had been written on page 237 of "ZaferWala".

49.Gujrat:

Dairahs of Gujrat are well known, about which Mulla Abdul Qader Badayuni had written that:

"Sheik Alaai (Rh) along with six or seven hundred families came to Gujrat just to know the Mahdavi culture and system of the residents of those Dairahs and resided for a short time among them and left after getting first hand information."

شیخ علائی به همان وضع و حالت که داشت باششصد و هفت صدخانه دار مردم ، به امید آنکه دراین سفر شاید باعیان و مقتدایان این طائفه صحبت داشته روش اهل دوائر بداند متوجه گجرات شد (منتخب التواریخ ، طبع کلکته ، جلد اول صفحه ۲۹۹)

Mir Gulam Ali Azad was of the opinion that Abdul Rahim Khan Khanan had favoured Mahdavia Faith. Sheik Mohammed Bin Taherul Fitni states that : "when the province of Gujrat came under the control of Abdul Rahim Khan Khanan, Mahdavis felt peace and liberty for them."

50. Palanpur:

Mahdavi Nawab was the ruler of Palanpur, where still lots of Mahdavis live here.

51. Khambayet:

One Mulla Saleh belonging to the family of Miyan Kabeer Khambati and Miyan Sheik Joe Khambati were staunch preachers of Mahdavia Faith, about whom"Author of "Khatim-e-Sulaimani" had written that:

"A learned and brave man by name Mullah Saleh had hoisted a flag on his Masjid, by inscribing the entire Tasbih from "Kalma-e-Tiyyaba to Amanna Sadqanna"on it with an intention that if anyone wanted to discuss and to know about the Faith he was welcomed with respect."

مردے بودبا علم و شجاعت ملا صالح نام یك علم بر مسجد فراه نموده و برآن تسبیح از كلمۀ طیب تا آمنا و صدقنا جمله نوشته بود جهت آنكه اگر كسی را آرزوی بحث و صحت دین باشد تانزد بنده رسد (گلشن دواز دهم چمن سوم)

52.Khanbel:

The Dairah of Bandagi Miyan (Syed Khundmir's elder son) Syed Shahabuddin (Rz) was here whose title was "Murshadul Murshadeen" given by Bandagi Miyan (Rz), as mentioned by Shah Burhan (Rh) in his "Daftar", "Bandagi Miyan (Rz) granted him this title." Author of "Tazkeratul Saleheen" had written that about him:

"There were eighteen Godly men in the Dairah of Bandagi Miyan Syed Shahabuddin (Rz) who were enjoying the company of Bandagi Malik Ilahdad (Rz) who had witnessed the Vision of Allah; apart from them there were hundreds of God Seekers."

نقل است بندگی میان سید شهاب الدین را مرشد المرشدین فرمودند (دفتر دوم ركن نهم باب اول)

This tells the grandeur of the Dairah of Khanbel. According to Shah Burhan (Rh), Miyan Sheik Mustafa Gujrati (Rh) had a deep devotion with Bandagi Miyan Syed Shahabuddin (Rz):

"Miyan Sheik Mustafa Gujrati (Rh), son of Miyan Abdul Rasheed (Rz) had proclaimed that if Allah granted permission to adopt another Qibla, I would adopt Khanbel as my Qibla, since Bandagi Miyan Syed Shahabuddin (Rz) resides here; thus Miyan Mustafa Gujrati (Rh) left his own Dairah and maintained his saintly connection by adopting the company of Murshadul Murshadeen (Rz)."

میان شیخ مصطفی بن شیخ عبدالرشید فرموده اند اگر بنده را بغیر از قبله قبلۀ دیگر مخیر سازند بنده قبله به طرف كهانبیل می كنیم كه بندگی میان سید شهاب الدین در آنجا هستند و نیز مشار الیه ترك دائره و مرشدی داده در صحبت مرشد المرشدین آمده بودند (حدیقته الحقائق دفتر دوم ركن دهم باب اول)

(Note: Khumbail was the main Daira of Hzt. Bandagi Miyan (Rz) from where he advanced along his 60 companions against Ainal's Army on 12th. Shawwal 930 H. and defeated the large Army, as prophesied by Imamana (As). The defeated army, while returning, slaughtered 40 Mahdavis who were posted for safeguarding the Daira and the womenfolk. Those martyrs were buried in a single large grave where they were slaughtered at the Eastern border of the Daira. Total area of the Dairah is 8 acres, still it runs in the name of Bibi Aysha (Rz) first wife of Hzt. Bandagi Miyan (Rz). There are 8 graves including Bibi Aysha (Rz), Shahabuddin Shahabul Haq and members of his family. The Rouza is well kept by the Mujawer. Just on the Eastern side some 100 yards, there is another Rouza of Bibi Fatima,Khatun-e-Vilayet (Rz), daughter of Imamana (As) second wife of Bandagi Miyan (Rz).

53.Surat Here, this author's (Hazrat Buzmi's) great Grand father Bandagi Miyan Syed Abdul Lateef (Rh), son of Miyan Syed Jalal (Rh) is buried. According to the Author of "Akhbarul Asrar" it is mentioned that:

"As instructed by his Murshid, Miyan Syed Abdul Lateef (Rh) had arrived in Gujrat, about whom his Murshid used to say that he was one of my arrows of my quiver whom I had sent to Gujrat."

نقـل اسـت کـه از حکـم مـرشد در گجرات تشریف آوردند میـان سید راجی محمد می فرمودند که بندگی میـان سیـد عبداللطیف تیـرے از ترکش من است کـه در گجرات فرستاده ام

Bandagi Miyan Syed Abdul Lateef (Rh) was the contemporary of Shah Burhan (Rh), about whom Shah Burhan (Rh) had written that:

Bandagi Syed Abdul Lateef (Rh) was the grandson of Hazrat Syed Abdul Lateef (Rz), son of Hazrat Bandagi Miyan Syed Sharief, Tashrifullah (Rz), Ibn Hazrat Bandagi Miyan Syed Khundmir (Rz).

Author of "Akhbarul Asrar" had written about him that he had been bestowed with such remarkable memory that he had memorised not only "Ummul Aqaaed" of Bandagi Miyan (Rz), but also memorised "Sirajul Absar" as well. He had such a strong mental capacity that no scholar could defeat him in dialectics discussions.

54.Bombay:

Bombay was also a city for Mahdavis.

55.Poona:

Poona had been the hub of Mahdavis. The dominating power of the Peshwa's army was the Arabs and Afghan Mahdavis who were under his employment. Author of " Khazanai-e-Rasool Khani" states that:

"At that time four thousand Arabs and ten thousand Mangadhi (Pathan) troops were under the command of that Rao".

در آن وقت هـمراه راو مذکور چهار هزار جوانان عرب ده هزار سوارمان گری همراه بود (خزانه رسول خانی ، تاریخ فارسی قلمی نمبر ٦٠٦ ، اسٹیٹ سنٹرل لائبریری حیدرآباد)

This proves that Peshwa was maintaining Arabs and Mahdavi Pathans in his army.

Author of "Hadia's" claims that after the ruin of Poona, Mahdavis migrated to Hyderabad Deccan is totally ill founded, since we had already stated above that Mahdavis who were living in Hyderabad, during the Qutub Shahi period and well before the advent of Asafia Dynasty in Hyderabad. His objection regarding Sardar Khan Ghadayzai is historically wrong. The real fact is that Sardar Khan Ghadayzai was the officer in the Cavalry of Huzur Nizam, maintaining 300 horsemen and 25 Camel driving men. On instructions by the English regime, Huzur Nizam sent one thousand troops for attacking at Poona. Sardar Khan also had been along with Nizam's contingents whose officer was Davis who wanted that Nizam's cavalry should be under the control of his Contingent to which Sardar Khan disagreed, under that pretext, he left Poona and came to Hyderabad to inform Nawab Sikander Jah about his decision. But Raja Chandulal did not permit him to visit Hyderabad. Then he went back to his Jagir; and after some time came to Poona and accepted Peshwa's employment. This fact had also been narrated by the author of "Rashidudin Khani":

"Alphinston, an English commander, who had started from Channapatna, arrived Poona and mingled with English forces, who were badly encircled from all directions by the Marhata armies of Holker, Sindhia, and Bhonsla Peshwas. In order to recognize his forces and his supporters, English commander planned an emblem for such recognition; then he wanted that the cavalry of his supporter Nizamul Mulk, should be controlled by the English command under Davis, who was the officer commanding of Hyderabad Contingent. But Sardar Khan Ghaday Zai, Mahdavi Pathan, did not agree since he had held a formidable position in the Nizam's government. He was against the English army and never wanted that Nizam's army, in which he had his own cavalry should go under the control of Davis; hence, he left the Nizam's Army, and preferred to join with the forces of Baji Rao Peshwa who was at war against English army".

Thus Sardar Khan really wanted to maintain the dignity of the Nizam's position. But Raja Chandul, prime minister, did not agree anti-English suggestion proposed by Sardar Khan. When Chandulal did not agree, he decided not only to leave the Nizam's employment, but he relinquished both Jagir and Mansubdari granted by the Nizam. He decided to support the Marhatas who were vehemently fighting against the English Army. Covertly the English commander was forcing Baji Rao Peshwa, to hand over the assassin Trimbak Rao, who killed their supporter Gangadhar. Further they wanted Baji Rao to surrender the post of Peshwa as well.

Author of Hadia had hatched up a wrong blame on Sardar Khan that he had instigated the Englishmen by calling them "Infidels" and unnecessarily intervened in the tussle between the Peshwa and the Englishmen with regard to Trimbak Rao and rebuked the English lawyer. On account of which the Englishmen became enraged; now they put pressure on Baji Rao Peshwa to relinquish his post and to hand over control of Peshwa's four thousand army as well. Under this scenario, here also, Sardar Khan was against the English demand for the merger of

Marahatta's four thousand army with the English army. Surprisingly, as against the suggestion of Sardar Khan, Marhatta officers were connivingly agreed to the English demand. This fact had been also reported by "Rashiduddin Khan".

Now the English were trying to get hold on Sardar Khan, not because he had abused the Englishmen by telling them infidels, as author of Hadia had blamed, but because, he was opposing their pressure for merging both the Nizam's and Marahtta armies with the English army. The blame of the auther of Hadia was baseless, since it was the Peshwa who rebuked the English Attorney and not Sardar Khan. It was also a fact that it was not Sardar Khan who ill treated the English Attorney.

According to "Mir'atul Akhbar" Baji Rao's army was not ready for the battle, but Mahdavi Afghans under Sardar Khan were ready for the battle, thus they proved their faithfulness to Baji Rao when he had decided to attack the English army. Thus Sardar Khan attacked the English Army under instructions of the Peshwa. Here again the author of Hadia puts blame on Sardar Khan that on account of his attack, Poona's kingdom was defeated, it is utterly wrong. Sardar Khan did what Baji Rao wanted. Baji Rao was defeated, because the Baji Rao's army, having hands in glove with Englishmen, did not join in the battle and refused to obey orders of their Peshwa. This all happened because the policy of the English commander was based on "grabbing the territories by hook or crook" and the Peshwa had no control over his own army on account of the duel policy"Divide and Rule" of the Englishmen. Thus, why should Sardar Khan be blamed?. The author of Hadia had his own rivalry with the Mahdavis, therefore he is blaming wrongly Sardar Khan for the defeat of the Peshwa, which is against the facts.

According to "Khazana-e-Rasool Khani" the reasons for the defeat of the Peshwa were:

1.Peshwa had strong hopes on his army but it proved wrong.

2. He did not plan any strategy for the battle and did not consult with his commanders

3. Only Mahdavi Afghans were ready to face the enemy because they were fighting for the honour of the country.

4. Finally the Peshwa decided to wage a war against the English army and requested Sardar Khan to join him and never consulted his commanders for the onslaught on the enemy.

5. When confronted with the opposing army, the Peshwa himself fled away from the battleground.

According to the "Mir'athul Akhbar" which was written during the beginning period of Nawab Nasirud Dowla (of Hyderabad) Mahdavi Afghan troops under the command of Sardar Khan Mahdavi were ready to fight when the Peshwa decided to fight, but the Peshwa's army did not join with Mahdavis and fled away. Thus the entire blame should go on to the Peshwa and his army alone for Peshwa's defeat. As against these facts author of Hadia blames Sardar Khan and his men who started the battle, which is entirely wrong since both "Mir'atul Akhbar" and "Rashid Khani" are the basic source for correct information which was written well before the Hadia's writing.

56. Shakkar War Pet, is a locality of Poona, where Mahdavis are still residing.

57. Belgaum:

Maindargi, Desnur, Pachapur, Sankeshwer are the localities of Belguam where Mahdavi resides dominantly.

58. Ahmadnagar:

A. It had already been discussed how Mahdavi Faith flourished during the kings of Ahmad Nagar, particularly during Burhan Nizam Shah and Ismail Nizam Shah. During the period of these two kings, father and son, this Faith got a strong hold. Whether it was a battleground or a session for discussion, Mahdavis were dominating in every field. Farishta had written about Ismail Nizam Shah that within a short spell of time, Mahdavis living all around India, had assembled around Ismail Nizam Shah.

B. It is stated in "Muntakhabal Bab" that during the period of Ismail Nizam Shah, more than ten thousand horsemen, all of them Mahdavis, and none else, marched towards Bijapur under the command of Miyan Jamal Khan.

Ismail Nizam Shah was himself a learned king, who used to arrange sessions for discussions and invite both Mahdavi and Non Mahdavi scholars. In such sessions Mahdavi scholars prevailed against the Non Mahdavi scholars with regard to Sharai jurisprudence and Mystic deliberations.

Sherza Khan: (of Adil Shahi Period):

Noorullah's history of Ali Adil Shah, the 2nd. is full with the references of bravery, demonstrated by Sharza Khan in many places, for instance:

"Salabat Khan and other eminent nobles knew that Sharza Khan was that lion whose awe-inspiring sword had terrified the legendary heroes of that period."	صــلابت خــاں و جميع امرائ نامدار هندوستان به يقين مـی داشتند كه شرزه خان شيرافگنی است كه شير فلك از دهشت نهنك حسامش شب و روز چون گاؤ زمين ترسان و هراسان است و كوه البرزوالوندار هيبت صدمهٔ گـرز گرانـش ليل و نهار همچو شاخ بيدلرزان وجنبان (تاريخ علی عادل شاهی)
"Syed Ilyas, titled as Sharza Khan whose bravery and manliness were well known among the nobles and the elites of the court. He was heavily awarded by Adil Shah with a robe of honour and he was usually deputed for crushing the revolts at any corner."	شـجــاعت نشان سيد الياس المخاطب شرزه خان را در جـميع وزرائ نصرت پير او امرائ ظفر آرا به دلاوری و مـردانـگی اختصاص و امتياز تمام دار و بخلعات شاهانه و بـه تشـاريف خسروانه كـه تار و پودش بافته و دست نصرت پيوست نساج تـائيد الهی بود مفتحرو مباهی فرمـوده بهـر تـنبيه و تاديب آن كم بخت برگشته طالع روانه فرمود (تاريخ علی عادل شاهی)

Author of "Khatim-e-Sulaimani" writes that:

1."Burhan Nizamulmulk was enthroned and declared as king on his father's throne, who became devotee of Bandagi Shah Nemat (Rz) and had invited many muhajirs from Gujrat whose presence made Ahmad Nager an envious place. Thus Chichond, Ahmad Nager Dowlatabad and many places were heavily populated by Mahdavis."

برهان نظام الملك به تخت پدر به شهر یاری مسلم شد و روے ارادت بـحضـرت شاه نعمت آورده بود و اکثرے مهـاجـران و صحابه را از گجرات طلبیده و ملك احمد نگر از تـوجهات قدوم ارباب مهدویه رشك خلد بریں کرده بـود چنـانچه در چچونڈ و احمد نگر دولت آباد وغیـره دیهـات آبـادی مهدویـان از سببش اکثر بود (گلشن دواز دهم چمن اول)

It is evident from the above that during the period of Muhajirs and companions Mahdavi Faith flourished in Ahmad Nager, Dowlatabad and elsewhere. "Khatim-e-Sulaimani" further states that:

"Nahnay Miyan was reared and trained by Bandagi Miyan (Shah Nemat (Rz)). He went to Nizamul Mulk and got a higher position, then became minister. He was a very Godly and pious man."

نهنی میـان تـربیت و تـلـقیـن از بندگی میان شده اند .... در ملك دکن رفته از امرائے کلاں نظام الملك شـده انـد و مـدار الـمهام گردید ندبسا بزرگ و صاحب کـمال بـودند (خـاتم سلیمانی گلشن دواز دهم چمن چهارم)

Kashful Asrar'" was written by Nahnnay Miyan in Arabic. Khaja Ibadullah Amratsari had written that Mahdavia Faith had established its dominance in the Deccan and they have settled on thousands everywhere and in Ahmad Nagar predominantly.

59.Bijapur:

Bijapur had been a center for Mahdavis. What influence Jamal Khan had in Ahmad Nagar, the same sort of influence Syed Ilyas Sharza Khan had in Bijapur. Every history of Bijapur has favourable references regarding Sharza Khan and his achievements.

A. "Mu'a siral Umara" states that Syed Ilyas went to Deccan from the North and got employed in Bijapur and was granted the title of Sharza Khan.

B. "Basateenus Salateen" (printed in Hyderabad) refers about Sharza Khan that he attacked Salabat Khan Dahalvi's army.

C. "Alamgir Nama" describes about Sharza Khan that: Ilyas Khan Mahdavi known as Sharza Khan had been acclaimed as a brave warrior and he had the superb ability to arrange his forces against unspeakable odds and gained victory.

D. "Author of "Akhbarul Asrar" states about Miyan Syed Saadullah (Rz) (died 1024 H.) that:

"It was a period when Bijapur was sparkling with the population of Mahdavis. Many Mahdavi Ministers had administered Bijapur. The Dairah of Hazrat (Bandagi Miyan Syed Sadullah (Rz), son of Hazrat Bandagi Miyan Syed Tashrifullah (Rz)) was extending leaps and bounds and was known as "Mahdavi Wada".

”انگـاه آبادی بیجا پور بسیار رونق وافی داشت و در آن شـاهی مدار المهام اکثر مهدویان بودند و در آنجا دائره آنحـضرت بسیار وسیع شده آن جائی را مهدوی واژه گویند (اخبار الاسرار ،قلمی، باب دوم فضیلت نهم)

E. According to "Akhbarul Asrar" The kings of Bijapur had complete confidence on Mahdavis who were made nobles of the court of the kings.

"Miyan Syed Ibrahim (Rh), son of Miyan Syed Abdul Wahab (Rh) was a very pious man. He was one of the eleven nobles who maintained king of Bijapur's treasure. Afterwards Miyan Syed Ibrahim (R) distributed his wealth comprising bags of gold coins and other household items among the poor and became devotee of Bandagi Miyan Syed Taher Ghazi (Rh), son of Bandagi Miyan Syed Raje Mohammed (Rz) (son of Hzt. Bandagi Miyan Syed Saadullah (Rz) who lived in his Diarah of Bijapur".)

”میـان سید ابراهیم بن میان سید عبدالوهاب بسیار متقی و پـرهیـزگار بودند و از جمله یا زده اشرافان که چوکید ار بادشاه بیجا پور عادل شاه بودند“

”کیسه هـائی زر و جمـله اموال خانه را براه خـدا بـذل کـرده عـلاقه از میان سید طاهر بن میان سید راجی محمد نمودند“

According to "Khatim-e-Sulaimani":

"Bijapur and its surrounding areas, villages, towns were swarming with twelve thousand Mahdavi weavers who had complete faith in Imamana (As)."

بـحـوالـی بـیـجا پور در دیهات و بلاد و قری مومنان یعنی بافندگان قدر دو از ده هزار مصدقان امام سعادت اندوز تصدیق اند (گلشن دو از دهم چمن چهارم)

F. This author's (Hazrat Bazmi's) great, great grandfather was Bandagi Miyan Syed Abdul Lateef (Rz) son of Hazrat Bandagi Miyan Syed Tashrifullah (Rz) (Died 989 H) was one of his confidant deputies. According to "Khatim-e-Sulaimani" and "Akhbarul Asrar" Hazrat Bandagi Miyan Syed Mahmood, Khatimul Murshad (Rz), on the occasion of the demise of his brother, Bandgi Miyan Syed Tashrifullah (Rz), sent his condolences to his nephew, Miyan Syed Abdul Lateef (Rz), along with his personal robe as a gift and granted him with the title "Lateefullah".

According to Shawahedul Vilayet" which was written at Farah in 1052 H. Shah Burhan (Rh) wrote: "Amir Syed Abdul Lateef (Rz) was the Seeker of Divinity and who was always immersed in meditation".

A third source is "Mu'arajul Vilayet" written by Bandagi Miyan Syed Mahmood (Rh), grandson of Khatim-e-Kar (Rz) about Bandagi Miyan Syed Abdul Lateef (Rz) that" with the blessings of Miyan Syed Abdul Lateef (Rz), his nephew Miyan Syed Raje Mohammed (Rh) (the only son of Bandagi Miyan Syed Saadullah (Rz) came to life. This fact also had been mentioned in "Khatim-e-Sulaimani", chapter 7, Section 4 that " On hearing the unfortunate demise of his adolescent nephew, Miyan Syed Raje Mohammed, Miyan Syed Abdul Lateef (Rz) was completely immersed in meditation and invoked the Almighty's Blessings for the life of his only nephew, miraculously came back to life. Such was his exalted position and his attributes are commendable. "Khatim-e-Sulaimani" had gone so far that "he was absorbed with the vision of Allah always."

(Note: This transltor's Great Great Great Grandfather was Haz.Syed Sadullah Asadullah Ghazi (Rz), the eldest son of Haz. Tashreefullah (Rz), I had the opportunity to visit Bijapur, very recently, on invitation by the Momin Brothers in Bijapur. Many bunkers are hereditary Mahdavi since long and residing in Momin Wada and have their own "Mahdavia Association, Bijapur "with a large membership. The president and the members of the Association informed that there are eleven Mahdavi Graveyards in and around Bijapur and they have been registered, recently, as the Waqf under the management of that association. These eleven graveyards prove that Bijapur was the hub of Mahdavis in the past.

One particular point requires to be mentioned that the grave of Hzt. Bandagi Miyan Syed Saadullah Asadullah Ghazi (Rz), was in a very dilapidated condition, abetting to the Jail Boundary, where a colony was illegally built on the Wakf Land of the Graveyard. The said grave was recently built with marble and had been sarounded with an iron mesh boundary, by one Br. Syed Najmuddin of Bangalore. Had he not built it in time, local Hindus would have dismantled it, and fresh houses would have been constructed illegally on the Waqf Land.

Another point of interest to mention is that: A long time back when the Government had decided to construct a prison on the Waqf lands of the graveyard, since there was no proper Association to safeguard and raise any objection some 125 years back. However when construction was started, they came across the grave of Hzt. Bandagi Miyan Syed Raje Mohammed (Rh), son of Hzt. Bandagi Miyan Syed Saadullah (Rz). It is said that on account of this venerable grave, they could not continue construction. The matter was brought before the Hindu priests, who after visiting the grave, advised to bring the grave within the prison boundary without dismantling the grave. Thus, now, it has become a respectable place within the prison boundary and this venerable grave is being looked after by the prison administration and every year the Urs ceremony is being regularly celebrated by the authorities, by inviting Mahdavis to arrange for the Urs in which the administration also takes part with respect and expenses of such Feast are borne on from the prison funds. Whenever Mahdavis go for offering respects, they are permitted properly and a Guide is provided to offer flowers and respects on that grave. This translator had the opportunity in the same manner to visit the grave. And had also visited all eleven grave yards which are well kept by the Bijapur Momin Association).

60.Gokak:

Author of "Matleul Vilayet" states that in 1061, there was a consensus in Gokak, in which one Mustafa Khan requested proof of the Mahdiath of Imamana (As). It means that there were Mahadavis living in Gokak well before 1061. When Alamgir invaded Bijapur, Mahdavis migrated to the surrounding areas.

61.Dharwad:

The Qazi of this place inquired the proof of the Mahdaviat. Aalim Maroof Miyan had answered properly in 1250 H. This answer was published in a "Risala" which became famous. "Akhbarul Asrar" mentions under the caption" Sons of Hazrat Bandagi Miyan Syed Saadullah (Rz)" written by Aalim Maroof Miyan, a learned scholar of that period, author of that "Risala".

62.Mysore:

When Hyder Ali of Mysore became the king, he established his capital in Sri Rangapatam, six miles away North of Mysore. He appointed many Mahdavis to different positions in his administration. Syed Mohammed Khan Mahdavi was the Qiladar who after handing over the charge of the Qila went along with his army, on account of a conspiracy hatched by Mir Asif against Mahdavis, they left Sri Ranga Patan in 1212 H.

Exodus of Mahdavis From Sri Rangapatam:

"A boy was born to the princess in the year 1212 H. the same year the prince of Iran, at the request of the nobles of the court, went out of the capital. The same year the Satan's kid, Mir Asif, Devan of Mysore poisoned the ears of Tipu Sultan against Mahdavis with a false cooked up apprehension that Mahdavis would revolt against the kingdom. Tipu Sultan expelled Mahdavis along with their families, even though, he knew that Mahdvis were trustworthy, loyal and faithful to the kingdom. But on account of much pressure from Asif who was not only the Devan but was also brother-in-law of Tipu. Thus Tipu did not give a second thought or consult with other confidants, had erroneously issued orders for the expulsion of all Mahdavis along with families en-block. Thus Mir Asif's plan to topple Tipu's government, became successful which was not possible in the presence of the loyal Mahdavi Commanders, since Asif had hands in gloves with the English commanders."

در سال یك هزار و دو صد دو از ده هجری خاتون خاصه سر اوقات حشمت و اجلال پسر زائیده ...... هم در آن سال شهزادهٔ ایران برجست استدعای امرائے هائے پائے تخت خود از حضور مرخص گردید.......... هم در آن سال آن نطفهٔ شیطان اعنی صاحب دیوان المخاطب به میر آصف شرارت و بیوفائی و بد خواهی قوم مهدوی كه آنهارا دائره و الـه گویند اگرچه آنها حسب ظاهر راست باز و حلال نمك بودند اما صاحب دیوان مذكور از آن قوم اندیشه تمام داشت و بیش ازین اكثر جنگ با از ایشان به ظهور آمده بود معروض داشته مزاج و هاج را بنوعی شورانیدند كه آنحضرت ازین قوم وسوسهٔ بغاوت پیدا كرده جملگی را بازن و بچه از قلمرو خود اخراج فرمودند (نشان حیدری صفحه ۳۷۸)

Author of "Khatimul Huda" writes that the reason of expulsion of Mahdavis from Sri Rangapatam had been that Mahdavis did not take part in the treacherous plan hatched by Mir Asif against Tipu sultan. Englishmen knew that unless Mahdavis were expelled from Sri Rangapatam, the treacherous plot of Mir Asif could not succeed. Therefore, on one hand, they were instigating Mir Asif to provoke Tipu for expulsion of Mahdavis, and on the other hand they were providing space to Mahdavis to inhabit in places which were under English control, if they were expelled. This all happened because they knew that Mahdavis were the backbone of the kingdom. Therefore they hatched this plan through Mir Asif who was hand in glove with the Englishmen. Thus the reason of their expulsion was nothing but their loyalty and trustworthiness.

There was yet another reason, which was a religious issue. On the 27th night of Ramzan, the Non Mahdavi troops objected Mahdavis for performing Dugana-e-Lailatul Qadr and they got orders for Mahdavis to offer prayers, away from the capital. Thus both political and religious issues caused their expulsion. But more important was the political Issue, since the English knew very well that unless Mahdavis who are loyal to the kingdom, if not driven away, they could not succeed in defeating Tipu Sultan. Thus politically they wanted Mahdavis to be expelled from the capital. When they were expelled Mir Asif played his treacherous plan and Tipu was defeated as planned and was surrounded by English army which was fighting against Tipu who was left alone by his own army on the orders of Mir Asif and the brave Tipu was ruthlessly murdered by the dubious tactics of English commanders and thus they conquered Mysore without any difficulty.

(Note: Ironically, it is a fact that, the same Mir Asif, after the murder of Tipu Sultan, when demanded his share in toppling the Tipu's Government, the commander of the English Army point blank fired on him saying "this is the share of a treacherous person who duped his own government and his own brother-in-law who was a brave king.")

The author of "Nishan-e-Hydri" is the contemporary of Tipu Sultan. He knew very well what was cooking up against Tipu Sultan. Now let us see what "Nishan-e-Hydri" had to say about these faithful, but helpless Mahdavis:

"Mir Asif, child of the Satan had poisoned the ears of Tipu Sultan by instigating him against Mahdavis by telling that they were treacherous and untrustworthy". That cursed man was afraid of these Mahdavis who were loyal and trustworthy. Tipu Sultan did not give a second thought and expelled them along with their kith and kins. Thus the treachery plan of Asif worked well, only after Tipu expelled them without giving a second thought. Thus this expulsion was without any bloodshed, as the author of Hadia blames that the reason of expulsion was bloodshed, which is wrong and a false accusation. It is a fact that if Mahdavis were not expelled, the treacherous plan of Mir Asif would not have succeeded and the brave Tipu would not have been murdered so ruthlessly and, of course the English would not have become successful in getting further hold on other territories, one by one and finally became so powerful to topple and crush the First Independence War of 1857, which they named it "Mutiny" against them. Thus the war against Tipu and his defeat became the cornerstone for the establishment of the British Raj in India.

"Karnamai-e-Hyderi" has also been an authentic history of Mysore. This book was written by Moulvi Abdul Raheem on the request of Tipu's son Prince Gulam Mohammed (born 1212 H) who wrote that since the year 1196 H. to 1211 H. Mahdavis were in the employment of the kingdom of Mysore and had a strong hold on the administration.

The information which comes from the nearest source of the kingdom is more reliable than any other sources. Hence we have to rely on such basic and reliable sources only and not on other dubious sources. Col. Wilks's history of Mysore cannot be relied upon which was written after the writing of "Nishan-e-Hydari". Thus the year 1212 H. was the correct year for expulsion of Mahdavis from Sri Rangapatam, as mentioned in the "Nishan-e-Hydari" while Col. Wilks had wrongly stated the year of the expulsion was 1208 H in his book.

The fact is that after the third battle of Mysore, the English had gained control on some portions of the kingdom of Mysore in which Dawazda Mahal also became under their control, to which place they offered Mahdavis to migrate to Dawazda Mahal after their expulsion. Thus the treachery was being hatched even from the year 1210 H because they knew unless Mahdavis are expelled from Sri Ranga Patam they could not conquer Mysore. Therefore they were pushing Mir Asif to poison the ears of Tipu against Mahdavis on one hand and they were instigating Mahdavis to migrate to the territory under their control.

Author of "Khatmul Huda" had stated that since Mahdavis did not take side of the conspirators, hence Mir Asif pressured Tipu for their expulsion from Sri Ranga Patam. Thus their expulsion was the result of two reasons: one political and the other religious. The word "Dairah Waley" had been used by "Nishan-e-Hydari", refers to Mahdavis who are called in Madras and in Mysore by the same nickname. Thus the Sultan ordered Mahdavis to, offer their Lailatul Qadr prayer in the outskirts of Sri Rangapatam.

Author of "Hadia" wrongly stated that only after the bloodshed, Mahdavis were pressured to leave Sri Rangapatam. As a matter of fact there was no bloodshed, as blaming by him falsely since none of the history of Mysore has recorded any such bloodshed. The author of "Nishan-e-Hyderi", a non Mahdavi Historian, was the contemporary of Tipu Sultan who wrote:

"Mir Asif, the satan's sperm, knew the trustworthiness and loyalty of Mahdavis towards the Kingdom, hence on the advice of Englishmen, instigated and poisoned the ear of Tipu for their expulsion on the wrong apprehension that Mahdavis were treacherous and they would revolt. Tipu did not give a second thought about the so called conspiracy, going to be hatched by the mahdavis against ther kingdom. Thus, his foolish order for expulsion of Mahdavis went against his own kingdom. thus he himself put his signature on his own death warrant by issuing orders for the mass expulsion of Mahdavis. There was no bloodshed as written by author of Hadia. Had Mahdavis not ordered to offer prayer outside Sri Rangapatam, they naturally became enraged and informed their firm desire to offer Lailatul Qadr prayer first and then to depasrt. Thus without any bloodshed they themselves left Sri Rangapatam which was wrongly recorded as expulsion. Had that not happened, Mir Asif's conspiracy would not have succeeded and Tipu would not have been defeated by the English army.

63.Kirgawal, 64.Channapatna:

However, Mahdavi population is still living not only in Mysore but many places like: Chital Drug, Bannur, Kirgawal, Bangalore, Channapatna and many more places of the than Mysore state. In Channapatna, about 80% of the population is Mahdavi, all business men and artisans. There is a graveyard of Hazrat Syed Raje Mohammed (Rh), Aaja Miyan (Rh), son of Miyan Syed Abdul Lateef (Rh), the great grandfather of the Author (Hazrat Bazmi). Author of "Akhbarul Asrar" informs that this pious man had been in the company of Bandagi Miyan Syed Miran Ghazi (Rh) (great great grandfather of this translator), son of Bandagi Miyan Syed Taher Ghazi (Rh), buried in Kirgawal, where another great grandfather of the Author (Hazrat Bazmi)

Miyan Syed Ashraf (Rh), son of Miyan Syed Abdul Lateef (Rh), also was buried. "Akhbarul Asrar" thus refers about Miyan Syed Ashraf (Rh) that:

"A man of high academic qualifications, memorized Devan-e-Mehri; and often over powered opponents in discussions, never allowed interpretation of the Sayings of Imamana (As) and he is famous for that and was buried in Kirgawal."

صاحب علم بودند و از دیوان مهری اکثر حفظ بود در اکثر مجلس ها غالب آمدندی برناجواز تاویل در نقل مهدی مدلل و مستحکم بودند ، مشهور و مدفون در کرگاول (باب دوم تفصیل نهم)

(Note: This Translator's four great great grandfathers by name Bandagi Miyan Syed Miran Ghazi (Rh), Bandagi Miyan Syed Ashraf Ghazi (Rh), Bandagi Miyn Syed Allah Bakhsh Ghazi (Rh) and Hazrat Syed Roshan Munawer (Rh) are buried in Kirgawal' one of the four Hazeeras (Graveyards) and Hzt.Syed Isa son of Haz.Syed Roshan Munawer (Kirgwal), the Great grand father of this translator was buried in the Bada Graveyard of Channapatna and his grand Father Hz. Syed Roshan Munawer was buried in the Chota Graveyard of Channapatna. Kirgwal is a village whose entire population is Mahdavi, some 40 miles south of Channapatna.)

65.Malabar:

a. Author of "Asaami Musaddaqueen" writes that Miyan Sheik Bhai Berari, was the personal secretary to the king of Berar. But on account of his being a Mahdavi, was expelled many a times. While preaching, he visited Malabar along with his companions where many men became Mahdavi and who arranged for the pilgrimage of Makkah for them.

b. Miyan Syed Abdul Qader Noorani (Rh), grandson of Bandagi Miyan Syed Saadullah (Rz) was buried in Kankoor, Malabar.

(He is the great great grandfather of Faqeer Abul Fatah Syed Nusrat Saheb, son of Mashaeq Hazrat Abu Sayeed Syed Mahmood, Murshad Miyan, Tashrifullahi (Chicago),and also of Dr.Nisar Syed and his relatives now living in Los Angeles, California.)

66.Palghat: Southern portion of Malabar, where Mahdavis are still living here.

67.Kochin: Here also Mahdavis lived.

68.Travencore: In Wadecheri, near Nager Koel, ten miles from Padmanath Puram, the old capital of Travencore, a Dairah was established in 12th. Century H. Now there remains a big graveyard of those Mahdavis who were residing there. When Trivendrum became the capital of Travencore, many Mahdavis moved to the new capital and some of them migrated to Pangudi of Taneveli area. In Tekad of Trivendrum still Mahdavis are living there.

Ras Kumari to Fathepur Saikri:

68.Pangudi: It is a part of Tanaveli some 32 miles to North of Tanaveli and 15 miles from

Ras Kumari, where many Mahdavi Families still live here.

69.Tichnalore: Just two miles from Tenaveli there remains a Grave Yard, reminding us about those Mahdavis who happened to be there in the remote past. Now it has become a part of history.

Trichnapalli: This city was a hub of Mahdavis, sometimes back. This author's (Hzt. Bazmi's) Grandfather, Miyan Syed Abdul Lateef (Rh), son of Bandagi Miyan Syed Raje Mohammed (Rh) was buried here. According to "Akhbarul Asrar" he was the disciple of Hazrat Bandgi Miyan Syed Ashraf Ghazi (Rh), son of Hazrat Bandagi Miyan Syed Miran Ghazi (Rz), was buried in Trichnapalli, where Mahdavis live in hundreds still.

Arcot: From Mangad to Arcot (a city of Tamilnadu) Mahdavis were living here in multiples.

(This humble Translator had the opportunity to visit Arcot, where Hazrat Miyan Syed Noor Mohammed (Rh), son of Hazrat Miyan Syed Aziz Mohammed (Rh) of Gokak, forefathers of Akailvi lineage was buried here (on Friday the 16th ZeeQaeda 1155 H. / 11th. January 1734 AD) . It is said that there had been many Grave Yards of Mahdavis reminding thousands had been living here in the remote past. The locality was known as Mahdi Wada. The people, might have been Mahdavis in the past, still carrying Mahdavi names and have some sort of natural affection with those Mahdavis buried here. But on account of lack of Tableegh, entire population had converted to Sunnat Wal Jamaat. Some ten years back a group of mahdavis along with this translator visited Arcot and offered flowers and respects to the graves of this graveyard. It was in a bad shape. Everywhere Andhra Babool plants had enveloped and wrapped upon the entire graveyard. By employing labour the plants were cut and burned. A barbed wire fence was arranged. The local people, particularly Janab Hakeem Saheb, his son Mr. Azad and his friends helped us in getting the graveyard fenced.

We visited the concerned authorities of Revenue and Municipality who helped us in tracing the survey No. of the graveyard and on our request the Patta was recorded in the name of Br. Syed Sultan Naseer, son of Hazrat Mashaeq Syed Mohammed Miyan Saheb Akhialvi (Rh), of Hyderabad. Hazrat Syed Noor Mohammed (Rh) is the tenth generation of Akhailvi Khanwada, buried in that graveyard of Arcot Masapet, Vellore District, Tamil Nadu.

There are still other graveyards in the vicinity of this graveyard. About which we shall again visit Arcot Masapet to point out other graveyard and take necessary action with the help of local people as well as concerned authorities who helped in locating the same and granted the Patta.

Yet on another occassion,on hearing from Mr. Azad, that very recently some miscreants and land grabbers had desecrated the holy graves and dismantled the entire graveyard and converted it into plots, this translator and Syed Sultan Naseer and others went and represented to the Collector of Vellore on 16th. March 2012, who very sympathetically investigated the matter on the spot and issued orders to deliver the physical possession along with Revenue Documents for Survey Nos.194, 195/1 & 195/2 as the Graveyard of Hazrat Bandagi Miyan Syed Noor Mohammed (Rh). Alhamdu Lillah we were successful in safeguarding the graveyard with the Help of Allah, first and then of the Collector, Mr. Ajay Yadav, IAS. Mr. Mohammed Jaan, Minister of Awqaf, Tamil Nadu also helped us in getting the grave yard registered under Awqaf.

Another town, Tirpatur, is in the vicinity of Arcot, where many Mahdavi families reside here carrying the sumptuous business of manufacturing T. Shirts which have an export value , as well as, it has a large consumption in India itself. Arcot is just five miles from Jolarpet Railway Junction of Madras Province. (Via Chittur District also reachable by bus.)

71.Chittor: One village in the vicinity of Voilpad of Chittor district is habituated by Mahdavis alone.

72.Coimbatore: The river Kaveri passes from here. On one side of the river Erode is situated and on the other side Palipallium is situated whose total population is Mahdavi. In Erode there is a big Grave Yard reminiscence of the remote past where Mahdavis used to live there and finally either buried or migrated to some other places from here.

73.Salam: Palakod is a town in Salam District where the entire population is Mahdavi.

74.Sidhot: This is situated 12 miles from Cudapah, a thriving place for Mahdavis.

75.Cudapah: Still It is a dominant place of Mahdavis.

76.Kurnool: Had been a hub of Mahdavis. Nawab Munawer Khan of Karnool was a Mahdavi who helped Mahdavis to flourish here under his patronage. On Exodus, when Mahdavis were driven away from Hyderabad, after the battle of Chanchalguda, many Mahdavis migrated to Kurnool in the year 1238 H. There were fourteen Dairahs in Kurnool. In 1255 H. Kurnool was merged into Indian Dominion, therefore many Mahdavis migrated either to Cudapah or other places, but mostly to Hyderabad. Still good numbers of Mahdavis reside there. Once Zuhra Pur was the center of Mahdavis, now there remain some graveyards and dilapidated remains of those flourishing inhabitants.

77.Machli Bander: Alamgir's invasion caused many Mahdavis to migrate from Hyderabad to Machli Bander. Hazrat Murshaduz Zaman (Rh) and his followers were taken care of by Malik Sharfuddin who arranged their residence in Machli Bander also known as Murtuza Nagar.

78.Adhoni: Miyan Syed Sharief (Rh), grandson of Miyan Syed Abdul Wahab (Rh) was the commissioner of Adhoni. He had a formidable position in the government and was controlling a huge army. He was buried in Adhoni. Author of "Tareekh-e-Mahadavian" writes that:

"Miyan Syed Ibrahim (Rh), son of Miyan Syed Abdul Wahab (Rh), Ibn Hazrat Syed Tashrifullah (Rz) was the closest confidant of Adil Shah. His son Miyan Syed Sharief (Rh) was a pious and un-matchable brave man. His wealth was increasing day in and day out. He was in the good books of the king, therefore he was appointed as the commissioner of Adhoni."

میـان سیـد ابراهیـم بن بندگی میان سید عبدالوهاب بن تشریف الله صاحب از معتمدان خاص عادل شاه بود و پسرایشان میان سید شریف بسیار متقی و در جوان مـردی عدیم المثال بودند دولت ایشان روز بروز در ترقی بود و از کمال عاطفت پادشاه صوبه داری اد هونی براوشان مفوض شد (تاریخ مهدویان ، سنٹرل ریکارڈ آفس ، حیدرآباد نمبر ۷۵۵)

79.Pindyal: Entire population except a few artisans all are Mahdavis. Miyan Syed Hasan Makki was the first to establish his Dairah here. Mahdavis maintain Mango gardens everywhere in Pindyal, which is their main source of living, who sell their produce in Bezwada and also export to many states of India.

80.Fursat Patan: Mostly populated by Mahdavis who maintain their own Dairah.

81.South of Deccan: According to "Khatim-e-Sulaimani":

"Be it known to all that Deccan is a vast territory. It is a place where four five kingdoms were established here. Except Malik Bureed and Nizam Shah, all kings were non Mahdavis. But most of the army men were Mahdavis. After the demise of Miran Syed Mahmood, Sani-e-Mahdi (Rz), majority of Muhajereen and Tabaieen migrated to many cities of South Deccan and adopted government jobs of high and low positions according to their calibre. Thus, most of the personnel in administration and the army, were Mahdavis who had their dominance."

بدان اے عزیز سراسر تمیز اقصاے دکن وسعتے کامل دارد و قدر پنـج شش سلاطین دراے مزرو بوم با قطاع جداگانـه رونق افزاے سریر سلطنت بودند و سواے سلاطیـن یکـی ملک برید دوم نظام شاه کسے مهدوی نبوداما افواج همگی اکثرے از مصدقان امام علیه السلام بودنـد جهت آن اکثرے مهاجران و تابعین بعد از وصال میـران سید محمود مهدی ثانی قدم در آن ملک سعادت لزوم بردند از طفیل خاک نعلین زمرۀ راشده کلمه گویان از وضـع و شریف و از امراء وغربا ممتـاز و سرافراز تصدیق شدند (گلشن دواز دهم چمن چهارم)

1. Thus spreading the mission of Imamana (As) was the responsibility of the preachers who systematically spread the mission in many regions of Deccan. The preaching was so impressive and heart touching which initiated not only the poor to accept Faith in large numbers but the elites also were fascinated to adopt it.

2. Bandagi Miyan Raje Mohammed (Rz) (Ibn Miyan Sharief Mohammed (Rz) Ibn Miyan Mahmood Shah (Rz)) was the maternal grandson of Badagi Miyan Syed Shahabul Haq (Rz), whose daughter Bibi Bua Salam (Rz) was married to Miyan Sharief Mohammed (Rz). Miyan Sharief Mohammed (Rz) was trained, nurtured and was brought up under the direct supervision

of Bandagi Miyan Syed Shahabul Haq (Rz). On account of which he had attained such sublime attributes which were not found in others. According to "Khatim-e-Sulaimani" Bandagi Miyan Syed Shahabul Haq stated that if Allah asked him on the Day of Judgment, as to what gift he had brought, he would present Sharief Mohammed (Rz) as his humble gift to Allah.

Bandagi Miyan Syed Raje Mohammed (Rz) arrived in Deccan during the period of Abdullah Qutub Shah (died 1083 H). Unfortunately at that time, king's kids, the prince and the princess, both had died on account of the Plague. Both the king and his queen were psychologically shattered down on account of the great loss and were mourning regularly and on account of which they were rarely attending to the functions of the government. Many Mahdavi elites happened to be in the court of the Qutub Shahi kings. Someone informed the king that one pious and godly man by name Syed Raje Mohammed (Rz) had come into the kingdom, if the king desired, they shall bring him here for his blessings. The king agreed and asked to request the Hazrat to pay a visit to the Darbar."Khatim-e-Sulaimani" narrates that:

"The writer heard the news from his Murshid that in order to pacify the Sultan on the death of his son and daughter, the Sultan had called Miyan Syed Raje Mohammed (Rz) who had come into the city."	مصنف از قبله گاه خود شنیده است که برائے بیان تعزیت و صبر بر رحلت پسر ودختر میان سید راجی محمد را که در آن بلده آمده بودند طلبیده بود (گلشن پنجم چمن چهارم)

Many Mahdavi nobles had been the devotees of Hazrat Raje Mohammed (Rz) who was buried in Chanchalguda in 1068H. Thus, even before 1068 H. Mahdavis were settled down in Chanchalguda and elsewhere in Qutub Shahi Kingdom.

Malkapur's hillock is known as "Noor Ghat" where Hazrat Shah Abdul Kareem Noori (Rh) was buried. According to "Khatim-e-Sulaimani" it is stated that:

"Miyan Shah Abdul Kareem Noori (Rh) Ibn Shah Abdul Lateef (Rh) was a very brave man who was employed by Sultan Qutub Shah. After relinquishing service he relinquished worldly affairs and established his Dairah in between Hyderabad and Golconda. He was buried in Noor Ghat, in Karwan area which was named after him.	میاں عبدالکریم بن شاه عبداللطیف مرد مردانه و شجاع یگانه و نوکر و مقرب سلطان قطب شاه بودند .... چند مدت ترک دنیا کرده مرشدی نیز نموده اند و دائره مابین حیدرآباد و قلعه گولکنڈه بود .... مرقد آنحضرت به کوه و آن کوه را نور گهاٹ می گویند یعنی از اسم آنحضرت مشهور و معروف است (گلشن نهم چمن اول)

Noor Ghat's fame was even older than writing of "Khatim-e-Sulaimani."

Qutub Shahi Army had many Ghulzai Afghans, who were Mahdavi Pathans. Manchappa (Nizamabad) was the Jaggir of these Ghulzai Afghans. Qutuab Shahi and Adil Shahi kings had granted many villages as Jagirs to many Mahdavis where they had established their Dairahs. Just four miles away from Manchappa there is Madak Palli, where Bandagi Miyan Syed Ali

Sutoon-e-Deen (Rh) was buried.

(Note: Hazrat Bandagi Miyan Syed Noor Mohammed, "Khatim-e-Kaar (Rz)" son of Bandagi Miyan Syed Mahmood "Khatimul Murshad (Rz)" was buried in Manchappa. The Mutawalli of this Hazeerah is Miyan Syed Abdul Jaleel Akhailvi, Son of HazratMashaeq Syed Mohammed Saheb Qibla Rh. Akailvi)

   Malik Yousuf (Rh) (died 1124 H) is from the lineage of Malik Hammad (Rz). He had written "Prem Sangram" about the martyrdom of Hazrat Bandagi Miyan Syed Khundmir (Rz).

   According to "Khatim-e-Sulaimani":

"In the beginning, he (Malik Yousuf (Rh) used to visit the Qutub Shahi king known as "Tana Shah", both in private or in the Court, since he had interest in the music and poetry. Tana Shah had great intimacy with Miyan Yousuf (Rh). Whenever a renowned poet or musician came to the court, Sultan used to send him to Miyan Yousuf (Rh) first. If Miyan Yousuf (Rh) liked him for his poetry and music, then Tana Shah too used to accept him as the poet or a musician of his court. If Miyan Yousuf (Rh) did not like him, then Tana Shah too disregarded him."

در اوائل حال بعضی اوقات نزد تانا شاه آمد و رفت بود در خلوت و جلوت قرب تمام داشتند چرا که او نیز در سرور و سخن دانی بهرۀ وافی داشت و به جناب حضرت عقیدت و اتحاد و صاف دلی کافی داشت و به حضورش از سرود سرائی و سخن دانے از هر ولایت و کشور که می رسید اول بخدمت آنحضرت می فرستاد و اگر پسند طبع و نظر شریف می شد تاشاه نیز پسند می نمود و اگر نامقبول به مزاج و الامی گشت شاه راهم مطبوع و منظور نمی گشت (گلشن دهم چمن چهارم)

   From the very early life Miyan Yousuf (Rh) was fascinated by poetry and music. According to "Khatim-e-Sulaimani":

"Hazrat' used to go in conveyance known as Palki arranged by Tana Shah, having 360 bells. He used to come out of the court very late in the night. When his Palki passed through the streets, the sound of the bells was heard for miles together and who ever heard, used to say "Mahdavi peerzadey was going, it seems that the Sultan had gone inside his chamber."

اکثر سواری آنحضرت بر گردون بود و محافه را موازی سیصد و شصت جرس و زنگوله آویخته بودند به وقت شب بعضی اوقات از بزم خاص بادشاه برمیخا ستندو در سواری گردون مجرس و در زمین مفرش حیدرآباد آواز اجراس و زنگوله هابکرده می رسید هر کس می گفت که پیر زادۀ مهدوی می رودشاید شاه از بزم خاص برخاست (گلشن دهم چمن چهارم)

"Malik Yousuf (Rh) had written many books on poetry pertaining to Elegies, Eulogies, Rubaaies, Masnavies, surth, soviya, chopaie etc.; and finally "Prem Sangram" was completed which became famous in public, particularly among the Mahdavis."

ملك يوسف در كبت ، دوهره ، سورٹھ وسويه و چوپائى و گڑگه وه چهند وغيرهم آن را تصنيف مى كردند تا جنگ نامه تمام شد و نام اوپريم سنگرام شد و منظور خاص و عام شد و مشهور در گرده امام عليه السلام شد (گلشن دهم چمن چهارم)

Makkhan Lal wrote in his "Nobles of Kingdom of Asafia" under chapter "About Muslims" that:

"Sultan Miyan of Khandela, belonging to the North Indian spiritual guides of Mahdavia Faith, migrated to Deccan as a tradesman, and established himself in Bhagiyanager now called Hyderabad."

كيفيت سلطان ميان از قوم پير زادهٔ مهدوى باشنده كهنڈيله موضع هندوستان در عهد غفران مآب آمده به صيغهٔ سوداگرى در بلدهٔ فرخنده بنياد اقامت مى داشت (يادگار مكهن لال ، طبع مطبع برهانيه ، حيدرآباد صفحه ٤٠)

Gulzar-e-Asafia describes about Sultan Miyan:

"Sultan Miyan was one of the highly intellectual and spiritual guides (of Mahdavis), who attained high positions by befriending the nobles of Deccan like Aazamul Omara, Arastu Jah, etc, and maintained 2000 troops and became owner of a palace granted by the Nizam to him." *(The adjoining vast area of the said palace, is now known as Sultan Bazar, named after him, a big locality in Hyderabad, was under his possession for a long time.)*

سلطان ميان يكى از پيرزاده هائے بزرگ منش ايشاں مرد بهادر صاحب قسمت بود بزور عقل رسائے خويش باعظم الامراء ارسطو جاه رشدبهم رسانيده بدو هزار سوار و بار و پياده ها محلات كنگ گيرى و گنگاوتى وغيره از سركار بهره مند شد (گلزار آصفيه صفحه ١١١ ١١٢)

Author of "Khatmul Huda" writes that: Hyderabadi Historians very well knew that Mahdavis, from the very inception of the Nizam's Dominion, had obtained higher positions in the administration. Even before Chandu Lal, Mahdavia nobles like Nawab Dildar Khan, Nawab Miran Yar Jung, Nawab Sultanul Mulk Bahadur and many more Jamadars were busy in the administration and they were granted the Jagirs and renowned titles."

Author of "Shamsul Huda" writes: " We Mahdavis had been granted Mansabs and Jagirs by both the Qutub Shahi and Asaf Jahi Sultans. The remains of Golconda, Tombs and other buildings remind our grandeur of that period. Particularly we are fellow riders of Asafia dynasty from its very inception and became trusted administrators like the late Nawab Mohammed Dildar Khan who enjoyed security of the State as well as he was welcomed openly in the court and in privacy in the chambers of the Nizams".

Author of "Tareekh-e-Mahdavian" writes about Nawab Dildar Khan that:

"On being trustworthy, loyal, shrewd, intelligent, pious and brave, Nawab Dildar Khan was appointed by Tegh Jung Bahadur under him; and slowly the number of troops was increased under him and on account of his honesty and loyalty he became confidant of Nawab Mir Nizam Ali Khan, Asif-e-Sani who also appreciated his manners and exalted his position still higher and fixed his sitting place in the Royal Palace and granted the Badi (Big) Akhaili (Now Zaheerabad) to him as Jagir; to which he developed it on the model of Jaipur."

چونکه دلدار خان بهادر بسیار هوشیار و جوان مرد و پرهیزگار وبه صفت امانت و وفاداری متصف بودند تیغ جنگ بهادر ایشان را به سلک ملازمان خود منتظم نمودند و باز رفته رفته تعداد سواران ایشان افزودند نخستین دو صد سوار بودند و پس از ان سه صدا فزودند و بکمال دیانت داری ایشان بدرگاه اشتباه آصف ثانی رسانید ندبندگان عالی را هم روش ایشان بسیار پسند آمد و مرتبهٔ ایشان را افزودند و نشست گاه ایشان بدیوڑهی خود مقرر فرمودند.......... اکیلی کلان درجاگیر شان بود بلکه بنا کردهٔ اوشان است بسیار خوش وضع و نمونهٔ جی پور است ـ الیٰ آخره

The fixing of sitting place in the Royal Palace was a great honour in those days, since those designated nobles only were supposed to become "King's Body Guards." *"Tareekh-e-Gulzar-e-Asafia" describes about Bazar-e-Eisa Miyan" a commercial hub was established by Isa Miyan known as Miran Yar Jung. The said bazaar is situated on the right side of the English Residency and adjacent to Sultan Bazar to its North, another commercial hub established by another Mahdavi Noble by name Sultan Miyan ."According to "Tareekh-e-Mahdavian":*

"When he (Malik Isa) became mature, he went to Sri Ranga Patam, where his cousin Nahnnay Miyan was under the employment of Hyder Ali Bahadur, through him, Isa Miyan also was appointed by Bahadur (Hyder Ali) and slowly he attained the position of the Nobles of the Court. He got well versed in the art of battleground and he took part in many battles along with Hyder Ali."

چون ایشان به سن بلوغ رسیدند در سریرنگ پڻن رفتند آنجا بنی عم ایشان نهنی میان که از ملازمان بهادر بودند بوساطت ایشان ملازم بهادر شاه شدند و شده ایشان هم به درجه امارت رسیدند و در آئین جنگ مهارت کامل پیدا نمودند و در جنگ ها همراه رکاب بهادر مانده بودند

It further states that:

"Nawab Isa Miyan carried the title of "Miran Yar Jung". His father Malik Macchoo was one of the pious men among Mahdavis. He had maintained his Dairah at (Chota) Nagpur which was 50 miles from Hyderabad, He used to celebrate the Urs Anniversary of Hazrat Ilahdad (Khalifa Giroh (Rz), who was his great grandfather, with pomp and glory, and used to invite all Mahdavis for the dinner."

در ذکر نواب عیسیٰ میان المخاطب میران یار جنگ بہادر نور الله مرقده نام اصلی ایشان ملک عیسیٰ است و پدر ایشان ملک مچهو از فقرای گروه مہدی علیہ السلام بودند دائره ایشان در ناگپور بود کہ از حیدرآباد بیست و پنج کرده است عرس بندگی ملک الهداد کہ جدامجد اوشان بودند بہ تکلف تمام می نمودند و ہمگی کسان قوم مہدویہ را مدعومی ساختند (تاریخ مہدویان ریکارڈ آفس ، حیدرآباد نمبر ۷۵۵)

According to "Tareekh-e-Mahdavian":

"8000 Troops were under his control. Many youngsters of the nobles of Hyderabad were working in his army. Mostly they were from his native place Chota Nagpur. He provided employment to all his companions and particularly he employed those who come from his native place."

فوج ایشان پیادہ و سوار ہشت ہزار بود ، اکثر عہدہ داران و سپاهیان اوشان از شرفا زادگان دکن بودند بیشتر ناگپوریان بودند کہ ہم وطنان اوشان اندو نواب صاحب ہمہ دوستان زمانۂ طفلی را بلکہ جمیع اهل وطن را ملازم خود داشتند

According to "Mahboobus Salateen", another history book:

"Nawab Musheerul Mulk's stay with the Marhattas was not appreciated by the Marhattas since within a short period Musheerul Mulk played such a devastating trick which caused disruption among the Marhattas. And upon his secret message to Isa Miyan, Miran Yar Jung, Mohammed Subhan Khan Bahadur, Raja Jeevant Rao, Sardarul Mulk Ghansi Miyan and Muzafferul Mulk and Syed Ali Bahadur dissociated with the Peshwa and joined with the forces of the Nizam along with their troops which resulted in disruption among the Marhattas who repented for their foolishness to have confidence in Musheerul Mulk."

There seems no link between Isa Miyan and his title Miran Yar Jung. It is said that when Nizamul Mulk Asif Jah-e-Sani wanted to grant a title to Isa Miyan, Isa Miyan, himself suggested his title "Miran Yar Jung"; when asked by Nizam its significance, Isa Miyan replied that"Our Imamana's title was "Miran Ji (As)" hence Nizamul Mulk awarded the same title. It shows the depth of Faith of Isa Miyan in Imamana (As) and the Nizam's liberal mindedness. It was in vogue to award titles to those nobles whose solidarity and integrity was tested and recommended by the administration. Thus many Mahdavi Nobles like: Nawab Naseeb Yar Jung, Kamal Yar Jung, Nawab Junaid Yar Jung, Nawab Bahadur Yar Jung and many more had been awarded such titles and jagirs.

82.Chanchalguda:

Hazrat Bandagi Syed Raje Mohammed (Rz) died in 1068 H and was buried in Chachalguda. It means to say that even before 1068 H. during Qutub Shahi period, well before the collapse of the Qutub Shahi dynasty, on the defeat of Tanashah, the last Qutub Shahi king, by Aurangzeb; Mahdavis were already living in Chanchalguda. Author of "Gulzar-e-Asafia writes that:

"During the period of Mir Nizam Ali Khan, Asif-e-Sani, the Nizam ordered for merging the ten thousand troop army of Paighah under Shamsul Omara Tegh Jung Bahadur with the State's army. Dildar Khan Mahdavi along with his 200 Mahdavi troops became part and parcel of Paighah. Thus. Dildar Khan settled down in Chanchalguda and used to present himself in the court. Thus within a short spell of time Chanchalguda's population swelled exorbitantly and the daily necessities were pouring in, in the shape of for merchandise in Chanchalguda and many traders started their business here and were pursuing a life of prosperity and tranquility. Some four thousand Mahdavi horsemen along with leaders, nobles and Jamadars were employed by Arastu Jah and other Nobles and Rajas. Thus Chanchalguda became famous all over India (Now it has become famous even around the world. The famous humorist, Mujtaba Husain of Hyderabad had penned an Essay on Chanchalguda, which gave much fame to it.)

One prominent Haji Zardar Khan of Karoli had mentioned the battle of Chanchalguda, 1238 H., in his book" "Saulat-e-Afghani" There are two Masnavies: (1) Masnavi-e-Nateq and (2) Masnavi-e-Irfan, known as "Akhbar-e-Shuhada" (about the Battle of Chanchalguda.)This "Muqaddama-e-Sirajul Absar" also was written in Chanchalguda."

در عهد حضرت غفران مآب میر نظام علی خان بهادر چوں جمیعت پائیگاہ بسر داری وسر کردگی شمس الامراء بهادر تیغ جنگ قریب دہ ہزار سوار ملازم رکاب ظفر انتساب سرکار دولت مدار گردید دلدار خاں نامی جمعدار مهدوی بادو صد سوار ان هم قوم خویش نیز نوکر بهادر معز گشت وبالائی چنچل گوڑہ مسکن ومقام خود ساخت وهر روز برائے سلام حاضر دربار میگر دید رفتہ رفتہ در چند مدت چنچل گوڑہ آن قدر آباد شد کہ همہ مایحتاج در آنجا بهم رسیدہ سو داگران این قوم ازهر چهار طرف اجناس فرد ختنی آوردہ خوش حال گذرا وقات می نمود ند قریب چهار هزار سوار ازین قوم باسردار ان وجمعدار ان وسپاهیان بیش قرار نوکر سرکار ورساله ارسطو جاہ ودیگر امیران وراجایان گردیدند (گلزار آصفیہ طبع حیدرآباد صفحہ ۱۱۱)

Battle of Chanchalguda:

The main reason for the escalation of the battle had been the murder of Moulvi Abdul Karim which was the result of a rivalry between Nawab Munirul Mulk and Moulvi Abdul Karim which has nothing to do either to Mahdavis, nor to the Sunnis, unnecessarily both communities, except the Shias, were forced to fight each other for no cause of their own and to suffer a lot on account the battle. Most Mahdavis were suffered on account of the exodus, while Sunnis suffered high casualties in thousands. Mohammed Qader Khan Munshi had written in "Tareekh-e-Asif Jahi" that:

"There had been an old enmity between Munirul Mulk, a Shia, and Moulvi Abdul Karim, a Sunni. Thus it pertains to the classic rivalry of Shia-Sunni conflict. It is said that in a Shia Ceremony the son of Munirul Mulk and Moulvi Abdul Karim entangled abruptly which was further culminated into a public riot which only cooled down when Munirul Mulk offered his apology to Abdul Karim."

از مولوی کینه دیرینه داشت که پیش از چند سال پسرش بعلت تقریب مشرب شیعه از مولوی رنجیدگی به میان آورد و مولوی باشتهار آن پرواخته بلوهٔ عام نموده بود آخربا ستعفائی منیر الملک به صلح انجامید (تاریخ آصف جاهی تاریخ فارسی قلمی نمبر ١٦٤٩ اسٹیٹ سنٹرل لائبریری آندهرا پردیش)

Mohammed Faizullah Munshi in his book "Khazanai-e-Rasool Khani" states that:

"Some three months ago, Nawab Sikander Jah, the Nizam, called Abdul Karim and asked his opinion about the marriage of a Sunni girl with a Shia boy. Abdul Karim gave opinion against the marriage telling as if the girl was being given to a pig. On that Sikander Jah kept quiet and the dialogue about the marriage of his daughter with Munirul Mulk'son was discontinued and that was the main reason of enmity between the two."

قبل از عرصهٔ سه ماهِ جناب مغفرت منزل مولوی کریم الدین (عبدالکریم) را پیش خود طلب داشته پر سید ندا گر کسی سنت جماعت حبیہ خودرا باهل تشیعہ (تشیع) عقد کرده بدهد دراین صورت چه مسئله است همان وقت مولوی صاحب فرمود که صبیہ خود رابه خنزیر سپرده برائی خانه داری خود بدولت واقبال سکوت کرده مولوی صاحب را رخصت فرمود ازیں سوال حاصل این بود که صبیہ خود انچه که از بطن زوجه (جهان پرور بیگم مالی میان سیف الملک کی بیٹی اورارسطو رجاه مشیر الملک کی پوتی ہے نواب ناصر الدوله کے بهائی میر تفضل علی خان المعروف میر بادشاه جهان پرور بیگم کے بطن سے تھی) جهان پرور بیگم متولد آن را در عقد پسر منیر الملک بهادر دادنی منظور بود باستماع این مسئله موقوف فرمود ازیں باعث بهادر موصوف را از مولوی صاحب عداوت قلبی بود (خزانہ رسول خانی تاریخ فارسی قلمی نمبر ٦.٦ اسٹیٹ سنٹرل لائبریری آندهراپردیش)

It is now clear that Muneerul Mulk had a personal grudge with Abdul Karim. One reason was that Munirul Mulk had openly apologized to Abdul Karim and the second reason was that

Nawab Sikander Jah, on the advice of Abdul Karim, did not agree to marry his daughter to Munirul Mulk's son.

Mohammed Faizullah Munshi had written in another Book:"Khazana-e-Gowher-e-Shahwar" about the episode of Abdul Karim and had mentioned that after hearing this problem, the betrothal ceremony was stopped by the Nizam, which act made Muneerul Mulk mad and consequently he cooked up a dirty plan which resulted in the murder of Moulvi Abdul Karim. At that time of this murder, Munirul Mulk was present in the Jilo Khana and had strictly ordered not to close the doors of Jilo Khana and not to help Abdul Karim at any cost where Arabs, Paltan troops and many more were present.

The ceremony which was mentioned was regarding the daughter of Jehan Perwer Begum, wife of the Nizam with the son of Munirul Mulk. The enmity became actively so grave that Munirul Mulk ordered to stop the Mansub of Abdul Karim. But later on it was granted by Chandulal.

Another Munshi by name Qader Khan had written"Tareekh-e-Asaf Jahi" which states that:

Although dialogue discontinued regarding the proposed marriage, but matter flared up and ended in Abdul Karim's murder.

The fact is that Munirul Mulk became very mad on breaking up of the betrothal ceremony of his son with the daughter of the Nizam, only on the suggestion given by Abdul Karim. Thus he planned to arrange the Abdul Karim's murder by keeping the doors of the Jilo Khana open from where Mahdavis could enter into the Masjid and thus the situation automatically should culminate into the murder of Abdul Karim by Mahdavis." His plan became successful in bringing the old rivalry of "Sunni-Mahdavi" to play. Thus Mahdavis were unfortunately involved in this murder. The details are as below:

Discussion between Abdul Karim and Miyan Yaseen Khan:

Zaberdast Khan and Yaseen Khan were two sons of Nawab Dildar Khan. According to "Tareekh-e-Mahdavian" after the demise of Nawab Dildar Khan both sons got their official responsible position as before in the court of the Nizam. But at the time of Chanchalguda Battle, both came from their Jagir Akhaili and mingled with those who were expelled.

One Sofi Miyan a resident of Razdar Khan Pet was the nephew of the Qazi of Dharoor (a non Mahdavi). There was a discussion between him and Miyan Yaseen Khan regarding equity between the holy Prophet (Slm) and Imamana (As). In that connection they both went to Abdul Karim to ascertain his view on this issue. This discussion took place in the evening of Tuesday, 30th. of Zil Hajj, 1237 H. It was mentioned in both "Masnavies of Irfan" and of "Natiq" that there was a discussion about a tradition mentioned in "Bukhari" in which a reference had been made regarding Imamana (As). In a previous meeting Abdul Karim had demanded Yaseen Khan to show that reference in "Bukhari". As per "Natiq", Abdul Karim asserted before Yaseen Khan that if the reference of Mahdi (As) is mentioned in "Bukahri", he would accept Imamana (As) as true Mahdi (As):

"Abdul Kareem told Yaseen Khan to "bring "Bukhari Sharief" on Tuesday and if I found the Tradition of Mahdi (As) in it, I shall surely become Mahdavi.

تو سہ شنبہ کے دن مجھ پاس آنا؛ بخاری لا کے میرے تیں دکھانا
اگر اس میں خبر مہدی کی پاؤں؛ تو صوفی کیا ہے میں ایمان لاؤ

Thus the discussion between them was about Equity between the holy prophet (Slm) and Imamana (As). According to Bukhari's narration "Imamakum Minkum", scholars of Sunnat Wal Jamaat had deduced the person of Imam Mahdi (As) as stated by Muhaddiss-e-Dehlavi regarding this tradition that:

"Imam for the prayer would be from you and Isa would follow him and that would be Mahdi (As)."

امام از کسے بود کہ از شماز و عیسیٰ اقتدا کنند
بوئے و آن مہدی است

But according to Mahdavia Faith "Imamakum Minkum" points out to Prophet Isa (As). However, the discussion went on between them in the Masjid-e-Mir Alam which was constructed in Jilo Khana of Munirul Mulk. In that reference, Abdul Karim became out of control and threw away "Bukhari" on the ground and slapped on Yaseen Khan.

Both Mahdavi and Non Mahdavi books confirm that Abdul Karim attacked first on Yaseen Khan:

Author of "Khazana-e-Rasool Khani" had reported that:

"Moulvi Saheb had slapped on the face of Yaseen Khan."

بر روئے نامورده مولوی صاحب طمانچہ زد

According to Vaquay Chanchalguda:

"Moulvi Saheb became enraged and slapped on his face."

جناب مولوی خشمگین شدہ طمانچہ بروئے زد

According to "Tareekh-e-Asif Jahi:

"Moulvi Saheb became enraged and slapped on his face."

جناب مولوی خشمگین شدہ طمانچہ بروئے زد

"Moulvi Saheb became enraged and slapped on his face."

مولوی صاحب موصوف بر دہنہ نامورده طمانچہ زد

After being slapped Yaseen Khan had put his hand on his sword, the very moment those who were present in the Masjid, ambushed on Yaseen Khan and wounded him. Yaseen Khan, after being attacked, was severely wounded, came out from the Masjid and sat down at the pond of the Jilo Khana. His servant carried the news of the wound to Chanchalguda. Some seventeen persons, 12 Afghan, 3 Saadaat and 2 Sheikh, went to help Yaseen Khan. By that time, Abdul Karim had called Arabs and Afghans, two of them were Dayem Khan and Hasan Khan (non Mahdavi Pathans, arch rivals of Mahdavi Pathans), both had grudge against Mahdavis and were zealous to fight against Mahdavis. The door of the Jilo Khana was closed when those 17

Mahdavis arrived to help Yaseen Khan. Meanwhile some 5000 persons had gathered inside the Jilo Khana.

Munirul Mulk's order:

On orders from Munirul Mulk the doors of Jilo Khana were opened. "Khazan-e-Rasool Khani" states that:

"Had Munirul Mulk not ordered to open the doors, there would not have arisen such a serious confrontation between the people (of two different faiths.)"	اگر بهادر موصوف حکم وا کردن جلو خانه نه کرده چه طاقت بود که بایں مرتبه هنگامه رونمود صریح واضح است

Not only he ordered to open the doors but he instigated Mahdavis to settle their account with Abdul Karim of Sunnatul Jamaat.

But even before Mahdavi attacked, the Arabs had ambushed on them, resulting in martyrdom of Moujdar Khan while another Mahdavi was wounded as narrated in "Irfan Masnavi":

"Suddenly a gun fire was heard; and someone was martyred in that gun fire. It was Allah's blessings that Moujdar khan was hit by the enemy's bullet and he became martyred and one Mahdavi became Ghazi, being wounded."	وہاں سے ضرب کے چلتے ہی گولی؛ شہادت کا یہاں پیغام بولی خدا کی اس قدر ہوئی سرفرازی؛ ہوا کوئی مردان میں سے غازی گئے موجدار خاں سلطان ہوکر؛ فدا راہ خدا میں جان کھوکر

According to "Vaquaey Chanchalguda", the Arabs started firing on Mahdavis and started battle in the Jilo Khana. On that Mahdavis deliberately broke open the door. There was only one passage from Jilo Khana to the Masjid.

Soon after Mahdavis entered the Masjid, Arabs attacked, one Mahdavi was martyred and the other was badly wounded. Now Mahdavis had no choice but to enter the Masjid by breaking the door, but the passage from the door was so narrow that the entrance was too narrow to enter easily. Still Inayet Khan and his friends tried to climb upward, suddenly Dayem Khan Manduzai (non Mahdavi Pathan) confronted Inayet Khan at the last step of the stairs and attacked cutting Inayet Khan's neck, but the brave Inayet Khan holding his neck in one hand and with the other hand struck Dayem Khan so vehemently that Dayem Khan fell down dead on the ground. Dayem Khan's brother Hasan Khan attacked Inayet Khan who finally became martyred in this encounter. On the murder of Dayem Khan, passage for entry was clear for Mahdavis and a fierce battle started in which Abdul Karim and his five friends were slaughtered by the Mahdavis. At this juncture every opponent fled away and Mahdavis saw that there was none to fight, they proclaimed Tasbih and came out of the Masjid.

Thus in this encounter two Mahdavis were martyred and fifteen wounded. One among the wounded succumbed to the injuries after twelve days. On the other side thirteen were either dead or wounded. In order to take wounded, some five hundred Mahdavis gathered at the Jilo Khana of Munirul Mulk.

Demand to produce Yaseen Khan:

It is a fact that what had happened it was just a coincidence in which there seems to be no rivalry or enmity involved between Mahdavis and Sunnis. None took seriously about the murder of Abdul Karim on that day. Even the next day, First of Muharram, Wednesday 1238 H., there was no hue or cry and silence was prevailed. However, since the murder of Izzat Khan, a close relative of the Sadras Sudoor, provoked the Sadrus Sudoor badly. Thus he and his friend, Syed Noorul Aoulia, had tried to instigate other scholars.

It is a fact that the said Sofi Miyan took Miyan Yaseen Khan to Abdul Karim. From it may be deduced that it might have been a conspiracy, since Sofi Miyan's name was not heard anymore, instead Miyan Yaseen Khan was blamed to be the key person in the said murder of Abdul Karim and five others in the battle of Jiloo Khana and the demand came from the other side to produce Yaseen Khan, whereas Miyan Yaseen khan was not at all involved in Abdul Karim's murder. Thus, finally Raja Chandulal sent word to Nawab Shah Alam Khan through Gajraj Singh that "if you want to settle the dispute, produce Yaseen Khan and hand him over to them". On that Nawab Shah Alam Khan wrote a Public Representation and handed over to the messenger. In which it was clarified that since Yaseen Khan was not involved in the murder of Abdul Karim, by Sharia he could not be handed over. (It was a confirmed fact that Miyan Mahmood Khan Moosa Khail had killed Abdul Karim and not Yaseen Khan.)

From the "Masnavi Irfan" it is stated that:

"Chandulal being perturbed with this episode called Gajraj Singh and asked him to go to Shah Alam Khan at Chanchalguda and tell him, if you want to come to any terms, you should surrender Yaseen Khan. Gajraj Singh accordingly met with Shah Alam Khan and whatever chandulal has asked him to tell him, informed to Shah Alam Khan, who informerd that Yaseen Khan would not be surrounded because he had not done any mischief.

زبس بچین چندو لال ہوکر ☆ بلا گجراج سنگھ کو اور کہو کر کہا چنچل گوڑہ کا راستہ لو ☆ یہ چل کر شاہ عالم خاں سے بولو اگر قصہ یہ تم کو توڑنا ہو ☆ تو ہاتھ ان کے کرو یسین خاں کو یہ سنکر کہو کر اور گجراج سنگھ ٹھیک ☆ چل آئے شاہ عالم خاں کے نزدیک کہے مہراج کا ہے حکم ایسا ☆ سنائے سب وہ سن آئے تھے جیسا کہے گر چاہتے ہو رفع شرتم ☆ کرو یسین خاں ان کی نذر تم کہاں یوں شاہ عالم خاں نے سن کر ☆ نہیں یسین خاں قاصر ذرا بھر

Raja Chandulal sent that Representation to the trouble mongers, advising them to keep quiet since it is a Law and Order problem, the government shall take action after 10th. Muharram and that was the order of Nawab Sikandder Jah. It was also ordered by the Nizam that there should be no ambush on the residents of Chanchalguda at any cost: As per "Masnavi Irfan":

339

شریعت سے وہ خارج ہوکے ٹولا ☆ ہواتھا مکہ مسجد بیچ گولا

سو اس حالت میں چند ولعل اظہر ☆ وہ قاضی پاس پھر بھجوا کہ محضر

کہا خاموش تم ہوجاؤ سارے ☆ جو کچھ ہو دہم کے بعد بارے

سوہ اک طور سے دریافت کہ ہم ☆ کریں گے فیصلہ بعد ازمحرم

کہوں سب سے صلاح یہ راہ کی ہے ☆ یہی مرضی سکندر جاہ کی ہے

Whatever was being asked was against sharia. In this situation, Chandulal asked everyone to keep quiet till 10th of Muharram because this is the order of Nawab Sikander Jah.

According to the "Vaquay of Chanchalguda", Nawab Sikander Jah ordered not to attack on Mahdavis at Chanchalguda:

****

"Even against Orders of the Nizam, some nobles like Niyaz Bahadur Khan, Mansur Khan, Saleh Mohammed Khan, Kaiqubad Jung, Sheik Hayatullah, Amir Khairullah Khan, Mir Gulam Ali Khan, many employees and a few Arabs, collected ammunition and cannons and gathered in the Masjid and declared Jihad against the infidels. (Mahdavis)"

بعضے نو ئینان دولت مثل نیاز بهادر خان بهادر ومنصور خاں و صالح محمد خان و کیقباد جنگ و شیخ حیات الله و میر خیر الله خان بهادر میر غلام علی خان هر دو برادر رفعت الملک بهادر و اکثر ملازمان رکاب انتساب و چند خیل بهادران عرب خلاف امر واجب الاذعان بارفقاے جان نثار و چندضرب توپ دشمن شکار تحریك عرق غیرت دین متین و احراز مثوبات جهاد فرقهٔ ملاعین مهیاے نبردو پیکار در مسجد مذکور درآمده(وقائع چنچل گوڑه صفحه ۱۷)

The author had used derogatory words: "infidels" about Mahdavis. However, it is important to note that "even against the orders of the Nizam" they had assembled". This Fact also had been reported by Hazrat Aalam Miyan Saheb:

"Finally, on competent orders, the Doors of the City were locked, but the trouble mongers had broken the locks and chains and invaded Chanchalguda and started battling."

آخرالامرحاکم وقت نے شہر کے دروازہ کو قفل بھی جڑوادیا تو ان ظالم باغیوں نے دروازہ بجمر کھولکر قفل سرکاری توڑ کر ہمارے مقابلہ آ کر جنگ شروع کردیا۔

It was a fact that Nizam's orders were not adhered to even by the Army Commanders, but instead, all assembled on Friday, the 3rd. Muharram 1238 H. in Makkah Masjid and declared Jihad and a Flag was erected and demanded to produce Miyan Yasin Khan to which absurd demand, Mahdavis flatly refused. At this point the opposing scholars instigated the participants that whoever joins and wage war and dies in the war against Mahdavis would be rewarded by (Allah) the same position as that of the battle of Badr and Hunain:

"On Friday, 3rd. Muharram, as soon as the doors of Makkah Masjid were opened multitudes along with Hafiz Haji Mir Shujauddin, Husain Haji, Syed Noorul Aoulia, Ghulami Saheb, Khateeb-e-Makkah Masjid and others entered the masjid. After Jum'a prayers, prominent scholars instigated the public that whoever wages war against that sect and if died in it, he would be rewarded by Allah the same position as was granted to the fighters of Badr and Hunain and he shall be in the sacred company of the holy prophet (Slm)".

صبح روز جمعه سیوم ماه محرم سندیك هزارودو صد سی هشت هجری همین که براے نماز جمعه دروازه مکه مسجد کشاده تمامی خلقت خدا و مولوی هامراه مولوی حافظ حاجی میر شجاع الدین حسین صاحب ، مولوی حاجی سید نور الاولیا و غلامی صاحب خطیب مکه مسجد و شریعت پناه و دیگران نیز داخل مسجد شدند بعد اداے فریضه مولوی هائے مسطور خلقت خدارا تحریص نمودند بدین نمط که هر کس امروز بر سر این قوم رودو کشته شود فرداے قیامت دربار گاه احدیت جل شانه فارغ البال در زمرهٔ شهدائے بدروحنین همراه رسول خدا صلی الله علیه و سلم محشور خواهد شد (گلزار آصفیه صفحه ۱۱٦)

The only fault of Mahdavis was that they did not hand over Miyan Yasin Khan because he did not kill Abdul Karim.

Sensing the gravity of the situation of a mutiny, the Nizam ordered for the closing of all doors of the City (There were 12 doors to enter the city from outside), and the doors were locked out so that these trouble shooters should not go and attack Chanchalguda.

"Every effort was made by the government to pacify them, but none cared and was bent upon to fight. So also was the fate of the advice given by Devan and the Peshkar. All assembled at the Makka Masjid on that afternoon, under the leadership of Moulvi Shujauddin and Noorul Aoulia, a sea of men followed them."

هر چند که از وزارت مآب ودیوان والا مقدار وپیشکار رفیع تبار باستعداد واصرار از اجتماع وبرزبان ناصحان وعظ گذار هوش عظمائی آن فساد بر آمودند اثرے نکرد وآن بحرخروشان به خاشاك اندر زبند نتوانست (وقائع چنچل گوڑہ صفحه ۱۶ در مسجد مذکور در رسیده قریب سه پهر مولوی شجاع الدین واولیاء صاحب که باعث این بلوائے قیامت بنیاد و دست آویز ارباب فساد بودند برداشته چوں بحر روان عالمی بدنبال آنهار داں گردید (صفحه ۱۷)

Author of " Tareekh-er-Asif Jahi" has written that ven after the Devan had reprimanded and the Yaqootpura door was locked, but the trouble mongers break opened the door on Friday, the 3rd. Muharram 1238 H., and invaded Chanchalguda and the battle started. It is estimated that more than 70,000 were the rioters. Then Shev Prasad sent a messenger to Anwar Khan to inform that more than 70,000 had gathered to attack on Chanchalguda and advised them to keep vigil at all sides. According to "Masnavi Irfan" it is stated that:

Shiv Prashad sent Anwar Khan to Adam Khan and informed him to be careful since the miscreants have gathered to attack chanchalguda. After hearing Adam khan told that we shall do whatever is required for our safety and if the miscreants attacked us, you will soon hear how fast they would be killed.

According to "Masanvi Natique": Shiv Prashad sent Anwar Khan to inform Adam Khan (Mahdavi) that more than one thousand cavalry have gathered to ambush Chanchalguda, thus the whole of the city is against you. Be careful and arrange your forces to check enemy's entry points leading to the entry routes to Chanchalguda."

اسی ساعت شیو پرساد باہم بھیجا پاس انور خاں کے آدم سلام اول کہا میرا تو کہنا پھر بہت ہوشیار رہنا لگا آدم سے پھر کہنے کو وہ خود تمہیں ہم نے کئے حق کے سپرد ہزار ہفتاد والی بند سارا قفص ہے چڑھا وہ کرکے تمہارا سوان کے لٹیرے چور نے بول تماشا ہیں نہایت باندھ کرغول کئے ہیں سب خیال خام ایا پھر آخر کس کا ہوا انجام کیسا وآدم واں سے آیا دوڑ ایک بار کیا سب آ کے انورخاں سے اظہار کہاسن کر کے انور خاں نے برجا اگر تو دیکھتا ہے تو ٹھہر جا یہ سب تو دیکھ کر احوال الناس خبر دے جاکر پھر مہراج کے پاس کہامہراج کا ہے حکم تعجیل سناکر آنہ کر کچھ راہ میں ڈھیل لکھا پھر اس قدر شفقہ وخاں نے دلاور شیر اس رستم جواں نے اگر ہم پر ہے یہ طوفان برپا گھڑی دو چار سے لیجیے گیا خدا کے حکم سے سرکاٹ ان کو ابھی کرتے ہیں بارہ باٹ ان کو

According to "Gulzar-e-Asafia":

"Shiv pershad sent Anwar Khan to inform Adam Khan (Mahdavi) that more than thousand cavalry have gathered to ambush chanchalguda, thus whole of the city has become against you. Be careful and arrange your force to check enemy's entry points joining to the entry routes to Chanchalguda.

سو ویسے میں شیو پرشاد دانا ☆ کیا ایک آدمی اپنا روانہ کہا چنچل گوڑہ کو جلد جا تو ☆ اور انور خاں کو ایسا بول آ تو دوالی بند سپہ ستر ہزار اسپ ☆ مسلح آپ اوپر آئے ہیں اب ہزاروں آدمی اجلاف مل کر ☆ لٹارے لوٹنے آویں مقرر یہ ساری قوم کا بلوہ ہے تم پر ☆ غرض بلدہ ایسا پلٹا ہے تم پر

According to "Gulzar-e-Asafia"

"About one lakh people fully equipped with arms and ammunition, holding flag were ready to wage a war"

قریب یک لک آدم مسلح و مکمل با سازو یراق و آلات حرب در سایہ لوائے مذکور جمع گشتہ بر سر جنگ مستعد گردیدند (گلزار آصفیہ طبع مطبع محمدی صفحہ ۱۱۶)

When they invaded Chachalguda, they had carried cannons too, and according to the map of the battle, they placed Cannons in the front. Behind the Cannons, cavalry led by Niyaz Khan and Tooti Khan, and behind the cavalry were the foot soldiers under the command of Mansur Khan and then the Arabs in the last row and finally the hoard of trouble mongers. But Mahdavis ambushed upon them all of a sudden from their behind, thus their whole strategy was disrupted and the scenario of the battlefield was altered in favour of Mahdavis. According to "Waquaey Chanchalguda" a non Mahdavi book:

"Thus, when they reached via Yaqoot Pura to a vast open ground which had paddy fields on both sides, they started planning for the battle and discussing the placement of sections of army at various points.; While Niyaz Bahadur Khan and others were busy in arranging cannons in the front and the brave Arabs behind the Cannons and cavalry to assist where necessary and how to surround the enemy and assault for the complete annihilation of all the infidels enblock. Such planning was still on the paper that suddenly the ill fated ones' (Mahdavis) cavalry ambushed on the Saleh Mohammed's Batallion from behind the elevated portion of land and the sword fighting started all of a sudden."

القصہ چون مردم بیرون دروازہ متصل بہ چنچل گوڑہ در میدان وسیع کہ ھر دو طرفین شالی زار بودہ رسیدہ قرار گرفتند در تعبیہ صفوف وطرح مبارزاں مصلحت نمودند ونیاز بھادر خاں بھادر ودیگر کلا نتراں نبر درا آراستن میدان کارزار وتقسیم مرد ان پیکار باہم دیگر کنگاش ومشتغل بودہ شہر یاں راپشت سر گرفتہ می خواستند کہ توپ ھارا پیش وفرقہ شجاعان عرب را در عقب آنھا مامور نمودہ بر وقت پیکار خود ھا با جمعیت سوار باعتضاد وامداد آنان مھیا ے نبرد با شند وبدین تدبیر صائب معاملہٗ گیر دارا پیش بردہ تنے را از آن ملاعین حی وقایم نگذار ند ھنوز این مصلحت دار آراء وترتیب صف ھار ونق قرار دا د نشدہ بود کہ درای اثنا جوق سواراں آن باطل سیر تاں ضلالت کیش فرصت دادہ (دیدہ) ازیس پشتہٗ کہ میا ن میدان بود آشکار ا شدہ بے محا بابہ سرعت ھر چہ تمام تر بر جمیت صالح محمد خان ریختند دیک بار جنگ تیغ واقع الی آخرہ صفحہ ۱۹،۱۵)

It seems author of that Book was present on the battlefield that is why he had described all the details of their planning. The vast land near Chanchalguda referred to above, in between the paddy fields, probably was the land known as Bagh-e-Samsamud Dowlah, and the elevated portion which is mentioned on its one portion, on which Chanchalguda High School was constructed. From the most elevated portion of where the Mahdavia Cavalry ambushed is the same on which the Central Jail is now standing. According to "Khazanai-e-Gowher-e-Shawar" there were only thirteen thousand Mahdavis who had blocked Chanchalguda on various entry points and established pickets for defense. Still the entire Mahdavia army did not take part in the battle since the battle was going around Yaqoot Pura Door, far off from Chanchalguda.

Mahdavia Army:

Our old sources "Akhbar-e-Shaheedan" and "Masnavi-e-Natiq" did not record total number of Mahdavis who took part in the battle. A very few Mahdavi horsemen ambushed at that place where actual battle was going on. Author of "Khatmul Huda" reports that approximately 80,000 Arabs, Ruhellahs, Kabali Pathans, Sindhi and Hindi comprising infantry and cavalry ambushed the houses of Mahdavis where about 150 Mahdavi were fighting. But "Khazana-e-Gowhar-e-Shawar" reported that about 13000 Mahdavi had blocked entry points of Chanchalguda who were ready for the battle. But all of them had no chance to engage themselves in the actual battle which took place far off from them all of a sudden.

According to "Gulzar-e-Asafia" the ringleader was Sheik Hayatullah who during the sword fight got two wounds on his face and hands, which he had never tasted before, and seeing blood is gushing out from his face, ran away from the battle field causing an unruly stampede in the rank and file and resulting their countless human casualties and a complete defeat at the hands of a few Mahdavia horsemen:

"Sheik Hayatullah and two or three brothers of Mir Muaani Khan, Jasaratud Dowlah who had never tasted the sword wounds, fled away from the battleground. When Niyaz Bahadur Khan, commander of the army, saw them fleeing, left his elephant and rode on a horse and ordered his companions to advance their forces".

دو سه تن از برادران میر معنی خاں جسارت الدوله که زد و خورد راگاهی به چشم خیال هم ندیده بودند دیده فرار رابر فرار داشتند شیخ حیات الله زخمی بردست رود برداشت پشت به جنگ داده گریزاں شد ۔

Meanwhile, he and his horse were badly wounded by a Mahdavi and he too wanted to flee, the same moment Miyan Shamshir Khan pounced upon him and attacked and killed the commander of that big army at the spot.

"Thus, Shamshir Khan and Mumrez Khan and their horsemen had ambushed at a time when the commander of the large army and his aides were still planning the battle strategy. Niyaz Bahadur Khan (Non Mahdavi) stroke with the sword at the head of Shamshir Khan (A Mahdavi), but was counter attacked, and his sword was broken and slipped from his hand and fell on the ground. His horse too did not move and fell down on the ground. Thus both Shamshir Khan and Niyaz Bahadur Khan fought hand to hand and killed each other".

دریں اثناء شمشیر خان همشیر زادهٔ شاه عالم خان کے در آن جماعہ کے به مزید معلوم اکند وکثرت جاه و جلال مخصوص وبتقریب کار کار پرده زاران این دولت ابد مدت کارش رونق بے حد داشت ودومی ممریز خان هر دواز سواران خود جدا شده به مقابل نیاز خان بهادر خان بقصد قتال درسیدند و خان مذکور نظر پر ولی وشیری به قصد طرف شدن آن هر دو گمراهان بادیه ضلالت اسپ سواری را جهاندیده و شمشیر سر شمشیر خان زداد و نیز بجواب پرواخت وسواران نمك حرام خان مسطور عار رسوائی بر خود پسندیده در خودداری وصیانت جان هائے خود کو شیدند خان مذکور ضربتی و گرفرور آورده میخواست که آن هر دورا مقتول سازد که تیغه شمشیر ش بدونیم واسپ از جائے خود حرکت نکردد و خان مذکور بر زمین افتاده هر دو باهم آویز شهائے رستمانه نمودومقتول الی آخره

When Niyaz Bahadur Khan was killed, his army fled away from the battleground.

Author of "Waquaey" had written that at that critical moment Niyaz Bhadur Khan's army betrayed the commander and fled away. It is clear that Shamshir Khan killed Niyaz Bahadur Khan who retaliated hard at Shamshir Khan and both died on the spot. From the Non Mahdvi books also it is confirmed that the army, seeing their commander was killed, fled away from the battleground.

"As soon as the 'one on one' sword battle started Niyaz Bahadur Khan's horsemen fled from the scene leaving behind their commander to fight alone and he too was killed. As per "Vaqua-e-Chanchalguda".

چنین که هر دو سمت رو به مقابلهٔ شمشیر رسیده سواران نیاز بهادر خان متوطن هند بود یکسر فرار کرده پشت نمود (خزانه رسول خانی (قلمی) ورق ۱۷۲)

According to "Khazana-e-Gowher-e-Shahi":

"The North Indians who were fighting along with Niyaz Bahadur Khan, as soon as Niyaz Bahadur Khan was killed, they too fled away."

سواران همراهی نیاز بهادر خان بهادر (که) ساکنان هند بودرو نهاده خان مذکور در آنجا شهید شده (خزانه گوهر شاهوار (قلمی) صفحه ۷۶۵)

"The effect of such a warrior's murder like that of Niyaz Khan was so severe that the whole strategy had changed in favour of Mahdavis."

از قتل چنین امیر نامدار و مرد کاردار آشوب قیامت در آن معرکه پدیدار آمد

And Shamshir Khan, Shaheed, changed the map of the battleground in favour of Mahdavis with his magnificent sword fighting.

The Stampede:

"When Mahdavis saw the battle ground had become empty, they ambushed on Mansur Khan, killed him and captured his cannons and brought to Chanchalguda and destroyed some of them."

مهدویان میدان ادخالی دیده توپ منصور خان راه که همراه خود اورده گوله ها سرداده بود به مقام خویش در چنچلگوڑه بردند (گلزار آصفیه ۱۱۷)

"Vaqua-e-Chanchalguda" states about this stampede:

"Mansur Khan was arranging his cannons that suddenly some Mahdavis arrived and attacked Mansur Khan and killed along with his nephew. Then Mahdavis took away the cannons and destroyed some of them."

منصور خان که بر سر توپ خود به یك سود ایستاده در آتش دستی ها به مبالغه و باکاری برد که ناگهان چند نفر از آنان از راه جرات بر سر خان مذکور رسیده به محاربه پیش منصور خان دلیرانه زخم کاری برداشته به قاهر زاده از پادر افتاد و آن خسران پشت دهان چالاکی به کرده توپ راه برداشت گردند و میخ زده باطل ساختند

This bravery shown by Mahdavis in snatching Cannons, is exemplary. Because when they snatched the cannons, they started bombardment on the enemy furiously. On account of which number of casualties of the enemy almost doubled. The dead ones were scattered all over the open land and the paddy fields whose counting was not possible. There is a big graveyard in between Yaqoot Pura and Dabeer Pura which reminds about these ill-fated ones who came with a zeal to kill Mahdavis to get reward of paradise, but were slaughtered ruthlessly by the Mahdavis.

It is said that during the period of Salar Jung those canons which were in good condition were called back from Chanchalguda.

Arab's defeat:

When the cavalry fled away leaving their cannons, Arabs too had to retreat and fled away.

"Khazana-e-Rasool" states that:

"It was Maghrib prayer time that the Arabs retreated badly."

درآن ضمن وقت مغرب رسیده جوانان عرب انچه بمقابله بواودند بعض گشت کردند

Saulat-e-Afghani" is a non Mahdivia source which reports that Niyaz Bahadur Khan's murder brought defeat to his army and the Mahdavis grabbed the flag from the fleeing forces till they reached the city gates. "Waqua-e- Chanchalguda" wrote:

"Such a brilliant commander's (Niyaz Bhadur Khan) murder brought tumult and disorder in the rank and file of the enemy. And thus those who had not heard the voice of the cannons and the rifles, fled away like typhoon and stamped disgrace on their foreheads and even their swords did not come out of the sheeth and fled away from the battle field."

از قتل چنین امیر نامدار و مرد کار زار آشوب قیامت درآن معر که پدیدار آمد و خلق انبوه شهر که چون خیل روباه دریس شیران جاگزیده عبث تهمت غیرت برخودبسته بودند عار گریز و فرار اختیار و به اندك صدائی توپ وتفنگ که گاهی به چشم خیال در خواب هم ندیده بودند منتشر شده نیل بدنامی برروی روزگار خود کشیدنده سیوف راهمچنان ودرنیام جاواده خود داری ها کردند ویك گل زخم نه شگفته روی از آن میدان بلا گردانیدند (وقائع چنچل گوڑه صفحه ۲۱)

Pursuing the fleeing Army:

It is stated that Mahdavis pursued doggedly against the fleeing army. "Saulat-e-Afghani" wrote:

When Niyaz Bahadur Khan was murdered by Shamshir Khan, the army became badly de-moralized which was the sole cause of the defeat that resulted in a stampede of a large army by a small group of Mahdavi Cavalrymen. "Irfan" wrote that Mahdavi snatched the flag and pursued them till the city gates.

By the evening of that Friday the battle was over. Correct number of casualties had not been recorded by the invaders, however they assume wrongly just one hundred might have been dead and the number of wounded were a few. That means to say that out of one lakh army just one hundred dared to face the death and the rest fled like a typhoon. This is nothing but false. Look at the just mentioned graveyard in between Dabeerpura and Yaqootpura and imagine how many might have been slaughtered by a small group of cavalry men who were Mahdavis. On the other hand Mahdavis had correctly recorded their casualties to be 59, name by name and the wounded ones were 110 and their names also had been recorded. "Saulat-e-Afghani" reports that: These people (Mahdavis) used sword only and showed their bravery by killing innumerable enemy and when Niyaz Bahadur Khan was slain, the whole army fled away like a whirlwind and Mahdavis even captured the fleeing army's cannons.

According to "Masnavi Irfan" total casualties of Mahdavies had been:

"Now we have to go to see how many of ours were martyred and how many were wounded, when counted there were 59 martyrs and 110 wounded, the names of each martyred has been recorded.

تھایاں تک فکر کا اوسان باقی ☆نہیں آتا نظر اب جان باقی
عناد رکھ ہاتھ عرفان اپنے غازی ☆چل اب اپنے شہید اور دیکھ غازی
شہید ۵۹ ویے اس روز از بس ☆ہوئے غازی سب بولوں ایک صد و دس
شہیدوں کی کہو تفصیل بارے ☆مفصل نام نام انسٹ و سارے

It shows that 59 were martyred and 110 were wounded, as said above.

"With much difficulty and with much pain Irfan counted again the wounded ones. He found out further 15 were wounded along with 110 already reported.

چل اے عرفان تو کر کے اس سواری ☆اٹھایا ہوں عزا کا بوجھ بھاری
یہ زخم درو خوش آتا ہے یارو ☆صدا مجروح غش کھاتا ہے یارو
جمع کس جستجو سے رات دن کر ☆کیا سب غازیاں کے نام گن کر
شمار اندر سب آئے صاحب جس ☆ہیں اول پانزدہ ایک سو دس

When this horrified news reached the Nizam and Chandu Lal they came to conclusion that it was not possible to over power Mahdavis. Then the Nizam called his English Officer and ordered him to kill Mahdavis en-block. (Nizam's such brutal order shows the severe classical rivalry and enmity between Sunnis and Mahdavis even existing among the kings.)

English Army Called For Help:

The battle was over on 3rd. Muharrum, Friday itself, by the evening. According to "Gulzar-e-Asafi" on the midnight of that day of the battle the English Army was called for. The reason was that Chandu Lal was very much disturbed and with an apprehension that Mahdavis may capture the city, he advised the Nizam for getting help from English Army for the safe-guard of the Dominion. Gulzar-e-Asafia" narrates that:

"Masnavi-e-Akhbar-e-Shaheedan" states that:

"The next day was Saturday, when Mahdavis were busy in funeral of their martyrs and taking care of their wounded ones, they saw two English Battalion coming to Chanchalguda against them. Then again Mahdavis were ready to confront the English Army also."

جمعہ گذرا سو دوسرا روز آئے ☆ زحل بن کر جراحت دوڑ آیا
شہیدوں کو ہوا مدفون روزی ☆ کریں تھے غازیاں کے زخم دوزی
پلک جو کجروی سے تیز آیا ☆ تولے دو پلٹناں انگریز آیا
خبر سن مہدوی سب کھاٹ باندے ☆ دوبارہ جنگ کا پھر ٹھاٹ باندھے
نظر کر دور سے دیکھا فرنگی ☆ کھڑے ہیں کر کے سب سامان جنگی

Gulzar-e-Asafia" wrote that:

"English battalion was comprised of Four thousand troops and ten cannons under the command of Barnett Saheb, Suderlane Saheb and Martin, Vakil, who came at 4.00 AM. the early morning of 4th Muharram 1238 Hijri At Chanchalguda.

بوقت نصب اللیل حکم جہاں باغ بنام راجہ چندو
لعل بہادر بکمال تشدد و تعصب شرف صدو ریافت
ہمیں وقت پلاٹین ہائے انگریزی ملازمان سرکار
برسرین ہا فریسند کہ صبح مقام چنچل گوڑہ راباہاک
برابر سازند (تاریخ گلزار آصفیہ صفحہ ۱۱۸)

Exodus of Mahdavis From Hyderabad:

These four thousand English troops came to overpower Mahdavis who had defeated an army of one lakh people. However the English knew very well about the bravery of Mahdavis. They did not forget how Mahdavi Pathans confronted the English army, which was fully equipped with amunition and cannons, in Poona. Here the problem was different which does not require any Military Action at all. The English Attorney got the brief and the nature of the Confrontation and came to conclusion that Mahdavis were not at fault, but their opponents defied the orders of the Nizam. The whole population of the city defied the orders and invaded Chanchalguda and when faced strong resistance from Mahdavis whole bunch of deserters fled away giving the battle field to the Mahdavis. The main fault of Mahdavis was that a few of them bravely defeated the entire one lakh army equipped with all sorts of ammunition, armory, cannons and rifles etc.

The Attorney of the English Army got complete information from Nawab Shah Alam Khan, he understood the problem and went to the Nizam, Nawab Sikander Jah and told that: "these people are very brave and they shall die for the cause of the kingdom. It was not fair to kill them and if you still want to kill them it would be a great loss of the kingdom. I had given them three days time for their exodus and I hope they would leave the kingdom."

According to "Irfan", one week time was given, thus it states:

"The English lieutenant came to the Mahdavis and sat on a chair and informed them that the government has given you one week time to go out of the boundaries of Nizam's Dominion. He further suggested to Mahdavis that their house affects shall be shifted by the Government where ever they wanted. Mahdavis accepted the order of government through the English lieutenant and agreed to go out of the boundaries within a week.

سپہوں نے شاہ عالم خاں پہ جھونکے ☆ کہے جانا برائے گفتگو کہ
اٹھا سن کر وہیں وہ خان مذکور ☆ چلا کر کے سپہوں کی بات منظور
سو اتنے میں خرد جو ہوا کٹھے ☆ کہا سب نے نہ کرنا بات بیٹھے
خدانخواستہ کچھ بیش و کم ہو ☆ تو پھر ہم کو تم اپنے پاس سمجھو
لگا کہنے کو خاں دکھلا کہ فاتح ☆ کروں تو جان پہ سردار ساتے
چلا کہہ کر وہ خان خونریز ☆ نے ہمراہ چاپراسی سوئے انگریز
جگر داری میں خاں ایسا گاڑھا ☆ ہوا جا کہ فرنگی پاس تھاڑا
وخاں جا کر سلام اس کو بجائے ☆ وہیں انگریز کرسی پر بٹھایا
بٹھا کر سی پہ وہ کرسی پہ کرسی ☆ لگا کرنے و احوال پرسی
وپرسش کر کے اس قصہ بنیاد ☆ کہا پھرسن کے سب اے آفریں بعد
نہایت آفریں کر کے کہا آج ☆ ہم تم صاحبوں کو حکم اخراج
مناسب تم کو اب آیا چلنا ☆ یہاں سے ۱۲ گھنٹوں میں نکلنا
لگا کہنے کہ تیں وہ خان کہ آرے ☆ ایک ہفتہ بیچ ہم جاتے ہیں سارے
اگر ہوا بار برداری یہ ہفتہ ☆ وگرنہ جائیں گے پھر رفتہ رفتہ

The crux of the problem was:

1. Abdul Karim was not killed by Miayn Yasin Khan;

2. There was no Sharai reason to hand over Yasin Khan, as per their demand, since Abdul Karim was not murdered by Miyan Yasin Khan. The Assassin was some other person who also was killed in the first confrontation at the Mir Alam Masjid.

3. The army, the public and everyone had defied orders of the Nizam and of the Devan.

4. It should have been done when the lock was broken, then only the English Army should have been deployed against lock breakers and stopped them, then and there, from marching towards Chanchalguda.

5. This wrong decision and maladministration resulted in heavy human loss of life mostly of the infiltrators.

6. It was an insult to the Nizam and to Chandu Lal and for the Administration since the whole Ryyot of Nizam defied his orders;

7. Innocent Mahdavis had to suffer for no reason. Alas! They became victims, finally they were expelled from the Nizam's Dominion.

Conspiracy of Izzat Yar Khan:

The son of Qader Nawaz Khan was the student of Abdul Karim and he was killed in the first encounter at the Masjid. Qader Nawaz Khan was the cousin of Izzat Yar Khan, the Sadrus Sudoor. This relationship excited the Sadrus Sadoor to take revenge from the Mahdavis by expelling them from the kingdom. For that purpose he went to the Nizam, Sikander Jah on the

Friday night itself, after hearing the shameful defeat of the entire Sunni population of the city of Hyderabad by a small group of Mahdavis, he poisoned the ears of the Nizam by instigating against Mahdavis that if they were not crushed now they would seize the reign of the government. Thus, the Nizam issued orders for deployment of the English Army. It was Raja Chandu Lal who opined the Attorney to suggest for the expulsion. Thus after hearing from Nawab Shah Alam Khan, the Attorney suggested for timely expulsion to reduce the tension, which they accepted. Hence it was the conspiracy of the Sadrus Sudoor and had nothing to do with either the Nizam or the Devan Chandu Lal.

This conspiracy is exposed in the "Masnavi-e- Irfan" in the following couplets:

"This all happened on account of poisoning the ears of Sikander Jah by instigating him that mahdavis are very brave and they do not care for their lives even. Therefore in order to saveguard the Dominion itself, exodus of Msahdavis from the boundaries of the Dominion is essential. Therefore Sikander Jah issued orders for exodus of Mahdavis."

یزیدی کو دہاں دے کر دک اندر ☆ یہاں ڈالا سکندر کو شک اندر
نبی کی آل واں تارک کرکے ☆ وہی اخراج کی یاں مشورت دے
کہا اب ملک سے ان کو نکالو ☆ ریاست اپنی ہے حضرت سنبھالو
جہاں تک کہ یہ قوم مہدوی ہیں ☆ بڑے رستم دلاور نر خوی
نہ اپنی جان کا ہے پاس ان کو ☆ وخاندان کا کب وسواس ان کو
کہا یہ ذات میں جن کے بل ہو ☆ نہ کیوں ان سے ریاست کو خلل ہو
کچھ اتنا بے حیا فتنہ تھا ظالم ☆ یزیدی سنگ دل تھا جتنا و ظالم
تھا ایسا کچھ و دارالحرب کفر ☆ سکندر کو رہا کرکے شک اندر

The English Captain told that it was an internal matter which does not come under their policy to confront a sect of the population of the Dominion. This also had been elaborated by "Irfan" in the following couplets:

"Chandulal asked the English lieutenant to bring two platoons of troops and fight against Mahdavis at Chanchalguda. After hearing the orders of Chandulal, the lieutenant told we do not take any military action against your own subjects since we can only fight against those who attack on you from outside.

و چندولعل کو کر حکم بد ظن ☆ کہا چنچل گوڑہ پر بھیج پلٹن
لگا کہنے کو اب انگریز جاوے ☆ پڑیوں سے جاکے وہ کھولا بجادے
یہ سن فرمان چندولعل ہو تیز ☆ وہیں پھر حکم بھیجا نزد انگریز
کہا دو پلٹنوں سے کر چڑھائی ☆ پڑیوں سے جلد اب لینا لڑائی
کہا انگریز یہ سن کر آخر انجام ☆ تمہارے ہم کو جھگڑوں سے نہیں کام
غنیم آ کر کرے تم پر چڑھاوی ☆ تو جا کر اس سے ہم لے ویں لڑائی
ہمیں کیا کام گھر گھر قصوں میں ہو ☆ آم آ ہوں آخر کمپنی کے گھر میں بدنام

"Then Devan Chandulal suggested to ask Mahdavis to go out of the kingdom for the time being: This is thus reported by "Irfan".

اگر چاہے تو کر دیں بندو بستی ☆ تمہاری طرف سے ہو پیش دستی
کہا چندولعل آرے ☆ کرو خاطر میں آوے سے تمہارے
ولیکن اس قدر کی چال ڈالو ☆ بہر طور ان کے تیں یہاں سے نکالو

According to the Author of "Gulzar-e-Asafia" it is said that Nawab Sikander Jah had ordered the English Army to destroy Chanchalguda to the ground level was not correct. This version is contradicted by Mohammed Faizullah Munshi who had written in his "Mir'atul Akhbar" that:

"It was Saturday morning, The Nizam issued orders for the expulsion of Mahdavis from the Dominion".

به وقت صبح روز شنبه بود احکام حضور پرنور صادر شد که این قوم را است سرحد ممالك محروسه بیرون نمایند

As had been said above, a relative of Sadrus Sudoor was the pupil of Abdul Karim, who was killed in the Masjid-e-Mir Alam debacle by Mahdavis. Makhan Lal thus said that:

"Qader Yar Khan's elder son was the pupil of Abdul Karim who died along with Abdul Karim in the first debacle occurred in Mir Alam Masjid."

فرزند کلاں قادر یار خان در مناقشه افغانان همراه هی حافظ عبدالکریم صاحب که شاگرد رشید حافظ بود به زخم گولی مرد

For that reason Sadrus Sudoor had a grudge with Mahdavis. Thus he poisoned the ear of Sikander Jah on which the Nizam ordered the English Captain during the midnight itself to ambush Chanchalguda. But as a matter of fact Sikander Jah had a good opinion about Mahdavis.

Nawab Sikander Jah And Mahdavis:

According to the "Tareekh-e-Asif Jahi" Mohammed Qader Khan Munshi had stated that:

"During the early period as the king, Sikander Jah was very much fascinated with hunting. Day in and day out he was busy along with his court companions in surveying the forests for possible games. He was very healthy with a built up body, used to go around the city some 10 to 15 miles every day along with necessary weapons and hunting implements. Incidentally two Mahdavi Pathans were attending the Nizam during his hunting activities. In view of their loyalty and services they were awarded titles of Qarawal Khan and Burq Andaz Khan. And they were permitted to become the Body Guards of the Nizam."

القصه نواب سکندر جاه بهادر در اوائل ریاست از بسکه شکار دوست واشت وشب وروز در جنگل وصحراء یا بعضی مصاحبان دمساز سیری نمود وباوجود تنومندی بدن وہ ' وہ پانزدہ 'پانزدہ کردہ عقب شکار آہو وغیرہ باساز وسلاح بندوق وسلاح دیگر گردونواحی بلدہٴ حیدر آبادی گشت وشکار را افگندہ آمادہٴ مسرت وابتهاج می گروید دو(۲) کسان افغانان پنی مهدویه بواسطهٴ آن که به همراهی این گوهر صدف آصفی باساز بندوق عقب شکاری گشتند یکی از آن بخطاب قراول خان ودیگرے به برق اندا ز خان سر افراز شدہ رساله دار سواران گشتند وباهمراهیان خود داخل چوکی خاص گردیدہ حاضر نوکری حضور می بودند (تاریخ آصفجاهی قلمی ورق ۶۷)

It all boils down to saying that Mahdavis were in the good books of Nawab Sikander Jah. Chandu Lal's instructions to Attorney were in compliance with the orders of the Nizam. However when Naasirud Dowla was enthroned, through the good offices of Chandu Lal, Mahdavis again got their previous position.

However just over six years or so the expulsion period was over through the good offices of Raja Chandu Lal who knew very well that Mahdavis were not at fault.

"Huzur Nizam (Naasirud Dowlah) accepted the request suggested by Raja Chandu Lal and issued orders for the end of the period of expulsion for Mahdavis and ordered them to come back to the city. When theuy came back, some of them were appointed as riders and cavalrymen. First of all Nawab Shah Alam Khan Jamadar was granted audience through the good offices of Raja Chandu Lal which practically ended the expulsion orders.."

حضـور پــر نور ادام الـلـه اقبـالـه ٬بـر طبق آرزو واستـدعـائـی مهـاراجه بهـادر اینهار او ر بلده طلبیده در رسـالـه٬ همـراهـی خویش ملازم و اشتند وزر خطیره درنـد رونـذرانه گـرفتنـد اول شاه عالم خان جمعدار آمـده باریاب حضور به سعی راجه چندولال مهاراجه بهادر گشت (گلزار آصفیه صفحه ٤٨١)

Thus all the responsibility to call the English Battalion and ordering for exodus of Mahdavis rest with Izzat Yar Khan alone. During the period of Nawab Sikander Jah he held a responsible position also.

Nawab Naasirud Dowlah and Mahdavis:

After the demise of Sikander Jaj, Nawab Naasirud Dowlah was enthroned in the year 1244 H. and Mahdavis attained their previous position as before."Tareekh-e-Gulzar-e-Asafia" was written during the period of Naasirud Dowla. Under the caption "Jamadar Afghan Mahdavis", thus written:

"Nawab Shah Alam Khan was first granted an audience by the Nizam on the recommendation of Raja Chandu Lal. Then slowly Mohammed Naseeb Khan and Mohammed Budhan Khan and afterwards 50 to 60 known Jamadars and further two thousand were employed who were living in Hyderabad's Begum Bazaar area and other localities and were permitted to offer respects daily by attending the court."

اول شاه عـالم خـان جمعدار آمده باریاب حضور به سعی راجه چندولال مهاراجه بهادر گشت بعد ازان رفتـه رفتـه محمد نصیب خان و دیگران و محمد بوڈهن خـان وغیـره پنـجـاه یا شصت جمعدار نامی قریب بادو هـزار مـردم ازیـں قـوم مـلازم و غیر مـلازم در بلـده ، حیدرآبـاد بـه مقـام بیگم بـازار مقام دارند هر روز جمـعـداران ایشان برائے سلام و مجرا حاضر دربارمی شوند(گلزار آصفیه صفحه ٤٨١)

The word "Jamadar" is used for an officer of an army. The above particulars denote that on account of Raja Chandu Lal, Mahdavis got their positions as before in the Dominion. Thus the episode of expulsion was the conspiracy of Izzat Yar Khan. Zaman Khan misrepresented these facts and had written in such a manner that Mahdavis would be blamed as rebels in order to create a bad opinion by persons who do not know the facts and conclude their opinion that Mahdavis fought against the kingdom. But ironically the fact is that whole Riyyat of the city defied the orders of the Nizam and fought against the peace loving Mahdavis.

When Mubarizud Dowla accepted the Wahabi Movement, Mahdavis, on orders by the Nizam, encircled Mubarizud Dowlah in his Kotla Aali Jah and produced him before the Nizam. Like that there are so many instances in which Mahdavis obeyed orders of the Nizam and of the administration. Thus they are not offenders, but defenders for the cause of the Dominion.

We had already stated what the English Officer informed about Mahdavis to the Nizam that Mahdavis are loyal who would stand for the cause of Dominion in its thick and thin. This came true during the period of Naasirud Dowlah. Had Nasirud Dowlah taken the 1238 debacle (Chanchalguda Battle) was against the Dominion, by the Mahdavis, he had not awarded so many Jagirs and Munsubs to Mahdavis. The same position was granted to them what Mir Nizam Ali Khan and Nawab Sikander Jah had given to them.

Nawab Naasirud Dowlah very well knew about the battle of Chanchalguda in which the whole city had defied orders of his father, the then Nizam, who had asked not to attack Chanchalguda, but the war-mongers broke the government locks which were put under special orders of the Nizam and then invaded Chanchalguda and finally were badly defeated by the Mahdavis. Thus these basic facts are the recorded historical events which no historian could dare to deny, but the author of Hadia had tried to presen

t Mahdavis as treacherous persons which is wrong. If that had been so, why did the Nizam grant Mahdavis respectable positions and employment and allowed them as his Body Guards?

Fate of Izzat Yar Khan:

The wicked Sadrus Sudoor, Izzat yar khan, the main culprit who caused exodus of Mahdavis could not remain in peace. Three brave men, Syed Qasim, Pir Saheb Miyan and Chaba Miyan left Kurnool in the guise of merchants arrived in Hyderabad. It is reported in the "Masnavi-e-Irfan" that these Mahdavis with an intent to kill Izzat Yar Khan arrived in Hyderabad and all three stamped their emphatic blow in such a manner that the culprit took his last breath and fell down. This culprit had caused to issue a fatwa that killing any Mahdavi was permissible by law. These three Mahdavis declared his killing was permitted by the Sharai law since the Fatwa was illegal.

1. It happened because Izzat Yar Khan and Noorul Aouliah, after the murder of Abdul Karim got prepared a public representation that killing of Mahdavis was legal.

2. All citizens defied the orders of the Nizam not to ambush at Chanchalguda. They had broken the locks of the City Doors which were locked under the orders of the Nizam just to prevent the public from ambushing Chanchalguda. When they were defeated by a few Mahdavis, it was Izzart Yar Khan who poisoned the ear of the Nizam for the Exodus of Mahdavis.

3. Izzat Yar Khan had a grudge against Mahdavis because his uncle, Qader Yar Khan's elder son, Taj Mohammed Khan was slain by Mahdavis along with Abdul Karim in Mandi Mir Alam Masjid.

4. On the orders of the Exodus, Mahdavis went many places beyond the limits of the Dominion and many reached Kurnool, where Nawab of Kurnool, Nawab Munawer Khan accommodated them with respect and provided them means of livelihood. This treatment of the Nawab of Kurnool still displeased Izzat Yar Khan, the main culprit. Therefore, he again poisoned the ear of the Nizam to write a letter to the Nawab of Kurnool not to facilitate Mahdavis, if he desires to have normal relations with the Nizam.

These are the facts which caused Izzat Yar Khan's death at the hands of three persons who came from Kurnool to take revenge.

What answer the Nawab of Kurnool had given to the Nizam had been written in the "Masnavi of Irfan":

لکھا یوں تم جو کرتے ہو بہانہ ☆ کسی نے تم کو شاید ورغلایا

نمک کا سب کے پاس کر ☆ وخاوندی کا پھر وسواس کرکے

رہے سارے پکڑا اپنا ٹھکانہ ☆ وگرنہ کرتے شہر اندر کرتے ٹھکانہ

گئی سب قوت عالی تمہاری ☆ ریاست ہوگئی خالی تمہاری

سخن جانو میرا پتھر کا کندہ ☆ شریک ہر حال ہے ان کا بندہ

"Whatever you have written is wrong because they are really faithful to you. On account of your orders these persons had left your kingdom and I think Allah is with them because they are not at fault.

In view of this answer, three Mahdavis came to Hyderabad to take revenge. Author of Hadia had mentioned that there were four Mahdavis who came to Hyderabad which is wrong. They were only three. According to "Irfan Masnavi", Izzat Yar Khan was escorted by many men when he was going through Sookha House where he was assassinated by these three Mahdavis. When the news of his murder by Mahdavis spread, there was a big tumult. But when they heard it was done by just three Mahdavis, public ran against them. The "Irfan Masnavi" thus states that:

یہاں تک شہر میں زیر و زبر ہوئی ☆ مہدوی تین شخص ہیں پھر خبر ہوئی

ہوئے جمع کھاتہ سن کے سب ☆ سدآئے تب کہیں اکل و شرب کے

گئے چھوٹے بڑے سارے چلاکر ☆ ہر ایک کوچہ عالم دوڑ آکر

زمانہ ہوگیا اطراف سارا ☆ ولے اتنا نہیں تھا کسی میں یارا

جو آکر سامنا باندھے انوں کا ☆ سو اس کو جان کر پیش آوے ہوکا

بھلا منہ پر قضا کے کیوں کراویں ☆ زمانے میں جو کر رستم کہاں میں

کہوں شیروں کا کیونکر سامنا لیں ☆ اگر ہولاکھ ہمت بکریاں میں

وہ شہزادوں کی دیکھے جہاں پیشانی ☆ جگران کے ہوے گل گل کے پانی

ارادہ کر جدھر شہزادے پھرتے ☆ ادھر کو ہاتھ سے ہتھیار کرتے

جدھر وہ دیکھتے کرکے ارادہ ☆ ادھر میدان ہوجاتا زیادہ

چلے لڑتے ہوے شہزادے ڈوب ڈوب ☆ مبارز کے پہنچے دیوڑھی تک

"Suddenly the news came that three Mahdavis have come from Kurnool and killed Izzat Yar Khan. On this news public became enraged and ran behind them and surrounded them but on account of their sword wielding power, nobody did come to confront them. Slowly these three persons came to the house of Mubarizud Dowlah.

From this it became clear that these three Mahdavis had to face the public wrath from

Sookha House to the Palace of Mubarizud Dowlah, at Aali Jah Kotla where these three Mahdavis were murdered and their bodies were hung on one of the Doors of the City.

Author of Hadia had wrongly stated that only one man killed those three Mahdavis which is wrong according to the "Tareekh-e-Khurshid Jahi" when they reached the Aali Jah Kotla Palace, the palace Sepoy's (Chowkidars) murdered them.

Since Izzat Yar Khan declared that killing of Mahdavis was legal, as an avenge for his So Called Fatwa, the three Mahdavis came to Hyderabad and killed him and stated that this was legal to revenge the man who decreed to kill Mahdavis.

(Note: The Translator had tried his best to translate the facts as reported in the "Muqaddamah" regarding the battles of Chanchalguda and Saidabad. But sometimes those facts had been narrated in lengthy paragraphs and poetic phraseology which had to be made consised for the sake of brevity. But the real facts of the battles in which Mahdavis were unnecessarily entangled, had been narrated, to show their bravery and skill. Thus all such readable details have been elaborately discussed and translated. As regards the "Masnavis of Irfan and Natiq", this translator could not translate the poetic phraseology narrated in the couplets because of his inability to translate correctly the poetic sense and the spirit inherited in these couplets, hence a few Urdu couplets which directly narrate the real facts have been copied down in Urdu as they are written in Urdu alone just in order to respect the workmanship of Hazrat Bazmi who had ventured to bring those priceless "Masnavis" which are un-noticed so far that they are such masterpiece so far unheard of, and when unearthed, it seems that the reader is witnessing the actual battle field where Mahdavi swords are demonstrating their savagery against the ernemy..")

----

83. Episode of Saidabad:

Author of Hadia had described with the same hypocrisy and distortion of the facts about the episode of Saidabad in these words:

"One day Nawab Sirajul Mulk arrived at his Palacde at Saedabad. His twenty or twenty two Mahdavi servants demanded salaries and fired on him, resulting in an iron ball stuck on the his face, which was noticed by his Arabs guards, and retaliated and murdered all of the agitators."

As a matter of facts, it is all wrong. The fact is that the Arabs opened the fire on the Mahdavis who did not have guns, except the swords. Consequently, Mahdavis took the defensive position and fought with their swords only and it is a fact that they did not carry any gun. According to "Tareekh-e-Rashid Khani" (a Non Mahdavi Source) the facts have been narrated about the debacle of 1268 H. that:

"The nawab visited Saroor Nagar for a picnic. It was 5th. of Jamadiul Awwal that Nawab

Sirajul Mulk was staying at Saidabagh. When the author (Rashid Khan, a non Mahdavi) heard about the arrival, he too visited to give company in the picnic. Mahdavi Pathans had pitched a tent at the entrance for the purpose of demanding unpaid salaries and thus created hurdles. The Nawab some how wanted to pacify them and tried to get some solution. Since no solution came out, he became furious. The same time a chair was presented to him, while he was occupying the chair the tumult started. He thought if he kept quiet it would be an insult to him. Being a warrior, he prepared himself to fight. There were some other persons, Dilawer Jung and Mohammed Khan who poured oil to flare up the situation, which resulted in sword fighting. The Arabs had encircled them and attacked them. I Salute to the bravery of the Mahdavi Pathans that even after being severely injured, they struck with sword and killed whoever came in front of them. Suddenly one iron ball from a gun (presumably from an Arab's gun) was struck on the cheek of Sirajul Mulk. The Palki men took him away and closed the door. The Police Head went into hiding in a pit. In this battle 19 Pathan were killed and four were injured and 40 Arabs were killed and 30 were injured. That day Pathan showed their bravery and strength to the best of their ability. Every one among them was a Rustum". (A Non Mahdavi writer praised the bravery of the Mahdavi Pathans, in these words.) (Pages 407, 408)

This was really a tragic episode which needed government action. Employees had worked many years without getting their remuneration and when they agitated they were confronted with rowdy elements who safeguarded the interest of the employer only, and fired bullets on the employees. No doubt Sirajul Mulk wanted to come to an amicable solution of the problem, but his rowdy aides made the situation worst and the situation turned to a dirty entanglement which resulted in 60 casualties and 100 wounded on both sides But the author of Hadia's contention that in this event only Mahdavis were killed by the Arabs was utterly false since actually 19 Mashdavis killed as against 40 Arabs.

According to the Author of "Khatmul Huda" another book:

The episode of Saidabad was a recent debacle and thousands knew that 20 to 25 employees who did not get their salaries for five years and in order to demand their salaries assembled before Nawab Sirjul Mulk at his Palace Saeedabad. Some rioters grabbed their swords and wanted to kill them, but these few Mashdavis showed their bravery in such a way that they killed at least 200 Ruhallahs and after seeing their bravery four to five thousand fled the scene and they left the Nawab alone. The Arabs too fled away and some drowned in the wells while fleeing.

As had been told the employees wanted their salaries and the Nawab too wanted to settle the dispute by pacifying them, but his coterie disrupted and tried to grab swords of the employees, which resulted in casualties on both sides. The commissioner of Police fell in a pit and the Nawab somehow was saved by his employees.

In this debacle neither the fault was of the Nawab nor of the Mahdavis. It all happened on account of Mohammed Khan Qaim Khani who had a grudge with the Mahdavis on account of the shameful defeat of the Qaim Khanis at the hand of Mahdavis in the Chanchalguda battle of 1238 H.

It is strange that the author of Hadia had arrived in Hyderabad just two years ahead of this debacle of 1268 H. and wrote wrongly in such a way that anyone who had no knowledge of this episode could draw his opinion that Mahdavis alone were killed and none other than Mahdavi was killed. According to "Tareekh-e-Rashiduddin Khani" forty Arabs were murdered and thirty were wounded. Thus the figure comes to 70 killed. Still they became so perturbed that they fought each other and became victims by friendly fire. It does not say how many Arabs were killed by Mahdavis and how many in friendly fire? But matters came to light that a few Mahdavis killed as many Arabs as they could and reached near the Palki of the Nawab. On such a bravery, Mahdavis were called "Rustam-e-Deccan"on account of their bravery against hundreds of Arab fighters.

As regards how the Nawab was wounded? It is also the act of those Arabs who started shooting and the Nawab got the wound by the Arab firing against Mahdavis, thus one of the iron balls inflicted a wound from their shooting, since Mahdavis were having swords only and not the guns.

84.Berar: (Khandes)

Syed Amjadul Mulk was the commander of Berar. As per Firishta: " After much discussion it was finally decided to appoint Syed Amjadul Mulk, a Mahdavi, as the commander of Berar and he should be deputed along with other nobles to confront Raja Ali Khan and Burhan Shah.

85.Balapur:

Author of "Ma'asirul Umara" states that Balapur and other territories of Berar were the Jagir of Syed Rustam Khan Deccani, son of Syed Ilyas Sharza Khan. And after Rustum Khan, his son became the Jagirdar of those places, this inheritance continued in his lineage for a long period.

86.Jalgaon jamood:

The authors' (and also this translator's) great great grandfather Bandagi Miyan Syed Sharief Tashrifullah (Rz) was buried here who was born in 926 H. Shah Burhan wrote:

" Bandagi Miyan's son Syed Sharief (Rz) was born in the midnight of 27th. Zil Hajj,926 H, , therefore that day was named"Youmatut Tashrief"; and the baby was named "Tashrifullah, on the commands of Allah Jalle Subhanhu. It is stated that:

"Bandagi Miyan (Rz) informed that :
"The command of Allah came that this son of yours is a gift from us; give him the name of "Tashrif-e-Haq (Rz)". Thus Bandagi Miyan (Rz)" named him Syed Sharief (Rz) and titled him "Tashrifullah (Rz)" by orders of the Almighty."

بندگی میاں فرمودند که حکم حق تعالیٰ می شود که اے سید خوندمیر این فرزند بر تو تشریف ماست و نام او شریف است لهذا بندگی میاں بامرالله اسم مبارک فرزند دلبند سید شریف نهاده و لقبش تشریف الله امر فرموده اند

Bandagi Miyan Syed Roshan Munawer (Rz) had written a letter to Bandagi Miyan Syed Sharief (Rz), addressing him as "Sharief, Ashraf, Musharraf, Tashrifullah:

"While Bandagi Miyan Syed Mahmood (Rz) wrote a condolence letter   on the demise of Hazrat Tashrif-e-Haq (Rz) addressing "We heard the news of the demise of our brother Syed Sharief, Tashrifullah (Rz) with much grief and pain."

خبـر وفـات بـرادرم سيـد شـريف تشـريف اللـه صاحب شنيدم بسيار درد و غم و اندوه شد

According to "Shawahedul Vilayet":

"Bandagi Miyan (Rz) had pronounced several good tidings, the best among them being "Tashrifullah (Rz)" and trained him under his personal guidance."

"According to" Mu'arijul Vilayet" Hazrat Tashrifullah (Rz) had miraculous powers, with which he brought back to life the daughter of a Raja and by a like supplication of his son, Miyan Syed Abdul Lateef (Rz), his nephew, Miyan Syed Raje Mohammed (Rh), came back to life, who was the only son of Hzt. Syed Saadullah Rz, his elder brother."

در حـق ميـان سيد شريف بشـارات بنـدگـی ميان بسيار است از آن جمـلـه بشارت خاص الخاص آن است کـه آن ذات را تشـريف اللـه فرمـوده تربيت خود کرده اند (باب سی و نهـم)
حضرت تشـريف الله نيز دختر راجه را زنده نمودند و بـدعـای ميـان سيد عبـداللطيف برادر زادۀ ايشان ميـان سيـد راجی مـحمد زنده شدند (باب يـاز دهم فصل دوم)

"According to" Akhbarul Asrar" Hzt Tashrief-er-Haq (Rz) died in 989 H. Hearing this news Bandagi Syed Mahmood (Rz) declared himself as the "Khatimul Murshid (Rz)".

وقتی کـه اخبـار رحـلت ميان سيد شريف رسيد همان وقت دعـوی خـاتم مرشدی فرمودند (باب دوم تفصيل دهـم)

The Opponents of Bandagi Miyan Syed Tashrifullah (Rz) had tried to malign by tampering the wordings of "Zubdatul Islam":

1. For the words "Buzargan Guftai-e-Raqam Karda Und" they changed as "Buzargan Gufta WA Raqam Karda Und".

2.For: "Khamoosh Bash Lub Mujniban" to "Kahmoosh Bash Muhibban"

3.for "Ba guftai-e-Rasool, Mahdi barabar Mohammed" to "Ba Guftand Rasool barabar Mohammed"

4. for "Ba Guftai-e-Mahdi, Miyan Wa Syed Mahmood Barabar" to Baguftai-e-Mahdi, Miyan Barabar Mahdi".

5. For:' Hazal Kalaam mervia-e-mun Tashrifulla….Wa ghairahum". To " Ilhaq Mua nidana",

these words are not available in "Zubdatul Islam".

Beliefs of Tashrief-e-Haq (Rz) and Imamana's Companions:

"Zubdatul Islam" states that the beliefs of the companions were the same as that of Hazrat Tashrifullah (Rz):

"Miyan Syed Shahabul Haq (Rz) and Miyan Syed Mahmood (Rz), Hasan-e-Vilayet, and Miyan Syed Sharief Tashrifullah (Rz) and their descendants and Bandagi Malik Ilahdad (Rz) and Miyan Malikji (Rz) and other companions of Imamana (As) accepted the excellence of Bandagi Miyan (Rz) according to the commands of Imamana (As) and they all believe on Imamana's dictates."	میاں سید شهاب الدین و میاں سید محمود حسین ولایت اور میاں سید شریف تشریف الله و فرزندان و نبیرگان ایشان رحمته الله علیهم اجمعین و بندگی ملک الهٰداد مرد ربانی و میاں ملک جی و دیگر صحابه رضی الله عنهم اجمعین چه طور فضل میاں به فرمودهٔ مهدی علیه السلام .... همان قبول کرده یقین در فرمودهٔ مهدی علیه السلام دارند

This confirms that the opponents manipulated the wordings of "Zubdatul Islam" to malign Hazrat Tashrifullah (Rz). Moreover, it is not at all written in" Zubdatul Islam"that, as equality is evident in between Rasool (Slm) and Mahdi (As), there exists an equality in between Mahdi (As) and Miyan (Rz)."But "Matleul Vilayet" had written "Bandagi Miyan proved his venerability as per the dictates of Imamana(As) which is an obvious fact.

The manner in which the Dairah of Bandagi Miyan Tashrifullah (Rz) was established, Shah Burhan (Rh) had narrated thus:

'When Bandagi Miyan Tashrifullah (Rz) arrived at Burhanpur, both Jalal Khan and Ba Yazid Khan, eminent nobles tried for his stay in Burhanpur which he did not like, and even denied their invitation for staying at their residence and rejected their gifts too. Then Jalal Khan handed over a shield and a sword to his minister and asked him to accompany him up to where he goes. When Bandagi Miyan Tashrifullah (Rz) arrived in Jalgaon, he approved it and told: "what a beautiful place is it if any body provides to him for his stay". When Jalal Khan heard of his choice, he called the landlord of that place and gifted him the Shield and the sword to him. He selected that piece of land and he stayed there till his demise."	چون به بلدهٔ برهان پور رسیدند جلال خاں و بایزید خاں امرائے کلاں از جملهٔ مصدقان ایشان نیز سعی اقامت در برهان پور بسیار کردند فاما قبول نه افتاد و در هر خانها هم بطریق مهمان داری نه رفته اند چنانچه خافی نیست و فتوح ایشان قبول نه کرده اند و یک سپر اعلیٰ و یک شمشیر خوب بابندهائے نقره بدست وزیر خود داده تادیه جل گاؤں یاران همراه فرستاده بود که تاهر جا که در خاطر مبارک بندگی میاں پسندمی آید همان جائے مقرر کرده و امداد نموده باش چوں قبله گاهی حضرت تشریف الله دردیه جل گاؤں رسیدند آن مکان شریف پسندیدند و فرمودند که چه خوب جائے گوشه ایست اگر کسی ماندن دهد چون وزیر جلال خاں را معلوم ش داربات دیه مذکور را آورده و آن سپرد شمشیر آن راداده در آنجا مقام کرده اند و چند سال در آن مانده اند (دفتر دوم رکن دواز دهم باب پنجم)

(Note: On receiving a legal notice from the Deputy Collector of Amrawati in April 1963

that the southern boundary wall of the Hazeera of Bndagi Miyan Syed Sharief (Rz) at Jalgaon Jamood has fallen, and if it was not constructed, land grabbers shall occupy the land of the Hazeera. Actually this notice was sent to Dhaboi. However this came to me by the Grace of Allah, since Haz. Tashreef-e-Haq is my great, great Grandfather. I took it to Hzt. Mohammed Miyan Saheb who advised me to collect funds. I collected funds to the tune of Rs.20, 000 from Hyderabad and Channapatna. Hzt. Mohammed Miyan Saheb himself accompanied me, along with another five persons and went to Jalgaon Jamood and with the help Mr. Sansaullah Baig and local people, a two hundred feet boundary wall was constructed within 15 days and thus saved the Hazeera. Still there was much work which was also carried in 2002. A large mausoleum and a Saray with all facilities was constructed from the funds provided by the Hyderabadis under the supervision of Br. Mohd. Ibrahim, Engineer of Amrawati. If Zareyeen like to go to the Massoleum, they have to go to Amrawati and contact Br.Ibrahim, who will guide in this respect. Otherwise they can directly catch a bus going to Jalgaon Jammod, from the Bus Stop, any person may lead to them to the Hazeera.   Translator)

85.Burhanpur:

This author's great grandfather Bandagi Miyan Syed Jalal Shaheed (Rh), son of Bandagi Miyan Syed Abdul Lateef (Rz) had maintained his dairah in Burhanpur and whose grave is near the Jamai-e-Masjid. Many Mahdavis still live in Nand Gaon, a village in Burhanpur.

86.Khandes:

Madarul Mulk of Khandes was a Mahdavi, according to "Khatim-e-Sulaimani":

"In Deccan some eminent nobles were Mahdavi; for example: Pir Mohammed Daccani was a minister of the king of Khandes. He might have come from Gujrat, since his brother Miyan Sheik Zainuddin known as Nahnnay Miyan was a Gujrati was already living there".

در دکهن بعضے کساں مهدوی امرائے کلاں شده مثل میاں پیر محمد دکهنی که مدار الملك بادشاه خاندیس بودند شاید در اصل گجراتی اند چرا که برادر شاں میاں شیخ زین الدین عرف نهنی میاں گجراتی اند (گلشن دوازدهم چمن چهارم)

87. Borkheda:

Borkheda also a town of Khandes where many Mahdavis lived and still there is one house of a Mujawer (Caretaker) (who looks after the mausoleum of Hazrat Bandagi Shah Dilawer (Rz).

بور کهیڑه در ملك خاندیس و پرگنه ، بهپال است ، از آنجا دو کرده سمت شمال است ، در آنجا بیشتر مصدقان بودند اکنوں یك خانۀ مجاور است (گلشن دواز دهم چمن چهارم)

(Note: In view of occurrences of rare miraculous incidents, the Hindus of this village have a great respect for Hazt. Bandagi Shah Dilawer (Rz). On account of which, the Mujawer, who is a Hindu, practices the Hindu rituals, by breaking coconuts at the doorstep of the Mausoleum, whenever anyone comes to offer their homage to the mausoleum. These

practices are not Sharie, hence must be forthwith stopped and a Mahdavi Mujawer should be appointed to safeguard the Shrine, otherwise, by the passage of time the shrine shall be owned and managed by Hindus, and it is apprehended that they may even change the name of Shah Dilawer (Rz) of their liking. Since very recently we have noticed how dubiously they had, with the connivance of Hindu Govt. Authorities, they had illegally constructed a temple adjacent to the famous Charminar . Like that these Hindus are trying to obliterate the Muslim monuments. At Iddgah of Mir Aalam, at Hydersabad also, they had constructed one mander illegally and Ayudia carnage is elf explanatary.).

87.Suhagpur is still a center for Mahdavis.

88.Ajmir:

"Miyan Sheik Mustafa Gujrati (Rh) had a dialectic Session in Ajmer who was brought by Asif Khan from Gujrat to Ajmer on orders of Akber; according to Badayuni.

چون خلیفه الزمانی بعد از تسخیر ولایت بنگ از پٹنه مراجعت نموده باجمیر رسیدند آصف خان ثانی میر بخشی اورا بحسب حکم از گجرات همراه آورد (منتخب التواریخ طبع کلکته جلد سوم صفحه ۵۰)

According to "Mua'sarul Omara":

"Syed Rustum Khan Daccani was the son of Syed Ilyas Sharza Khan whose forefathers belong to Bukhara. One among them came from Bukhara to India and stayed in Ajmer and on account of the company of Mahdavis, he adopted Mahdavia Faith."

"سید رستم خان دکنی پسر شرزه خان سید الیاس است ، وطن ناگانش بخارا است ، یکی از آنهما به هندوستان وارد گشته چندے درنواحی اجمیر جاگرفت و به صحبت سکنۂ آنجابه مذهب مهدویان برآمد (مآثر الامراء جلد دوم صفحه ۲ ۵۰۲،۵۰۳)

Thus it comes to light that in the vicinity of Ajmer many influential observers of Islamic jurisprudence were living and under whose influence many became Mahdavi, among them were peoples who migrated from Bukhara and elsewhere.

89.Nagore:

It is stated that Miyan Ali of Dholqa migrated to Nagore in the dairah of Bandagi Shah Nemat (Rz), which was the birthplace of Sheik Mubarak (Rh), father of Abul Fazal and Faizi.

90.Khawaspur (Jodhpur):

According to Badayuni, when Sheik Alaai (Rh) arrived at Khawaspur, which is near Jodhpur, Khawas Khan asd an Officer appointed at its border, came and welcomed him and became one of his devotees. If the officer became Mahdavi, there should be no doubt about the public to follow the officer. But the author of Hadia had written that Khawas Khan reverted to his old Faith. The fact is that the author of Hadia had based his wrong allegation on Farishta's writings which are not completely authentic. Even otherwise the author is against Mahdavis. Apart from this, his writings are distorted from the facts. He wrote Imamana's year of Demise to be 960 H. Whereas the actual year was 910 H. Further he wrote that Sheik Alaai (Rh) was unable to face the Scholars with reference to Imamana (As) and the faith; whereas other prominent scholars and historians had testified that Sheik Alaai (Rh) had always overpowered upon all his opponent scholars. Thus Farishta had become an unreliable author because he was arrested by Mahdavis for his wrong and unbearable behavior in Ahmed Nager. Farishta also wrongly reported that Khawas Khan reverted to his Faith, (God forbid). The facts are that Sheik Alaai (Rh) had maintained his preachings particularly on the principle of "Amr Bil Ma'roofi Wa Tanhauna Anil Munkar" "Enjoin virtue and abhor evil". That was the sublime dictates of the Holy Qur'an. These strictures were harsh for Khawas Khan, because unfortunately, Khawas Khan was appointed in such a place where these dictates were hard to apply, and sometimes Khawas Khan in view of his duty he was unable to adhere to the Dictates of the holy Qur'an. In these circumstances, he had to comply orders of his superiors, therefore he had to neglect some of the Sharai strictures, in the interest of his service. This cannot be said that on account of his such act he had reverterd from Mahdavit. This fact of the conditions of service, both Farishta and author of Hadia had purposely kept hidden to deceive others. Author of "Muntakhabatut Tawareekh" thus wrote:

" Sheik Alaai (Rh) arrived in Khawas Pur, where Khawas Khan was posted at the border, he warmly welcomed and finally entered into his company. Since he was very interested in hearing sermons, Sheik Alaai (Rh) used to go to his house and deliver his sermons based on "enjoin virtue and abhor evil". Thus he (Khawas Khan) could not digest since it was not practicable for him on account of his post at such a place where he could not stop soldiers from what they were doing and could not reprimand them. Thus Sheik Alaai's strict strictures could not be followed by Khawas Khan. This was the main point of objection to Khawas Khan and never took it as a mischief as reported by Farishta. The author of Hadia had blindly copied what Farishta had written.

According to Eliot :"He (Sheik Alaai (Rh)) set forth, accompanied by six or seven thousand followers, with the intention of performing the pilgrimage to Makkah. When he arrived at Khawaspur which is in Jodhpur territory, Khawas Khan came forth to welcome him and intended to be in his company. When Saleem Shah heard that Khawas Khan had become Mahdavi on the hands of Sheik Alaai (Rh), he called back Sheik Alaai (Rh) from Khawaspur. In a like situation when Bahadur Khan of Deccan had become the devotee of Sheik Alaai (Rh), on that occasion also, Saleem Shah called back Sheik Alaai (Rh) from Deccan as reported by "Muntakhabut Tawareekh".

Sheik Alaai (Rh) and "Tareekh-e-Dawoodi":

Except "Tareekh-e-Farishta", nowhere it was written that Khawas Khan had reverted to his original faith. Farishta's version is based on his enmity towards Mahdavis because he was arrested by Mahdavis at Ahmed Nager. Thus Author of Hadia, another arch rival of Mahdavis, joined him with the sole purpose of disgracing Khawas Khan and Mahdavis together.

According to the author of "Khatmul Huda":

91.Jodhpur: also was a center of Mahdavis. In many cities, towns and villages of every province of India (and Pakistan) tens of thousands of Mahdavis are still living in peace and harmony along with other residents.

92. Jalore:

Jalore is situated on the West- Southern side of Jodhpur at a distance of 71 miles. Bandagi Shah Nemat (Rz) had maintained his dairah here. From the 10th century to 12th Century, Jalore had been a dairah of so many venerable and religious personalities and now it has two sacred shrines of Hazrat Malik Miyan Maroof (Rz), Sahaabi-e-Mahdi (AS) and Bandagi Miyan Syed Mahmood Khatimul Murshid (Rz).

93. Dongerpur (Mewad):

Bandagi Malik Ilhadad (Rz) had established his dairah here where Humayun, Hindal, Kamran and Mirza Askari had come along with Malik Pir Mohammed (Rh) to meet Bandagi Malik Ilahdad (Rz).

94.Udaipur:

After the martyrdom of Miyan Syed Raju (Rh), Miyan Syed Ibrahim (Rh) arrived in Udaipur and settled down here.

95. Jaipur:

Author of Hadia had written that on account of the pressure from Akber, the Afghans came from Delhi to Gujrat and adopted Mahdavia Faith and settled down, then on the recommendation of the Raja of Jaipur they settled down in Jaipur. Author of "Saulat-e-Afghani" very well knew about genealogies of these Afghans, therefore he had a doubt about Hadia's version. Therefore he wrote a letter to the author of Hadia asking him the source of his information about the Afghans to which he did not get any reply. Thus, neither Mahdavia books nor non Mahdavia books state the arrival of Afghans from Jaipur to Gujrat on pressure from Akber. According to "Khatim-e-Sulaimani" Afghan tribes, after converting to the Mahdavi faith, had gone to Jaipur from Gujrat. Akber was born in 949 H, and long before Akber's birth, Afghan tribes had converted to Mahdavia Faith at the hand of Bandagi Miyan Syed Khundmir (Rz) (Mrtrd. 930 H):

"These Afghan tribes arrived in Gujrat and on hearing sermons of Amir Kabir Bandagi Miyan Syed Khundmir (Rz) they became Mahdavi on his hands. When they felt uneasiness for living in Gujrat, they left for North India and when Raja of Amber heard and found them warriors, had offered them employment to them and provided them boarding and lodging facilities. They were about 12,000 in all".

ذكر افاغنه پنی هدوی كه اى افغانان در عهد سلطنت گجراتیان باقبائل در گجرات آمده بودند از بیان كلام حضرت امیر كبیر بندگی میان سید خوندمیر از سعادت تصدیق كامیاب و مشرف شدند پس از چند گاه از گجرات سبب سكونت صورت نه پذیر فت از آنجا نقل مكان نموده عاز هند شدند تاراجه آنبیر ایشان را دلاور و شجاع دریافته بنوكری هر گزیدو مسكن و مامن دادایشان خورد و كلان قریب دواز ده هزار بودند (گلشن دواز دهم چمن چهارم)

This testifies that Afghan tribes after becoming Mahdavi in Gujrat, went to Amber in Jaipur. According to "Khatim-e-Sulaimani":

"After the demise of Miyan Mustafa (Rh), (his son) Sheik Abdullah (Rh) lived in Biayna for some time, then lived in the vicinity of Biyana and then went to Akberabad and finally settled down in Anber and established his dairah here."

بعد از وفات میان مصطفیٰ شیخ عبدالله چند ایام در بلدۀ بیانه و چندگاه بحوالی آن و چند ایام بحواله اكبر آباد گذرانیـد نـد و بعد از آن در قریۀ آنبیر آمده دائره بستنـد و در آنجا سكونت مدتی واقع شد (گلشن نهم چمن چهارم)

Miyan Sheik Mustafa Gujrati (Rh) died in 984, then Miyan Sheik Abdullah (Rh), his son, established his dairah at Anber (Jaipur) and according to Professor Mahmood Shirani Miyan Sheik Abdullah (Rh) lived in that dairah for 15 years and left at 999 H. and arrived in Khandela along with his wife and children. Anber was the old capital of Jaipur. Thus even before 1000 H. Gujratis had established their dairah in Khandaila of Jaipur. Miyan Mahmood (Rh) had established his dairah at Amersir and some Afghans of that place became Mahdavi at his hand. As reported by Miyan Syed Fazlullah in " Sunnatus Saleheen" that:

"In the territory of Dhondar, Miyan Mahmood Shah (Rh) son of Miyan Syed Budha (Rz) had his dairah at village Amersir who was living in the company of Bandagi Miyan Syed Mahmood, Khaatimul Murshid (Rz). After the demise of Khatimul Murshid (Rz), he went to Bandagi Miyan Syed Miran (Rz) and with his permission, he established his dairah, where some Afghans became his disciples.

در ملك دهنڈار دائره میان محمود شاه ولد میان سیدبڈه در موضع امرسر بود ایشان صحبتی حضرت بندگی میان سید محمود خاتم المرشد بودند و بعد از رحلت خاتم المرشد به حضور بندگی میان سید میران در جالور رفته رضائی میان سید میران طلبیده آمده برضائی ایشان در آن شهر با دائره بودنـد و در شهر امر سر افغانان مریدان ایشان بودند

1. Miyan Mahmood Shah (Rh) son of Miyan Syed Budha (Rz) has founded his dairah at

Amersir, where some Afghans became his disciples.

2. Miyan Mahmood Shah (Rh) gained beneficence from Hazrat Khatimul Murshid (Rz).

3. After the demise of Khatimul Murshid (Rz), Mahmood Shah (Rh) went to Jalore and obtained permission from Khatimul Murshid's son Bandagi Miyan Syed Miran (Rz) and founded his dairah at Amersir.

4. Hazrat Khatimul Murshid (Rz) died in 996 and his son Miyan Syed Miran (Rz) died in 1015 H.

From the above, it is clear that Miyan Mahmood Shah (Rh) was busy in preaching in Amersir of Dhondar territory. Miyan Sher Mohammed (Rh) had founded dairah in village Tigrea who happened to be from the lineage of Maqdoom Bahauddin Naqshbandi. Thus, Gujratis were the first to establish dairah at Amersir, Anber (Jaipur) and after many years, Deccanis went to Jaipur and founded their dairahs. Thus, Author of Hadia's contention is utterly wrong that Afghans of Jaipur went to Gujrat and became Mahdavi. The fact is that Afghans after becoming Mahdavi in Gujrat went to Jaipur.

96. Khandela: Regarding dairah of Khandela, Professor Mahmood Shirani had written a thesis which was already referred to above in connection with Miyan Sheik Mustafa Gujrati (Rh) whose son Miyan Abdullah established his Dairah at Khandela.

97. Belikhun (Jaipur):

Author of "Tareekh-e-Mahdavian" states that the disciples of Fujju Miyan were more than six thousand Afghans and at the time of his sermons big gatherings were seen. This Fajju Miyan was none but Miyam Syed Fazlullah (Rh).

98. Kalpi:

Mullah Abdul Qader Badayuni had written about Miyan Shah Burhanuddin (Rh) of Kalpi that:

"Shah Burhanuddin (Rh) of Kalpi was an ascetic, having full trust in Allah and God fearing also, who was living a life in seclusion and separation. Had attained beneficence and excellence in a 3 day company of Hazrat Miyan Ilahdad (Rz), who in turn was the disciple of Mir Syed Mohammed (As) Juanpuri, Qudasallahu Ruha. Thus Shah Burhanuddin (Rh) had attained complete beneficence, austerity and always be in the presence of the Almighty. He was living in a narrow, dark room, being immersed in remembrance of Allah's names, meditating and guarding his incoming and outgoing breaths; (Paas-e-Anfaas) pursuing the Mahdavia way of life. Although he was not well versed in Arabic, but used to comment Qur'an in such an eloquent and pleasing manner that everyone present to hear his sermons could understand their meaning completely. The author had the opportunity to visit him one night while returning from Chinar, during the period of Abdullah Uzbeck and had the occasion of high ranking discussion and read to his high sounding poems and matters relating to amenable good counsel and religious matters."

برهان اهل زهد و توكل و تقوئ و سلطان ارباب عزت و
تجريد و استغنا است مى گويند كه سه روز صحبت
ميان الهداد ـ بارى وال كه بيك واسطه بمير سيد محمد
جونپورى مشهور قدس الله روحه مير سد داشته اين
فيض حاصل كرده و بدرجه كمال رسيده مرتاض و
باحضور بود.......... در كالپى حجرۀ داشت بسيار تنگ
و تاريك پيوسته در آن بذكر و فكر و مراقبه اشتغال
داشته ، اوقات به پاس انفاس بطريق مهدويه ميگذرانيد
و باآنكه علوم عربيه هيچ نخوانده بود ، تفسير قرآن
بوجه بليغ ميگفت وصاحب كشف قلوب بود و فقير در
وقت مراجعت از سفر چنار در شهور ٩٦٧ء نهصدو
شصت و هفت در زمان حكومت عبدالله خان اوزبك
شبى بملازمت شيخ رسيدم سخنان بلند فرمود و پارۀ از
اشعار هندى خود كه مشتمل بروعظ و نصيحت و
تصوف و ذوق توحيد و تجريد بود بتقريب خواند
(منتخب التواريخ جلد سوم صفحه ٦ تا ٧)

"The second day, I, along with Mehar Ali met Shah Burhasnuddin again. That day before embarking on travel, Mehar Ali had ill treated his servants and kicked and abused them vehemently. When we entered into his presence, the very first sentence we heard from his mouth was that the holy Prophet (Slm) said "the Muslim is one who does not hurt other Muslims, either by hand or tounge." The holy Prophet (Slm) had reprimanded those who used to abuse and ill treat his Muslim servants. Then he discussed about matters relating to mystic knowledge and piety related topics. Hearing all, Mehar Ali stood up before him and humbly requested his forgiveness and offered some gifts which the Shah did not accept. The Shah reached one hundred years and died in 970 H. Badayuni told the date of demise, in Chronogram by the words" Dil Guft Ke Shah was a Vali." My heart tells that shah was a vali. (970)"

روز دیگر مهر علی .... بدر قگئی فقیر شریف ادراك ملاقات شیخ را دریافت اتفاقاً چوں پیش از آں بیك ساعت بعضی خدمتگاران و ملازمان خود را لت ولكدم محكم و مضبوط زده دشنام و فحش بسیار نامربوط برزبان رانده سوار شده بود در آن مجلس اول كلمهٔ كه برزبان شیخ گزشت ایں بود قال النبی صلی الله علیه و سلم المسلم من سلم المسلمون من یده ولسانه و بتقریب ایں نكات ارجمند و معارف بلند فرمود مهر علی بطریق عذر خواهی برپای خاست و اظهار ندامت و خجالت نموده فاتحه التماس كردو پارهٔ نذرے گزرانید قبول نه شد ، عمر شریف شیخ قریب به سن صد سالگی رسیده در سنه نهصدو هفتا و محمل رحلت بست و ایں تاریخ یافتم ع ــ دل گفت كه شیخ اولیا بود (منتخب التواریخ طبع كلكته جلد سوم صفحه ۷)

Badayuni concludes that a place where such a God fearing, pious and such a venerable personality was living, how is it possible that this place should not have Mahdavis. While discussing about Malik Jaaisi and his religious guide Hazrat Bandagi Malik Ilahdad (Rz), we had also mentioned about his disciple Shah Burhan. Thus he was the same Sheik Burhan (Rh) who lived in Kalpi and had a large gathering of his disciples. This fact had also been confirmed by Sheik Abdul Haq, Muhaddis-e-Dahlavi, who opined that he had heard Shah Burhan (Rh) was also a Mahdavi.

99. Fath-e-pur Saikri:

On orders of Akber, Asif Khan brought Miyan Mustafa (Rh) from Gujrat to Ajmir and then Akber took him to Fatehpur Sekri and then Akber asked Miyan Mustafa (Rh) to stay with Abdul Samad, Musawwer-e-Sheereen Qalam.

Professor Mohammed Shirani states that: The inclination of people to see Miyan Mustafa Gujrati (Rh) was so immense that on every Thursday sweets were out of stock in the bazaar and when asked, the owners of the sweet shops used to say: "Do not you know that the public had gone to listen Sheik Mustafa (Rh) and to become his disciple?, Therefore it is hard to get

Beetles and sweets today." It indicates that the entire population had become Mahdavi. When Akber reached FathePur, he called scholars for discussion, which ran for many days and the details of just five sessions, Miyan Mustafa (RH) himself had written.

The flame of Mahdavit made scholars envious of its grandeur. From Mahdavi literature it came to light that before and after the Discussions, Miyan Mustafa Gujrati (Rh) was being ill treated and subjected to harassment and torture. Mulla Abdul Qader Badyuni had written his eyewitness episodes of Miyan who was being tortured even though he was very weak and during the discussion a pot was brought in which Miyan Gujrati (Rh) spat blood.

Mahdavi faith in cities of of India:

Bandagi Shah Burhan (Rh) had written a letter to his contemporary from Farha that:

"Followers of Imamana (As) live in many parts of India like Bahut (Jehlum), Bhakker, Multan, Dhondar, Jalore, Nagore, many parts of Gujrat and Deccan, Samana, Delhi, Agra, Juanpur, etc"

"مقتدایان حضرت خلیفته الرحمنؐ که در ولایت هندوستان ساکن اند خصوصاً در بهت و بهکر و ملتان و دهنڈار و جالور و ناگور و گجرات کلاں و جملهٔ دکنؔ و سماناؔ و دهلیؔ و آگرهؔ و جونپورؔ و جزآں (خاؔتم سلیمانی گلشن یاز دهم اول)

100. "Bahut" had been used which is none but Jehlum of Punjab. Thus Mahdavis spread from Bengal to Khurasan and from Deccan to Punjab.

101. Makkah-e-Moazzamah:

A. According to "Shawahedul Vilayet": Imamana (As) had stayed in Makkah for some months where many Arabs became his followers."

حاصل الامر چند روز حضرت خاتم ولایت در شهر مکه مبارک اقامت کردند در آنجا بسیار اهل عرب منقاد شده سر بر آستانه شریف نهادند

B. From the translation of "Makhzanul Dalael" it comes to light that there were many Arabs who had accepted him as Mahdi (As).

C. According to the Risala "Asaami Musaddaqeen" it is said that Miyan Sheik Berari (Rz) had stayed one year in Makkah and preached our Mahdavia Faith with full zeal and enthusiasm. He had that much convincing ability to speak and refute Sheik Ali Muttaqi's allegations against Imamana (AS) who also was living in Makkah, an arch rival of Imamana (As). Before writing his "Risalatur Rudd" Sheik Muttaqi obtained Fatwas from scholars of Makkah and sent to India. These Decrees are recorded by him in "Al Burhan Fe Alaamath-e-Mahdi Akhiruzzam" which had been replied by Hazrat Syed Isa, known as Aalam Miyan Saheb who wrote in his book "Shubhatul Fatawah".

D. According to "Khatim-e-Sulaimani" a copy of "Sirajul Absar" was sent to Makkah.

E. "While replying to the author of Hadia, Author of "Khatmul Huda" had categorically written that our Mahdavi scholars had gone to Makkah and preached Mahdavia Faith, but none could dare to hurt any one of them or stop them from preaching, leave aside killing.

F. Syed Jalal son of Syed Sayeed Khan was traveling from Madras to Hyderabad. During the journey, Syed Mohammed Maqdoom, a fellow traveler, had put some questions about Imamana (As) to Syed Jalal who answered in Persian language. Fifth question pertains to "Makkah and Mahdavi Preachings". Which states that:

"Miyan Malik Sujawandi (Rz), Sheik Bhai Berarai (Rz) and Miyan Syed Hasan Makki (Rz) were the perfect scholars who used to attend Sharief-e-Makkah's Assembly, where some scholars of Makkah along with Sheik Ali, the slanderer, were present. They were badly defeated by our said scholars in dialectic discussions. The questions and answers ar recorded in "Risali-e-Chahar Sanad" which is famous in Makkah."

میان عبدالملك سجاوندی و شیخ بهائی براری و میان سید حسن مکی این قسم کاملان این گروه در مجلس شریف به عالمان مکه وبه شیخ علی مفتری مباحثه نموده ملزم ساختند سوال و جواب در رساله چار سند مشهور است اور مکه چوں ظاهر نباشد (بیاض قلمی)

That Miyan Hasan Makki (Rz) returned from Makkah to Pindyal, then went to Jaipur and to Faraha Mubrak and then to Khurasan. Aftetrwards his whereabouts are not known. Thus it comes to light that Mahdavi Scholars had gone even to Makklah and had dialectic discussions, the details of the discussions are recorded in "Risal-e-Chahar Sanad."

102. Madinah-e-Munawwara:

A. According to "Tareekh-e-Sulaimani" there had been a Dialectic discussion in Madinah at the Shrine of the holy Prophet (Slm) with scholars of Madinah and Miyan Syed Husain Makki (Rz).

B. Mohammed Ji Miyan (Rz) had a dialectic discussion in Madinah about Imamana's proclamation of Mahdiat, about which professor Mahmood Shirani wrote that:

"We donot know about Mohammed Ji Miyan (Rz), but we have one of his letters which he wrote from Madinah which is famous in dairah. He was 80 years old when he wrote that letter which was forwarded by one of his friends in 1190 H. which reads as below:

"Disclosure of Imamana's proclamation of Mahdiat by the late Mohammed Ji Miyan (Rz) at Madinah-e-Munawwara which was heard by all who were present there.

Different Cities And Shah Burhan (Rh):

"Khatham-e-Sulaimani" states that "scholar-guide Miyan Shah Burhanuddin (Rh) had traveled many countries of the World and spread the message of Mahdavia Faith. After reaching Farah Mubarak he disclosed his desire for the pilgrimage of Makkah. He went to Syria and Baitul Muqaddas and performed pilgrimage of Makkah and Madinah and offered respects at the shrines of Ahl-e-Bait, companions of the holy Prophet (Slm) and mystics and venerable personalities. His journey details have been mentioned in the preamble of "Shawahedul Vilayet" that:

"As a matter of fact, with Beneficence from Imam Mahdi (As) this weak and meek, became the world trotter for the cause of spreading Imamana's message, started his Mission from Deccan to Gujrat, from Gujrat to Indian cities, like Lahore, Punjab; then to Kabul, Balakh, undkhud, Chachakto, from here to Maimana, Maroojaaq, Herat, then to Farah Mubarak, on Monday, the 7th. of Ramazanul Mubarak, 1052 H. had the unique opportunity of performing pilgrimage on the holy shrine of our Mentor, Hazrat Syed Mohmmed Juanpuri, Mahdi-e-Mauood Alaihis Salaam.Then went to Shiraz of Persia, Basra of Iraq, then to Makkah for performing Hajj and from Makkah to Madinah to offer humble pilgrimage on the shrine of Huzoor Sarswer-e-Kayenat, Sall-e-Ala wasallum, then back to Baghdad, Iraq, and Farah Mubarak. Then reached to the Fort Buss and Qandhar. I had carried some 300 Pamphlets, regarding Imamana (As) which were distributed at various places where I had dialectic discussions with scholars of those places which I visited in order to inculcate them the Teachings of Imamana (As). Then I came back to the holy shrine of Imamana (As) and started writing "Shawahedul Vilayet, at the feet of my Mentor.

Peoples of different cities:

Different peoples of different cities and countries accepted Mahdi Faith like Khurasan, Turkistan, India, a few references are being given here:

"This indegent and despicable had been vested with globe trotting fate, therefore from Deccan to Gujrat to Delhi, to Lahore then to Kabul, to Balakh, to Undkhud, to Chichaktu, then to Maroojaq, then to Herat and lastly to Fraha at the Mausoleum of Imamana (AS), performed pilgrimage on Monday the seventh of Ramazan 1052 H. and after that went to Basra of Iraq and Shiraz of Persia and after that performed pilgrimage of Kabatullah and Madinah-e-Munawwara, then to Baghdad of Iraq to Farah Mubarak and then fate drove him to Fort Buss, then to Qandhar. We had some three hundred pamphlets written by scholars regarding proof of Mahdiat. We happened to read some among the scholars and distributed them and where necessary we had discussion about Mahdavia Faith and spread the Message finally and wrote "Shawahedul Mahdi."

في الجمله چون قسمت اين فقير حقير ذره مقصر كمينه كمترين سگ آستانه امام البرو البحر مسافرت بود لهذا از ملك دكن به گجرات از گجرات به هند و از هند به لاهور يعنى پنجاب و از لاهور به كابل و از كابل به بلغ و از بلخ به اند خو و از اند خوبه چچكتو همين قدر از آنجا به ميمنه و مارو جاق و به هرات و فراه رسيديم و بزيارت روضهٔ مبارك روز دو شنبه بتاريخ هفتم ماه مبارك رمضان سنهٔ يك هزار و پنجاه و دوء از هجرت مشرف شديم و از زيارت شهنشاه به عراق و فارس چو شيراز و بصره رفتيم و از آنجا به طواف كعبه الله و بزيارت مدينه مسكينه حرسهما الله عن الآفات والبليات سر افراز كشتيم و باز از عربستان به عراق و به بغداد شده به بلده فراه رسيديم و از فراه بتقدير الله به قلعه بس رسيديم از آنجا به قندهار فتيم و برابر خود از علمائ مصدقان سه صد رساله معتبر داشتيم و بااكثرے علماے زمان ملاقات واقع شد و مباحثه ها روى نموده و ظاهر است كه در يك مجلس اين جمله رساله ها خواندن ممكن نبود ازين موجب در جواب علمائے زمان به حكم دلائل عيان از كتب علماے مصدقان بعون الله الملك المنان انتخاب كرده اوراق چند بهره مند نوشته يعنى رساله شواهد المهدى

From the above, it is clear that Shah Burhanuddin had started his journey from Bijapur of Deccan to Balakh of Turkistan, Herat and Farah of Khurasan, then went to Persia, Iraq, Baitul Muqaddas to Hijaz and returned to Qandhar and wherever he went, he spread the Message of Imamana (As) Thus after listening his convincing arguments regarding proof of Mahdiat, some of the residents of the above mentioned cities had accepted Mahdiat. Thus the credit goes to Miyan Shah Burhanuddin for the furtherance of the Faith to its entirety. He was the only World Trotting Preacher who boldly and painstakingly spread the Sublime Message of Imamana (As) single-handedly without fear in those days when the sources of conveyance were very few still his zeal and enthusiasm was such that he never cared for the troubles occurred in the course of his deliberations in befitting manners.

Now still there are some more cities he had visited whose details are available from other sources, as under:

103. Qabchaq:

According to "Tazkeratul Saleheen" in the Dairah of Bandagi Miyan Syed Shahabuddin (Rz) there were 18 prominent spiritual guides, among them one was Malik Mohammesd Ishaaq

Qabchaqi (Rz) who claimed to have vision of Allah by his naked eyes.

104. Khattah:

According to "Tareekh-e-Mahdavian " Manju Ji (Rh) was one of the nobles of Gujrat who came from Kahatta/Khattan who was among the disciples of Bandagi Miyan Shah Nizam (Rz). Kahtta is a place in China and Khattan is near Kashgar of Turkistan .

105.Sherwan:

According to "Asaami Musaddaqeen", when Imamana (As) reached Farah, scholars of Herat Mullah Ali Fayyaz, Mullah Mohammed Shirwani, Mullah Maqdoom, Mulla Ali Gul, all scholars accepted his Mahdiat and some kept quiet; among them Mullah Mohammed was from Sherwan.

106. Shiraz:

Author of "Asaami Musaddaqeen" had narrated about Miyan Sheik Mustafa Gujrati (Rh) that:

"Miyan Sheik Mustafa Gujrati (Rh) had been a devout scholar of Islamic Jurisprudence, proficient in mysticism and a godliman, having miraculous convincing powers who influenced many scholars for example Alauddun Shirazi who was a noted scholar of his period, Qazi Bakhan, Pir Mohammed, Baba Hasanji, Qaiser Khan, Miyan Nasir and many more like them and officers of Gujrat, administrators, Osman Khan Surju, nephew of Sher Shah Suri and Sherkhan Pouladi and many among the commoners had accepted Mahdavi Faith.

میاں شیخ مصطفی از علمائ شریعت و مقتدائ طریقت و صاحب معاملات بودند ، بسبب ایشان بسیار علماء مثل ملا علاء الدین شیرازی که علامه زمان بود و چند سال در حرم محترم درس داده بودند قاضی بخن و پیر محمد و بابا حسن جی و قیصر خان و میاں ناصر و مثل ایشان بسیار علما و خوانین و ملوك گجرات مانند عثمان خان سور که خواهر ناده شیر شاه بود و شیر خان پولادی امیر گجرات و مثل ایشان بسیار خلائق روی به تصدیق آوردند ۔

From the above it comes to light that Alauddin Shirazi was a Mahdavi.

107. Gazron:

Gazron is a city towards West of Shiraz. Miyan Syed Naseer belonged to Gazron as reported in "Akhbarul Asrar".

108. Hamdan:

Miyan Abdul Rahman had mentioned the name of Miyan Abdul Samad Hamdani who happened to be one among the scholras of Herat who came to Imamana (As) and accepted Imamana (As) as Mahdi (As).

109. Mazandran:

Miyan Hissamuddin Mazandarani was one among the 41 Martyrs who were killed while they were safeguarding the Diarah of khambail lon 12th.Shwwal 930 H.

Khambail. *(On 12th. Shawwal 930 H. when Bandagi Miyan prepared himself to go for the battle against Ainal, he drew a line and asked forty compnions not to cross that line. They were so obedient that in order to safeguard the women folk of Dairah, they did not cross that line and were massacred by the enemy's fleeing troops.)* Thus Miyan Hissamuddin was from Mazandran who was martyred among them. .

110. Bukhara:

Syed Ilyas Sharza Khan's great grand father was from Bukhara, who migrated to India and settled down in Ajmer and accepted Mahdavi Faith. And many scholars from Bukhara migrated to India and settled down in many parts of India and particularly in Gujrat and have accepted Mahdiat and their descendants are living in many parts of India and they are Mahdavis.

111. Baghdad:

Miyan Abdullah Baghdadi was one of the companions of Imamana (As). (As per Abbdul Rahman 's "Moulood").

112. ROME:

Miyan Abdu Shah Romi was one of the companions of Bandagi Miyan Shah Dilawer (Rz).

Spread of Mahdavia Faith And Khaja Hasan Nizami:

Khaja Hasan Nizami had written about the spread of Mahdavia Faith that:

"During the period of Sher Shah Suri, In india, a venerable person of Juanpur, Syed Mohammed Saheb (As) had proclaimed his Mahdiat. Hundreds and thousands of Muslims had accepted him as Imam Mahdi (As).

Even today there are thousands of Mahdavis still living in Hyderabad, Palanpur, Jaipur, Mysore,Baluchistan and North Western Frontier Province of India (Now in Pakistan)". Khaja Hasan Nizami had mentioned Sher Shah Suri, instead of Sikander Lodhi. However even during the period of Sher Shah Suri also Mahdiat was at its heights.

Spread of Mahdavia Faith and Mahmood Shirani:

In the same manner, Professor Mahmood Shirani had written that:

"Nowadays, this sect has lakhs of followers. Gujrat is just like its birth place. Therefore in Bombay and Gujrat they are found in large numbers. There are many populated places of these people in Rajputana, Central and Southern India. The religion of Palanpur is Mahdavi since many generations and thousands of Mahdavis reside in it. Madras presidency, Deccan, Karnataka, Maharashtra, Telangana, Malaybar are the places where Mahdavi live in large numbers. It may be said that they may be living even in out of India and at different places of the World.

Thus Mahdavi Faith spread in many provinces of India. Its propagation had reached apart from India to Badakhshan, Balkh of Turkistan, Herat and Farah, Kabul of Khurasan,

Qandhar, Keech, Makran and also in Arabian territory and in other Muslim countries. Kings, nobles, ministers,Godlimen, learned ones, unlettered ones accepted Imamana (As) as the Promised Mahdi-e-Mauood (As). Thus persons of every walk of life accepted this Faith. Those who have accepted it are Gujrati,Dhondari,Sherwani,Mazandrani,Bukhari, Hamdani,Romi,Bengali,Punjabi, Deccani, Sindhi, Malabari,Makrani,Qandhari,Baghdadi,and Bulkhi all including.Whatever we have written about this Faith's propagation it is not in a complete shape, but written by few persons, that too very short and cursory. It is a fact that whatever propagation has been done it is just through "Narration of the Holy Qur'an" and never "through sword wielding or coercion". It is a fact that when Mahdavis were martyred, they had to kill the assassins only in revenge. The references of those places given above are correct, if now no Mahdavi resides there, it does not mean that they never inhabited there. Iran till 900 H. was the center of Sunnath wal Jamaath and a hub of mysticism. Now the entire population is Shia.

******

CHAPTER VII
Traditions About Mahdi
And Ibn Khaldun And Others

The author of the tract Ar Rudd believed in the Traditions about Imam Mahdi (As). But some of the opponents of Mahdiat with reference to Ibn Khaldun, and others say that the Traditions about Mahdi (As) are incorrect. Hence an investigation is in order.

Ibn Khaldun has first examined the traditions that have been narrated about Mahdi (As), then tried to prove that they are not reliable. Ibn Khaldun died in 808 H. It seems that those traditions had been accepted without any objection from the period of the holy Prophet (Slm) up to the Eighth Century Hijri without any reservations. However, after Ibn Khaldun, Sir Syed Ahmed Khan through his "Tahzibul Akhlaq" and Margoliout, the renowned English Orientalist in his thesis "Mahdis and Mahdism" tried to prove that the concept of Mahdiat did not at all exist in the beginning of Islam.

At first we shall investigate the doubts of Sir Syed Ahmed Khan and Margoliout. Sir Syed Khan in his thesis "Mahdi Akhiruz Zaman (As)" had maintained that Bani Fatima (Rz) and Bani Abbas (Rz) used to run a propaganda campaign against Bani Umayya. However in their predictions they could not say that another prophet would come whose obedience was obligatory on every body. Hence they coined the term Mahdi (As). It means a person who is (rightly) guided by Allah and who would establish equity and justice and therefore he should be obeyed by all.

Margoliout said that:

"For a quarter of a century after the demise of Mohammed (Slm), the Islamic World prospered exceedingly, while constant succession of victories was crowning the Muslims. Hence a Deliverer and Restorer was not required. But when this period reached to its end, and the sky began to cloud over and in the year 35 we hear the Doctrine that Mohammed (Slm) himself was to return…….. a name was at that time, coined for the expansion of this idea, they coined the word Mahdi (As). (On Mahdis and Mahdism by D.S.Margoliout).

That means to say that after more than a quarter century from the demise of the holy Prophet (Slm), the Muslims were enjoying prosperity on account of continuous victories and therefore there was no necessity of a Deliverer, but when this period ended, and the sky began to cloud and in the year 35 H., we hear the doctrine that Mohammed (Slm) himself would come back. Thus in order to propagate this idea a word was coined and it was "Mahdi (As)".

Margoliout had related the tradition regarding Mahdi (As) to the year 35 H., but from what source he had adopted the year 35 no body knows. And Sir Syed Ahmed Khan had asserted that when the Khilafat was permanently shifted to Bani Omayyah and Imam Husain (As) was martyred, Bani Abbas (Rz) and Bani Fatima (Rz) used to run a propaganda against Bani Ummayah. However in their prediction they could not say that another prophet would come, whose obedience is obligatory on every body. Hence they coined the word Mahdi (As). It means that a person who is (rightly) guided by Allah and who would establish equity and justice, therefore he should be obeyed by all. Thus, according to him the traditions about Huzoor Mahdi (AS) had been coined after 61 Hijri. However, both Margoliout and Sir Syed Ahmed Khan agree at one point that the word "Mahdi (As)" was coined, but they differ in the era.

Period of the Prophet (Slm):

The reality is that during the period of the holy Prophet (Slm) the word Mahdi (As) was already widely known to all (Except to Sir Syed Ahmed Khan and Margoliout).

According to "Seerath-e-Ibn Hisham" (Abdul Malik Ibn Hisham), Umr Bin al-Jumuh was one of the leaders of Bani Salma. His son Mu'az Bin Umr had accepted Islam at the hand of the holy Prophet (Slm) in Aqbah. After coming to Madinah, other youngsters also accepted Islam. But Umro, their father, had installed a wooden idol of Manath to worship in his house. Those who were converted to Islam, used to take away that idol and throw it in the latrine. Umro used to bring it back from the latrine and used to wash and apply scent over it. This had been a continuous practice that the youngsters used to put it in the latrine and Umro used to bring back and wash. One day Umro attached a sword and told the idol "if there is good in you, defend yourself with this sword against those who treat you like this". The youngsters took away the sword and tied the idol with a dead dog and threw it in the latrine. Umro as usual searched the idol out in the latrine, being attached to a dead dog. The people of his clan spoke to him then he too accepted Islam. He wrote a poem in which he decried the idol and praised Allah and the holy Prophet (Slm): The poem is as below:

انـت و كـلـب وسـط بـئـر فى قـرن	(ا) والـلـه لـو كـنـت لهـا لـم تـكـن
الآن فتشنــــاك مـن سـؤ الـغـيـن	(ب) أف لـمـلـقـاك الهـامستـدن
الـواهـب الـرزق ديّـان الـديـن	(ج) الـحـمـد لـلـه الـعـلـى ذى الـمـنـن
أكـون فـى ظـلـمة قبـر مـرتهن	(د) هـو الـذى أنـفـذنـى مـن قبـل أن

باحمد المهدى النبى المؤمن

Translation of the above couplets:

A."By God, had you been a deity worth worshipping, both you and the dead dog would not have been tied to a rope and thrown in the well";

B. "Pity that you being a god was thrown in a pit. We had investigated about you and we had saved us from the evil from you";

C. "All praise be to Allah who is the Sustainer, Pardoner and Custodian of the religions;

D. "The same Allah who saved me from the darkness of the grave before I become of the group with others".

E. "Because of Ahmed (Slm) who is Mahdi (As), Nabi (Slm) and Trustworthy".

The last line of the poetry states that "with the help of Ahmed (Slm) who is Mahdi (As), the Apostle and trustworthy." The word Mahdi (As) was used for the holy Prophet (Slm). This episode pertains to a period before the Migration. From this It may be inferred that after the Migration, the Muslims of Makkah and Madinah had recognized the word Mahdi (As) and it was being used for the holy Prophet (Slm) even by the Mulims of Madinah. Thus the word Mahdi (As) was in use even among the masses from the very early period of Migration.

Seerat-e-Ibn Hisham is an abridgement of Seerat-e-Ibn Ishaq. Hence it should be accepted that this Elegy (Encomium) and these couplets were there in the Seerat-e-Ibn Ishaq. Ibn Ishaq died in the year 151 Hijri. History of Islam bears witness that there is no book that is older than this regarding the Seerat of the holy Prophet (Slm). Apart from this, in the Gabb Memorial Series, an approved old Devan of Hazrat Hissan Bin Sabit (Rz) is available which was published in the year 1910 AD in Europe and on its page No.58 this Elegy is available and that couplet also is available in which the word Mahdi (As) was used for the holy Prophet (Slm).

Thus from this oldest and authentic source, it is proved that the word Mahdi (As) was well known both in the periods of the holy Prophet (Slm) and that of the companions who were fully acquainted with the word MAHDI and its meanings..

2. On the demise of the holy Prophet (Slm) Hazrat Hisham bin Sabit (Rz) had written an elegy (Marsia) which was copied by Ibn Sa'ad in "Tabqaat".

كحـلـت مـأ قيهـا بـكـحل الا رمـد   (ا) مـــا بـــال عـينـك لا تنــام كــانـمـا

يـا خيـر مـن وطـى الـحصـى لا تبـعـد   (ب) جـزعـاً عـلـى الـمـهـدى اصبـح ثـاويـا

بـعـد الـمـغيّـب فـى سـوأ الـملـحـد   (ج) يــاويـح انـصـار الـنـبـى ورهـطـه

كنـت الـمـغيّـب فـى الـضـريـح الـملـحد   (د) جـنـبـى يـقيـك الـتـرب لهـفـى يتنـى

Translation of the above couplets:

A. "What has happened to your eyes which do not sleep as if they are filled with kohl" (Surma that is used by those who are suffering from inflammation of the eyes).

B. "You are lamenting for that "Mahdi (As)" who had passed away, the one who tramples over the small pieces of sand do not go far."

C. "Alas for the Ansaar! Group took the news of his demise with profound regret those who had been buried in the grave".

D. "I yearn to save you from the grave dust. How good would it have been that I had gone in the grave before you." (to save you from the dust of the grave).

The second line of the elegy states "Mourning for that "Mahdi" (As) who had passed away". The word Mahdi (As) was used in the elegy for the holy Prophet (Slm). Had that word"Mahdi" if was not in usage, then how could Hazrat Hishsam Bin Sabit (Rz) write the word "Mahdi" in the elegy for the Prophet (Slm)? The word "Mahdi"(As) denotes, "the one who is Guided by Allah, deputed by Allah." Ibn Sa'ad had copied some eighteen lines from that elegy. It is also available in "Seerat-e- Ibn Hisham" and also it had been copied particularly that line in which the word "Mahdi" (AS) had been used for the holy Prophet (Slm).

3. Period of Khulfa-e-Rashedeen (Rz): From the Arabic literature also it comes to light that during the period of the Khulafa-e-Rasheda" the word "Mahdi" (As) was in use. Hazrat Bandagi Miyan Syed Khundmir (Rz) had mentioned the poetry of Hazrat Ali (Rz) in his "Maktoob-e-Multani":

The very first line of the poetry refers the word "Mahdi"(As).

(ا) بُنَيّ اذا مـا جـاشـت الـتـرك فـانـتـظـر   ولاية مهـدى يـقـدم فـيـعـدل

(ب) وذلّ مـلـوك الـظـلـم من آل هـاشـم   وبـويـع مـنـهـم مـن يـلـذ ويـهـذل

(ج) صبـى مـن الـصبيـان لا راى عـنـده   ولا عـنـده جـدّ ولا هـوا يـعـقـل

(د) فثـم يـقـوم قـائـم الـحـق مـنـكـم   وبـالـحـق يـاتيـكـم وبـالـحـق يعـمل

(ه) سـمـى رسـول الـلـه نـفـسى فـداه   فـلا تـخـذلـوه يـا بـنـى وعـجلـوا

The translation of above couplets:

A. "Oh my sons: when the Turks start fighting, wait for "Mahdi's Sainthood, who would arise and establish justice."

B. "And the tyrant kings of Ahle Hashim shall be disgraced and fealty (Bai'ath) would be taken out of them of a person who would be an hedonist and buffoon".

C. "There would be one boy who would not have an opinion of his own. He was not intelligent, but a simpleton".

D. "Then would emerge among you who would establish justice".

E. "And he would be the namesake of the Messenger of Allah. Let my life be sacrificed for him. Hence my children! Do not be deficient in giving help to him. Be quick in helping him".

This is a recognized fact in Islam that whenever the word Turk had been used it connotes to the infidel Turks. Thus it was the prophecy that the Tataries (Infidel Turks) would attack Baghdad. It did happen in the year 656 H., when Mu'tasim Billah was the Caliph who was not an intelligent one, but a simpleton, (As per the prophecy) to whom his minister gave a wrong suggestion that in order to increase the revenue, the army should be demolished and he did it without giving a second thought. Thus the prophecy suggests to wait for the advent of "Mahdi"(As). The period is not mentioned when that would happen. Thus after 190 years of the fall of Baghdad, Imamana Mahdi (AS) was born in Juanpur in 847 H. Here we have only to denote that the advent of Mahdi (As) was being awaited while the signs of Mahdi (As) were being informed.

Period of Bani Umayyah: Sir Syed Ahmed Khan has said that after the tragic event of Karbala, the traditions relating to Mahdi (As) were coined. But it is an historical proof that even before that tragic event, Bani Hashim had faith on the advent of Mahdi (As). Author of "Al uqdul Fareed" had narrated what Hazrat Ibn Abbas (Rz) had stated to Hazrat Umayyah and his followers that:

"And I witness that Allah did send Mohammed (Slm) from Qureysh and Qureysh are noble who were born to Bani Abdul Muttalib, who came from Bani Hashim and they are good among all. Allah desires that the thing on which you take pride, we too take pride on you. It is a proven fact that we had begun, the end too would come from us."

واشهدان الله لم يجعل محمد امن قريش الا و قريش خيـر البـريـه و لـم يـجعله فى بنى عبدالمطلب الاوهم خيـر بنى هاشم يريد ان يفخر عليكم الا بما تفخرون بـه ان بـنـا فتح الامروبنا يختم الـعـقد الفريد . (طبع مطبع عامر مصر ١٣٩٣ه الجزء الثانى صفحه ١٣٦)

The word "Fatha ul Amr" according to the tradition connotes "Guidance". Thus from the above it comes to light that "Mahdi (As) would guide the Ummah in the manner we (Bani Hashim) had begun it and it is certain that Mahdi (As) would be born to us and Allah would complete it through us."

From the oldest historical record it is proved that fifty years from the demise of the holy Prophet (Slm), the traditions relating to Mahdi (As) had already spread in the Muslim World. And upon the basis of those traditions a group of people had tried to accept Mohammed bin Hanfia (Rz) as the Mahdi (As). "Tabqaat-e-Ibn Sa'ad" narrates that:

"Moosa Ibn Ismail narrated what he heard from Abu Awana who told Abu Hamza that people used to salute by telling "Ya Mahdi" to Mohammed Bin Ali and he too asserted that he was Mahdi who calls towards virtue and rectitude. My name is that of the holy Prophet (Sm) and my patronymic name is that of the prophet's. If any person wants to salute, tell Oh Mohammed Salamun alaik; oh Abul Qasim (Salamun alaik.)"

حـدثنـا موسىٰ ابن اسمعٰيل قال ثنا ابو عوانه عن ابـى حمـزه قال كانوا يسلمون علىٰ محمد بن علىٰ سلام علـيك يـا مهدى فقال اجل انا مهدى اهدى الى الرشد والخير اسمى اسم نبى الله و كنيتى كنية نبـى اللـه فـاذاسلـم احد كم فليقل سلام عليك يا محمد السلام عليك يا ابا القاسم

Whatever is recorded in the "Tabqaat", the same is narrated in "Tareekhe-e-Tabri" in chapter "Mukhtar" while discussing about the year 64 H. it is stated that:

"Mukhtar had praised Allah and passed on Darood to the holy Prophet (Slm); then he told that "Mahdi (As) son of Wasi whose name is Mohammed Bin Ali had selected me and sent me to you as trustworthy, minister and leader and ordered me to wage a war against infidels and to avenge the blood of Ahl-e-Bait (Rz)."

فحمد اله و اثنى عليه و صلى على النبى صلعم ثم قال اما بعد فان المهدى ابن الوصى محمد بن على بعثنى اليـكـم امينـاً وزيـراً و منتخبا و امير اوامرنى بقتال الملحدين والطلب بدماء اهل بيته

Author of "Tabri" also has written that:

"Mukhtar began to send people who were gathered near Sulaiman bin Omr with the words stating that "I was sent by Imam Mahdi (As) who is all powerful and virtuous."

و اقبـل المـختار يبعث الى الشيعه وقد اجتمعت عند سليمـان بـن صرو فيقول لهم انى قد جئتكم من قبل ولى الامـر معـدن الـفضـل و وصى الوصى والامام المهدى

Margoliouth had mentioned the oldest source in which the word "Mahdi"(As) was used:
"We seem to have traced the name "Mahdi"(As) in this context to its actual source, our main

authority being a poet who preached the sovereignty of Ibnul Hanafiah in the century after his death, a doctrine associated with a sect called the Kaisanis. (On Mahdis and Mahdism by D.S. Margoliouth- page 3-4)."

From this we get the original source in which the word "Mahdi"(As) had been used. Our authority on this issue is a poem of a poet who after the death of Ibnul Hanafiah used to preach the leadership of Ibnul Hanafiah. That is a belief of a sect which is known as Kaisania. The poet, Kaseer, who died in 105 H., as mentioned in "Kashful Zannoon" at page 303 , printed in Europe, volume 3.

Somehow it comes to light from the passage of Margoliouth that at the very first time the word "Mahdi"(As) was used for Ibnul Hanafiah but as a matter of fact, as had been mentioned previously that, this word was actually used for the holy Prophet (Slm) during his life time only which was used by Umro Bin al-Jumooh in his poem. It is not a point of issue whether Mukhtar was right in calling Ibnul Hanafiah as Mahdi (As) or not, but from these old sources it came to light that even before the year 64 H this word Mahdi (As) was already recognized in the world of Islam.

Ibn Sa'ad had reported in "Tabqaat" that:

"Thus Ibn Hanafiah intended to go to Kufa and this news reached to Mukhtar who did not like that Ibn Hanafiah should go to Kufa, thus he said that "Mahdi who was arriving in your city; whose symbol was that a person would inflict a blow on him, but it would not affect him". When this news reached, Abu Hanafiah stopped going to Kufa."

فهم ابن الحنفيه ان يقدم الى الكوفة و بلغ ذلك المختـار فثقل عليه قدومه فقال ان فى المهدى عـلامة يقدم بلدكم هذا فيضربه رجل فى السوق لا تـضره ولا تحيك فيه فبلغ ذلك ابن الحنفية فا قام الى آخره

From this it comes to light the signs pertaining to Mahdi (As) were known to all. And Banu Umayyah also knew about Mahdi (As). Masoodi had written that on orders from Hisham, Yousuf Bin Umeral Shaqi had hanged Zaid bin Ali bin Al Husain bin Ali ibn Abi Talib and his naked body was hanged on to a date palm tree. On this a poet says in his poetry that: "We had hanged Zaid on a palm tree and did not belief that Mahdi (As) would be hanged on a palm tree". This episode dates back to 122 H. From this it is clear that Banu Umayyah were well versed with the belief that the true Mahdi (As) would be that person who would never be subdued, killed as was hanged like Zaid. They were also waiting for Mahdi (As) and they denied Zaid Bin Ali Bin Husain to be Mahdi when they saw that Zaid was hanged on a palm tree which was unbelievable for a real Mahdi (As) being hanged like that. That means to say that according to their belief Mahdi (As) could not be subdued or hanged. On that a poet of Bani Umayyah read a couplet: which reads that:

"We had hanged Zaid for you on a palm tree knowing that real Mahdi (As) could not be hanged like that." (This event took place in 122 Hijri)

صلبنالكم زيد اعلىٰ جذع نخلة
ولم ارمهديا علىٰ الجذع يصلب

From the couplet by an Ummaid poet it comes to light that Bani Umayyah had faith about the advent of Mahdi (As) and they were also waiting for Imam Mahdi (As). However, the poet had not accepted Zaid Bin Ali Bin Husain as Mahdi for the only reason that he was hanged and according to his belief Mahdi (As) could not be hanged like Zaid.

Period of Bani Abbas.

Margoliouth had asserted in his thesis that the traditions of Mahdi (As) were coined when Mansur Abbasi had designated his son as his heir apparent. His narration is that:

"Mansur presented his son to the public as the heir of the throne, when a courtier arose and declared that the Prophet (Slm) had foretold that Mahdi (As) is from us, he shall fill the earth with justice even as it has been filled with injustice. The courtier called on someone who was present to attest this tradition and just being afraid of Mansur made him do so". (On Mahdis and Mahdism page 7)

Before this, it was proved that even before the Khilafat-e-Abbasia, belief regarding Mahdi (As) was perpetuated and the Ummah was waiting for the arrival of Mahdi (As).

Masoodi had narrated about Khilafat-e-Saffah that after the murder of Imam Ibrahim, Abu Salma Hafs bin Sulaiman had written a letter to Abu Abdullah Jafer Bin Mohammed Bin Ali Bin al Husain Ibn Ali (Rz) Bin Abi Talib, that in their name oath of allegiance would be taken in Khurasan. Abu Abdulla Jafer Bin Mohammed (Imam Jafer-e-Sadeq) burned the letter before the messenger, but Abu Mohammed Abdullah was inclined to accept it. What was written in the letter to Abu Salam can be ascertained from the wordings of the letter written to Abu Mohammed Abdullah Bin al Hasan (Rz), which was revealed during the discussion with Abu Abdullah Jafer bin Mohammed (Rz):

"Abdullah Bin al Hasan (Rz) argued with Abu Abdullah Jafer and even told that the Ummah had belief in his son that he was Mahdi of the Ummah. But Abu Abdullah Jafer (Rz) did not accept by swearing on Allah and told that he could not be the promised Mahdi. If he drew the sword, he would surely be killed. To this Abdullah did not accept and even he told that on account of prejudice, you do not accept. Still Abu Abdullah Jafer (Rz) told that it was only his advice."

فنازعه عبدالله بن الحسن الكلام الى ان قال انما يريد القوم ابنى محمداً لانه مهدى هذه الامة فقال له ابو عبدالله جعفر و الله ماهو بمهدى هذه الامة و لئن شهر سيفه ليقتلن فنازعه عبدالله القول حتى قال له و الله مايمنعك من ذلك الا الحسد فقال ابو عبدالله والله ما هذا الا نصح منى

The words "Mahdi Hazal Ummati" (Mahdi of this Ummah) points out to the promised

Mahdi (As) alone. Abu Salama had written in his letter that Abdullah Bin al Hasan's son, Mohammed would be declared Mahdi and the oath of allegiance would be taken on his hands. Here Ummat means Muslims only. Abu Salama's writing was based on reality or it was just to divert the attention from the movement of Bani Abbas (Rz); whatever it may be, but it proves the belief of Muslims about Mahdi (As) was confirmed and this pertains to even before Mahdi Abbasi.

"Tareekh-e-Yaqoobi" reports that an Aerabi came to Safah Abbasi through Abul Jaham and read a poem:

A. "Foundation of the country has become strong on account of the brave men of Bani Abbas (Rz)."	(١)اصبح الملک ثابت الاساس بالبهاالیل من بنی العباس
B. "Oh thou that is pure from any vulgarity and the leader of pure persons."	(٢) یا امیر المطهرین من الرجس ویار اس منتهیٰ کل راس
C. "You are Mahdi of Bani Hashim and those who had become hopeless, now they have faith in you."	(٣) انت مهدی هاشم و سواکم اناس رجوک بعد ایاس

That Aerabi read about 18 couplets, out of which we have just copied three. In the third couplet that Aerabi had mentioned Safah as Mahdi of Bani Hashim and these words are used as a respect. It denotes that the fact of Mahdi had become a common talk about which even Aerabi too knew very well. Second point is that even after becoming the Caliph they were waiting for Mahdi. Had the fact of Advent of Mahdi (As) not been recognized by Bani Abbas (Rz), the Aerabi would not have used the word Mahdi for Safah. "Tareekh-e-Yaqoobi" covers the period upto 259 H. Pertaining to Mu'atamad-Allah.

It had been proved from the oldest sources that the fact of Advent of Mahdi (As) was a recognized fact even before declaration of Mahdi Abbasi as the heir apparent.

The fact was ascertained from the historic sources that even before proclamation of Mahdi Abbasi to be the crown prince, the fact of Mahdi's reality was an accepted fact by the Bani Abbas (Rz). Hence Margoliouth's contention that just to appease Mansur Abbasi, a courtier had read the tradition and another one had affirmed it, was baseless. To think or regard it as the beginning of the belief regarding Mahdi had no validity. The fact is that which had been written by Hafiz ibn Timia in his "Minhajus Sunnath": it says:

"Both predecessor and descendants had recognized the tradition in which the holy Prophet (Slm) informed that his (Mahdi's) name would be on prophet's name and his father's name also would be on prophet's father's name. After hearing many persons were desirous that the Prophet (Slm) himself would born as Mahdi (As). Hence Mansur Abbasi named his son Mohammed, so as his name should tally with the prophet's name, and his father's name to be like his father's name. But he surely was not Mahdi."

كـان الحديث المعروف عند السلف والخلف ان النبى صـلـى الله تعالىٰ عليه و سلم قال فى المهدى يواطى اسمه اسمى واسم ابيه اسم ابى صاريطمع كثير من الناس ان يكون هو المهدى حتى سـمـى الـمـنـصـور ابنـه محمد اولقبه بـالمهدى مواطأة اسمه باسمه و اسم ابيه باسم ابيه و لكن لم يكن هوا الموعود به

Thus, Mansur Abbasi had given his son the title of Mahdi so that he could prove the traditions which were present in the Ummah and were already spread in the Islamic world.

Authors of Sihah

When the authors of "Sihah" started collecting traditions, the traditions relating to Mahdi were already spread in the Islamic world; and the Ummah was waiting for the arrival of Mahdi. But Imam Bukhari (Rh) did not collect any record of the traditions of Mahdi which became proof to the opponents of Mahdi (As). Therefore Sir Syed Ahmed Khan had written that "His contention about Mahdi got more strength since Imam Malik was born in 95 and died in 179 and these incidents happened during his life time, but in his "Muatta" no tradition about Mahdi was recorded, nor in Bukhari or in Muslim. "Margoliouth does not refer Muatta or Muslim, but states about Imam Bukhari that: "Only the most critical of the Traditionalists, Imam Bukhari (Rh) had omitted them altogether. (On Muatta") (Mahdis and Mahdavism) That means to say among the traditionalists Imam Bukhari (Rh) omitted to record the traditions regarding Mahdi. Before discussing about the "Sihah", we shall discuss about "Muatta" first.

When Imam Bukhari (Rh) started collection of Traditions, "Muatta" was very famous and was very important in the Muslim world. Zarqani wrote about "Muatta" that:

"Muatta": (Book on Traditions)

When Imam Bukhari (Rh) started collection of Traditions, "Muatta" was very famous and very important in the Muslim world. Zarqani wrote about "Muatta" that:

"Ibn Fahar had deduced from Imam Shafai (Rh) that after the Holy Qur'an, there is no book which is authentic except "Muatta", the book of Malik, in the Muslim world."

اخـرج ابن فهر عن الشافعى ماعلى ظهر الارض كتاب بعد كتاب الله اصح من كتاب مالك

As regards the subject matter of "Muatta", Ibn Khaldun had written in his Muqaddama that:

"Imam Malik (Rh) had written "Muatta"
in which he included those accepted
Traditions which pertain to principles,
doctrines and jurisprudence only."

و كتب مـالـك رحـمـة الـلـه كتـاب المـوطا اودعـه
اصـول الاحكـام من الصحيح المتفق عليه ورتبه على
ابواب الفقه .

Thus the book of Imam Malik (Rh) contains problems of jurisprudence and orders regarding worship. Shah Valiullah also had written on "Muatta" that: "Imam Malik (Rh) had compiled those traditions which pertain to jurisprudence and he named it "Muatta."

In a book which deals with jurisprudence and if it lacks those traditions relating to "Mahdi", it does not mean that the author did not give importance to other traditions, particularly about Imam Mahdi (As). Those who criticize the traditions regarding "Mahdi", they try to argue from the historical literature of Traditions. The most classical book is Ibn Sa'ad's "Tabqaat" (died 230 H.) which proves that many years before the birth of Imam Malik (Rh), a group had recognized Mohammed Bin Hanafiah as "Mahdi" which proves the existence of the traditions of "Imam Mahdi". Imam Malik (Rz) did not include traditions of "Mahdi", because his subject matter was Islamic Jurisprudence and not the prophecies regarding "Mahdi."

"Imam Bukhari" & "Muatta":

Imam Bukhari (rh) had referred "Muatta". Ibnul Arabi Maliki had written commentary on "Tirmizi" that: "Muatta" is the base for "Bukhari" and "Muslim." Zarqani too had accepted Ibnul Arabi's contention by telling that Qazi Abu Baker ibnul Arabi had written that "Muatta" is the base for "Bukhari" and both became the source for "Muslim" and "Tirmizi." Saheb Musaffa had written that the books of "Siha Sitta" are the commentary of "Muatta". In this way "Sahih Bukhari" is the commentary of "Muatta" since Qazi Abu Baker had ranked "Muatta" as the first one and the Bukhari" is the second one. That is why Imam Bukhari (Rh), following "Muatta", had recorded the traditions regarding jurisprudence and principles only, and avoided to record prophecies and events.

Imam Bukhari (Rh) and Prophet's traditions:

When Imam Bukhari (Rh) started compilation of "Bukhari", he had one lakh correct traditions and two lakhs incorrect traditions. Thus Imam Bukhari (Rh) had recorded only correct traditions, but what about those correct traditions which he had not recorded as reported by Hazimi, that:

"Narrated Abul Fazal Abdullah Bin Ahmed bin Mohammed to Ibn Talha who in his book wrote about Abu Sayeed Almalini that he told to Abdullah Ibn Addi who told as narrated by Mohammed bin Ahmed that he heard Mohammed Bin Ismail that he had memorised one lakh correct traditions and two lakhs incorrect ones."

اخبـرنـا ابو الفضل عبدالله بن احمد بن محمد
انبـاء ابن طلحه فى كتابه عن ابى سعيد المالينى
انبـاء عبـدالله بن عدى حدثنى محمد بن احمد
قال سمعت محمد بن اسمعيل يقول احفظ مائة
الف حديث صحيح و احفظ مائتى الف حديث
غير صحيح

It is a fact that "Bukahri" pertains the correct traditions, but does not record other correct traditions. They are more in numbers. As reported by Hazimi:

"Abu Masood Abdul Jaleel ibn Mohammed had written in his book about what had been said by Abu Ali Ahmed bin Mohammed bin Shaharyar who heard Abul Farj Mohammed bin Abdullah bin Ahmed that he heard from Abu Baker Ismail who heard from the man who was speaking to Imam Bukhari (Rh) who said to him that "I had recorded the most correct traditions and left another correct traditions which are more than what I had recorded."

ابنـأ ابـو مسـعـود عبـدالـجليل بن محمد فى كتابه انبأ ابو على احمد بن محمد بن شهريار انبـأ ابوالفرج محمد بن عبدالله بن احمد انبأ ابـو بـكـر الا سماعيل قال سمعت من يحكى عن البخارى انه قال لم اخرج فى هذا الكتاب الاصحيحا و ما ترك من الصحيح اكثر

Now we have to see why Imam Bukhari (Rh) had left such correct traditions also in his "Bukhari"? This has been explained by Hazimi:

"Imam Bukhari (Rh) wanted to compile a small book on such traditions and for that reason, he never tried to record all traditions."

فقد ظهر بهذا ان قصد البخارى كان وضع مختصر فى الـحديث و انه لم يقصد الاستيعاب لا فى الرجال و لا فى الحديث

Thus, it is now clear that, Imam Bukhari (Rh) wanted to record those traditions pertaining to biography, jurisprudence and commentary only. Regarding this "Zahedul Kausari" reports that:

"Thus Imam Bukhari's intention was to record those traditions which are authentic and relating to jurisprudence, biography and commentary."

فغرض البخارى تخريج الاحاديث الصحيحة المتصلة و استنباط الفقه والسيرة والتفسير الى آخره

Now it is clear that Imam Bukhari (Rh) never had an idea to record all authentic traditions in his book; for example he did not record traditions which tell about the Holy Prophet (Slm) that he was the most distinguished prophet. Other books have recorded it, but this important tradition is not available in "Bukhari". From other sources also it came to light that Imam Bukhari (Rh) was of the opinion to compile a brief book and did not like to have a detailed book. About this Ibn Hajar Asqalani had written in "Muqaddama-e-Fathul Bari" that:

"Reported Abu Ahmed Bin Addi that he heard from Al Hasan Bin al Husain al Bazaar that he heard Ibrahim Bin Mu'aqilin Nafsi that he heard Imam Bukhari (Rh) was telling that he did not record any tradition which was not correct and also left such correct traditions for the sake of brevity."

"Muqaddama Ibn Salah" describes that:

"We have heard from Imam Bukhari (Rh) that he had recorded those traditions which are authentic and even left such correct traditions for the purpose of brevity."

و قال ابو احمد بن عدى سمعت الحسن بن الحسين البزار يقول سمعت ابراهيم بن معقل النسفى يقول سمعت البخارى يقول ما ادخلت فى كتابى الجامع الاماصح و تركت من الصحيح حتى لا يطول

فقد روينا عن البخارى انه قال ما ادخلت فى كتاب الجامع الاماصح و تركت من الصحاح لملال الطول

The same has been reported by Sheik Abdul Haq, Muhaddis-e-Dehlvi in his "Safarus Sa'adath" that:

"Imam Bukhari (Rh) had reported that he did not include in the book which was not correct and left even some correct traditions so that the book should not become bulky."

مگر انچه صحيح است و ترك كرده ام بسى از صحاح را از ترس طول كتاب

From these extracts it is proved that Imam Bukhari (Rh) had left even some authentic traditions due to the fear that his book may become bulky.

It is a fact that authors of "Sihah" had collected some traditions pertaining to Mahdi (As), therefore it must be accepted that Imam Bukhari (Rh) avoided to record Mahdi's lengthy traditions in order to make "Bukhari" a brief one, although they would fit to his principle for the sake of brevity. It may be said that he had included the tradition regarding Hazrat Esa (As), the answer to this point is that it came under the chapter "Kitabul Anbia" and not under "Kitabul Fitan" which includes news and prophecies. It is also wrong to suggest that Imam Bukhari (Rh) did not repeat any tradition, since "Bukhari" contains many repetitions as mentioned by the author of "Ash'atul Lam'aat" That:

"All traditions which are recorded in "Bukhari" are 7275 which have repetition and 4000 without repetition."

مبلغ انچه از احاديث در اين كتاب آورده باتكرار هفت هزار و دو يست و هفتاد و پنج حديث و بعد از حذف تكرار چهار هزار

Imam Bukhari (Rh) & Narrators of Mahdi's Traditions:

If Imam Bukhari (Rh) did not record any tradition from any narrator of the traditions of Mahdi (As), it does not mean that those narrators have become belittled, because other Imams had believed them. Imam Muslim (Rh) was with Imam Bukhari (Rh), but he had not taken any tradition from him pertaining to Mahdi (As). Kausari had written that" Imam Muslim (Rh) had not copied any tradition from "Bukhari", although they were living together and was dependant on Bukhari."

Imam Muslim (Rh) and "Sahih Bukhari":

"Had there been no "Bukhari", there would have been no "Muslim." It is a proven fact that "Muslim" had deduced from "Bukhari" and added some more traditions in his book."

و قال ابو الـحسـن الـدار قـطـنـى الحافظ لو لا البخارى لمـا راح مسلم و لا جاء و قال ايضا انما اخذ مسـلـم كتاب البخارى فعمل فيه مستخرجاً وزادفيه احاديث

Imam Muslim (Rh) confirms that those traditions which he had omitted were not weak. Sheik Abdul Haq says in his"Safarus Sa'adat" that "Whatever he had included in his book, they are authentic traditions, but those traditions which he had omitted to record should not be considered as weak. This fact Imam Bukhari (Rh) too confirmed by telling that he had avoided to record even authentic traditions in order to keep "Bukahri" brief. It seems Imam Bukhari (Rz) had limited his scope, for his book, pertaining to items like jurisprudence, commentaries and biographies and avoided those Traditions pertaining to prophecies, historical events and news. Thus if "Muslim" lacks in the traditions of "Mahdi" it is just because Imam Muslim (Rh) was following Imam Bukhari (Rh). Thus the contention of Sir Syed and Margoliouth that traditions regarding Mahdi (As) are not true because they do not find place in either "Bukhari" or "Muslim". It is meaningless in view of the above findings.

Bukhari's Tareekhul Kabeer:

Imam Bukhari (Rh) had avoided to mention about eminent elites of Hanafiah in his "Tareekh ul Kabeer". Author of "Muqaddama-e-Anwarul Bari" had criticized by telling Imam Bukhari, out of prejudice and displeasure, he had not mentioned about hundreds of eminent elites of Hanafiah. But can anybody deny their existence? Then on the same premise if Imam Bukhari (Rh) had not recorded any Tradition of "Mahdi" can anybody deny the sanctity of those traditions regarding Imam Mahdi (As)?

B. "Muqddamah-e-Anwaar-e-Bari" wrote that the contemporaries of Imam Bukhari (Rh) like eminent muhaddiseen, Imam Zahbi (Rh), Imam Abu Zar'a (Rh) and Imam Abu Hatim (Rh) decided on certain disputed problems, not to refer Imam Bukhri (Rh). Thus on that decision how could the importance of traditions of Imam Mahdi (As) belittled?

Mahdi's traditions and conditions of Sheikhain:

In "Mustadrik" Hakim had extracted such traditions which fit to the conditions of the Sheikhain, (Imam Bukhari (Rh) and Imam Muslim (Rh). Further "Kitabul Fitan" and "Malhem" contain many of the Mahdi's traditions which fit on the conditions of the Sheikhain. Following is a tradition worth mentioning:

"Reported a tradition by Abu Abdullah Suffar who heard from Mohammed Bin Ibrahim Bin Arooma who heard from Husain bin Hafs who heard from Sufian and Sufian heard from Khalid Hamza who heard from ibn Qalaba who heard from Abi Asma who heard from Soban (Rh) who narrated that the holy Prophet (Slm) told that three people would fight for the treasury (throne), who would be the sons of a Khalifa and none would succeed. Then would emerge black flags from the East and they would fight such a fiercely battle that none had fought like that before. After telling some thing, He (Prophet Slm) told that when you see him, offer allegiance to him and go to him even if you had to crawl through the snows, because he is the Khalifa Mahdi (As)." (This tradition fits to the conditions of the Sheikhain).

This tradition which directs Mahdi (As) to be the Khalifa had been accepted as true and correct by both Hakim and Zahbi who say that it fits to the conditions of the Sheikhain also."

اخبرنا ابو عبدالله الصف رثنا محمد بن ابراهيم بن ارومه ثنا الحسين بن حفص ثنا سفيان عن خالد الحذاء عن ابى قلابة عن ابى اسماء عن ثوبان رضى الله عنه قال قال رسول الله صلى الله عليه و آله و سلم يقتتل عندكنزكم ثلاثة كلهم ابن خليفة ثم لا يصيرالى واحد منهم ثم تطلع الرايات السود من قبل المشرق فيقاتلونكم قتالا لم يقاتله قوم ثم ذكر شئيا فقال اذارأيتموه فبايعوه ولو حبوا على الثلج فانه خليفة الله المهدى .(هذا صحيح على شرط الشيخين)

Ibn Khaldun:

As had been stated before, the Traditionalists have corrected Mahdi's traditions in the books of "Sihah". Thus the commentator of these books also did not find out any flaw in Mahdi's traditions. Ibn Khaldun was the first to criticize about Mahdi's traditions. He seems to have been perturbed on the criticism of the narrators. He wrote about "Amr-e-Fatimi" that:

"The Traditionalists agreed for the purpose of proper functioning and balancing, critical examination (of the traditions) is more important. Therefore, if any narrator neglects or shows leniency about any tradition, then the tradition becomes doubtful and becomes unacceptable. Then nobody can say that this sort of blame also existed in those books of "Sihah" and "Muslim" which are famous and accepted by sall. Thus there is a general consensus of the Ummah about their authenticity."

المعروف عند اهل الحديث ان الجرح مقدم على التعديل فاذا وجدنا طعناً فى بعض رجال الا سانيد بغفلة او بسوء حفظ او ضعف او سوء راى تطرق ذلك الى صحة الحديث واوهن منها ولا تقولن مثل ذلك ربما يتطرق الى رجال الصحيحين فان الاجماع قد اتصل فى الامة على تلقهما بالقبول والعمل بما فيهما و فى الاجماع اعظم حماية و احسن دفع الى آخره

Ibn Khaldun accepts availability of the blame expressed by the narrators about the traditions of Mahdi (As), and the same blame had been expressed about some traditions recorded in "Sihah". Still general consensus favoured for "Sahihayen". In such cases, it is proved that the blame regarding some traditions can be ignored if there is favourable consensus. Hence, even the eminent narrators of the traditions about Imam Mahdi (As) should not become blameworthy. Thus such baseless blames should be disregarded; since, these traditions have a series of numerous chains of narrators and had become continuously unbroken and are designated as "Mutawathir". Sheik Abdul Haq Muhaddiss-e-Dehalvi had written that:

"These Traditions (of Mahdi As) support each other to the extent of continuity and a series of traditions particularly regarding the context that Mahdi (As) comes from the Ahl-e-Bait, and from the genealogy of (Bibi) Fatima (Rz) is exemplary. The same is written in "Ash'atul Lam'aat."

"قد تظاهرت الا احاديث البالغة حد التواتر معنا فى كون المهدى من اهل البيت من ولد فاطمة

Author of "Abrazul Wahamul Maqnoon" states that: "There are eminent persons who had said that these Traditions (of Mahdi) have a definite and unequivocal order of continuity (Mutawatir) in series. They are Hafiz Saqavi (Rh) who had elaborated in his "Fathul Mughees", Hafiz Jalaluddin Seyouthi (Rh) in his "fawaedul Mutakasira, Allama Ibn Hajar (Rh) in his "Sawamiq-e-Muharriqa" and many more who have memorized those traditions."

فممن نص على تواتر احاديث المهدى ايضاً الحافظ شمس الدين السخاوى فى فتح الغيث والحافظ جلال الدين السيوطى فى الفوائد المتكاثره وغيرهما من كتبه والعلامة ابن حجرا لهيتمى فى الصواعق المحرقة وغيره من مصنفاته والحدث الزرقانى فى شرحه للمواهب اللدنيه و جم غفير من الحفاظ النقاد

If continuity is not objectionable, then how could consensus be objected? When the traditions of Mahdi (As) had been accepted as continuously unbroken series, then discussing narrators' weakness is not worthwhile. In view of these basic facts, Ibn Khaldun's criticism do not belittle the importance of the traditions regarding Imam Mahdi (As). We have to verify what eminent commentators like Ibn Hajar Asqalani wrote in his "Najbatul Fikr" and Mulla Ali Qari in his commentary regarding these Continuous, Unbroken traditions of Mahdi? They say "Mutwatera" regarding Mahdi, since they are bound for implementation without any discussion."

Ibn Khaldun had criticized on the manner of the traditionalists, but had not deduced on that:" No blame should be discussed about the attributes of the narrators of traditions of Mahdi. If we agree on his criticism we have to accept the weakness of a tradition, but how can you prove that it had been fabricated. To some traditionalists it is not possible to prove any fabrication even in the unauthentic traditions. Sheik Abdul Haq had stated in his "Safarus Sa'adath" that:

"In the phraseology of the traditionalists any tradition which seems to be unauthentic, may come under this category, still fabrication is impossible to be proved. It may be kept in mind that if any tradition is suggested to be unauthentic or deceptive it is simply because they are based on suspicion or doubt; lacking in certainty. Sometimes it happens that the liar too says the truth."	مراد بحديث موضوع در اصطلاح محدثين اين است نه آنكه البته ثابت شود وضع و كذب د خصوص اين حديث و بايد دانست كه حكم بوضع و افترابحكم ظن غالب است نه بقطع و يقين فان الكذوب قد يصدق

When the fabrication in the unauthentic tradition is not proved, then how can the fabrication is proved in those traditions which had been corrected by the traditionalist? Thus according to the principles of the traditionalists, if some of the narrators of the traditions of Mahdi (As) may be blamed; still the fabrication cannot be proved. Then how can we believe that Ibn Khaldun was perfectly correct when he ignored to accept the basic facts. The reality is that in order to disregard those sects who believed in different peoples' Mahdiat or Imamat, particularly about the Ismailites: He thus states:

"And among them Ismailia who claim Imam's divinity on the basis of possessing some divine spirit in him. Among them there are some others who believe in the incarnation of those Imams who had already died. And also those who are waiting for the resurrection of the Caliphate of Ahl-e-Bait (Rz). They argue on those traditions which we have presented in connection with Imam Mahdi (As)."	وجاء الا سما عليلية منهم يدعون الوهية الامام بنوع من الحلول و آخرون يدعون رجعة من مات من الائمة بنوع التناسخ وآخرون منتظرون مجئى من يقطع بموته منهم و آخرون منتظرون عود الا مرفى اهل البيت مستدلين على ذلك بماقد مناه من الاحاديث فى المهدى

Thus Ibn Khaldun thought that if he condemned and disregarded the traditions of Mahdi (As) as baseless, then all such sects and their whims would be automatically shattered. But his whim was hundred percent wrong. Since the traditions relating to Imam Mahdi (As) are hundred percent correct and have been accepted by the Muhaddeseen (Rh) as mentioned below:

Traditions of Mahdi (As) and Hafiz Ibn Timia (Rz):

Even before Ibn Khaldun, Hafiz Ibn Timia (Rh) had accepted the Traditions of Mahdi (As) stating that they are recognized by Imam Ahmed (Rh), Abu Dawood (Rh) and Tirmizi (Rh). His acceptance that they are the recognized traditions, describes that he had believed in the sanctity of Mahdiat and to him traditions of Mahdi (As) were the basic proof of Mahdiat. He had accepted the correctness of these traditions in these words:

"Thus those traditions which are presented as the proof for the advent of Mahdi (As) are perfectly correct which have been reported by "Abu Dawood", "Tirmizi" and "Ahmed" etc."	”فـالـجـواب ان الاحـاديث التى يحتج بهاعلى خروج المهدى احاديث صحيحة رواها ابو داؤد والترمذى و احمد وغيرهم	

This is the opinion of that authority in respect of the traditions of Mahdi (As) who was born one hundred years ahead of Ibn Khaldun, and who was far better in the faculty of Traditions than Ibn Khaldun.

Traditions of Mahdi (As) and Allama Ferozabadi (Rh):

The contemporary of Ibn Khaldun (died 808), Allama Mujaddeddin Ferozabadi (Rh) (died 817) had objected regarding some traditions which were recorded in "Safar-e-Sa'adaat" which pertains to worship and events. Some examples are as follows:

1. In the chapter referring preference to meat: the meat which is preferred in this world and hereafter for eating has not been proved (Page 551 of Safarus Sa'adat)

2. Whether the myrtle leaves are preferred, for that no proof was available. (Page 556)

3. Whether Consensus is an Hujjat, there is no such tradition is existing. (Page 572).

4. Guess should it be taken as an Hujjat? Also not proved. (Page 572,573)

5. Appearance of the signs of Doomsday just after two hundred years has no sanctity. (Page 571)

But Allama Ferozabadi (Rh) did never object about the traditions of Mahdi (As). Had there been any doubt or if they were not authentic, Allama Ferozabadi (Rh) would have not hesitated to object and explained his objections about them which are recorded in "Safarus Sadfaath"also.

Traditions of Mahdi (As) and Historical Evidence:

Sir Syed Ahmed Khan had accepted under chapter "Books on Traditions" that the proof of a fabricated tradition is that which is against a historical event. He says that:" in order to recognize an unauthentic or a fabricated tradition, Shah Abdul Aziz had stated that such tradition would have no relevance to historical events of facts. One such example is that Sheik Ali had claimed in Rudd to have narrated that Mahdi would be the king of the whole world which is certainly against a historical fact, therefore Sheik Ali had presented a fabricated and a false tradition which should not be rejected as baseless in view of the following tradition:

"The emperors of the whole world would be four persons; two from the Momins and two from the infidels. From Momins would be Zul Qarnain (As)) and Sulaiman (As) and from the Infidels would be Nimrod and Bakht-e-Nasr and from my Ahl-e-Biat (Rz) one person would be the king of whole world who would be the fifth (Sirajul Absar p.36.)

مـلـوک الارض اربـعة ، مـومنـان و کـافران
فـالـمومنان ذوالقرنین و سلیمان و کافران نمرود
و بـخـت نـصـر و سـیـمـلـکها خامس من اهل بیتی
(سراج الابصار صفحه ٢٦)

The names of four persons mentioned in this tradition did never govern the entire world and particularly such places like Hijaz and Tuhama were not under their governance. This tradition should not be related to an informer of a veritable intelligence that is the holy Prophet (Slm). Thus any tradition which has a relevance to an historical evidence it may be taken as a correct tradition. Thus the condition of the traditions of Mahdi (As) is like that.

From the oldest sources of literature and history we have tried our best to prove that the very word Mahdi (As) was already in use even during the period of the holy Prophet (Slm) and even before the birth of Imam Malik (Rh), a group of persons had recognized Mohammad bin Hanafiah as Mahdi (As). It proves that the traditions relating to Imam (As) were already existed in the Muslim world. Thus any blame of any narrator is therefore nullified with the help of historic evidence. If those sources are not the proof, then the names of the narrators on which Ibn Khaldun had based his criticism does not have any value; because these sources have no historic importance. Apart from this, it is difficult to point out the temperaments of the narrators. Finally it is asserted that the fact of the advent of Mahdi (As) is proved from all sources of the history, literature and even from the books of traditions.

Cross Examination of the Traditions:

For criticizing traditions relating to Imam Mahdi (As) how far Ibn Khaldun had kept in view the principles relating to scrutiny of the traditions, shall become clear from the following examples:

1. Narrated Abu Baker bin Abi Sheeba, who heard Ahmed bin Abdul Malik, who heard Abul Maleeh al Rafeeh Bin Ali Bin Nafeel who heard Sayeed Bin Al-Musayib (Rz) "We were with Umme Salma (Rz) discussing about Mahdi (As) then she said, I heard the Holy Prophet (Slm) telling Al-Mahdi is from the progeny of Fatima (Rz)".

(١) حـدثنـا ابـوبـکر بـن ابی شیبه حدثنا احمد بن
عبدالـمـلـک حـدثنا ابو الملیح الرفی عن زیاد بن
بیان عن علی بن نفیل عن سعید بن المسیب قال کنا
عـنـدام سلـمـه فتـذاکـر نـا المهدی فقالت سمعت
رسـول الـله صلی الله علیه و سلم یقول المهدی من
ولد فاطمة (ابن ماجه)

He had criticized this tradition by saying that since Abu Jafer Aqeeli was unbelievable, his tradition should not be accepted as correct, because it came from a single source.

Ibn Khaldun's statement that Abu Jafer Aqeeli's tradition is a weak tradition; is not true because Abu Jafer Aqeeli had not elaborated the weakness of this tradition. Aqeeli's statement is mentioned in "Tahzeebul Tahzeeb" as below:

"Aqeeli had written in his book that this tradition is unable to be accepted in the chapter of Mahdi, because he (Ali Bin Nafeel) is recognized through this tradition only. Aqeeli further said that there are confirmed and strong traditions available with reference to the chapter of "Mahdi" and they are confirmed, even otherwise.

ذكره العقيلى فى كتابه و قال لايتابع على حديثه فى المهدى ولا يعرف الابه قال و فى المهدى احاديث جياد من غير هذا الوجه

Author of "Abrazul Wahamul Maqnoon" had reported the full text of Aqeeli's statement:

"Aqeeli had said in his book that Ali Bin Nafeel Harani has reported to Sayeed Binul Museeb about this tradition in the chapter of Mahdi (As), that he is known through this tradition only and he had spread this tradition as well. Then he said that for Mahdi (As), many strong and confirmed traditions are available and the words" Rajulum Ahl-e-Bait" had come briefly. This is the statement of Aqeeli."

قال فى كتابه على بن نفيل حرانى و هو جدالنفيلى عن سعيد بن المسيب فى المهدى لا يتابع عليه ولا يعرف الابه و ساق هذا الحديث ثم قال و فى المهدى احاديث جياد من غير هذا الوجه بخلاف هذا اللفظ فلفظ رجل من اهل بيته على الجملة مجملا هذا كلام العقيلى

From this statement it becomes clear that Aqeeli's statement tells that whatever traditions are available in reference to Mahdi (As) they point out about a person who would come from Ahl-e-Bait (Rz). But Ali Bin Nufail had asserted particularly that person would be from the "Progeny of Fatima (Rz)". Since it is the only statement of Ali Bin Nufail, it becomes unreliable. However, to say "coming from the genealogy of Fatima (Rz), by implications it means Ahl-e-Bait only." It all boils down to say that Ali bin Nufail may be the lone and single narrator, still "Tahzeebul Tahzeeb" reports about Ali Bin Nufail that:

"Abdullah Bin Jafarul Raqee told that he had heard Abul Maleehul Raqee was praising Ali Bin Nufail by saying him to be a righteous man, about whom Abu Hatim had asserted that there is no harm in taking any tradition from him. Ibn Habban had reported about Ali bin Nufail and Abu Arooba had reported about the date of his demise being 125 H."

قال عبدالله بن جعفر الرقى سمعت ابالمليح الرقى ثينى على على بن نفيل و يذكرمنه صلاحاً قال ابو حاتم لا باس به و ذكره ابن حبان فى الثقات و قال ابو عروبة الحرانى مات سنة خمس و عشرين و ماية

If those persons who had memorized (Traditions) had recognized someone to be righteous and trustworthy, then even if he narrates a single tradition, how could anybody prove that this particular tradition was a weak one? Further Abu Jafer Aqeeli's contention that Ali Bin Nafeel's narration was unique is incorrect, because in other traditions too Progeny of Bibi Fatima (Rz) has been reported. Hafiz Ibn Timia (Rh) too had confirmed Mahdi (As) to be from the progeny of Bibi Fatima (Rz). Ibn Timia's version is that:

"In a certain tradition it has been mentioned that Mahdi (As) is from my progeny, the descendant of Fatima (Rz)."

و ایضاًفیه المهدی من عترتی من ولد فاطمه

Before this it has been asserted that Imam Mahdi (As) comes from the descendants of Bibi Fatima (Rz); these are continuous unbroken Mutawatir series of traditions. This continuity had been confirmed by Mulla Ali Qari in his "Risala-e-Mahdi" thus, this continuity is noted both in the chapter of Mahdi (As) that Imam Mahdi (As) belongs to the descendants of Bibi Fatima (As). Ibn Khaldun, by referring to Abu Jafer Aqeel, is trying to prove the narration of Ali Bin Nafeel being untrustworthy and on that score trying to nullify Mahdiat itself. On the other hand Aqeeli himself had accepted the accuracy of the traditions of Mahdi (As) and he was fully convinced about the advent of Mahdi (As).

His criticism is based on the books of the names of the Narrators. The oldest among them is "Tabqat-e-Ibn Sa'ad" (Author Died in 230 H) and through it we have tried to prove that on the basis of these Traditions of Imam Mahdi (As) which are continuously asserted by the holy Prophet (Slm) that Imam Mahdi (AS) comes from the Ahl-e-Bait and these traditions are unbroken and continuous. A group of people had tried to accept Mohammad bin Hanafiah as Mahdi even before 65 H. And Ali Bin Nafeel to whom Ibn Khaldun had tried to criticize, died in 125 H.

Margoliouth had stated that Kaseer had accepted Ibn Hanafiah as Mahdi and had used the word Mahdi for him. Kaseer was the contemporary of Ali Bin Nafeel, and his year of death was 105. The contemporaries of Ali Bin Naqeel vouchsafe about the commonality of the Mahdi's traditions. Thus Ibn Khaldun's attempt to rank the tradition of Ali Bin Naqeel in the category of being weak, is nothing but to emphasize his assertion to nullify the very issue of Mahdiat; it is utterly against the facts, since Aqeeli himself had accepted the correctness of the traditions of Imam Mahdi (As) as well as advent of Mahdi (As) and had expressed that they are very strong.

2. Osman bin Abi Sheeba narrated that he heard from Abu Dawood Hazri who had heard from Yaseen who had heard from Ibrahim bin Mohammad Bin Al Hanafiah who heard the Prophet (Slm) telling that "Allah would give him mandatory power in a single night. Allah would give him plenipotentiary."

(٢) حـدثنـا عثمـان بـن ابـی شیبه حدثنا ابو داؤد الـحـضـری حدثنا یا سین عن ابراهیم بن محمد بن الـحـنفیه عن امه عن علی قال قال رسول الله صلی الله علیه و سلم المهدی منا اهل البیت یصلحه الله فی لیلة (ابن ماجه)

Ibn Khaldun had criticized this tradition in these words:

"Although Ibn Moin (Rh) tells that there is no harm in accepting the tradition of Yasin Ajli (Rh), but Imam Bukhari (Rh) remarked about it "Fih-e-Nazr" that means "very weak", whereas Ibn Adi in his "Kamil" and Zahbi in his "Mizan" had contradicted this tradition and say that their weakness had been recognized by all."

وياسيـن العجلى و ان قال فيه ابن معين ليس به بـاس فقـد قال البخـارى فيه نظر و هذه اللفظة فى اصطلاحة قوية فى التضعيف جد او اورد له ابن عدى فى الكامل والذهبى فى الميزان هذا الحديث على وجه الا ستنكار و قال هو معروف به

Ibn Khaldun's assertion that Ibn Addi in his"Kamil" and Zahbi in his "Mizan" had contradicted this tradition is utterly wrong; because Zahbi in his "Mizan"had only mentioned Ibn Addi's statement about Yasin that he is recognized through this tradition and no other tradition had been narrated by him. If the narrator is a righteous man, then his narration of this tradition should not be taken as weak. About Yasin, "Tahzeebul Tahzeeb" reports that:

"Douri had reported to Ibn Moin (Rh) that there is no harm in getting a tradition from Yasin (Rh), since Ishaq Bin Mansur (Rh) had reported that Yasin (Rh) is a righteous man in reporting traditions. The same had been reported by Abu Zar'ah (Rh) that there is no harm in taking tradition from Yasin (Rh). Imam Bukhari (Rh) had remarked about him by stating "Fih-e-Nazr"and also said that except this tradition, I do not know any other tradition from him. Yahya bin Moin (Rh) had said that he had heard Sufian Soori was inquiring about this tradition. Ibn Addi told that he was recognized through this tradition only. Ibn Maja (Rh) had reported about Yasin (Rh) without giving any reference. Therefore the modern writers presumed Yasin to be Yasin Bin Mu'aaz ziat (Rh), thus they tried to weaken it, and then rejected."

قال الـدورى عـن ابن معين ليس به بـاس و قـال اسـحـق بـن منصور عن ابن معيـن صـالح و قال ابو زرعه لا باس به و قـال البخارى فيه نظر ولا اعلم حديثاً غير هـذا قـلـت و قال يـحـيـٰى بـن يمان رايت سـفـيـان الثورى يسئـال يـاسيـن عـن هـذاالحديث قال ابن عدى و هو معروف بـه انتهـى و وقـع فـى سنن ابن ماجه عن يـاسيـن غيـر منسوب فظنه بعض الحفاظ المتاخرين ياسين بن معاذ الزيات فضعف الحديث فلم يصنع شيئا

This version makes it clear that Ibn Moin (Rh) and Zar'aa (Rh) had moderated and Imam Bukhari (Rh) had criticized Yaasin (Rh). Abu Zar'aa (Rh) and Ibn Moin (Rh) are eminent Imams of traditions. Even Imam Ahmed Hunbal (Rh), an acclaimed Muhaddis, had accepted mastery of Ibn Moin (Rh). In this connection Mohammed Bin Rafay had narrated that he heard Ahmed Bin Hunbal (Rh) saying "the tradition which is not recognized by Ibn Moin (Rh), should not be taken as tradition. Khateeb had even admitted Ibn Moin (Rh) as Imam-e-Rabbani (Rh), eminent scholar, trustworthy. Abu Zar'aa (Rh) and Ibn Moin (Rh), masters on traditions had recognized Yasin (Rh) as trustworthy in respect of traditions and had asserted that there is no harm in accepting his tradition. Thus in this way they had sided with Yasin (Rh). While Imam Bukhari (Rh) had criticized him by saying "fihe Nazar", but he had not given any reason for his criticism as to why he had said Yasin (Rh) lacked trust which is creating doubt. Further Imam Bukhari's contention that except this tradition there is no other tradition from him; any way his contention does not make this tradition a weak one. Thus Imam Bukhari's criticism is ambiguous and it is a fact that the criticism which is dubious is not acceptable. Abu Zar'aa (Rh) and Ibn Moin (Rh), masters on traditions had recognized Yasin (Rh) as trustworthy in respect of traditions and had asserted that there is no harm in accepting traditions from him. Thus in this way they had sided with Yasin.

Badruddin Aini says that:

"Sahih Bukhari had a group of narrators on whom the predecessors had criticized and their criticism is under certain conditions and unless those conditions are not fulfilled, that criticism is not acceptable by the people, because people accept that criticism when it is clear and the purpose of the criticism should be made clear."

فى الصحيح جماعة جرحهم بعض المتقدمين و هو محمول على انه لم ثيبت جرحهم بشرطه فان الجرح مايثبت الامفسّرا مبين السبب عندالجمهور

From this it becomes clear that the criticism which is explicit and its purpose is clear then only it is acceptable by the people, if it fails that criterion, then it is not acceptable by the people. Thus it came to light that according to Imam Bukhari (Rh) too dubious criticism is not acceptable. Abu Zar'aa (Rh) and Ibn Moin (Rh) had corrected Yasin (Rh) and Imam Bukhari's assertion by just telling "Fih-e-Nazar" is ambiguous, hence it cannot make the tradition weak.

3. It is clear in Fiqha and principles as stated by Khateeb Hafez that, it is the correct religion which has been consented by commentators of Hadees and the critics as Bukhari, Muslim and others.

هذا ظاهر مقرر فى الفقه وااصول وذكر الخطيب الحافظ انه مذهب الائمة من حفاظ الحديث و نقاده مثل البخارى و مسلم و غيرهما (٣٢)

Abu Dawoodul Hazri (Rh) was accepted by Ibn Moin (Rh) as trustworthy and Abu Dawood (Rh) who had been acclaimed as eminent narrator of traditions, had referred Yasin (Rh). Thus only because he had narrated just one tradition, therefore that tradition should not be deemed to be as weak.

3. Three persons will fight for the treasury who are the sons of the Khalifa. But none would get it. Then shall rise black flags from the East and then they will be killed in such a manner that none would have been killed like them. Then he told something which I did not remember. Then he said if you see him offer your allegiance to him even if you have to crawl the snows, because he is Khalifa Mahdi of Allah.

Criticism on this tradition is made in these words:

"The narrators of this tradition are the narrators for the traditionalists but Abu Qalaba Jarmi and Zahbi refer him as a Mudallis. Sufian Suri also is the narrator of this tradition and who is known as a Mudallis, the concealer. Both of them had made this tradition ambiguous and audition is not clear. Therefore it cannot be accepted. Abdul Razzaq Bin Hummam also is the narrator who is famous as Shia who became blind in his last days and he used to create confusion by mixing traditions. According to Addi he had narrated traditions regarding excellence which were not accepted on account of the narrator being a Shia."

(٣) حدثنا يحيى احمد بن يوسف قال حدثنا عبدالرزاق ان سفيان ثورى عن خالد الحذاعن ابى قلابه عن ابى اسما الرجى عن ثوبانؓ قال قال رسول اللّٰه صلى اللّٰه عليه وسلم يقتل عندكنزكم ثلاثة كلهم ابن خليفه ثم لا يصير الى واحد منهم ثم تطلع الرايات السود من قبل المشرق فيقتلونكم قتلالم يقتله قوم ثم ذكر شيئًا لا احفظه فقال اذا رايتموه فبايعوه ولوحبو اعلى الثلج فانه خليفة اللّٰه المهدى (ابن ماجه)

ورجاله رجال الصحيحين الا ان فيه ابا قلابة الجرمى و ذكر الذهبى وغير انه مدلس و فيه سفيان الثورى و هو مشهور بالتدليس و كل واحد منهما عنعن ولم يصرح بالسماع فلا يقبل و فيه عبدالرزاق بن همام و كان مشهوراً بالتشيع و عمى فى آخروقته فخلط قال ابن عدى حدث بالاحاديث فى الفضائل لم يوافقه عليها احد و نسبوه الى التشيع انتهىٰ

A. Ibn Khaldun had criticized on Abu Qalaba (Abdullah Bin Zaidul Basri) and Sufian Suri on the basis of this criticism. He had declared that to say that Traditions of Mahdi (AS) are null and void is against reality. The oldest Book on Narrators is "Tabqaat-e-Ibn Sa'ad" in which Abu Qalaba (Rh) was mentioned as trustworthy. His name was Abdullah Bin Zaid (Rh), trustworthy, who was the narrator of many traditions.

Author of "Tahzeebul Tahzeeb" writes that Ibn Sa'ad had included Abu Qalaba among the second tier of Basra and said that he was trustworthy and had narrated many traditions. Here it is not mentioned that he was a Mudallis. Ibn Sa'ad died in the year 230 H. Zahbi had written "Mizan" in 745 H in which it is written that Abu Qalaba (Rh) was a scholar among the successors. He is acclaimed as trustworthy, but he is a Mudallis. Ibn Hatim (Rh) had repudiated this by telling Abu Qalaba (Rh) was not a Mudallis (deceiter). And Ajli (Rh) has accepted him to be trustworthy. He died in 104 H.

B. In this manner Sufian Suri (Rh) too was accepted as the Imam of Traditions. According to "Tahzeebul Tahzeeb" Shu'ba Ibn Ainia (Rh), Abu Aasim (Rh) and Ibn Moin (Rh) and many other scholars have said that Sufian (Rh) is Ameerul Momineen for Traditions.

Ibn Mubarak (Rh) had stated that he had written traditions from one thousand one hundred shuyukh, but Sufian (Rh) was the most prominent sheikh from whom I wrote the traditions.

Yahya Ibn Moin (Rh) had written that in matters of jurisprudence, traditions, asceticism and all other things none was supreme to Sufian (Rh).

Abu Qatan had told about Shuba who informed me about Sufian (Rh) that he was the leader of all in piety and knowledge.

Khateeb had told about Sufian that Sufian (Rh) is one of the Imam of the Muslims.

Zahbi too had accepted Sufian (Rh) as a man of literary talents and a great critic of his time whose reliability and credibility nobody can doubt. Now the matter of discussion is that whether the statement of Mudallis is acceptable or not, particularly as stated about Abu Qalaba (Rh) and Sufian (Rh) who are acclaimed as trustworthy and superior among the traditionalist. Kausari had written in "Shrutul Aimma-e-Khamsa:"

"Hafiz Abu Sayeed Salahuddin Al-Alaaie, after stating about persons who come under the category of Mudalliseen, had written in "Jamaiut Tahsilul Akamul Murasil" that all these Mudalliseen are not of the same status that whatever had been told about them should be accepted. One group among them used to state so on and so, which lacks details of the source. There are many categories of them. One of the category is that very rarely they are qualified for Tadlees; therefore they should not be categorised as Mudalliseen. For example Yahiya Bin Sayeed, Hisham Bin Urwa, Moosa Bin Uqba. Second category is of those whose tadlees is doubtful. Therefore whatever they state, their statements are examined because they were Imam or whatever they said lacks in tadlees or those who do it with trustworthiness, they come in second category. They are Zuhri, Sulaiman Alamash, Ibrahim Nakhayee, Ismail Bin Zabi Khalid, Sulaimanul Yatmi, Hamidut Taweel, Hakam Bin Utba, Yahya bin Ibn Kaseer, Ibn Jareeh, Suri, Ibn Oyainah. Traditions of these persons have been recorded in "Sahihain" which lack in details of their sources and some have accepted that tradition with reservation that since the Sheikhain (Rh) knew it very well about them, hence accepted."

قال الحافظ ابو سعيد صلاح الدين العلائى فى جامع التحصيل لا حكام المراسيل بعد ان اسرد اسماء من ذكر بالتدليس من الرواة هؤلا و كلهم ليسوا على حد واحد بحيث انه يتوقف فى كل ما قال فيه واحد منهم (عن) ولم يصرح بالسماع بل هم على طبقات اولها من لم يوصف بذلك الا نادر اجدا بحيث انه لا ينبغى ان يعدفيهم كيحيى بن سعيد و هشام بن عروه و موسىٰ بن عقبه و ثانيها من احتمل الائمة تدليسه و خرجوا له فى الصحيح و ان لم يصرح بالسماع و ذلك اما لامامته اولقلة تدليسه فى جنب ماروى اوانه لا يدلس الا عن ثقة و ذلك كالزهرى و سليمان الاعمش و ابراهيم النخعى و اسمعيل بن ابى خالد و سليمان التيمى وحميد الطويل والحكم بن عتبة و يحيىٰ بن ابى كثير و ابن جريح والثورى و ابن عيينة و شريك و هشيم ففى الصحيحين وغيرهما لهؤلاء الحديث الكثير ممماليس فيه التصريح بالسماع و بعض الائمة حمل ذلك على ان الشيخين اطلعا على سماع الواحد لذلك الحديث الذى اخرجه بلفظ عن و نحوها من شيخه

With the above version it comes to light that those who are recognised as Imam of traditions and who perform less tadlees and who are trustworthy their statements are accepted, among them come Sufian Suri (Rh) about whom Ibn Khaldun has objections. Author of " Abrazul Wahamul Maktun" had written the names of some such Mudallaseen. They are: Zahri, Sulaimul

Aiash,Ibrahimul Khatmi, Ismail Bin Abu Khalid,Hamidut Taweel, Yahiya Ibn Kaseer, Ibn Jareeh,Sufian Suri, Ibn Ainina,Shariek Hasham. Then he wrote that traditions reported by these Imams have been written in "Seheheen" as well as in other books, although they lack their original sources. When the Sheikhain (Rh) had accepted their traditions, it may be taken that they were based on trustworthiness.

Traditionalists very well knew that Hazrat Abdullah Bin Abbas (Rz) was a minor during the time of the Prophet (Slm). One of the conditions for the narrator is that the narrator should be a major, intelligent and who is able to understand, still, the traditionalists have taken those traditions reported by Ibn Abbas (Rz) in which they say "told by the Prophet (Slm)" without link and they do not say the name of the companion. There is a possibility of tadlees, but who could criticise? Sheik Abdul Haq had stated that "Tadlees" and "Irsal" are the same. Thus the statement of Ibn Khaldun that the narrations of Sufian (Rh) and Abu Qalaba (Rh) are not acceptable, because there is a possibility of being a "Tadlees" and that they lack in the details of their sources. Whereas all scholars accept Tadlees when there is the possibility of trustworthiness; as has been written by Sheik Abdul Haq in his "Safrus Sa'adat."

C. Ibn Khaldun had stated that Abdul Razzaq was a Shia, therefore his narration is not acceptable. But the traditionalists do not accept the narrations of the extremist Shia regarding the excellence of Ahl-e-Bait. Author of "Tahzeebut Tahzeeb" had written that:

"Ahmed Bin Saleh Misri told that he said to Ahmed Hanbal (Rh), Whether you had seen a person who is better than Abdul Razzaq (Rh) in respect of traditions? He replied "No". Like that Abu Zar'aa Damishqi (Rh) told that Abdul Razzaq (Rh) comes under that category whose narrations are accepted."

قال احمد بن صالح المصرى قلت لاحمد بن حنبل رايت احمد احسن حديثا من عبدالرزاق قال لا و قال ابو زعه الدمشقى عبدالرزاق احد من ثبت حديثه

Abdullah Bin Ahmed states in"Tahzeebul Tahzeeb" that:

"Abdullah Ibn Ahmed (Rh) asked his father whether Abdul Razzaq was a Shia? Whether he used to exaggerate? His father told that he had not heard about Abdul Razzaq that he was a Shia. Abdullah Ibn Ahmed further reported to have heard from Muslama Bin Shabib that he had heard Abdul Razzaq (Rh) was telling that he did not get temptation to prefer Hazrat Ali (Rz) over Abu Bakr (Rz) and Omer (Rz). Allah May pardon those who do not respect Abu Bakr (Rz), Omer (Rz) and Osman (Rz). Such persons who do not respect all Khulafa-e-Rashida, are not Momin. Abdul Razzaq (Rh) further told that he respects them all equally."

قال عبدالله بن احمد سالت ابى هل كان عبدالرزاق يتشيع و يفرط فى التشيع فقال اما انا فلم اسمع منه فى هذاشيئاد و قال عبدالله ابن احمد سمعت مسلمة ابن شبيب يقول سمعت عبدالرزاق ما انشرح صدرى قط ان افضل عليا على ابى بكر و عمر رحم الله ابابكر و عمر و عثمان من لم يحبهم فما هو مومن و قال اوثق اعمالى حبى اياهم

These are the facts about Abdul Razzaq's Shism. Mohammed bin Ismail Alfazari reports in "Tahzeebul Tazeeb" that:

"Mohammad Bin Ismail Fazari reported that he heard in San'aa that Ahmed and Yahiya had removed traditions of Abdul Razzaq, for which action he felt much. I met Moin (Rh) during Hajj and informed to him about Razzaq (Rh). Thus Ibn Moin (Rh) told : Oh, Abu Saleh, if Abdul Razzaq (Rh) even becomes an apostate, even then we would never drop his traditions."

قـال مـحـمد بن اسمٰعيل الفزارى بلغنى و نحن بصنعا ان احـمـد و يحيى تركا حديث عبدالرزاق فدخلنا غم شـديـد فـوافيت ابن معين فى الموسم فذكرت له فقال يـا ابا صالح لوارتد عبدالرزاق ماتركنا حديثه (تهذيب التهذيب جلد ٦ ، صفحه ٣١٤، ٣١٥)

This indicates that Abdul Razzaq (Rh) was not an extremist Shia and was treated to be a trustworthy man. Traditionalists have taken traditions from him. Ibn Moin (Rh) believed him to be a most honest man. In these circumstances how the tradition of Mahdi (As) narrated by Abdul Razzaq (Rh) should not be accepted? Did Ibn Khaldun know all about Abdul Razzaaq (Rh)? Whether he had not adopted this behaviour just to create suspicion among the masses about traditions of Mahdi (As)? Ibn Hajar Asqalani (died 852) says that except one person, all have accepted Abdul Razzaq (Rh) a trustworthy man. Ibn Hajar's statement:

"Abdul Razzaq bin Hummam bin Nafey Alhameri (Rh) is one of the writers whom all have accepted him except Abbas Bin Abdul Azeem ul Anbari who had said against him too much to which no body favoured."

عبدالرزاق بـن هـمـام نـافـع الـحميرى الصنعانى احدالـحفـاظ الا ثبات صاحب التصانيف و ثقه الائمه كـلـهـم الا الـعباس بن عبدالعظيم العنبرى وحده فتكلم بكلام افرط فيه ولم يوافقه عليه احد

As regards Ibn Khaldun's statement that Abdul Razzaq (Rh) had become blind in his old age and used to mix up traditions. Then from where it can be proved that the tradition under discussion he had heard or narrated after he had become blind? Date of birth of Abdul Razzaq (Rh) was 1126 H. and date of demise being 1211 H.

(Note: Point to note is that Ibn Khaldun died in the year 808H., then how could he criticize about Abdul Razzak who was born in 1126, after three hundred years? Hence it is doubtful.)

We have already proved that many hundred years before his birth that is in the year 65 H. Traditions of Mahdi (As) were famous in the Islamic World. For the traditionalists if any tradition has more than two or more narrators, then it becomes acceptable. We have proved three such traditions which relate to the holy Prophet (Slm) in which the word Mahdi (As) has been mentioned. In this way even during the period of the holy Prophet (Slm) traditions of Mahdi (As) were well known and for that reason only Hazrat Umr Bin al Jumooh (Rz) and Hazrat Hissan Bin Sabit (Rz) had used the word Mahdi (As) for the holy Prophet (Slm) during

Prophet's lifetime. This is a fact and no body Can dare to deny this historically proved fact?

☆☆☆

CHAPTER VIII

Confirmation of obligation

Allah commands:

"Allah who had made Qur'an an obligation onto you, He will make you reach to your native country."

From it becomes clear that Qur'an was made an obligation for the holy Prophet (Slm). Thus it is also an obligation on the Ummah and those commands which are confirmed by the Qur'an, must become obligatory. Imam Fakhar-e-Razi (Rz) had commented on"Farza Alaikul Qur'an."

"Told Abu Ali: "Allah had made His commands as obligatory on you." Thus His orders and His dictates must be adhered to without any reservations. So also, if Allah had prohibited anything for the Muslims, then it is obligatory on them to forbid and relinquish it. Following are some examples of the obligations as mentioned in the Holy Qur'an:

1. Then set not rivals unto Allah, while you know (the truth) 2:22 (Last Part)

(۱) فلا تجلوالله اندادا وانتم تعلمون (البقرة ع ۳)

2. And cover not truth with falsehood, nor conceal the truth when ye know it. (2:42)

(۲)لا تلبسوا الحق بالباطل و تكتموا الحق و انتم تعلمون (البقرة ع ۵)

3. Then complete your fast till the night appears, and do not associate with your wives. (2:187 Part)

(۳) ثم اتموا الصيام الى الليل ولا تباشروهن (البقرة ع ۲۳)

4.Do not marry unbelieving women (idolaters) until they believe. (2:221 part)

(۴)ولا تنكحوا المشركت حتیٰ يؤمن (البقرة ع ۲۷)

5. Conceal no evidence. (2:283)

(۵)ولا تكتموا الشهادة (البقرة ع ۳۹)

6. Oh.Ye who believe: Devour not usury, doubling and multiplying. (3:130)

(۶) يا ايها الذين آمنوا لاتا كلوا الربوا اضعافا مظاعفة (آل عمران ع ۱۴)

7. And Marry not women whom your father married. Except what is past. (4:22)

(۷) لا تنكحوا ما نكح اباؤكم من النساء الاماقد سلف (النساء ع ۳)

8.Do not kill or destroy your selves (4:29)

(۸) ولا تقتلوا انفسكم (النساء ع ۵)

9. Ye who believe: approach not prayers when you are intoxicated (4:43)

(۹) يا ايها الذين آمنوا لا تقربوا الصلوٰة و انتم سكارىٰ (النساء ع ۷)

10. Kill not your children on a plea of poverty.(6:151)

(۱۰) ولاتقتلوا اولادكم من املاق (الانعام ع ۱۹)

11. And never be one of the unbelieverers. (10:105)

(۱۱) ولا تكونن من المشركين (يونس ع ۱۱)

12.And give not short measure or weight.(11:84)

(۱۲) ولا تنقصوا المكيال والميزان (هود ع ۸)

13. Nor come near adultery, For it is a shameful deed and an evil. (17:32)

(۱۳) ولا تقربوا الزنىٰ انه كان فاحشة (بنى اسرائيل ع ۳)

14.Ye, Who believe: enter not houses other than your own, until you have asked permission and saluted those who are in them. (24:27)

(۱۴) يا ايها الذين آمنوا لا تدخلوا بيوتا غير بيوتكم حتىٰ تستانسوا و تسلموا علىٰ هلها (النور ع ۳)

15..Obey not the idolaters and hypocrites. (33:48)

(۱۵) ولا تطع الكٰفرين والمنٰفقين (احزاب ع ۶)

16.Oh Ye Believers: Obey Allah and obey the Apostle, and make not waste your deed. (47:33)

(۱۶) يا ايها الذين آمنوا اطيعوا الله واطيعو الرسول ولا تبطلوا اعمالكم (محمد ع ۴)

17. Oh. Ye. Who believe: Do not raise your voice above the voice of the Prophet (Slm) and never speak aloud to him as you speak with each other (49:2)

(۱۷) يا ايها الذين آمنوا لا ترفعوا اصواتكم فوق صوت النبى (الحجرات ع ۱)

18. And spy not one another, nor backbite each other . (49:12)

(۱۸) ولا تجسسوا ولا يغتب بعضكم بعضا (الحجرات ع ۳)

19. And do not follow Satan. (2:168)

(۱۹) ولا تتبعوا خطوٰت الشيطٰن (البقره ع ۲)

20. And do not break your oath when you confirmed it. (16:91)

(۲۰) ولا تنقضوا الايمان بعد توكيدها (النحل ع ۳)

21. Do not help sin and tyranny.

(۲۱) ولا تعاونوا على الاثم والعدوان (النساء ع ۱)

From these examples it became clear that whatever deeds which have been prohibited by Allah must be abandoned. Particularly those must be stopped for whom hellfire is the punishment.

Migration:

For those who avoid migration, Allah had reprimanded, therefore migration is an obligation. Thus Allah commands:

"When Angels take the souls of those who die in sin against their souls they say: In what plight were you? They reply: weak and oppressed, were we in the earth. They Say: Was not the earth of Allah spacious enough for you to move yourself away from evil. Such men will find their abode in Hell. (4:97)

ان الـذين تـوفهم الملائكة ظالمى انفسهم قالـوا فيـم كنتـم قالـوا كنا مستضعفين فى الارض قالـوا الـم تكن ارض اللـه واسعة فتهـاجـروا فيهـا فـاولئک مـأوٰهم جهنم (النساء ع ١٣)

1. Author of "Kashaaf" had commented on it:

""If any person feels that in any city it is not possible for him to carry peacefully his religious obligations, then he should not try to live there at any cost, when he knows that there is another city where these obligations can be carried out without any fear and disturbance, then migration is an obligation for him."

وهـذا دليـل عـلى ان الرجل اذا كان فى بلد لا يتمكن فيـه مـن اقامة امـر دينـه كـما يجب لبعض الاسباب والـعوائق عن اقامة الدين لا تخصرا و علم انه فى غير بـلده اقوم بـحق الله و ادوم على العبادة حقت عليه المهاجرة

2. Author of"Tafseer-e-Baizavi" writes regarding "Fathu Haajeru Fiha."

"In this verse it has been argued that when a man can not continue his religious obligations at any place it is imperative for him to leave that place."

و فى الآية دليـل عـلى وجوب الهجرة من موضع لا يتمكن الرجل فيه من اقامة دينه

3. Imam Zahed had written in his "Tafseer-e-Zahedi"regarding"Al Lazeena Hajeru WA Jahedu Fi Sabilillahi"That:

"Some say that migration has not been abolished. They have argued on the basis of a Saying of the holy Prophet (Slm) that migration is lasting till the Day of Judgement."

قال بعضهم الهجرة باقية غير منسوخة واحتجوا بقول النبى صـلى اللـه عـليـه و سلم الهجرة باقية الى يوم القيامه

4. Author of "Tafseer-e-Madarik" had commented on"Fatuhajeru Fiha":

"This verse is for that person who could not maintain his religious obligations in any city and when he knows that there is one place where he can perform the religious obligations, then migration is mandated. According to a Tradition, if a person moves to a place for the purpose of his religion, and that place is even at the distance of a palm, he deserves paradise and he would accompany Prophets Ibrahim (AS) and Mohammad (Slm)"

والآية تـدل على من لم يتمكن من اقامة دينه فى بـلد كـما يجب و علم انه يتمكن من اقامته فى غيـره حقت عليه المهاجرة و فى الحديث من فـربـدينة من ارض الى ارض و ان كان شبرامن الارض استوجبت لـه الـجنة و كان رفيق ابيه ابراهيم و نبيه محمد صلى الله عليه و سلم

B. In "Madarik" it is stated for"Al Lazeena Hajeru" that:

"And he migrates from his country for the cause of Allah and for his religion, where peace is available for religion. Thus migration shall be performed in the last days as had been performed in the beginning."

هى المهاجرة عن اوطانهم الى الله بدينهم الى حيث يا منون عليه فالهجرة كاينة فى آخر الزمان كما كانت فى اول الاسلام

5. Author of "Tafseerur Rahman" states regarding"Alam Takun Arzullahi Wasia":

"Thus it is imperative for a person who could not express his religion at a place peacefully, then he should move to a place where he could do."

فهى واجبة على كل من لا يمكنه اظهار الدين بمكان الى مكان يمكنه فيه

Migration & conquering Makkah:

Sheik Abdul Qader Muhaddiss-e-Dehlavi wrote about"Fa hijratuhu Ila Ma Hajara Ilaih":

"And the tradition which declares no migration after victory over Makkah, it is only regarding migration from Makkah only; because after the victory it became "Darus Salam" and migration is performed from a Darul Kufr." And who ever is able, it lasts for him till the Day of Judgement. This was the intent of the holy Prophet (Slm) that Migration is not terminated until Repentance is not terminated. It means to say that order of Migration is not terminated till the door of Repentance is not closed. That is Day of Judgement""

فهى

فيه

The holy Prophet (Slm) also said this:

"Verily, Migration demolishes the past sins and Hajj demolishes those sins which pertain to previous period."

ان الهجرة تهدم ما كان قبلها و ان الحج يهدم ما كان قبله

That means to say that for demolishing the sins, Hajj and Migration are equal. Thus when there arise a reason for migration it becomes mandatory.

It may be kept in mind that just migrating from a Darul Kufr to Darul Islam is not alone migration, but it includes migration from a terrifying place to a peaceful place also. At the inception some companions had migrated to Ethiopia (Hubsha-Africa), although it was not a Darul Islam,. still not against Muslims, hence the Holy Prophet(Slm) directed them to migrate. In the same manner some companions had migrated to Madinah from Makkah, although Madinah had not become Darul Islam at that time.

Thus Migration, in view of the holy Qur'an, is an obligation. Author of Hadia doubts that the verse " La Yastawi Alqaedoon" does not mandate migration, is not correct. This point is researched here.:

"Not equal are those Believers who sit (at home) and receive no hurt, and those who strive and fight for the cause of Allah with their goods and their lives. Allah had granted a grade higher to those who strive and fight with their goods and lives; than to those who sit (at Home), Allah has promised with those who strive and fight. He had distinguished above those who sit (at home) with a special reward." (4:95)

لا يستوى القاعدون من المومنين غير اولى الضرر والمجاهدون فى سبيل الله باموالهم و انفسهم فضل الله المجاهدين باموالهم و انفسهم على القاعدين درجة وكلا و عدالله الحسنىٰ و فضل الله المجاهدين على القاعدين اجراً عظيما (النساء ع ١٣)

In this verse the word "Al Mujahedoon" is used in contrast with who perform jehad and Qaedeen (those who sit in home) it means who fight in the battle and provide wealth to those who perform jehad, thus they also come under the category of performers of jehad. Further, in this Verse two times the word "Qaedeen" had been used. They are those who sit in their homes but they had intent for jehad.

For Mujahedeen there are two issues. One: those who use wealth for jehad, and second: those who performs jehad in person. With this verse Jehad becomes mandatory and incidentally migration also becomes mandatory.

The holy Prophet (Slm) stated that migrant is he who had migrated from the thing which had been prohibited by Allah. Here migration means relinquishment or abandonment of a thing which is prohibited by Allah. Further when asked which migration is preferable, he said that the migration of that person who has separated himself from a thing which has been prohibited by Allah.

It comes to knowledge that Jehad is based on migration whether it is external or hidden. External Jehad is proved for those companions who accompanied the holy Prophet (Slm) in the Ghazwas (battles) against the infidels. They had to leave their family and homes. Hidden is that without any reason relinquishing or distancing from a thing which is prohibited by Allah. Thus a person who is migrating from a thing which is prohibited by Allah is the real Migrant. Thus this verse mandates both Jehad and migration as an obligation. Because without external migration it was not possible for the companions to take part in the Jehad (Gazwath),.

If any person participates in jehad, instead of sitting in house without any reason, he would be regarded as a migrant, because he has relinquished to stay at home, according to the commands of Allah.

Abu Dawood (Rh) has narrated that mujahid is the one who fights with his self (Nafs)."

Author of Hadia's contention that Imamana (As) had not performed Jehad is not correct. We have already asserted that Imamana (As) had fought against Raja Dalpat of Gaud. As regards Jehad Fin Nafs, it is also proved through traditions.

"Muhajir is one who should not act against which Allah has prohibited."

المهاجر من هجر ما نهى الله عنه

Author of "Ash'atul Lam'at" had written about this tradition that:

"The real and perfect mujahid is he who under the dictates of Allah fights with his own passions (desires), because the self refuses to obey dictates of Allah. Thus he fights with his own self and suppresses it, and kills it."

مجاهد حقیقی کامل کسی است که کارزار میکند نفس خود را در طاعت خدا که نفس او بامی آرد و اطاعت فرمان نمی کند پس بادی جنگ می کند و اسیر میگرداند و می کشداورا

Author of "Madarik" states that:

"Hazrat Ali (Rz) stated that enjoining virtue and abhorring evil is a superior Jehad."

عن علی رضی الله عنه افضل الجهاد الامر بالمعروف و النهی عن المنكر

Perfect Jehad, real Jehad and superior Jehad were all the attributes of Imamana (As), but to say that his entire life was served in Jehad is the befitting tribute to him.

It may also be pointed out that if any person without any reason does a work against Shariat, then he is a hypocrite. The same is applicable to the one who abandons jehad or avoids migration.

Renunciation of World: (Tark-e-Duniya)

The punishment of a person who is immersed in the worldly life is Hell Fire:

"Those who desire the life of the present and its glitter, to them we shall pay the price of their deeds therein without diminution. They are those for whom there is nothing in the Hereafter, but the Hell fire". (11:15,16)

من کان یرید الحیوة الدنیا و زینتها نوف الیهم اعمالهم فیها و هم فیها لا یبخسون اولئک الذین لیس لهم فی الآخرة الاالنار (هود ع ۲)

Fakhruddin Razi (Rz) has written about these verses that:

"We would obviously keep the meaning of this verse common to all and would say that this verse is for even those momins who do deeds for show and for those infidels who too have this quality. Allah Says"Nothing is there for them in Hereafter, except Hell Fire. This verse is for those who are hypocrites."

(والقول الثانى) و هوان نجرى الاية على ظاهرها فى العموم و نقول انه يندرج فيه المومن الذى ياتى بالطاعات على سبيل الرياء والسمعة و يندرج فيه الكافر الذى هذا صفته و هذا القول مشكل لان قوله اولئك الذى ليس لهم فى الآخرة الاالنار لا يليق بالمومن الا اذا قلنا المراد اولئك الذين ليس لهم فى الآخرة الاالنار بسبب هذه الاعمال الفاسدة والافعال الباطلة المقرونة بالريا

Imam Fakhruddin Razi (Rz) took the meanings of "Mun Kana" as "whoever" commonly for all and did not specify it for the infidels only. "Tafseer-e-Baizavi" also has taken "Mun Kana" for generally and not specifically. Thus Imamana (As) too had taken for general purpose as mentioned in "Insaf Nama" in chapter 5 that:

"One scholar by name "Rukn" came to Imamana (As) at Naherwala. Imamana (As) gave sermon on "Mun Kana Yureedul Hayathud Duniya" and kept the word "Mun" in general sense. The Scholar told that the word Mun is for infidels. Imamana told that Allah had said "Mun Kana" for all, whether he is a momin or an infidel, who ever has that quality he is an Infidel. Then the scholar reported that here at this place the Qazi, scholars and the king have this quality. Imamana (As) told that Allah had said for all, hence we too take for all and do not limit for infidels. Then the scholar told that he too had that quality. Imamana (As) told that this quality should not be attributed to a Muslim. Then again the scholar told that he had that quality. Then Imamana (As) told that you are a Muslim who recite the Muslim Creed, then how can you have that quality. Then the scholar said the same words for a third time. Then Imamana (As) said that Allah declared you to be an Infidel."

نقل است که در شهر نهرواله از علمائے که نام او ركن بود برائے ملاقات حضرت میران آمد حضرت میران آیں آیت من کان یرید الحیوة الدنیا الآیة بیان کردند و لفظ من را بروجه عموم داشتند پس آن عالم مذکور گفت که من را مفسران خاص بر کافران داشته اند ، میران فرمودند که خدائے تعالیٰ من کان فرموده است یعنی هر که باشد خواه کلمه گو خواه غیر آں هر که دروے ایں صفت باشد او کافراست و ایں صفت جز درکافر نباشد ، پس آن عالم گفت که اینجا قاضی و علما و بادشاه ایں صفت دارند حضرت میران فرمودند که خدائے تعالیٰ من کان فرموده است ماهم من کان گوئیم و اسم کسے مقید نه کنیم ، پس آن عالم گفت که درمن ایں صفت موجود است میران فرمودند که در مسلمان ایں صفت نبا شد باز ایں عالم کرت دوم همیں گفت که ورما ایں صفت موجود است میران فرمودند شما کلمهٔ رسول الله میگوئید ایں صفت درشما چوں باشد ، باز آن عالم کرت سوم همان کلمهٔ مذکور گفت ، پس حضرت میران فرمودند اگر در تو ایں صفت است و خود را بر آں قرار دادی پس خدائے تعالیٰ تراکا فرمیگوید

This event pertains to Naherwala and to a period prior the Emphasised Proclamation (Daawai-e-Mue'da). From this event it is not correct to argue that "Munkir-e-Mahdi" is not kafir, because, here the argument is about the seeker of the world and not about "Munkir-e-Mahdi". From this event it is proved that Imamana (As) had regarded the seeker of the world as an infidel according to the Holy Qur'an. Thus it is obvious that "Mun Kana"(Whoever) is absolute, i-e; common to all and not limited to the infidels only. Thus "Mun kana" is generalised and not limited to the infidels. Hence to denounce the worldly life and its glitter is mandated by Allah. The holy Prophet (Slm) had said: "Leave the world to the worldly people". This world or Duniya in comprised of both "Wajood-e-Hayt-e-Duniya" and "Mata-e-Hayat-e-Duniya" means possessing worldly life and worldly materials. Therefore both should be abandoned. According to Imamana (As), the existence of this mortal life is your "self" or your entity, if it is mixed with worldly material and fanfare it is called "Wajood-e-Hayath-e-Dunyia" which gets you the title of infidelity. Thus renunciation of worldly life means renunciation of self, your entity, your egotism and your nafs. Who ever is immersed in the worldly material life becomes unmindful of Allah and the life Hereafter which leads him towards infidelity. Thus which ever thing draws your attention from the righteous life, leads you away from Allah and the life Hereafter. Therefore renunciation of worldly life is an obligation. Hence it is obligatory for everyone to abandon each and everything which hinders you from remembrance of Allah.

Some scholars criticised Imamana (As) by telling that Imamana (As) prohibits from getting education. Imamana (As) told that he follows Mohammad Rasoolullah (Slm). When the holy Prophet (Slm) had not prohibited it, how can he prohibit. Imamana (As) told that he emphasises continuity of remembrance of Allah is an obligation. Whichever hinders that obligation He prohibits from it, whether it is education or service to earn livelihood or even to be busy with the public in discussion other than Allah's remembrance.

The opponents of Imamana (As) criticised about the renunciation of the world (Tark-e-Duniya) as Ruhbaniat as adopted by the Christians and others. But it must be clarified that Ruhbaniat even denies a man or woman from his or her natural desires, for example marriage is not permitted for them (Raheb) which may drag them towards immorality and illegal relationship which is prohibited in Islam and where marriage is a lawful engagement of man and woman as husband and wife. In "Turk-e-Duniya" marriage is permissible, but it prohibits intentional desires which leads to Asceticism or Zuhad Fil Nafs. Being immersed in worldly life, engaged with wife and children and the fanfare, neglecting the remembrance of Allah leads one to infidelity. But to have wife and children and earning for livelihood is not infidelity and always permitted even by Sharia..

Then the scholars told Imamana (As) that he had forbidden earnings. Imamana (As) told that earning for livelihood is permitted for a momin. But you have to ponder who is a momin according to the holy Qur'an.

Opponents of Mahdavis criticised for relinquishing the earnings for the purpose of propagation of religion. It is a fact that the holy Prophet (Slm) lived in Makkah for thirteen years after becoming prophet (Slm), but no record is available to show what was his source of livelihood during that period and even after migration to Madinah.

Desire for vision of Allah:

Allah commands:

"Thus whoever is desirous of the vision of Allah, he must do righteous deeds and should not associate any body with Allah."(18:110) 80

فـمـن كـان يـرجـوالـقـآء ربه فليعمل عملا صالحا ولا يشرك بعبادة ربه احدا (الكهف ع ۱۲)

About this verse Imam Fakhr-e-Razi (Rz) told that:

"Our friends have asserted "from the word "Liqa-e-Rab" means Vision of Allah."

واصحابنا حملوا القاء الرب على رويته

Another Verse tells that whoever does not have desire of the vision of Allah, his abode is Hell:

"Those who are not desirous of Our Vision, but are pleased and satisfied with the life of the present and those who heed not Our signs; their abode is Hell, because of the evil they had earned during their life."(10:7,8)	ان الذين لا يرجون لقآء نا ورضوابالحيوة الدنيا واطمانوا بها والذين هم عن اٰيٰتنا غٰفلون اولئك ماواهم النار بما كانوا يكسبون (يونس ع ۱)

We have clarified that when Allah prohibits Muslims from any deed, it becomes obligatory on Muslims to relinquish it. No desire for the vision of Allah, is to agree with the worldly life and to neglect the signs of Allah, the punishment for all these acts is Hell Fire. When not having the desire to have the vision of Allah causes Hell Fire, then is it not an obligation to have the desire of the vision of Allah? Thus desire for the "Vision of Allah" is an obligation.

Man was born for the worship of Allah. How should this worship be performed? The holy Prophet (Slm) said:

"In Ta'budullaha Kana Tarahu" Worship Allah as if you are seeing Him. Allah Says "I created human beings and Jinns, to worship Me". It means that man was born to see Allah; then is it not an obligation to have the desire for the "Vision of Allah"? When Allah commands Muslims for anything, then it becomes obligation to achieve it. Some examples are presented here:

1.Oh.People: Worship Allah Who had created you. .(2:21)	(۱) يا ايها الناس اعبدواربكم الذى خلقكم (البقرة)
2.Thus if they attack you, kill them. Such is the recompense of the disbelievers". (2:191)	(۲) فان قٰتلوكم فاقتلوم كذلك جزاء الكافرين (البقرة ع ۱۴)
3. During the menses do not go to your wives. (2:24)	(۳) فاعتزلوا النساء فى المحيض (البقرة ع ۲۴)
4. Do not fear them (idols), but fear Me alone. (2:8)	(۴) فلا تخشوهم واخشونى (البقرة ع ۸)
5.With pleasure give away woman's dower (Mehar)(4:4)	(۵) وآتوا النساء صدقٰتهن نحلة (النساء ع ۱)
6. Oh.Faithfuls honor your promises. (5:1)	(۶) يا ايها الذين آمنوا اوفوابالعقود (المائده ع ۱)
7. Fight for the cause of Allah, certainly you shall be prosper.	(۷) و جاهدوا فى سبيله لعلكم تفلحون (المائده)
8. Thus remember Me, I shall remember you. Be thankful to Me. Do not become infidel.(2:152)	(۸) فاذكرونى اذكركم واشكروالى ولا تكفرون (البقرة ع ۱۸)

9. You obey to that which had come to you from you Creator. (7:3)

(۹) اتبعوا ما انزل اليكم من ربكم (الاعراف ع ۱)

10. And give full measure with justice.

(۱۰) واوفوا الكيل والميزان بالقسط (الانعام ۹)

11. Worship Allah with humility and in secret. Verily He disowns transgressors. (7:55)

(۱۱) ادعواربكم تضرعا و خفية انه لا يحب المعتدين (الاعراف ع ۷)

12. Abstain from open and hidden sins. (6:120)

(۱۲) وذروا ظاهرالاثم و باطنه (الانعام ع ۱۴)

13. Fight against the polytheists, with all, as they used to fight with you all. (9:36)

(۱۳) وقاتلوا المشركين كافة كما يقاتلو نكم كافة (التوبه ع ۵)

14. If you do not have knowledge, then ask others who knew it. (Learned Ones) (16:13)

(۱۴) فسئلوا اهل الذكران كنتم لا تعلمون (النحل ع ۶)

15. Thus get away from the evils of idol worship and from lieing. (22:30)

(۱۵) فاجتنبوا الرجس من الاوثان واجتنبوا قول الزور (الحج ع ۴)

16. Oh Faithful, remember Allah's beneficence. (33:9)

(۱۶) يا ايها الذين آمنوا اذكرو انعمة الله عليكم (الاحزاب ع ۲)

17. Oh. Ye, who believe! Fear Allah and speak always truth. (33:70)

(۱۷) يا ايها الذين آمنوا اتقوا الله و قولوا قولا سديدا (الاحزاب ع ۹)

18. Oh. The faithful: spend from your chaste earnings and from that which We have produced for you from the land. (W2: 267)

(۱۸) يا ايها الذين آمنوا انفقوا من طيبت ماكسبتم و مما اخرجنا لكم من الارض (البقرة ع ۳۷)

19. Assist virtue and righteousness.(5:3)

(۱۹) و تعاونوا على البروالتقوى (المائده ع ۱)

20. Oh.Faithfuls. Fear Allah and search for His help.(I5:38)

(۲۰) يا يها الذين آمنوا اتقوا الله و اتبغوا اليه الوسيلة (المائده ع ۶)

21. Bow down along with those who are bowing (for prayers) (2:43)

(۲۱) واركعوا مع الراكعين (البقرة ع ۵)

Imam Hissas Hanafi (Rz) (D 370) had described that every command of Allah is an obligation. That means every command creates an obligation. That is why Allah has mentioned one pillar of prayer which is Bowing, thus it is an obligation to bow in the prayer. Allah had made it imperative to bow down in the prayer. Thus Bowing down in the prayer is an obligation. In the same way "remembrance of Allah", "Trust on Allah", "relinquishment of worldly affairs- i.e."Tark-e-Duniya" and "To be in the company of righteous persons " etc., also are obligations as per the wordings of the Holy Qur'an. Because Allah had emphatically ordained positively for performance by the Muslims.

Company with virtuous people:

"Allah states that: Oh the Faithfuls Fear Allah and be in the company of the virtuous people."

هم الذين صدقوا فى دين الله نية و قولا و عملا

Author of "Kasshaaf" has said about this verse that: These are the people who are true in religious duties, with their heart and mind, in their precept and practise. Thus such people who are true in their resolve, precept and practise may be born till the Day of Judgement and the commands given in the Qur'an are eternal, without any limitation of time and space. Therefore the statement of commentators that such virtuous people were only the companions and migrants is not correct. Hazrat Anas states:

"Said Anas that he heard the holy Prophet (Slm) telling that the example of my Ummah is like the rain, we can not say whether its beginning is good or its end."

قال قال رسول الله صلى الله عليه و سلم مثل امتى مثل المطولا يلذى اوله خير ام آخره

From this tradition two issues emerge. is good: Which one part of the Ummah, swhrether firest or the last is good? It is alo difficult to designate good to which one? First one or the last one. Another is that whole of the Ummah is best, from the beginning to the end. Whatever you take the meanings, it is certain that like the companions of the holy Prophet (Slm) virtuous people would always born in the world. Since the holy Prophet (Slm) also said that:

"Those who come after me, would love me with intensity. Every one of them would desire to see me with my family and with my grandeur."

من اشد امتى لى حبا ناس يكونون يعدى يودا احد هم لورأباهله و ماله

Regarding this tradition Sheik Abdul Haq wrote:

"Be it known that the explicit meaning of this tradition, and other traditions which may come, may indicate that in future some peoples may come who would be equal in excellence to the Holy Prophet's companions, or even would exceed in excellence of those companions. Ibn Abdul Burr who is one of the celebrities among the traditionalists had the same opinion and is clinging to the same tradition."

بدانكه ظاهر اين حديث و بعضى احاديث كه درين باب بيايد دلالت درد بر آنكه تواند كه بعد از صحابه رضوان الله عليهم اجمعين كسى بيايد كه مساوى باشد ايشان را در فضل يا افضل باشد از ايشان و ابن عبدالبر كه از مشاهير علماى حديث است باين جانب رفته و تمسك باين احاديث نموده است

This proves that like the companions of the holy Prophet (Slm), truthful people may emerge any time in future. Imam Fakhr-e-Razi (Rz) also did not specify about the truthful people to be only those who were the companions of the holy prophet (Slm). This proves two issues. One is that truthful persons are not those specific people known as the companions of the holy Prophet (Slm). Second being those to whom Imam Fakher-e-Razi (Rz) had maintained that if we have to accept consensus of the Ummah then we must be with the truthful people of the Ummah and not otherwise.

Author of "Tafseer-e-Madarik" says that:

"The verse argues that consensus is a proof, therefore, it is commanded to be with the truthful people, thus, we are bound to accept and obey."

والآية تـدل عـلـى ان الاجـمـاع حجة لانـه امر بالكون مع الصادقين فلزم قبول قولهم

Author of "Tafseerur Rahman" stresses that Company with the truthful is an obligation:

"Be with the truthful people to help the continuity of your righteousness, because company of truthful people is an obligation."

(وكـونـوا) لـلاستعانة على استدامة التقوىٰ (مع الصادقين) ولوجوب التقوىٰ و ملازمة الصادقين

If it is said that "Konu M'as Sadequeen" is to follow the truthful, then it would be said that best following would only be possible when the company of the truthful people is available, but preferably it may be taken as the company only and not the following.

In another tradition the holy Prophet (Slm) says:

"Whoever loved me, will be with me in the Paradise." 110

من احبنى كان معى فى الجنة

Here also 'Kana M'aie' means the company of Huzoor Rasoolullah (Slm). The religion teaches "avoid bad people's company, and adopt 'good peoples' company". Imam Fakhr-e-Razi has taken the word "Konu" as command. According to him: "Be with the Ummah" means "Be with the truthful people of the Ummah" only and not otherwise. The holy Qur'an too tells us:

"And Allah had revealed Qur'an on you stating that when Allah's signs become the point of mockery and utterances of profane words, then avoid their company, till they change the topic, otherwise you would judged as one among them."

و قـد نـزل عـليـكم فى الكتب ان اذا سمعتم ٰايت الله يـكفر بها ولستهزا بها فلا تقعدوا معهم حتى يخوضوا فى حديث غيره انكم اذا مثلهم (النساء ع ٢٠)

In this verse "Fala Taq'udo M'aahum" tells "not to sit with them" means "with those people who ridicule the verses of Allah". Thus leaving their company becomes obligatory. In the same sense" Konu M'as Sdequeen" "be in the company of Sadequeen" also is an obligation as

"Warkaoo Ma'ar Rakeyeen" is an obligation for prayers. The holy Prophet (Slm) advises:

"When you see such a person who has adopted asceticism from the worldly affairs and has reserved himself, then be near to him, because he was granted wisdom."

اذا رأيتم الرجل قد اعطنى زهدا فى الدنيا و قله منطق فاقتربوا منه فانه يلقى الحكمة

Imamana (As) has explained "with whom to live":

"Sixth is that to be in the company of Godly people."

ششم صحبت بندگان خدا بكند

"And further said: "If some one breaks these conditions, then his becoming a momin is difficult."

اگر اين حد هارا كسى به شكند اورا ايمان شدن محال است

The fact is that the manner in which completion of an Islamic obligation is required it is possible only in the company of the pious people.

Perpetual Remembrance of Allah:

"Allah ordains:"Thus be with remembrance of Allah, while sitting, standing and lying"

فاذكروا الله قياما و قعود او على جنوبكم (النساء ع ١٥)

1. Mohammad Ibn Jareer Tabri (Rz) had mentioned in his"Tafseer-e-Jameul Qur'an" that:

"Narrated a tradition by Mussna, by telling that Abu Saleh had stated to Muaviya and Muaviya to Ali Bin Talha and he heard Ibn Abbas (Rz) telling the assertion of Allah "Fazkurallaha Quiaman WA Qauoodan WA Ala Junoobihim".....,about this verse, Hazrat Abbas (Rz) said that Allahfixed a part of some obligation, as obligation, but He accepted no excuse for remembrance which is mandated on every one,man and woman, except the lunatic. Thus Allah ordained to be always with remembrance of Allah while sitting, standing, lying, in the day or in the night, on the land or on the sea journey, in travelling or staying in house, even in sickness or in good health, in poverty or riches, hidden or open thus in every condition remembering Allah is a must, which becomes an obligation."

حدثنى المثنى قال ثنا ابو صالح قال ثنا معاويه عن على بن ابى طلحه عن ابن عباس قوله فاذكروا الله قياما يقول لا يفرض الله على عباده فريضة الا جعل لهاجزأ معلوما ثم عذرا هلها فى حال عنه غير الذكر فان الله لم يجعل له حد اينتهى اليه و لم يعذرا حد فى تركه الا مغلوبا على عقله فقال فاذكروا الله قياما و قعود او على جنوبكم بالليل والنهار فى البرو البحر و فى السفرو الحضر والغنى والفقر والسقم والصحة والسروا لعلانية و على كل حال

"Allah commands : O. Ye who had testified Allah and His Rasool, remember Allah with your heart and tongues, with every bit of your body, so that your body should not be empty with Allah's remembrance."

يقول تعالىٰ ذكره يا ايها الذين صدقوا الله و رسوله اذكروا الله بقلوبكم والسنتكم وجوارحكم ذكرا كثيرا فلا تخلوا ابدانكم من ذكره فى حال من احوال الى آخره

Ibn Jareer Tabri (Rz) also said according to Abbas (Rz) the remembrance of Allah is an obligation.

2. Imam Hassas in his"Kitab-e-Ahkaamul Qur'an's part one has stated in a chapter regarding "Obligation of Remembrance of Allah" that it is "Akbar min Afzalus Salath" means Remembrance is superior than Prayer, therefore it is an obligation in all respects.

(Note: Zikri Mahdavis, in view of the above Saying : "Remembrance of Allh is Akber, min Afzalus Salath" have taken as a MANDATE and clinging to it and thus they are neglecting Salath. It is an exageration, therefore wrong. Salath is a second piller of Islm, which cannot and should not be avoided in any manner whatsoever, because Allah commands : When you complete prayers, then be busy with His remembrance,sitting, standing or lying down.")

3. Author of "Mu'aallimul Tanzeel" writes for this verse that:

"All Commentators are of the opinion that purpose of Allah is continuous and constant for His remembrance in all situations, since man always has these three positions, therefore Allah ordains in Chapter 4,"Al Nissa"that when you complete your prayer, remember Allah while sitting, standing or lying down."

و قال سائر المفسرين ارادبه المداومة على الذكر فى العموم الاحوال لان الانسان قل ما يخلو من احدى هذه الحالات الثلث نظيره فى سورة النسا فاذا قضيتم الصلوة فاذكروا الله قياما و قعودا و على جنوبكم

Author of "Mu'aallimul Tanzeel" commenting on this verse had referred Ibn Abbas' Saying which had already been referred by Ibn Jareer (Rz), but with a little difference that Tibri had written"La Yaf Rizullaha" and in "Mu'aallimul Tanzeel" it refers to Lum Yaf Rizullaha" somewhere Tibri says "Juz Ma'aluma" and Tanzeel says "Huda Ma'aluma". Thus the tradition is that:

"Told Mujahid about "Zikr-e-Kaseer" that you should not forget Allah at any moment of a time."

قال المجاهد الذكر الكثير ان لا تنساه ابدا

4. Author of "Kashaf" says:

"At all times; Prophet (Slm) told that Allah's zikr rests at every Muslim's tongue and at all times; and also in the heart of every Muslim."

اى فى كافة الاوقات قال رسول الله صلى الله عليه و سلم ذكر الله على فم كل مسلم و روى فى قلب كل مسلم

5. Fakhr-e-Razi (Rz) comments about this verse that:

"With reference to this verse, Commentators have two assertions: First: Its aim is that man should be always absorbed in Zikr as he has three postures only. Second is that: Zikr also represents Prayer, but first contention is preferable since many verses determine the supremacy of Zikr."

للمفسرين فى هـذه الآية قولان الا ول ان يكون المراد منه كون الانسان دائم الذكر لربه فان الاحوال ليست الاهذه الثلاثة ثم لما وصفهم بكونهم ذاكرين فيها كان ذلك دليلا على كونهم مواظبين على الـذكر غير فاترين عنه البتة والقول الثانى ان المراد بـالذكر الصلوة.......... والحمل على الاول اولى لان الآيات الكثيرة ناطقة بفضيلة الذكر

Fakhr-e-Razi (Rz) had reported what Ibn Abbas (Rz) was telling about "La Takun Minal Ghafeleen."

"Ibn Abbas (Rz) reported the assertion of Allah about:

"Yaz kuroonallaha........." that if Ibn Adam had any other posture apart from those three ones, then Allah would have ordained for that also. Thus it is certain that Allah had commanded for perpetual Zikr."

عن ابن عباس انه قال فى قوله الذين يذكرون الله قياما و قعود او على جنوبهم لوحصل لابن آدم حـالة رابعة سوى هـذه الاحوال لا مر الله بالذكر عندها والمراد منه تعالى امر بالذكر على الدوام

Imam Fakhr-e-Razi (Rz) in this connection further says that:

"Allah's assertion "Bil Ghuduwi wal Aasaal"refers to zikr which is an obligation. Allah's assertion: La takun Minal Ghafeleen" proves perpetual remembrance in the heart is obligatory. And that Allah's majesty and grandeur should always be on one's tongue, heart and mind."

قوله بـالغدوو الآصـال دال على انه يجب ان يكون الـذكر حاصلا فى كل الاوقـات و قوله لا تكن من الغـافلين يـدل على ان الذكر القلبى يجب ان يكون دائمـا و ان لا يغفل الانسـان لـحظة واحـدة عن استحضار جلال الله و كبريائه بقدر الطاقة البشرية والقوة الانسانية

6. "Baizavi"stresses for perpetuity of Zikr, day in and day out in every posture, sitting, standing and lying. Author of "Tafseer-e-Madarik" states:

"Its aim is to remember Allah in all circumstances, because man has those three postures and whoever desires Paradise, he must be busy with perpetual remembrance."

اوالمـراد الـذكر على كل حال لان الانسان لايخلو عـن هذه الاحوال و فى الحديث من احب ان يرتع فى رياض الجنة فليكثر ذكر الله

7. Tafseer-e-Madarik" stresses for perpetual remembrance in every situation and in every position. Further says that remembering Allah with perpetuity and firmness of mind and heart day in and day out is a must. Author of "Tafseerur Rahman" comments:

8. "Be not with the negligent, but it is imperative to remember Allah from the depth of your heart, while your tongue may be busy with things unrelated to Allah."

(ولا تكن) فيمابين ذلك (من الغافلين) بالكلية بل لا بدوان تكون ذاكر ابا لقلب و ان اشتغل لسانك بالغير

Thus it is affirmed from the statement of venerable commentators that "perpetual remembrance is an obligation". Therefore to act on it is a must. Apart from this, Allah had stressed it by making it an imperative and ordained as an emphasised order. If such an order is not an obligation then how the order asking "Wark'aoo Maur Rakeyeen" which is one of the pillars of the prayer becomes obligation?

9. One of the traditions proves the perpetuity of remembrance. Hazrat Abdullah Bin Busar (Rz) reports that the holy Prophet (Slm) said to keep your tongue moist with remembrance of Allah:

"Ya Rasoolullah which act is superior? Said: leave the world in such a condition that your tongue is moist with remembrance of Allah".

لا يزال لسانك رطبا من ذكر الله
يا رسول الله اى الاعمال افضل قال ان تفارق الدنيا ولسانك رطب من ذكر الله

Bibi Ayesha (Rz) reports that the holy Prophet (Slm) used to perform Zikr in all circumstances and in all situations.

(Note: The difficulty is that, human mind does not accept two thoughts at a time. You either pray or be busy with remembrance. Thus both are impossible at a time. Time is the essence here. It may be possible if you take prayer also as the remembrance. That is why Allahn Has clarified that "After prayer, be busy with remembrance".)

Extermination/ Seclusion:

Allah commands:

"Remember the name of Allah and devote yourself to Him with complete attention."

اذكر اسم ربك و تبتل اليه تبتيلا

This verse is addressed to the holy Prophet (Slm). Still this command is general to all Muslims. Imam Khassas (Rz) comments that:

"We are obliged to follow the holy Prophet (Slm) for those acts which have been ordered by Allah, even if it pertains to the Prophet (Slm) particularly."

علينا اتباع النبى صلى الله عليه و سلم فيما امره الله به

1. Mohammad Ibn Jareer (Rz) had commented on "Tabattal Ilaihi Tabteela" that:

"For your wants and prayers, be with Him alone and get secluded from others, except Allah. It is usually used in Arabic"tabattalat hazal amar" meaning : "I am spared for that work". In that sense Bibi Maryam (As), mother of Jesus Christ (AS) was called "Butool"because she had secluded herself from every one and spared herself to Allah alone. Thus a worshipper who "exterminates every worldly connection and spares himself for Allah's worship", he is called "Tabattal", who had separated from worldly affairs with the sole purpose of being with Allah always alone.

انقطع اليه انقطاعا لحوائجک و عبادتک دون سـائـر الا شيـا غيــره و هومن قولهم تبتـلت هـذا الا مـرومنه قيل لام عيسٰی ابن مـريـم البتـول لا نـقـطـا عها الی الله و يقال لـلعـابـد الـمـنقطع عن الدنيا و اسبابها الی عبادة الله قد تبتل

Author of "Mu'allimul Tanzeel" had commented on "Tabattal Ilaih" that:

"Ibn Zaid (Rz) had told the meaning of "Tabatul" is to abandon every worldly thing and request Allah to grant whatever He Wishes to grant."

قال ابن زيد التبتل رفض الدنيا و مافيها و التماس ما عندالله

Imam Fakhr-e-Razi (Rz) had commented on it That:

"Fara told that "Tabattal" is said for a worshipper when "he abandons everything and turns himself towards worship of Allah": i-e; has become attentive towards obedience of Allah by exterminating himself from every thing. Zaid bin Asaam (Rz) has said the meaning of "Tabattul" is "to abandon the world and whatever is in it and request from Him all your needs."

قـال الـفـراء يـقـال لـلعـابـدا ذا تـرک کل شـئـى و اقبـل علـى العـبـادة قد تبتل اى انـقطع عن کل شئى الى امر الله و طاعته و قـال زيد بن اسام التبتل رفض الدنيا مع کل مافيها و التماس ما عندالله

Reliable commentators have taken the meaning of "Tabattal"as exterminating every worldly affair for Allah or seclusion from world. Therefore whoever has relinquished the world (became Tarik-e-Duniya) is called "Tabattal Illallah".

Allah ordained:

"Withdraw from those who have made the Religion a matter of sport and those who are immersed in worldly life."

وذرالـذيـن اتخذو ادينهم لعباولهوا وغـرتهم الحيواة الدنيا (الانعام ع ٨)

This verse commands the people to get away from those who had made religion a thing of sport. Imamana (As) had termed the worldly life as Kufr(Infedility). Therefore why should not we exterminate from those who are busy in worldly affairs? The Prophet (Slm) told "not to give up seclusion, since it is itself a sort of worship". Hazrat Sayeed Binul Musayb narrated that Huzoor Prophet (Slm) had said that" Seclusion is incumbent on you, because it is itself a

Worship. So, never leave seclusion (Uzlat) for it is a kind of worship for you."

In Mahdavia Faith Seclusion means in pursuance of the commands of Allah to withdraw from worldly people and be with the remembrance of Allah alone.

Trust in Allah:

"Thus have trust in Allah; it is certain that Allah befriends those who resigned to the Will of Allah."

فتوكل على الله ان الله يحب المتوكلين (آل عمران ع ١٤٧)

1. Mohammad Ibn Jareer Tibri (Rz) has commented:

"But; Oh Faithfuls, have trust in Allah alone., leaving every creation."

ولكن على ربهم ايها المومنون فتوكلوا دون سائر خلقه الى آخره

2. Author of "Ma'allim-e-Tanzeel"had commented on this verse that:

"To have trust in Allah means you should not desire any help from other than Allah. Should not demand even meals from any one, except from Allah alone and believe that Allah is witnessing all your deeds."

قيل التوكل ان لا تعص الله من اجل رزقك و قيل ان لا تطلب لنفسك ناصرا غير الله ولا لرزقك خازنا غيره ولا لعملك شاهدا غيره

"Kasshaf" has commented on it that: Believers must have complete trust in Allah and must leave all affairs to Him alone, because He is alone to help them. Hence to have trust in Allah without reservations is an obligation.?"

وليخص المومنون ربهم بالتوكل والتفويض اليه لعلمهم انه لا ناصر سواه ولان ايمانهم يوجب ذلك و يقتضيه

Further states that:

"Leave all affairs to His judgement with firm faith on His deliberations and make Him your solicitor and protector in such a way that all your affairs must be surrendered to Him alone for solution and for fulfilment."

واسند امرك اليه و كله الى تدبيره (وكيلا) حافظا موكولاً اليه كل امر

"Thus it becomes obligatory to trust in Allah, since none would help, except the One who has created us."

فليخصوه بالتوكل عليه لما علموا ان لا ناصر سواه و آمنوا به

Wa Ala Rabbihim Yatawakkaloon" is the attribute of faithfuls which determines our belief and the thing on which our belief is based, nothing but complete Trust in Allah which becomes an obligatory. But it has many channels. Here we refer back to a tradition reported by Abu Huraira (Rz) regarding Hazrat Bilal (Rz) who was holding a bag full of dates on which the holy Prophet (Slm) retarded by telling to spend it without fearing for the future. Hazrat Sheik Abdul Haq wrote regarding this tradition that:

"This determines your trust in Allah and complete belief in Him for the supply of provisions for you in future."

ایں ارشاد است به مقام توکل و اعتماد بر حق سبحانه تعالیٰ

Imam Fakhr-e-Razi (Rz) has commented about this verse that: "Allaha Fal Yatawakulul Momineen". "It is a must for a momin to trust on Allah alone". Allah Says: "Believers trust only on Him and not on any other being." Thus it becomes an obligation.

5."Tafseer-e-Baizavi" has commented about this verse that: "Have trust in Allah in all your affairs as you know not, but Allah Knows each and every thing for you.

In the same "Tafseer" it occurs:

It is a must for them to have trust in Allah , when they have known that none is there to help them except Allah, therefore they must have faith on Him alone."

The same was the practise in the Daira-e-Mahdavia about which Mulla Abdul Qader Badayuni states:

"Having complete faith in Allah to the extremity on His attribute of Sustenance that they never used to keep anything pertaining to means of livelihood with them and their motive was to earn daily and spend daily."

هیچ چیزے از اسباب معیشت با خود از غایت اعتماد بر رزاقی حق تعالیٰ نمی گذاشتند وروز نوروزی نودستور العمل ایشان بود

Those obligations are based on the verses of the holy Qur'an: reprimanding from doing anything which will lead you to the Hellfire. So it is an obligation leave that work.

Principles of Islamic Jurisprudence & Commands: Their Types:

From the traditions mentioned above, we come to know that there is no difference in the terminology of Obligation and Necessity. Both carry equal meanings. Qur'an presents commands of "To do" and "Not to do". Both are inevitable obligations. The scholars agree as a principle that Qur'anic dictates are clear obligations which necessitate you to perform or not to perform as the case may be. If some one hears any Qur'anic command, then it is obligatory on him to work accordingly. These are called lasting and unshakable orders known as "Aayat-e-Muhakkamat"whose meanings cannot be changed through allusion, comparison or figurative expression. Those verses like "Kuno Ma'as'sadequeen" or "FataWakkal Alallah" or "Fazkrulaha," "Warkauoo Ma'ur Rakeyeen" are such which carry direct and unambiguous meanings and one who hears them, can he change their meanings? From those verses commands and orders are derived.

There are several types of Commands reported in the books of jurisprudence. These obligations are based on two kinds of verses. In some verses it is mentioned about those acts which brings Hell Fire. Therefore to abandon those acts is obligation. In the same way, some commandments have been made incumbent on the Muslims. Hence these commandments must necessarily be carried on. To say that these commands are only desirable (Mustahab) is against the intent of the Almighty. Hence to leave unattended them is an offence (Makrooh). It is unlawful. Some examples:

1. Al Wajoob: "Aqi mus salaath" (Establish prayer) It is a religious duty to establish prayer which is related to worship. Therefore for any command regarding religion, if order is given in a positive sense, its performance is an obligation.

2. Al Abaha:"Oh. Ye. The faithful: do not disgrace the signs of Allah, nor to the month which is forbidden and also not to the animal which is being sacrificed and not to those animals who bear girth around their necks and also for those who have intended to go for pilgrimage to Kabatullah and request for Allah's mercy and Pleasure. And when you come out from Ehram, then you may go for hunting,"(5:2) 142

(٢) الا بـاحة . يا ايها الذين آمنوا لا تحلوا شعائر الله ولا الشهـر الـحـرام ولا الهـدى ولا القـلايد ولا امين البيت الـحـرام يبتـغـون فضلا من ربهم رضوانا و اذا حللتم فاصطادوا (المائده ع ١)

It is said :"When you come out of Ehram, then go for hunting": Here "go for hunting" is a permission for hunting, now the question arises whether before Ehram is there any prohibition for the hunting? If before Ehram there is a permission, then why permission is being given specifically after removing Ehram? Here Allah is not giving permission through this verse, but asserting that when you are in Ehram you cannot go for hunting. Therefore avoidance from hunting while in Ehram, is an obligation. Obligation should not be taken as permission which is a sin.

3. Al Andub: If you find any virtue in the slaves let them go under certain conditions."(24:33 Part)

(٣) الندب. فكاتبوهم ان علمتم فيهم خيرا (النور ٠ ع ٤)

Allah said at another place:

4. Al Tahdeed: "Do whatever you want to do. No doubt, Allah is looking your deeds."

(٣) التهديد . اعملوا ماشئتم انه بما تعلمون بصير (حم السجده ع ٥)

Here Allah's assertion that :"Do whatever you want to do; Allah is looking your deeds" stresses towards an obligation for "to leave bad deeds and adopt good deeds" if they do not adhere to it they would get punishment.

5. "Al Taskheer: And you know those people who had transgressed on the day of Sabath, therefore We decreed them to become monkeys."(2:65)

(٥) التسخيـر. و لقد علمتم الذين اعتدوا منكم فى السبت فقلنا لهم كونوا قردة خاسئين (البقره ع ٨)

Allah decreed to them (Jews) to become monkeys who transgressed on the day of Sabath (Saturday). Here the previous warning is being mentioned. Thus that order was a clear obligation. Hence that order was made perfect and they became monkeys.

6."Al Irshad: "Al Irshad:"And make two witnesses who have the quality to do justice."(65:23 Part)

(٢) الا رشـاد . واشهدوا ذوى عدل منكم (الطلاق ع ١)

7. Al Ta'jeez: "If you doubt about this Book which We have Revealed on Our servant, then bring one verse just like this"(2:23 Part)

(٤) التعجيز . و ان كنتم فى ريب مما نزلنا على عبدنا فاتوا بسورة من مثله (البقرة ع ٣)

This verse is not in our discussion. We are discussing those verses in which particular order had been given to Muslims. Here address is to the infidels. However there is a clear command not to doubt on the Qur'an and if anyone has a doubt, it is imperative on him to bring at least one verse like that.

8. Al Imtanan:"Whatever Allah had given to you eat it and do not follow Satan step by step."(6:142)

(٨) الامتنـان . كلـوا مـما رزقكم الله ولا تتبعوا خطوات الشيطن (الانعام ع ٤١)

Allah's advice is to eat and do not follow Satan, denotes that not only in eating, but also in all deeds do not follow Satan and whatever is eaten is legitimate and there is no restriction. Author of "Tafseer-r-. Husain" points out about this verse that:

**9.Eat from which it is provided by Allah is legitimate."

(٩) بخوريـد از انچه روزى داد خداى و حلال كرد برشما

Those who believe prohibitory orders in the words "Kilo-Eat" we have to ask them, whether, before this verse was revealed, Muslims were not being satisfied with the meals provided by Allah? If so, then what is the purpose of now being stressed to eat now? It is clear from this verse that Allah is asking not to follow the Satan so that you may leave the legitimate thing and adopt illegitimate thing.

10. Al Ikram: "No doubt that pious people will live in gardens with flowing canals. They will be told to enter with peace and security."(15:45)

(١٠) الاكـرام . ان الـمتـقيـن فى جنـت و عيـون ادخلوها بسلم امنين (الحجر ع ٣)

This verse is for future for pious people to enter paradise. It is obligatory on them to enter with peace and security.

11. Al Tasvia: :"Enter here. Whether you show patience or not, it is equal. You will get the reward for which you have done."(52:16)

(١١) التسـويـه . اصلوها فاصبروا اولا تصبروا سواء عليكم انما تجزون ماكنتم تعملون (الطور ع ١)

This verse also is not for our discussion since we are concerned with that verse in which if Allah ordains to Muslims, then it becomes obligation to Muslims to do. Or not to do according to the order.

12. Al Dua::"Oh my Allah, forgive me"(14:41)

(١٢) الدعا . ربنا اغفرلى (ابراهيم ع ٦)

This verse relates to past where Prophet Ibrahim (As) is asking Allah's forgiveness which is out of our discussion, since we are discussing in which Allah commands to Muslims and it becomes obligatory to Muslims to do.

13. Al Tamanni: ""And they will call: Oh. Cherisher: Kill and destroy us. Answer would be given to them: You would be in the same position."(43:77)

(١٣) التـمنى . ونادوا يا مالك ليقض علينا ربک قال انکم ماکثون (زخرف ع ٤)

This verse is for the future. Residents of the Hell who will tell and the Angel would reply accordingly that the abode for the infidels is Hell.

14.Al Ahtakhar: "Prophet Musa (As) demanded the magicians to throw whatever they wanted to do."(10:60)

(١٤) الاحتـقـار . قـال لهم موسى القواما انتم ملقون (يونس ع ٨)

This also relates to the past. Prophet Musa (AS) asked the magicians to do whatever they want to do. From the words of Prophet Musa (As) it comes to light that the magic of the magicians is going to become ineffective and the faithful with their power of the faith would be able to fight against the slight of hand (Jiggling tricks) of the magicians. Thus it was obligatory on the faithful to act against the magicians.

15. Al-Takveen: "When We desire to create any thing, We ask it "to be"; thus it gets life." (16:40)

(١٥) التـکوين . انما قولنا لشئى اذا اردنه ان نقو ل له کن فيکون (النحل ع ٥)

This verse emphasises the importance of Allah's command. When Allah Asks anything to become, it is imperative to that thing to obey the command. Therefore in the same manner when Allah Commands the Muslims, then it is an obligation on them to obey the Command. When Allah Commands "Waz Kurallha zikr-e-kaseer." Whether any person can avoid this command?

16. **Al Tadeeb:** "Holy Prophet (Slm) told Abbas (Rz) to eat which is before you."

(١٦) التـاديـب . قـولـه عـليـه السلام لا بن عباس رضى الله عنهما کل ماليیک

In Arabic culture, a few persons gather for dinner and used to eat in a common big utensil. Prophet's telling to Abbas (Rz) was to eat that which is before you, and do not encroach on other People's portion. It is just to teach manners. It is a social obligation which must be adopted.

17.Al Ihanata. Taste you (this)! Verily, you were pretending to be mighty and generous." (44:49)

(١٧) الاهانة . ذق انک انت العزيز الکريم

Thus according to principles of Jurisprudence, a command takes many categories which have been discussed above. We have to see what is the intention of Allah in issuing these commands.

The above verses relate to the past or to the future. Some relate to infidels only and some say it relates to Muslims. Scholars have accepted it as an obligation for prayers only, but there exist obligations for other issues as well which we have tried to prove in detail while discussing those verses one by one.

Even if anyone agrees to the above principles, there is no harm in accepting them since the verses "Koonoo Ma'as Sadeqeen, Uzkurullaha Qyaaman Wa-Quoodun, Wa-Tabtilu ilaihi Tabteela, and Fatawakkal Allalah" are implicit obligations on which no other condition has been described in which other examples fits. This is also implied that whoever avoids, bears the responsibility and gets proper punishment; as mentioned below:

لاتجعلوا دعاء الرسول كدعاء بعضكم بعضا قديعلم الله الذين يتسللون منكم لواذا فليحذر الذين يخالفون عن امره ان تصيبهم فتنة اويصيبهم عذاب اليم (الطور ع ٩)

"You should not treat Prophet's call as if you call each other; and Allah knows very well those who by taking cover move away. Thus who ever oppose Allah, they should fear from so doing to avoid any punishment or torment."

Such objections are available in many sects. For example the Company of pious persons and perpetual remembrance of Allah are obligations which Mahdavis accept as an implicit order from Allah, hence they practise them without reservation , but if other sects of Muslims do not adhere to them; they should not ascertain that these obligations are abolished in Sharia. Then they must show proof for such abolition. We are firm in our opinion that if they declare as abolished and do not adhere to the clear commands they are not following the dictates of Sharia.

Question of" Eid Prayers." About which Sheik Abdul Qader had written that:

صلوٰة عيدين فرض است برقول امام ابو حنيفه مثل جمعه در روايتے واجب است و تسميه او به سنت از جهت ثبوت اوبه سنت است نه بكتاب و نزد صاحبيه سنت است و نزد شافعى نفل است و گردانيده اند اورا افضل نوافل و درقولے سنت موكده است و مالك گفته است كه سنت واجبه و شايد كه وجوب بمعنى تاكيد است و احتمال دارد كه مراد چيزے باشد كه درمذهب ابو حنيفه گفته شد و مشهور نزد امام احمد فرض عين است چنانچه مذهب ابو حنيفه است و صحيح نزدوے فرض كفايت است مثل صلوٰة جنازه و جهاد و درروايتے از ابو حنيفه نيز همچنين آمده

"Eid prayers are obligatory. According to Imam Abu Hanifa (Rz) it is like the prayer of Friday. Some say it is a binding, worth following, and some say Sunnat. If it is a sunnat, it had not been proved either by book or by traditionalists. Whereas Imam Shaafaie (Rz) declares it as Nafil-/supererogatory. Some say they are superior to supererogatory and some say they are emphasised Sunnat. Imam Malik (Rz) says them to be Sunnat worth following as being emphasised. However according to Imam Ahmed (Rz) it is obligatory, the same is the decree of Imam Abu Hanifa (Rz). Still some say it is an adequate obligation comparing to funeral prayer and Jehad."

Thus Eid prayers are obligation,

adequate obligation, wajib, Sunnat, emphasised Sunnt, supererogatory, superior to supererogatory and so many attributes have been attached to these prayers and name them any one of the above. There exist some differences regarding the performance also. Some people offer them in Masjid and it is said that it is against Sunnat. Therefore Author of "Madarijul Nabuwat" had written that:

"In some cities, Eid prayer is performed in Masjid, which is against the tradition."	در بعض امصار که در مساجد میگذارند خلاف سنت است

With these differences, just imagine how many objections may not arise in several religious issues in performance of other religious matters. Imam Hissas (Rz) had reported Hazrat Omer (Rz) as telling; that:

"Reported Hazrat Omer (Rz) that the verse regarding Riba/interest was revealed very lately, that is why by the time its explanation could be ascertained, the holy Prophet (Slm) passed away."	قال عمر ایضا ان آیة الربا من آخرمانزل من القرآن و ان النبی صلی الله علیه و سلم قبض قبل ان بینه لنا الیٰ آخره

It is clear that explanation could not be obtained from the holy Prophet (Slm) regarding Riba/usury or interest. But as regards other obligations regarding company of pious persons (Suhbat-e-Sadequeen), migration (Hijrat), Trust in Allah (Tawakkul), Zikirullaha Kaseer etc. there are so many explanations from the holy Prophet (Slm).

(Note:Regarding Riba/Interest: One Verse ordains and prohibits Muslims from earning or taking interest. Another Verse states, "Avoid Interest, doubling and tripling". The second verse emphatically prohibits to earn interest by doubling or trippling. Does it means to say, take simple interest, but not doubled one or trippled one?. It requires thorough investigation and Fiqhi clarification. Another aspect is that the interest which is earned from the amounts given as a loan to a person who is in distress in performing his responsibilities, like, marriages of a daughter or payments for the bills for health etc., in my opinion, have been strictly prohibited, but interest for such loans or deposits with the commercial banks who invest their amounts for business, should that earniung be avoided? when income from the investments in legal business, or the rents from houses are legitimized, where risk is involved. Should Bank Deposits also may not be taken as legal Investment, and their earnings should be allowed, since the investments done by banks also have the risk factor? While it is a different issue that the deposits of the Banks earn a fixed income, I enquire, should all such fixed incomes be declared as prohibitted? A Fiqhi consensus is necessary to avoid ambiguities. Khundmiri)

Regarding Mazmaza (gorgling) and Istenshaque (cleaning the nostrils) are obligatory for some . But is it possible that any person proves that these items of ablution were obligatory at the early period of Islam? The same is the problem of Witr prayer (in Isha). Some have accepted it as obligatory and some did not take it as an obligation. Thus such differences are not taken as to have been abolished in Shariat.

The opponents of Mahdavis, when they could not trace any fault in performance of Islamic obligations, then they enquire about the obligatory position of Migration (Hijtrat), Company of the pious people (Suhbat-e-Sadequeen), Trust in Allah (Tawakkul) etc. and claim that they are abolished in Sharait. Whereas, for Mahdavis, these obligations are based on clear dictates from the holy Qur'an. As regards their obligatory status it has been proved from the earliest sources that Imamana (AS) had declared their being obligations with firm commands of Allah based on the dictates of the holy Qur'an. Hazrat Bandagi Miyan Syed Khundmir (Rz) had recorded in "Aqueedai-e-Sharifa" by obtaining clarifications from Imamana (As) himself personally.

"The purpose is that I, Syed Khundmir (Rz) son of Syed Moosa alias Chajjoo, had heard these obligations from the mouth of Imamana (As)."	الـمـقـصـود بنـده سيـد خوندمير بن سيد موسىٰ عرف چهـجو ايـن احكـام از زبـان سيـد محمد مهدى عليه السلام شنيده است۔

Further at the end of "Aqueedai-e-Sharifa" he asserts that:

"Be it may be known that the obligations which have been mentioned, from the beginning till the Demise of Imamana (As) I had been in his company and never heard any difference about them."	معلوم بعد كه اين احكام كه مذكور است از اول تا آخر وقت رحلت آن ذات مادام كه اين بنده در صحبت وے بود ر هيچ حكم از آن احكام تفاوت نيا فتم

Thus whatever the obligations which had been dictated by Imamana (As) they are all based on the holy Qur'an and clarified by the Holy Prophet (Slm) through traditions.

PART TWO
CHAPTER I
Doubts of decliners about
Imamana's Characters & Their Answers

There are so many traditions about Imam Mahdi (As). Sheik Ali's contention is that Mahdi (As) is the one who should fit on to the traditions. If even a few of them fit on Imam Mahdi (As), there is no use to discuss about all. ("Sirajul" Absar P.156)

Author of 'Sirajul Absar" argues that those traditions which are reported with reference to Imam Mahdi (As) have minor differences. It is a religious issue which relates to beliefs. The jurists are not clinging to all traditions. They relied on some traditions and commented on them and omitted others from their scrutiny.

Author of Hadia had maintained that so many traditions have been reported regarding Imam Mahdi (As); they must fit on to the person of Mahdi (As). And in order to poison the minds of the masses he had presented an example: "The example thus may be perceived that rope if made of hair, imagine how strong would it be when every hair is so weak".

If we follow the fault finder's principle and gather all the subjects and all the traditions which pertain to Fasting, Hajj and Poor's tax, then we have so many ropes which will be of no use. For example; Sheik Ali, author of "Kanzul Ummal" had recorded more than 4500 traditions in "Kitabus Salah". If we read and follow, it would become difficult to offer prayers. Thus, the same is the situation for the traditions regarding Imam Mahdi (As). Since it is not possible that all the implications of all these traditions are found in one person. Apart from this all those traditions which are mentioned in "Sihah" relating to the chapter of Mahdi (As) or those that have been recorded in the journals of "Uqdurer Durer" or "Al Ariful Wardi" represent many differences. They point out the differences of faith and beliefs of those scholars regarding the signs pertaining to Imam Mahdi (AS).

All the traditions which have been reported in respect of Imam Mahdi, author of Hadia, in order to declare them authentic, had referred"Insaf Nama's" contention that denial of a single information is infidelity.

The assertion regarding antecedents which had been recorded in the second chapter of "Insaf Nama", the decliner could not grasp its true meanings. Here single Information means which had occurred once and had become absolute. Here guess is in the sense about whom it is being guessed that is also absolute. Author of Sirajul Absar's contention is that if we try to consider on the interpretation of the jurists, we will not find them all to have agreed on Islamic issues and on those differences which arose later on, were not objected. In that connection he had stated that if the jurists try to consider about the signs of Imam Mahdi (As), they would never form a firm opinion about them. Thus they had formed different opinions, because there was no ascertainment and permanency in the signs of Imam Mahdi (As). Therefore a group had avoided to declare its opinion. Author of "Sirajul Absar" had referred an assertion in the "Shu'bul Iman" of Baihiqi (Rh) (D. 458) that:

"Differences have arisen among people regarding Imam Mahdi (As). Therefore one group delayed to announce its verdict; still it had a belief that (Imam) Mahdi (As) will be a person from the progeny of Bibi Fatima (Rz) and Allah would depute whenever he would wish for the betterment of the religion."

اختــلف الــنــاس فى امــر الـمـهـدى فتـوقـف جـمـاعـة واحـالـواالعلم الى عالمه و اعتقدوا انه واحد من اولاد فـاطـمة بـنـت رسـول الله صلى الله عليه و سلم يخلقه الـلـه متى شـاء و يبعثه نصرة لدينه (سـراج الابصـار مـع مقدمه طبع اول صفحه ٢)

(And it is a fact that the Ninth Century was filled up with innovations and bid'aths which required a personality to eradicate them and made the Ummah Clean. That was a period when the Almighty deputed Imam Mahdi for the betterment of the religion.)

Delay occurs only when there is some inconsistency and when preference could not be given to one over another. The contention of "Shu'bul Iman" had been seconded by Taftazani (d. 791) who says at the end of "Sharah-e-Maqasid" that:

"Scholars believe that Mahdi (As) is from the progeny of Bibi Fatima (Rz). Allah shall depute whenever He would wish for helping the religion."

فـذهب العلماء الىٰ انه امام عادل من ولد فاطمة يخلقه الله متى شاء و يبعثه نصرة لدينه

Author of "Sirajul Absar" argues to adopt the beliefs of the scholars. Traditions also have a common stand what had been stated above. Now arises the problem of examining the truthfulness of Imam Mahdi (As). Miyan Aalim Billah (Rh) is of the opinion that whatever the criterion had been adopted for judging the truthfulness of the prophets (As), the same should be adopted for Imam Mahdi (As), since he is also one among the commissioned personalities.

Author of "Sirajul Absar" had maintained that characters are absolute and sufficient proof. And whose characters have been proved there should be no dispute. In this connection he had produced sixteen arguments from Qur'an, traditions and narratives of the eminent scholars. (vide "Sirajul Absar" P.166, 204).

Author of Hadia had objected to this argument and wrote that "when Abdul Malik Sujawandi (Rh) found that the traditions are against his Sheik (As), then he started arguing with Imamana's characters.

It is a fact that the traditions recorded in the "Sihah" justifiably fit to the person of Imamana (As). However his reluctance to accept characters as proof shows his evil minded malice, because the Prophet (Slm) himself told that Imamana's characters should be like his characters. Thus, why the argument regarding characters should become inappropriate for Imamana (As)? Particularly when characters had been one of the conditions for proof of prophethood, same way characters should become one of the conditions as an absolute proof of Mahdiat also. Religious scholars have based characters of the holy Prophet (Slm) as the proof of his Nabuvwat. While discussing the proofs of Mahdiat, we have clarified that even Qur'an had presented the characters of the holy Prophet (Slm) and his life before Prophethood as the proof of his being a prophet (Messenger of Allah), and the verses "Um Lum Ya'rafu Rasoolohum" and "Faqad Ba'sa Feekum Omera" that characters can be taken as a proof.

When author of Hadia found hard for himself to negate Mahdiat of Imamana (As) from the traditions reported in "Sihah" and also to nullify the argument of Characters of Imamana (As), he wrongly ventured by creating doubts about the characters of Imamana (As); and these doubts are also as weak as those doubts of the Christians in respect of the holy Prophet's characters.

Surprisingly he had referred Sheik's "Risala-e-Al Burhan". How can we presume that he had not gone through the Review on it; in which the sheik had used the words" Noble and Magnificent"with regard to the characters of Imamana (As).

In order to nullify the argument of characters, he had created doubts regarding Imamana's characters in chapter 3, Argument No. 17 of his book; and in the preamble he had accepted "Akhlaq-e-Nasiri" as the book on Characters and wrote that the gist of the comments on reality of characters as confirmed by Islamic scholars and philosophers of Greece is that the books on characters like "Ahyaaul Uloom" and "Akhlaq-e-Nasiri" are filled with examples. ("Hadia-e-Mahdavia" p.148)

The decliner had accepted "Akhlaq-e-Nasiri" as a book on characters. One of the headings of this book is "Characters for Drinking Wine" in chapter 4, of his thesis determines characters of the drinkers of wine. Pity on him that he praises a book which describes about the characters of the drinkers while Imamana's characters are at issue; thus the fault finder argues by presenting such a book, which proves his maliciousness and his love for wine. However for the purpose of justice we would submit some narrations in order to investigate his doubts.

Performing Migration, Punishment for Turning back from migration:

Chapter eight of "Insaf Nama" reports:

نـقـل اسـت از بنـدگی مـیـان سید خوندمیر و از بنـدگی
مـیـان نـظـام آن روز کـه بـی بـی شـکر خاتون و چند
کسـان دیـگر از کـاهه ولایت تهته بـاز گشتند و لب
آب رسیدند بندگی مـیان نظام فرمودند که بنده برابر
رفتـه بـود تـا ایشـان را کرایه کرده در سفینه نشاند و
ایشـان دو گـره بـرائـی کـرایـه بنده را داده بودند بنده
کشتی کرایـه کرده کرایه ایشان راداد ، آن دو گره پیش
بـنـده بـفـرامـوشـی مـانده بود ، بنده وقت مغرب بـاز
گشت نجانه آمد ، چون سپر از کتف خود فرو کردم
دو گـره جنبیده بنده رایاد آمد که دو گرهائی ایشان
پیـش مـا مـاندند، چون صبـاح شد و دوسه ساعت روز
بر آمد بنده مستعد شده از حجره بیرون آمد تادو گره
هـائـی ایشـان بدیشان رفته برسانـدچون از خانه بدرم
آمـدم بـنـدگی میـران همان وقت بیرون آمدند بنده
را دیـدنـد که مستعد شده میـرود، دست جنبانده اشارت
کردند که کجا میروید بنده پیش میرانؑ آمد و گفت که
میرانجیو دو گرۀ شکر خاتون که برائی کرایه کردن داده
بـود بفراموشی پیش بنده چند دو گره مانده اند میروم تا
ایشـان رابـرسانم بندگی میـران فرمودند که میان نظام دو
گـره هـا بـخوریـد اگر حق تعالیٰ به پرسد دامن مابگیرید
ایشـان از خـدائـی تـعـالـیٰ روی گردانیده میروند اگر حق
تعالیٰ قوت دهد از ایشان انچه هست زده بستانم

"Reported by Hazrat Bandagi Miyan (Rz) and Hazrat Shah Nizam (Rz) that the day when Shakkar Khatoon and some people returned from Kaha of Thatta (now in Pakistan) and reached near the banks of a river, Hazrat Shah Nizam (Rz) told that he had gone along with them to negotiate rent and arrange for them a boat for which they gave money to him. He arranged for them the boat; but the money they had given to Hazrat Nizam (Rz) was left with him and he returned at Maghrib prayer. When he took out the shirt he heard the noise of money which he recalled it to have been given by those people. In the morning he came out from his house and started to go to hand over

that money to them. At the same time Imamana (As) came out and asked Shah Nizam (Rz) as to where he was going? Shah Nizam (Rz) told to hand over the left over money to Shakkar Khatoon. Imamana (As) said: "keep that money for your use and if Allah asked, refer my name. If Allah gave strength I would take over whatever they had."

It is reported that Shakker Khatoon and others had turned away from the migration and returned back. On that Imamana (As) decreed to punish them by usurping their money and asked Shah Nizam (Rz) to use it for himself.

In the above mentioned narration the words" If Allah Gives the strength" are described by the author of "Insaf Nama" thus:"It should be known that the meanings of "Strength" means "Command of Allah." Similarly Allah Says: "Oh! Musa (As) catch him with force and give command to your nation".

Like that, during the period of the holy Prophet (Slm) a group of people had migrated from Makkah to Madinah, then they deviated and returned back about which details are given below:

(Note : Mohammad Ibn Jareer Tibri (Rz) has commented on the verse "fama lakum fil munafiqeen", which we have referred here and we had omitted other narratives for the sake of brevity since, it represents what ibn jareer Tibri (Rz) had narrated that:)

"It was told that a group came from Makkah to Madinah and they boasted themselves to be migrants. Then they asked permission from the holy Prophet (Slm) for going back to bring some funds to establish trade, thus returned back. There were difference of opinion about them: some said they were hypocrites and some said they were faithful. But Allah revealed their hypocrisy in this verse and ordered to kill them"

قـوم خرجـوا مـن مـكة حتـى أتوا المدينة يـزعمـون أنهـم مهاجرون ثم ارتدوا وبعد ذلـك فاستـاذنوا النبي صلى الله عليه و سـلم الى مكة لياتوا ببضائع لهم يتجرون فيهـا فاختـلف فيـهـم الـمؤمنون وقائل يـقـول هـم منـافقون و قـائل يقول هم مؤمنين فبين الله نفافقهم فامريقتالهم.

B. Author of "Mo'alim-e-tanzeel" under this verse said that:

Mujahid told some people came to Madinah and have accepted Islam then they converted and went back to Makkah after taking permission from the Holy Prophet (Slm), contending to go to Makkah to bring some cash for establishing some business, but they settled down in Makkah instead. In this matter Muslims have difference of opinion. Some were saying still they are Muslims, others were saying they were hypocrites.

قـال مـجـاهـد قـوم خرجـوا الى المدينة واسلموا ثم ارتـدوا واستـاذنـو رسول الله صلى الله عليه وسلم الـى مكة لياتوا ببضائع يتجرون فيها فخرجوا وقامو بـمكة فاختـلف الـمسلمون فيهم فقائل يقول هم منافقون وقائل يقول هم مؤمنون وقال بعضهم نزلت فى النـاس مـن قـريش قـدموا المدينة واسلموا ثم نـدمـوا عـلـى ذلـك فـخرجوا كهيئة المتنزهين حتى تبـاعـدوا مـن الـمدينة مكتبوا الـى رسول الله

"At this moment this verse was revealed about those people who came to Madinah and became Muslims and then pretended by telling that they were going back for sight seeing, and they reached Makkah. They wrote to the holy Prophet (Slm) that "when we left for Madinah we were Muslim, but we became afraid of the climate of Madinah and went to Syria. This news was heard by Muslims, some Muslims insisted to go to Syria to kill them and snatch away whatever they had. But some Muslims objected by telling that how can you kill them they are still Muslims and they left their houses in Makkah. This all came to the knowledge of holy Prophet (Slm) and also the difference of opinion. The holy Prophet (Slm) kept quiet, soon after this verse was revealed."

وانـا عـلـى الـذى فـارقـناك عليه من الايـمان ولكنا اجتوينا المدينة واشتقنا الـى ارضنـا ثـم انهـم خرجوا فى تجارة لهم نحو الشام فبلغ ذالـك المسلمين فقـال بـعضهـم نـخرج اليهم فنقتاهم ناخـذنا معهم لاتهم رغبوا عن ديننا وقـالـت طـائفة كيف تقتلون قوما على دينكم بان لم يذروأ ديارهم وكان هذا بعين النبى وهو ساكت لا هنهى واحدا من الفريقين فنزلت هذه الآية.

C. Author of "Tafseer-e-Kashaf" has commented under this verse that:

5. It is stated that a group of hypocrites asked permission from the holy Prophet (Slm) to allow them to go to ba'diah (a jungle nearby) in view of Madinah's harsh climate. They started to go and finally met with the infidels of Quraish. At that occasion Muslims had different views against them, some said they became infidels and some said they were still Muslims. These were the people who after becoming Muslims migrated to Makkah and wrote to the holy Prophet (Slm) that they are still Muslims and we left you only because of the harsh climate of Madinah.

روى ان قوما من المنافقين استاذنوا رسول الله صلى عليه وسلم فى الخروج الى البدو معتلين باجتواء المدينة فلما خرجوا لم يزالوا را حدين مرحلة حتى الحقوا بالمشركين فاختلف المسلمون فيهم فقال بعضهم هم كفار وقال بعضهم هم مسلمون وقيل كانوا قوما هاجرو من مكة ثم بداء لهم فرجعوا وكتبوا الى رسول الله صلى الله عليه وسلم انا على دينك وما اخرجنا الا اجتواء المدينة والاشتياق الى بلدنا .

D. Imam Fakhr Razi (Rz) had commented under the verse 'fama lakum fil munafiqeena' that:

6. The verse is revealed against those Quraish who became muslim and migrated to Madinah. They resided there till Allah desired; then they asked permission from the holy Prophet(Slm) to go to Ba'diah, a place near to a jungle. On getting permission, they started going till they reached Makkah, on that, some Muslims said that those people are still muslim like us, and they would have surely borne on such difficulties as we are bearing in Madinah, and some people have the opinion that they had converted and became hypocrites. In order to settle the difference of opinion among Muslims, Allah ordained by informing that "why should you fight about those people who have deceived you and became hypocrites."

انها نزلت فى قوم قدموا على النبى صلى الله عليه وسلم و آله مسلمين فاقاموا بالمدينة ماشاء الله ثم قالوا يا رسول الله نزيد ان نخرج الى الصحراء فاذن لنا فيه فاذن لهم فلما خرجوا لم يزالوا يرحلون مرحلة مرحلة حتى لحقوا بالمشركين فتكلم المومنون فيهم فقال بعضهم لو كانوا مسلمين مثلنا لبقوا معنا وصبروا كما صبرنا وقال قوم هم مسلمون وليس لنا ان ننشيهم الى الكفر الى ان يظهر امرهم فبين الله تعالى نفافقهم فى هذه الآية .

E. Jalaluddin Seyouti(Rz) had mentioned these traditions under the commentary of this verse:'munafiqeena' that:

7. Imam Ahmed Bin Hunbal(Rz) has reported from Abdul Rahman bin Aouf(Rz) that a group of Arabs came to the holy Prophet(Slm) in Madinah, and accepted Islam, but they pretended that they have been affected by the epidemic fever of Madinah, thus they left Madinah. Some Muslims met with them when they left Madinah and asked as to why they had gone from Madinah, they told that on account of epidemic fever we came back. The Muslims asked them whether they did not believe in the beneficence of the holy Prophet(Slm). Thus some of the Muslims branded them as hypocrites and others still believed that they were muslims. On this differences of opinion Allah revealed the verse stating "why you have difference of opinion about those people who had become infidels.

اخرج احمد بسند فيه انقطاع عن عبدالرحمن بن عوف ان قوما من العرب اتوا رسول الله صلى الله عليه وسلم بالمدينة فاسلموا واصابهم وباء المدينة حماها فاركسوا خرجوا من المدينة فاستقبلهم نفر من الصحابة فقالوا لهم مالكم رجعتم قالوا اصابنا وباء المدينة فقالوا امالكم فى رسول الله اسوة حسنة فقال بعضهم نافقوا وقال بعضهم لم ينافقوا انهم مسلمون فانزل الله فما لكم فى المنافقين فئتين الآية .

Ibn Abi Hatim (Rz) had commented with some difference about the statement of Abi Salma bin Abdul Rahman(Rz).

8. A group of Arabs migrated towards Madinah to meet the holy Prophet (Slm). They lived in the company of holy Prophet till Allah desired: then they became frustrated (on account of the climate of Madinah) and went back to Makkah and met their relatives. Some companions of the holy Prophet (Slm) recognised them and questioned them as to what problem made them to come back to Makkah. They lied to the companions. On that some of the companions branded them as hypocrites and some had opined that they were still Muslims, however their hypocrisy became known through the verse which was revealed about their status: "why you should have a difference of opinion about those who had converted and became hypocrites.

اخرج ابن ابى حاتم من وجه آخر عن ابى سلمة بن عبدالرحمن ان نفرا من طوائف العرب هاجروا الى رسول الله صلى الله عليه وسلم فمكثوا معه ما شاء الله ان يمكثوا ثم ارتكسوا فرجعوا الى قومهم فلقوا سرية من اصحاب رسول الله صلى الله عليه وسلم فعرفوهم قالوا هم ماردكم فاعتلوا لهم فقال بعض القوم لهم نافقتم فلم يزل بعض ذالك حتى' فشا فيهم القول فنزلت هذه الآية فما لكم فى المنافقين فئتين .

From the above commentaries it is clear that a group of people who accepted Islam and migrated to Madinah, and then went back to Makkah on false pretension that they want to go to

Makkah to bring some amount for establishing trade in Madinah, but really they went back to Makkah and after meeting their relatives they converted and became hypocrites. Therefore Allah's command came to the holy Prophet that:

"Thus do not make friend from any one of them until they migrate for the cause of Allah. If they evade, then catch them and slaughter them whereever you find them. Do not make them friend or helpers any more (to you)". (4:89)

فلا تتخذوا منهم اولياء حتىٰ يهاجروا فى سبيل الله فان تولوا فخذوهم واقتلوهم حيث وجدتموهم ولا تتخذوا منهم وليا ولا نصيرا (النساء ع ١٢)

Thus Allah's clear mandate had come to imprison them and kill them as a punishment for their evasion from migration. Thus in the case of Shakker Khatoon also the same verdict of Allah befits on her and her companions, therefore, Imamana's advice to Shah Nizam (Rz) "not to refund their money, and use for yourself" was a lawful decision, since they became hypocrite. Thus Imamana's orders could not be objected. Further, Imamana (As) had also decreed about Shakker Khatoon and others as hypocrites as per "Shawahedul Vilayet" which Decree is correct according to Qur'an. For example: It is a sin not to fast (during Ramzan), but after fasting, breaking before time is a severe sin. Same way, although not to convert to Islam is a sin, but after becoming Muslim, reverting back becomes a greater sin whose punishment is killing. This is also the case of migration. After performing migration, reverting back is a great sin. Allah's decree is to imprison them and kill them where ever they were found.

Now the question is, whether Migration has been mandated for all times? We have already discussed that orders of Qur'an are universal without limitation of time and space. If reasons for Migration became known then migration is an obligation and it is continued till the Day of Judgment. Whereas specific migration had been discontinued. Imam Fakhr-e-Razi (Rh) had opined that:

"Hasan (Rz) had said that migration is not terminated. Now the assertion of the holy Prophet (Slm) that after the conquest of Makkah there is no migration, refers to that specific migration. This migration was terminated after the conquest of Makkah."

قال الحسن الهجرة غير منقطعة ابدا واما قوله عليه السلام لا هجرة بعد الفتح فالمراد الهجرة المخصوصة فانها انقطعت بالفتح

When Migration is not terminated for ever then all orders regarding this are applicable. Hence, it is very irreligious to say that Imamana's direction to confiscate her amount can not be branded as "Rude", because Shakker Khatoon turned away from migration after starting it. This confiscation of her money was a punishment to her, therefore it is malicious on the part of the author of Hadia to remark the order of Imamana (As) as a "Rude" one.

2. Kisan-e-Mahdi to meet Jesus Christ:

Miyan Vali Yousuf (Rh) had narrated in chapter 18 of his "Insaf Nama" that:

A. When asked whether companions of Mahdi (As) would meet Jesus Christ (As)? Imamana (As) had confirmed it. Question was regarding companions; but answer was given about Kisan.

B. In chapter 19 it is stated that all the Muhajirs, particularly Bandagi Miyan Syed Mahmood (Rz), Bandagi Miyan Syed Khundmir (Rz), Bandagi Shah Nemat (Rz), Bandagi Shah Dilawer (Rz) and others wanted to know whether Kisan-e-Mahdi (As) would meet Jesus Christ (As)? Answer was given by Imamana (As) in positive.

Author of Hadia had objected that from these narrations it comes to light that during the period of the companions of Mahdi (As), Jesus Christ (As) would emerge, but actually it did not happen?

From both narrations stated above it was confirmed that Imamana (As) had prophesied about the Kisan-e-Mahdi (As) who would meet Jesus Christ (As). Here the word Kisan is used in an absolute sense, directly and indirectly both inclusive. If Kisan-e-Mahdi (As) denotes to companions of Mahdi (As) then the explanation of that narration is a prophecy. The same has been asserted by the holy Prophet (Slm) that:

"What would be your position when Esa (As) would descend among you?"
كيف انتم اذانزل فيكم ابن مريم الىٰ آخره

The Arabic word "Fikum" points to the companions of the Prophet (Slm). Could any body object about the tradition that the holy Prophet (Slm) had informed about the descending of Jesus Christ (As) among the companions of the holy Prophet (As)? However, Imam Ahmed Hanbal (Rh) had referred Hazrat Abu Huraira (Rz) as telling:

"The holy Prophet (Slm) informed that whoever would be alive among them, had a chance of meeting Esa (As)."
عـن النبى صلى الله عليه و سلم قال يوشک من عاش منكم ان يلقى عيسىٰ ابن مريم الىٰ آخره

In this tradition the words "Mun Aash" denote to" whoever would be alive". It does not say about Ummah, but it refers to the companions of the Prophet (Slm) only. Thus the manner in which the explanation had been given for that tradition, the same answer shall be for the assertion of Imamana (As), because this question relates to a period of Jesus Christ (As) when he would descend.

The assertion mentioned in" Insaf Nama" is a translation of the tradition. Both the holy Prophet (Slm) and Imamana (As) knew that Jesus Christ (As) would descend before the Day of Judgment. Therefore they have predicted that their followers would be available till the descention of Jesus Christ (As). Author of "Insaf Nama" in its chapter 17 had narrated that:

"Asserted by Imamana (As) that Beneficence of Mahdi (As) shall last till the Doomsday." Imamana (As) asserted: "Mahdi and Mahdavis ta Qam-e-qiamat bashand". Meaning ""Mahdi (As) and Mahdavis shall be living till the day of Judgment."
"نقـل است که حضرت ميراں" فرمودند پس از بنده تاقيامت فيض مهدى باشد"

This assertion predicts Mahdavia Faith would last till the Day of Judgment.

Miyan Sheik Mustafa Gujrati (Rh) had written in his letter that Imamana (As) had asserted that our people would live till the Doomsday. From this assertion two points emerge: One is that Mahdavia Faith would last till the Doomsday; second: the word Kisan denotes to Mahdavis. It is not particular for the companions.

"Dafter-e-Shah Burhan" narrates that:

"Imamana (As) had narrated that our people, mostly from the group of Brother Syed Khundmir (Rz), would be living till the Doomsday."

نقل است حضرت امامؑ فرمودند که کسان ما تاقام قیامت باشند در گروه برادرم سید خوندمیر (دفتر اول رکن هشم باب سوم)

Naqliat-e-Miyan Syed Aalam" reports Imamana's assertion that:

"My people would meet Esa (As) and my Beneficence would last till Doomsday."

کسان من با عیسیٰ ملاقات کنند و فیض من تا قیامت بماند

The same is mentioned in "Hashia-e-Sharief":

"My people would meet Esa (As) and my Beneficence shall last till Doomsday"

کسان از من ملاقات کنند فیض بنده تا قیامت بماند

These assertions clarify that the word "Kisan" is used for Mahdavis in general and not for companions particularly.

3. Descending of Esa (As) is near:

""Bandagi Miyan Syed Khundmir (Rz) said that once he was sitting with Imamana (As) at night and asked Imamana (As) as to when Isa (As) would come. Imamana (As) told "near". I asked whether after sixty years since his departure. Imamana (As) again said "Near". Then asked over fifty years, the answer was "near". Then asked after forty years, Answer was"near". Then questioned after 30 years. Answer was "near". Then Imamana (As) said " Here is Isa (As), ask him". Bandagi Miyan (Rz) said that he spoke to Hazrat Isa (As) on many subjects, but forgot to ask as to when he would arrive?"

بندگی میان فرمودند که امشب به توجه تمام نشسته بودم بچشم حضرت میران رامیدیدم وپر سیدم که میرانجیو مهتر عیسیٰ کدام وقت بیایند ، میران فرمودند که نزدیك ، پس از شما شصت سال یایند فرمودند که نزدیك باز پرسیدم که پس از شما پنجاه سال ، باز فرمودند که نزدیك باره پرسیدم پس از شماده سال باز فرمودند که نزدیك اینك مهتر عیسیٰ حاضر اند بهر سید میان فرمودند که بنده مهتر عیسیٰ رابسیار چیز ها پرسیدم این فراموش شد که شما کے خواهید آمد

It was a divination reported by Bandagi Miyan (Rz). On such divination raising objections is nothing but a malice and trying to negate it, is mere foolishness. Further, his remark is meaningless that why Bandagi Miyan (Rz) questioned about six times, since Imamana's answer was "Near" for those questions. It has an analog according to Qur'an and traditions. Allah says:

A."Perhaps Doomsday is near" 14

(الف) لعل الساعة قريب (الشورىٰ ع ١)

B.Perhaps Doomsday is near.(33:63)

(ب) لعل الساعة تكون قريباً (الاحزاب ع ٨)

These verses denote that Doomsday is near, the holy Prophet (Slm) said:

"The day of my Advent and the Doomsday are like these two fingers.' (He showed his two joint fingers.)."

بعثت انا والساعة كهاتين و يقرن بين اصبعيه السبابة والوسطى

This tradition tells that the nearness of the Doomsday is obvious like the joint fingers that is to say very near. Traditionalists have agreed that emergence of Anti Christ and appearance of Jesus Christ (As) are the two major signs of the Doomsday. Therefore the author of "Mishkat"had stated that "Deputation of the holy Prophet (Slm) and appearance of Jesus Christ (As) both are very near". After one thousand years in the episode of Divination, it was stated that appearance of Jesus Christ (As) was near. That is correct according to the holy Qur'an and the traditions. To raise objections on that episode tantamount to raise objection on the Qur'an and the traditions, which is clearly his irreligiousness. Now, the fault finder utters that:

"The questioner was familiar with the disposition; then why should he go reducing from 60,50,40,30; he could have asked a single number. The answer from Miran (As) would be nearer only. It has nothing to do with temperament. The answer was given according to the Qur'an and traditions. Imamana's repeating the word "near" directs us to keep the faith that the appearance of Jesus Christ (As) is near which may happen near to the Doomsday and this word, "Near" is the translation of the Arabic word "Qareeb"and if anything is said according to Qur'an and traditions and if branded as rude, it merely points out to be a hypocrisy on the part of the fault finder. Thus that assertion only confirms the Appearance of Jesus Christ (As) is near, which is correct according to Qur'an and Traditions.

(Note:It is a warning to be ready with your wherewithals for final requital by Allah. And it is a fact that the final hour may come any time sooner than imagined. It is also a fact that the day of a man's death is his Doomsday as the saying goes, no-one knows his or her last day when would come?)

The holy Prophet (Slm) had informed about the appearance of Hazrat Isa (AS), he too had said "near", Imam Ahmed Hanbal (Rz) had reported that:

"The Prophet (Slm) had said that it is very near and whoever would be living, he would meet Isa son of Maryam (As)."

عن النبى عليه السلام قال يوشک من عاش منكم ان يلقى عيسىٰ ابن مريم الى آخره

Whether on the basis of this tradition anybody would object that no body would meet Jesus Christ (As)? "The "Insaf Nama" tells about "near"and tradition refers "Youshak"; thus whatever had been reported in "Insaf Nama" interprets the tradition.

4. Imam's Prophecy and His Demise:

Qazi, a public speaker, inquired Imamana (As) about Imamana's day of birth, day on which he proclaimed his Mahdiat and the day of his demise: Imamana (As) answered : "Monday".

Objection is raised that according to "Matleul Vilayet", the day of demise of Imamana (As) had been mentioned as "Thursday". Thus Imamana's prophecy seems to have been wrong:

"Nobody knows what he would earn tomorrow and nobody knows on which land he would die"

ما تدری نفس ماذاتکسب غدا و ما تدری نفس بای ارض تموت

As regards day of demise all books of biography are not unanimous. For example "Matleul Vilayet" and "Shawahedul Vilayet" reported "Thursday" as the day of Imamana's demise. Other books are unanimous on date of demise was 19th. Zi Qaeda 910 H, but there exists disagreement regarding the day of demise. The oldest biography"Moulood" written by Miyan Abdul Rahman (Rh) mentioned the day being "Monday" and "Khatim-e-Sulaimani" too agrees on "Monday" being the day of his demise:

"As narrated, Monday afternoon had been confirmed as the day of demise."

وبروایتے وقت ضحیٰ یوم الاشنین هذا القول فی اسناده صحیح

Thus the objection was wrong. Such differences are not new. There is a difference even on the day of demise of the holy Prophet (Slm) also. Author of "Ash'atul Lam'aat" had referred Ibn Jozi (Rz) who had written in "Kitbul Wafat" that:

"In the beginning illness started in the month of Safar when just two days left and he passed away on 12th. Rabiul Awwal."

ابن جوزی در کتاب الوفا گفته که ابتدائ مرض در شهر صفر بوده که دو شب از آن مانده بود وفات وے دو از دهم ربیع الاول بود

"Sulaiman Timi who was a social worker said with determination that the illness started on Saturday the 22nd. Safar and passed away on Monday the 2nd. Rabiul Awwal and that had been confirmed."

و سلیمان تیمی که یکی از ثقات است جزم کرده است بآں که ابتداے مرض در روز شنبه بود بسیت و دوم صفر و وفات در روز دوشنبه دوم ربیع الاول والله اعلم و این قول را ترجیح داده اند

If 2nd. Rabbiul Awwal was Monday then 12th. Rabbiul Awwal falls on Thursday. Thus there is a difference not only for the day, but for the date also, whereas Mahdavia literature just differ on the question of the day, but the date is confirmed with all sources. If there is a difference in narration, on the basis of narrators, objector cannot put blame on Imamana (As).

No person except Allah determines the date of demise and those who could predict they do it on the strength of inspiration from Allah alone. It is a fact that the holy Prophet (Slm) had predicted about his demise when he was addressing at Hajjatul Wida, it is reported in "Uqdul Fareed" that:

"Oh the people! Listen to me what I am saying to you that I do not know whether would I meet you next year at this place?."

ایها الناس اسمعوا منی ابین لکم فانی لا ادری لعلی لا القاکم بعد عامی هذا فی موقفی هذا

Whether this assertion of the holy Prophet (Slm) should become a point of objection for the author of Hadia too?

However Seyuoti (Rz) had written some assertions of the holy Prophet (Slm) in his "Alqasasul Kubra":

A. "Abu Nayeem had narrated what Maqall Bin Yasar (Rz) had heard the holy Prophet (Slm) telling that: "from all of the portions of the world, Madinah is my migrated place and also the resting place."

اخرج ابو نعيم عن معقل بن يسار قال قال رسول (ا)
الله صلى الله عليه و سلم المدينة مهاجرى و مضجعى
من الارض

Another tradition is:

B. "Zubair Bin Bakkar (Rz) had narrated about Hasan (Rz) who heard the holy Prophet (Slm) telling that: "Madinah is the place of my migration and Madinah shall be the place where I shall die which is my resting place". Further he also reported the same version from Ata Bin Yasar (Rz)"

اخرج الزبير بن بكار فى اخبار المدينة عن (ب)
الحسن قال رسول الله عليه و سلم المدينة مهاجرى و
بها وفاتى و منها محشرى و اخرج ايضاً من مرسل عطا
بن يسار مثله

C. The Prophet (Slm) had also predicted that his burial place shall be near the Masjid-e-Nabavi as had been reported by Imam Ahmed Hunbal (Rz):

"The holy Prophet (Slm) informed: "Oh Muaz, it is certain that shortly you would not find me after this year and perhaps you may pass through my grave in this masjid."

يا معاذ انك عسى ان لا تلقانى بعد عامى هذا
ولعلك ان تمر بمسجدى هذا و قبرى

The scholars wanted to know the days of birth and demise of Imamana (AS) because they knew the days of birth and demise of the holy Prophet (Slm) as reported by Seyuoti, that:

"Ibn Asaker (Rz) heard from Mak'hool (Rz) who heard the holy Prophet (Slm) was telling to Bilal: "Do not leave fast on Monday because I was born on Monday and I received revelation on Monday and I migrated on Monday and I shall die on Monday."

اخرج ابن عساكر عن مكحول ان رسول الله صلى
الله عليه و سلم قال لبلال الا لا تغادر صيام الا ثنين
فانى ولدت يوم الا ثنين و اوحى الى يوم الا ثنين و
هاجرت يوم الاثنين واموت يوم الاثنين

Day of Imamana's Demise:

As had been mentioned, the holy Prophet (Slm) had indicated the place of his burial, and the day of his demise. According to Ibn Jozi's narration the holy Prophet (Slm) passed away on 12th. Rabbiul Awwal and according to Sulaiman Taimi (Rz) it was 2nd. Rabbiul Awwal

Monday, and 12th. Rabbiul Awwal was Thursday. The news given by the holy Prophet (Slm) regarding his day of demise could not be objected because 12th was not accepted generally to be the date of his demise. This fact is seconded by author of "Ifadatul Ifham" that:

There is a difference even about the date of demise. Some say it was 2nd. Rabbiul Awwal, some say 13th,. And some say 14th.

As regards Imamana's date of demise being Monday, was correctly mentioned by the oldest source of Miyan Abdul Rahman (Rh) in his "Moulood" . However, there appear to be differences regarding the day of demise, which are insignificant in view of the oldest biography"Moulood". Therefore raising objection on Imamana (As) is baseless and futile.

Nasikh-o-Mansookh

A detailed discussion is available in chapter six.

5. Accusation of Tampering Qur'an:

Author of Hadia had accused that in Mahdvia Faith even they tried to tamper the holy Qur'an and presented some such verses through which good tidings had been given by Imamana (As) to particular companions. The author of Hadia does not know even the meaning of tampering, otherwise he would not have made silly objections of indictment to the good tidings which are mentioned in the holy Qur'an to his companions.

The circumstances of the revelation is misunderstood by telling that it is the cause of the revelation of a particular verse, but actually the revelation points out the state of affairs and position of the people at a proper time, according to Moulvi Hameeduddin, previous principal of Darul Uloom.

Therefore Imamana's giving good tidings to his companions by applying meanings of some verses does not mean a contradiction to the circumstances of the revelations and it should not be mischievously branded as tampering.

Mullah Mohsin Kashani has written his "Tafseer-e-Shafi", in its preamble he states that:

"When this verse was read before Ali Abu Abdullah (Rz) they say "O Lord provide us coolness of our eyes through our wives and siblings and provide one Imam from us" then, Abu Abdullah (Rz) asked what they requested was a superb thing to make Imam from the pious people, then they ask Ibn-e-Rasululah (Rz) in what manner this verse was revealed, he told "wajal Lana lilmuttaqeena Imama" (make one Imam from us of the pious people).

قـرى على ابى عبدالله الذين يقولون ربناهب لنا مـن ازواجـنا و ذرياتنا قرة اعين واجعلنا للمتقين امامـا فقـال ابـو عبدالله عليه السلام لقد سالوا الـلـه عـظيما ان يجعلهم للمتقين اماما فقيل له يا ابـن رسـول الـلـه كيف نـزلـت فقال انما نزلت واجعل لنا من المتقين اماما .

It is obvious from this narration of Sheites that according to the verse"WA Ja'alna "Lil" Muttaqeena Imama" was tampered by the words "Wajal "Lana Min al" Muttaqeena Imama."

If the book "Fasal Fil Tahreef Kitab Rubbul- Arba'a", written by Shia Muhaddis Noori, had the objector read that book, he would not have accused Mahdavis for the tampering the verses of Qur'an.

A. The objector had referred to a narration regarding Bandagi Miyan Syed Mahmood (Rz), the verse being "Fa Aowha Ila Abdihi", but it is not recorded in"Tazkeratul Saleheen". Through this a good tiding was given to Bandagi Miyan Syed Mahmood (Rz) to have delectable experience of the Prophethood.

B. For Bandagi Miyan Syed Khundmir (Rz) the verse "Al Kauser" had been referred which suggests that the beneficence of Shah-e-Khundmir (Rz) shall flow like a canal.

C. The verse "Allahu Noorus Sama Wati Wal Arz" referred to Bandagi Miyan Syed Khundmir (Rz) who gets Beneficence without any connection (direct from Allah).

D. Bandagi Miyan Syed Khundmir (Rz) was given the good tidings of "Sultanun Naseer" (Help - provider).

Author of Hadia took "Sultanun Naseer" in the sense of" Owner of a kingdom" which is wrong, because the word "Sultan" had come in the Qur'an at various places, but it was not used at any time"Sultan" for a "king . Hence "Sultanun Naseer" means "Helper of Mehdi (As)".

Allah tells about the companions of the holy Prophet."

"(They) Help Allah and his Rasool (Slm)"(59:8)	ينصرون الله و رسوله (حشر ع ١)

"Tafseer-e- Madarik" comments on this verse that:

"That is to say they provide help to Allah's religion and assist His Rasool (Slm)."	اى ينصرون دين الله و يعينون رسوله

The holy Qur'an testifies that the companions of the Prophet (Slm) were the (Ansars) helpers of the holy Prophet (Slm). Therefore if Bandagi Miyan (Rz) who was the companion of Imamana (As) if declared as "Nasir-e-Mahdi (As)" Helper of the Imam (As)" what is wrong in it? Particularly when in the"Naqliat-e-Miyan Syed Aalam", Bandagi Miyan Syed Khundmir (Rz) was granted the tidings of "Nasir-e-Deen" Helper of religion"

D. Imamana (As) had also given the tidings of "Hamalahul Insaan" to Bandagi Miyan (Rz).

Author of Hadia had raised three objections on it:

No.1. Imamana (As) had commented about this verse, by mentioning "Samawat" to the prophets, for "Arz" "aulia" and for "Jibal" to scholars. This is not against the Arabian proverb or idiom.

"Naquliat-e-Miyan Syed Aalam" refer about the good tidings of Imamana (As) to Bandagi Miyan (Rz):

"Allah's assertion" "Man lifted the burden of Vilayet-e-Mustafavi", Imamana(As) informred Bandagi Miyan that Man is You".(Bhai Syed Khundmir)"

قوله تعالیٰ حملها الانسان این نیز ذات شما است

Here Samawat had not been referred for the Prophets.

Whereas in the "Tazkeratus Saleheen" it is stated that:

"It is reported that Hazrat Miran (As) had referred the verse "Hamalahul Insan" in favor of Bandagi Miyan Syed Khundmir (Rz)."

نقل است حضرت میراںؑ آیت حملها الانسان در حق بندگی میان خواندند (باب اول)

When the assertions of Imamana (As) have no reference to prophets, Aulia and scholars, then how can anybody raise such silly objections against a person who had not referred them at all. However, for the sake of discussion even if we agree, then also it should not be a point of objection, since the meanings of "Samawat" may be taken as "height", here Sky is not taken particularly. Then it may be taken as the "prophets" who were being benefited from the "extra-sensory height" of the invisible world. Now the word "Arz" comes which may be taken for the "people of the world". For example: Allah has referred "Ahl-e-Qaria (village)" in Sura "Yousuf". Author of "Mu'aheb Aliah"has commented with reference to this verse, by using the words "Residents of land and mountains." Then for the residents of land and mountains means "Aulia and scholars" which is applicable, then what is the harm in it? Author of Hadia's objection is that such explanation of the verse is against the Arabic idioms. When the Arabic idiom for "KURSI" (chair) refers to "Knowledge", then what is the harm in applying "prophets for Samawat" and "Aulia and scholars" as residents of land and mountains.

Author of "Kashshaf" had written regarding "Wasi-a-Kursi-e-hus samawat wal Arz" that:

"And knowledge was given the name of "Kursi."

و سمی العلم کرسیا

Author of Madarik has written for "Wasia Kursia" that:

"His Kursi means His knowledge."

ای علمه

Author of 'Ad-Durre Manshoor" had reported that Ibn-e-Abbas (Rz) said about 'Kursi' means 'Ilm' (knowledge).

Author of "Muahebul Aliah" had written that:

"Allah's Ilm (Knowledge) has surrounded the skies and everything in and between the earth and the skies."

فراگرفته است علم اوهمه آسمان هاراو انچه در آن است

Thus Kursi has been mentioned as Knowledge. When Kursi has been mentioned as knowledge and it is not against the Arabic Idiom, then what is the harm in mentioning "Samawat" (Skies) for prophets".

Author of Hadia's seconds objection is that: in the said Verse "Innahu Kana Zalooman Jahoola"points out for disgrace, therefore Imamana's tiding to Bandagi Miyan (Rz) was unfair.

On the other hand Imam Fakhr-e-Razi (Rz) had said about this verse that the angels had suspected about man that he would become tyrant on the basis of his ignorance. Fakhr-e-Razi's statement is this:

"It was a fact that the angels suspected man may become a tyrant on account of his ignorance."

انه كان ظلوما جهولا فى ظن الملائكه

Author of "Muahib Aliah" had said that: "In chapter 46 "Ahqaf"(of Qur'an) it had been mentioned that man's tyranny and ignorance is before the mankind and not before Allah."

دراحقاف آورده كه ظلول و جهول است نزد خلق نه نزد حق

Ruhul Arwah" mentions that: "Tyranny and ignorance is not a disgrace, but praise."

ظلو موجهولا اينجا مدح است نه ذم

It is clear that man was a tyrant on account of his passions and was ignorant about other things for his lack of knowledge, then how these faculties of a man be taken as a disgrace?

Author of Hadia's third objection is that Trust (Amaanat) had been taken as martyrdom. On the other hand in Mahdavia literature: Trust is meant "vision of Allah" as well as "martyrdom" both had been accepted as its meanings. Author of Madarik had written about it that:

"Trust means obedience of Allah."

يريد بالا مانة الطاعة لله

The final purpose of obedience is "vision of Allah" and the final purpose of acceptence is "to be assassinated" for the cause of Allah. Thus Shah Khundmir (Rz) was proficient about his both excellences. Thus he had the vision of Allah, and he was martyred for the cause of Religion. According to the "Daftar-e-Burhan", part one, chapter 4, that day (14th. Shawwal, the day of martyrdom of Hazrat Bandagi Miyan (Rz) is known as the day of "Nearness to Allah i.e; Yaumul Fatha".)

(Note: What we have read earlier is that battle started on 12th.Shawwal 930 H. It is a historian proven fact that on that day Hzt.Bdagi Miyn(Rz) defeated the Enemy and that day was declared as "Youmil Fatha" which day is still being observed as Youmul Fatha by Mahdavis of different places. In Hydrabad Hazt. Mohmmed Miyan Saheb of Akhaili(Rh) started to celebrate 12th. Shawwal as the "Youmul Fatha" by inviting hundreds for the dinner in his Masjid at Chanchalgud. Hence to designate 14th.Shawwal as "Youmuil Fatha, contradicts earlier statemdent, therefore 12th.Shawwal should be rtecognized as the "Youmul Fatha".)

Bandagi Miyan's martyrdom had occurred according to the tradition mentioned in "Kitabul Fitan" by Nayeem Bin Hammad (Rz) that after 20 years from the date of demise of Imam Mahdi (As), one person would be killed by the sword. The words of the tradition is as mentioned below:

"" (That person) would have Mahdi's faculties, shall live for 20 years, then his demise would come through the sword"

عـلـى سيرة المهدى بقاء ٥ عشرين سنة ثم يموت قتيلا بالسلاح (كتاب الفتن)

The details have already been discussed earlier and it has a backing of the tradition of Nisai.

A. Abu Huraira (Rz) narrated that the holy Prophet (Slm) had pointed out about the "Battle of Hind". Thus "If I (as Abu Huraira (Rz) wished) get the chance (to take part in it) I shall sacrifice myself along with my property and shall have the distinction to be included in the list of supreme martyrs, and if returned alive, then I shall be that Abu Huraira (Rz) who had been freed from the fire of the Hell." (Sunan-e-Nisai, printed in Lahore, volume 2, p. 32).

B. Soban, the slave of the holy Prophet (Slm) told, he heard the holy Prophet (Slm) was telling that there would be two groups in my Ummah, both would be saved by Allah from the Hellfire who would fight in India and the other would be with Hazrat Isa (As)."(Sanan-e-Nisaai page 34, volume 2, printed in Lahore.)"

Both "Kitabul Fitan" and "Sunan-e-Nisai" if read together it comes to light that advent of Imam Mahdi (As) should take place in India, and the news of a battle which would take place after 20 years was such a supreme battle about which Hazrat Abu Huraira (Rz), a very righteous personality had expressed his desire to be martyred in it .

Thus Imamana's giving good tidings to his companions is in no way to be considered as a literal or intrinsic distortion and neither it can be said to be rude ones.

Ibn Abdul Birr (Rz) reported about Mua'z bin Ibn Jabal (Rz) that:

"Narrated Shu'bi to Fadwa Bin Nofil al Ashjaee and Masrooq who reported that I was sitting with Ibnul Masood who told that really Muaaz (Rz) was very powerful and obedient to the Almighty, lived in seclusion, never associated anyone with Allah. Thus I told him 'oh Muaaz! Allah had stated that "Inna Ibrahim Kana Ummathun qaanatallahi Hanifa". Thus Ibn Masood repeated and said. When Muaaz (Rz) heard him repeating the same, I recognized that he had purposely read, so I kept quiet. Then he asked me: "do you know what is Ummah and what is Qaanat"? I answered Allah knows better. He told that Ummat is that which teaches virtues and whose leadership must be recognised and followed. Qaanat is the one who is obedient to Allah. In this manner Muaaz (Rz) Ibn Jabal used to preach virtues and was obedient to Allah and his apostle."

روى الشعبى عن فروه بن نوفل الاشجعى ومسروق ولفظ الحديث لفروه الاشجعى قال ان معاذا كان امة قانتالله حنيفا ولم يكن من المشركين فقالا ياابا عبدالرحمٰن انما قال الله تعالىٰ ان ابراهيم كان امة قانتالله حنيفا فعاد قوله ان معاذا فلما رايته اعاد عرفت انه تعمد الا مرفسكت فقال اتدرى ما الامة وماالقانت قلت والله اعلم قال الامة الذى يعلم الخير ويوتم به يقتدئ والقانت المطيع لله وكذلك معاذ ابن جبل معلما ومطيعالله ولرسوله

The same version had come in "Madarijul Nabuwwat" and at its end it is written that:

"Thus Ibn Masood told that he had not forgotten and I had compared him to the Prophet Ibrahim (As) and we also used to compare Muaaz (Rz) to Prophet Ibrahim (As)."

پس گفت ابن مسعود فراموش نه كرده ام بلكه بطريق تشبيه معاذ به حضرت ابراهيم عليه السلام گفته ام وبوديم ماكه تشبيه ميداديم معاذ رابا ابراهيم

Holy Prophet (Slm) had used the words "Khairul Baria" (Best of the creation) for Hazrat Ibrahim (As). Inspite of this to read "Inna Muaza Kana Ummat" is neither the literal distortion nor distortion in the meaning. So, can it be taken as a distortion, if Imamana (As) gave the "Glad Tidings" to his companions with reference to any of the verses of the holy Qur'an?

Thus the author of Hadia could not differentiate between comparison and distortion.

What Shah Dilawer (Rz) had commented about " Yalad WA yulad" will be disused in Part 3, under the chapter "Characters of Shah Dilawer (Rz)".

Traditions and Sufis:

Author of"Insaf Nama" in chapter one had stated that Mulla Moinuddin Patni had sent two scholars to Imamana (As) with some questions, the third question was that:

"You prefer Vilayat (Sainthood) over Nabuwwat (prophet hood); Imamana (AS) answered that he did not tell, but the holy Prophet (Slm) himself had said that his Vilayet is supreme to his Nabuwwat. The mullahs said that Rasool's vilayet is supreme to his Nabauwwat, not of any other person's. Imamana (As) asked them "had I ever uttered that I am supreme to the holy Prophet (Slm)?."

شما ولايت را برنبوت فضل ميدهيد گفتند بنده
مى دهد يا رسول الله فرموده اند الولايت افضل
من النبوة ملايان گفتند كه ولايت نبى برنبوت
فاضل است نه ولايت ديگرے فرمودند بنده كه ام
وقت گفته است كه بنده را بر نبى فضل است
الىٰ آخره

Author of Hadia had translated the above tradition in these words:

"Al-Vilayet is supreme to Nabuwwat. "It is not a tradition and it was not proved as a tradition from any book of the traditions". Imamana's answer has two parts. He was asked by the Mullahs "whether he had preferred Vilayet over Nabuwwat"?, Actually it was said by the holy Prophet (Slm) himself. Hence as a matter of fact, by implications, it is clear that the holy Prophet (Slm) had himself asserted about his vilayet.

In the second part the faith of the mystic scholars has been described that they too accepted Vilayet to be supreme over Nabuwwat. Mulla Abdul Rahman Jami (Rh) had narrated in "Shawahedul Nabuwwat" that:

"If you hear any Godly man or any narration is heard through him (the Godly Man) that "Vilayet is supreme to Nabuwwat", then his intent is nothing but to say that Nabi's Vilayet is supreme to his Nabuwwat."

اذاسمعت احدا من اهل الله اوينقل اليک انه قال
الولايت اعلىٰ من النبوة فليس يريد ذلک الا ان ولاية
النبى اعلى من نبوته

By telling "Al Vilayet Afzal Minan Nabuwwat," the faith of the mystics had been described; then how could it be ascertained that the words "Rasoolullah had said", points out to which tradition? As a matter of fact the supremacy of Vilayet over Nabuwwat is well known to the mystics and on account of its being famous, Imamana (As) had pointed it out specifically.

Syed Mohammad Ibn Jaferul Mulki (Rh) (Disciple of Khaja Naseeruddin, Chiragh-e-Dehalvi (Rh) in his "Bahrul Mua'ani's" letter No. 14 had written that:

"Thus, my friend: Moosa Kaleemullah (As) and Jesus Christ (As) had desired for the Vilayet of the holy Prophet (Slm), because the holy Prophet (Slm) had asserted that "Vilayet is my domain". Thus my friend, do not be in doubt, that I had given preference to Aulia over the Prophets."

پس اے محبوب اين خواستن موسىٰ كليم و تمنا
بردن عيسىٰ مسيح عليه السلام همين ولايت
حضرت رسالت عليه السلام است كه حضرت
خواجه عالم فرموده است الولايت منى و اے
محبوب گمان نبرى كه اوليا را برانبياء افضل
ميكنم

This narration is clear that "Al Vilayet Minni" is the tradition of the holy prophet (Slm). The letter of "Bahrul Mua'ani" was written in 824 H. This means to say that this tradition was well known and famous even before the birth of Imamana (As) (847 H.) that is why Imamana (AS) had just pointed out but not explained.

The venerability of Syed Mohammad Jaferul Makki (Rh), had been proved by Sheik Abdul Haq in his "Akhbarul Akhiyar" that:

"Syed Mohammad Ibn Jafer Al Makki ul Husaini (Rh) was one of the prominent disciples of Sheik (Khaja) Naseeruddin Mahmood (Rh). He had a high rank for his divine life and he was a perfect monotheist, and belongs to the Aoulias."	سیـد مـحمد ابن جعفر المکی الحسینی از اعاظم خلفائ شیـخ نـصیـر الـدین محمود است در توحید و تفرید مقام عالی وارد ، از افراد اولیاء است

Apart from this Syed Mohammed Ibn Jaferul Makki (Rh) has been benefited by obtaining beneficence from almost 382 Aoulias. "Bahrul Mua'ani's letter states:

"This faqeer after taking permission from his mentor, met 382 Aoulias and served them. Every one of them had gifted me one divine blessing. Those who seek apparent meanings and who like outward conditions, think it to be a very simple job."	ایـن فقیر بر حکم اجازت فرد حقیقت پیر خود قدس سره سیـصد وهشتا دودو ، ولی را دریافته ام و خدمت کرده ام و هـریـکی نـعمتی در حق این فقیر ارزانی داشته اندو اهل سـلوك ظـاهـر جـو واهـل ظـواهر دانسته اند که این کار آسان است

Author of Hadia's contention had been recorded previously, in which it was asserted that if any reliable mystic accepts any narration as a tradition, then no body should hesitate to recognize it as a tradition.

Now we have to ask the author of Hadia and his coterie whether Syed Mohammad Ibn Jafer Makki (Rh) can be regarded as a reliable mystic or not?

The book "Bahrul Mua'ani" in which the tradition "Al Vilayet Minni" is recorded, Sheik Abdul Haq had written that:

"Bahrul Mua'ani" is written by him, in which the intricacies of monotheism, the teachings of the mystics and the realities of Divinity had been recorded. These assertions are staggering."	اور اتصنیفی است مسمی به بحر المعانی دروے بسیارے از حقـایـق تـوحیـد و عـلـوم قوم و اسرار معرفت بیان کرده سخن را مستانه می گوید

Whether the statement of the Sheik Abdul Haq does not point out that those traditions which are recorded in it, are accepted by the mystics? However, the tradition "Al Vilayet Minni" was recorded by a reliable mystic which cannot be branded as untrue. Because traditions of the mystics are approved by all and the objector too had himself agreed that any tradition reported by a reliable Godly Man is acceptable. Shah Valiullah Dehalvi's assertion points out that the traditions of the mystics have the same status what the jurists have narrated. In "Hujjatul Balegha's seventh chapter he says that:

"Here is the fifth category of the traditions which pertains to the jurists, mystics, historians and people like them."

ههـنـا طبـقة خـامسة مـنها ما اشتهر على السنة الفقهاء والصوفية و المورخين و نحوهم

If the traditions of the mystics are rejected only because they do not relate to the books of the traditions, then all the narrations of the jurists should be rejected whose links are not available in those books of traditions (Sihah).

The meanings of "Al Vilayet Minni" are clear. The holy Prophet (Slm) in spite of being supreme among the prophets, did not refer to his Nabuwwat but asserted that Vilayet belongs to his person. Not referring to his Nabuwwat, but relating his Vilayet to himself speaks its supremacy and status of the Vilayet what it possesses, which can be judged by the statement referred in "Bahrul Mua'ani" regarding the desire of Musa Kaleemullah (As) and the Jesus Christ (As) to get beneficence from the holy Prophet's Vilayet.

According to "Insaf Nama", chapter 12:

"According to"Miratul Arifeen" some people tell that Vilayet is superior to Nabuwwat."

درمرأة الـعـارفـيـن آورده اسـت كه بعضى گويند الولايت افضل من النبوة

From this, it becomes clear that the author of "Insaf Nama" accepts "Al Vilayet Afzal Minal Nabuwwat" were narrated only because it was accepted by many venerable people. Whatever discussion we have made in this regard is correct. Imamana's answer in this connection has two issues: 1. Referring the tradition of "Al Vilayet Minni;" and 2. Faith of the mystics was stated.

Even if it is accepted that the narration of "Insaf Nama" "Al Vilayet Afzal Minal Nabuwwat" is nothing but a repetition of what the holy Prophet had asserted by telling "Rasoolullah (Slm) farmooda und", still there should arise no objection, because the opposing scholars have already accepted it. Here, what scholars say that, Prophet's Vilayet is superior to Prophet's Nabuwwat. Points out that they had accepted it as a tradition.

Ibrahim Bin Mohammad bin Arab Shah Asfaraini (Rh) had commented regarding "Sharah-e-Mulla Jami"that:

"Thus bringing Vali before Nabi as had been mentioned creates an indication that it is a tradition stating "Vilayet is superior to Nabuwwat."

ثم فى تقديم الولى على النبى حيث اشيربه اشارة دقيقة الى الماثور المشهور من ان الولاية افضل من النبوة

Ibrahim Bin Asfaraini is famous as Mullah Asamuddin. He was one of he student of Abdul Rahman Jaami. He passed away either in the year 943 or 951 H.

From this it is proved that even during the 10th. Century "Al Vilayet Afzal Minal Nabuwwat" had been accepted as a tradition, which was pointed out by Imamana (As) that it was an approved fact of even by the opponent who had also admitted this fact. Author of "Shawahedul Nabuwwat" had written that:

"Nabi had two status: one is Vilayet which is heart of Nabuwwat and the other is Nabuwwat which is a manifestation of Vilayet. Nabi obtains Blessings and Beneficence from Allah through Vilayet and transfers it through Nabuwwat (to the Ummah). There is no doubt the attention towards Allah, is more appreciable and far better than comparing to his attention towards the public. Thus for that reason, the status of Vilayet is superior to the status of the Nabuwwat."

نبی را دو جهت است یکی جهت ولایت که باطن نبوت است و دیگر جهت نبوت که ظاهر ولایت است و نبی به جهت ولایت از حق تعالیٰ عطا و فیض می ستاند و شک نیست که روے که در حق است سبحانه اشرف و افضل است ازروے که در خلق است پس مراد آن است که جهت ولایت نبی از جهت نبوت وے افضل است

Thus it is obvious and clear to assert that Vilayet of the Prophet (Slm) is superior to his Nabuwwat (prophet hood).

There are two narrations regarding Nabuwwat of the holy Prophet (Slm): The Prophet (Slm) himself informed that:

"At the time when Adam (As) was still in water and mud, I was designated as the last of the prophets."

(١) قال انی عند الله مکتوب خاتم النبین و ان آدم لمنجدل فی طینته

This narration is available in "Sharh-e-Sunnat" and Imam Ahmed Hunbal (Rz) also had narrated.

Abu Huraira (Rz) narrates in "Tirmizi" regarding Nabuwwat of the holy Prophet (Slm); that:

A. "The companions asked the holy Prophet (Slm) when was your Nabuwwat commissioned. Replied: "At a time when Adam (As) was in between body and soul."

قال قالو یا رسول الله متیٰ وجبت لک النبوة قال و آدم بین الروح و الجسد

The holy Prophet (Slm) is the descendant of Hazrat Adam (As). In spite of this authentic traditions, it proves that the holy Prophet (Slm) was enjoying the position of Nabuwwat and was designated as the Last of the Prophets (Khatemun Nabbiyeen) even before Hazrat Adam (As) was created. When the rank of the Prophethood of the holy Prophet (Slm) is so high, then what would be the position of his Vilayet?, particularly when the holy Prophet (Slm) asserted that."

"I am from Allah, and the faithfuls (Momineen) are from me."

انا من الله و المومنون منی

Now we have to see what was the belief of the Mahdavia predecessors? This had been written by Malik Ji Mehri (Rz) in his four stanza poem. Hazrat Malik Ji Mehri (Rz) was the muhajir-e-Mahdi (As) and also the son of a Muhajir, because his father Bandagi Malik Taha (Rz) was also a Muhajir. He is also the son in law of Bandgi Miyan Syed Khundmir (Rz). Thus

Bandagi Malik Mehri's poem which he had written in a few couplets are presented on the right side written as it is in Persian and its translation on the left side.

Almighty Allah was a hidden treasure. When He desired to come out from that concealment, the light of the Prophet (Mohammad (Slm), came into the being. It is the manifestation through vilayet.

When Allah separated a segment from this light for all affairs, vilayet came into being. Whatever it is, it is manifested through vilayet.

(۱) کنت کنزا که بدقدم مستور ☆ چوں کتمان صرف خواست عبور
(۲) کرد نور نبی زغیب حضور ☆ هرچه هست از ولایت از ظهور
(۳) چوں که از ذات خویش قطعه نور ☆ حق جدا کرد بحر کل امور
(۴) آں ولایت شده زغیب حضور ☆ هرچه هست از ولایت است ظهور

The poem is in Persian, presented as it is. This refers to the holy Prophet's saying" Ana Minallah"(I am from Allah). Thus the word "Ana" represents holy prophet's three status: Abdiath, Nabuwwat and Vilayet, for which there are traditions written both in "Sahih" and "Sihah Sittah" which tell that even before Prophet Adam (As) was in the making, the holy Prophet (Slm) was designated as Prophet and that too the Last of all Prophets. Thus holy Prophet's vilayet could not be termed as "Created" like the creation of Adam.

(Note: This point "Creation" requires thorough research- Translator.)

It may be pointed out that Malik Ji Mehri was martyred in 930 H. and it is obvious that the poem was written well before 930 H. Thus it becomes clear that during the period from the demise of Imamana (As) till 20 years, this belief was acclaimed by the Muhajirs of Imamana (As). Further Allah had said that the holy Prophet (Slm) possesses "Khulqu-e-Azeem" the sublime characters. "Allah had declared that the holy Prophet (Slm) is an embodiment of magnificent characters, were clarified by Bibi Ayesha (Rz) by telling "His characters represent the very holy Qur'an" The tradition in "Madarijul Nabuwwat" states that:

"Qur'an is the word of Allah which determines His attributes, thus Ayesha (Rz) took Allah's attributes as that of Mohammed's character which points out her mystic understanding since she knew it."

قرآن کلام خدا وصفت اوست پس گردانید عائشه صفت خدا راخلق محمد صلی الله علیه وسلم وداد معرفت خود داد بداں جهت اطلاع وے برآن

For Bibi Ayesha (Rz) the holy Prophet's characters were the attributes of Allah, and Imam Mehdi's characters are also described to be the attributes of Allah. Since the tradition "Khulquhu Khulqi" describes Imamana's characters as well. When Imam Mahdi's characters represent the holy prophet's characters, then it proves that the Vilayet of the holy Prophet (Slm) is also manifested in Imam Mahdi (As). However by telling that the Holy Prophet's Vilayet is superior to his Nabuwwat, is just to brand the opponent as accused, Imamana (As) has presented the confirmed narration as his argument which is in total confirmity with the way of the holy

Qur'an.

Allah made Ibrahim (As) to tell by saying :

"Verily, they are enemy for me."

فانهم عدولى

A. The infidels, think idols may become friends or enemies to them. But how could a Nabi also could tell that the idols were his enemy. Here Prophet Ibrahim (As) Just in order to make understand his opponents, had said according to the belief of the opponents. He said "Since you think that one idol is an enemy to you, in the same manner those idols are enemy to me also. But it is my belief that I am the friend of Allah alone and not of the idols".

Thus Imamana (As) had presented confirmed narration to brand opponents as accused one.

B. When Hazrat Abu Bakr (Rz) when demanded proof of holy Prophet's Nabuwwat, the Prophet referred to that Sheik with whom Abu Bakr (Rz) had met in Yeman, because what that Sheik had told to Abu Bakr (Rz) became true, word by word:

"By the time Abu Bakr (Rz) arrived in Makkah, the holy Prophet (Slm) had already declared his prophethood that he was the apostle of Allah not only for you, but for all people of the World. Thus I say: "believe in Allah". Then Abu Bakr (Rz) asked what is the proof? "Proof is that man, whom you have met in Yeman."

قال يا ابابكر انى رسول الله اليک والى الناس كلهم فامن بالله فقلت دليلک على ذالک قال الشيخ الذى لقيته باليمن

The holy Prophet (Slm) had referred what that Sheik Yamani had said:

"I found that a trustworthy man shall become Nabi, to whom a young man and an older man would help that Nabi. The young man would help him in his thick and thin and the older man, a weak and white colored man who would have a sign on his stomach and a sign on his left thigh; (he too would help)."

اجد فى العلم الصحيح الصادق ان نبيا يبعث فى الحرم يعاون على امره فتى وكهل فاما الفتى فخواص غمرات ودفاع معضلات وامالكهل فابيض نحيف على بطنه شامة وعلى فخذه اليسرى علامة (اسد الغابه)

From the above the holy Prophet (Slm), after becoming prophet, had given proof of that man who had prophesied about him and at that time he (the Yamini) was not a Muslim. Still the holy Prophet (Slm) granted his prophecy the status of divination. There should be no objection to present such instances. Apart from this the holy Prophet (Slm) had accepted the saying of a physiognomist (Qiyafa Shinas). The fact is that Asama's color was not that of his father Zaid Bin Haris, but had his mother, Aiman's color. The hypocrites used to taunt Asama's genealogy on the basis of the difference of color of the father and the son. This displeased the holy Prophet (Slm). One day both father and son were sleeping while their heads were covered with a cloth, but their feet were not covered. A physiognomist saw their feet and told that these feet are of the father and of his son. The holy Prophet (Slm) heard it and joyfully said about this event to Ayesha (Rz). Thus to accept a physiognomist's claim was just to defeat the enemies who were taunting Asama.

The cause of pleasure of Huzoor (Slm) was that the Arabs used to belief in the "sayings of the physiognomist" as reliable. Thus it was to treat the enemies as accused. The author of "Madarijul Nabuwwat" has written about this "It does not make necessary that the words of physiognomist should be reliable in Shariat also."

According to Holy Qur'an and tradition, to defeat the enemy, enemy's admitted facts may be presented to satisfy him. From the tradition of Bibi Ayesha (Rz), the holy Prophet (Slm) had furnished the admitted fact of the enemy to defeat him, although according to Shariat he was not reliable. Thus in view of this analogy, if Imamana (As) had presented the admitted fact of his opponents, then there should not arise any objection. The episode which was referred to by Bandagi Miyan (Rz) shall be discussed in the chapter" Bandagi Miyan Syed Khundmir (Rz)".

8. Ta'iyyeyun is Layeen: (Donation of a Fixed amount regularly is disgraceful)

Author of "Insaf Nama" had reported in chapter 9 that:

حضرت میران تعین را لعین فرمودند

"Imamana had decreed any fixed amount if given for more than three times to a Godly man is disgraceful (a curse)."

Author of Hadia had objected to determine this fixation as disgraceful if offered third time. It may be made clear that earning is lawful in Mahdavia Faith. Imam (As) said that "Momin's earning is lawful", thus he did not prohibit it. But if a fixed amount is given to a Godly man repeatedly, it does not come under the purview of lawful earnings. An example of such fixed income is given in "Insaf Nama" in its chapter 9:

نقل است که در موضع بهیلوٹ یك ملا سی تنگه کهنه پیش میران سید محمود آورد قبول کردند و بعد از آن همان شخص بعد از یك ماه بازسی تنگه آورد ، باز قبول کردند باز سیومی کرت آورد بعد از یك ماه حضرت میران سید محمود قبول نکردند و فرمودند مگر فتح خان مارا تعین گرداند

"Reported that one Mullah had donated 30 gold coins to Bandagi Miyan Syed Mahmood (Rz) in Bhelote which were accepted by him. Then after 30 days the same Mullah had donated again 30 coins, which also were accepted. Third time again 30 coins were donated which were not accepted by telling "Fatah Khan had fixed that much amount for us" (every month; hence rejected).

From this the condition of fixation can be understood easily. A fixed amount at a fixed period without obtaining any service, is called fixation. For two months it was taken as a gift and accepted, but when the like amount after a fixed date was given which became a fixed income for the third month that was not accepted by telling Fixation is a curse. Thus such fixation was not acceptable both by the holy Prophet (Slm) and by Imamana (As)

The holy Prophet had fixed annuities for his wives from taxes received from Khyber and other places just to provide sustenance for them during a year. But how could it be said a fixation? This only proves that the holy Prophet used to get from the booty of any Jihad which was lawful for distribution as sustenance. *(When Allah had fixed one fifth of the booty to the holy Prophet (Slm). How could this be called a fixation?)*

In order to make fixation lawful, author of Hadia had presented the daily earnings of the Caliphs. The author of Hadia does not know that these daily earnings were lawful since they were performing duties of the state. Again he had cited another example of fixed annual incomes from the Baitul Maal allowed by Hazrat Omer (Rz) to Muhajereen, Ansars and Ummahatul Momineen. This example does not fit for his purpose since nobody can prove that it was permitted by the holy Prophet (Slm). However it cannot be regarded as a fixation.

Apart from this, Jihad was obligatory for Muslims. The Caliph had the authority to depute any one for any expedition. Therefore such annuities provided a sense of security for the families of those who were to be deputed for any Jihad and also it was a remuneration for them to be ready for "on call" duties. How can anybody prove that such annuities were equivalent to those fixed incomes allotted by the kings without extracting any services from the courtiers? It is strange that the author had referred this tradition which proves his absurdity and lack of common sense. *(Since he himself was receiving fixed incomes from various sources).*

"After completion of an obligation it is lawful to claim remuneration." طلب كسب الحلال فريضة بعد الفريضة

But the meaning of this tradition had been wrongly mentioned that after completion of a religious duty earning is lawful. It is a fact that the holy Prophet (Slm) had lived in Madinah for ten years. Can anybody prove that after administering religious responsibilities could he get the chance to earn any thing for him? Then what was his lawful source of income for maintenance of his family?

That tradition does not prove the obligatory position of the earnings, but it proves that every earning must be lawful. Thus the annuities fixed by the kings to nobles without extracting any services are unlawful earnings and which come under the category of regular fixed incomes which Imamana had decreed as disgraceful. These infallible words of Imamana (As) that "Fixation is a curse" point out the utmost excellence of Imamana (As) in pursuing Sharai deliberations.

Author of "Insaf Nama" had narrated that Imamana (As) had accepted dinner invitations from those who had fixed incomes. Author of Hadia objects that Imamana's action was against his own words. This author had no knowledge that there are so many traditions which tell that the holy Prophet's actions sometimes were apparently against his words. Can anybody dare to argue against Rasoolullah (Slm)? Following is an examples:

"Ibad Bin Tameem (Rz) narrated that he asked his uncle who told that the holy Prophet (Slm) was lying on his back in the masjid in such a condition that his one leg was over another leg".

(١) عــن عبــاد بــن تـميـم عن عمه قال رايت رسول الله صـلـى الـلـه عـليـه و سلم مستلقيا و اضعا احدى قدميه على الاخرى

This has been accepted by both "Muslim" and "Bukhari" that while lying the holy Prophet (Slm) kept his one leg over another.

"Jaber (Rz) had narrated that the holy Prophet (Slm) advised not to keep one leg over another while some one was lying on one's back."

(ب) عـن جـابـر قال نهى رسول الله صلى الله عليه و سـلـم ان يـرفع الرجل احدے رجليه على الاخرى وهو مستلق على ظهره

" The same, Jaber (Rz) narrated that the holy Prophet (Slm) had asserted that nobody should lie down on his back and keep one leg over his another leg."

(ج) و عـنـه ان الـنبى صـلـى الله عليه و سلم قال لا يستلقين احدكم ثم يضع احدے رجليه على الاخرى

According to "Muslim" the above two traditions the holy Prophet (Slm) had advised Muslims not to keep one leg over other leg while lying down on the back. But against it, the first one states that the holy Prophet (Slm) himself was lying on his back and had kept his one leg over another. Thus, here also could the fault finder dare to raise any objection on the holy Prophet (Slm) as to why he had acted against his own assertions?

Imamana (As) had always asserted that Fixation (of any amount being received consecutively for three times) is disgraceful. But it is stated that Imamana (As) had accepted dinner invitations from those who were in receipt of such fixed amount. In what sense it can be said that he had gone back against his own assertion?

If there is any difference between the precept and practice of the holy Prophet (Slm), then we have to base our actions on his dictates only. In this connection author of "Asheathul Lam'aath" stated that:

"When found any difference in precept and practice, then we have to act on dictates, because they are more powerful than practice. This had been accepted by Imam Abu Hanifa (Rz) for the sake of jurisprudence."

چوں قول و فعل متعارض آمده تمسك به قول كرديم و قـول اقـوى اسـت از فـعـل نـزد امـام ابـو حنيفه چنانكه در اصول فقه ثابت شده است

There is one more instance that the holy Prophet (Slm) had prohibited to keep "Saum-e-Visal", but he himself had kept. However, Muslims have to follow what has been dictated by the holy Prophet (Slm), since it pertains to Islamic Jurisprudence.

The point of consideration is that when the action of holy Prophet (Slm) i-e; by keeping his one leg over the other, while lying on his back, and he was himself keeping "Saum-e-Visal" and this difference in precept and practice of the holy Prophet (Slm) cannot and should not be pointed out as objectionable, then how Imamana's decree that "Fixation is disgraceful" and accepting dinner from those who were in receipt of fixed amounts could be objected?

It may be pointed out that Imamana (As) himself had never acted against his assertions, but rarely he had accepted dinner from a person who was in receipt of fixed income.

9. Earning for Livelihood is Lawful-Kasab is Halal:

Author of Hadia had stated that relinquishing lawful earnings-Turk-e-Kasab-e-Halal-was the habit of the Sheik (Imamana (As) and also of his disciples. But author of "Tabqaat-e-Akbari" had stated that Mahdavis were engaged in lawful earnings. With reference to Sheik Alaai (Rh) it has been written that:

"If busy in agriculture or trade, he would give ten percent for the cause of Allah."

کشت یا زراعت و تجارت میکرده وہ یك در راہِ خدا صرف می نمود

That instance had already been discussed above and the author of Hadia too had referred in his book, chapter 8 that:

"Ushr is that if Allah had provided anything through land, skills, or through service, ten percent should be given to the needy ones." This proves that Mahdavis were engaged in lawful earnings. The author of "Insaf Nama" in chapter 5 had written that:

"Then Mullahs inquired by telling that he (Imamana(AS)) had declared earnings are banned? Imamana (As) replied that: "momin is eligible for Lawful Earnings", thus you must investigate whom Qur'an declares Momin?"

باز ملایان سوال کردند که شما کسب را حرام می گوئید میران فرمودند که مومن را کسب حلال است مومن باید و در قرآن تامل باید کرد که مومن کرامی گویند

This is enough to prove that Mahdavis were busy in skillful services and lawful earnings. They were never had been prohibited from services and their remunerations. In order to negate Mahdiat, someone had asserted that Mahdavis had relinquished earnings and branded them rude is itself rude on the part of objector himself, since earnings is neither a condition of the Prophet hood nor for the Mahdiat. However, the holy Prophet (Slm) had stated that:

"No revelation was given to me to collect money or to become a trader."

Still can anybody show what was the source of income of the holy Prophet (Slm) during thirteen years in Makkah and ten years in Madinah?

Those who (Mahdavis) relinquish earnings they know the benefits of the earnings. They do not avoid their children's earnings. When the earnings of their children come under their disposal, they think it to be like their earnings. There is a tradition in this connection:

"It is proved that your children are the result of your earnings."

ان اولادکم من کسبکم

"Ashatul Lamaat" comments on this tradition that:

"Whatever your children spend for you, it is lawful for you to accept it as if you have earned by your skill."

پس انچه انفاق کند به شما اولاد شما نیز حلال طیب است و در حکم اکل از کسب یداست

It all boils down to say that whoever had relinquished earnings, he too gets benefits from Allah's blessings.

10. Relinquishing Worldly Affairs:

There should be no objection for those Mahdavis who relinquish the worldly life with their own will and pleasure even before their last breathings. Author of Hadia had presented this tradition:

"The way you live, in the same manner you will die and as you die, in the same condition you shall be raised."

کما تعیشون تموتون و کما تموتون تبعثون

It seems he had some difficulty in understanding this tradition. That is why he had wrongly translated it. Just on account of enmity with the Mahdavis, he had not hesitated to translate the tradition wrongly. In order to refute him, we would like to refer Abdullah Ibn Abi Sarha, writer of traditions, as an example Sarha's life passed through four periods which has been described in " Madarijul Nabuwwat" that: "As an infidel, as a Muslim, as an apostate, (and again) as a Muslim". According to the author in what position he would be raised on the day of Judgment (since he was murdered)?

Apart from this "Tirmizi" has reported what Abdullah bin Amr has said:

"The end of a Jannati is occurred on the actions of the inhabitants of Jannat, irrespective of his actions through out his life." (Clarification needed)?

صاحب الجنة یختم له یعمل اهل الجنة وان عمل ای عمل .

As mentioned in "Mouahib Alaih" "Summa Yattabbaoona Min Qareeb" that:

"The commentary of "Ainul Muaani" states that even if one who is remorseful even for a moment before his death and repents, the angels praise him for his repentance and say to him how soon you have come and how best you die."

توبه کند ملائکه بطریق استحسان می گویند که چه زود آمدی و چه خوش مسارعت نمودی (جلد اول صفحه ۹۳)

Thus relinquishing the worldly life, just before the death of some Mahdavis is also in conformity with the traditions of the holy Prophet (Slm).

11. Invitation for Feast:

Author of Hadia states that avoiding to attend feast is against tradition. In the Chapter 8 of "Insaf Nama" it has been written that Mahdavis had even avoided to go to dinners if offered even by Mahdavis out side the dairah. It may be pointed that this chapter is not regarding avoidance of going to dinners, but it relates to the avoidance to visit the houses of those who refused migration; incidentally it included avoidance to go to the dinners outside the dairah. It seems the author tried to tell that Imamana (As) had prohibited attending dinners. But it is a fact that Imamana (As) himself had attended dinners offered by Mir Zunnoon. According to "Matleul Vilayet" when Mir Zunnoon tried to offer dinner for more than three days, Imamana (As) denied his offer stating that the holy Prophet (Slm) never agreed for more than three day's hospitality.

"The holy Prophet (Slm) did not accept hospitality beyond three days. When he insisted, Imamana (As) said that the holy prophet's habit was not to accept hospitality beyond three days."	آنحضرت بعد از سه روز قبول نه کردند وقتیکه کوشش بیغایت کردند فرمودند که سنت مصطفی صلی الله علیه وسلم مهمان داری بیش از سه روز قبول نه کردند

Thus by referring the tradition, Imamana (As) refused to accept Mir Zunnoon's offer beyond three days. This action is nothing but revival of the tradition of the holy Prophet (Slm), then how could this be objected?

Author of Hadia had referred that companions of Imamana (As) did never go for dinner, or to see ailing persons beyond dairah.

A. ."It is stated that Imamana (As), Bandgi Syed Mahmood (Rz), Bandagi Syed Khundmir (Rz), Bandagi Shah Nemat (Rz), Bandagi Shah Dilawer (Rz), never went to any person's invitation for dinner or for visiting a sick man or for offering condolences, outside the Daira.	(ا) نقل است از حضرت میران وبندگی سید محمود و بندگی سید خوندمیر میان نعمت و میان دلاور که در خانه کس نه جهت مهمانی ونه در معذرت رفتند مگر درون دائره برفتند

B. It is stated in "Insaf Nama" that once Imamana (As) was coming back from Jamai-e-Masjid to Daira in Khurasan. On the way there was a house of a Khurasani who invited Imamana (As) for a dinner, to which Imamana (As) excused, but allowed his companions to attend. Thus going outside the daira for dinners was not prohibited. Thus it is a fact that even outside the daira also companions were allowed to go if invited for dinner. Author of Hadia had referred to two traditions:

"The holy Prophet (Slm) said that if a person is invited for a dinner and he does not go, he has become disobedient of Allah and His Rasool (Slm)."	(الف) قال رسول الله صلی الله علیه و سلم من دعی فلم یجب فقد عصی الله و رسوله
"The holy Prophet (Slm) remarked that it is a worst wedding party in which nobles and elites are invited and poor are neglected. And whoever did not attend dinner he had committed disobedience to Allah and his Prophet (Slm)."	(ب) قال رسول الله صلی الله علیه و سلم شر الطعام الولیمه یدعی لها الا غنیاء و یترک الفقراء من ترک الدعوة فقد عصی الله و رسوله

In both the traditions the invitation is meant for the valima specifically. In both the traditions the invitation was meant for valima dinner. The author of "Mishkat" has also included these traditions under the chapter "Valima":

12. General Dinners (not the valima):

Author of "Tiesiral Qari" has written that:

"It is a consensus that general dinners are desirable, but valima dinners are mandated."

جمهور براین اند که دعوت غیر ولیمه مستحب است و دعوتے که امر بر آں واقع شده ولیمه است

There is not a single incidence in which Imamana (As) had prohibited to accept the valima dinner.

In "Asshatul Lam'at" it is written that:

"Apparently it refers to the necessity or as an"emphasized Sunnat" or just "desirable (Mustahab)"and that too when it is assumed that nothing is unlawful."

ظاهر در وجوب است یا مبنی بر تاکید سنیت و استجاب است و این بر تقدیر عدم وجود موانع است

It was a custom in dairahs that if there was any prohibition for avoiding dinners, then they did not attend dinners. Except valima Dinners, other dinners are desirable to attend. If they are not attended, it does not mean to neglect the tradition. Thus author of Hadia's contention that Mahdavis avoid traditions by not attending dinners is unfair and baseless.

Apart from this, the author of "Tiesiriul Qari" had written that:

"Some take its meanings that, someone avoided the dinner, because the poor were not invited."

بعضے معنے چنیں می گویند کسی که ترک کند دعوت و نخواهند هیچ کس را

Not accepting the dinner because poor have not been invited is desirable since Holy Prophet (Slm) did not like such dinners in which poor were neglected.

12. Attainment of Learning:

The evil mindeness of the author of Hadia is obvious in the following lines:

In chapter 10 of "Insaf Nama" it is written that Imamana (As) was against learning is not correct. One person asked Imamana (AS), if he would permit him to read something, instead of taking afternoon nap? On that Imamana (As) said" go to sleep". It does not mean that Imamana(As) was aginst learning. It was an advice, so that he can woke up early in the morning for the Morning prayer. The wording of "Inssaf Nama" are as below:

B."One of the brothers asked permission from Imamana (As), if permitted he would read some thing. Instead of taking a nap, Imamana (As) asked him "go to sleep instead of reading."

(ب) نقل است حضرت میران را از برادران کسی پر سید میرانجیو اگر رضائے خوندکار باشد وقت قیلوله چیزے بخوانیم حضرت میران ؑ فرمودند ایں وقت ھم مخوانید بخسپید

The author of Hadia translated the narrations of "Insaf Nama"very dishonestly.

The fact is that great scholars have confirmed Huzoor Mahdi (As) and had mentioned even in their books although they were not Mahdavi, but had narrated about the sublime attributes of Imamana (As). The detailed discussion about this had already been presented earlier. Thus the Sayings of Imamana (AS) that it is better to sleep in the afternoon, is in total conformity with the traditions in order to wake up in the early mornings to perform the Fajr prayer before sunrise.

A person who asked permission to read and Imamana (As) asked him "to go and have a nap", since daytime nap had been a custom in the dairah. "Kanzul Ummal" refers that:

"Saeb Bin Yazeed narrates that Omer Binal Khattab (Rz) used to come at midday and say: come and have a nap, anything if left it is for Satan."

(ا) عن السائب بن یزید قال کان عمر بن الخطاب یمر علینا عند نصف النھار و قبیلہ فیقول قوموا فما بقی فھو للشیطان (ھب)

Behiqi wrote in "Shubul Eman" that:

"Narrated Mujahid that it was brought to the notice of Omer (Rz) that one of his administrators does not go for a nap. Hazrat Omer (Rz) wrote to him "for having a nap in the afternoon, since I found a tradition that Satan does not take naps in the afternoon."

(ب) عن مجاھد قال بلغ عمران عاملالہ لا یقیل فکتب الیہ عمر قل فانی حدثت ان الشیطان لا یقیل (ش)

It is obvious from it that the one who takes a nap in the afternoon, can perform worship at night easily and wakes up early in the morning also for the Fajr prayer.

Thus it is a fact that "Satan does not take nap" and the one who objects for taking a nap, is just like Satan.

Abu Nayeem has reported that::

"Take a nap because Satan does not take naps (Qailoola)."

قیلوا فان الشیطان لا یقیل

This tradition has been mentioned by author of "Kanzul Ummal" under this subject.

"It helps for night prayers."

الاسباب المعینۃ علی قیام اللیل

Thus Imamana's asking him to go for a nap (Qailoola) and avoid reading was in accordance to the traditions. And it also helps one to wake up before sunrise and offer prayers on time.

Author of Hadia had objected on Imamana's assertion that to understand Qur'an "Noor-e-Eman" is enough. Author of Hadia has translated one narration of the "Insaf Nama", and had avoided to translate another narration. Both the narrations are as under:

"Imamana (As) told Miyan Lad Shah (Rz) that the basic knowledge was essential to perform prayers, keeping fast and following the religious duties as mentioned in Shariat, then he said:" to understand the meanings of the holy Qur'an when being described "Noor-e-Eman?" is sufficient."

نقل است از میان لاڑ شاه که حضرت میراںؑ نیز فرمودند علم لابدی می بایدتا نماز و روزه مانند این افعال دردین رسول علیه السلام درست شود و نیز حضرت میران فرمودند که برائے فہم کردن معانی قرآن وقتے که بیان کرده شود نور ایمان بس است (باب دہم)

In the "Naqliat-e-Miyan Abdul Rasheed" it is stated that:

"Narrated Imamana (As) that the basic knowledge is necessary to follow Sharaie dictations and to perform religious duties. Then he told "to understand the meanings of Qur'an "Noor-e-Eman" is enough."

فرمودند علم لابدی بایدتا نماز و روزه و مانند این درست شود و نیز فرمودند برائے فہم معانی قرآن نور ایمان بس است الیٰ آخره (باب ہشتم)

Thus, how can it be deduced that Imamana (As) was against learning? From this assertion it comes to light that Imamana's intention was that if anyone is well versed in the basic knowledge and at the time when a sermon is being given about the Qur'an, if the listener has "Noor-e-Eman" he could understand the meanings of the Qur'an very well. Thus basic knowledge is essential along with firm belief then only the meaning of the holy Qur'an can be understood and not otherwise. There is no reason for author of Hadia to raise unwanted silly objections against Imamana (As)

Imamana (As) has first emphasized for gaining essential knowledge. Secondly it is asserted that "Noor-e-Eman"is enough to understand the meanings of the holy Qur'an. The words of the Narration"Waqt-e-ke Biyan Karda Shawad", means that when the meanings of the holy Qur'an are being explained and if the listener has concentration in hearing the sermon attentively and if he is bestowed with Noor-e-Eman,by Allah, he can easily understand it completely. Thus author of Hadia has no reason to raise any silly objection, if he was able to understand the meanings of "Noor-e-Eman".

Mulla Abdul Qader Badayuni refers about Sheik Burhanuddin of Kalpi that:

"Miyan Sheik Burhanuddin (Rh) of Kalpi was following the way of life of Mahdavis; always busy in remembrance of Allah, and had no basic knowledge in Arabic; still he used to comment on Qur'an eloquently."

اوقات بیاس انفاس بطریقۂ مہدویہ میگذرانید و با آنکه علوم عربیہ ہیچ نخوانده بود تفسیر قرآن به وجه بلیغ می گفت

Even having no proficiency in Arabic, he was still commenting on Qur'an eloquently, should it not be considered as it was "Noor-e-Eman" only on account of which he was able to understand the meanings of Qur'an and describe them eloquently?

From these narrations can it be deduced wheather, was there any prohibition for getting basic knowledge? Of course at particular times and situations it might have been advised otherwise just in order that such work or reading should not hinder the important duty of remembrance of Allah.

It is narrated in 'Insaf Nama' that:

"It is narrated that Miran Syed Mahmood (Rz) was reading "Tamheed" (name of a book). Imamana (As) asked him: what was he reading? Miran Mahmood (Rz) replied that he was reading "Tamheed". Imamana (As) asked him to leave reading and be busy with the remembrance of Allah so that you get that capacity to understand it."

(الف) نقـل است كه يك روز ميران سيد محمود تمهيد مى خـوانـدنـدحـضـرت ميرانؓ پـر سيدندچـه ميخوانيد بـنـدگى سيد محمودؓ عرض كردند كه تمهيد ميخوانيم بـنـدگى حضرت ميرانؓ فرمودند بگذاريد و كوشش ذكر بكنيد تاحالتى پديد آيد كه اين را فهم كردن بتوانيد

From this, it comes to light that according to Imamana (As) remembrance of Allah was preferable to reading the "Tamheed". Last words "Ien Ra Faham Kardan Bathawneed" means "to understand it." It points out that when you start understanding, then read it. Thus from it nobody can say that Imamana (As) had prohibited reading. In the same way Imamana (As) had objected Bandagi Shah Nizam (Rz) when he was reading "Kanz". Imamana (As) advised him to read a book of traditions, because "Kanz" was the book on Fiqha. Therefore he preferred the book on Traditions over the book on jurisprudence.

There is another narration that Imamana (As) advised Miran Syed Mahmood (Rz) not to go to Miyan Abu Bakar (Rz) and Miyan Salamullah (Rz) for gaining knowledgde, instead asked him to be busy in remembrance of Allah to get the innerself broadened. This does not imply that Imamana (As) had prohibited Miran Syed Mahmood (Rz) to visit Miyan Abu Baker (Rz) and Salamullah (Rz) for gaining knowledge. But Imamana (As) had prohibited those who were well educated in learning, asked them not to read "Kanz" and "Tamheed" and preference was given to remembrance of Allah instead. Thus basic knowledge was necessary as mentioned in "Insaf Nama":

"Miyan Lad Shah (Rz) narrated that Imamana (As) had asked everybody to read books on basic knowledge regarding Shariat for the purpose of performing tenets of Islam properly."

نقل است از ميان لاڑ شاه كه حضرت ميران نيز فرمودند كه عـلـم لابدى بايد تا نماز و روزه و مانند اين افعال در دين رسول عليه السلام درست شود

This is clear that Imamana (As) emphasized to obtain basic Sharie knowledge. Thus Imamana (As) had prohibited those books which were not essential. Thus how can it be said that Mahdavis were prohibited by Imamana (As) from acquiring learning?.

Even if we take it for granted, as alleged that there was a prohibition on reading of general books, we would like to substantiate the standard of learning provided by Imamana (As) to his followers, on that basis they became proficient in dialectic discussions and providing intrinsic meanings of the holy Qur'an. A few instances of the descendants and their followers are furnished to understand what they learned from the teachings of Imamana(As)? On account of his teachiungs only, the knowledge of the companions was very effective and bountiful. Abdul Qader Badayuni had met Sheik Burhanuddin (Rh) in Kalpi and what he had written about him, its translation is given here: "Sheik Burhanuddin (Rh) was pursuing the life of the Mahdvi Faith, always busy in remembrance of Allah. Although he did not have perfect knowledge in Arabic, still his commentary of the holy Qur'an was perfectly well versed and eloquent". This statement is of that person regarding Sheik Burhanuddin (Rh) of Kalpi who during the period of Akbar had the company of several eminent scholars of Iran, Turan and India. The opponents used to raise objections on Mahdavis just for their explicit meaning by telling that gaining knowledge was prohibited on Mahdavis. These opponents do not know about Mahdavis who were perfect and well versed to offer commentary of the Qur'an. They should know that knowledge is not dependent on acquired learning only, but mostly on inherent and inspired knowledge which was provided by Allah alone through Imamana(As)..

Aalim Billah (Rh) in his book"Minhajul Taqweem" had recorded regarding the fifth question of Miyan Sheik Mubarak Nagori (Rh) that:

"Thus, it may be known that companions of Imam Mahdi (As) were of three categories:

1."They were philologist and they knew well the very circumstances of revelation of Qur'an.

2. Were masters on Commentaries and used to comment from beginning to the end with their implicit and explicit knowledge.

3. Thus may it be known that the companions of Imamana (As) were of three categories who knew the language well and the circumstances of the revelations and had mastery over commentary of the Qur'an from the beginning to the end with the inner meanings and some were even unlettered and could not read, still they acquired beneficence through Imamana's teachings and were able to discuss Sharai problems. Although they were unlettered, still had the capacity to describe Qur'anic verses perfectly well who were living till this author's time."

ثم اعلم يا اخى ان اصحاب المهدى كانوا ثلثه اقسام قسم منهم كانوا عارفين باللغات و شان النزول قادرين على مطالعة التفاسير فهوء لا ء فسروا القران من اوله الى آخره بقوة الظاهرة والباطنة و قسم منهم كانوا اميين ما كانت لهم قدرة على المطالعة فحصل لهم بصحبة المهدى و فيضه قوة المطالعة والبيان فبينوا على وقف الشرع و قسم منهم كانوا اميين الى زماننا هذا.

Miyan Aalim Billah (Rh) had referred to these Ummis/unlettered people, who never faulted in epilogue for commentaries nor did they declare a prohibited thing was halal. He further says:

"Rather those companions who were Ummis, I had heard from them the answers for even difficult problems, although they did not know even the A, B, C alphabets. This is all on account of Allah's inspiration to them"

بل سمعت من بعضهم جواب اشكال سنين مع انه لا يعرف حروف التهجى ثم وجدت ذلك بعينه فى الكشاف ذلك نتيجة الهام الحق

Author of "Sirajul Absar" had written answer to Sheik Ali's question, that:

A. "Our brothers would never stop any of us from acquiring knowledge;

B. Those who are commentators, their sermons are perfect in Arabic grammar.

C. Our brothers do not comment their views, but they do read commentaries and then they take that much which is correct."

(الف) اخواننا لا يمنعون احد امن التعلم (سراج الابصار مع مقدمه طبع اول صفحه ٥٨)
(ب) لان المبينين من اخواننا الذين يعتمد عليهم يقرؤن التفاسير و يبينون على قاعدة العربيه الى آخره (سراج الابصار صفحه ٢٣)
(ج) اخواننا لا يفسرون برائهم بل يطالعون التفسير فياخذون باحسن مافيها من الوجوه الى آخره (سراج الابصار صفحه ١١٨)

If, the meaning of the narrations of "Insaf Nama's chapter 10 had been what the author of Hadia has taken, then companions of Imam Mahdi (As) would not have written at all. But as a matter of fact Hazrat Bandagi Miyan (Rz) had written several journals in Arabic with regard to proof of Mahdiat (As). One of the Tabe-e-Tabaeen, (Miyan Abdul Malik Sujawandi (Rh)) had written "Sirajul Absar" in Arabic. The disciple of Hazrat Shah Nemth (Rz), Allama Muntakhabuddin (Rh) had written "Makhzanul Dalael" in Arabic and also "Kashful Asrar" in Arabic too. This was the standard of learning of the companions and the descendants of Imamana (As).

Imamana (As) had actually emphasized on acquiring basic knowledge; it does not give room for objections, which are raised by the author of Hadia foolishly. It is just on account of his malicious, false and absurd accusations against Mahdavis that he has raised the objections. There are so many books of Hadiths on one subject. But giving verdict just on the basis of "Single" tradition and keeping quiet about other traditions is nothing but dishonesty.

13. Performance of Hajj and Not Visiting the Grave of the holy Prophet (Slm):

Miyan Abdul Rahman (Rh) had stated in "Maulood" that:

"Then he (Imam Mahdi (As) intended to visit Madinah and paid for the camel fair, but when got inspiration from the holy Prophet (Slm) directing Imamana to: "proceed to Gujrat where you would proclaim your Mahdiat at that place also". Thus Imamana (As) took back the amount paid as rent of camels and paid for the boat's fare (to return back to India)."

بعده عزم زيارت مصطفى كردند و كرايه نيز بـه شتران داد نـد كـه ازروح مقدس حضرت رسالت پناه معلوم شد كه اى سيد محمـد شمـا در بـلاد گجرات برويد كه دعوت مهديت شمـادر گجرات منتج خـواهـد شـد ، پـس زر كـرايه باز گرفته بكرايه سفينه دادند

On that issue, author of Hadia had objected that:"Injustice was done to the Holy Prophet (Slm)" thereby Imamana (As) hurt his venerable soul by performing Hajj and not visiting Madinah.

From the above mentioned report in"Maulood", it is clear that Imamana (As) intended to go to Madinah and had even paid the rent for camels, but on account of instructions from the soul of the holy Prophet (Slm) he did not go to Madinah. The author took Prophet's directions as wrong inspiration and thus he had belied the Prophet's narration that:

"Whoever saw me, has seen the truth."

من رأنى فقد راى الحق

Because Satan cannot impersonate the holy prophet (Slm). As per tradition:

"Whoever saw me in the dream, he would soon see me while awoken and Satan cannot impersonify me" (Bukhari & Muslim)

مـن رأنى فى الـمنام فسير انى فى اليقظة ولا يتمثل الشيطان بى متفق عليه

Thus, to tell that the directions given by the Rooh-e-Mubarak was a wrong inspiration is nothing but ignorance and hypocrisy on the part of the biased author of Hadia. He had also objected for obeying orders of the holy Prophet (Slm). It is a fact that most venerable Godly people hear the voices of the prophets (As) and get benefited. Author of "Muaheb-e-Ludannia" states that:

"Hujjatul Islam Al Ghazali (Rh) had written in his book "Al Mutaqadameenul Zalal" that the saints while awakening they contemplate souls of prophets (AS) and angels and hear their voices and get benefits out of them."

و قـال حـجة الاسلام الـغـزالـى فى كتابـه المنقذمن الـضـلال وهم يـعنـى اربـاب الـقلـوب فى يقظتهم يشاهدون الـملائكة و ارواح الانبياء ويسمعون منهم اصواتا و يقتبسون منهم فوائد انتهى

Not only this, the scholars of traditions even corrected traditions asking from the soul of the holy Prophet (Slm). Sheik Abdul Haq Muhaddis-e-Dahalvi had written that:

"Many scholars of traditions had corrected the narrated traditions from the soul of the holy Prophet (Slm). They used "to inquire and correct from the Holy Prophet (Slm) that someone had narrated this tradition to have been told by you". The holy Prophet (Slm) used to answer "yes or no according to the situation."

بسیارے از محدثین تصحیح احادیث که مروی است از حضرت وے نموده عرض کرده که یا رسول الله فلاں این حدیث از تو روایت کرده است پس فرمود آنحضرت نعم اولا

Pity on the author of Hadia who did not accept the directions to have been given by the Prophet (Slm) to Imam Mahdi (As).

The author had further objected that without going to Madinah, Imamana (As) had returned to Gujrat for propagation of Mahdiat and to this he uttered that it was a discourtesy shown to the holy Prophet (Slm) by Imamana (As).

It is a fact that Imam Husain (Rz) without performing Hajj went to Kofa just on the starting day of the Hajj Rituals on 8th.Zil Hajjah, just for taking the so called oath of allegiance of the residents of Kofa. Whether the author would brand this action of Imam Husain (Rz) also as impoliteness one? Since Hajj was mandated at any cost. Ibn Aseer had written that:

"Thus started Husain (Rz) from Makkah on the day of Tarviah, 8th of Zil Hajj, (the starting day of Hajj rituals)."
The day of Tarviah is 8th. Zil Hajjah.

ثم خرج الحسین یوم الترویه

Those two traditions presented by the author are:

"It becomes necessary for me to intercede for him who visited my shrine."

(۱) من زار قبری وجبت له شفاعتی

Author's argument by presenting this tradition is futile, since it is not proved that the holy Prophet's intercession is restricted to the visitors only and not to all among the Ummah.

The holy Prophet (Slm) had asserted that:

"Thus I am elected to intercession and my intercession is for them who died and did not associate anything with Allah."

فاخترت الشفاعة وهی لمن مات لایشرک بالله شئیا (رواه الترمذی و ابن ماجه)

It is clear from this tradition that Prophet's intercession is not limited to the visitors only. Thus if any one (Muslim for any reason) had not visited, would he not be recommended?

Sheik Abdul Haq, Muhaddis-e-Dehalvi had written in this regard that:

"Good Tidings for the visitors and those who died on the religion of Islam, since the holy prophet (Slm) would intercede for them also."

بشارت بود به موت زوار اسلام به برکت سید انام که استحقاق شفاعت متفرع به آن است

Intercession will be for those also who send Darood on the Holy Prophet (Slm).

Tabrani reports the tradition that came from Abu Darda:

"Whoever sends 10 times Darood on me surely on the day of Judgment intercession would search him out." مـن صـلـى عـلـى حين يصبح عشرا وحين يمسـى عشرا ادركته شفاعتى يوم القيامة

If the visitor of the Mausoleum only gets intercession, how can those who see in dreams or awaken be left?

"Whoever had visited my grave after my death, he would be like one who met me in my life." (ب) من زار قبرى بعد وفاتى كمن زارنى فى حياتى

From this tradition it cannot be said that whoever visits should be recognized as companion. The visitor cannot be said as a companion, nor the visitor is preferred over a non visitor, but it comes to light that the visitor's coming to the holy shrine is as if meeting the holy Prophet (Slm). It proves that the holy Prophet (Slm) is alive, even after his demise.

"Whoever performed Hajj and did not visit me, he had affected injustice to me." (ج)   من حج البيت ولم يزرنى فقد جفانى

This tradition is the one which was made the basis for the author's malicious argument and through this he wants to prove that after performing Hajj, not visiting the shrine of the holy prophet (Slm), is like doing injustice to the holy Prophet (Slm). But the fact as narrated earlier is that Imamana (As) had intended for the visit. How can it be called injustice when Imamana (As) was directed to go to Gujrat by the holy Prophet (Slm). Even after clear directions from the soul of the holy Prophet (Slm), if Imamana (As) had gone to Madinah would have caused rather disobedience.

However Author's argument from this tradition is wrong because after performing Hajj, not visiting the Shrine at Madinah was not mentioned in it. Two kinds of traditions have been narrated.

One is that which refers to visiting the grave of the holy Prophet (Slm) is reported but the words "after performing Hajj" is not mentioned.

In others, performance of Hajj has been mentioned, but "visiting the grave" is not mentioned. This tradition needs one to meet the holy Prophet (As) during his life time only. Thus Injustice is referred to those who during the life of Holy Prophet (Slm) did not meet after performance of Hajj. Thus, we have to accept that on account of holy Prophet's directions, Imamana (As) did not go to Madinah. Therefore the word "Injustice" does not apply to him.

Here the words "Zar-e-Qubri" are available. There are still some more examples:

Holy Prophet(slm) asserted:

قال رسول الله صلى الله عليه وسلم نهيتكم عن زيارة
القبور

1.I prohibit you from visiting graves(*?*) *(Requires clarification)*.

قال زار رسول الله صلى الله عليه وسلم قبر امه

2.I had visited my mother's grave.

فزوروا القبور

3. Visit the graves.

من زار قبر ابويه

4.I had visited my father's grave.

لعن الله زوارات القبور

5. Women who visit graves are cursed by Allah.

Thus wherever "Ziarat-e-Qubur" is mentioned the word grave has come. If absolute Ziarat is meat, there must be a likelihood of the grave of a died person. Thus to take the meanings of "Lam Yazurni" as "Lam Yazur Qabri" is not correct.

(1) "And perform Hajj and Umrah for the sake of Allah.

(ا) واتموا الحج والعمرة لله (البقره ٢٤)

(2) And for the sake of Allah, Hajj is mandatory on Muslims who are capable to perform it."

(ب) ولله على الناس حج البيت من استطاع اليه سبيلا(آل عمران)

Thus Hajj is an obligation and its completion based on the performance of its rituals which does not include visiting the shrine of the holy Prophet (Slm) in Madinah. After performing Hajj, if any person is not engaged in immorality, he becomes clean from all sins, as if he was born afresh from his mother's womb. The tradition thus states:

"Holy Prophet (Slm) said whoever performs Hajj for the sake of Allah and does not engage himself in immorality, then after the Hajj he becomes so clean as if he was born afresh from his mother's womb."

قال رسول الله صلى الله عليه وسلم من حج لله فلم يرفث ولم يفسق رجع كيوم ولدته امه

If a person performs Hajj for the sake of Allah and does not engage in any immorality, but had not visited the shrine of the holy Prophet (Slm), he cannot be judged as an impolite person. And if it is said so, it decreases the sanctity of the Hajj, as if he is deprived of the benefits of the Hajj.

The answer for those who argue from another tradition" Mun Hajja Baiti walum Yazurni"(It means that after perfomence of Hajj, you did not visit me" is said to be unauthentic according to Sanaai and Jozi who said "that it is an unauthentic tradition" and Mohammad Bin Taher Fatni (Rz) says that:

"Sanaai had termed it as unauthentic tradition, while in "La'aali"Zarkashi said it is a weak tradition and Jozi too said it is a fabricated one."

قال الصنعانى موضوع فى اللآلى قال الزركشى هو ضعيف وبالغ ابن جوزى فذكره فى الموضوعات

"Whoever, after my death, visited my grave, it is as if he met me during my life; and if did not visit my grave, it is just like an injustice to me." من زار قبری بعد موتی فکانماز ارفی حیاتی ومن لم یزر قبری فقد جفانی

Hence it is baseless to argue about those traditions which have been regarded as inauthentic.

Author of Hadia should not have referred this fabricated and unauthentic tradition, because it does not mention the period "whether after Hajj one should visit the grave of the Prophet (Slm)"? It may be pointed out that there are two types of traditions in this connection. In some the Hajj is not a condition. Some traditions refer Hajj, but visiting the shrine is not mentioned in it. But it refers to visiting during the life time of the holy Prophet (Slm). The admonition of injustice is for those who during the lifetime of the holy Prophet (Slm) had not visited him personally after performing the Hajj.

In the second type of traditions, persuasion is made to visit the shrine of Rasoolullah after his demise. There is a difference between these two traditions. It is wrong to arrive at a single opinion. It had been stated that if not visited the shrine it becomes injustice, whether you perform Hajj or not. It is clear that if any person without any reason did not visit the shrine, certainly it is injustice. Therefore another tradition substantiate this argument. The tradition is as below:

"A person even after having capacity to visit my shrine, and had not visited, then it is mere injustice to me." من وجد سعة ولم یزرنی فقد جفانی

From this it becomes clear that even after having the capacity if any person does not visit the shrine, he renders injustice to the holy Prophet (Slm).

As a matter of fact Ibn Jozi had termed this tradition presented by the Objector as an inauthentic one. Mohammad Bin Tahar Fatni had commented that many Muhaddiseen had termed this tradition as an inauthentic one. Thus after performing Hajj if someone did not visit the holy Prophet (Slm) it should not be termed as injustice.

From this argument nobody should deduce that Mahdavis avoid going to the shrine of the holy Prophet (Slm) after performing Hajj. This assertion is supported by Mahdavi literature in which instances have been recorded of those persons who had gone to Madinah after performing the Hajj. Bandagi Miyan shah Burhan's and Bandagi Miyan's performance of Hajj and going to Madinah had been mentioned. Professor Mahmood Shirani had also mentioned in his thesis that Mohammad Ji Miyan (Rz) had visited both Mandinah Mubarak and Farah Mubarak. Nisaai had recorded the narration of Abu Huraira (Rz) that:

"Do not make my grave Eidgah, but send Darood on me, which would reach me where from you are sending." لا تجعلو اقبری عید اوصلوا علی فان صلوتکم تبلغنی حیث کنتم (اشعته اللمعات جلد اول صفحه ۴۰۸)

This tradition is from "Sihah", and its rank is far greater than the one the author had quoted. It means to say that for sending Darood it is not necessary that somebody should be present at the holy shrine in Madinah.

****

14. NAUBAT-E-IZDEAJ:

The day Imamana(As)got high fever and became very weak, he was in the house of Bibi Buwan(Rz). It was his routine, in order to check the turn, he used to plant pegs to watch time.

He felt that it was the turn to move to Bibi Malkan's house, he asked his companions to help him to move to her house. At that time, Bibi Malkan(Rz) was also present at the house of Bibi Buwan(Rz).Noticing Imamana's precarious health condition and weakness, Companions pleaded Imamana(AS) to be at the same place, since Bibi Malkan(Rz) also was present there.

At this, Imamana(As) expressed his anger that the Companions are not helping him to keep his routine which was according to the Shariath. Still he asked to help him to move. Then Bibi Malkan(Rz) also advised to continue to stay at the place where was he. For that she volunteered to give her turn to Bibi Buwan(Rz).

Imamana(As) sensing that Bibi Malkan's such gesture was not from her own, but she had withdrawn her turn in view of the Companions' request. Hence, Imamana (As) reprimanded the Companions that they were showing courtesy to Bibi Buwan (Rz), but he could not go against the dictates of Shariath and then got up from the bed and started to go to Bibi Malkan's House. He knew by inspiration that it was his last place, where he had to take his last breath. There was a mat, not even a cot, in the house of Bibi Malkan(Rz) on which he lied down and passed away after some time, proclaming the Tradition that "We are not the heir of any one, nor any one is our heir."

(*Note: It is doubtful, since it was given to understand that Imamana(As) did never repeat the words" "We are not the heir of any one, nor any one is our heir."It requires thorough search whether such words were ever asseted by Imamana(As) at any time during his life time."*)

Thus, even at his last breath, he maintained the Naubat-e-Izdewaj as per Sharaie dictates and thus followed the Holy Prophet's practice in toto..

It is a fact that the Holy Prophet(Slm) also asked her wives about his turn. He was told to move to that house of his choice. On that he asked them to help him to move to Bibi Ayesha's house, since he knew that her house was his last place, where he had to take his last breath and passed away by proclaming, "We are no the heir of any one, nor any one is our heir". Thus, Imamana(As) also passed away at his designated place, by toeing to the foot prints of the Holy Prophet(Slm), Imamana(As) and moved to Bibi Malkan's house and maintained the Sharaie dictates and took his last breath.

Author of Hadia here too objected by saying, when the holy Prophet (Slm) had accepted suggestions of the companions, Imamana (As) who claimed to follow the Prophet (Slm) in all respects, should have accepted suggestions and stayed where he was. In this connection he had referred two traditions:

"The holy Prophet (Slm) inquired at whose (Bibi's) house he would be residing the next day? Azwaj-e-Mutahharat permitted him to decide where he was willing to reside? Thus he went to Bibi Ayesha's house, where he passed away."

(ا) ان رسول الله صلى الله عليه و سلم كان يسئل فى مرضه الذى مات فيه اين انا غدا يريد يوم عائشة فاذن له ازواجه ان يكون حيث شاء فكان فى بيت عائشة حتىٰ مات عندها

"(Bibi) Sauda (Rz) was old enough, therefore she gave up her turn in favor of Bibi Ayesha (Rz). Thus the holy Prophet (Slm) used to stay with Bibi Ayesha (Rz) for two days, one of Bibi Aysha's turn and the other of Bibi Souda's turn."

(ب) ان سودة لما كبرت قالت يا رسول الله جعلت يومى منك لعائشة فكان رسول الله يقسم لعائشة يومين يومها و يوم سودة

From the first tradition it comes to light that the holy Prophet's all wives had given him permission to stay at his choice. And the other mentions that Bibi Sauda (Rz) had given permission to stay with Bibi Ayesha (Rz) in place of her turn. Author's reference to these two traditions is useless, since both are different in purpose. According to "Shawahedul Vilayet", at Farah, the companions had suggested, and not the Azwaj-e-Mutahharat, and also that Bibi Malkan (Rz) too was present at the house of Bibi Buwan (Rz). Then only Bibi Malkan (Rz) asserted that she had forgiven her turn in favor of Bibi Buwan (Rz). But Imamana (As) felt that Bibi Malkan's permission was not from her heart, therefore he preferred to go and stay with Bibi Malkan (Rz). Instead, had he preferred to live with Bibi Buwan (Rz), then it was an act of injustice to Bibi Malkan (Rz). Thus even after Bibi Malkan's forgiveness in favour of Bibi Buwan (Rz), Imamana (As) preferred to go and stay with Bibi Malkan (Rz). Thus raising objection on Imamana (As) was not correct and unwarranted.

Author Of "Madarijun Nabuwwat" had reported that:

"Holy Prophet (Slm) was once staying in the house of Bibi Ayesha (Rz), when Umm-e-Salma (Rz) sent meals. Bibi Ayesha (Rz) struck on the utensil which was broken and the food was thrown on the ground. The holy Prophet (Slm) picked up the broken pieces of the utensil and collected food and kept in it. This Self justification was told to others and said that "your mother (Bibi Ayesha (Rz) had envied."

يكبارے آنحضرت صلى الله عليه وسلم در خانه عائشه بود ام سلمه طعام فرستاد عائشه دست به كاسه بشكست وطعام برزمين ريخت آنحضرت پاره هائے كاسه بر چيد طعام برداشت ودر آن نهادوقصه اعتدار رابه حاضران گفت غيرت كرد مادر شمار الى آخره

When such envying was not objected then why should Bibi Malkan's envying be objected?

Had Bibi Malkan (Rz) expressed her opinion before suggestion was offered by the companions, it represents her offer was from her heart. Author of Hadia had erroneously referred to what had been written in "Shawahdul Vilayet" that Bibi Malkan (Rz) had offered first, then the companions had suggested. Objections reported that Bibi Malkan (Rz) was present there and suggested to Imamana (As) that "you are suffering hardship and I am present here and I had volunteered to forego my turn in your (Imamana') favor, the companion too suggested the same thing. But according to "Shawhedul Vilyet" the companions first suggested then Bibi Malkan (Rz) seconded the suggestion. The words" suffering from hardship"were spoken by the companions and not by Bibi Malkan (Rz). On that Imamana(AS) expressed his opinion that "companions are soft with me, but their suggestion was against Shari'at." It means to say that persuasion was from the companions and not from Bibi Malkan(Rz). When Imamana (AS) noticed that Bibi Malkan (Rz) was not telling from her heart, then Imamana (As) did not like to live in the house of Bibi Buwan (Rz). Even otherwise had he decided to live in Bibi Buwan's house then it would have been against justice. The verse in this connection states that:

"Thus if you feel you cannot do justice, فان خفتم الا تعدلوا فواحدة (النساء ع ا)
then rest with one (wife) only."

In these circumstances, Imamana's decision to go to Bibi Malkan's house was justifiable on the basis of Qur'anic dictation. How can it be said that it was against the holy Prophet's precepts?

From the fault finder's first tradition, the Holy Prophet's inquiry was ambiguous and what Azwaj-e-Mutahharat told was also ambiguous. Neither holy Prophet (Slm) pointed out about Bibi Aysha (Rz) nor his wives clarified it and when they permitted the holy Prophet (Slm) to stay with whomever he desired, then the holy Prophet (Slm) did according to his desire. In the same manner even when Bibi Malkan (Rz) volunteered to forego her turn, Imamana (As) did according to his desire.

As regards the tradition of Bibi Sauda (Rz) who had forgone her turn in favor of Bibi Ayesha (Rz), in which the right of turn was not given to the holy Prophet (Slm), but to Bibi Ayesha (Rz). Like that if Bibi Malkan (Rz) had foregone her turn to Bibi Buwan (Rz) and had Imamana (As) not staying in the house of Bibi Buwan (Rz), then it could be said that Imamana (As) did not follow the holy Prophet (Slm) and still not staying with Bibi Buwan (Rz) tantamount to injustice for Bibi Buwan (Rz).

Here Bibi Malkan (Rz) had forgiven her turn to Imamana (As), and Imamana (As) did what he desired as the holy Prophet (Slm) did according to his desire. Thus to object on the action of Imamana (As), the fault finmder is really pointing out his silly objection towards the holy Prophet (Slm). Shame, shame!

His second objection was that naubat (Turn) is meant for the night and not for day. This particularity is wrong. Since according to Qur'an, justice is desirable. Here justice is absolute; therefore its applicability may be daytime, including night and day. Bibi Ayesha (Rz) had narrated that:

"The holy Prophet (Slm) used to fix turns for his wives with justice. He used to say: "Khudawanda, this is my distribution on which I am the owner. Do not disgrace me for which you are the owner and I am not the owner."

ان النبی علیه السلام کان یقسم بین نسائہ فیعدل و یقول اللھم ھذا قسمی فیما املک فلا تلمنی فیما تملک ولا املک

Holy prophet's assertion "Fima Amlak" points out that all those which are under our control, we have to administer justice because it is mandated. Thus as sleeping in the night is under our control, day also is under our control. Justice is mandated for both.

It is but natural that when a person was busy during the night, he could adjust his time in the day; according to "Ashatul Lam'at":

"Distribution of time rests with the person. If he is busy in the night, he can allot time of the day for his purpose."

عماد ر حق مقیم شب است وروز تابع است مرد اگر مرد است کہ در شب کاربار دار دپس عماد قسم در حق او روز است

According to "Shawaahedul Vilayet" Imamana (As) used to be busy during the night in remembrance of Allah and during the day he was busy in religious teachings. Then the question of avoidance of any Sharai obligation does not come at all as mentioned below:

"On dictations from the Almighty, Imamana (As) after Isha prayer till Fajr prayer, used to stay in Hazrat Bandagi Miyan's room. Thus it continued for three months and some say four months; Imamana (AS) trained Bandagi Miyan (Rz) minutely in detail during his stay in Farah Mubarak.

حضرت ولایت پناہ بفرمان اللہ پیاپے سہ ماہ بعد از نماز عشاء تا صبحگاہ در حجرۂ بندگی میاں آمدہ یکجا بودند و از برائے نماز صبح بیرون آمدند این قدر پیاپے سہ ماہ پرورش نمودند و بعضی یک صدو بست شب می گویند یعنی چار ماہ

This narration belongs to the period when Imamana (As) was staying in Faraah.

From this it is clear that Imamana (As) was very busy in transmitting religious teachings during the nights, therefore he had no time for Naubat /turns for the wives in the night, that was the reason for fixing the turns during daytime for the Izdewaj. Author of Hadia raised a third objection that this distribution of time on the day is not justifiable. As a matter of fact this distribution of timings had not been written in any of the biographies. Even it is not mentioned in the"Moulood" of Miyan Abdul Rahman (Rz) which is the oldest source, which was written even before "Shawahdul Vilayet".

There is no consensus over a distribution of time in the books of biography. However we have proved that according to the Qur'an he had maintained justice among wives taking it as an obligation hence he minutely maintained the justice, thus Imamana (As) took it as a worship to get the pleasure from Allah.

15.Justice Among Wives:

Author of "Uswa-e-Sahahba" has written that:" Hazrat Maaz bin Jabal (Rz) had two wives. He had maintained strict justice for them. He used to be strict so much that he never drank even water from the other, even he did not take water for ablution." Whether the decliner would raise any objection on Hazrat Maaz (Rz) too?

The holy Prophet (Slm) in view of his severe health problem, it is but natural that he might have forgotten the routine of of the naubat-e-izdewaj, hence he inquired from other wives about the next day whose naubat/turn was? Wives understood his intention and permitted him to stay with Bibi Ayesha (Rz). Does this verification by the Prophet (Slm) called unnecessary by the author? The author should know that this is all done to teach the Ummah. In the same manner Imamana (As) had done to show that whatever shrewdness is used in compliance of obligations is nothing but worship to get approval from the Almighty, whether it relates to Naubat/turns or distribution of hours during the day.

His fourth objection lacks his proficiency in Arabic and also in Persian. "Shawahedul Vilayet" thus states:

"Well, you had forgiven your right of turn, but who can pardon me for not following the limits (Hudd) of Shariat-e-Mohammadia which have been commanded by the Almighty Allah?"	خوب شماحق خود بخشیدید فاما حد شرع محمدی را که خداوند تعالیٰ حکم کرده است کدام کس باشد که به بخشد

In the above passage the word "Hudd" is used whose plural is "Hudood" (limits) as mentioned in the Verse as below":

"And whoever transgresses the limits (Hudood) ordained by Allah, then such are the wrongdoers (Zalemoon)."	من یتعد حدود الله فاولئک هم الظالمون (البقره ع ۲۹)

Earlier it has been mentioned that Bibi Malkan (Rz) had unwillingly forgiven her turn. So in reply, Huzoor Mahdi (As) had spoken the above mentioned words. Hundreds of pages of Fiqha can be written on this topic "Justice between the wives" and hundreds of pages can be written on their commentary, but who can present the precept of justice between the wives following the Command of Allah and the practice of the holy Prophet (Slm) except Huzoor Mahdi (as) as the Khalifatullah?.

Thus "Shawahedul Vilayet" had mentioned about the practice adopted by the holy Prophet (Slm). In obedience of the holy prophet (Slm) it was only Imamana (As) who could maintain that sort of justice among his wives.

Thus the action of Imamana (As) was in accordance with the practice of the holy Prophet (Slm). So Imamana (AS) went to that house where his turn was."According to"Hashia-e-Insaf Nama."

"Imamana (As) instructed to take him to that house where his turn was. Companions suggested in view of high temperature, better to stay there where he was. Imamana (As) said that it would be against Shariat. Thus he went to that place where he had to take his last breath, that is how he maintained the limits of Shariat."

میراں ؑ فرمودند مراآنجا بیرید آن کس نوبت است برادران عرض کردند خوندکار رابسیار حرارت است اینجا بمانید میراں ؑ فرمودند خلاف شریعت رسول می شود جائے کہ نوبت بود رفتند این چنیں حد ہائے شریعت داشتند

Knowledge of the future is the domain of Allah alone. But if He wishes to provide that knowledge to His choicest Godlimen, He provides it to them. Hence the Holy Prophet (Slm) got the knowledge where he would take his last breath through revelation, therefore he desired to go to the house of Bibi Ayesha (Rz).

Imam Mahdi (As) is the seal of the religion. Is it not a fact that Allah had also informed him his place of demise? If we look into the matter minutely we can understand that nothing is against the Saying "Nobody knows where he would die"? Still the holy Prophet (Slm) said:

"Madinah is my place of migration and the place of demise."

المدینۃ مہاجری وبہاوفاتی

16. Takfeer-e-Munkereen:

Author of Hadia objected on branding kafir to the one who did not accept Imamana's Mahdiat and told that it is impolite.

If branding any one as infidel is an act of impoliteness, then what about whom Allah had branded Kafir in many verses of the Qur'an. The holy Prophet (Slm) had said Kafir to his non believer, the tradition says:

"Whoever witnesses that there is no god, but Allah, and I am his Messenger, he would not enter the Hell and Fire would not consume him."

لا یشہدداحد ان لا الہ الا اللہ و انی رسول اللہ فیدخل النار او تطعمہ

From this assertion of the Prophet (Slm) all holders of the holy Scriptures become infidels, although they believe in the Oneness of Allah and believe in other prophets too, but they had denied the prophethood of the holy Prophet (Slm). Can anybody put a question that simply because they had not accepted the Holy Prophet Mohammad (Slm) as the last Messenger, how the follower of other prophets becomes infidel?

As regards advent of Imam Mahdi (As), there are two types of traditions. Some of them assert that the denial is infidelity; for example: "Mun Kazabal Mahdi faqad kufr" meaning whoever belies Mahdi (As) is an infidel ("Sirajul Absar" p.138)

1. Sheik Ali in his "Risala-e-Rudd" has written while arguing the tradition that "Mahdi's

denial brands someone as infidel, according to the Shaik and his own teacher Ibn Hajrul Haitami, both had accepted the above said traditions.

2. Some traditions assert Mahdi's denial results in infidelity. For example the holy Prophet (Slm) asserted: Since "Mahdi (As) is the Khalifatullah, and he is my disciple as well". Further he said that "Mahdi's characters shall be like that of my own". Holy Prophet's assertions are true. Thus whoever denies Mahdi (As), as the Khalifatullah possessing Rasool's characters, is an infidel. If the denial of such a venerable personality, who is the caliph of Allah, should it not be considered as infidelity? Then how can any prophet's denial be called infidelity? If the first tradition has some weakness, then with the introduction of the true traditions that weakness should have gone.

3. The Holy Prophet (Slm) had specified that Imam Mahdi (As) shall come after him and before Prophet Isa (As) and all are the Saviours of the Ummah from its extinction; thus the following tradition determines the above statement:

"How that Ummah would be perished, when I am in its beginning and Isa (As) is at the end, and Mahdi (As) is in the middle."

كيف تهـلك امة انا اولها والمهدى وسطها والمسيح آخرها

Now if denial of the holy Prophet (Slm) and that of Isa (As) if branded as infidelity, then on what grounds Mahdi's denial should not be described as infidelity, because he comes in the middle ?

4. Imam Mahdi's appearance is a fact according to the repeatedly unbroken (Mutawatir) traditions, as had already been discussed, then the denial of continuous traditions why should not be called infidelity as mentioned in the books of principles?

5. Sheik Ali had obtained Fatwas from the scholars of Makkah against Mahdavis which had been published in "Risali-e-Burhan's last chapter in which also it is stated that the denial of Mahdi (As) is infidelity.

6. Sheik Ali had himself accepted that denial of Mahdi (As) is an infidelity which is written in his "Rudd". ("Sirajul Absar" P.148)

7. Author of "Hadia-e-Mahdavia" also had admitted that denial of Mahdi (As) is an infidelity; it states:

"Thus the signs of Mahdi (As) as had been mentioned in the traditions if present in the claimant (of Mahdiat) for the purpose of verification and if found correct (on his person) then "his denial becomes infidelity".

The reality is that whatever the signs had been mentioned in the books of "Sihah", all of them were present in the person of Imamana (As). (Vide Part one)

Why go so far, Ahl-e-Sunnat Wal Jama'at have maintained that even denial of Hazrat Abu Bakr (Rz) and Hazrat Omer (Rz) is an infidelity, as mentioned in the "Fatawa-e-Alamgiri":

"Whoever had denied the leadership of Abu Bakr (Rz) is an infidel. Some have named him a beginner/mubtadi not an infidel, but correctly he is an infidel and in the same manner, if Hazrat Omer's Caliphate if denied, then also such person who denies would be branded as an infidel."

من انكر امامة ابى ابكر الصديق رضى الله عنه فهو كافرو على قول بعضهم هو مبتدع و ليس بكافروالصحيح انه كافر و كذالك من انكر خلافة عمر رضى الله عنه فى اصح الاقوال كذافى الظهيريه (الفتاوى عالمگيرى)

Both Shaikhain (Rz) are deputies of the holy Prophet (Slm), when their denial as Caliphs makes the decliner infidel, on the same criterion the denial of Imam Mahdi (As), who according to the traditions is designated as the "Khalifatullah and Repeller" from the extinction of the Ummah, as prophesied by the Holy Prophet (Slm), should the decliner of that person be not called an infidel?

The proofs of the Mahdiat of Imamana (As) are much stronger than the proofs of khilafat and Imamat of the Shaikhain (Rz). Now we have to verify what Imamana (As) had said about his denial through the following:

Hazrat Bandagi Miyan Syed Khundmir (Rz) had written "Aqueedai-e-Shariefa" in which what he had heard from Imamana (As), he had recorded. Aqueedai-e-Shariefa's narration is as below:

"Thus, I, Syed Khundmir (Rz) son of Syed Moosa alias Chajjoo, had heard these dictates from the tongue of Imamana (As), who had stated that "Whatever orders I state, these are the Commands of Allah. Thus whoever denies even a word of mine, he would be called to account by Allah."

المقصود بنده سيد خوند مير بن سيد موسىٰ عرف چهجو ميان مى احكام از زبان سيد محمد مهدى عليه السلام شنيده است و او فرموده است هر حكمى كه بيان مى كنم از خداو به امر خدا بيان مى كنم هر كه ازيں احكام يك حرف را منكر شوداد عند الله ماخوذگردد

The last words are worth considering that whoever denies the orders of Imamana (As) shall be held accountable before Allah. Before Allah those only are held accountable who deny Allah's designated persons. Allah says:

"They Denied our signs, thus Allah held them accountable for their sins and Allah is He who punishes them severely."

كذابوابآيتنا فاخذهم الله بذنوبهم والله شديد العقاب (آل عمران ع ٢)

Thus, now we understand the meanings that whoever denies Imamana's orders, he is contradicting the signs of Allah, since these orders are given under the orders of Allah, therefore the denier will be accounted for and punished accordingly, as others are accounted for. It may be pointed out that whatever had been written in "Aqueedai-e-Shariefa" had the consensus of all companions of Imamana (As).

Bandagi Shah Dilawer (Rz) also had written those orders of Imamana (As) in his letter which he had heard from Imamana (As) and he further states that:

"And another narration is that one day Miyan Syed Salamullah's brother Syed Karimullah asked Imamana (As) "Is your (Imamana's) denial entails one to infidelity? Imamana (As) replied: Yes whoever denies us he is an infidel. And then he pointed out his skin and said this personality's denier is an infidel."

و دیگر یك روز میان سید کریم الله برادر میان سید سلام الله میرانؐ را پرسید که انکار شما کفر است فرمودند آرے انکار ما کفر است و اشارت برذات خود کردند و ذات خود را نموده فرمودند که انکار این ذات کفر است

Whatever Bandagi Shah Dilawer (Rz) had written in his letter, the same had been written in "Insaf Nama" and at the end it is written that:

"This too was heard (by me) from the tongue of Imamana (As)."

این هم از زبان میرانؐ شنیده است

This narration confirms the words spoken by Imamana (As) in which it is mentioned that the denier is an infidel.

Author of "Insaf Nama" had written that:

"Imamana (As) picked up a portion of his skin and said: "this skin and flesh is of this person, whoever denies this person he is an infidel."

نقل است که حضرت میرانؐ بهردوانگشت خود پوست خود گرفتند و فرمودند که این پوست و گوشت از بنده است هر که از مهدیت این ذات منکر شود او کافر است (باب دوم)

Imamana's proclamation that "his denial is infidelity" is positively true, particularly when it is based on the traditions; and the fundamentals of his proclamation are based on the holy Qur'an and the traditions of the holy Prophet (Slm).

There are some narrations in which it is mentioned, "Do not call the denier as an infidel without giving the reference of any tradition or the verse of the Holy Qur'an, he suggested. Author of "Insaf Nama" states:

"At Village Bhadra Vali all companions gathered and adopted a Mahzara/public proclamation and came to conclusion that without giving a reference (of the tradition or the Qur'an) we must not call anyone as an infidel. Then Bandagi Miyan Syed Khundmir (Rz), Shah Nemat (Rz) and the others asked if any person does not know the reference, then what should he do? Should he hide the truth? Then it was unanimously agreed and suggested that you must memorise one or more traditions and explain to the person who is questioning, and inform him what the holy Prophet (Slm) had specifically told and asserted that whoever denies Mahdi (As), the denier is a proven infidel and his abode is Hell. In that meeting I (Miyan Vali (Rh) was present."

نیز معلوم باد که در موضع بهدری والی همه یاران مهدی محضره کرده بودند پس همه مهاجران فرمودند که ما را باید که بغیر عبارت کسی را کافر نه گوئیم بعده میان سید خوندمیرؓ و میان نعمتؓ و مهاجران دیگر فرمودند که اگر کسی بیچاره را عبارت نمی آید اوچه کند حق پوشی کند بعده بعضے مهاجران فرمودند اگر بسیارند اندایں مقدار حدیث رایاد کند و نجواند کما قال علیه السلام من انکر المهدی فقد کفر و قوله تعالیٰ و من یکفر من الاحزاب فالنار موعده دران مجلس این ناقل حاضر بود (باب دوم)

This narration directs Mahdavis to refer any tradition or any verse before calling the decliner of Imamana (As) as an infidel. It means that you should not call someone as an infidel, on your own, without referring to the Qur'an and traditions. But you should say that "in view of the Qur'an and the traditions the decliner of the Khalifatullah, Mahdi (As) is an infidel". This method is adopted because the opponents may not get the chance of telling that Mahdavis regard the common people as infidels without presenting any proof. From the above argument the infidelity of any person has not been denied, but it is being advised that "do not brand any one infidel without giving any reference of the Holy Qur'an and the traditions". Thus infidelity is not being denied but it is proven on the basis of the Qur'an and traditions.

Author of "Insaf Nama" in chapter 2 reports:

"While in Khurasan, someone complained about those Mahdavis who openly declare others as infidels. Imamana (As) asked them to teach them and then stated that "they do not know how to say and what to say."

نقل است که در خراسان پیش حضرت میراں بعضے
یاران عرض کردند که بعضی برادران دراں شهر می
روند و خلق را کافر می گویند میراں فرمودند که ایشاں
رابز، نیدو نیز فرمودند که بیچارگان را ازیں جهت می
زنند که گفتن نمی دانند

The words "Guftan Nami Danand" means "do not know what to say" it means that the way they were telling others as infidels was wrong. It does not mean that "Don't tell infidel", but convince anybody properly why he is an infidel. Thus Imamana's deliberations point out that whoever does not believe him as Imam Mahdi (As), he renders himself to be called an infidel and he would be bound to be called to account for before the Almighty. From the consensus and as per commands of Imamana (As) no person should be called an infidel, but convince him through traditions and verses of Qur'an that according to the traditions if any one does not believe Imamana (As) as the Promised Mahdi (As), he becomes an infidel.

It is obvious from the infallible words of Imamana (As) which were heard by his companions, that whoever denies Imamana (As) is an infidel and he will be answerable to Allah.

Miyan Abdul Rahman (Rz) in his "Moulood" had copied the wordings of Imamana's Proclamation of Mahdiat in these words:

"After Zuhar prayer in a gathering Imamana (As) asserted that "I am Mahdi-e-Mauood (As), follower of Mohammad Rasoolullah (Slm). Whoever follows me he is a momin and whoever denies me he is proved to be an infidel"

بعد از نماز ظهر در اجماع فرمودند انا المهدی الموعود
خلیفة الله و انا تابع محمد رسول الله من اتبعنی فهو
مومن و من انکر بذاتی فقد کفر

For the purpose of understanding, this proclamation, we come across two issues:.

l. Imamana's declaration of Mahdiat; and 2. Nonbeliever to be called an infidel.

That proclamation is recorded in the "Aqeedai-e-Shariefa". Hazrat Bandagi Miyan (Rz) had already asserted in the beginning that "whatever had been written are the words of Imamana (As) which I heard from the holy tongue of Imamana (As)".

The same thing has been stated and written by Bandagi Shah Dilawer (Rz) that he had heard Imamana (As) was saying that his non believer is an infidel. This narration has been recorded in the Mahzara/public declaration of Shah Dilawer (Rz) and also referred in chapter two of "Insaf Nama" with a clarification that Miyan Syed Karimullah (Rz) had heard these wordings also from the holy tongue of Imamana (As). What had been written in "Moulood" had been authenticated by the above two oldest sources, therefore there should arise no doubt about it as per the contention of the Muhaddiseen.

Thus the objection that "Moulood's narration is a "Mursil" written after hearing from a companion, why should it become unreliable and untenable? Since that narration is based on two old authentic sources which vouchsafe Moulood's version.

It has an analogy. Imam Ahmed (Rz) accepts this reported narration with one condition, but Imam Malik (Rz) and Abu Hanifa (Rz) accept it without reservation as mentioned in "Ashatul Lam'aat" that:

"Imam Abu Hanifa (RZ) and Malik (Rz) accepted it absolutely and they say that what has been reported has authenticity, therefore acceptable because it has authority. Had there been any doubt he would not have reported it by just saying that "the holy Prophet (Slm) has said" to such statement Imam Ahmed (Rz) had accepted to have been said by the holy Prophet (Slm)" hence "Irsaal" is acceptable"	نزد امام ابو حنیفه و مالک رحمۃ اللہ علیهما مقبول است مطلقاً و ایشان گویند کہ ارسال بجهت کمال و ثوق و اعتماد است زیر اکہ کلام ورثقہ است و اگر نزدوے صحیح نمی بودارسال نمی نمود قال رسول اللہ نمی گفت ...... از امام احمد دو قول است بقولے قبول (اشعتہ اللمعات جلد اول صفحہ ۳)

If the "Emphasised Proclamation" (Dawa-e-muwakkedah) of Imamana (As) had not been declared by Imamana (As) himself, then Miyan Abdul Rahman (Rz) would not have asserted that Imamana (As) had proclaimed his Mahdiat in those words.

Imam Bukhari (Rz) and others have declared that the weak traditions are unacceptable. Reason being that he himself started collecting traditions after two hundred years from the demise of the holy prophet (Slm) and that too from different sources. Apart from it, the political situation was very turbulent on account of the happenings after the Banu Umayyai's fall which brought a period of change thus created so many hardships in collecting the true and accurate traditions, since thousands of inauthentic traditions were circulating among the Ummah. Therefore his stand in rejecting such weak traditions was not without tenable circumstances.

However, even in the "Sahih Bukhari" there are a number of "Taaleeqaat" which come under the category of "terminated narrations" like "Mursil"(whose chain of links is broken) But the difference between these two is that in "Taaleeqaat" where the chain is broken in the inception, but finally the broken chain is found at the end. If the narrator does not lack the continuity of the sources and had the links, then it must be taken as a contiguous (Muttasil) tradition, but if the sources are disconnected then they are called terminated. If this capitulation occurs from the beginning to the end, then it is called suspended. This suspension is called "Taaleeq". These "dropped off traditions" may be one or more; and sometimes the authority becomes doubtful, hence it is rejected. Just by informing: "Said by the holy prophet (Slm)" the narration becomes as "Mursil" hence acceptable.

As stated in "Ashatul Lm'aat":

"Sahih Bukhari"contains translations of many "Taaleeqaat" and they had been accepted as correct, as connected ones. Imam Bukhari (Rz) has made it necessary for himself not to include any unauthentic tradition ever."	تعليقات در تراجم صحيح بخاري بسيار است وهمه آن صحيح است وحكم اتصال دارد زير اكه وے التزام كرد است ودرىن كتاب جز صحيح نيارد (اشعته اللمعات)

However it is certain that if the narrator is reliable than his "taleeqaat" also would be regarded as "adjoining" meaning "Muttasil", thus those may be accepted. Miyan Abdul Rahman (Rz), author of "Moulood" was born during the lifetime of Imamana (As) and had Imam's good tidings as reported in "Tazkeratul Saleheen" that:

"When Abdul Rahman (Rz) was born, Imamana (As) went to his house and proclaimed Azan in his ears and said that Allah has given a son to brother Nizam (Rz) who would become an immortal creeper (Amrat Bail)"	چونكه بندگى ميان عبدالرحمن به حضور حضرت ميران متولد شدند آنحضرت خود آمده در گوش ايشان بانگ نماز گفتند و فرمودند كه خدائ تعالىٰ بهائ نظام راپوت داده است و امرت بيل شده است (باب ياز دهم)

He is regarded as a Muhajir: Thus he had the company of Muhajereen also. He had memorized the holy Qur'an and was well versed in Arabic and Persian languages. Author of "Khatim-e-Sulaimani" had maintained that:

"It is reported that he (Miyan Abdul Rahman (Rh) had memorized the holy Qur'an and was proficient in both Arabic and Persian languages."	نقل است كه آنحضرت حافظ قرآن بودند در علم عربى وفارسى دستگاه وسيع داشتند

Muhaddiseen had confidence on "Bukhari" and had given "Taaleeqaat" the grade of a continuous narration. Therefore if we are satisfied about a person like Miyan Abdul Rehaman, who carried Glad Tidings of Imamana (As) and if we accept his asserted narrative as contiguous, particularly when other such contiguous narratives support it, then there should be no objection as per the rule of the Muhaddisseen.

Thus as per Imamana's assertion the non believer is a proved infidel based on the tradition of the holy prophet (Slm). Now it remains to investigate as to why Imamana (As) had not mentioned this fact in his letters sent to various kings?

The first point is that the holy prophet (Slm) wrote a letter to Kisra of Persia, and the holy prophet (Slm) did not brand Kisra, as a non believer or an infidel. His letter states that:

"In the name of Allah, the most Beneficent and Merciful: From Mohammad Rasoolullah (Slm) to the great Kisra of Persia: Salutation to the one who followed the guidance and who believed in Allah and His Messenger and gave witness that "there is no god, but Allah and that I am His Messenger" for all and deputed to reprimand every living being, thus I call upon you to accept Islam for your safety. If you deny you would become the cursed one by (Zorastra)-Majus."

بسم الـله الـرحمن الرحيم من محمد رسول الله الىٰ
كسرىٰ عظيم فارس سلام علىٰ من اتبع الهدىٰ و آمن
بـالله و رسوله و اشهدان لا اله الا الله و انى رسول الله
الى الـنـاس كـافة لينـذر مـن كان حيا اسلم تسلم فان
ابيت فعليك اثم المجوس

Next letter was to Hirql, in which also he did not mention the word infidel if he (Hirql) denied the holy prophet (As) to be the Last Messenger of Allah.

"In the name of Allah, the most Beneficent and Merciful: From Mohammad Abdullah (Slm) who is His Apostle, to Hirql, Emperor of Rome. Salutation to him who follows the guidance: Now I call upon you and invite you towards Islam. Accept Islam so that you become safe and may Allah double your rewards. If you deny, you will bear the punishment of your subjects as well. O! The bearer of the Scripture, come towards the truth which is common between us that we should not worship other than Allah and should not associate with Him anything and should never make anyone Sustainer other than Allah. Thus if they deny: tell (O, Faithful) be a witness (O Ahl-e-kitab) that we are Muslims."

بسم الـله الرحمن الرحيم من محمد عبدالله و رسوله
الى هـرقل عظيم روم سلام علىٰ من تبع الهدىٰ اما بعد
فانى ادعوك بـداعية الاسلام اسلم تسلم و اسلم
يوتك الله اجرك مرتين و ان توليت فعليك اثم الا
ريسيين ويـا اهل الكتاب تعالوا الى كلمة سواء بيننا و
بيـنكم ان لا نعبد الا الله ولا نشرك به شيئا ولا يتخذ
بـعضنـا بـعضـا اربابـا مـن دون الله فان تولوا فقولوا
اشهدوا بانا مسلمون

From these letters whether can it be argued that the one who had denied the holy prophet (Slm) was not an infidel?

Imamana (As) had thus stated in his letters written to the kings on the lines adopted by the holy Prophet (Slm) that:

"We have declared our Mahdiat on commands of Allah and the witnesses are the holy Qur'an and the following of Mohammad Rasoolullah (Slm). You are called upon to investigate (our Claim of Mahdiat), otherwise faces of those kings will be rendered black in both worlds."

به فرمان خدائے تعالیٰ دعوت مهدیت اظهار کردیم و برآن شاهد کلام الله و اتباع رسول الله آوردیم تا شمارا باید که تفحص کنید و گرنه بهر دو جهان حاکمان سیاه روی گردند الیٰ آخره

From these words it is proved that whoever does not accept him as Mahdi (As) his face would be darkened in both worlds. Now the discussion is whose face would be blackened, whether Momin's or infidel's? The imam's assertion is that of a Khalifatullah, therefore it must be described according to the holy Qur'an only. Allah says:

"Thus whose faces will be blackened, (they would be asked): Did you reject the faith even accepting it? Thus taste the torment for your infidelity."

فاما الذین اسودت وجوههم اکفرتم بعد ایمانکم فذوقوا العذاب بما کنتم تکفرون (آل عمران ع ۱۱)

This verse proves that whoever became infidel after accepting the faith their faces would become black and for that they had to taste the wrath of the Hellfire. It is obvious from"Bima Kuntum Takfuroon" that blackened face denotes the attribute of an infidel. Imam (As) has said that his non believers would be rendered with black face, therefore his non believer is a proven infidel.

Imamana's reference to black face points out the said verse of the Qur'an which refers to those people who after accepting the Holy prophet (Slm) had denied to accept Imamana (As) they are rendering themselves to infidelity and causing for themselves torment of the Hellfire.

Apart from this Imam Mahdi (As) is a designated Narrator (of Qur'an). If his denier is not termed as infidel, then how a decliner of other commissioned ones by Allah be termed as infidels?

Now remains author of Hadia's doubt that Imamana (As) although had been lenient towards Muslims, still named them infidels, which require investigation. Author of "Insaf Nama" had mentioned a narration that:

"Imamana (As) had stated: if any person proclaims the tenet of "La Ilaha Illallah - Mohammadur Rasoolullah" then neither (Jazia) infidelity tax should be collected, nor should they be made forced labourers. Without performing matrimony rituals their women should not be used. In this way the dignity of Muslim creed should be observed."

فرمودند که کسے کلمۀ لا اله الا اللّه محمد رسول اللّه بگوید از ایشان جزیه نباید گرفت و بکار ایشان را نباید گرفت و زنان ایشان را بغیر نکاح تصرف نباید کرداىں چنیں حرمت کلمه باید داشت

Islam allows to observe the dignity of those who have holy Scriptures and allows matrimony with their girls and also allows their sacrificed animals, still, because they had not accepted the holy prophet (Slm) as designated Apostle of Allah, they are considered as infidels. Although their dignity is observed but their infidelity cannot be repudiated. Same is the case with Muslims who do not recognize Imamana (As) as the promised Mahdi). Author of "Minhajut Taqweem" states that:

"Here nothing is annulled from the jurisprudence, because Mahdi (As) is the follower of Shariat and not the repudiator of Shariat. Thus orders remain as they are. But matrimony and eating their Zabiha, offering prayers on Friday and Eid behind a person whose infidelity has not been proved is permitted."

وهٰهنا لم ينسخ شئی من شريعة النبی لان المهدی تابع الشريعة لانا سخه فبقيت الاحكام كما كانت فالمنا كحة و اكل الذبائح والتسليم وصلوٰة الجمعة والعيد خلف من لم يعلم انكاره لا تمنع تكفير المنكر

Chapter 4 of "Insaf Nama" states:

"It is narrated by Bandagi Miyan Syed Khundmir (Rz) that Miran (As) had arranged a feast to one mullah who brought his son to Miran (As) and asked him to bless him. Miran (As) asked Shaik Sadruddin to hear what the mullah was asking. If Allah gave power, Jazia could be demanded, provided Allah wished."

نقل است از بندگی میان سید خوندمیرؓ حضرت میراںؑ در شهر تهته دعوت می کردند ملاے پسر خود را پیش میراںؑ آورد و گفت که پسر ما را دعا کنید حضرت میراںؑ فرمودند شیخ صدر الدین به بینید که ملاچه می گوید و فرمودند که اگر حق تعالیٰ قوت دهد از ایشان جزیه بستانیم یعنی اگر امر شود

In that narration the words "Agar Amar Shawad" "Provided Allah Wished" are added by the author of "Insaf Nama". A description as per Qur'an. Allah States:

"Oh. Yahya grab book with strength, that order (Al Hakam) was given to him in his boyhood"

یا یحییٰ خذا الکتاب بقوة و آتیٰنه الحکم صبیا (مریم ع ۱)

Author of "Kasshaf" had written under "Alhukm" the word Nabuwwat, thus it came to the knowledge that apostle's strength is under "Allah's wish". Before this "Insaf Nama" reported that Imamana (As) told "not to demand Jizia from a person who proclaims "La Ilaaha Illallah". In this narration Imamana (As) had particularly addressed to the mullah. It is clear from the narration that during the dinner the Mullah requested Imamana (As) to bless his son. Regarding Mullah there are two situations: Whether his request for thde blessings wass genuine or not. Had he demanded blessings from his heart, then it may be taken that he must have accepted Imamana's Mahdiat. But if he was not convinced with Imamana's Mahdiat and still asking for the Blessings then he's asking was a joke.

Thus he was creating obstacles and whoever creates obstacle is bound to be dealt with accordingly. Therefore Imamana (As) said, if Allah wished, he would demand jizia from him.

This author had an old copy of "Insaf Nama" in which the following is recorded:

"Verily, if a wise man denies Mahdiat (of Imamana (As) and then through him requires Allah's blessings, he is an infidel, thus it becomes the touchstone for him, therefore he should be dealt with accordingly."	آرے چونکه دانشمندے انکار مهدیت شخصی کند و باز واسطه از حضرت حق تعالیٰ شفاعت جوید هم نزد خود کافر است و ایں محك تمام عمرش باشد و آں کس معیار امسال هیش است فی الجمله حرك دیده و دانسته کفر اختیار کند لائق حربست

Author of Hadia had written that Hazrat Bandagi Miyan Syed Khundmir (Rz) did not take booty from the enemy after the battle (First day battle at Khambail in which he became victorious against army.) Its answer is that Bandagi Miyan (Rz) disregarded the booty, but had ordered to pick up just ammunition and nothing else. As mentioned in"Matleul Vilayet"

Bandagi Miyan (Rz) warned his followers: "whoever takes other than ammunition, he would be deprived off from the reward of this battle."

"Bandagi Miyan (Rz) followed the enemy up to one and half mile. After the defeat the enemy left many things as booty which was a reward of this battle but Bandgi Miyan (Rz) sternly ordered his followers not to take anything except ammunition, otherwise one who collects other than ammunition would be deprived of from the rewards of this battle."	بندگی میاں قدریك و نیم میل معاقبۀ ایشاں نمودند دریں میدان غنائم بسیار از هزیمت ایشاں هریك نوع یافته شدامـا بندگی میاںؓ فرمودند هر که یك خاشاك را از امتعۀ ایشاں جز آلات حرب بردارد از جزاے ایں كار زار محروم ماند (صحه ۱۳۸)

Thus keeping in view the dignity of "Kalema" (La Ilaaha Illallah) does not mean that who had not accepted Imamana (As) as Mahdi (As), is he or she not the infidel?, same way as keeping the dignity of the holders of the Scriptures, does not mean that they are not infidels.

Author of Hadia maintains that refusing Imamana (As) as the promised Mahdi (As) is not called infidelity and sarcastically states that there are so many people who had claimed themselves to be Mahdi, before Syed Mohammad Juanpuri (As), so who is to be confirmed as the Promised Mahdi (As)?

"When the Holy Prophet (Slm) returned from Hajjatul Vida, then some wretched ignorant yearned for Nabuwwat. Among them were: Musailama Bin Samam, Aswad Bin Ka'ab Ansi, Tulaiha bin khuwailad Asadi, and one woman Sabah Bintal Haris bin Sued Tamima."

From what arguments the Nabuwwat of the aforesaid claimants was refuted in favor of the holy prophet (Slm), the same arguments are sufficient to prove Imamana's Mehdiat (against the fake claimants of Mehdiat).

17. Leadership (for prayers) of Non Believers:

Author of Hadia's contention is wrong that Imamana (As) offered prayers under the leadership of non believers, even after branding them infidel.

From the statements of "Insaf Nama" referred by the Author of Hadia it does not prove that Imamana (As) had any time offered prayers on Friday or Eidain under the leadership of a person whose infidelity was known. In Chapter 3, author of "Insaf Nama" narrated that:

"It is narrated that In the village of Bhadravali many Muhajireen like Bandagi Miyan Syed Khnudmir (Rz), Miyan Shah Nemat (Rz), were present and after Zuhar prepared a public declaration "not to offer prayers behind the non believers" (decliners of Imamana (As)". Some companions argued that Imamana (As) had offered prayers of Friday and Eidain behind the non believers, if it was not legitimate, then why Imamana (As) had offered? Bandagi Miyan (Rz) and Shah Nemat (Rz) told that they would not indulge in such unauthentic versions, but we shall do what Miran (As) had said to us and we shall avoid for which Miran (As) had forbidden. Author of "Insaf Nama" was present in this gathering."

نقل است که در موضع بهدر یوالی اکثر مهاجرین همچو بندگی میان سید خوندمیرؒ و میان نعمتؒ بعد از ظهر محضره کرده بودند و گفتگو همی بود که بدنبال مخالفان و منکران مهدیؑ نماز نگذار ند بعده بعضی یاران فرمودند که میرانؑ نماز جمعه و هر دو عید ـــــــ مخالفان گزارده اند اگر روا نبودے چرا گردار دندے بعده بندگی میان سید خوندمیرؒ و میان نعمتؒ و بعضے کسان فرمودند که مادراین کیفیت نیفتیم انچه میرانؑ کردند آن بکنیم و آنچه منع کردند از ان باز مانیم دراین مجلس این ناقل حاضر بود

From the above narration it is clear that many muhajereen had gathered to prepare a public declaration that Imamana (As) had not offered prayers behind any non believers. When some had argued that Imamana (As) had offered Friday and Eidain prayers, to which statement Bandagi Miyan (Rz), Shah Naimat (Rz) and others did not accept and told that they would not indulge in hearsay gossips and we shall follow to what Imamana (As) has asserted. If anything had been forbidden, they will avoid such thing and shall strictly follow what is proved from his precept and practice.

It is a fact that when both precept and practice are one and the same then following is possible. The delicacy of the answer given by Bandagi Miyan (Rz) and other Companions can be understood by those who are familiar with the technicalities of the traditions.

It is commonly accepted that if any practice of the holy prophet (Slm) was different to his dictates then it is implied on the Ummah to practice according to his dictates only. Autor of "Madarijul Nabuwwat" states that:

مـروی اسـت کـہ رسول الله صلی الله علیہ و سلم نجانۀ
زینبؓ رفت در حالیکہ وی سربرہنہ بود گفت یا رسول
الـلّـہ بـے خـطبـہ و بـے گواہ حضرت فرمود الله المزوج و
جبرئیل الشاہد پس طعام ولیمہ ترتیب نمود

"It is narrated that the holy prophet (Slm) went to Zainab's house, although she was without head scarf. Zainab (Rz) reminded: "Ya Rasoolullah (Slm), without Khutba and without witnesses? Prophet (Slm) told Allah arranged matrimony and Gabriel is the witness. Thus holy Prophet (Slm) arranged for the Walima dinner next day."

This narration proves two issues.

1. Bibi Zinab's inquiry: Whether without Khutba and witness? It proves that the holy Prophet (Slm) might have informed the Muslims that offering wedding Khutba before the Witnesses was essential for marriage and this fact was well known verbally even before Bibi Zainab (Rz) became the wife of the holy prophet (Slm).

2. Holy prophet's narration that Allah administers (marriage) and Gabriel is the witness indicates that perhaps Khutba and witnesses were not in vogue at that time yet. Therefore it is now clear that Khutba and witnesses are necessary for marriages.

(ب) عن ابی ہریرہ قال نہی رسول الله صلی الله علیہ
و سـلـم عـن الـوصـال فـی الـصـوم فقال لہ رجل انک
تـواصـل یـا رسـول الـلّـہ قـال و ایکم مثلی انی ابیت
یطعمنی ربی ویسقینی (متفق علیہ)

"Narrated by Abu Huraira (Rz) that the holy Prophet (Slm) had prohibited from keeping "Saum-e-Visal" (fasting for more than two or more days without taking food) when one person inquired "do you keep Saum-e-Visal"?, the Prophet (Slm) asked "who is among you like me? During the night Allah feeds me and provides water."

It proves that the holy Prophet (Slm) used to keep "Saum-e-Visal", but he had prohibited for Muslims. That means to say it is not permitted. Author of "Madarijul Nabuwwat" states that:

"Many believe that Saum-e-Visal is not permitted. Imam Hanifa (Rz) and Imam Malik (Rz) endorse it as "not allowed."

اکثر بر آنند که جائز نیست و امام ابو حنیفه و امام مالک رحمهما الله براین اند

Whenever there is a difference in precept and practice of the holy Prophet (Slm), the Ummah had to follow his dictates. Author of "Ashtul Lam'at" narrates that "Azwaj-e-Mutahharat" were more than nine, but at the time of demise there were only nine. But Ummah has to follow his dictate that Muslims should not marry more than four wives, if he is able to justify among them.

18.Difference In Precept And Practice:

Author of "Taiseerul Qari" wrote: When there is a difference in between precept and practice then we adopted precept because precept is stronger than practice. This also had been accepted by Imam Abu Hanifa (Rz).

Author of "Ashatul Lamaat" has written that:

"When the difference arises between precept and practice, we have adopted precept only because precept has more strength upon practice, the same has been accepted by Imam Abu Hanifa (Rh). Thus it is accepted as a matter of Fiqha."

چوں قول و فعل متعارض آمده تمسک به قول کردیم و قول اقوی است از فعل نزد امام ابو حنیفه چنانکه در اصول فقه ثابت شده

"When there is a difference in precept and practice, they prefer precept only."

وقتی که قول و فعل تعارض کنند ترجیح مرقول راست

In "Sifrus Saadat" has written that:

"Prophet's precept is stronger than practice, hence becomes perfect, because practice sometimes becomes particularized for him."

قول از فعل قوی و اتم است چه فعل احتمال اختصاص دارد

In the "Insaf Nama" there are so many narrations on this subject that Imamana (As) had prohibited offering prayers behind adversaries. Some more have been recorded in "Insaf Nama"in chapter 3, they are:

1. Imamana (As) had ordered people to repeat prayers who had offered prayers behind the adversaries if they come to know that the leader for the prayers was a non believer.

2. Muhajereen of Imamana (As) had a consensus that whoever had offered prayer behind an adversary he may be regarded as an outsider means he is a Khariji.

3. Imamana (As) inquired why should anyone go to that place where it becomes compulsory to offer prayer behind an adversary?.

4. Shah Nizam had also repeated the above narration.

When Sheik Ahmed Muhr-e-Siah wanted to lead Maghrib Prayers, Bandagi Miyan (Rz) dragged him out by saying that he was a non believer, hence his Imamat was wrong.

6.Mulla Mahmood Khund Shah wanted to lead the prayers in Bhelote while Miyan Syad Mahmood (Rz) was present, then a brother caught him by the hand and dragged him out by saying that he was a non believer.

7. Some companions of Imamana (As) told that Imamana (As) had offered prayers of Friday and Eidain behind non believers, on that Hazrat Bandagi Miyan (Rz) and other companions told that they do not want to indulge in such things (which are unable to prove the so called unfounded and hearsay gossips against Imamana (As)) and we shall follow whatever commands Imamana (As) had given, we shall follow his precepts and not his practice.

The narration that Imamana (As) had offered prayers on Friday and Eidain even behind non believers is not authentic since it is not written in any old sources.

Regarding Imamana's practice, the authentic source is that letter of Shah Dilawer (Rz), which is regarded as public declaration which has been accepted by the companions and their descendants; its last line tells that;

"Be it known that this letter had been approved by the companions and descendants including Miran Syed Mahmood (Rz), Bandagi Miyan Syed Khundmir (Rz), Miyan Shah Nemat (Rz), Miyan Shah Nizam (Rz), Miyan Shah Dilawer (Rz), Malik Maroof (Rz), Miyan Yousuf (Rz) and Miyan Syed Salamullah (Rz). Malik Burhanuddin (Rz) also had signed on this declaration who died in 915 H. That means to say that Public Declaration belongs to the year 915 H. or even earlier. The beginning of this letter starts with these words:

"Miyan Lad Shah (Rz) came from Gujrat and asserted that denial of Mehdi (As) is not an infidelity."

میاں لاڈ شاہ از گجرات آمده اند از برائے ظهور کردن آنکه انکار مهدی کفر نیست

Lad Shah's arrival from Gujrat had been mentioned, therefore it is not correct to argue that Shah Dilawer (Rz) was not in Bhelote of Radhanpur area. While the author of "Tazkeratus Saleheen" had reported Shah Nemat's arrival from Gujrat to Radhanpur has been reported:

"When Shah Nemat (Rz) arrived from Gujrat and stayed at Radhanpur, then Bandagi Miyan Syed Mahmood (Rz) demanded some money from him."

چونکه ایشان از گجرات مراجعت نموده در موضع رادهن پور منزل ساختند بندگی میران سید محمود چیزے خرچ از ایشاں طلب نمودند (باب دوم)

Here it had been stated that Shah Nemat (Rz) had arrived from Gujrat to Radhanpur. And in the letter of Shah Dilawer (Rz) it had been reported that Miyan Lad Shah had arrived from Gujrat. It means to say that before the year 915 H. Shah Nemat (Rz) was with Miyan Syed Mahmood (Rz) in Radhanpur. In that Mahzara/Public Declaration it has been mentioned that:

A.."After proclamation of Mahdiat (at Badhli), Imamana (As) never did offer prayer behind any opponent."

(ا) میران از وقتیکه ظهور مهدیت کرده اند بدنبال هیچ مخالف نماز نگزارده اند (صفحه ۲۰)

In this declaration the word "Prayer" has come which includes a Friday and Eidain prayers as well. Still it can be asserted that Imamana (As) had never offered prayers of Friday and Eidain behind his adversaries after Badhli's Declaration. It is clear from the Declaration that:

B.."If the king and the Qazi were adversaries then it does not imply that the Imam of the Masjid also was an adversary."

(ب) به مخالفت بادشاه و قاضی لازم نمی آید که تاخطیب آن مسجد هم مخالف بودے

Where Imamana (As) had offered prayers, whether the Imam was an adversary or not, Mahzara mentions that:

C. .."The status of the Imam of a masjid was reticent and ambiguous, where Imamana (As) did not offer any prayer, but at other places if favourable to him, for example at Kaha (Sindh) sons of Qazi Qadan (Rz) were agreeable he has offered prayers behind him"

(ج) حضرت میران هرجا که نماز گزارده اند خطیبان آنجا ساکت بودند بلکه در بعضے جاموافق هم بودند چنانچه در کاهه ابنائے قاضی قاضن موافق بود

Thus it is certain that Imamana (As) had never offered prayers behind any such person about whom it was known that he was an adversary. This is what has been written in the Public Declaration.

"I ask every person to present a leader /Imam of prayer who had openly denied or argued about Mahdiat and Imamana (As) had offered prayer behind him?"

بنده هر کس رامی گوید که خطیب رابیارید که اوبا مهدی و یاران وے حجت و انکار کرده است پس ظهور شدن مخالفت بدنبال او حضرت میران نماز گزارده اند

So, it is not proved that, even from the oldest source 0f 915 H., Imamana (As) had offered prayers behind any adversary. And this fact is approved by the companions and descendants. Hence if some companions or as reported by a single companion (Miyan Lad Shah (Rz) who reported against the facts should be rejected as untenable. Particularly when the names of certain companions, who had wrongly spoken like Miyan Lad Shah, have not been revealed. On the other hand the name of Miyan Syed Salalmullah (Rz) was mentioned who had been with Imamana everywhere from the beginning (Juanpur) to the last Resort (Farah Mubarak).

It may be pointed out that those who were arguing against the joint declaration of the companions and descendants are those who were the followers of Miyan Lad Shah (Rz) who did not accompany Imamana (As) from Pattan, Naherwala, upto Farah Mubarak, which is apparent from the letter of Miyan Shah Dilawer (Rz):

"He, Miyan Lad Shah (Rz), did not accompany Imamana (As) even from Patan to Farah."

ایشان از نهرواله تافره دنبال نبودند

Thus he did not know that after the Proclamation of Badhli, Imamana (As) never offered prayers behind any adversary, hence he is misled by hearsay gossips.

The Declaration of Miyan Shah Dilawer (Rz) has been mentioned in "Minhajut Taquweem", in which Miyan Abdul Malik Sujawandi (Rh) had answered the letter of Miyan Sheik Mubarak (Rh) Nagori:

"But, It is wrong to suggest that Imamana (As) had offered Farz prayers behind his adversary, because Imamana (As) had never offered prayers behind other than an agreeable Imam."

اما الصلوٰة المفروضة خلف امام غیر امامهم قط فغیر صحیح لانه ماصلی خلف غیر امامه قط

Thus, it cannot be proved that Imamana (As) had offered five times prayers as well as Friday or Eidain prayers, behind any adversary.

In the same way, Imamana (As) had offered Friday and Eidain prayers, behind an imam whose infidelity was not known. As had been reported by Miyan Abdul Malik Sujawandi (Rh):

"But Friday and Eidain prayers, favouring Islamic customs, Imamana (As) might have offered prayer behind such an Imam whose infidelity was not known. So also no companion of Imam (As) had reported that Imamana (As) had even offered prayer behind an Imam whose infidelity was known."

اما صلوٰة العیدو الجمة فخلف امام لایعلم انکاره رعایة لشعار الاسلام وما نقل احد من اصحابه علیه السلام انه صلی خلف امام ظهر انکاره (منهاج التقویم)

Thus, it cannot be proved that Imamana (As) had offered five times prayers as well as Friday or Eidain prayers, behind any adversary.

Now remains Imamana's precept, which has been recorded by Hazrat Bandagi Miyan (Rz) after listening (as stated) from the holy tongue of Imamana (As) in his "Aqeedai-e-Shariefa" and to which all companions of Imamana (As) had consented :

"And asserted that do not offer prayer behind any adversary, if offered, then repeat that prayer."

نیز فرموده است که بدنبال منکران مهدی نماز مگزارید اگر گذارده باشید باز بگر دانید (عقیده شریفه)

This is the precept of Imamana (As) which Hazrat Bandagi Miyan (Rz) had heard from the mouth of Imamana (AS); therefore it is compulsory on Mahdavis to follow without any reservation. In contrary, if it is proved, by some source, that Imamana (As) had offered prayers behind an adversary, then this is not acceptable, because when there is a difference in precept and practice, we have to follow the precept only, since dictation is stronger than the practice which had been discussed in the previous chapter in detail. What Bandagi Miyan Shah Khundmir (Rz) had reported, the same is reported in "Insaf Nama" as mentioned below:

"It has been reported that there appeared an opposition in Thatta, and the matter reached to the extent that the army was called for. Some companions said to Imamana (AS) that when we went into the city we had to offer prayer behind an adversary. Imamana (As) instructed them to repeat that prayer. Again requested to Imamana (As) that if they happened to go alone, or in twos, then what should we do? Imamana (As) told them to go in a group and offer prayer in your group only."

نـقـل است در شهر تته مخالفت ظاهر شده تابه حـدے که لشکر هانامزد کردند در آن روز بعضے ازیاران مهدی پیش میرانؑ عرض کـردند که امروز در شهر رفته بودیم و نماز بـا امـام مـخـالف گزاردیم حضرت میرانؑ فـرمـودنـد کـه نـماز باز گردانید بعده یاران عـرض کردند که اگر یگاں و دوگاں برویم چـه کـنیـم فـرمـودنـد جماعت شده بروید و نماز با جماعت بگذارید (باب سوم)

"Naqliat-e-Miyan Abdul Rasheed" states that:

"Asserted (Imamana (As) if by mistake prayer was offered (behind an adversary), then repeat the prayer."

فـرمـودنـد اگـر بـه سهو گزارده باشد بازبگردانید (باب سوم)

Imamana's assertion that to repeat the prayer is such which does not require any further clarification. Now remains the episode of Qhandhar which is recorded in the oldest source "Moulood" of Miyan Abdul Rahman (Rz) which does not refer that the Imam of that place had said anything against Imamana (AS) and neither it mentions that Imamana (AS) had offered prayers behind him or any adversary. It may be pointed out that Miyan Syed Salamullah (Rz) had accompanied Imamana (AS) from the beginning to the last leg and was also present in Qhandhar. If Imamana (AS) had offered prayers behind his adversary, then Miyan Syed Salamullah (Rz) never would have agreed with the letter of Miyan Shah Dilawer (Rz) written in 915 H., which stresses that after the proclamation of Badhli, Imamana (AS) had never offered prayers behind any adversary.

"Khatim-e-Sulaimani" reports that:

"Miyan Syed Salamulla (Rz), brother of Bibi Alahdadi (Rz), and first cousin of Imamana (As), accompanied Imamana (As) from Juanpur to Farah and never was absent from the company of Imamana (As) during this long period."

نـقـل اسـت کـه میان سلام الله برادر حقیقی بی بی الـهـدیتی پسر عـم میراں علیه السلام از بلدۀ پُر نور جونپور در سـفر و حضر همراه حضرت امام بود و گاهی از آنحضرت جدانشده

The decliner's contention that Miyan Syed Salamullah (Rz) had offered prayers, following Imamana (As), behind the adversary, is utterly wrong. The decliner had referred the following narrations as reported in"Insaf Nama":

"It is narrated that in the village Bhadravali, all Muhajereen were present under a tree, namely, Miyan Syed Khundmir (Rz), Miyan Shah Nizam (Rz), Miyan Nemat (Rz), Miyan Dilawar (Rz), Miyan Syed Salamullah (Rz) , Miyan Abu Baker (Rz). The discussion was regarding a person who had offered prayer behind an adversary, thus that man was branded as an "Outsider or a Khariji". Then Miyan Nizam (Rz) inquired Miyan Syed Salamullah (Rz) and Miyan Abu Baker (Rz) what was their practice when many non believers live in your Daira? Miyan Syed Salamullah (Rz) told that he had done according to the situation. Then Miyan Nizam (Rz) smilingly told that they had become outsiders. In that gathering, I was also present there"

نقل است کہ در موضع بھدری والی بوقت عصر ھمہ مھاجران مھدی حاضر بودند بزیر درخت بُرھمچوں میاں سید خوندمیرؓ و میاں نظامؓ و میاں نعمتؓ و بندگی میاں دلاورؓ و میاں ابو بکرؓ و میاں سید سلام اللّٰہؓ بلکہ ھمہ مھاجران و گفتگو ایں بود کہ اگر کسی بدنبال منکران مھدی نماز گزارده اور اخارجی گوئیم بعده بندگی میاں نظامؓ فرمودند کہ میاں ابو بکر و میاں سید سلام اللّٰہ حال شما چوں است درون دائره شما مخالفان مھدی می ماند میاں سید سلام اللّٰہؓ فرمودند مارا انچہ خواھد افتاد آں خواھم کرد بعده میاں نظامؓ تبسم کردند و فرمودند کہ شما در حضور مجلس خارجی شدید درایں مجلس ایں ناقل حاضر بود (باب سوم)

At that gathering except Miyan Syed Mahmood (Rz) every Muhajir's name had been mentioned. It means to say that this gathering was arranged after the demise of Miyan Syed Mahmood (Rz) that is after 920 H.

Miyan Syed Salamullah (Rz) and Miyan Abu Baker (Rz) were the companions of Imamana (As) who had consented in 915 H. For the facts written in the letter of Miyan Shah Dilawer (Rz), stating that Imamana (As) did never offer prayer behind any adversary after the Proclamation of Badhli. In such circumstances how could it be ascertained that after 920 H. they would have offered prayers behind an adversary?

Two issues come out from the said narration: 1. All consented to declare that Mahdavi who offers prayer behind an adversary becomes an "Outsider"

2. After discussion Miyan Nizam questioned Miyan Syed Salamullah (Rz) about his practice.

Miyan Syed Salamullah (Rz) was asked what was his practice when many non believers were residing in his Dairah?

If in any Daira, non believers were residing, then, how anyone can guess that the head of the Daira would allow a non believer to lead the prayers?

From this narration it comes to light that just because non believers were living in those dairahs, Miyan Nizam (Rz) might have remarked as a joke and the answer also was given accordingly corresponding to the joke. Thus it cannot be deduced from this joke that Miyan Syed Salamullah (Rz) and Miyan Abu Baker (Rz) could presume that offering prayers behind an adversary was lawful, particularly when both of them in 915 had consented not to offer prayer behind an adversary since Imamana (As) had not offered any prayer behind an adversary after proclamation of Badhli.

And after that proclamation Imamana (As) had pronounced that the non believers are infidels, then how could it be said that companions of Imamana (As) used to offer prayers behind any adversary?

Author of Hadia's contention that there is no difference in the five times prayers and the Friday and Eidain prayers is utterly false and wrong; since the author does not know that while five times prayers require lapsed prayers should be offered later as Qaza prayers, Friday or Eidain prayers do not require any Qaza prayers, instead the Holy Prophet had advised:

"If any person failed to offer Friday prayer, he is required to pay one Dinar or Half Dinar in charity; as narrated by Samra bin Jandab that:

"Narrated that the holy Prophet (Slm) had advised to those who had not offered the Friday prayer without any reason to pay one Dinar or half a Dinar as a Charity. This has the consent of Imam Ahmed Hanbal (Rz), Abu Dawood (Rz) and Ibn Maja (Rz)."

قـال قـال رسول الله صلى الله عليه و سلم مـن تـرک الجمعة من غير عذر فليتصدق بـدينار فان لـم يـجد فنصف دينار (رواه احمد و ابو داؤد و ابن ماجه)

Author of "Safar-e-Saadat" had written that:

"Stated that whoever had missed Friday prayer without any reason, he had to pay charity of one Dinar or half Dinar; One Dirham or half Dirham or
2 ½ kilo wheat or half of it."

گفته انـد که هر کرفوت شود جمعه بے عذر باید کـه تصـدق کند بدينار يا نصف دينار يادرهم يا نصف درهم يا صاع حنط يا نصف صاع حنطه

But if any of the five times prayers is missed for any reason, there is no charity for it, but you have to offer prayer for the Lapsed one.

19.Friday Prayer and Conditional Obligations:

Five time prayers can be offered by a single man alone, but Friday or Eidain prayers always have to be offered in congregation only. However, Friday prayer is not an obligation for slaves, women, kids and the sick. It is narrated in "Sanan-e-Abu Dawood" by the holy prophet (Slm). With reference to this tradition Author of "Ashatul Lamaat" had written that:

"On the travelers, blinds, and lame persons Friday prayer is not an obligatory prayer. The same has been stated in other traditions."

برمسـافر و اعـمىٰ واعـرج نيز فـرض نيست چنانچه در احاديث ديگر واقع شده است

But as far as five times prayers are concerned they are obligated on residents, as well as on travelers, on women, on slaves, the sick and on the disabled ones.

If heavy rain is there, Friday prayer can be postponed .(Abu Dawood, (Rz) Abu Huraira (Rz), but for Zuhar prayer there is no such provision.

Apart from this Taibi (D.773) had written in "Al Khashif un Haquequl Sunan" that

"Some scholars have maintained that Friday prayer is a sufficiency obligation. Mulla Ali Qari too had accepted what Taibi had stated. But nobody had taken Zuhar prayer as the "sufficiency obligation".

Author of "Insaf Nama" in chapter 4 narrated that:

"Many Muhajereen-e-Mahdi (As) had never gone to opponents' masjid for hearing even a sermon or to get learning."

اکثر مهاجران مهدی را دیدیم که برائے وعظ شنیدن در مسجد و یا برائے خواندن علم پیش مخالفان رفته بودند

When the companions of Imamana (As) disliked to go to any non Mahdavi masjid even for hearing any sermon, then how could it be said that for offering prayers of Friday or Eidain they would have gone?

20.Idolatary and Hypocrisy- Clarified:

Author of "Insaf Nama" in chapter 11, had written that:

"Imamana had described Remembrance of three Pass (three hour period) is a short remembrance and four Pass to be a remembrance of the polytheists."

میرانجیو سه پاس را ذکر قلیل فرمودند و چهار پاس ذکر مشرکان فرمودند

In chapter 17 of Insaf Nama it is written that:

"Short remembrance is an attribute of hypocrites (three Pass)."

میرانؑ فرمودند بودند که ذکر قلیل صفت منافقان یعنی سه پاس

We have proved earlier, in the Part One, chapter 8, of "Insaf Nama" that Perpetual Remembrance is an obligation according to the holy Qur'an. Imamana's narrations point out towards it. As regards the word" Polytheist and Hypocrites" they are used in a literal sense and not in conventional or real sense.

Hypocrite is the one whose precept and practice are against each other. For example:

A. A person who considers perpetual Remembrance is an obligation still he does not follow, then he is called a hypocrite literally.

B. In the same way a person practices four Pass in Remembrance and other four Pass without remembrance, then he is called a polytheist literally, because he served four passes without remembrance.

Commentary of "Insaf Nama" also accept it:

"Four Pass remembrance is called polytheism. It means to say four pass served in Allah's remembrance and four pass served with other than Allah; it means to say that he served four hours with Allah and four hours with Satan"

چهار پاس ذکر کننده را مشرک فرمودند یعنی چهار پاس در یادِ خدا باشند و چهار پاس بغیر خدا مشغول شوند و دوستی حق و دوستی شیطان برابر کنند

This does not mean to say that this sort of man had taken a stone and plant as his idols. However the warnings of Imamana (As) should not be objected, otherwise same objection would arise on the traditions of the holy Prophet (As).

About hypocrisy, Abu Huraira (Rz) narrates that:

"There are three signs of hypocrisy ("Muslim" had added this) that he offers five times prayers, keeps fast then he is a Muslim, while "Bukhari" and "Muslim" agree that: 1. Whenever he tells, he tells a lie; 2. And when he promises for something, he did not keep the promise and 3. Breaches the trust."

آية المنافق ثلث زاد مسلم وان صام وصلى وزعم انه مسلم ثم اتفقا اذا احدث كذب واذاوعد اخلف واذا او تمن خان (متفق عليه)

From this tradition, a person who is a Muslim, who offers prayers and keeps fast, but tells lies, does not keep promises and breaches the trust, may be branded as a hypocrite for example: Abdullah Ibn Abi was a known hypocrite.

But according to Sheik Abdul Haq, such a man cannot be declared a hypocrite, but it means that such attributes are found in the hypocrites.

In this way if it is said that in lieu of perpetual remembrance, if a person is just busy in three Pahar zikr, if he is called a hypocrite, why there be any objection?.

It all boils down to say that Imamana's assertion was just to be with Allah as long as possible thus it is Asserted that "to be engaged in remembering Allah always either sitting, standing or lying. To be precise" Be with Allah, where you are" Imamana (As) advised to his son, Miran Syed Mahmood, Sani-e-Mehdi (Rz) when he asked permission for going to adopt a course for earning a livelihood.

"Shaddad Bin Aous narrated to have heard the holy Prophet (Slm) telling about a person who offers his prayers just for show, he may be branded as a polytheist, it applies also to fast and charity if being given just for show."

شرك. عن شداد ابن اوس قال سمعت رسول الله صلى الله عليه و سلم يقول من صلى يرائى فقد اشرك و من صام يرائى فقد اشرك و من تصدق يرائى فقد اشرك

While commenting on this tradition, author of "Ashatul Lamat" said that:

"Its purpose is that polytheism has two phases. One is conspicuous and the other is concealed. Idol worship is open. It includes any worship done for other than Allah. Thus anything which hinders anyone from Allah, is his idol."

غايت آنكه شرك دو قسم جلى و خفى مى باشد ، شيرك آشكارا، بت پرستى كردن و مرائى كه برائى غير خدا عمل ميكند نيز بت پرستى ميكند ليكن پنهائى چنانچه گفته اند كل ماصدك عن الله فهو صنمك

Hidden polytheism is called short polytheism/Shirk-e-Asghar in traditional language:

"Mahmood Bin Labeed (Rz) narrated that the holy Prophet (Slm) said that the thing which is more dangerous is "Shirk-e-Asghar". When the companions asked what is that? He told it was to act with the purpose to show off." (narrated by Ahmed Hunbal (Rz)

عن محمود ابن لبید ان النبی صلی الله علیه و سلم قال ان اخوف ما اخاف علیکم الشرک الا صغر قالوا یا رسول الله و ما الشرک الا صغر قال الریا رواه احمد

Wherever Imamana (As) had used the word"Shirk" it does not mean real Idoltary for example a person who worships plants and stones is called a Mushrik.

Now we have to see what the author of Hadia tells about Mahdavis: He states:" Now look up at Mahdavis who have fallen to such a bad thing? They ran away from us for obtaining mystic position and getting the vision of Allah, but the tables turned on them and they were named polytheists and hypocrites, and even they were designated as the worst of all."

The same objection can be labeled to those Muslims whom the Prophet (Slm) declared about them that even after becoming Muslims, they are still living the way of the polytheists.

21.Jinn Became Dog, as per tradition:

Miyan Vali Bin Yousuf (Rh) has narrated in "Hujjatul Munsifeen" that:

A. It is reported that a dog was shadowing Imamana(As) and used to stay where Imamana (As) stayed and used to give Azan five times on which the muwazzin used to get up at the proper time daily, from early morning to one pahar (three hours) the dog was busy in remembrance of Allah. If food was kept, it never ate. Sawwiat was given to it. Some persons used to ask about its future. It was said that it would be with the "Ashab-e-Kuhaf(men of the cave)."

روایت کرده است (اند) دنبال امام مهدی سگے اختیار کرده بود همیشه هرجاکه فروشدے این هم فرشدے و پنج وقت بانگ نماز گفتی و بغیرت موذن ازننگ این سگ از خواب بیدار گشتی و هر صبح تاربع روز، زانو نشسته ذکر خفی می کردی کرات و مرات (برائے) آزمودن پیش او طعام نهادے (نهادندے) درآں وقت هرگز نخوردے بعده، اوراهم سویت کسے را حواله کردے بعضے کسان گفت (گفتند) که حال این سگ کدام است فرمودند این یار سگ اصحاب کهف خواهد شد

Author of Hadia had questioned as to how was it possible that a dog could give Call for Prayers? It may be pointed out that this episode had been recorded under miracles of Allah. Miyan Wali Ibn Yousuf (Rh) had referred those miracles which were caused by Imamana (As) in his "Hujjatul Munsifeen". Therefore he himself wrote that:

"I had written in "Hujjatul Munsifeen" with regard to Imam Mahdi's miracles and some extraordinary things which had been reported by the companions; and had been recorded just to test what the adversaries have to say; and whether the followers treat them as a Proof."

بعض آیت هائے مهدی ونقل هائے یاران مهدی شنیده بودم نبشته ام و نام ایں حجة المنصفین نهاده ام تادیده شود که مخالفان براین چه میگویند و موافقان را حجت باشد

The opponents could not inquire "how and in what manner it happened". If they indulge in such questions, then any miracle of any Apostle could not become authentic, but objectionable. An example of the holy Prophet (As) is recorded hereunder:

ازیں باب است حدیث ضب یعنی سو سمار و کلام کردن او دریں حدیث مشهور است روایت کرده است آں رابیهقی در احادیث کثیره و ذکر کرده است قاضی عیاض در شفا از حدیث عمر رضی الله عنه که بود رسول خدا صلی الله علیه و سلم در محفلی از اصحاب خود ناگاه آمد اعرابی از بنی سلیم که شکار کرده است ضب راو گردانیده است اور ادر آستین خود برد اور در منزل گاه خود بریان کندو بخور و چون دیداعرابی جماعه را گفت این کیست که باجامه نشسته است گفته رسول خدا است ، پس بیرون آوردضب را از آستین خود و گفت سو گند بلات و عزی ایمان نمی آرم به توتا ایمان آردایں ضب دانداخت ضب را پیش آنحضرت صلی الله علیه و سلم پس ندا کرد آنحضرت ضب را فرمود یا ضب ، پس جواب داد ضب بزبان متین که شنیدند قوم همه لبیك و سعدیك فرمودند آنحضرت اے ضب کسی آید قیامت را گفت ضب تمام خلق پس فرمود آنحضرت کرا عبادت میکنی گفت خدائی را که در آسمان است عرش اوودر زمین است سلطنت او و در دریا است راه او وودر جنت است رحمت او و در آتش عتاب او ، فرمود آنحضرت من کسیتم گفت رسول خدا ، رسول رب العالمین ، خاتم النبین قدافلح من صدقك و خاب من کذبك پس اسلام آورد اعرابی الحدیث و اشعار نیز نقل کرده اند که ایں ضب نعت آنحضرت خواند صلی الله علیه و سلم

From the same category is the tradition of Soosmar (Ghod-phod) and it had spoken as well. Behaqi had narrated and also there are many traditions available on it.

Narrated Omr (Rz) that the holy Prophet (Slm) was sitting in a gathering. All of a sudden an Airabi came. He had captured a Soosmar and had hidden it in his sleeves with an idea to take it to home, roast and eat. On seeing the gathering he murmured and asked who was that person wearing a gorgeous clothing? He was told that he was the holy prophet (Slm). He took out the Soosmar and threw it in front of the holy Prophet (Slm), swearing in the name of Lott and Uzza (Two Idols of Pagan Arabs), by declaring that he would not accept Islam until the soosmar accepts Islam.

The holy Prophet (Slm) addressed to soosmar. The soosmar replied politely which was heard by all present. The Prophet (Slm) inquired it whether Doomsday would occur? Soosmar told that Doomsday is for all creations. Prophet (Slm) asked whose worship it performs. It answered: Of that Sustainer whose throne is in the skies and whose dominion is on the Earth and the seas are his pathway and paradise is filled with his blessings and the Hell is the manifestation of his punishment. The prophet asked it to tell who he (holy prophet (Slm) was? Soosmar told that he is the Apostle of the Creator of this universe and the Seal of the Prophethood. Whoever accepted him he would become prosper and whoever belied him earned nothing but calamity. Hearing it, the Aarabi accepted Islam., The soosmar had spoken "Encomium" in honor of the Prophet (Slm) which was recorded."

Thus soosmar was in dialogue with the holy Prophet (Slm) and offered poem, praising the Prophet (Slm). Author of Hadia had objected on dog's calling for prayers five times and asked what was the language of the dog and who understood it? Now we have to ask the author about the language of the soosmar in which he announced its "Encomium" and what was its rhyme and its versification? Pity on the author who does not know that plants and stones too had addressed the Holy Prophet (Slm). Author of "Madarijul Nabuwwat " had written that:

"Narrated Hazrat Ali (Rz) that while in Makkah, the holy Prophet (Slm) and he went around the outskirts of Makkah, he noticed that there was no tree and no hillock which did not offer salutation to the holy Prophet (Slm) by name. Reported in "Tirmizi."

از عـلـى رضـى الله عنه آمده که فرمود بودم من با پیغمبر صـلـى الـلّه عـلـيه و آله و سلم بمکه پس بیرون آمدیم در بعضے نواحی آن پس پیش نیامد کوه و نه درخت مگر آن که می گوید السلام علیک یا رسول الله رواه الترمذی

This is also certified by the Holy Qur'an, in which Allah states:

"And there is none who does not praise Allah and proclaims His chastisement."

و ان من شئي الا يسبح بحمده

(بنی اسرائیل ع ۸)

A. If Soosmar's dialogue and plants and stones' addressing the holy Prophet (Slm) is a fact that animals, plants and stone speak and praise, and this fact is an accepted by all, then what is the trouble for the author to accept the dog's calling for the prayers and worshiping Allah?

B. According to "Hujjatul Munsifeen" the said dog might have been with the dog of "Ashab-e-Kahaf"(Men of the cave referred in the Qur'an)). Thus it would be appropriate to tell about that dog of the "Ashab-e-Kahaf."

"And their dog was there in the cave spreading its legs in between the cave."

و کلبهم باسط ذراعیه بالوصید (الکهف ع ۳)

Author of "Mu'allamul Tanzeel" had narrated that:

"Narrated Ka'ab Ahyar that Khalid bin Sa'ad was telling that there would be no animal in the paradise, except the dog of the "Ashab-e-Kahaf and the donkey of Bala'am."

قال کعب احبار قال خالد بن سعدان لیس فی الجنة شئی من الدواب سوے کلب اصحاب الکهف و حمار بلعام

Thus it came to notice that the dog of the "Ashab-e-Kahaf" would get a place in the paradise and dog's traits would vanish on account of the company of the "Ashab-e-Kahaf."

Imam Fakhr-e-Razi (Rz) also had narrated about this verse that:

"Narrated Ka'ab that they passed across a dog who barked on them. They dragged it off and it happened many a time. Then the dog asked them: "what they want from me"? And advised them: "do not fear from me since, I keep friendship with Allah's friends. Thus go to sleep, I shall protect you."

قال کعب مروا بکلب فنبح علیهم فطردوه ففعلوا مرارا فقال لهم الکلب ماتریدون منی لا تخشوا جانبی انا احب احباء الله فنا مواحتی احرسکم

Thus it is clear from this that the dog had a dialogue with them. Had Author of Hadia, any objection for that dialogue of the dog? And had he asked what was its language?

From the traditions it is said that in houses where dog was kept angels do not visit and it is said that the holy Prophet (Slm) never visit a house which had a dog. But the author of Hadia had not read such traditions, and for his information we present it:

"Maimoona narrated that the holy Prophet (Slm) was very sad and kept quiet for the reason that Gabriel (As) even after promising to visit, did not come. Suddenly he felt the presence of a dog's kid in his tent. The Prophet (Slm) asked someone to drag it out and the holy Prophet (Slm) cleaned that place with water. During the night Gabriel (As) came to visit him. The Prophet (Slm) inquired as to why he had not come even though promised?. Gabriel (As) told that we (angels) do not visit houses where dog or an idol is kept. Then in the following morning the holy prophet ordered to kill the dogs. While he ordered to kill the dogs of the small gardens only, but to spare dogs of the big gardens narrated by "Muslim."

عـن ميمـونه ان رسول الله صلى الله عليه و سلم اصبح يـومـا و اجـمـا و قال ان جبرئيل كان وعدنى ان يلقانى الـليـلة فـلم يلقنى والله ما اخلفنى و قع فى نفسه جرد كلـب تـحت فسطاط فامربه فاخرج ثم اخذ بيده ماء فـنـفح مكانه فلما امسى لقيه فقال وعدتنى ان تلقانى الـبـارحة قال اجل ولكنالا ندخل بيتا فيه كلب او صورة فـاصبـح رسـول اللّـه صـلـى اللّـه عليـه و سلم يومئذ فـامـربقتل الكلاب حتى انه يامربكلب الحائط الصغير ويترك كلب الحائط الكبير رواه مسلم

Abdul Haq, Muhaddis-e-Dehalvi, had commented on the words "Tahat-e-Fustat" that:

"The kitten was near the tent of the holy Prophet (Slm). Fustat is the name of that tent which was kept in a journey, but here it is meant for curtain which is kept in house. Another narration says that the kitten was under the cot of the house and the holy Prophet (Slm) did not have any knowledge about it."

زيـر خيـمـه بـود آنحضرت را فسطاط در اصل نام خيمه اسـت كـه در سـفر باشـد ومراد ايں جاپرده ايست كه در خـانـه مـى بـاشـد چنـانچـه حـجـله ومانند آن كذاقيل ودربـعـضى رعـايت آمده كه در خانه آنحضرت بود زير سرير واز خاطر شريف وے رفته بود

It is said that the kitten was of Imam Hasan (Rz) or Imam Husain (Rz):

"And the dog was either belonging to Hasan (Rz) or Husain (Rz) sitting under the cot of the holy Prophet (Slm), later on was driven away on the instructions of the holy Prophet (Slm)."

واذا الـكـلـب بـحسن واوحسين كان تحت نضد لهم فامربه فاخرج

According to Ahmed Bin Hunbal (Rz), Hasan Bin Ali (Rz) used to play with that kitten:

"When the house was opened, I did not ???? find anything except the kitten, with which Hasan (Rz) was playing."

فـفتـحـت البيت فلم اجد فيه شيئا غير جرد كلب كان يلعب به الحسن

Thus it is certain that Gabriel (As) did not visit on account of the presence of the kitten in the house, as promised to the Holy Prophet(Slm).

There is no information that any dog was kept by Imamana (As) in his house. From the objection of the author it cannot be proved that Imamana (As) was keeping a dog in his house. He had written: "Wherever Imamana (As) stopped, the dog too used to stop." This does not prove that any dog was kept by Imamana (As) in his house. However it is reported in the "Insaf Namaa" that:

"There was a dog in the Diara of Imamana (As) when it saw a snake rushed towards it."

در دائره میران سگے بود مار دیده و دویده الیٰ آخره

It means to say that Imamana (As) did not keep any dog in his house. But a dog was living in Imamana's Daira. Daira was like a locality where houses or huts were constructed temporarily since Imamana (As) never stayed for more than 18 months at any one place. In such circumstances, the author had remarked that the holy Prophet (Slm) did not visit any house which had a dog, is simply useless and unwarranted.

Apart from this in the chapter of Bibi Ayesha (Rz) it is said that:

"Ayesha (Rz) used to play with the dolls in the house of the holy Prophet (Slm)".

کانت عائشه تلعب بالبنات فی بیت النبی صلی الله علیه وسلم

"Bukhari" and "Muslim" had reported that:

"I used to play with the dolls when the holy Prophet (Slm) was with me and there were my girlfriends who were also playing along with me." Reported Bibi Ayesha (Rz)

قالت کنت العب بالبنات عندالنبی صلی الله علیه وسلم وکان لی صواحب یلعبن معی الیٰ آخره

In a previous tradition it was said that if the dolls are kept in a house, angels do not visit. It is a fact that Bibi Ayesha (Rz) used to play with dolls along with her girlfriends in the presence of his holy Prophet (Slm). It may be pointed out that those dolls were never figured like a man but just a playing thing without resembling a man. Abdul Haq thus reports that:

"These dolls did not possess particular faces like photos."

مرآں لعبت ها را صورت مشخص نبود چنانچه تصاویر را

Author of "Tuhfa" also had stated that:

"How can the dolls be attributed to having a face. We have to guess what is in vogue at that period."

لفظ بنات را چرا به صورت حمل باید کرد و برانچه دراین وقت معروف و مروج است قیاس باید نمود

When the word "face" cannot be attributed to those dolls, then how the word "Baith" could be applied on a Daira which is like a locality?. Thus it is clear that the dog was in the Daira and not in the house of Imamana (As).

Now we like to discuss about those traditions which are not the traditions but the author had preferred to present them.

"Whoever had kept a dog except for protection of a herd, or for the purpose of a game or for agriculture, it is said that Allah's blessing is reduced for him daily to an equivalent of a Qeerat."	(ا) من اتخذ كلبا الا كلب ماشية او صيداو زرع انتقص من اجره كل يوم قيراط

This tradition too is not appropriate for the purpose of the decliner. There is a warning for those who rear the dogs. But if a dog itself followed any person this warning is not for him. Here the beginning words of "Hujjatul Munsifeen" is that:

"It is reported that a dog used to follow behind Imamana (As)."	روایت کرده است دنبال امام مهدی سگے اختیار کرده بود الٰی آخره

From this it is clear that the dog was not kept, but the dog for getting blessings from Imamana (As) used to follow him. So this was the act of a dog and has nothing to do with Imamana (As). Thus "Mun ittakhaza" does not apply to Imamana (As). Author of "Mirqat" had written under "Mun ittakhaza Kalban"; that "Iqtanahu wa Hafizahu" and "Mun Iqtana Kalban" and had described that:

"It Means: Kept safe, tied and stopped."	ای حفظ وحبس وامسک

The second tradition states: to bind the dogs (Yartabitoona Kalban). Thus the dog was following Imamana (As) by itself. Therefore neither "Mun ittakhaza Kalban" nor "Yartabitoona Kalban" apply to Imamana (As).

Another tradition presented by the author is this:

"It is a fact that the holy Prophet (Slm) ordered to kill the dogs except those which were reared for hunting or for protection of the herds."	(ب) ان النبی صلی الله علیه و سلم امر بقتل الكلاب الا كلب صيداوغنم اوماشية

The decliner's presentation of this tradition is simply senseless, because the previous tradition tells that the holy Prophet (Slm) had not ordered to kill those dogs which were kept for the safety of the big gardens. For his information, the wordings of the tradition are:

"Thus the holy Prophet (Slm) ordered to kill the dogs of the small gardens, but not of the big gardens and asked to let them live (for the specific purpose.)"	فامريقتل الكلب حتٰی انه يامريكلب الحائط الصغيرويترک كلب الحائط الكبير .

The commentators had stated that the holy Prophet (Slm) did not order to kill the dogs of the big gardens because safety of those gardens was imminent.

The position of the daira also was like a big garden, hence keeping dogs for the sake of safety cannot be said to be a hindrance for the angels to visit that place.

Author of "Ashatul Lam'aat" had written that:

"And were left alive those dogs of the big gardens because they were kept for the purpose of safety and security. That means to say that those dogs which required to be reared for the sake of security do not hinder the angels to enter."

ومی گذاشت سگ بوستان بزرگ را که درو زیارت احتیاج است به محافظت وپاسبانی دراینجا ظاهر می شود که سگے که احتیاج است به نگهداشتن وے مانع نیست از دخول ملائکه

Thus there is no record that any dog was kept by Imamana (As) in his house. If it is accepted that the dog did not come into the daira by itself, but was reared for the purpose of security of the daira, then also in view of the tradition, there should be no objection.

However the author of "Madarijul Nabuwwat" had explained that it is permissible to keep a dog for the protection of a house.

"Keeping a dog for protection of a house, or game or for gardens is permissible."

نگاه داشتن سگ برائے شکار و حراست خانه و کشت و باغ جائز است

"Ashatul Lama'at" narrates:

"Keeping the dogs for the purpose of protection of house or the herds is permitted."

نگاه داشتن کلب برائے پاسبانی و حفظ مواشی مباح است

Now we like to review the absurd opinion of the author of Hadia against Imamana (As):

"He had neither a garden, nor he played games and had not any herd of lambs that required the need for keeping a dog, without these three reasons, keeping a dog was a sin." This silly objection indicates that the decliner was unaware of the religion of the traditionalists. It proved from the traditions that keeping a dog for protection of a big garden or a house is permissible and it is not a cause of hindrance for the angels to visit those places, particularly when the dairah was just like a locality.

The author had written that the Saints (Aouliah Allah) never kept dogs. This information is also baseless since Mulla Abdul Rahman Jami (Rh) had narrated that Sheik Najmuddin Kubra (Rz) had a dog and Sheik Abdul Qader Jeelani (Rz) too had a dog. Mulla Abdul Rahman Jami (Rh) reports about Sheik Najmuddin Kubra (Rh) that:

"One day there had been a discussion regarding "Men of the Cave", Sheik Saaduddin Hamavi, one of the disciples of the Shaikh, began to think whether there was any person in the Ummah whose traits affect any dog. Sheik Najmuddin Kubra (Rz) by inspiration got his idea and went to the door of his monastery. At the same time a dog appeared and stood up before him, Sheik looked at it. Then the dog became senseless and when it came to senses ran towards a graveyard. It is said that wherever it went 50 to 60 dogs used to encircle it and used to keep one hand before another and kept quiet without creating any noise and not eating anything and used to stand up for paying respect to that dog. Finally that dog died and was buried under the orders of the Sheik, a building was constructed over its grave."

روزی تحقیق و تقریر اصحاب کهف می رفت شیخ سعد الدین حمومی را رحمه الله تعالیٰ که یکی از مریدان شیخ بود بخاطر گزشت که آیا درای امت کسی باشد که صحبت وے در سگ اثر کند بنور فراست بدانست برخاست و بدر خانقاه رفت و بالسیت و ناگاه سگے آنجا رسیده بالیتادو دنبال جنبانید شیخ را نظر بروے فتادو در حال بخشش یافت و متحیر و بیخود شده روی از شهر بگردانید و بگورستان رفت و سربر زمین مالید تاآورده اند که هر کجا که می آمدومی رفت قریب پنجاه و شصت سگ گرداگرد او حلقه میکردند و هیچ نخوردے و بحرمت بایستادندے عاقبت بدان نزدیکی بمرو فرمودتاوے رادفن کردند و برسر قبروے عمارت ساختند

From this episode it comes to light that with the beneficence of that glance of the Sheik, the dog was so much affected that other dogs too got the blessings from the company of that blessed dog. Sheik's order for constructing a building was to initiate his disciples, including Sheik Saaduddin Hamavi, to get beneficence by visiting its grave.???? The significance of this episode gets more important when Mullah Abdul Rahman Jami, a godly man and a mystic had reported this episode without any objection.

Author of "Khazinatul Asfiah" had written a couplet regarding this episode: The Saying of Moulana Rome vouchsafe this episode:

"Put a glance on me that I become contented. When the dog got blessings from Najmuddin Kubra (Rz), it became the leader of the dogs."

چنانچه قول مولوی روم درای باب شاهد حال است
شعر : ایک نظر فرما که مستغنی شوم زابنائے جنس
سگ چو شد منظور نجم الدین سگان را سروراست

Yet another fact against the baseless assertion of the jealous decliner that "the saints never kept dogs". For this ill-informed decliner we like to bring to his notuice that Hazrat Shaikh Abdul Qader Jeelani (Rz) had also kept a dog for protection of his monastery. It is reported that when Sheik Ahmed arrived at the monastery riding on a tiger, the dog attacked the tiger and cut down it into pieces. This episode had been narrated in an eulogy, which is as follows:

"When Hazrat Ghous-e-Azam (Rz) heard about the arrival of Sheik Ahmed riding on a tiger, he sent a cow for the tiger's meal, but before the tiger jumped on the cow, the dog of the monastery jumped on the tiger and cut it into pieces."

حضرت غوث اعظم رضی الله عنه را معلوم شد پس انگاه در عقب فرستادن ماده گاو سگے که همیشه بر در خانقاه عالیجاه افتاده بود بموجب حسب الامر عالی روان شد به مجرد دیدن ماده گاو شیخ شیر خود را براو داشت و ماده گاو استاده ماند سگ آنحضرت از عقب گاو زغن کرده شیر را گرفت و پاره پاره کرد

From the above narration it is clear that Hazrat Sheik Abdul Quader Jeelani (Rz) used to keep a dog at his monastery. On orders of the Sheik (Rz) it jumped on the tiger which tell that the dog had the Blessings of the Sheik (Rz), on account of that Blessing only, it attacked the tiger and cut into pieces, as mentioned above..

Thus the author's contention is absolutely wrong that the saints never kept the dogs. Before raising foolish allegations, he must consult others, if he has not read about those Saints. It is his illiteracy and lack of knowledge.

Be it Najmuddin Kubra (Rz) or Sheik Abdul Quader Jeelani (Rz), if they reared a dog for security of their houses it cannot get the sanctity in view of the traditions of the holy Prophet (Slm).

Apart from this the author had narrated an incomplete translation that: " Miyan Syed Mahmood, Sani-e-Mehdi (Rz) kept a dog whose name was Lala. One day Bibi Malkan (Rz) threw a piece of brick on it. Miyan (Rz) informed her that if it was a dog, your throwing the brick was correct, but it was not a dog. Bibi inquired: Miranji (Rz) is it not Bhai Kalo, but Kalo's brother. The portion the author had omitted is this:

"One day a dog by name Lala came to the house of Bibi Malkan (Rz), whom Bibi Malkan (Rz) bet it with a piece of brick."

روزے پیش صحن خانه بی بی ملکان لاله آمد بی بی برو خشت پاره زوند الی آخره

From this event it comes to light that even just looking at a dog entering the house, Bibi hit the dog with a piece of brick , then the question of keeping a dog in houses does not arise.

That portion was purposely omitted by the author which points out how Mahdavis used to hate the dogs.These points come to light from the above narrations:

1. It is stated that the dog had entered into the courtyard, tells that the dog was not living in the house but came from outside in the daira which was like a locality.

2. The wording of the narration reported by the biased decliner was that it was not a dog. It tells that it was not a dog but a jinn.

3. Bibi Malkan's remark that it is like Bhai Kaloo, tells that the Kaloo named dog used to live in Imamana's daira, was also a Jinn.

4. It was known that the dog which was living in the daira was a Jinn, that is why Bibi Malkan (Rz) referred it, and Miran Syed Mahmood (Rz) testified that it was its brother.

According to a tradition it is stated that the Jinns changed themselves into the face of a dog.

"Ibn Sa'albital Khishni narrated that the holy Prophet (Slm) said there are three types of Jinns. One type has feathers upon them, through those feathers they fly in the air. The second type is that of the snake and dogs. The third type is that they come down on the earth and travel, but nobody recognizes them."

عـن ابى ثـعلبة الخشنى يرفعه الجن ثلثة اصناف صنف لهـم اجنحة يطيرون فى الهواء وصنف حيات و كلاب و صنف يحلون و يظعنون رواه فى شرح السنة

There should be no objection if the Jinns convert themselves as dogs. However, dogs have no filthy faces, but its entity is filthy. After all Jinns and men are created by the Almighty for His worship only:

"I did not create the Jinn and men, but for worship"

ماخلقت الجن والانس الا ليعبدون (ذاريات)

Thus in this way if a Jinn in the face of a dog indulges in worship, how could it be said that it is against Qur'anic Version?

22.Obligation of Hajj - Capacity to Perform:

Author of Hadia on account of his crookedness had said that "Sheik Juanpuri (As) used to prohibit people from performing Hajj, even though Hajj is one of the tenets of Islam, hence it is an obligation, if people were capable to perform. Thus he reports that: " a pious woman approached Imamana (As) and informed that she had intended to perform Hajj, "if permitted, I shall proceed". Imamana (As) asked her to be with remembrance of Allah. After some time she again went to Imamana (As) and told that she had enough money to go and perform Hajj. There is peace and no troubles also. Imamana (As) asked her to go to Miyan Dilawer (Rz) and circumuambulate three times around his room. She did as was told and she had the vision of Allah on the third round and she became absorbed and senseless. Imamana sent "puskhurda" (left over water after drinking) to her, by consuming it, she came to her senses.

The fact is that it was a young lady having no male person along with her and went to Imamana (As) and asked his permission. Ladies are prohibited to perform Hajj when no eligible male person was available to go along with them.

"Without a Mahram no woman should travel."

(ا) لا تسافرن امرأة الا و معها محرم

Here Mahram, close relation, is one with whom matrimony is unlawful, (except husband).

"Abu Huraira (Rz) narrates that the holy Prophet (Slm) prohibited women from performing travel even for one day or one night, except when a Mahram (or husband) also traveling along with her."

(ب) عن ابی هریرہ قال قال رسول اللہ صلی اللہ علیہ و سلم لا تسافر امراۃ مسیرۃ یوم ولیلۃ الا و معها ذو محرم

Sheik Abdul Haque, Muhaddis-e-Dehalvi states with reference to this tradition that:

"Some say it is for three day's journey. But a traditionalist state that there is no limitation of days, it is for any time, whether a short journey or a long one."

در بعضے روایات مسیرۃ سہ روزہ واقع شدہ و گفتہ اند بر ہر تقدیر مراد تحدید نیست بلکہ مطلق سفر است طویل یا قصیر

Thus, in view of the traditions, Imamana's prohibition was correct for that young lady who desired to perform Hajj without having a Mahram, or husband, any male person along with her.

The first thing is that a pious woman asked permission for Hajj. Imamana (As) asked her to be with remembrance of Allah, and he had never told not to perform Hajj.

Second is that when she went to Imamana (As) second time and told that she had amount and there is peace for the journey. It proves that the lady felt the conditions for Hajj were not fulfilled, hence she went second time and asked permission by telling she had money to perform Hajj and there was peace for the journey. Still she had no Mahram person along with her. Then Imamana (As) asked her to go to Miyan Shah Dilawer's room, who was her spiritual guide and to circumambulate three times of the room of her Murshid, means to get beneficence from Shah Dilawer (Rz). Such sort of assertion is well known in Arabic and Persian. Examples:

"Then came Abu Bakr (Rz) and he had brought whatever he had with him. The holy Prophet (Slm) asked if he had left some stock for the family? He answered that he had Allah and His Rasool (Slm) for him."

بعد از آن ابو بکر آمد ، ہر چہ داشت تمام بر آوردبہ وے نیز فرمود ، بـرائے عیال چہ ذخیرہ کردۂ گفت اذخرت اللہ و رسولہ

The holy Prophet (Slm) asked about Stock. The answer was accordingly given. It was Trust in Allah. Here Abu Bakr's answer was regarding the stock, but he referred Allah and His Rasool (Slm) for that.. There should be no objection for his answer.

Author of "Mukhtasarul Muaani" had written this couplet whose translation is:

"Asked: Demand anything. We shall cook good food for you. Then I said cook for me Shirt and a robe."

Here cooking shirt and robe means to stitch a shirt and a robe.

In case of that lady who asked permission for Hajj, the relevant word for Hajj was circumambulation. But purpose was to be in the company of Shah Dilawer (Rz). But if the lady actually took the meanings in reality and circumambulated, then it is her action. In Persian sometimes it is said" Khak Shudan"as an idiom, but could it be taken as to become earth?

Author of "Muntahiul Arab" states that" After knowing conditions then perform Tawaf-e--Kabah" that means if you do not know the rituals of the Hajj, then performance of Hajj is not complete. Therefore if a person does circumumbulate for thousand times of a room, it is not a Tawaf, then how could it be called a Hajj? It may be pointed out that the word Tawaf has two meanings. Literary meaning is to go around a thing. The conventional meanings are two: One going around the Kabatullah and second is to go around the grave of a Saint or godliman. According to the author of "Farhang-e-Asafia":

"To go round and round of a thing" or to go around Kabatullah or around the grave of a saint."

In the same sense "Bahar-e-Ajam" states that "Tawaf" means to go around a thing for example going around the graves of saintly people also, apart from Kabatullah.

It all boils down to say that the author of Hadia's contention that going around the room of Shah Dilawer (Rz) was deemed to have performed the Hajj, which is senseless and meaningless, maliciously and derogatorily uttered by the author of Hadia against Imamana (As).

However, In "Tazkeratus Saleheen" it has been mentioned about Shah Dilawer (Rz) for a person and not for a lady.

"Narrated that a brother requested Imamana's permission for going to Hajj; Imamana (As) asked him to circumambulate the room of Miyan Dilawer (Rz), you will get your purpose accomplished."

نقل است که برادر پیش میرانجی رخصت حج خواست فرمودند کـه سـر طـواف حـجـره میان دلاور بکنید تا مقصود حاصل خواهدشدد (باب هفتم)

Here instead of a young lady, a brother is mentioned and it was not clear whether he had meant to perform the Hajj or not. Therefore Imamana's advice to him was to circumambulate the room of Shah Dilawer (Rz) in order to get beneficence of Shah Dilawer (Rz) to get his desire of going to Hajj accomplished. In the same sense the young lady was also asked to circumambulate. But it was not clear whether the person or the lady had actually circumambulated around the room of Shah Dilawer (Rz)? From it comes to light that the person had guessed the meaning of the word according to the context. Imamana's words "Maqsood hasil Khawhed shawad" means you will attain your purpose solved. Therefore asking a lady or a brother to attend to the service of Shah Dilawer (Rz) and get his beneficence in order to get his or her purpose solved.

It may be pointed out that no Mahdavi disciple had tried to go around the room of an alive mentor leave aside any grave. Although it had been a practice of some mystics. For example:

Hazrat Abu Sayeed Abul Khair (D.440) was an eminent saint. His custom was that whenever a disciple intended to go to Hajj, he used to direct him to circumambulate the grave of Peer Abul Fazal for seven times. This had been reported by Mullah Abdul Rahman Jami:

"Thus if any disciple intended to go to Hajj, Shaik Abu Sayeed used to direct him to the grave of Pir Abul Fazal and asked him to circumambulate seven times so as to get his purpose solved."

بعد از آن هر مرید را که اندیشهٔ حج بودے شیخ وے را بسر خاك پیر ابوالفضل فرستادے و گفتے آن خاك را زیارت کن و هفت باز گرد آن خاك طواف کن تا مقصود حاصل شود

However Mahdavis do visit the graves which is according to the traditions, but never take rounds of any grave. Author of "Shawahedul Vilayet" in chapter 12 had referred what Imamana (As) said to Malik Barkhurdar (Rz):

"If out of love, even I give you my skin to you, and you did not practice what I taught during the prayers of Asr and Maghrib, then my Allah has that power to take out my skin from your body and give it back to me and punish you."

اگر بنده محبت کرده پوست خود بپوشاند انچه بنده درمیان عصر و مغرب میگوید نه کنید خدائے من قادر است پوست بنده به بنده بپوشاند و شما را عذاب کند

In "Naqliyat-e-Miyan Abdul Rasheed" the same episode has been written with some difference:

"It is narrated that if a person out of benediction requested for a shirt or shoes, Imamana (As) used to say: even if you wear my skin, you would not get salvation, until you practice what I say. Then he said that on the Day of Judgment Allah would not ask your caste or creed or whose son you are, but ask for your practice and sincerity in the worship."

نقل است اگر کسی از حضرت میران بطریق تبرك جامه یا کفش طلبیدے فرمودندے اگر پوست من بپوشید نجات نیابید تاکه عمل نه کنید انچه بنده می گوید ، باز فرمودند که روز قیامت از نسب نخواهد پرسید که این پسر کسیت از عمل با اخلاص خواهد پرسید (باب هفتم)

When such instances are reported about Imamana (As) for practice, then how could it be accepted that Imamana (As) had directed the lady or the brother to circumambulate the room of Shah Dilawer (Rz) for three times in lieu of the Hajj?

In these circumstances, the word "Tawaf" shall be deemed to have been used to serve the purpose and obtain beneficence which are in accordance with the Qur'an and the traditions:

The Holy Prophet (Slm) said:

"One thousand servants circumambulate around me, as if they are hidden eggs or scattered pearls"

یطوف علی الف خادم کانهم بیض مکنون اولولو منثور

Can any person argue on this tradition that the person of the holy Prophet (Slm) may be taken as Kabatullah and those who are circumambulating around him are actually circumambulating the Kabatullah?

About this tradition author of "Ashatul Lam'at" had written that:

"Circumambulate around me and serve me" گرد من گردند و خدمت می کنند مرا

The Qur'an even tells "Circumambulate around you" it also means to serve you. "Tafseer-e-Baizavi" mentions about "Yatoofu Alaihim" means service only. In this manner the meanings of "to circumambulate the room of Shah Dilawer (Rz)" may be construed to serve Miyan Shah Dilawer (Rz) to get his beneficence and nothing else.

Thus nobody can argue that Imamana (As) had prohibited anyone from performing Hajj. (And it is a fact that he himself had performed Hajj.) Therefore prohibiting the lady who was alone for going to Hajj was just in accordance to the tradition and was perfectly correct. A man who is malicious only can attribute this action as impolite.

Apart from this "Tirmizi" had reported about Umroo Bin Shuaib that:

"The holy Prophet (Slm) told that whoever repeats Allah's Greatness for 100 times in a day and again in the night, it tantamount to have performed 100 times Hajj." قال رسول الله صلى الله عليه و سلم من سبح الله مأته مرة بالغداة و مأته بالعشى كان كمن حج مائة حجة

How can it be said that just by telling 100 times "Subhanalla", actually he had performed Hajj? It is just to indicate the excellence for repeating the Greatness of Allah.

In the same sense the circumambulation of the room of Shah Dilawer (Rz) means to serve Shah Dilawer (Rz) and get his beneficence through serving him.

23. Jinn and Punishment:

This narration is regarding Shah Dilawer (Rz), which shall be dealt in Part 3 under Shah Dilawer's narratives.

24: 1. Previous Learning 2. Sikander's Episode:

This episode pertains to Shah Nizam (Rz). This also shall be discussed in Part 3.

25. After Farz, Lifting Hands for Blessings: Against tradition:

Author of Hadia had branded as rude not to lift hands for blessings after the Farz prayers by Mahdavis, and had insisted that it is a tradition to lift hands after the Farz prayers and this is in vogue from the time of the holy Prophet (Slm) to this day by the Ummah., but it seems it is prohibited for Mahdvis.

We have argued about the Obligatory functions and had proved that when Allah commands Muslims an order, then it becomes an obligation to him.

"Call your Sustainer with humility and in a hidden manner, Allah does not hold dear who transgress." ادعوا ربكم تضرعا و خفية انه لا يحب المعتدين

According to the verse it requires humility in a hidden manner for calling Blessings from Allah and this is a fixed limit from Allah. If any person did not call with humility he had crossed that limit, his call has no value before Allah. The call for blessings is completed in prostration only since prostration itself is a perfect act of humility and the call which is being made in the prostration is a hidden one. Therefore the holy Prophet (Slm) had advised to invoke the Blessings while prostrating. "Muslim" had narrated Hazrat Abu Huraira (Rz) that:

"Narrated that in prostration, one is nearer to Allah, thus call him while prostrating."	قـال قـال رسـول الـلّـه صـلى الـلّـه عليه و سلم اقرب مايكون العبد من ربه و هو ساجدفاكثروا الدعافيه

The holy Prophet (Slm) not only advised his followers for calling the blessings while prostrating, but he himself was practicing as narrated by Bibi Ayesha (Rz) in "Muslim":

"Narrated Ayesha (Rz) that one night, when I did not find the holy Prophet (Slm) in his bed, then I searched him out when my hands touched his sole, I heard him uttering slowly while prostrating: "Oh Allah with your permission I am seeking your protection from your wrath and claiming peace and tranquility from your wrath and seeking your refuge from you with your permission and I cannot count your Blessings."	قـالـت فقدت رسول الله صلى الله عليه و سلم ليلة من الـفـراش فـالتمسته فوقعت يدى على بطن قدميه و هو فـى السـجـدة و هـمـا منصوبتان و هو يقول اللهم انى اعـوذبـرضـاك مـن سـخـطـك و بـمـعـافـاتـک من عقوبتك و اعوذبک منـک لا احصىٰ ثناء عليک رواه مسلم

There are two conditions for benediction. The holy Prophet (Slm) had clarified that calling for the blessings while prostrating shows humility in a hidden manner. Therefore Mahdavis do not lift their hands in benediction, because the purpose to hide is nullified by making it openly, which is against the Qur'anic injunctions and against the tradition also. Since the holy Prophet (Slm) had ordained categorically in this respect.

Apart from this Author of "Madarik" had stated that:

"Narrated by Hasan (Rz) that in between hidden benediction and open one, there are seventy weaknesses."	عن الحسن بين دعوة السر والعلانية سبعون ضعفا

It is clear that invoking benediction by lifting hands means calling openly, therefore prone to have 70 weaknesses.

There is no tradition that the holy Prophet (Slm) had called a benediction by lifting his hands. No-one can prove that lifting hands in benediction had been adopted on the basis of a tradition. Author of Hadia had presented the following traditions to justify his so called claim:

1. 1."Call his benediction with hidden palms and do not call vice versa, when completed run over your faces with your palms."

(۱) سلوا اللّه بطون کفکم ولا تسئلوه بظهورها فاذافرغتم فامسحوابها و جوهکم (ابو داؤد)

2. "It was the practice of the holy Prophet (Slm) who used to call for benediction by lifting his hands then he ran over his palms over his face."

(۲) کان رسول الله صلی الله علیه و سلم اذا رفع یدیه فی الدعاء لم یردهما حتّی یمسح بهاوجهه (ترمذی)

The holy Prophet (Slm) had never lifted his hands after the Farz prayer according to this tradition. It comes to light that the holy Prophet (Slm) whenever he lifted his hands, he used to run over his face with the palms of his hands. It does not prove that after Farz prayers he had lifted hands for benediction.

3. It is said that the etiquette of calling the Blessings has been described in "Tirmizi" that both hands should be lifted with palms opened; while Haakim mentions that lifting of both hands toward the sky. But both do not refer lifting is necessary after farz prayer.

4.."People asked the holy Prophet (Slm) as to which benediction is mostly granted? Prophet asserted "between the last quarter of the night and before completion of the Farz prayer of Fajr."

(۳) قیل یا رسول الله صلی الله علیه و سلم ای الدعاء اسمع قال جوف اللیل الاخر ودبر الصلوات المکتوبات (ترمذی)

It is regarding best timings for acceptance of the benediction by Allah.. There is no peculiarity of the Farz prayer. Even that benediction which is invoked during the last quarter of the night may be mostly accepted. The benediction which is invoked after Farz prayer which is recited in between Durood and Salaam. The holy Prophet (Slm) had clearly stated that between the last quarter of the night. Therefore it is not necessary to invoke benediction only after completion of the Farz prayer, but he asserted to invoke before completion of Farz prayer of Fajr. Any time during the night it may be invoked which may be accepted by the Almighty mostly. But no where it was stated that you have to lift hands for acceptance after farz prayer.

5. In Chapter "Al Anbiah" of "Sahih Bukahri", it is mentioned that when Hazrat Ibrahim (As) left his wife and son near Kabatullah under the command of the Almighty, he went far enough that he could not see them, then he invoked benediction facing towards Kabatullah. Here also it is not mentioned that after completion of the Farz prayer he lifted hands for calling the Blessings from the Almighty .

However it cannot be proved that only by lifting hands, benediction is accepted by Allah.

It may be said that the narrations regarding calls for Blessings by lifting hands might have been in vogue, before orders came for the benedictions to be invoked while prostrating. And these are according to the categorical Qur'anic injunction.

"The Holy Prophet (Slm) never raised his hands for the blessings of Allah, except for calling for the rain, he raised his hands to the extent of his armpits."

ان النبى صلى الله عليه وسلم كان لا يرفع يديه فى شئٍ من دعائه الا فى الاستسقا حتىٰ يرى بياض ابطيه (مسلم)

Author of Hadia had maintained that after Farz prayer lifting of hands is in vogue as per traditions, but he never presented a single tradition in which lifting hands were essential.

However he had tried to cut and amend according to suit his purpose by quoting a tradition of "Bukhari" so that general public may assume that after Farz prayer lifting hands for benediction was directed. What he had tried to present the same is presented hereunder:

"It is reported in "Sahih Bukhari" that one day the holy Prophet (Slm) went to patch up some differences among Bani Amr. When he reached masjid, he saw Abu Baker (Rz) was leading the prayer. The holy Prophet (Slm) by crossing the prayer mats came to the first row. Abu Baker (Rz) guessed the presence of the holy Prophet (Slm) and in order to provide him the leader's position, started to come back, but the holy Prophet (Slm) hinted Abu Bakr (Rz) to continue leading the prayer. But, instead, Abu Bakr (Rz) lifted both his hands and praised Allah and turned back and after completion of the prayers, the holy Prophet (Slm) asked him as to why he had not continued the prayers even after he had hinted? Abu Bakr (Rz) told: the son of Abu Qahafa was not so great to lead the prayers in the presence of the holy Prophet (Slm)!

In presenting this tradition, the author of Hadia had shown his dishonesty. It is mentioned in the tradition that when Abu Bakr (Rz) came back, the holy Prophet (Slm) went forward and led the prayer, which fact the author did not mention and presented this tradition in such a way that the public should think that Abu Bakr (Rz) had completed the prayer and lifted his hands for the benediction and came back. In order to prove his deceit the true version of the tradition as mentioned in "Bukahri" is submitted below :

ثنا سعيد بن ابى مريم ثنا ابو غسان ثنا ابو حازم عن سهل بن سعد ان انا سا من بنى عمرو بن عوف كان بينهم شئى فخرج اليهم النبى صلى الله عليه و سلم فى اناس من اصحابه يصلح بينهم فحضرت الصلوٰة لم يات النبى صلى الله عليه و سلم فاذن بلال بالصلوٰة و لم يات النبى صلى الله عليه و سلم فجاء الى ابى بكر فقال ان النبى صلى الله عليه و سلم حبس و قد حضرت الصلوٰة فهل لك ان تؤم الناس فقال نعم ان شئت فاقام الصلوٰة فتقدم ابو بكر ثم جاء النبى صلى الله عليه و سلم يمشى فى الصفوف حتى قام فى الصف الاول فاخذ الناس فى التصفيح حتى كثر و اوكان ابو بكر لايكاد يلتفت فى الصلوة فالتفت فاذاهو بالنبى صلى الله عليه و سلم وراءه فاشار اليه بيده فامره ان يصلى كما هو فرفع ابوبكريديه فحمد الله ثم رجع القهقوىٰ وراءه حتى دخل فى الصف فتقدم النبى صلى الله عليه و سلم فصلى بالناس فلما فرغ اقبل على الناس فقال يا ايها الناس اذا نابكم شئى فى صلوتكم اخذتم بالتصفيح انما التصفيح للنساء من تابه شئى فى صلوة فليقل سبحان الله سبحان الله فانه لايسمعه احدالا التفت يا ابابكو ما منعك حين اشرت اليك لم تصل فقال ما كان ينبغى لا بن ابى قحافه ان يصلى بين يدى النبى صلى الله عليه و سلم

"Sayeed Bin Abi Maryam narrated this tradition that Abu Ghissan reported that Abu Hazim told to Suhail Bin Sa'ad that some persons belonging to Bani Umroo had cultivated some differences. Thus the holy Prophet (Slm) went to patch up those differences. Some companions too accompanied him. Time for prayer had come, Call for prayers was given but the holy Prophet (Slm) did not arrive. Bilal (Rz) went to Abu Bakr (Rz) and told that the holy Prophet (Slm) might have been stopped at that place and may not come early for the prayers. So would he lead and complete the prayer. He agreed on being pressed. Bilal (Rz) started Takbeer and Abu Bakr (Rz) went forward to lead. Then the holy prophet (Slm) came and somehow managed to go into the front row and stood behind Abu Bakr (Rz). People started their hands clapping till the noise increased. Abu Bakr (Rz) as per his habit never cared for it. When he sensed that holy Prophet (Slm) was behind him who had hinted Abu Bakr (Rz) to continue prayer. Abu Bakr (Rz) lifted his both hands and praised Allah and gave leader's place to the holy Prophet (Slm). Then the holy Prophet (Slm) advanced and started leading the prayer. After completion, he addressed the people and remarked "if anything happens you people start beating on one another. This is the habit of women. If anything occurs during prayer you have to say "Subhan Allah, Subhan Allah" and whoever heard it would become attentive". Then addressed Abu Bakr (Rz) and asked: "when I hinted you to continue the prayer then why you had stopped the prayer?" Abu Bakr (Rz) told that the son of Abu Qahafa felt inappropriate to lead in the presence of the holy P r o p h e t (S l m) . "

This tradition tells that Abu Bakr (Rz) had yet to start the prayers and when he sensed that holy Prophet (Slm) had come, he lifted his hands and praised Allah and came back, then the holy Prophet (Slm) completed the prayer. It does not speak that after completion of the Farz prayer, Abu Bakr (Rz) lifted his both hands and called for the Blessings. Hamidi narrated that Abu Bakr (Rz) did not lift his hands but raised his head in gratitude. In another tradition it is stated that:

"Thus Abu Bakr (Rz) lifted his both hands and praised Allah. It means that he outright exclaimed Allah's Greatness. Safian had reported in Hamidi that for offering gratitude Abu Bakr (Rz) lifted his head and came back. Ibn Jozi claimed that Abu Bakr (Rz) showed hand in gratitude but did not tell anything. Holy Prophet (Slm) asked as to why he had lifted his hands when he hinted him to continue. Then what was the hindrance to continue the prayer? Abu Bakr (Rz) said that when I guessed your presence I exclaimed Allah's Greatness and came back."

فرفع ابو بكر يديه فحمد الله ظاهرة انه حمد الله تعالىٰ بلفظه صريحا لكن فى رواية الحميدى عن سفيان فرفع ابو بكر راسه الى السماء شكر اللّٰه و رجع القهقرىٰ وادعى ابن جوزى انه اشارا لى الشكر والحمد بيده ولم يتكلم وليس فى رواية الحميدى مايمنع ان يكون بلفظه و يقوى ذلك مارواه احمد من رواية عبدالعزيز الماجشون عن ابى حازم يا ابابكر لمارفعت يديك و ما منعك ان تثبت حين اشرت اليك قال رفعت يدى لانى حمدت الله على مارايت منك

Thus, if Hazrat Abu Bakr Siddiq (Rz) had lifted his hands or his head it is nothing to do with the completion of the Farz prayer. And it is a fact that when the holy Prophet (Slm) arrived he simply praised Allah in gratitude. Ibn Jozi had said that he did not utter anything from his mouth. Hence the holy Prophet (Slm) led the prayer.

Author of Hadia hopelessly failed to submit a single tradition which points out that after the Farz prayer the holy Prophet (Slm) had ever lifted his hands and invoked benediction. His assertion that lifting hands for benediction after farz prayer was in practice following any tradition is null and void since it is baseless. Particularly when the claimant failed to submit any concrete proof about the existence of any tradition.

Author of "Safer-e-Saadat" had said that:

"There is no tradition regarding running of both palms of the hands on face."

درباب مسح الوجه باليدين بعد الدعا حديثى صحيح نشده

When running hands on face after benediction is negatived thus the question of lifting hands for benediction does not arise at all.

Regarding the practice of Mahdavis author of "Proofs of Mahdi" has written that:

"Thus what blame could be framed against the sect of Imamana (As) who in every rak'at recite sura-e-Fatiha, and before completion of prayer, and before Salaam, recite Darood and Massora and after performing Tahiathal Wazoo go in prostration and call for benediction secretly. Thus because of not lifting hands after Farz prayer how any blame could be inflicted upon them and how can it be said that they do not call for the benediction?"

پس چگونه طعن لازم آید بر قوم مهدی علیه السلام که سورۀ فاتحه در هر رکعت می خوانند و دعاء ماثوره بعد از درود قبل تمام ، الصلوٰۃ یعنی قبل السلام می خوانند بعد از دورکعت تحیتہ الوضو در خلوت گذارده بہ سجده رفتہ مناجات و دعوات کہ بایآت و احادیث ثبوت یافتہ اند بہ طریق راز و نیاز باخالق خود می خواهند پس محض بر نابرداشتن دست بعد از هر نمازے برایشان چگونه طعن لازم آید وایشاں راچگونه توان گفت کہ دعانمی خوانند

Author of "Isbat-e-Mahdi" had still narrated that:

"Imamana (As) had particularly directed his followers to request secretly Allah's Blessings . They should do it secretly after completion of ablution, offer two rak'ats of "Thiathal Wazoo" and invoke benediction secretly while prostrating. There is no tradition that the holy Prophet (Slm) had lifted hands after farz prayer for calling benediction or had ordered to act like that.

26. Mairaj of Imamana (As):

Author of Hadia had objected about the version of Mairaj of Imamana (As) at the end of the chapter 3.

There is no such version even in the oldest sources, and even if available it can be said to have been spiritual mairaj and not at all the physical one. Author of "Khatim-e-Sulaimani" reports regarding Miyan Syed Salamullah (Rz) that:

"Narrated by Miyan Syed Salamulla (Rz), brother of Bibi Alahdadi (Rz) and first cousin of Imamana (As) that he had been along with Imamana (As) from Juanpur and wherever Imamana (As) went he was with him and even when he was in the Mairaj."

نقل است کہ میاں سید سلام اللہ برادر حقیقی بی بی الهدتی و پسر عم میراں علیہ السلام از بلدۀ پرنور جونپور در سفر و حضر همراہ حضرت امام بود و گاهی از حضرت جدانشدہ بحدے کہ در معراج نیز در کاب شریف بود (گلشن چهارم چمن سوم)

How could Miyan Salamullah (Rz) have physical Mairaj when he was not the Khalifatullah, nor innocent?, thus the mairaj of Imamana (As) was spiritual only and not physical one. Now as regards Mairaj of Imamana (As), when the Mairaj of the holy Prophet (Slm) was not objected, how objection would arise on Imamana's Mairaj?.

Author of Hadia had reported an Arabic narration and pretended it to be that it was a Revelation and that is a description of Allah. This had been discussed in Part 4 under the chapter Imamana's attributes.

(Note: "Since the issue of Mairaj had never been stated by Imamana (As) personally, as

the holy Prophet (Slm) had declared in detail and which is revealed in two Sooras, "Al Asra and Al Najam" in the Holy Qur'an, as a concrete proof, therefore it seems unnecessary to compare it to that of the Holy Prophet's Mairaj. Hence better to drop this issue to avoid undue criticism by the decliners since mere Hzt.Syed Salamullah's saying was not seconded by any other companion, leave aside even by Immana(As)! Translator)

27. Tradition of Grazing Goats:

Author of Hadia had presented this tradition at the end of chapter 3 of his book:

اکنت ترعی الغنم قال نعم وهل من نبی الاوقد رعاها

"Asked whether you too grazed the goats; replied Yes: Was there any Prophet (As) who did not do that?"

The decliner had asserted that all prophets had caused the goats to graze according to that tradition; but there is no legend to certify that all the prophets had adopted this profession.

Author of "Mirqaat" under this tradition reports that:

روی ان ایوب کان خیاطا و زکریا کان نجارا

"It is narrated that Ayyub was a tailor and Zakaria a carpenter."

Then could any body doubt about the Nabuwwat of Ayyub and Zakaria,because they did not graze the goats? Further author's contention that grazing goats was a tradition for getting the Nabuwat ! is utterly wrong, since there is no record as to show that the prophets, after being designated as prophets, all of them had performed this profession. The legend is that some shepherds, who were performing that job, were honoured by Allah and commissioned prophet hood upon them. The following version proves that the act of grazing goats was an act done prior to their prophethood only and not after becoming the prophet.

"Reported that Allah had asked Moosa (As) that "did he know why he had been granted the prophet hood"? Replied Moosa (As) that Allah knows better. He was asked by Allah to remember that day when the goats were grazing in the valley of Aiman, and a goat ran away and you too ran after it which caused you trouble and pain and when you reached that goat, you did not beat the goat nor you became mad on it, instead you showed affection and informed it that it had caused trouble and pain both for it and yourself. And when We noticed this act of kindness to the goat, We too showed kindness to you and bestowed upon you the prophethood and made you exalted."

در روایـات آمـده است کـه پروردگار تعالیٰ وحی کرد بـه مـوسیٰ کلیم الله علی نبینا علیه الصلوٰة والسلام میدانی یا مـوسیٰ کـه بـچـه صـفت دادم ترا نبوت را گفت موسیٰ پروردگارا تو دانا تری بدان فرمود یا دکن آن روز را کـه مـی چـرانیدی غنم را درد وادئ ایمن پس گریخت شاتی و دویـدی تـو در دنبـال آن و رنـج و تعب کشیدی در آن و چـون بـرسیـدی تـوبـآں شـاتی هیچ نزدی آن را و خشم نگرفتی بـر آن بـلـکـه شـفقت کـردی و گفتی در تعب انـداختی تـوابے بیـچـاره خودرا و مراو چون دیدیم ما ایں نرمی ورحمت و شفقت از تو برآں حیوان رحمت کردیم ما نیز برتو و نبوت دادیم و بر گزیدیم

This episode is a proof that Hazrat Moosa (As) was grazing goats even before he got the prophethood. The same is true with regard to the holy Prophet (Slm) as reported in "Sifr-e-Saadat" that:

"Before the Nabuwwat, he was grazing the goats for compensation."

پیش از نبوت خود را باجاره واد برائے گوسفند چرانیدن

The Author's malicious accusation against Imamana (As) as if Imamana(As) had branded the act of grazing goats as blasphemy is utterly wrong and unfounded. As a matter of fact such version is no where available in any Mahdavia literature or elsewhere, on the other hand Imamana (As) had stressed by saying "Earning is legitimate for a faithful. "It is reported in "Hayat-e-Masih" that the author of Hadia came to Hyderabad from ShahJehanPur and had studied under Karamat Ali the lessons regarding traditions, but he never cared to understand traditions in the manner of the traditionalists. Further, what was his intention in presenting an unauthentic tradition regarding 'Grazing of goats'? The act of grazing goats cannot be called a tradition, because this was an act which was performed well before gaining the prophethood (by some prophets). Hence it does not require to be followed by all other prophets. However, except some, all prophets did not perform that act. Hzt. Ayyub (As) was a tailor and Hzt. Zakaria (As) was a carpenter. The details are given by Jozi:

"Hazrat Adam (As) was a cultivator, Hzt. Noah (As) (and Zakaria (As) were carpenters; Hzt. Idrees (As) used to stitch clothes; Hazraat Ibrahm (As) and Lott (As) were cultivators; Hzt. Saleh (As) was a businessman; Hzt. Dawood (As) used to manufacture ammunition; Hazrat Moosa (As), Shoeb (As) and the holy Prophet (Slm) were shepherds."

کـان آدم حراثا و نوح و ذکریا نجارین و ادریس خیاط و ابراهیـم و لـوط زراعین و صالح تاجرا و کان داؤد یعـمـل الـخوص بیده و یا کل من ثمنه و کان موسیٰ و شعیب و محمد رعاة

In the words of the author if "grazing goats' is a tradition, then why not cultivation, carpentry and tailoring be taken as a tradition?.

Holy Prophet's assertion is that Nabuwwat was not granted to the worldly men or kings, but to the shepherds, artisans, cultivators and men of hospitality. But the author's contention is that shepherding was one of the conditions of Nabuwwat is unfounded. On the other hand hospitality and humility are the attributes of Nabuwwat.

Author of "Mirqaat" wrote under this tradition that:

"What Qattabi told, it means that Allah did not grant prophethood to any worldly man or kings, but it was granted to the shepherds and artisans."

قـال الخطابی یرید ان الله تعالیٰ لم یضع النبوة فی ابناء الـدنیـا واملوکها ولکن فی رعاء الشاء واهل التواضع من اصحاب الحرفت

From this it is clear that Prophethood was not granted to kings but to such persons whose hospitality was proven. But the author of Hadia had mistakenly tried to emphasise that the shepherds only were given the prophethood. Alas! His knowledge is too poor to be reckoned!!

"Jubair Bin Nufeer reported that the holy Prophet (Slm) told that the Revelation was not sent to him for hoarding the stock and to become a businessman, but it was sent to praise Allah and his greatness and to become one of the prostrating persons and to worship Him till death."

عـن جبیـربـن نفیر مرسلا قال قال رسول الله صلی الله علیـه و سـلم ما اوحی الیٰ ان اجمع المال و اکون من التـاجرین و لکن اوحی الی ان سبح بحمد ربک و کن من الساجدین و اعبدربک حتی یاتیک الیقین

This is clear that after becoming Apostle of Allah, the holy Prophet (Slm) did not hoard any stock, neither he was a merchant, but the purpose of his life was to praise Allah and propagation of Islam. The same was the situation of Imamana (As) before the proclamation of the Mahdiat. Pity on the author who prefers shepherding over the propagation of Islam.

28. Last Prayer of Imamana (As) in a Masjid:

On Friday Imamana (As) got the mortal disease. After Friday prayer he offered Vitr prayer. "Insaf Nama" asserts that:

"Reported that when death was presumed soon, Imamana (As) offered his Friday prayer in the Jama Masjid, and offered Vitr prayer as the holy Prophet (Slm) too had performed."

نقل است بروقت که رحلت حضرت میراں ؑ نزدیك آمد در جامع مسجد رفته نماز جمعه گذارده فارغ شده بعده و تراداکردند حضرت رسالت پناه هم وتراداکرده بود (باب نوز دهم)

The Vitr prayer had been the last prayer of the holy Prophet (Slm). But it is an accepted fact that the last prayer was Maghrib. And in some traditions Maghrib prayer had been accepted as "Vitrun nahaar."

"Maghrib prayer is known as Day's Vitr."

صلوٰۃ المغرب وترالنهار

Since both Maghrib and Vitr prayers have three Rakats, therefore Vitr has been used in a literal sense. Thus the word Vitr is used in "Insaf Nama" in its literal sense only. The excellence for Vitr is according to its having odd number of Rakats, hence the tradition:

"Proved that Allah, who is odd and single, He likes the odd numbers."

ان اللّٰه و تریحب الوتر

The holy Prophet (Slm) also liked the odd figures only as mentioned in" Madarijul Nabuwwat":

"Among all things Holy Prophet (Slm) always accustomed to prefer odd numbers."

رعایت عدد و تر درهمه چیز عادت آنحضرت بود

Thus the holy prophet's last prayer was Vitrun Nahaar. And Allah had brought this fact to the notice of Imamana (As) that mortal disease had engulfed him which has been accordingly reported in "Maoulood" of Abdul Rahman (Rz):

"The same day he felt weakness and felt fever."

همان روز حضرت را اثر زحمت پیدا شده تپ بیاید

Imamana offered three Rakats of Vitr. Thus scholars knew very well that the holy Prophet (Slm) had also offered Vitr prayer after the Friday prayer, hence they deduced that Imamana (As) also would pass away before the next Friday. These words were spoken by them:

"Among the gathering of scholars, there were Moulana Gull, Moulana Mahmood and Abdul Shukoor, and others who were unanimous in their conclusion that Imamana (As) was the promised Mahdi (As), and he would not survive till the next Friday."

در آن مجمع علماء مولانا گل و مولانا محمود و مولانا عبدالشکور حاضر بودند ، میان خود گفتند این ذات مهدی موعود حق است آئینده نخواهد آمد (مولود میان عبدالرحمن صفحه ۱۳۲)

The similarity was neither in the Friday prayer nor the Vitr prayer, but it is in the Odd number of Rakaats. Thus "Insaf Nama" used Vitr in its literal meanings.

29.Description of the Verse of Holy Qur'an:

The scholars of Farah inquired Imamana (As) whether he is included in the Ummah? Imamana (As) answered positively that the holy Prophet (Slm) also was included in the Ummah. This has been mentioned in Chapter 24 of the"Shawahedul Vilayet":

"One day the scholars inquired Imamana (As) whether he is included in the Ummah of the holy Prophet (Slm)? Imamana (As) answered that he is included in the Ummah as the holy Prophet (Slm) too was included. For which Allah informed that there would be no wrath to them, since he is among them."

نقل است که روزے در فراه علماء یا حبیب ذوالجلال این سوال کردند که شما داخل درامت رسول الله صلی الله علیه و سلم هستید .... فرمودند من درین امت داخل ام چنانچه آنحضرت درای امت داخل است کما قال الله تعالیٰ و ما کان الله لیعذبهم و انت فیهم

The scholar's intention was to declare him in the Ummah and thus brand him as an ordinary man of the Ummah. Imamana (As) answered in the same manner and confirmed that he is in the Ummah, as the holy Prophet (Slm) was included in his Ummah.

The words "Included" are told by the scholars. And Imamana (As) had just repeated their words, but asserted by firmly telling them that what relationship of the holy Prophet (Slm) was with the Ummah, the same is that of mine. Thus real purpose was to show the relationship with Ummah par with that of the holy Prophet (Slm).

What relationship the holy Prophet (Slm) had with the Ummah, Imamana (As) asserted the same is with him. Then he recited a tradition":

"How would the Ummah be perished when I am in the beginning, Mahdi (As) is in the middle and Jesus Christ (As) is at the end."

کیف تهلک امة انا فی اولها والمهدی فی واسطها والمسیح آخرها

It proves that Imamana (As), the holy Prophet (Slm) and Jesus Christ (As) all the three venerable personalities are the saviours of the Ummah. And the holy Prophet (Slm) had two entities as mentioned by Allah which were reported by the holy Prophet (Slm) himself:

"As I was ordered, I am the first Muslim."

وبذالک امرت وانا اول المسلمین

Imam Fakhr-e-Razi (Rz) had commented on this Verse that:

"It is an imperative fact that he, (the holy Prophet (Slm), among the Muslims of that period was the first among them."

فیجب ان یکون المراد کونه اولا لمسلمی زمانه

Author of "Ashatul Lam'aat" wrote that:

"And I am the first Muslim of the Ummah, since every Prophet (As) is the first mermber of his particular Ummah."

ومـن اول مسـلمـان ایں امتم چه هره پیغمبر اول مسلمان است نسبت به امت خود

The second entity is that he is the predecessor of the Ummah. Author of "Tafseer-e-Husaini" narrated:

"I was ordered that to be the pioneer and to be the first Muslim in the Ummah, because I am the guide and leader of the Ummah, in the present life and also in the Hereafter."

فـرمـوده شـده ام به آنکه باشم اول گردن نهادگان ازیں امت زیراکه من پیش رو ایشانم در دنیا و آخرت (جلد ثانی ۲۱۱)

According to the tradition, it is correct to say that the Nabi is the originator of his Ummah, but to say Ummah is in the Nabi, is rather a joke and against the Qur'an and tradition. Author of "Muallamul Tanzeel" had commented on this verse:

"Said Qatadah that the holy Prophet (Slm) is the first Muslim among the Muslims of the Ummah."

قال قتاده وانا اول المسلمین من هذه الامة

Thus the holy Prophet (Slm) is the Narrator and had been commissioned as the Apostle of Allah.

In the same sense, on account of his being the perfect follower (of the holy Prophet (Slm)), Imamana (As) is in the Ummah, and also the Narrator of the Qur'an being the Khalifatullah holding the position of a Guide and the Promised Mahdi (As).

What connection the holy Prophet (Slm) had in the Ummah, Imamana had recited this verse:

"And Allah would not inflict wrath on them (Ummah) because the holy Prophet resides among them, who is always busy in begging His pardon for all."

و مـا کـان الـلّـه لیـعـذبـهـم و انـت فیهم و ما کان اللّه معذبهم و هم یستغفرون (الانفال ع ۴)

The illiterate decliner had tried to specify the word "Hum" (Arabic) with 'Kaferoon' That means to say that the holy Prophet (As) is also among them. Before this we had clarified that 'To be among them" are not the words of Imamana (As), but were told by the opponent scholars, and Imamana (As) had just repeated their words to clarify his purpose. That means to say what relation the holy Prophet (Slm) had with the Ummah, the same position is of Imamana (As) in the Ummah. This type of narration cannot be objected.

Author of "Madarijul Nabuwwat" had stated that:

"After that came Abu Bakr (Rz), whatever he had with him, he had brought. The holy Prophet (Slm) asked what did you leave for the family? He answered I had hoarded Allah and his Rasool (Slm) (for Family).

بعد ازاں ابو بکر آمد هر چه داشت تمام آورده بوے نیز فرمود برائے عیال چه ذخیره کرده گفت اذخرت الله ورسوله

This is clear that Abu Bakr (Rz) had repeated what was asked for, that is to say he had firm trust on Allah and the holy Prophet (Slm) (who would provide sustenance to his family).

Thus Abu Bakr (Rz) just repeated the words what the holy Prophet (Slm) had told that he had full faith on Allah and his Messenger (Slm) (for providing sustenance to his family).

Could there be any objection that Abu Bakr (Rz) felt Allah as a thing of hoarding?

Thus Imamana (As) also had repeated what had been told by the opponents, just to clarify his relationship (with Ummah). Thus what relation the holy Prophet (Slm) had with the Ummah, the same relation Imamana (As) had with the Ummah.

Further the word"Hum" should not be linked to the infidels.

Author of "Kasshaf" had commented on " Wahum Yastaghferoon" in these words:

A.."Among them there are people who are seeking forgiveness from Allah, and they are Muslims who were with him, those who were weak and old, stayed behind and did not go for Jihad along with the holy Prophet (Slm)."

وفیهم من یستغفرو هم المسلمون بین اظهر هم ممن تخلف عن رسول الله ﷺ من المستضعفین

B. "Baizavi" narrates about this verse that:

"Among the remaining Muslims, they were those who were asking forgiveness."

وهم یستغفرون یعنی المسلمین

Thus from this verse it is clear that "Hum Yastaghferoon" points out to those Muslims and not to the infidels. Imam Fakhr-e- Razi (Rz) had written about this verse that:

"Although, Allah would never inflict wrath on the infidels, because the Muslims who beg pardon from Allah are among them. The word although denotes in general meanings, but actually it denotes to a few. For example, when it is said that the residents of the locality had killed some one of a city and were engaged in arson, means some among them and not all of them."

و ما كـان اللـه مـعـذب هـؤلاء الكفار و فيهم مومنون يسـتغفرون فاللفظ و ان كان عاما الا ان المراد بعضهم كـمـا قـال قتـل اهـل الـمـحـلة رجلا واقدم اهل البلدة الفلانية على الفساد والمراد بعضهم

This proves that the words "Hum Yastaghferoon" means Muslims and not the infidels, because infidels do not beg for pardon, and if they also beg, then they could not be branded as infidels.

Author's assertion that " Hum" means Infidels only. But it had been already proved that "Wahum Yaztaghferoon" denotes Muslims and faithful, among whom the holy Prophet (Slm) was living. But still the decliner stresses that the words " Anta Feehim" denotes that the holy Prophet (Slm) was among the Infidels which is utterly wrong. Particularly, when the holy Prophet (Slm) was not alone and there were many Muslims too. Therefore the meanings of "Anta Feehim" is explained hereunder: "Oh Mohammad (Slm) you are with that group which is asking forgiveness" including the infidels too".

Thus it is asserted that he is the first among the Muslims, therefore included among the Muslims as well as the infidels. Therefore on account of these Muslims, wrath of Allah was not inflicted on those infidels who were living among the Muslims. As mentioned by "Muaheb Alaih":

"Just because they beg for pardon and they are faithful, therefore on account of their auspiciousness, wrath was not inflicted even on the infidels, since they were mingled among the Muslims."

و حـال آنـكه ايشان استغفارمى كنند يعنى درميان ايشان مستـغـفـرانـد از مومنان ، پس به بركت ايشان بلائى نمى رسد

The Word "Hum" has come in the said verse which means Ummah in which both Muslims and infidels were living and the holy Prophet (Slm) was among them. Hence his position was double folded. One as the first in muslameen and the other as the Last of the Prophets..

Thus Imamana's answer was correctly based on the Qur'an and the traditions. Hence raising filthy objections on Imamana (As) and thereby trying to disbelieve Imamana's Mahdiat is just nothing but absurd and baseless objection .

In order to emphasize the greatness of the holy Prophet (Slm), Imamana (As) would have presented another verse, but in presenting the verse "Anta Feehim" particularly to make those scholars ashamed who were hesitating to accept Imamana's Mahdiat, by pointing out that their peculiar habit is not that of the faithfuls but that of the infidels. And also to impress that even after pertinently demanding by the infidels for the wrath from Allah, miraculously it did not occur. It has nothing to do with Prophethood of the Holy Prophet (Slm) and it is not a condition of Nabuwwat. Thus it is not against the prophet's Nabuwwat and through this no proof could be presented against the Nabuwwat. Because miracles are not the proof of Nabuwwat. In the same manner, proof of Imamana's Mahdiat is not dependent upon any miracle.

30. Glad Tidings to Bandagi Miyan (Rz)

Imamana (As) had said about Bandagi Miyan (Rz) that:

بـرادرم سیـد خـونـدمیر ماوشما یك وجود هستیم هر كه انکـار جـامه بند شما كند او و منكر ذات بنده است (دفتر اول ركن سوم باب پنجم)

"Brotherum (My Brother) Syed Khundmir (Rz) I and you are one entity. Whoever denies even a particle of yours is an enemy of my person."

An opponent had maliciously objected on imamana's characters stating that Imamana (As) had equalized the particle of cloth of Bandagi Miyan (Rz) to his Mahdiat.

It may be pointed out that Bandagi Miyan (Rz) is a bearer of glad tidings from Imamana (As) and Imamana (As) had prophesied with certainty that Bandagi Miyan's martyrdom, is a perfect proof of his Mahdiat(Badal-e-Zat-e-Mahdi(As). **In this connection, Imamana (As) had even asserted as a challenge that "if that martyrdom does not take place in twenty years from my demise and that there are not three shrines of Bandagi Miyan (Rz) after his martyrdom, take me as an impostor, and if that happen as prophesied by me, accept my Mahdiat and believe me I was the true Mahdi-e-Akhiruzzaman (As).**

Thus in such circumstances whatever news had been prophesied by Imamana (As) about Bandagi Miyan (Rz), if anyone denies, it is to deny the very Mahdiat of Imamana (As).

The reference of a piece of Bandagi Miyan's robe was given by Imamana (As) is just to emancipate Bandagi Miyan's position in the Ummah. Such kind of assertion is well known in Persian literature. In this regard, Mullah Abdul Qader Badayuni had written about the companions of Imamana (As) which is recorded in"Najatur Rasheed":

چند از اهل الله از دامن ایشان برخاسته

"Some Godlimen have sprung from their lap (their auspicious company)."

Here "lap" refers to the beneficence of the companions of Imamana (As). In the same sense "Piece of the robe of Bandagi Miyan (Rz) mentioned by Imamana (As) is to emphasize the excellence of Bandagi Miyan (Rz).

According to a tradition:

"Allah Shall get down on His throne which will create noise like a new saddle creates the noise on account of its tightness."

ينـزل اللّٰه تعـالـیٰ على كرسيه فياط كما ياط الرجل الجديد من تضائقه

This is just to praise Allah's greatness. Thus Imamana's version of "Bund Jama" is to praise Bandagi Miyan and nothing more.

As Malik Mehri had written:

"Whoever is against the greatness of Bandagi Miyan (Rz), he is really against Imamana (As)."

هـر كـه مـخـالف شود از فضل آن ☆ گشت مخالف ز امام جهاں

In this connection Allah states:

"Thus let him free whose neck is burdened with faith."

فتحرير رقبة مومنة

Here neck means "neck of a faithful" a faithful means perfect Momin. Thus the reference of "Bund Jama" is just to give eminence to Bandagi Miyan (Rz). Thus whatever Imamana (As) had asserted in favour of Bandagi Miyan (Rz) if anyone raises objections, it tantamount that the biased decliner does not understand the Persian language and the style of the holy Qur'an and traditions.

CHAPTER TWO
Imamana's Commands
About the Saints.

In contradiction to the proof regarding characters written in the" Sirajul Absar" the author of Hadia had created doubts with the commands of Imamana (As) regarding the saints in his chapter 4 of Hadia. The following are the real narratives and their translations presented to refute the author's doubts.

1. Imamana (As) at the grave of Khaja Gaysoo Daraz (Rz) (Gulbarga)

Author of "Shawahedul Vilayet" in chapter 11 had mentioned that:

"It is reported that some companions inquired Imamana (As) as to why so much time he had taken in the tomb? He replied that the soul of Syed Mohammad Gaysoo Daraz (Rz) welcomed him and requested to tread over the grave with shoes in order to cleanse the stain of wrongly claiming Mahdiat by him. He repeated his request many a times. Then I had to tread over his grave three times, thus he was pleased and bid me goodbye. That was the reason for the delay."

نقـل اسـت کـه در ایـن بـاب از امـام اولی الالباب یـاران پرسیـدنـد کـه درنـگ در گنبـد بسیـار فرمودنـد ، چـه مـوجب بود گفتند کـه روح سیـد محمد استقبال کرده بـاحتیـاج تمام بـر سـر قبر خـود آورده سعی بلیغ فرمود کـه گـرد نعلین بـر سر قبر مـاتا نیقـد خجالـت دعوی مهدیـت کـه از مـا صدور یافتـه بـود دورنگر دد ، بـرایـن معنی چنـد بـار تکرار شـد تا آرزوے ایشان قبول نمودیم وسه کرت بـالائ قبرشان بـاکفش هـآمـدورفت کردیـم بنا برخوش حال شـده رخصـت کردنـد، مـوجب درنـگ ایـن بود

Author of Hadia had remarked in his book's chapter 4 page 209 that Imamana (As) had trodden the grave of Hazrat Gaysoo Dasraz (Rz).

There is no unanimity on the episode of treading the grave in any of the biographies of Imamana (As). The oldest source is the biography written by Miyan Abdul Rahman (Rz) "Moulood" which does not mention any such treading over the grave by Imamana (As); except that he went inside the tomb with his shoes as mentioned below:

"Wearing shoes he went inside the tomb. Attendants remarked that the grave was of a saint, therefore they asked Imamana (As) to leave shoes outside. Imamana (As) questioned them as to whom should he hear, to him or to their Pir?

بـانـعـلین بگنبد میرفتند ، خادمان آنجا عرض کردند کـه ایشان ولی الله انـد حضرت نعلین واگذارنـد ، فرمودنـد کـه سخن تو بشنوم یا سخن پیر تو

The same is written in "Janatul Vilyet":

"Miran (As) went inside the tomb with shoes."

میران علیه السلام مع کفشها رفته در گنبد

Imamana's going with shoes should not be objected as stated in "Bukhari" and "Muslim" that:

"Anas (Rz) reported that the holy prophet (Slm) informed, when any one is buried in the grave and when his companions start to return, he hears the rattling noise of their shoes."

عن انس رضی الله عنه قال قال رسول الله صلی الله علیه و سلم ان العبداذا وضع فی قبره تولی عنه اصحابه انه یسمع قرع نعالهم الی آخره

""Hashia-e-Sharief" also reports that the grave was not spoiled:

" The soul of Syed Mohammad Gaysoo Daraz (Rz) came three farlang (miles) ahead to welcome Imamana (As) and took him inside (the tomb) with his shoes and asked him to cross over his grave."

ارواح سید محمد گیسودراز سه فرسنگ پیش حضرت میران آمده میران را باکفش درون گنبد بروند و گفتند بالائ قبر شده بیائید

Here it is not mentioned that Imamana (As) had spoiled the grave.

In the event of difference of narratives how could this be related to Imamana (As)?

However it cannot be proved from any source of biographies that Imamana (As) had trodden the grave.

It is narrated that the soul of Hazrat Gaysoo Daraz (Rz) welcomed Imamana (As) and took him to the grave. This proves that at that moment the soul was outside the grave and not in the grave. However if it is proved that Imamana (As) had trodden the grave, then also how could there be an objection when the soul is outside the grave, since without the soul there is no significance to the heap of a mud (grave).

The gist of this narration is that Imamana (As) had accepted the request of Hazrat Gaysoo Daraz (Rz), and went inside. That is all. the question of spoiling the grave does not arise. Author of Hadia had submitted some traditions in this regard:

"Thus you have seen a person who was wandering in the Muslim graveyard wearing shoes. He was ordered to throw away his shoes ."

فرای رجلا یمشی بین المقابر بنعلیه فقال یا صاحب السبتتین القهما

The decliner states that this tradition is from "Maja". Before this we have submitted the tradition of both the Sheikhain (Bukhari and Muslim) that when the person is buried, and when people start to return, then the buried one hears the rattling sound of the shoes of his friends. This proves that wearing shoes, one can go to the graveyard. Therefore it becomes useless for him to submit Maja's tradition in lieu of Sheikhain's traditions.

On the other hand, it is a fact that Imamana (As) had actually respected the graves, even in those graveyards where the marks of the graves were not existing. Miyan Abdul Rahman (As) had written about Doulatabad graveyard that:

"From the shrine of Syed Raju (Rz) to the shrine of Syed Mohammad Arif (Rz), Imamana (As) was walking on his toes, without touching full legs. On that Miyan Syed Salamullah (Rz) pointed out: "Miranji (As) why are you going like that"? Imamana (As) replied: "from this place to that place many saints are buried."

از روضه سید السادات سید راجو تا به روضهٔ اشرف سید محمد عارف بر نرانگشت پامی رفتند و تمام قدم مبارک بر زمین نه داشتند میان سید سلام الله عرض کردند که میرانجی چنین چار می روید و برمرکب سوار نمی شوید فرمودند از آنجا تا اینجا همه اولیاء الله به کمالیت اعظم هستند ......

The same is narrated in "Hashi-e-Sharief": "Imamana (As) went to Doulatabad and visited the graves of all saints. At one place he was going on his toes, when companions asked why he was treading like that, Imamana (As) replied that there are many graves of the saints."

نقل است حضرت میران در دولت آباد رسیدند بالائی کهتکه سوار شده ، زیارت همه اولیاء کردند بعده یک جا عقب پائے مبارک بر زمین رسانیده به پهلوی چلیدند برادران عرض کردند خوندکار چگونه می چلند میران فرمودند اینجا بسیار اولیاء الله هستند

(Note:At one place Imamana (As) was walking on his thumbs and at another place he was walking on his toes. That means to say that he was not wearing shoes at all. (Then how can the decliner say that in Gulbarga he had gone into the tomb of Hazrat Gaysoo Daraz (Rz) wearing his shoes? Just it is absurd, malicious and unimaginable propaganda against Imamana (As)!!

In the first episode Miyan Salamullah (Rz) asked the reason and in another episode companion asked the reason. In both cases Imamana (As) told that in those places eminent saints are buried. From this, it comes to light that even signs of the graves were oblitrated and there were no signs of the graves, still he had respect for them.

The third point is that with much difficulty he was not putting full legs as a mark of respect. Thus he was following practically the narration of the holy prophet (Slm) that complete respect must be shown to the graves. His practice always was to follow the traditions. to their entirety.

Thus it is a fact that all biographies are not unanimous that Imamana (As) had trodden the grave of Hazrat Gaysoo Daraz (Rz). (And just now given examples of showing respect to the eminent saints he did not walk over the places where he felt that there may be graves . Then to think of treading the grave of Gaysoo Daraz (Rz) is just false and unfounded and not acceptable by any sane man).

(Note: "Thus the unwanted narration of "Shwahedul Vilayet"in chapter 2, regarding treading the holy grave of Hazrat Gaysoo Daraz (Rz) by Imamana (As) must be deleted and erased to avoid wrong and unholy objections by the adversaries." Translator.)

When the holy prophet (Slm) migrated from Makkah to Madinah, he stayed in the house of Abu Ayub. Abu Ayub did not feel good that he himself stayed on the upper floor, while the holy

Prophet (Slm) staying on the ground floor, so he requested :

"Ya Rasoolallah (Slm), my parents be sacrificed for you, I am feeling much shame that Sarwar-e-Anbiah (Slm) reside on the ground floor and we reside on the upper one. Therefore Ya Rasoolallah (Slm) better you come and sleep on the upper floor and we come down."

يا رسـول الله مادر و پدر من فدائے تو باو من درسكونت بـالا خانـه بسيار حرج و كلفت مى كشم كه سرور انبيا درزير بـاشـد و ما بربالا خانه نشينيم يا رسول الله تو بالا خانه اختيار كن تابزيرآيم

This shows what respect the companions had for the holy Prophet (Slm). But it is a fact that Hazrat Ali (Rz) had kept his legs on Prophet's shoulders. This could not be criticized because this was done only on orders of the holy Prophet (Slm), as narrated in "Madarijul Nabuwwat"

"Thus Ali (Rz) following orders, kept his legs on the shoulders of the holy Prophet (Slm)"

عـلى امتشالا للامرپائے بركتف رسول الله صلى الله عليه و سلم نهاد

On orders of the holy Prophet (Slm) if Hazrat Ali (Rz) kept his legs on the shoulders of the holy prophet (Slm), therefore it could not be criticized, then how Imamana's action of keeping his legs on the grave of Hazrat Gaysoo Daraz (Rz), "only at the request of Gaysoo Daraz (Rz)" (as stated above is still doubtful) could be criticized? Particularly when the soul of Hazrat Gaysoo Daraz (Rz) was out from the grave, consequently the grave was just a heap of mud having no sanctity.

2. Ranks of Seven Saints:

Chapter 24 of "Shawahedul Vilayet" states that:

""Once Imamana (As) by turning to his back said that "you too are not bad, since you pertain to this group also". After some time companions inquired: when there was no person visible behind you, then to whom you had said those words. Imamana (As) replied seven souls of saints had visited and were lamenting that: "had they been in the period of Imamana (As), then they too would have the beneficence of Imamana (As), then he convinced them that they are not bad since they too are in that group."

آن شهنشـاه قبلـه گاه بفرمان حضرت اله پس پشت مبارك نگـاه كـرده بزبان مبارك مى فرمودند كه شما هـم بـد نيستيـد شما هم بدنيستيد داخل اين جماعت هستيـد بعـد از ساعتـى يـاران به آنحضرت استفسار كـردنـد كـه ميرانـجى پس پشت مبارك خدام كسـى ظاهر انبوداىس سخن مبارك كرافرمودند گفتند ارواح هـفـت سلطان حاضر شده بودند و آرزومى بردند كه كـاشكے مـادر عـصر ميران سيد محمد مهدىّ ختم ولايت مـحـمـدى بـودمـى تـا از فيض ولايت مقيده مستفيض شدمى بنا برايشان در جواب داديم كه شما هم بدنيستيد داخل اين گروه هستيد

On this, the author of Hadia in his chapter 4 on page 210 had criticized that Imamana (As) disgraced the saints. It was an inspiration that souls of the seven saints arrived (Sultan Shibli was one among them) and were lamenting that they had not been alive during the period of

"Khatim-e-Vilayet-e-Mohammedi (As)". Then Imamana (As) said even otherwise they are in that group. This shows their greatness and not a disgrace. The same narration is found in "Insaf Nama" in its chapter 17 it is stated that::

"Imamana (As) had said that even after him, guided persons will be born till the Day of Judgment. Thus after the holy Prophet (Slm) and his companions, many saints were born. For example Baayazeed-e-Bustami (Rh), Sultan Ibrahim (Rh) and Sheik Shibli (Rh) and many more who did not have the company of the companions of the holy Prophet (Slm), still they gained excellence. In the same manner after Imamana (As) and his companions, many people had arrived and became saints."

نیز معلوم باد که حضرت میراں فرمودند که پس از من تا قیامت مهدی شوند چنانچه پس از مصطفیٰ و یاران مصطفیٰ بعضے اولیاء الله شدند چنانچه بایزید بسطامی و سلطان ابراهیم و شیخ شبلی ، مثل ایشان چند کسان بغیر صحبت یاران مصطفیٰ کامل شدند همچنان بعد از مهدی و بعد از یاران همچنان اولیاء شوند

"Insaf Nama" lacks the words "You are not bad", but the common ground of both"Insaf Nama"and"Shawahedul Vilayet" is that Sultan Shibli (Rh), Sultan Ibrahim (Rh), Baayazeed-e-Bustami (Rh) etc., were perfect in their sainthood, therefore there should be no objection. Now remains to discuss about the ranks of the companions of Imamana (As). In this regard, author of "Uqdur Durar" had mentioned, what Hazrat Ali (Rz) had said about such saints who would be born afterwards, as had been prophesied by the Holy Prophet (Slm):

""(They are those persons) that neither the earlier people had surpassed them, nor the persons who hereafter come shall get such status."

لم یسبقهم الاولون ولا یدرکهم آخرون (الباب الرابع)

"Shawahedul Vilayet" had described about the "cherished Sainthood" (Vilayet-e-muqaida) to which the Prophets (As) too had wished to acquire it. The author of "Bahrul Muaani" had stated that:

"Thus, Oh! My friend, Moosa Kalimullah (As) and Jesus Christ (As) had wished to acquire this Sainthood of the holy Prophet (Slm)."

پس اے محبوب خواستن موسیٰ کلیم الله و تمنا بردن عیسیٰ مسیح علیهما السلام همین ولایت حضرت رسالت علیه السلام است

There are certain traditions which vouchsafe about such eminent personalities in the Ummah who are neither martyr nor Nabi, but the martyrs and the prophets are envious of them:

"Narrated holy Prophet (Slm) that there are among godly people who are neither martyrs nor they were Nabi, still Nabis and martyrs would become envious of them at the Day of Judgment."

قال قال رسول الله صلی الله علیه و آله و سلم ان من عباد الله لا ناساماهم بانبیاء ولا شهداء یغبطهم الانبیاء والشهداء یوم القیامة الیٰ آخره

Thus the rank of the companions of Imamana (As) is greater than those eminent people stated above.

3. Saints Supported Pilgrims' Ship:

Author of "Shawahedul Vilayet " had reported that:

"The day Imamana (As) sat in a ship for the purpose of Hajj, one companion who was accompanying him thought in mind that during the journey, there had been a shrine of a Saint to which Imamana (As) did not visit, had he visited, it would have been better. Suddenly Imamana (As) looked sharply towards him and directed him to look at the ship. With the effect of Imamana's powerful glance, he looked that all the saints and mystics buried in India were supporting the ship by tightening the rope over their shoulders. When that companion saw this all happenings he became ashamed and repented. Imamana (As) asked him not to behave impudently."

روزے کـه در کشـی نشسـته به طرف کعبته الله روان شـده بـودنـد کـه یـک مهاجر آنحضرت در دل خطره آورد کـه روضۀ فلاں اولیاء الله درمیان راه بود حضرت امیـر زیـارت نـه کـردنـد، اگر زیـارت کـردنـدے خوب بـود، اکنـوں آں روضـه کـجا آمدن بایں طرف کجا، در آں میـان نـاگـاه آن شهنشـاه تندنگـاه کـردنـد و فـرمـودنـد کـه نیکو به بیں چوں به تاثیر آن نظر مبارک آں مهـاجـر را پـرده از غیـب دور کـرده شد ، چه مـی بینـد کـه همـه اولیـاء اللـه کـه در هندوستان آسوده انـدرسـن هـائے کشتی بـر کتف خـود نهاده میکشند چـوں چنیـں معاملـه دید بسیار شرمنده گـردیـد و عذر خـواهی بحضرت قبله گاهی کـرد آنحضرت فرمودند بعد ازیـں چنیـں گستاخی مکن .

Author of Hadia had also objected on this episode telling that it tantamount to disgrace the mystics.

This is clear that Imamana (As) was going in a ship to Makkah for Hajj. At that juncture to think that someone's visitation was missed is hypocrisy. Imamana (As) tried to eradicate that hypocrisy and perpetuated the greatness of the intention of the Hajj that whoever is going with an intention of Hajj to Makkah, then he gets the good wishes of all Mystics for him.

Here attempting to save a drowning ship of the pilgrims by keeping the tightening rope on the shoulders is not a thing to be objected.

We get two lessons from this episode. One: the eminence of pilgrimage to Makkah for Hajj.

Second: the eminence of the Indian Mystics who helped by supporting a drowning ship of those pilgrims, is itself a worship.

4. Legs of Abdul Qader Jeelani on the Necks of All Mystics:.

It is narrated in "Shawahedul Vilayet" that:

"It was reported to Imamana (As) that Sheikh Abdul Qader Jeelani (Rz) had once said that "his legs were on all the necks of the mystics", to which Sheikh Sanan (Rh) objected by saying that "he did not accept his (Sheik's) legs on my neck. Imamana (As) on commands of Allah asserted: "Of course, Sheik Abdul Qader (Rz) was an eminent person of his period, that when Sheik Sanan (Rz) did not accept his legs on his neck, it brought the wrath by having a pig's leg over his shoulders. Then Imamana (As) commented that Sheik Abdul Qader (Rz) had put his burden on the mystics, instead he would have told that the "legs of all mystics are on my neck."

نقـل اسـت کـه در حـضـور پر نور امام البروالبحر ذکر سلطان عبدالـقـادر گیـلانی رحمته الله گزشت ایشان فرمودند ان قدمی هذه علی رقبة کل اولیاء الله یعنی بـدرستی کـه ای قدم من بر گردن همه اولیاء الله باشد و ذکر شیخ صنعـان رحمته الله علیه هم مذکور شد کـه ایشان گفتند که ما قدم شاه بر کتف خود قبول نمی کنیم آن امـام زمرۀ اولیٰ الالباب قائل بامر ملک الوهاب فرمود کـه آرے سید عبدالـقادر در همچنان کامل بودند و در عـصـر خـود صـاحب زمـان بودند چنانچه شیخ صنعا کـه قـدم ایشان قبول نکردند بنا بر قدم خوکان بر کتف خویـش نهاده خوک بـانی کـردبـاز فرمودند کـه سید عبدالـقادر گرانی خود که بر کتف اولیاء نهادند بهتر آن بودے کـه فرمودے کـه قدم هائے اولیاء الله بر کتف من باشد

Author of "Nehaya" has written that:

To put the legs on anything is to pulverize it"

وضع القدم علی الشئ مثل للروع و القمع

Author of "Muntakhab-ul-Lughat" has written about the word Rida' that:

"To stop and rub anything.

باز ایستادن از چیزے و مالیدن چیزے برجائے

And for the word "Qum'aa" it is written that:

"To abuse and disregard." 17/2

قهر کردن و خوار گردانیدن

Author of "Taj-ul-Uroos" has written that:

"To put the leg on anything is to pulverize, abuse and disregard that thing.

وضع القدم علی الشئ مثل للردع و القمع

The said remark of Imamana (As) about Sheik Abdul Qader Jeelani (Rz) was taken by the author of Hadia as a disgrace. But how it is a disgrace?, when Imamana (As) had praised Sheik Abdul Qader Jeelani (Rz) by saying that " he was an eminent person of his period"?

The Holy Prophet (Slm) addressed Muslims at Hajjatul Wida (Farewell Address):

"Be it known that everything which pertains to paganism had been kept under my feet."

الا کل شئی من امر الجاهلیة تحت قدمی موضوع

Sheik Abdul Haq had commented this tradition that:

"Pagan rituals had been made null and void therefore abandoned."

پست و پامال است یعنی خوار و باطل و متروک است

Thus in Arabic when a thing kept under the feet or if that thing comes under the feet, both have the same meanings. Sheik Abdul Qader's statement was also in Arabic and its meaning would be taken as if he condemned all the saints. We have to ask the author whether he also endorses that statement of the Sheik (Rz)?

Imamana (As) had said that if Sheik Abdul Qader (Rh) had instead told that the feet of all Saints are on his neck, would have been better which shows humility instead of boasting (by saying that his legs are on all the necks of the mystics); and which is according to the Qur'an and traditions:

"Do not praise your passions".   فلا تزكوا انفسكم (النجم ع ١)

Because when the words "Khairul Baria" (Best among creations) were used for him, the holy Prophet (Slm) referred them to Prophet Ibrahim (As), saying : it was his (Prophet Ibrahim's) attribute.

"Narrated by Anas that a person came to the holy prophet (Slm) and addressed him "The best of the creation". The holy Prophet (Slm) pointed out that it was Prophet Ibrahim's attribute (Not Mine)." ("Muslim").

عن انس قال جاء رجل الى النبى صلى الله عليه و آله و سلم فقال يا خير البريه فقال رسول الله صلى الله عليه و سلم ذاك ابراهيم رواه مسلم

Another tradition states about humility:

"Narrated by Mutraff what was told by his father when he went with a delegation led by the holy Prophet (Slm) to the people of Bani Aamir, they welcomed the holy Prophet (Slm) by addressing "you are our leader." The holy Prophet (Slm) replied "Leader is Allah."

عن مطرف قال (ابى) انطلقت فى و فدبنى عامر الى رسول الله صلى الله عليه و آله و سلم فقلنا انت سيدنا فقال السيد هو الله الى آخره

Yet there is one more tradition related to humility:

"Narrated by Aiyaz Bin Hamarul Mujashai that the holy Prophet (Slm) said that Allah had sent him the revelation to be polite so that nobody should boast on each other and go beyond the limits."

عن عياض بن حمار المجاشعى ان رسول الله صلى الله عليه و سلم قال ان الله تعالىٰ اوحى الى ان تواضعوا حتى لا يفتخر احد على احد ولا يبغى احد على احد . (رواه مسلم)

From these traditions we come to know, when it was told to the holy Prophet (Slm) that you are the best of the creation, holy Prophet (Slm) said it was the attribute of Prophet Ibrahim (As). Also he told that he was not the leader, but Allah. Thus what Imamana (As) had said it was according to the holy Qur'an and the traditions. This proved that the remark of Imamana (As) maintained the dignity of both of Sheik Abdul Qader (Rh) as well as of the saints.

What Sheik Abdul Qader Jeelani (Rh) had said, it is available in the oldest source"Awariful Muarif" in which the wordings of Sheik Abdul Qader Jeelani's remarks are criticized:

"Such wordings were copied by a group of great persons which had crossed the limits of boasting, hence surprising. This is because they had not come out of their intoxication and had uttered such words. But when those insightful persons consider with their short sightedness they would come to realize that it was all on account of the passions. When their heart inspires something they imagine that they are exalted. In such a situation they do not realize what were they telling, consequently they start boasting: Thus in such circumstances they cross the limit of boasting. Thus someone said "is there any person like me under this blue sky?" or someone said "My legs are on the necks of all saints."

لقد نقل عن جمع من الكبار كلمات موذنة بالاعجاب و كل ما نقل من ذلك القبيل عن المشايخ لبقايا السكر عندهم و انحصارهم فى مضيق سكر الحال و عدم الخروج الى فضاء الصحو فى ابتداء امرهم و ذلك اذا صدق صاحب البصيرة نظره يعلم انه من استراق النفس السمع عند نزول الوارد على القلب والنفس اذا استرقت السمع عند ظهور الوارد على القلب ظهرت بصفتها على وجه لايجفر على الوقت و صلافة الحال فيكون من ذلك كلمات موذنه بالعجب كقول بعضهم من تحت خضراء السماء مثلى و قول بعضهم قدمى على رقبة جميع الاولياء الى آخره

This version is of Sheik Shahabuddin Suherwardi (Rh) (D. 632). From this version following points emerge":

1. Sheik Abdul Qader's saying pertains to his initial stages as a saint;
2. This utterance pertained to be under the influence of intoxication;
3. This shows boasting and self pride;

It may be pointed out that Sheik Abdul Qader (Rh) is related to Sheik Shahabuddin Suherwardi (Rh) by two links: 1. Sheik Shahabuddin (Rh) was the disciple and was trained by his uncle Sheik Abul Najeeb Suherwardi (Rh) (D. 563) and Sheikh Abul Najeeb (Rh) is one of the companions of Sheik Abdul Qader (Rh) (D.562) and one of his confidants. 2. And the second is that Sheik Shahabuddin (Rh) himself had the company of Sheik Abdul Qader Jeelani (Rh) and had uttered Good Tidings for him, which had been recorded by Mulla Abdul Rahman Jami (Rh) in his "Nafkhatul Uns" about Sheik Shahabuddin Suherwardi (Rh) that:

"He comes from the lineage of Hazrat Abu Bakr Siddiq (Rh) and had mystic training under his uncle Sheik Abul Najeeb Suharwardi (Rh) and was in the company of Sheik Abdul Qader Jeelani (Rh) and many other eminent persons. Some say that he was with many saints in the Island of Ibadan where he met Khaja Khizr (As) and to whom Sheik Abdul Qader Jeelani (Rh) had said that he was the last among the celebrities of Iraq."

از اولاد ابو بكر صديق رضى الله عنه و انتساب وے در تصوف بعم وے ابو النجيب سهروردى است و به صحبت شيخ عبدالقادر گيلانى رسيده غير ايشان از مشائخ وقت بسيارے رادريافته است و گفته اند كه مدتى با بعضى از ابدال درجزيرۀ عباد ان بود و خضر عليه السلام رادريافته و شيخ عبدالقادر وے راگفته است كه انت آخر المشهورين بالعراق

Thus, Sheik Shahabuddin Suherwardi (Rh) had the blessings of Sheik Abdul Qader Jeelani (Rh), therefore what he had written about him cannot be objected.

As regards the narration in the "Nafkhatul Uns" about the date of birth of Sheik Shahabuddin (Rh) as mentioned is 539 H, and Sheik Abdul Qader's date of demise was 562 H, that means to say that Sheik Shahabuddin (Rh) was just of the age of 23 years when Sheik Abdul Qader Jeelani (Rh) passed away. It is still out of our comprehension that what Sheik Shahabuddin (Rh) had written about Sheik Abdul Qader's narration, should he not have consulted with his uncle? And that too how could he write such remarks without any investigation about the Sheik (Rz)?

Sheik Ali bin Ahmed Al-Muhami () (D. 835) has written in Shar-he-Awarif" that:

The word "Subdued" points out to whether Sheik Abdul Qader Jeelani (Rh) had been under the influence of intoxication? "Hashia Sharief" informs what Imamana (As) had commented:

"He could not digest his inner strength, he would instead have said, "the legs of all saints are on my neck?"

هضم نه کردند چرا این چنین نه گفت که پائے همه اولیاء بر گردن ما است

The words "Could not digest" point out two meanings: one: this narration relates to the initial stage of the seeker. Second: Such utterance is the result of being under the influence of intoxication. (Not on account of drinking of wine etc., but on account of being immersed in mysticism)

Sheik Ahmed Sar-e-Hindi (D.1034) has written regarding it that:

"The author of "Awarif" is the disciple of, and was trained by Sheik Najeeb Suherwardi (Rz), who had been in the company of Sheik Abdul Qadar Jeelani, (Rz)who had taken that saying of Sheik Abdul Qader Jeelani (Rh) to be one of the utterances which come under the category of boasting and arrogance and they occur when the Sheik (Rh) was still under the influence of the intoxication."

صاحب عوارف که مرید و مرباے شیخ ابو النجیب سهروردی است که از محرمان و مصاحبان حضرت شیخ عبدالقادر بوده است این کلمه را از آن کلمات ساخته است که مشعر عجب اند که از مشائخ دربدایت احوال بواسطه بقایاے سکر (صدور) یافته اند

What Sheik Ahmed Sar-e-Hindi has commented on the sayings of the author of "Awarif" seems to have been consented completely.

Thus whatever Imamana (As) had stated about the utterances of Sheik Abdul Qader Jeelani (Rz) could not be objected. "Shawahedul Vilayet" had mentioned that:

"His own burden he had put on the shoulders of the Saints."

گرانی خود بر کتف اولیاء ، نهادند

Imamana's contention that it would have been better "if Sheik Abdul Qader Jeelani (Rh) would have said that the burden of all saints I am bearing, instead of saying that my burden is on the shoulders of the saints".

" Madarijul Nabuwwat" states that the holy Prophet (Slm) stated that when Hazrat Ali (Rz) kept his legs on the shoulders of the Prophet (Slm) for dismantling the idols of Kabatullah, the

Prophet (Slm) had addressed Hzt. Ali (Rz) in this manner:

"Oh Ali (Rz)! For what better purpose of Allah your time was served, and what better is my position that I am holding the burden for the purpose of Allah."

اے علی خوش وقت تو که کار حق می کنی و جندا حال من که بار حق می کشم

From the above tradition it comes to light that it is better to bear one's burden than to make others to hold our burden.

5.Sheik Akber's Manifestation:

The decliner had written on page 99 and 306 of his Hadia about the narration of Imamana (As) in respect of Sheik Akber (Rh) that he used to look into "Divine Tablet" before writing something. This proves that Sheik Akber (Rh) was a man who got inspirations. How can it be said that Imamana (As) had made him an innocent person?.

It is possible that any sayings of an inspired person may not be always true.

Imamana (As) not only had informed about Sheik Akber's being an inspired person, he had also objected Sheik Akber's so called interpretation about the Pharaoh.

When someone told that Sheik Akber (Rh) was of the opinion that the Pharaoh too may get salvation. On this Imamana (As) told that:

"What happened to Ibn Arabi (Rz) to tell that the Pharaoh and his men would get salvation? As if he had not read what Allah had spoken to him: "Thus Allah caught him (Pharaoh) for the wrath of the hereafter and also in the worldly wrath."

چه شده بود ابن عربی را که نجات فرعون و فرعونیاں خبر داد چرا براین آیت نظر نه کردند که حق سبحانه و تعالیٰ در حق وے چنیں می فرماید فاخذه الله نکال الآخرة والاولیٰ یعنی پس بگرفت اور اخدائے تعالیٰ به عقوبت آنجهاں و این جهاں (شواهد الولایت باب ٢٤)

From that verse, Imamana (As) had argued that Pharaoh not only had been punished in the world, but he deserved punishment in the Hereafter too. It says that in the world he was punished by drowning in the sea and in the thereafter he would get the wrath of the hellfire.

Imamana's narration vouchsafe by a tradition of the Prophet (Slm) when the head of Abu Jahal was brought to him (at the battle of Badr) he said that:

"The Pharaoh of this Ummah was dead."

مات فرعون هذه الامة

Thus it is confirmed that both Abu Jahal and Pharaoh belonged to the same category of infidelity. Thus Sheik Akber's narration that Pharaoh could get salvation was wrong as per the tradition and Qur'an.

Imamana's narration that Sheik Akber (Rh) writes after looking the Divine Tablet was just to proclaim him a person of manifestation, and it does not in any way to brand him an innocent man. Therefore whatever Sheikh Akber had said about Pharaoh's salvation became wrong according to the Holy Qur'an and tradition.

****

Chapter Three
Imamana's Commands about his Companions.

Author of Hadia, in order to refute an argument regarding characters of Imamana (As) as described in "Sirajul Absar" had pointed out some doubts on the commands of Imamana (As) about his companions. He had claimed in his book's chapter 5 that:"For them "Vilayet" is superior to "Nabuwwat" and they are the office bearers of the Vilayet, and that they are far superior to the companions of the holy Prophet (Slm) and even to the progeny of the holy Prophet (Slm)."

This is not the belief of Mahdavis that companions of Imamana (As) are superior to the companions of the holy Prophet (Slm).

As a matter of fact, there are two beliefs regarding companions of the holy Prophet (Slm). One belief is that companions are superior to the Ummah. This belief is based on those traditions relating to the excellence of the companions.

Another belief is that after those companions some people would emerge in the future who would be equal to them or even superior to them. The basis of this belief is based on those traditions narrated about the excellence of someone who would be born in the future among the Ummah.

Author of Hadia had mentioned about the first category of traditions only, while overlooking the other category. For example a few traditions of the second category are presented:

1."Narrated by the holy Prophet (Slm) as regards faith, for me, those people are better who come after me and who would follow those books in which commands of religion have been written and who would accept whatever is written in those books"

(١) فقال رسول الله صلى الله عليه و سلم ان اعجب الخلق ايمانا لقوم يكونون من بعدى يجدون صحفا فيها كتاب يؤمنون بما فيها

The said narration reported by Razeen (Rz) points out about a group of people who would be born after the holy Prophet (Slm) and their faith would be perfect according to the holy Qur'an and traditions.

2."At the end-time of the Ummah there would arise a group of people who would get same benefits what the first Ummah got and that (group) "enjoins virtue and abhors evil"(Amr Bil Ma'aroof-e- wa Nahi Unil Munkir).

(٢) سيكون فى آخر هذه الامة قوم لهم مثل اجراولهم يامرون بالمعروف و ينهون عن المنكر الى آخره

The said tradition had been narrated by Behaqi (Rz) who had recorded in

"Dalael-e-Nabuwwat" which had been accepted by Ahmed Bin Hunbal (Rz) which is as below:

3 ."Abi Umama (Rz) narrated that the holy Prophet (Slm) said that blessedness for that person who had seen me and seven times more for that person who had not seen me and still he had accepted me".

عـن ابى امامه ان رسول الله صلى الله عليه و سلم قال طوبى لـمـن رانى و طوبى سبع مرات لمن لم يرانى و آمن بى

4.."Narrated Abi Mahreez (Rz) that I asked Abi Juma'a (Rz) who was one of the companions to tell a tradition which he heard from the holy Prophet (Slm), and which you thought to be the best of the traditions. He thus narrated: "We were at the breakfast with the holy Prophet (Slm), when Abu Ubaida (Rz) inquired : "oh holy Prophet (Slm) is there anyone better than us; since, we had accepted Islam, we had waged Jihad along with you". The holy Prophet (Slm) answered positively and asserted that "There would be a group of people who would come after me and accept me even though they had not seen me." narrated by Ahmed Hunbal (Rz) and Darmi (Rz)."

(۴)عن ابى محير يزقال قلت لابى جمعة رجل مـن الـصـحـابة حدثنا حديثا سمعته من رسول الـلّـه صـلـى الـلّـه عـليـه و آلـه و سلم قال نعم احـدثك حديثا جيدا تـغـذينا مع رسول الله صـلـى الـلّـه عليه و آله و سلم و معنا ابو عبيدة بـن الـجـراح فقال يا رسول الله احد خير منا و سـلـمـنا وجا هدنا معك قال نعم قوم يكونون مـن بعد كم يومنون بى و لم يرونى رواه احمد والدارمى

This tradition confirms that a certain group of people who would come afterwards, who would be better than those companions who had accepted Islam and had joined for Jihad along with the holy Prophet (Slm). This is also supported by a tradition from "Muslim":

5. "Narrated Abu Huraira (Rz) that he heard the holy Prophet (Slm) saying that "Those people would love me most who would come after me and every one of them would desire to see me with my family and my grandeur."

(۵)عـن ابى هريره ان رسول الله صلى الله عليه و آله و سـلـم قـال مـن اشـد امتى لى حبا ناس يكونون بعدى يودا حدهم لورأنى باهله و ماله

It is a fact that love of the holy Prophet (Slm) is the criterion of the faith. Whoever had a deep love with the holy Prophet (Slm) he alone is supposed to be the perfect Muslim. Both "Bukhari" And "Muslim" confirm what the holy Prophet (Slm) had stated that:

6. "No person would become a perfect believer unless he loved me more than his parents and everyone."

(۲)لايومـن احد كم حتىٰ اكون احب اليه من والده و ولده والناس اجمعين

Sheik Abdul Haq Dahlavi had commented on this tradition as mentioned below:

"The symbol of a perfect believer is that the holy Prophet (Slm) should be the most favourite and respectable among all to him."

نشان مومن کامل آن است که پیغمبر خدا صلی الله علیه و سلم محبوب تراز همه چیز وهمه کس باشد نزد مومن الی آخره

Do not those two traditions confirm that the perfect believers are those who come after him? Haakim (Rh) had narrated in "Mustadrik" that:

7. "Narrated (Holy Prophet (Slm) that group of people who would come after me they are still in people's backbone (yet to born), they would accept me even though they had not seen me. They would get suspended leaf(???) and whatever is written on it they would act on it. Thus among the believers they are most supreme" . This tradition was accepted by all the Sheikhain (Rz)."

قال اقوام یاتون من بعدی فی اصلاب الرجال فیؤمنون بی ولم یرونی ویجدون الورق المعلق فیعملون بما فیه فهؤلاء افضل اهل الایمان ایمانا هذا حدیث صحیح الاسناد ولم یخرجاه

Reported "Tirmizi" about Anas who narrated:

8." My Ummah's example is like a rain, we do not know its inception is better or its end."

مثل امتی مثل المطرلایدری اوله خیر ام آخره

From the above traditions it is clear that after the companions of the holy Prophet (Slm) some others would emerge who would be equal to the companions or even better than them.

Nayeem Bin Hammad (Rz) narrated in "Kitab-e-Fitan" which supports the above tradition:

9. " Abu Ayub (Rz) had narrated from "Artat" that Abdul Rahman bin Jubair bin Nafeer (Rz) had heard the holy Prophet (Slm) telling that "It is certain that my people will meet Masih Ibn Mariyam (As), who would be like you or they would be better than you."

حدثنا ابو ایوب عن ارطاة عن عبدالرحمن بن جبیر بن نفیر قال قال رسول الله صلی الله علیه و سلم لیدرکن المسیح ابن مریم رجال من امتی هم مثلکم اوخیر هم مثلکم اوخیر

10. "Asshatul Lumaat" had commented on the words "Ashhadu Ummati" that: "The clear meaning of this Tradition and those which are reported in this connection have argued that after the period of the companions of the holy Prophet (Slm) such people would emerge who would be either equal to them or even better than them". Reported by Ibnul Burr (Rh) who was a known traditionalist and whose faith also supports these sayings."

ظاهر این حدیث و بعضی احادیث دیگر که درایس باب بیاید دلالت داردبرآنکه تواند که بعد از صحابه رضوان الله علیهم اجمعین کسی بیاید که مساوی باشد ایشان رادرفضل یا افضل باشد از ایشان و ابن عبدالبر که از مشاهیر علمائ حدیث است باین جانب رفته و تمسك باین احادیث نموده است

Apart from this Abu Dawood Tayalsi (Rh) has reported with reference to Ibn-e-Abbas (Rz):

"It is nearly possible that this Ummah may become Anbiya completely".

كاوت هذه الامة ان تكون انبياء كلها

The same narration has come in "Durr-e-Manshoor": *(Rather it may be taken as an exaggeration)*

"It has been inferred by Ibn Jareer (Rz) that "On the Day of Judgment all other Ummahs will say indeed it is correct that this Ummah (of the holy Prophet (Slm) would become Anbiya completely."

اخرج ابن جرير عن زيد بن اسلم ان الامم يقولون يوم القيٰمة والله لقد كادت هذه الامة ان يكونوا انبياء كلهم .

From the above traditions we come to the conclusion that in the future a group would arise who would be either equal to the companions of the holy Prophet (Slm) or even better than them. Thus it can be deduced that these companions are none but of Imamana's alone.

Author of "Iqdud Durer" had reported about Hazrat Ali (Rz) who had said presumably about the companions of Imam Mahdi (As) that:

"Neither the beginners took the lead over them nor the last ones would reach to their rank."

لم يسبقهم الاولون ولا يدركهم آخرون

In such circumstances if Imamana (As) had implied that his companions are like that of the companions of the holy Prophet (Slm), then how could this statement goes against the above mentioned traditions? Thus author of Hadia's contention that "These officers of Vilayet (Companions of Imam Mahdi) are better than the companions of the holy Prophet (Slm) and even better than the progeny of Ahl-e-Bait (As)" becomes a senseless criticism, hence stands null and void.

Now we present those narrations pertaining to Imamana (As) which the author of Hadia has mentioned in chapter 5 of his book:

Author of "Shawahedul Vilayet" had narrated that:

1. ."One day the attributes of Siddiq-e-Akber (Rz) (Hazrat Abu Bakr Rz) were being mentioned and which were counted to be about 300.Bandagi Miyan Shah Nizam (Rz) inquired Imamana (As) whether someone among us had those attributes? Imamana (As) pointed out to Shah Nizam (Rz) and said that those attributes (of Abu Bakr (Rz) are with you."

روزے بيان صفات صديق اكبر بود رضى الله عنه كه سيصدو چندغات هستند ، بندگى ميان نظام فرودند كه هيچ يكى از آن صفات درماهست آنحضرت بزبان مبارك فرمودند بل هو كل فيك (باب دهم)

If the attributes of Siddiq-e-Akber (Rz) also pertain in Shah Nizam (Rz), how Shah Nizam (Rz) would become superior to Siddiq-e-Akber (Rz)?

2. Author of Hadia had referred an inauthentic "Saying" which states that at a certain time when Hazrat Abu Bakr (Rz) had worn a blanket, Gabriel (As) also had become a blanket clad. Referring this it is stated that when Shah Nizam (Rz) had worn blanket over him the angels had taken clothes like that of Hazrat Shah Nizam (Rz). But the fact is that such narrations are not recorded in any of the mahdavia literature.

A. However, we find some good tidings given by Imamana (As) to some of his companions which are mentioned in "Insaf Nama" chapter 17: In that also this narrative regarding Shah Nizam's clothing is not mentioned at all. It states that:

"Fifth Good Tiding: all attributes (of Hazrat Abu Bakr Rz) are with you (Shah Nizam Rz)".

پنجم بل هو کل فیک

B. Shah Nizam's fifth Tidings is stated in "Hashia-e-Inasf Nama" that:

"Thus, all, of them are in him (Shah Nizam (Rz)".

بل هو کل فیه

C. Narrations mentioned by Miyan Syed Aalam (Rh) did not mention about Gabriel's blanket cladding. The Sixth Tiding is that:

"Sixth Good Tidings: All such attributes are in you (Shah Nizam Rz).

ششم بل هو کل فیک

This also points out about Abu Bakr's attributes.

D. "Shawahedul Vilayet" (Written in 1052 H.) also refers many narratives, but nothing about Gabriel's blanket cladding.

Author of "Tazkeratul Saaleheen" (D.1104) has narrated in chapter 11 that:

"Inquired by Miyan Salamullah (Rz) whether any one of the companions has that rank? Imamana (As) pointed towards Shah Nizam (Rz) and said that all such attributes are in Shah Nizam (Rz)."

(ھ) میان سید سلام الله عرض کردند که میرانجی دریاران خوندکار بایں مرتبہ کسے ہست آنحضرت سوے شاہ نظامؓ اشارت نمودہ فرمودند کہ بل کلھا فیہ

Nothing is mentioned about the blanket cladding of Gabriel (As) in any of the above five sources, then author of Hadia if refers an unknown source, then who will prove that it was really said by Imamana (As) and how could Imamana (As) be blamed for it?

However, this Blanket Cladding had been referred to Bandagi Miyan (Rz) as mentioned in "Insaf Nama":

"It is narrated that at the time of an unfortunate happenings, Miyan Syed Khundmir (Rz) had clad himself with a blanket and whatever was available to him he distributed among his companions and thus he followed what Hazrat Abu Bakr (Rz) had once done; Thus Siddiq-e-Mahdi (As) also had done accordingly."

بندگی میان سید خوند میر گلیم پوشیدہ انچہ در خانہ بود ھمہ داندند چنانچہ ابوبکر صدیق گلیم پوشیدہ بود ھمچنیں صدیق مھدی کردند

Here too it had been said that Bandagi Miyan (Rz) had clad himself with a blanket, and not by Shah Nizam (Rz). But it is not at all mentioned that the angels have also done the same thing. Miyan Syed Alam's writings also support this. Thus no source refers that the angels had clad themselves with the blanket when Bandagi Miyan clad himself with a blanket.

(It seems this is an absurd allegation by the author of Hadia, since it is a proven fact that angels were ever having been seen by human eyes, except by the prophets and inspired persons.)

"At a time of distress Bandagi Miyan Syed Khundmir (Rz) clad himself with a blanket and distributed whatever he had among his followers. Thus he followed Hzt. Abu Bakr (Rz)."

نقل است که میان سید خوندمیرؓ در وقت ابتلاء در دائره خود گلیم پوشیده بود هرچه درخانه بود به فقراء کردند در راه خدائے تعالیٰ صدیق ولایت متابعت صدیق اکبر کردند

Here also it is mentioned that Bandagi Miyan (Rz) clad himself with the blanket and there is no reference as to the angels too had clad with blankets. As regards cladding with blanket is concerned it pertains to Bandagi Miyan (Rz) and not to Shah Nizam (Rz).

Further no books of Mahdavia had any reference of that the angel had clad with the blanket when Bandagi Miyan (rz) had clad himself with the blanket. As a matter of fact during the period of the holy Prophet (Slm) the reference of cladding blankets by the Angels had been accepted by the non Mahdavi sources when Hzt. Abu Bkr (Rz) had clad with a blanket.

However, Jalaluddin Seyuoti (Rz) had mentioned also in "Tareekh-e-Khulapha" about this tradition pertaining to Hzt. Abu Bakr (Rz).

Thus, the referred tradition of cladding of blanket by Angels has no reference in Mahdavia books, therefore it does not have any bearing to Imamana (As) then how characters of Imamana (As) could be questioned? Further Imamana (As) had never equaled his companions to the companions of the holy Prophet (Slm) as reported by the biased decliner.

3. Author of Hadia had also presented another narrative that Imamana (As) had one day came from his room and stated among the muhajereen that if anyone wants to see Abu Bakr (Rz), then he can see Miyan Dilawer (Rz). Here similarity might have been deduced in facial complexion or characters, but this does not in any way degrades Hzt. Abu Bakr (Rz) nor enhances Shah Dilawer's eminence.

A. Author of "Tazkeratul Saleheen" mentioned a narrative that:

"Imamana (As) told that Bhai Nemat (Rz) is the Eliminator of Innovations and also that both of us had driven horses for (obtaining) Trust in Allah, there was no difference (except that of horses') ears."

فرمودند که بھائی نعمت مقراض بدعت اند نیز فرمودند که بنده و بھائی نعمت درمیدان توکل اسپھادوانیدیم هیچ فرق نه شد مگر گوشواره (باب پنجم)

This tells that the trust in Allah of Imamana (As) was greater than Shah Nemat's, but is there any point for any objection?

It may be pointed out here what the holy Prophet (Slm) had addressed to Hazrat Bilal (Rz):

"For the reason that I heard the rattling sound of your shoes in the paradise before I was there."

فـانـی سـمعت دف نعلیک بین یدی فی الجنة (اشعته اللمعات جلد اول صفحه ۵۵۴)

This points out that Hazrat Bilal (Rz) was ahead in the paradise and the holy Prophet (Slm) was following him. When this is not objectionable, then how the narrative of Imamana's trust on Allaah had been ahead of the Shah Nemt's trust on Allah, comparing to that of Shah Nemat (Rz), then we do not know why such a silly objection should be raised?

It is reported that Imamana (As) had said about Miyan Shah Nemat (Rz) that he was Omer (Rz) of Vilayet and Miyan Nemat was second to Hazrat Osman (Rz) in modesty. These narratives do not prove that Shah Nemat (Rz) was made superior to either Hazrat Omer (Rz) or Hazrat Osman (Rz). Thus, it is a fact that, there is no such written proof to ascertain that the companions of Imamana (As) had been, any time, asserted by any one to be superior to the companions of the holy Prophet (Slm).

Now remains another objection of the author of Hadia that when there were only four companions of the holy Prophet (Slm) why there were five for Imamana (As) and further that when there were ten Mubasshirs of the holy Prophet (Slm) how could there be twelve in Mahdavis? This objection is just absurd, senseless and highly malicious and prejudiced one, hence not tenable. Because the higher number has nothing to do with the superiority of the rank. For example during the life time of the holy Prophet (Slm) only 120,000 Arabs had accepted Islam. In the case of Imamana (As) how dare he can object as to why the entire world had not become Muslim during the period of Mahdi (As)?

Thus, it may be admitted that, wherever the discussion of the companions of Anbiya has been written in "Matla-al-wilayat", the companions of the holy Prophet (Slm) are exempted. The example of this exemption is given as below.

"It is narrated by Abdullah bin Omer (Rz) that "I heard the holy Prophet (Slm) saying that heaven has not shed its shadow and the land has not created any person who is more truthful than Abu Zarr (Rz)."

عـن عبـدالله بن عمر (Rz) وقال سمعت رسول الله صـلـی الله علیه وسلم یقول ما اظلت الخضراء وما اقلت الخبراء باصدق من ابی ذر (رواه الترمذی)

With reference to this tradition Abdul-Haq Muhaddis Dehalvi has commented that:

"Traditionalists have stated that what the holy Prophet (Slm) has said, is just an exaggeration, or it may be particularized (for Abu Zarr (Rz) but Anbiya and the companions, comparing to Abu Zarr (Rz), are exempted."

گـفتـه انـد کـه ایـں قول از آنحضرت برسبیل مبـالـغـه اسـت یا مخصوص است بغیر انبیاء و صحابه که فاضل تر انداز دے ۔

It is also wrong to say that there were only four Caliphs, because the holy Prophet (Slm) had already prophesied that caliphate would run for a total period of thirty years.

"The period of caliphate will be thirty years after me". الخلافة بعدى ثلاثون سنة

This thirty year period includes the period of Imam Hasan (Rz) also, about which Sheik Abdul Haq, Muhaddis-e-Dehalvi, had commented that:

"Four Caliphs had ruled for 29 years, seven months and nine days, still there remained less than five months which was the period of the Caliphate of Imam Hasan (Rz). Thus Hasan Bin Ali (Rz) too was the Caliph for the remaining period of 30 years." خلافت خلفائى اربعه بست ونه سال نه روز هفت ماه تمام مى شود وپنجم ماه از سى سال باقى ماند كه بامام المسلمين حسن بن على تمام ميگردد وپس وى نيز از خلفا باشد

Thus there were five Caliphs and not four.

Author of Hadia had based his false objection on an unauthentic narration that the purpose behind five Caliphs in Mahdavi faith is just to prove the superiority of Vilayet over Nabuwwat. Whereas such a thing has never been mentioned in any of the previous narrations. Therefore the author of "Tazkeratul Saleheen" had stated what Imamana (As) had spoken that:

"Allah ordains that Miran Syed Mahmood (Rz), Miyan Syed Khundmir (Rz), Miyan Nemat (Rz) and Miyan Nizam (Rz) and fifth Enquirer (Shah Dilawer (Rz) are the Caliphs of Imamana (As)." فرمودند كه فرمان خدائى تعالى مى شود كه ميران سيد محمود و ميان سيد خوندمير و ميان نعمت و ميان نظام و پنجم سائل است (باب هفتم)

This is clear that there are five Caliphs of Imamana (As). But there had been no reference regarding Vilayet or Nabuwwat. The Author had also objected for the twelve Mubasshirs of Imamana (As), whereas Allah had mentioned fourteen companions of the holy Prophet (Slm). Hazrat Ali (Rz) had narrated that:

A."There was no Prophet (As) to whom more than seven companions had been given, but for me fourteen are given. Seven from the Quraish: Ali, Hasan, Husain, Hamza, Jafer, Abu Baker and Omer; seven from Migrants: Abdullah Ibn Masood, Salman, Abu Zarr. Miqdad, Huzaifa, Ammar and Bilal." (ا) ما من نبى الا قد اعطى سبعة نقباء وزراء نجباء رفقاء واعطيت انا اربعة عشر وزيرا نقيا نجيبا سمبعة من قريش على والحسن والحسين و حمزه و جعفر و عمر و سبعة من المهاجرين عبدالله ابن مسعود و سلمان و بوذر وحذيفة و عمارو مقداد و بلال

B. There was no Prophet (As) before me to whom more than seven companions were given and to me fourteen: Hamza, Jafer, Ali, Hasan, Husain, Abu Baker, Omer, Abdullah Ibn Masood, Abu Zarr, Miqdad, Huzaifa, Ammar, Bilal and Suhaib."

(ب) لـم يكن نبى قبلى الاعطى سبعة رفقاء نجباء وزراء و انى و قد اعطيت اربعة عشر حمزه و جعفر و عـلـى و حسن و حسين و ابوبكر و عمر و عبدالله ابن مسعود و ابوذر والمقداد و حذيفه و عمارو بلال و صهيب

"Tirmizi" also stated what Hazrat Ali (Rz) had narrated:

"Narrated holy Prophet (Slm) that every Nabi had seven persons of noble birth as friends, but to me fourteen have been awarded. When asked who were they, he replied: me and my two sons, Hasan, and Husain, Jafer, Hamza, Abu Baker, Omer, Musab Ibn Umair, Bilal, Salman, Ammaar, Abdullah Ibn Masood, Abu Zarr and Miqdad".

(ج) قـال قـال رسـول الله صلى الله عليه و آله و سـلـم ان لكل بنى سبعة نجباء و اعطيت انا اربعة عشر قلنا فمن هم قال انا و ابناءَ و جعفر و حمزه و ابوبكر و عمر مصعب ابن عمير و بلال و سـلـمـان و عمـار و عبدالـلـه بن مسـعـود وابوذروالمقداد رضى الله عنهم

Abdul Haq Muhaddis-e-Dehalvi had stated in" Manaqib Ashra" that:

"It may be known that Good Tidings is not for them alone, because it is for Ahl-e-Bait-e-Nabawi, Izdewaj-e-Mutahharat and also for other companions as well."

بـايـددانست بشارت مخصوص به ايشان نيست از جهـت و رود آن بـاهل بيت نبوت از ازواج و جزايشان را از اصحاب

From the above narratives, it becomes clear that the Good Tidings were not for the ten alone, because there were fourteen nobles who were provided by Allah to the holy Prophet (Slm); therefore they are all mubasshirs. Now if there are twelve mubasshirs of Imamana (As) why should there be any objection?

Imamana (As) had said about Shah Dilawer (Rz) that:

"Imamana (As) said that there are twelve mubasshirs of mine, like me there are twelve are with Shah Dilawer (Rz).".

حضـرت ميراںؑ فرمودند كه اثناء عشر مبشر چنانچه به حضور بنده شده اند همچنان پيش بهائى دلاورؓ خواهند شد (تذكرة الصالحين)

This narrative refers to twelve disciples, it does not mean that Shah Dilawer's disciples are in any way equal to Imamana's disciples? Or equal to the companions of the holy Prophet (Slm)?.

What Imamana (As) has forecasted about the disciples of Shah Dilawer (Rz), it became a true word by word that:

"Disciples of Shah Dilawer (Rz) became caliphs and the successor of Shah Dilawer (Rz) and became spiritual guides. They were twelve, out of them well known were: Miyan Abdul Karim, Miyan Yousuf, Miyan Abdul Malik Sujawandi etc."

نقـل است خـلـفائى بندگى ميان شاه دلاورؓ كه پـس ايشان خـلافـت و مـرشدى برايشان است دوازده كس اند چنانچه ميان عبدالكريم و ميان يوسف و ميان عبدالملك الى آخره

The holy Prophet (Slm) stated:

"Whatever Allah had revealed to me, I had revealed to Abu Bakr (Rz)."

ماصب اللّٰه فى صدرى شئًا الا وصبته فى صدر ابى بكر

From this tradition if Hazrat Abu Bakr (Rz) does not become superior to the holy Prophet (Slm), then with equal number of caliphs, how Shah Dilawer's Caliphs become equal to Imamana (As)?

Author of Hadia also had objected about the two Siddiqs. But renowned books of Mahdavia accept only one Siddiqu-e-Akber by the name Abu Baker(rz). But Bandagi Malik Mehri (Rz) had written in his couplet That:

"One like Abu Bakr (Rz) among them is special, Shah-e-Khundmir (Rz), who is the sun of the later period."

يك ابو بكرؓ سان اخص همه
شاه خوندمير مهر دور پسين

From the above couplet it is clear that the last period means the period of Mahdiat, in which Shah-e-Khundmir (Rz) became Siddiq-e-Akber of that period, because he was the first to declare 'Amanna Saddaqna' at the "Emphasized Proclamation" of Mahdiat by Imamana (As) at Badhli.; on which Shah Burhan (Rh) had narrated that:

"On declaration of Mahdiat, Syed Khundmir (Rz) became known as "Siddiq-e-Akber."

بعد از اظهار دعوى مهديت امير سيد خوندمير صديق
اكبر شد (دفتر اول ركن دوم باب دوم)

However, the author himself had admitted that there were two Siddiq-e-Akber (Rz) among the companions of the holy Prophet (Slm), as narrated in "Ibn Maja" by Hazrat Ali (Rz) that:

"I am Abdullah, and brother of the holy Prophet (Slm) and Siddiq-e-Akber."

انا عبدالله واخورسول الله صلى الله عليه و سلم وانا
الصديق الاكبر الى آخره

Author of Hadia had presented some traditions on this issue;

Now some traditions pertaining to the excellence of the companions of the holy Prophet (Sm) are submitted.

These traditions pertain to "Sawamiq-e-Muharraqa." And it is known that it addresses to the Shietes and those traditions accordingly are related to the excellence of the companions of the holy Prophet (Slm).

Author's foolishness could be seen that he is presenting the same narratives with regard to Mahdavis and it is a known fact that Mahdavis have the same faith about the beginning of Islam as mentioned in true traditions.

Ibn Hajar had presented traditions regarding the excellence of the companions of the holy Prophet (slm) because the Shietes had not accepted the ranks of other three companions, except Hzt. Ali (Rz).

Those traditions which are particularly mentioned about the attributes of the companions of the holy Prophet (Slm) had been accepted by Mahdavis. But these traditions could not negate those traditions in which it is mentioned that the ensuing group shall get the same status as that of the first one.

Previously we have submitted some traditions mentioned in the "Muslim" which state that those who would come after wards would have an intense love with the holy Prophet (Slm). Along with that we have presented the accepted traditions of "Bukhari" also which mention that loving the holy Prophet (Slm) was a part of faith are the real faithful. Does not this prove that perfect faithfuls are those who would come after the companions of the holy Prophet (slm), it is also an accepted fact of Ibn Abdul Barr (Rz), who was the most respected muhaddis.

From those traditions which the author of Hadia had presented, we shall only discuss about those which are mentioned in "Sihah".

"Anyone of you who spends gold to the size of Uhad Mountain, cannot reach to a Mud (Equal to two Iraqi Rattal) or even to its half)"

(١) لو ان احد كم انفق مثل احد ذهبا ما بلغ مداحدهم ولا نصفه

This tradition compares to the beginning period of Islam when people were very poor and their sacrifices have no match. This tradition speaks about distribution of wealth. During the period of Hzt. Osman (Rz) the muhajereen had become wealthy. Even if that wealth was distributed among the Muslims, still that could not be compared to that wealth which was distributed in the beginning period of Islam. How could you argue with this tradition regarding the faith of the people who would come after wards? His objection is absurd and untenable. Particularly when the holy Prophet (Slm) had declared that the faith of those who would accept him as the Prophet (slm) without seeing him is better than of those who accepted him as the Prophet (Slm) after seeing him and had accompanied him in Jihad.

Author of Hadia had shown his dishonesty by presenting this tradition by deleting the first para of the tradition. The correct tradition as mentioned in "Bukhari" and "Muslim" is presented below:

"Abu Sayeed khudri (Rz) reported that the holy Prophet (slm) had stated that do not abuse my companions, if any one of yours spend gold to the extent of Uhad mountain it would not reach to a Mud or even half of it."

عن ابى سعيد الخدرى قال قال النبى صلى الله عليه و آله و سلم لا تسبوا اصحابى فلو ان احد كم انفق مثل احد ذهبا مابلغ مد احدهم ولا نصيفه

It is clear that one who abuses the companions, his spending could not tally the spending of the companions of the early period of Islam. This only emphasizes the extent of spending during the initial period and not to compare the ranks as regards faith is concerned. It is evident from what the holy Prophet (Slm) had asserted:

"The best people are those who are nearest to me; then those who are nearer to them, and then those who are nearer to those who are further to them".

(٢) خير القرون قرنى ثم الذين يلونهم ثم الذين يلونهم

It is not clear as to what should be the purpose of the author to present this tradition? This tells that the period of the companions was better than the period of the descendants. This means that the period was free of innovations.

Author of "Ashatul Lamaat" had stated that:

<table>
<tr>
<td>

"The period of the followers of the companions of the holy Prophet (Slm) is reckoned up to 260 years, then innovations emerged and rare things appeared, like Philosophers rebelled, rationalists spoke out and the educated ones were tested by the faith regarding creation of Qur'an."

</td>
<td dir="rtl">

قرن اتباع تابعین از انجاتا صدودویست و شصت سال و درایں وقت ظاهر شد بدعت هاپیدا شداشیائی غریب و برداشتند فلاسفه سرهائ خودرا و کشادند معتزله زبان هاراو ممتحن گشتند اهل علم بقول خلق قرآن الی آخره

</td>
</tr>
</table>

If we take this tradition in the sense of degradation, then the period which would be far from the first one, the grip of faith would decrease simultaneously. Then those who would accompany Jesus Christ (AS) would be having the lowest grade of faith. Thus as presumed by the author the faith of Mahdi (As) would be like that. He submits a tradition in this connection reported by Abu Nayeem (Rz).

<table>
<tr>
<td>

"The first and the last period of this Ummah is best because in the first the holy Prophet (slm) was there and in the last Jesus Christ (As) would be present. Thus in between these two periods there may come crooked people who would be neither from me nor I am from them."

</td>
<td dir="rtl">

(۳) خیر هذه الامة اولها و آخرها اولها فیهم رسول الله و آخرها فیهم عیسیٰ ابن مریم و بین ذلک فیج اعوج لیسوا منی ولا انا منهم

</td>
</tr>
</table>

This tradition is not found in "Sihah", therefore we would not like to comment such unauthentic tradition. However the claimant's purpose is not served from the version of this tradition, because he had neglected to present another tradition reported by Razeen (Rz) in "Mishkot":

<table>
<tr>
<td>

"How could this Ummah be perished when I am at its inception, Mehdi (As) is in between and Jesus Christ (As) is at the end", but as prophesied by holy Prophet (Slm), it is possible that such crooked people may exist, and to make them correct, Promised Mahdi had been commissioned.

</td>
<td dir="rtl">

کیف تهلک امة انا اولها والمهدی وسطها و المسیح آخرها و لکن بین ذلک فیج اعوج لیسوا منی ولا انا منهم رواه رزین

</td>
</tr>
</table>

Razeen's rank is far greater than that of Abu Nayeem (Rz). Because narrators of the tradition of Razeen (Rz) were accepted by Mulla Qari (Rz). The decliner had not pointed out this tradition, because it pertains Mahdi's name and as regards repelling the Ummah from destruction, all the three periods are equal. Thus his presentation of that tradition does not help him for his dubious and malicious purpose. Further, Mahdi (As) has been mentioned in between two prophets (As), thus Imam Mehdi (As) comes under the category of commissioned personalities by Allah.

"Except Prophets and Nabis, on account of having the company of the holy Prophet (slm), none could claim a better position than Abu Bakr (Rz)".

ماصحب النبين والمرسلين اجمعين ولا صاحب ليس افضل من ابى بكر (حاكم نے روايت كى ہے)

This tradition too is out of our discussion since it is not from"Sihah". We have just mentioned it here because the biased decliner wants to take wrong meanings out of it, by telling that among the companions of the holy Prophet (Slm) Abu Bakr (Rz) alone is supreme. Here the supremacy of Hazrat Abu Bakr (Rz) is negated but not the equality. Thus this tradition does not prove that in the future nobody will get the rank of Abu Bakr (Rz).

"Neither the sun rose or set on any person who is superior to Abu Bakr (Rz) excepting the prophets."

ما طلعت الشمس ولا غربت على احد افضل من ابى بكر الا ان يكون نبى .

This tradition does not prove that in future none would claim his rank. It is a fact that the holy Prophet (Slm) had informed that those who come in the future they would have perfect faith.

Same sort of narration had been asserted about Hzt. Omer (Rz). Hzt. Jabir had narrated in "Tirmizi" about Omar (Rz) that:

"Verily I had heard the holy Prophet (Slm) telling that the sun did not rise on a person who is better than Omer (Rz)."

فلقد سمعت رسول الله صلى الله عليه وسلم يقول ماطلعت الشمس على رجل خير من عمر

The narration of "Tirmizi" is far better than Abu Nayeem's and Abd bin Hameed's. Therefore supremacy of Abu Bakr (Rz) becomes doubtful for the muhaddiseen.

If arguing with Abu Nayeem's narration, then what mistake Tabrani had committed who had reported Hzt. Jaber's narrative that among the companions of the holy Prophet (Slm) Abu Bakr (Rz) is supreme; but not among the Ummah of the future about whom the holy Prophet (Slm) had said"

"Verily, Hasan (Rz) and Husian (Rz) are the leaders of the youngsters of the paradise."

ان الحسن و الحسين سيد الشباب اهل الجنة (ترمذى)

It is a fact that peoples of the paradise shall be of younger age according to a tradition:

"Those among the residents of paradise who die in the world whether old or young, they would be of the of age of thirty and would never be more than that."

من مـات مـن اهـل الجنة من صغير او كبير يردون بنى ثلاثين فى الجنة لايزيدون عليها ابد ا

According to this tradition Imam Hasan (Rz) and Imam Husain (Rz) would become leaders of the inhabitants of the paradise except prophets and Khulafa-e-Rashedeen. Sheik Abdul Haq had commented on this:

"Tayyabi had told that they are supreme to those who died in the cause of Allah at their younger age, but it is doubtful because their supremacy is not particularized. But they are supreme to those who died at an old age. Thus they are leaders of the inhabitants of paradise because they shall younger, except prophets and Khulfa-e-Rashedeen."

طيبى گفته كه مراد آن است كه ايشان افضل انداز كسى كه جوان مرد در راه خدا و دراىن سخن نظر است زيرا كه نيست وجـه تـخصيص مرفضل ايشان را بر كسى كه جوان مرد بلكه ايشـان افضل انداز بسيارے كسان كه پير مرد اندپس اولىٰ آن اسـت كـه بـعضى گفته اند كه مراد آن است كه ايشان سيد اهـل الـجـنـة انـد زيـراكـه اهـل جـنـت همه جوانانند ليكن تخصيص كنند بغير ابنياء و خلفائ راشدين

From this it is ascertained that they are the leaders of residents of paradise except the prophets (As) and Khulafa-e-Rashdedeen (Rz), because they (Hasan (Rz) and Husain (Rz) had been given the glad tidings that they will be the leaders of the youngsters in the Paradise. In the same manner the glad tidings also had been given to the predecessors; that group also would be exempted about whom the holy Prophet (Slm) had ordained that their reward would be like that of the predecessor or that their faith would be better (than others).

"Abu Bakr (Rz) and Omer (Rz) shall be leaders of those who died at the old age either before them or after them except the prophets (As) and apostles (As)."

ابـو بـكرؓ و عمرؓ سيد ا كهـول اهـل الجنة من الاولين والآخرين الا النبين و المرسلين

From this it is clear that Abu Bakr (Rz) and Omer (Rz) are the leaders of those who died at the old age, except prophets and apostles. Sheik Abdul Haq states that:

"It means that they (Abu Bakr (Rz) and Omer (Rz) are leaders of those who died at their old age."

پـس مـعنـى اسـت كـه سيد كسانى اند كه كهل مردند در دنيا

Author of "Qamoos" had written about the word "Kuhal" that:

"That person is called "Kuhal" whose age has exceeded 30 years or still exceeded between 34 and 51.

مـن جـاوز الثـلاثين او اربـعـا و ثلاثين الـىٰ احدى و خمسين

On the other hand Sheikhain (Rz) are the caliphs of the holy Prophet (Slm) and Imam Mahdi (As) is Khalifatullah therefore this tradition does not apply to him (Imam Mahdi (As) because he did not die at the age of "kuhal" that is 51, but he died at the age 63 like that of the holy Prophet (Slm) who also died at the age 63.

According to another tradition "Kuhal" denotes to tolerance and intelligence. From this tradition the Shaikhain (Rz) are tolerant and intelligent people. Thus it cannot be argued that they would become leaders of the residents of the Paradise.

Sheik Abdul Haq Muhaddis Dehelvi has commented on this tradition that:

"Some have taken the meaning of "Kuhal" as tolerant and intelligent. It means to say that Allah would bring tolerant and intelligent people in the Paradise."	بعضے گفتہ اند کہ مراد بہ کہل اینجا حلیم و عاقل است یعنے مے در آرد ایشان را خدائے تعالیٰ در بہشت حلیم و عاقل ۔

Further in respect of the excellence of the companions of Mahdi (As), Hazrat Ali (Rz) states that:

"Neither the first ones took lead over them nor the last ones reached to their rank."	لم یسبقھم الاولون ولا یدرکھم آخرون

Such is the rank of the companions of Mahdi (As). Therefore according to the tradition the words" Minal Awwaleen WA Akhereen" do not apply to the companions of Imam Mahdi (As). Ibn Masood had narrated what the holy Prophet (Slm) was telling about a person who would enter the paradise at the end and who would tell That:

"Allah had given me that thing which was not given either to the beginners nor to the last ones."	لقد اعطانی اللہ شیئا ما اعطاہ احدامن الاولین والآخرین

However, the author of Hadia was trying to stress that the Sheikhain (RZ) (Hzt. Abu Bakr and Hzt. Omar) were superior to every one of the Ummah and he is unable to contain himself by uttering that they are even superior to Imam Mahdi (As) about whom we have presented the tradition of Razeen (Rz) above and about whom the holy prophet (slm) had ordained that he is the Khalifatullah.

Author's ignorance can be seen that he is giving preference to the Sheikhain (Rz) who are the caliphs of the holy Prophet (Slm), whereas Imam Mahdi (As) is the Khalifatullah and comes under the category of the commissioned ones.

According to Razeen (Rz):

"How could the Ummah be perished in whose beginning I am, and at the last Jesus Christ (As) is there and in between Imam Mahdi (As) exists."	کیف تھلک امتی انا فی اولھا و المھدی فی وسطھا وعیسیٰ فی آخرھا

Apart from this Imam Mahdi's reference had come in between two prophets, thus he becomes one of the commissioned ones. On the other hand the Sheikhain (Rz) are not the commissioned ones, thus according to the tradition Imam Mahdi (As) is exempted from the words "Minal Awwaleen Wal Akhereen". Further according to Ibn Maja (Rz) Imam Mahdi (As) comes from the lineage of Saadaath who belongs to paradise as mentioned below:

"Anas Bin Malik (Rz) reports that he heard the holy Prophet (Slm) was telling that we the descendants of Abdul Muttalib are leaders of the residents of Paradise, including Hamza, Ali, Jafer, Hasan, Husain and Mahdi."

عـن انس بن مالک قال سمعت رسول اللهّ يقول نحن ولـد عبدالمطلب سادة اهل الجنة انا و حمزه و علی و جعفر الحسن والحسين والمهدی (ابن ماجه)

From this tradition Imam Mahdi (As) is one of the leaders of the inhabitants of the paradise. But if the excellence of the Sheikhain (Rz) is asserted only on one narrative than from the following traditions, Hzt. Abu Zarr (Rz) surpasses even to all of the prophets (As), Sheikhain (Rz) and even the holy Prophet (Slm):

"Narrated By Abdullah Bin Amar that he heard the holy Prophet (Slm) telling : neither sky shed a shadow nor the Earth lifted such a person who is superior to Abu Zarr (Rz) for his trustworthiness."

عن عبدالله بن عمرو قال سمعت رسول الله صلی الله عـليـه و آلـه و سلم يقول ما اظلت الخضراء و ما اقلت الغبراء باصدق من ابی ذررواه الترمذی

This tradition tells that there was no man superior to Abu Zarr (Rz) in truthfulness. This tradition is also available in "Tirmizi", and "Tabquat-e-Ibn Saad". Now we have to ask the biased decliner:should he declare Abu Zarr (Rz) to be superior to all prophets (As), on the basis of this tradition? But, to us, the Prophets and the companions of the holy Prophet (Slm) have been excluded because they are superior to Abu Zarr (Rz).

With reference to this tradition Sheik Abdul Haq Muhaddis Dehalvi has commented that:

"Traditionalists have commented that the Saying of the holy prophet (Slm) is nothing but exaggeration since prophets (As) and companions are more superior to Abu Zarr (Rz).

گفته اند که ایں قول از آنحضرت بر سبیل مبالغه اسـت یـا مخصوص است بغی انبیاء و صحابه که فاضل تر انداز دے ۔

Apart from this, there is a good tiding for Hzt. Ali (Rz):

"Undoubtedly, the combating of Ali (Rz), at the battle of Khandaq, is superior to all actions of the Ummah till the Day of Judgment."

لمبارزة علی بن ابی طالب یوم خندق افضل من اعمال امتی الٰی یوم القیامه

Whether in the actions of Ummah the Sheikhains' actions are not included? There is one more tradition about Bibi Maryam (As) and Aasia (Rz):

"No one woman was perfect except the Imran's daughter, Maryam (As), and Pharaoh's wife Aasia (Rz)."

لـم یـکـمـل مـن الـنسـاء الا مریمّ بنت عمران و آسیةّ وامراة فرعون

Even otherwise the traditionalists had excluded Bibi Fatima (Rz), because she had been given many more good tidings by the holy Prophet (Slm). In the same manner wherever the excellence of the companions had been mentioned we have to exclude those to whom the holy Prophet (Slm) had given Glad Tidings already over those companions who were accompanying the holy Prophet (Slm) in the battle. Among them the Sheikhain (Rz) were also present.

Thus the traditions regarding the beginners of Ummah do not negate those traditions referring to those people who were equal to the companions of the holy Prophet (Slm) or even better than them. Allah States:

"Remember, oh Bani Israel, my favours on you which I bestowed and that I gave you (Israelites) superiority over all the inhabitants of the world."

يـا بنى اسرائيل اذكروانعمتى التى انعمت عليكم وانى فضلتكم على العالمين (سوره البقرة ع ۵)

This verse gives superiority to the Israelites over all the Ummahs of the world until the Day of Judgment. Thus, whether Israelites are even superior to the Muslim Ummah? But the fact is that the Muslim Ummah is excluded from this verse, since Allah had given another good tidings about the Muslim Ummah:

"You are the best Ummah for the world."

كنتم خيرامة اخرجت للناس (آل عمران ع ١ ١)

Even the holy Prophet (Slm) too had given glad tidings to the beginners of the Ummah and also had described their attributes, but from these attributes those are excluded about whom in many traditions the holy Prophet (Slm) had asserted that they would be perfect in Faith comparing to the beginners.

Thus, Imaman's assertion that his companions are Second to Omer (Rz) or Second to Abu Baker (Rz) could not be criticized. He had just equalized his companions to Omer (Rz) and Osman (Rz), but he did not make his companions superior to the holy Prophet's Caliphs. Thus it cannot be argued against Imamana (As), because the caliber of Ibn Abdul Barr (Rz) too had been accepted that even after the holy Prophet (Slm) such people would emerge who would be better than the companions of the holy Prophet (Slm).

It may also be pointed out that Ikhwan/ brothers are superior to the companions, because the holy Prophet (Slm) had desired to see them. Abu Huraira (Rz) had narrated that:

"I did desire to see my brothers": the companions inquired: "whether we are not your brothers"? Replied: "you are my companions, and my brothers are those who have not yet born (from among the Ahl-e-Bait (Rz)."

وددت انا قدراينا اخواننا قالوا اولسنا اخوانک قال انتم اصحابى و اخواننا الذين لم ياتوابعد

Behaqi had narrated in "Shubul Iman" what Hzt Omer (Rz) said about Abu Bakr (Rz) that:

"Omer Ibnil Khattab (Rz) said that if Abu Bakr's faith is compared to the faith of the entire Ummah, his faith is greater than the faith of the Ummah"

و اخرج البيهقى فى شعب الايمان عن عمر قال لو وزن ايمان ابى بكر بايمان اهل الارض لرجح بهم

Under these circumstances author of Hadia's contention that the faith of Hzt. Abu Bakr (Rz) is heavier to the faith of the entire Ummah has no value since this is not a tradition, since it was the saying of Hzt.Omer (Rz). Further this statement of Hzt. Omer (Rz) is nothing but exaggeration; because the holy Prophet (Slm) had prophesied that there are certain people in the Ummah who are distinguished on the basis of their faith.

Dailami had narrated to Ibn Omer (Rz) thus:

"If the entire earth and skies are kept on one side and the Faith of Ali (Rz) on the other side, then Ali's faith would be heavier."

لـولا ان السـمٰـوٰات والارض موضوعتان فى كفة و ايمان على فى كفة لرجح ايمان على

Prophets (As) and Nabis (As) are all included in the inhabitants of the world then whether Hzt. Ali's faith would be heavier to their's also?

The fact is that this sort of tidings, point out to the perfectness of their faith. This is the way of description about someone in Arabic . Before this we have referred to the tradition regarding Brothers whose rank is greater than the rank of the Caliphs. Now we have to ask whether Abu Bakr (Rz) comes under the category of Brothers or Companions?

Further "Tirmizi" has reported that:

"The holy Prophet (As) said that Allah has stated that those people who love each other on account of my splendour they are like Minar-e-Noor, thus even the prophets and martyrs would be envious of them.

قـال يـقـول الله تعالىٰ المتحابون فى جلالى لهم من بر من نور يغبطهم النبيون و الشهداء .

Haakim had narrated in "Mustadrik" that:

"Asserted (holy Prophet (Slm) those people who would come after me, they are yet to be born and who would accept me, eventhough they had not seen me. Whatever they find in the book they would practice it. As regards Faith, they would be superior to all the faithfuls. Haakim states that this tradition is accepted by all."

قال اقوام ياتون من بعدى فى اصلاب الرجال فيومنون بـى ولـم يـرونى و يـجـدون الـورق الـمعلق فيعملون بـمـافيـه فهؤلاء افـضل اهل الايمان ايمانا هذاحديث صحيح الاسناد و لم يخرجاه

This tradition points out that as regards faith, the faith of those who would come after wards would be heavier.

2. Caliphs of the Prophet (Slm) and Khalifatullah:

Hazrat Abu Bakr (Rz) had testified that he is the Caliph of the holy prophet and not the Khalifatullah.

Thus Imamana's assertion about his companions as being Second to Omer (Rz) or Second to Osman (Rz) should not be made a point of unnecessary criticism.

CHAPTER IV
Imamana's Assertions And the Prophets

In order to negate the argument regarding the characters of Imamana (As), as mentioned in "Sirajul Absar", author of Hadia had created some doubts about the Sayings of Imamana (As) about the Prophets (As) which are hereby being presented to refute in the following passages.

Imamana (As) had given glad tidings to his companions mentioning the ranks of some prophets, on which author of Hadia had raised objections by saying that every companion had been granted the position of the prophets (As). But as a matter of fact it is only a comparison, based on the Qur'an and the traditions. It is reported in the chapter 19 of "Shawahedul Vilayet" that:

"Reported that during a Sermon, Imamana (As) had granted the position of Hazrat Ibrahim Khalillullah (As) to Miyan Azizullah (Rz) and Miyan Maqdoom (Rz) stating that if both were alive they would be granted an extra position. After finishing the dinner both brothers kissed the hands of every brother of the Daira and went out. One died after three days and the other after nine days".

(١) نقـل اسـت کـه یك روز حضرت میراںؑ بوقت بیان قرآن در حق هـر دوشـان (یعنی میـاں عزیز الله و میان مـخـدوم) می فرمودند که هر دورا مقام ابراهیم خلیل الله صلوٰۃ الله علیه السلام داده شده است ، اگر حیات بودے بیشتـر بـاشنـد و لاکـن ایشـان سـفـر می کنند چونکه از دعـوت فـارغ شـدند آں هر دو برادران باهر یکی برادران دسـت بـوس کرده وداع کردند یکی برادر بعد سیوم روز نقل شد و برادر اولی بعد نهم روز وفات یافت ۔

In this narrative it is reported that Miyan Azizullh (Rz) and Miyan Maqdoom (Rz) were granted the position of Prophet Ibrahim (AS). Therefore the word "position" requires clarification:

In the "Insaf Nama" the Sayings of Imamana (As) are based on a single source. The same narrative had been recorded in chapter 17 , that:

"It was reported at the time of Asr Prayer, Imamana (As) had said regarding Miyan Maqdoom (Rz) and Miyan Azizullah (Rz) both were granted the rank of Prophet Ibrahim (As). If both were alive, they would get extra rank. Both, after finishing the dinner, kissed the hands of the brothers of the Dairah and went out. One died after three days and the other after nine days."

نقـل است میـان مخدوم را و میان عزیز الله را در وقت عـصـر در حـق هـر دو کسـان فرمـودند که هر دو را سیر ابراهیـم است اگـر حیـات بـاشـد بیشتر باشند و لیکن ایشـان سفـر کـردند چـونکه از دعوت فارغ شدند و هـریکـی برادران دست بوس کردند باآن کسان ، بعده سیوم روز نقل شد و دیگر نهم روز نقل شد

From this narrative of "Insaf Nama" "Muqam-e-Ibrahim (As)" and "Sair-e-Ibrahim"(As) are equal in meanings. Whoever gets the "Muqam-e-Ibrahim (As)" or "Sair-e-Ibrahim (As), he is called "Officiating to Hzt. Ibrahim (As)." In Chapter 27 of "Shawahedul Vilayet" it is stated that:

"Narrated by Imamana (As) that Allah asserted that : "at the point where "Vilayet-e-Mustafavi" ends, there emerges someone who would officiate Prophets (As). Someone gets Sair-e-Ibrahim (As), someone would get "Sair-e-Moosa (As), and someone gets "Sair-e-Iesa (As)."

فـرمـودنـد که فرمان حق تعالیٰ می شود که ائ سید محمد هـر جـاکه ختم ولایت مصطفیٰ شود آنجا بعضے قائم مقام انبیـاء بـاشند و بعضے راسیر ابراهیم و بعضے را سیر موسیٰ و بعضے را سیر عیسیٰ تعین فرمودند

This narrative confirms that whoever is officiating any Nabi (As), he is having the "Sair" of that Nabi (As). The meanings of the "Sair-e-Ibrahim (As)" is that he is having such attributes which were related to Prophet Ibrahim (As)". And the person who has such attributes shall be considered to officiate to Prophet Ibrahim (As). The narrative describes that if he gets the attributes of a particular prophet, it surely does not mean that someone is designated as that prophet or nabi, but just describing the similarity of that prophet's attributes in him. Therefore, "Sair-e-Ibrahim) (As)" and Sair-e-Iesa (As) can only be achievable by someone who is born under the Blessings of that Nabi (AS) or any Prophet (As). Ibn-e-Masood relates that the holy Prophet (Slm) had stated that there will be such people in his Ummah as if they were born with the Blessings of Prophet Ibrahim (As).

"Their hearts have been created on the heart of Ibrahim."(As).

دل هـائے ایشان را بر دل ابراهیم پیدا کرده است (مدارج جلد اول صفحه ۱۵۳)

Born in the Heart of Ibrahim (As):

In"Kanzul Ammal", it is reported that In"Kanzul Ammal", that,

"Their hearts would be on the heart of Ibrahim (As)."

قلوبهم علی قلب ابراهیم

"The holy Prophet (Slm) also said that
"Abu Bakr (Rz) is my minister, therefore
he is officiating me."

ابو بکر وزیری یقوم مقامی

The objection made by the author of Hadiya that "could it be said that officiating the Holy Prophet (Slm) means that Abu Bakr (Rz) becomes Nabi? Before this, it has been stated what Abdullah Ibn Masood had stated:

"Thus, Ibn-e-Masood has said that he has
not forgotten that Ma'az (Rz) has been
given similarity to Hazrath Ibrahim (As)
and thus, Ma'az (Rz) was similar to the
Prophet Ibrahim (As)."

پس گفت ابن مسعود فراموش نکرده ام بطریق تشبیه
معاذ بحضرت ابراهیم علیه السلام گفت ام و بودیم
ماکه تشبیه میدادیم معاذرا با ابراهیم

This proves that this is only a similarity of Ibrahim (As) and the Holy Prophet (Slm) also has designated some of his companions by giving similarity to some prophets (As). Reported by Anas that :

A. Whoever wishes to see the friendship of Ibrahim (As) (with Allah), he must look to Abu Bakr (Rz) for his generosity and whoever wants to see Noah (As) in his troubles, he must see Omar (Rz) for his bravery. Whoever wants to see Idris (As) in his exalted position, he must see Usman (Rz) for his piety. Whoever wants to see Yahiya (As) for his worship, he must see Ali (Rz) for his chastity."

من احب ان ینظرالی ابراهیم فی خلته فلینظر الی ابی
بکرفی سماحته و من احب ان ینظر الی نوح فی شدته
فلینظر الی عمر فی شجاعته و من احب ان ینظرالی
ادریس فی رفعته فلینظر الی عثمان فی رحمته و من
احب ان ینظر الی یحییٰ ابن زکریا فی عبادته فلینظر
الی علی فی طهارته

From this it proves that whoever gets the position of any prophet, he may be said that he is officiating that Nabi.

From these traditions it comes to light that to get immersed in the personality of Prophet Iesa (As) does not msake him Jesus Christ (As).

Abu Huraira (Rz) has said that he has heard the Holy Prophet (Slm) Saying:

B."Whoever wants to see Iesa (As) in
his humility, he must see Abu Zarr
(Rz)."

من سرّه ان ینظر الی تواضع عیسیٰ فلینظر الی ابی ذر

Hazrath Jaber reported that he heard the Prophet (Slm) Saying:

C. "Abu Bakr (Rz) and Omar (Rz) are similar to prophets Noah (As) and Ibrahim (As), one of them is very hard in matters of Allah and the other is very soft, like the milk."

مثـل ابـى بـكـر و عـمر مثل نوح و ابراهيم فى الانبياء احـدهـمـا اشـد فـى اللـه مـن الحجـارة و هو مصيب والآخرالين فى الله من اللبن و هو مصيب

The Holy Prophet (Slm) has said about Jarir bin Abdullah (Rz), as reported by Hazrat Omar (Rz) that:

D. "Jarir (Rz) is the Yusuf (As) of this Ummah."

جرير يوسف هذه الامة

Based on the above traditions, whether the fault-finder would dare to conclude that the Holy Prophet (Slm) has made all his companions the prophets? As a matter of fact, Imamana's assertion describes just the similarity of the attributes of those companions to the attributes of some such prophets and nothing more.

It can also be deduced from the Qur'an that whoever follows Allah and any of His Prophets (As), he gets similar attributes of that prophet (As). An example is given below, as per Qur'an:

"Whoever follows Allah and his prophets, thus those people would be along those to whom Allah has awarded His blessings, they are: prophets, Faithfuls, Martyrs and Pious persons."

و مـن يـطع الله والرسول فاولئک مع الذين انعم الله عـليـهـم مـن الـنبيـن والصديقين والشهداء والصلحين (النساء ع ٩)

From this verse of the Holy Qur'an it cannot be argued that whoever follows Allah and His Prophet (Slm), he may be called faithful, martyrs and pious man, but how can he be designated as a prophet. It tantamount to say that whoever follows Allah and His Prophet (Slm) he would get the friendship of that prophet, that means he would be granted position of that prophet.

Where ever according to the tradition, if someone is designated as a prophet, it means that he is having the position of that particular prophet. Abu Dawood Tayalsi (Rz) has reported that Ibn-e-Abbas (Rz) has said that:

"It is possible that the whole of the Ummah gets the position of prophethood."

كادت هذه الامة ان تكون انبياء كلها

This tradition also speaks about the ranks of those prophets and it does not say that the every one of the Ummah becomes the prophet. In Mahdavia literature, nowhere has it been written that Imamana (As) has given glad tidings to his companions as a Nabi, but Imamana (As) had only said that someone is having the attributes of some such prophet. In that sense he had only asserted that someone had the position or rank, even officiating to any prophet, but never designated someone as the prophet.

1. Author of "Matlaul Vilayet" had written with reference to Imamana's stay in Sindh that:

"On command by Allah Imamana (As) had given Glad Tidings to his companions of imminent prophets."

به فرمان حق تعالیٰ بشارت هائے مقامات اولوالعزم انبیاء
و مرسل فرمودند (فصل هفتم)

It is all just to say that whatever positions and attributes have been mentioned for the companions, it does not mean that on the basis of those attributes, someone had been designated also as the prophet or Nabi.

2. Author of "Shawahed-ul-Vilayat" has narrated that:

"Imamana (As) said about Miyan Shaikh Bheek (Rz) as officiating to Hazrath Iesa (As)" (since Miyan Bheek (Rz) had invoked the Blessings of Allah, and a child became alive, on which basis people of that place took him as an Aouthar to worship and followed him."

نقل است که حضرت امام علیه السلام میان شیخ بهیکؓ
را قائم مقام مهتر عیسیٰ علیه السلام فرمودند

Officiating means getting the same position and having the same attributes, but it does not mean that he had become a prophet.

The Holy Prophet (Slm) also has designated Abu Bakr (Rz) to officiate the Holy Prophet (Slm) himself, this does not mean that he has designated Abu Bakr as a Nabi, or a prophet.

3. Author of "Shawahedul Vilayet" had narrated that:

"One day Imamana (As) asserted that perhaps Allah after designating him as Promised Mahdi (As), might have described my attributes to be that of a certain prophet, that is why many prophets had aspired for my company."

نقل است که روزے امام علیه السلام فرمودند که بنده را
خدائے تعالیٰ مهدی موعود کرده و صفت بنده به پیغمبران
خبرداده بود بناء بر اکثر پیغمبران تمنائے صحبت بنده کرده
بودند (باب ۲۶)

The above narration does not disgrace the prophets, but it shows the exaltation of the holy Prophet (Slm). Apart from this, Imamana's excellence is not only because he is the one who was commissioned by Allah, but because of his character to be like that of the holy Prophet's.

To aspire for the company of Imamana (As) by some prophets, it can be deduced that the position what Imamana (As) had acquired from Allah, that position was not given to the aspiring prophets, it cannot be objected because the holy Prophet (Slm) had said that:

"Narrated by Omer (Rz) that he heard the holy Prophet (Slm) saying: "Among the people there are certain who are neither Nabi nor martyrs, but on the Dooms Day after seeing their ranks before Allah, prophets and martyrs may envy for their position."

عـن عـمر رضى الله عنه قال قال رسول الله صلى الله عـليـه و آلـه و سـلـم ان من عبادالله لانا ساماهم بانبياء ولا شهـداء يـغبـطهـم الانبيـاء و الشهدأ يـوم القيـامة بمكانهم من الله الٰى آخره

From this tradition also the excellence of the holy Prophet (Slm) is proved in the sense that from the Ummah certain people would emerge who were neither Nabi nor Martyrs but the prophets and martyrs would envy for the position they may have before Allah on the Day of Judgment.

To envying means, when any person had some sublime attributes, and when the same are not possessed by others, then to yearn attributes for them also is called enving. This tradition points out that there would be such eminent people in the Ummah who would be superior to all except the prophets.

This is the position of general persons, but what about Imamana (AS) who is according to the traditions having the characters of the holy Prophet (Slm) and designated as the Repeller/Saviour from destruction of the Ummah, as well as her is the Khalifatullah, if it is said that even the prophets had aspired for his company; why should there be any criticism? Particularly when, according to the traditions, even the prophets had aspired by such eminent people belonging to the holy prophet's Ummah!!

Abu Nayeem Isfehani (Rz) had referred what Hazrat Omer (RZ) had informed about the desire of Prophet Moosa (As):

A. "My Lord make me (a person) of the Ummah of Mohammed (Slm)."

يارب فاجعلنى من امة محمد

Author of "Uqdud Durer" had mentioned in its chapter 12 that:xs

B."Narrated by Abdullah Bin Jafer (Rz) that when Allah showed the grandeur of this Ummah to Prophet Moosa (As), Moosa (As) aspired to become one of that Ummah."

عـن عبـدالـلـه بـن جـعفـر قال لماقص الله تعالٰى على مـوسىٰ عـليـه السـلام شـان هذه الامة تمنى ان يكون رجلا منهم الٰى آخره

Imam Fakher-e-Razi (Rz) with reference to the verse "Ishrah Li Sadri" has narrated that:

C. "Asserted Moosa (As): Oh Lord make me disciple of Mohammed (Slm)"

قال اللّٰهم اجعلنى من امة محمد صلعم

Author of "Madarijul Nabuwwat" had reported that:

"It had been mentioned in another tradition that the holy Prophet (Slm) inquired: "Are you not pleased to have Prophets Ibrahim (As) and Moosa (As) among you" Then informed that "they would be among the Ummah on the Dooms Day". But Ibrahim (As) would say that "Although Holy Prophet (Slm) was his disciple and the son; still make me one among his Ummah"

در حـدیث دیگر آمده که فرمود آیا شما خرسند نیستید که بـاشد ابراهیم و عیسیٰؑ درمیان شما بعد از آن فرمود کـه ایشـان داخـل امـت انـد روز قیـامـت اما ابراهیم می گویـد تـو دعـوت مـنی و ذریت منی پس بگردان مرا از امت خود

It is not only prophets Ibrahim (As) and Moosa (As), but all prophets aspired to become the part of this Ummah of the holy Prophet (Slm), as reported in "Ashatul Lam'at" that:

"All prophets had aspired to become the part of the Ummah of the holy Prophet (Slm)."

تـمـامی انبیاء و رسل آرزو کرده اند که کاشکے امتان او بودند

Imamana's assertion that many prophets aspired for the company of Imamana (As), thus the excellence of the Ummah comes to light through this tradition.

4. The decliner had presented a narration in which it is stated that one of the muhajirs of Imamana (As), Miyan Sheik Mohammed proclaimed himself to be the Jesus Christ (As) and was murdered in Thatta (Sindh). Then Hazrat Shah Dilawer (Rz) gave glad tidings to him, since at the time of gasping/last moment, he repented, thus his repentance at the last moment was granted. At that Miyan Syed Mahmood (Rz) informed that because he had accepted Imamana (As), how could he be rejected?

Miyan Sheik Mohammed's episode was also reported in old books that his repennce was granted at his last hour, was not mentioned. Miyan Syed Aalam in his Memoirs has written that:

"One day Imamana (As) was going somewhere. Someone asked: "When Jesus Christ (As) would arrive after Imamana's departure"? Imamana(As) replied: "After us". Miyan Shaik Mohammed was one of the Muhajirs who was standing behind Imamana (As). He felt Imamana (As) had suggested about him to be Jesus Christ (As). Therefore, he after the demise of Imamana (As), proclaimed himself to be Jesus Christ (As) to whom many people accepted and he collected a cavalry of 500 horsemen. This news was heard by Miran Syed Mahmood (Rz). He sent three muhajirs, Miyan Nizam Ghalib, Miyan Hyder and Miyan Soomar. While they were on the way to reach him, they heard that the administrator of Thatta murdered him along with his disciples."

نقل است روزے میرانؑ براه می رفتند شخصی گفت کہ پس از خوندکار عیسیؑ کے خواہند آمد فرمودند کہ عیسیؑ پس ماخواہد آمد ، میان شیخ محمد نام مہاجر بود اوشان پس پشت میران استادہ بودند بر خود گمان کردند کہ میران مرافرمودند بعد رحلت در سند رفتہ دعوی عیسیؑ کردند بسیار کسان گرویدند و پنج صد سوار جمع شدند خبرش بہ میران سید محمود رسید فرمودند وسہ مہاجران رابکشتن اوفرستادندیکی میان نظام غالب دوم میان حیدر سوم میان سومار ، ایشان میان راہ خبرش یافتند کہ سرش بریدند با جمیع توابعان حاکم آنجائی

This narrative points out four issues:

1. Imamana's assertion that Jesus Christ (As) would come after him.

2. Sheik Mohammed's proclamation as Christ and was killed.

3. Last time repentance was not granted.

4. The episode pertains to the daira of Miyan Shah Nizam (Rz).

Regarding Sheik Mohammed Muhajir Shah Nizam (Rz) states that:

"After this, he went from my Daira to Sindh, and proclaimed himself to be Jesus Christ (As) and was murdered."

بعد از آن از پیش بندہ رفتند در ملک سندھ دعوی عیسیؑ اظہار کردہ متقول گشتند (باب یاز دہم)

Thus in either books nowhere it was mentioned that at the last hour his repentance was granted."Khatim-e-Sulaimani" also does not mention that his repentance was granted.

From these traditions it comes to light that to get immersed in Prophet Iesa (As) is different to actually claiming to be Jesus Christ (As).

The portion of the assertion regarding Shah Dilawer (Rz) was not available either in the Memoirs of Miyan Syed Aalam, nor in "Khatim-e-Sulaimani" or in "Tazkeratul Saleheen"

However, Shah Dilawer's Glad Tidings for Sheik Mohammed Muhajir could not be objected since Sheik Mohammed's proclamation of Christ was based on misunderstanding that Imamana (As) had said that Christ (As) would come behind him and at that time Sheik Mohammed heard it who was just behind Imamana (As) and after Imamana's demise he proclaimed, since he misunderstood the meaning of "behind", instead of "after" because he was "behind" Imamana (As) and wrongly took for himself and proclaimed as Jesus Christ (As) and was murdered.

At the last hour he might have repented and this fact might have been known to Shah Dilawer (Rz) by inspiration, and on that basis Shah Dilawer (Rz) might have given the tidings about his salvation, then how he could be blamed?

Now remains the matter of repentance by Sheik Mohammed Muhajir who at the last hour repentance for his mistake and it was up to Allah to accept and pardon him, because that proclamation was made on misunderstanding only. Allah thus states that:

"It is up to Allah to accept repentance at the last moment of those who had done wrong on the basis of misunderstanding."	انـمـا الـتـوبة على الله للذين يعملون السـوء بجهالة ثم يتوبون من قريب (النساء ع ٣)

From this verse it comes to light that if a person commits some mistake on misunderstanding and if he even at the last moment (at death bed) repents with sincerity, then Allah accepts such repentance and grants salvation to him. Sheik Mohammed's proclamation was just based on misunderstanding, hence he might have repented at the last hour and his last moment repentance might have been granted by Allah. It is mentioned in "Ashatul Lamat" that:

"Under coercion acceptance of faith is not permitted, while repentance on account of fear is accepted."	ايمان باس غير مقبول است و توبه باس مقبول

According to a tradition:

"Muaaz Bin Jabal (Rz) narrated that he heard the holy Prophet (Slm) saying that if a person's last words are "La Ilaaha Illallah" he is admitted to the Paradise". Reported by Abu Dawood (Rz)."	عن معاذ ابن جبل قال قال رسول الله صلى الله عليه و سـلـم مـن كـان آخـر كـلامه لا اله الا الله دخل الجنة رواه ابو داؤد

When the Last words of the Kalema "La Ilaaha Illallah" are accepted then why should not the last time repentance of Sheik Mohmmed be accepted by Allah?

Another tradition says that:

"Abi Sayeed (Rz) and Abu Huraira (Rz) both had narrated that the holy Prophet (Slm) had advised to pronounce the creed to the dying person and ask him to repeat."	عـن ابى سـعيد و ابى هريره قالا قال رسول الله صلى الله عليه و سلم لقنوا موتاكم لا اله الا الله

The Holy Prophet (Slm) said that:

"Every person would be raised in the condition in which he died". يبعث كل عبد على ما مات عليه

The word "Mouthakum" in the above first tradition denotes for those persons who repeat the Kalemah at their deathbed. Therefore the last hour pronouncing the creed to a dying man helps him for his future journey, then why the last hour repentance of Shaik Mohammed would not be accepted?

Thus Imamana's assertion that: "Jesus Christ (As) would follow him" is correct according to the holy Qur'an: Allah ordains that:

"Later on, we brought our prophets on their feet." ثم قفينا على آثارهم برسلنا (الحديد ع ٣)

Here also "Later On" means after wards.

5. The decliner had maliciously accused on the basis of an unauthentic narration that Mahdavis, out of all prophets, claim Jesus Christ (As) as the perfect Muslim. As a matter of fact no where it is written that Jesus Christ (As) was a complete Muslim.

A. Bandagi Malik Mehri (Rz) had composed a Persian couplet in this connection, translation is as below:

""None was Muslim from top to toe, with whole body and soul, except the holy Prophet (Slm) and Imamana (As)." مسلمان زسر تا قدم جسم و جان ـ نشد کس جز آن مرسل و این امام ـ

B. Author of "Insaf Nama" had reported that::

"We heard Bandagi Miyan (Rz) was telling many a time that he asserted before Imamana (As) that there are only two Muslims. Imamana (As) asked as to where from he heard that thing? Bandagi Miyan (Rz) said, yes Miranji (As) it is correct. Again Imamana (As) asked as to where from he heard that? Bandagi Miyan (Rz) told that Imamana (As) had informed him. Then Imamana (As) asked who are they? Bandagi Miyan (Rz) asserted that one is the holy Prophet (Slm) and the second being Imamana (As). Imamana (As) had again consented that some Prophets were Muslim up to their head, some were up to their bellies, some up to their right hand and some with their left hand only. But the above said two were complete Muslim."

از بندگی میاں سید خوندمیر چند بار شنیدیم فرمودند که یك روز پیش بندگی حضرت میراںؑ عرض کردم که در تمام عالم دو مسلمان معلوم می شوند بعده حضرت میراںؑ فرمودند که سید خوندمیرؓ شماچه می گوئید ایں سخن بندگی میاں فرمودند آرے میرانجیو همچنیں است بعده میراں فرمودند از کجا می شود بعده میاں فرمودند کـه از میرانجی معلوم می شود حضرت میراںؑ فرمودند که کدام دو کساں میاں فرمودند ایك محمد رسول الله صلعم ثانی محمد مهدی مراد الله بعده میراں فرمودند آرے همچنان است بعضی انبیاء را سر مسلمان شده بود بعضی تاناف و بعضی راتا پهلوئی راست و بعضی را هر دو پهلو مگر همیں دو تن سر تا پا مسلمان شدند (باب دواز دهم)

From the above two narrations, it proves that only two are complete Muslim and about Jesus Christ (As) nothing was mentioned.

C. "Hashi-e-Insaf Nama" also mentions about the two being complete Muslims, they are holy Prophet (Slm) and Imamana (As). Here also nothing was mentioned about Jesus Christ (As).

D. Bandagi Shah Burhan's Dafter also mentions that:

"It is narrated that Imamana (As) had many a times asserted that some prophets' head was Muslim, some up to their chest, some up to the bellies and out of all prophets and saints only two were complete Muslim, the holy Prophet (Slm) and I (Imamana (As))."

نقل است که حضرت امام کائنات علیه الصلوٰۃ کرات و مرات فرمودند که بعضی انبیاء را سر مسلمان شده بود و بعضی تاسینه و بعضی تاناف و درمیان جمله انبیاء و اولیاء از سر تا پا همیں دو تن مسلمان شدند یکی محمد رسول الله دوم محمد مهدی صلی الله علیهما (دفتر دوم رکن چهارم باب اول)

From these old sources it is proved that the holy Prophet (Slm) and Imamana (As) are two complete Muslims and nowhere it is written about Jesus Christ (As).

From this tradition it is reported that there exist grades for the prophets. Details are as below:

"Narrated by Ibn Masood that the holy Prophet (Slm) was telling "there is none with whom a Jinn or an angel has not been appointed". The companions asked "whether with you too"? The holy Prophet (Slm) asserted positively by saying that "one is with me also, but Allah made me overpowered on to him and he accepted Islam and he has no power whatsoever to mislead me". Reported by "Muslim".

عـن ابـن مسـعـود قـال قـال رسـول الـلـه مـا منكم احـدالاوقـد و كـل بـه قـرينـه من الجن و قرينـه من الـملائكة قالوا وایاک یا رسول الله قال و اياى ولكن الله اعاننى عليه فلا يامرنى الا بخير (رواه مسلم)

From this tradition it came to light that everyone has a Jinn and the holy prophet's jinn had become Muslim. Thus Jinn is also known as "Humzad". Abdul Haq Muhaddis-e-Dehlavi had commented that:

"It is said that man does not give birth to a child, but of course he bears his like which is called Hamzad."

در بـعضے روايات آمده است که زائیده نمی شود آدمی زاد را فـرزنـدے مگر آن كه زائیده می شود از جن مانند آں وے را همزادوے گويند

Traditions also tell that this Hamzad had been mentioned as the Satan. As per "Kanzul Ammal:

"None is there among you to whom no Satan had been appointed. When asked whether with you too? Answered "yes, but Allah helped me to overpower him" and the holy Prophet (Slm) had also said that the "Satan of Hazrat Adam (As) was a Satan and remained Satan forever, while my Satan had become Muslim . As mentioned in "Nihaya."

مـامنـكم مـن احدالا وله شيطان قال ولک یا رسول الله قال ولى و لكن الله اعاننى عليه فاسلم الىٰ آخره

Author of "Nihaya" reported that:

"Every person has his own Satan. When inquired what about you (holy Prophet (Slm)? He confirmed it and said that "by the grace of Allah I overpowered him and my Satan became Muslim."

مـا مـن آدمی الا و مـعه شيطان قيل و معک قال نعم ولكن الله اعاننى عليه فاسلم و رواية حتىٰ اسلم

"Adam's Satan was an infidel, my Satan is a Muslim".

كان شيطان آدم كافراو شيطانی مسلما

That means to say that it is not peculiar with Hazrat Adam (As), other prophets' Satans were also never became Muslim. Only holy prophet's Satan had become Muslim. Seyuoti had reported in "Khsais-e-Kubra" that:

"Buzar had narrated from Abu Huraira (Rz) who heard the holy Prophet (Slm) saying that " I had been made superior to all other prophets in two qualities. My Satan was an infidel, but Allah helped me to overpower him and he became Muslim". Abu Huraira (Rz) had said that he forgot about the second quality".

اخرج البزار عن ابی هریرة قال قال رسول الله صلی الله علیه و سلم فضلت علی الانبیاء بخصلتین کان شیطانی کافرا فاعاننی الیه حتیٰ اسلم و نسیت الخصلة الاخری

From these traditions, it is proved that the Satan of the holy Prophet (Slm) had become Muslim, but not of others. It means to say that the holy Prophet (Slm) in every sense he was a complete Muslim, other prophets were not complete Muslim. Therefore Allah had ordained about him that is why he possessed the best characters. According to the traditions, Imamana (As) also had been bestowed with like characters as that of the holy Prophet (Slm). Another narration about Imam Mahdi (As) is that:

"Same would be his name as my name and his characters would be as of mine."

یواطی اسمه اسمی و خلقه خلقی

Imamana (As) had said that his Satan also had become Muslim. The details are as below:

A. Bandagi Malik Sujawandi (Rh) had written in "Minhajut Taqueem " that:

"Among all narratives about Imamana (As), the one is that Imamana's Satan had become Muslim, like the one of the Holy Prophet (Slm)."

منها ماروی عن المهدی انه قال اسلم شیطانی کماروی ذلک عن النبی علیه السلام

B. Bandagi Ilahdad Hameed (Rz) also said that:

"Every one's Hamzad (Satan) is an infidel, except holy prophet's and Imamana's hamzad (Satan) who had become Muslim".

مانده همزاد ایں و آں کافر شد مسلمان به هر دو تن همزاد

C."Hashia Insaf Nama" had stated that:

"Narrated that Holy prophet's Satan and Imamana's Satan, both had become Muslim."

خناس رسول علیه السلام و میراں علیه السلام ایں هر دو خناسان مسلمان بودند

It is reported by "Shawahed-e-Wilayat" that:

"The 30th peculiarity of Imamana (As) is that his Satan also has become Muslim, like that of the holy Prophet (Slm).

خصوصیت سی ام آنکه فرموده اند که خناس بنده مسلمان شده است ـ

Thus Imamana's satan's becoming Muslim is a well known fact as mentioned by Abdul Malik

Sujawandi (Rh) that it was Imamana's famous attribute:

"In the same way, Imamana (As) had
informed that his Satan had converted to
Islam which is a well known fact.   "

هكذا اخبر المهدى عليه السلام ان شيطانه ايضا اسلم
عنده وهوالخبر المشهور بين الناس منه

Thus except the Satan of two, the holy Prophet (Slm) and Imamana (As), none others' Satan became Muslim. Thus whose Satan had become Muslim their stages of the vision of Allah would be more.

And now remains that example which has been described about Islam and the prophets, this also cannot be objected.

The holy Prophet (Slm) stated that:

"The holy Prophet (Slm) asserted that
"the example of mine and other prophets
is that a building whose construction
was done on a good scale but in which a
place for one brick was left, around
which people inspected and became
surprised as to why one brick's place
was left empty. Thus I closed that space
with a brick.

مثلى و مثل الانبياء كمثل قصر احسن بنيانه ترك منه
موضع لبنة قطان به النظار يتعجبون من حسن بنيانه الا
موضع تلك اللبنه فكنت انا سددت موضع اللبنة

6. Author of "Shawahedul Vilayet" had narrated thus:

"Bandagi Miyan (Rz) inquired Imamana
(As) "what was that position"? Imamana
(As) asserted "the souls of the firsts and
the lasts were presented and Allah
ordained me to lead them. I looked at
myself and told: "My Lord I am so weak
that I am unable to lead them." Then
again I looked over me and replied: "Oh
Lord with Thy help which You had
bestowed on to me I accept to lead them
and if there are still more, then also I
shall lead them all."

بندگى ميان سيد خوندمير حضرت امام الابرار رادر اين
باب استفسار كردند كه ميرانجى اين چه احوال بود ،
فرمودند كه ارواح اولين و آخرين حاضر كرده شد از
طرف حق تعالىٰ فرمان شد كه اى سيد محمد كه
اينهمه ارواح رابه پيشوائى قبول كن بنده در اين مشت
خاك نظر كرديم و گفتيم كه خداوندا اين ضعيف راچه
طاقت و قدرت باشد كه پيشوائى اينها تواند كرد و باز
به فضل خدا عنايت خدائى تعالىٰ نظر كرديم براى بنده
دار و گفتيم خداوند به فضل تو و عنايت توانچه تو
فرمائى به پيشوائى قبول كرديم و اگر صدچندان ديگران
باشند بفضل تو قبول كنيم

From this it is clear that Imamana (As) had led all souls as commanded by Allah. Why should any objection arise? As regards ranks of the companions, it is asserted by Imamana (As) that:

"Neither the first ones, nor the followers could reach to the rank of those persons."

لم يسبتهم الا اولون ولا يدركهم آخرون .

Ibn Masood had narrated that:

"Asserted holy Prophet (Slm) that "whoever enters in the paradise at the end, he would go forward then comes back. The hell fire looks after him and then he goes through that fire and while seeing at the fire , he asserts that Allah is Great Who had liberated me from the fire. Allah had bestowed on to me that thing which was not given to either the first ones or to the last ones."

عـن ابـن مسعود ان رسول الله صلى الله عليه و آله و سـلـم قـال آخر من يدخل الجنة رجل فهو يمشى مرة ويكبـومرة وتسفعه النار مرة فاذا جاوزها التفت اليها فقـال تبارک الذى نجانى منک لقدائطانى الله شيئا ما اعطاه احدامن الاولين و الآخرين الى آخره

This tradition confirms that one who enters paradise at the end, Allah would grant him more than what was granted to his predecessors. It does not say whether he would be Khalifatullah, or a prophet. If this tradition creates no objection, then how the narrative of "Shawahedul Vilayet" that Mahdi (As) would lead the first and the last would become a point of objection. Particularly when no one could reach the status of the companions of Imamana (As).

7. Author of "Shawahedul Vilayet"states in chapter 3 that:

"Asserted by Imamana (As) that "Allah had provided me with information about the ranks and status of all prophets, saints, faithful men and women as clear as one keeps a grain of mustard on the palm."

حضـرت امام عليه السلام فرمودند كه حق تعالىٰ بنده را مراتبات و مقامات جميع انبياء و اولياء و مومنين و مـومـنـات و احـوال جمله موجودات همچنان معلوم كـرده اسـت كـه چنـانچـه كسى دانه خردل ددست داردو هر طرف بگرداند تاكماحقه‘ شيناسد

Allah stresses in the holy Qur'an that:

"Allah knows everything what is in the Earth and in the skies."

والله يعلم مافى السمٰوٰت و ما فى الارض (الحجرات ع ٢)

Even otherwise, it is reported about the holy Prophet (Slm) who stated that:

"Thus I came to know what is in the Earth and what is in the skies."

فعلمت ما فى السمٰوٰت والارض

Whether anyone could argue if the holy Prophet (Slm) knew the Divine knowledge of Allah? Since Allah had provided him that sort of knowledge which was provided to Hazrat Ibrahim (As)

Again Allah asserts:

"In this manner We used to inform Ibrahim (As) about our kingdom of the earth and of the skies."

وكذلك نرى ابراهيم ملكوت السموات والارض (انعام ع ٩)

However, the holy Prophet (Slm) had the knowledge of everything which is available in the holy Qur'an and as mentioned in the traditions; and Imamana (As) too had that knowledge, because he also was from the category of the Commissioned ones; that is why the holy Prophet (Slm) had placed Imamana (As) in between two prophets as mentioned in the tradition of "Kaifa Tahleka Ummati".

Author of Hadia had objected about Imamana's assertion that he knew everything of the earth and of the skies by the Grace of Allah. The words of his objection are mentioned below:

"Invisible knowledge is the attribute of Allah. And whenever it is necessary Allah provides it to any one Who likes. "Sheikh-e-Mousoof" (Imamana (As) participated in it; and tells as if he knew that knowledge also."

"Shawahedul Vilayet's version "Allah........Banda Raa Hum Chunan Maaloom Karda asth" means "Allah had informed me" (as had informed others). Does this version indicate that (Naozoo Billah) Imamana (As)became partner of Allah? The source of knowledge which Allah possesses, Imamana (As) too knew that source by the Grace of Allah.

How could the biased decliner presume that obtaining knowledge from Allah makes Imamana (As) Allah's participant (Naozoo Billah)?

"Insaf Nama" was written prior to "Shawahedul Vilayet", its wordings are as below:

"It is narrated by Imamana (As) that "Allah had informed me about the ranks of all the prophets, saints, faithful men and women and about all creation with clarity as if a man keeps a thing in his palm to test it completely as a jeweler tries to distinguish purity and impurity of gold."

حضرت میران فرمودند که حق تعالیٰ بنده را مراتب انبیاء و اولیاء و مومنین و مومنات و احوال جمله موجودات همچنان معلوم کرده است که چنانچه کسی چیزے دردست دارد به هر طرف آن چیز را میگرداند تا کما حقهٗ بشناسد چنانچه صرافی می کند تا واقف شود به حیات دوروات، مهره نقره (باب پنجم)

Here the example of jeweler had been given which indicates about his being perfect in his avocation. In the same manner in "Shawahedul Vilayet" the example is given of a grain of mustard to describe about having complete information and nothing else.

The words "Huq Ta'la Banda Ra..... Hum Chunan Maloom Kurda Asath" are clear that Allah had informed Imamana (As) about everything. It does not mean that Imamana (As) knows everything, without the help of Allah.

If the decliner thinks to get information from Allah, makes some one participant of Allah (Naoozoo Billah) then he must accept the first man, Prophet Adam (As), to be the first participant of Allah (Naoozoo Billah).

"Adam (As) was taught all attributes (of every creation)". علم آدم الاسماء كلها (سوره بقره ع ٣)

In that sense the holy Prophet (Slm) too becomes a participant of Allah, as per wrong thinking of the decliner. Because Allah had addressed the Holy Prophet (Slm):

"And taught you which you did not know". علمك مالم تكن تعلم (سوره النساء ع ١١)

It cannot be said that Prophet Adam (As) was the only one to have the knowledge of every creation, and the holy Prophet (Slm) had little knowledge. It is just unthinkable. Because the holy Prophet (Slm) himself admitted that " I came to know everything about the Earth and the skies with the help provided by Allah Subhana Wat Ta'allh."

Now remains " knowledge of invisible" Allah states that:

"Verily, Allah knows what is in the skies and what is hidden under the Earth." ان الله يعلم غيب السموات والارض (الحجرات ع ٣)

This confirms that knowledge of the invisible is the attribute of Allah alone. Still Allah confirms that:

"Verily Allah does not inform about the invisible knowledge to all, except to a few prophets whom he likes." فلايظهر على غيبه احد الامن ارتضى من رسول (الجن ع ٢)

It means to say that whomever Allah likes He informs about the knowledge of the invisible. Further Allah states that:

"Whoever had been commissioned he is on the right path." انك لمن المرسلين على صراط مستقيم (يسٰين ع ١)

Regarding Imamana (As) the holy Prophet (Slm) had informed that Imamana (As) is Khalifatullah and Repeller from Destruction of Ummah who possesses holy prophet's characters; then should not Imamana (As) also be on the right path? Unless Imamana (As) is not on the right path, how could he save the Ummah from destruction?

Thus as regards the knowledge of invisible is concerned, Imamana (As) had stated that when Allah commands him, in turn, he informs to others. In chapter 12 of "Shawahedul Vilayet" it is written that:

"What can I do? When did I say to you that whatever I am saying it is based on Allah's commands"? Then Syed Salamullah requested Imamana (As) to say that he does not possess the keys of Allah's treasures. Imamana asserted : "If the owner of the treasure hands over the keys; I still have no authority to open them without his clear commands."

حضرت میران علیہ السلام فرمودند کہ بندہ چہ کند و بکدام وقت بہ شما گفتہ بود حکم بندہ بر حکم خدائے تعالیٰ جاری است ، بندگی میان سید سلام اللہ عرض کردند کہ میرانجی بگوئید کہ بدست شما کلید خزائن خدائے تعالیٰ نیست انگاہ حضرت ولایت پناہ فرمودند اگر صاحب کلید خزائن خود بہ بندہ خویش بدھد فاما بندہ راچہ طاقت باشد کہ بغیر رضائے صاحب قفل خزائن بکشاید

From the above it is clear that Imamana (As) without firm command from Allah, never gave any information to others. In these circumstances the decliner's assertion that Mahdavi believe Imamana (As) to be the participant (Naozoo Billah) of Allah as far as knowledge of invisible is concerned, is malicious, unfounded and based on bias and prejudice.

Even the holy Prophet (Slm) used to tell that any information comes only on Allah's Will and command; as mentioned in "Ashatul Lamaat" that:

Disappearance of Prophet's camel and taunting:

"Narrated that when Holy Prophet's camel disappeared and nobody knew where it went? Then the infidels sarcastically said that he (holy Prophet (Slm) used to tell that he knew even the facts about the skies, what happened to him that he did not know where his camel had gone? The Prophet (Slm) then and there asserted that "By Allah he does not know, except when Allah lets him know. Now Allah informs me that it is somewhere and its nose string is stuck to a tree."

در خبر آمده است که چون ناقهٔ آنحضرت گم شد و دریافت که کارفت منافقان گفتند که محمدمی گوید که خبر آسمان می رسانم و نمید که ناقهٔ او کجا است پس فرمود آنحضرت والله من نمید انم مگر انچه بداناندمرا پروردگار من اکنون بنمود مرا پروردگار من که وے درجائے چنیں و چنان است و مهاروے در شاخ درختے بند شده است

Author of Hadia had presented another narration: "Imamana (As) had spoken about Shah Dilawer (Rz) who knew everything from empyrean throne of Allah to the interior of the Earth, just like a mustard seed in his palm"

It was a confirmed fact that even Imamana (As) did not know anything until Allah made known to him, how could he say that Shah Dilawer (Rz) knew all about the invisible knowledge? This narration is just to inform Shah Dilawer's excellence, just like the holy Prophet (Slm) had said about Abu Zarr (Rz) that:

"Abdullah Bin Omer (Rz) said that he heard the holy Prophet (Slm) telling "neither the sky clamped its shadow on anyone, nor the Earth held any one, who was more truthful than Abu Zarr (Rz)".

عن عبدالله ابن عمر و قال سمعت رسول الله صلی الله علیه و سلم یقول ما اظلت الخضراء و ما اقلت الغبراء با صدق من ابی ذررواه الترمذی

This tradition confirms that Abu Zarr (Rz) was more truthful than (so to say) the prophets and even to the holy Prophet (slm). Therefore traditionalists have taken this tradition as an exaggeration. Sheik Abdul Haq, Muhaddis-e-Dehlavi stated that:

"Whatever was told by the holy Prophet (Slm) was just an exaggeration".

و گفته اند که ایں قول از آنحضرت برسبیل مبالغه است

As Abu Zarr's truthfulness had been described by the holy Prophet (Slm), in the same sense Shah Dilawer's knowledge was described by Imamana (As). When there arises no objection to the holy prophet's assertion about Abu Zarr (Rz), then why should there be any objection for Imamana's narration regarding Shah Dilawer (Rz)?

There is one narration in "Moulood" of Miyan Abdul Rahman (Rh) which states that:

"Imamana (As) answered: "I am deeply immersed in the continuous manifestation of the Entity of Allah that if even a single drop from this Divine Sea is given to any prophet he would become senseless for the rest of his life". Thus Allah Informs: "Oh Syed Mohammed (As) we have commissioned you to hold the seal of the "Vilayet-e-Mohammedi (Slm)" Thus our Grace is for you and we make you to perform obligatory prayers and verily it is our Benevolence and Favour to you."

حضرت در جواب فرمودند که چنان بے دریے تجلی ذات حق می شود که بحر عمیق ، اگر ازیں بحریك قطره بولی کامل یا به نبی مرسل داده شود در تمام عمرش ، هیچ آگاهی نماندو فرمان حق تعالیٰ می شود کہ اے سید محمد از سبب آنکہ تراخاتم ولایت محمدی گردانیدیم فرض ادامیکنانیم این منت و فضل ما است

Thus, the said statement has two points, one about the manifestation of Allah and second is that some prophets do not have the capacity to bear those manifestations of Allah. Here the purpose is just to mention the greatness of Allah and nothing else.

Such sort of statement also is mentioned in traditions, when Bibi Ayesha's acquittal was declared in a verse then Hazrat Abu Bakr (Rz) said to Bibi Ayesha (Rz) that:

"O Ayesha! Offer your thanks to the holy Prophet (Slm)."

یا عائشہ اشکری رسول الله صلی الله علیه وسلم

Then Bibi Ayesha (Rz) answered to her father that:

"I shall not offer my thanks (to the holy Prophet (Slm) but to Allah."

انا لا اشکر الا ربی

That episode when Imamana(As) was in Trance for 12 years, pertains to the period when Imamana (As) had an inspiration in Juanpur, before migration. The words told by Imamana (As) "even a prophet could not bear a single drop from this Divine Sea" describes its intensity and does not entail to disgrace the prophets and such kind of narration is in use in literature.

To say that even prophets could not bear the intensity of the manifestations, cannot be objected because it was already clarified that from the Ummah such people would emerge that by seeing their ranks, even prophets would envy for their status. They would only envy with those who had the capacity to bear and absorb the intensity of those manifestations but never indulge in utterances like "Anal Haq Subhani". Another point is that of a status of complete annihilation. At that moment of time the man who speaks his entity is immersed into the Entity of the Almighty and whatever he says, it is not from his tongue (but by Allah). As said in a tradition:

"Some moments with Allah are such to me as if I feel Allah is within me."

لی مع الله وقت لا یسعنی فیه غیر ربی

This is that time when the Seeker's hand becomes Allah's hand. As mentioned in a tradition that:

"I (Allah) become his audition from which he hears; and become his vision, through which he sees, and become his hand, through which he holds, and become his legs, through which he treads".

كنت سمعه الذى يسمع به و بصره الذى يبصر به ويده التى يبطش بها ورجله التى يمشى بها الى آخره

10. The author had objected even on the narration in which Imamana (As) had asserted the features of the holy Prophet (Slm) to be like that of Prophet Ibrahim (As). Although this is a reported fact by the holy Prophet (Slm) himself who said that he had a complete resemblance of prophet Ibrahim (As). "Bukhari" and "Muslim" have reported what Abu Huraira (Rz) had said that:

"Abu Huraira (Rz) narrated what the holy Prophet (Slm) was telling about his dream that "I had seen Ibrahim (As). In his progeny, I am alone to have likeliness to him."

رايت ابراهيم و انا اشبه ولده به

Another tradition:

"I saw Ibrahim (As), then I saw that man who had an exact resemblance to Ibrahim (As), and that man was I" (the holy Prophet (Slm)."

رايت ابراهيم فاذا اقرب من رايت به شبها صاحبكم يعنى نفسه

Regarding Imam Mahdi (As) it is stated that:

"He would resemble not only in character but in the face also."

يشبه فى الخلق ولا يشبه فى الخلق

Sheik Abdul Haq had commented on this Tradition that:

"He would not resemble exactly to the face of the holy Prophet (Slm), but to an extent and also in all respects would resemble as per the traditions."

مشابهت ندارد آنحضرت را در صورت ظاهر يعنى در همه چيز و همه وجوه والا در احاديث مشابهت به صورت نيز به بعضى جهات ثابت شده است

Sheik Abdul Haq had taken the meaning of "La Yashbahu", as not completely, but to an extent. Thus here "La" denotes to peremptory or emphatically. That means: "ofcourse resembling completely."

Really in "La yashbahu" the word 'La' does not come for denial as Allah has stated in a verse that:

"For the Scripture holders should know."

لئلا يعلم اهل الكتاب

Author of "Tafseer-e-Madarik" had written about 'li-alla yalam' as 'li-yalam'. and the author of "Kashshaf" has described the 'li-alla yalam' that:

"This noun denotes emphasis and a sort of research on which the word 'la' is attached. Thus it was emphasized on the People of books about it.

توكيد معنى الفعل الذى تدخل عليه و تحقيقه كانه قيل لتحقيق علم اهل الكتاب (تفسير آيه ما منعك ان لا تسجد)

Thus the words 'la-yashbahu' the word 'la' does not negate but emphasizes that means to say it will be similar.

Then how could he (the Holy Prophet (Slm) say about his son (Imamana (As)) that he would not resemble?.

Apart from this the holy Prophet (Slm) had said that he (the Holy Prophet (Slm) resembles to the face of Hazrat Ibrahim (As). Thus it cannot be said that he would have suggested that his son (Imam Mahdi (As)) would not resemble to him? Particularly as it was known to all that Imam Hasan (RZ) and Imam Husain (Rz) both had a resemblance to the holy Prophet (Slm). "Bukhari" recorded what Anas (Rz) had said that:

"No-one had a resemblance to the holy Prophet (Slm) except Hasan (Rz) and also Husain (Rz) that was the same opinion of all".

قال لم يكن احدا اشبه بالنبى صلى الله عليه وآله و سلم من الحسن بن على قال فى الحسين ايضاً كان اشبهم برسول الله صلى الله عليه و سلم

If it is objected that how could there be any resemblance when there had been a long lapse of time? Then there shall arise same objection as to how should there be any resemblance between the holy Prophet (Slm) and Prophet Ibrahim (As) since comparatively a much longer period had lapsed?. *(With a difference of thousands of years)*

Author of "Madarik" had stated that:

"In between Ibrahim (As) and Musa (As) 1000 years and in between Ibrahim (As) and Isa (As) 2000 years".

بين ابراهيمٓ و موسىٓ الف سنة و بينه و بين عيسىٓ الفان

Thus in between Prophet Ibrahim (As) and Hazrat Isa (As) there is a gap of 2000 years. If the period of Hazrat Isa (As) and the holy Prophet (Slm) is added, the period comes to 2571 years. (2000+571=2571years)

The holy Prophet (Slm) passed away in 11 H. and Imamana was born on 847 H. When even with such a long period (2571) the possibility of resemblance exists between Hazrat Ibrahim (As) and the holy Prophet (Slm), there should not be any objection to have a resemblance between the Holy Prophet (Slm) and Imamana (As) since the period is just 836 years (847-11=836 years, compared to 2571 years.

Generally speaking with a generation gap any two persons resemblance becomes unimaginable. Therefore emphatically it is mentioned that there may be a resemblance between the holy Prophet (Slm) and Imamana (As) as there had been a resemblance in between the holy Prophet (Slm) and Hazrat Ibrahim (As).

(Note: Allah is alone to decide who should have a resemblance to whom. Since Allah, the Almighty, emphatically Asserts:" We know alone who is in the womb of his or her mother". Thus it is Allah alone who made the resemblance in between Prophet Ibrahim (As) and the Holy Prophet (Slm) on one hand, and to create a resemblance between the holy Prophet (Slm) and Imamana (As) on the other hand, since it is the domain of Allah alone. Hence Allah alone inspired the holy Prophet (Slm)) to prophecy that Imam Mahdi (As) shall have the resemblance to him as well as the characters of Imamana (As) to be like that of the Holy Prophet(Slm).

Author of Hadia had accused of presenting some excerpts from the later published books of Mahdavis that "there had been a resemblance in between the holy Prophet (Slm) and Imamana (As). As a matter of fact in the old sources like "Moulood" of Miyan Abdul Rahman (Rh) (Born 908 H) is mentioned that:

"Imamana (As) had stated that if Hazrat Ibrahim (As), the holy Prophet (Slm) and I were at one place none could find any distinction among us."	آنحضرت فرمودند اگر بنده و حضرت ابراهیم خلیل الله و حضرت محمد مصطفیؐ دریك زمانه بودندے هیچ کس درمیان ما تمیز کردن نتوانستی

The Imamana's assertion is according to the traditions, hence objection is untenable.

11. The decliner had raised doubts about verification also and as a matter of fact according to the traditions there should be no doubt about such verification.

A. Regarding verification it had been reported in "Aqueeda-e-Shariefa"" that:

"Narrated that rectification (of each person) is done before me. Whoever is acceptable here, he is accepted by Allah. And if he is not correct with me than he is reprobate before Allah."	یز فرمودند که پیش این بنده تصحیح می شود هر که اینجا مقبول شدا و نزد خدا مقبول است و هر که پیش این ذات صحیح نشداوعنداللہ مردود است

B. It is narrated in "Hashia-e-Sharief" that:

"Rectification has been done before me since Allah ordains that "Oh Syed Mohammed (As) whoever is right with you, he is accepted by Us and whoever is not correct with you he is a reprobate."	حضرت میراںؑ فرمودند پیش این بنده تصیح میشود و فرمان می شودائے سید محمد هر که پیش توصحیح شداومقبول حضرت ماست و هر که پیش تو صحیح نشداوعند اللہ مردود است

C. Bandagi Malik Sujawandi (Rh) had given details of this:

"Asserted Imamana (As) that "Allah had corrected me. And Allah rectifies faithful before me. He shows me all faithful who had passed away and those who would come after me till the Dooms Day. I knew everyone of them who had benefited from mysticism and at what stage he was benefited."

قـال الامـام المهدى وضع التصحيح من الله عندى و ان الـلـه تـعـالـىٰ يـصـحـح المومنين يرينى جميع اهل الايـمـان الـذيـن كـانـوا قبلى ويكونون بعدى الى يوم الـقـيـامة و انـا اعـلـم لـكل واحد ممن اخذوا فيضامن مشكوٰة الولاية باى مقدارا خذوا

This confirms that all the first and the last were shown to Imamana (As) whom Imamana (As) came to know them very well.

How the predecessors and the successors were shown to Imamana (As) is reported in "Matleul Vilayet":

"Among the companions, one companion asked what is Rectification? Imamana (As) narrated when a king is dead and another king takes place, the military passes before him. When asked what is Correction? Narrated:" The officer presents all; cadre of the army to the new sovereign.

كسى از صحابه عرض نمود كه تصحيح چه فرمودند چوں يكے پادشاه بگذرد ويجاى وے ديگرے بنشيند پس همـه لشكر بحضور او مى گذرد و صحيح مى شود آن را چـه مى گويند گفتند كسى آں عرض ولى مى گويند و كسى آمده نيامده هـم خوانند ـ

Thus if the military passes before the commander or the king, in Deccan it is called Enlisted.

Thus all the Awwaleen and Akhereen were brought before Imamana (As) as the army men are brought before a king (for inspection).

Had the fault finder deep knowledge of the traditions, then he could easily understand the word "Arz" spoken by Imamana (As) which represents the holy prophet's assertion. Author of "Muntakhabatul Lughat " had explained about the word "ARZ" means: "to present military". And "Aariz" is one who presents the military, before the commander-in-chief or the king.

Thus what Imamana (As) had said the word "Arz" which was used in the following tradition:

"Narrated by Jaber (Rz) who heard the holy Prophet (Slm) telling: "verily, presented before me all prophets. Among them I suddenly saw Musa (As) and men belonging to the tribe of Shannah, and then I saw Isa Ibn Mariyam (As) with whom Urwah Bin Masood had a resemblance to him and then I saw Ibrahim (As), in resemblance to him was your Friend that is me (the holy Prophet (Slm)."

عـن جـابـر ان رسول الله صلى الله عليه وسلم قال قد عـرض عـلى الانبـيـاء فـاذا مـوسىٰ ضرب من الرجل كـانـه مـن رجـال شـنـوـة ورايت عيسىٰ بن مريم فاذا اقـرب مـن رايت بـه شبـها عـروه بن مسعود و رايت ابـراهـيـم فـاذا اقرب من رايت به شبها صاحبكم يعنى نفسه

The words "Arz Alal Anbiah" denote that all prophets were presented before the holy Prophet (Slm) as a commander presents his military before a king. As the prophets were presented their Ummahs also were presented before the holy Prophet (Slm). As reported in "Bukhari" and "Muslim:

"Narrated that one day the holy Prophet (Slm) came out and informed that before him all ummahs were presented. Thus when a Nabi was passing one person followed him. Then another Nabi passed, two persons followed him. Then one Nabi passed and a group followed him. Then another Nabi passed and none followed him. Then I saw blackness which covered the entire horizon. On it I surmised that this is my Ummah."

قـال خـرج رسول الله صلى الله عليه وسلم يوما فقال عـرضـت عـلـى الامـم فـيجعل يمر النبى و معه الرجل والـنبـى و معه الرجلان و النبى و معه الرهط و النبى و لـيـس مـعه احد فرايت سوادا اكثير اسدالافق فرجوت ان يـكـون امتـى فـقيل هذا موسىٰ فى قومہ ثم قيل لى انظـر فـرايت سـواد اكثيرا سد الافق فقيل لى انظر هكـذا وهكـذا فـرايت سـواد كثيرا سد الافق فقيل هولاء امتك الى آخره .

From this it is clear that all prophets and their Ummahs were presented before the holy Prophet (Slm) as the commander presents his military before the king. This is not enough, all the Ummah of the holy Prophet (Slm) was presented and every one of the Ummah was before him. "Kanzal Ummal" reports that:

"Presented before me my Ummah near that room last night and I know every one of the Ummah including you and your friends in flesh and blood."

عـرضـت على امتى البارحة لدى هذه الحجرة حتى لانا اعـرف بـالـرجل مـنهـم من احدكم بصاحبه صورہ وافى الطين

It is clear that the first and the last were shown both to the holy Prophet (Slm) and. Imamana (As). The words. "Arz-e-Wali", and in the tradition the words "Arz-e-Alal Anbiah" and "Arzat alal Ummah" and "Arzat ala Ummati" had been used, It is reported in "Ashatul Lamaat" that:

"Narrated holy Prophet (Slm) that presented before me all prophets and shown me as presented any army before the Commander-in-Chief.".

گفت آنحضرتؐ به تحقیق عرض کرده شدند برمن پیغمبران و نموده شدند چنانچه لشکر را عرض می کنند برسردار

Now it remains to see how the holy Prophet (Slm) looked at them. It is mentioned in "Ashatul Lamaat" that:

"Presented and shown before me through revelation with clarity."

ظاهر کرده شدند و نموده شدند مرا امت هابطریق کشف و عیان

Thus to Imamana (As) also shown all the faithful from the first and the last to come till the Dooms Day in the same manner through revelation. Imamana (As) knew everyone who was benefited by mysticism and to what extent; as the holy Prophet (Slm) knew every one of his Ummah.

When Allah took a covenant from the prophets (As), He referred about the holy Prophet (Slm) to them:

"He is the one who would certify what you had."

مصدق لما معکم (آل عمران ع ۹)

In the same manner Imamana (As) had certified about the holy Prophet (Slm) and other prophets (As).

Allah had also stated that:

"Came Mohammed (Slm) with Huq (Allah) and certified all prophets (AS)."

جاء بالصدق و صدق المرسلین (الصفت)

In the same manner Imamana (As) the Khalifatullah who had the same characters of the holy Prophet (Slm) had affirmed all the prophets (As) including the holy Prophet (Slm) also.

In"Aqueda-e-Shriefa" and "Hashia-e-Sharief" it is clearly written that whoever was accepted by Imamana (As), he was accepted by Allah. It is clear that the person who fits on "Mussadiqul Lima Ma'akum" and "Saddaqal Mursaleen" whose affirmation is an obligation of the Ummah and whoever denies him how could he be accepted by Allah?

Here the Ummahs are being informed and not the prophets as the decliner thinks.

Now we have to discuss about another objection as to whether Bandagi Miyan Syed Khundmir (Rz) also had the same authority? Bandagi Miyan (Rz) is the caliph of Imamana (As), so in the capacity of Imamana's deputy he also invites towards the programme what Imamana (As) had been destined with.

Shah Valiullah Muhaddis-e-Dehlavi had stated in his "Hujjatullahul Baaligha" that:

"(In the Mairaj) all prophets (As) met with the holy Prophet (Slm) and their attendance before him was just to show their intimacy and each other knew every one's position."

امـا مـلاقاته مع الانبیاء صلوٰت الله علیهم و مفاخرته معهم فحقیقتها اجتماعهم من حیث ارتباطهم بحظیرة القدس و ظهورمـا اختـص بـه مـن بینهم من وجوه الکمال .

The decliner had further presented a narrative that the souls of the prophets (As) attended to know their status and for what purpose they were commissioned? It means to say that the purpose for which they were appointed was depicted in the personality of Imamana (As) and whatever was the program of the prophets (As) the same program was manifested in the personality of Imam Mahdi (As) as the Khalifatullah.

CHAPTER V

Imamana's Assertions About Monotheismn And Interpretations

The decliner in order to negate the argument presented in chapter 9 of "Sirajul Absar" regarding characters of Imamana (As), had raised certain doubts for the assertions of Imamana (As) in connection with monotheism and interpretations of dreams, stating that these assertions are rude for Allah. The following are the narratives through them we want to repudiate those unwanted doubts.

1. Author of "Shawahedul Vilayet" had reported that while Imamana (As) was in Jaisalmir, he ordered to slaughter a cow, when Raja heard about it, went to Imamana (As) to revenge, but when he heard Imamana's sermon he was subdued, this is also mentioned in it that:

"Thus the great infidel met Imamana (As) and heard Qur'an's sermons and fell down at the feet of Imamana (As) and surrendered by saying: "the Creator of the cow had killed it, whom should we complain"?

القصه آں کافر بزرگ با حضرت ملاقات کردو بیان شنید سـر خود برپائی مبارک حضرت میراں نهاده منقاد گشته می گفت آفریـدگـار گاؤ ، گاؤ را کشته است مابکه جنگ کنیم (باب ۱۹)

The objection is "on hearing the sermon, the Raja had spoken those words "the Creator of the cow had killed it, whom should we complain"? Imamana (As) did not say anything to him.

The answer to the objection is that in "Hujjathul Munsifeen" also the words "Afridgar-e-Gaao, Gaao Ra kushta" (Parverdigar-e-Gaao (Creator of cow) had slaughtered the cow" had been reported, which is as below:

"That Godliman is such that we had not seen him and not even heard of him when he shows his glamorous sight, neither a faithful had the strength nor the infidel to see."

آں مرد خدا چنان است که گاهی ندیده ایم و نه گاهی شنیده ایم هرگاه که تجلی آن ذات باشد نه قوت مومن ماند و نه قوت کافر

The same is the version in "Naqliat-e- Syed Aalam." In both the narratives the words "Creator of the cow killed the cow" are not mentioned in them. When there are differences in narration, how could the blame go to Imamana (As)?

As a matter of fact killing of the cow is the act of the Almighty, none other could claim that act done by him. Allah states:

"You did not throw (pebbles in Badr Battle), but really we did."

وما رمیت اذ رمیت و لکن الله رمی (انفال ع ۲)

The meanings of this verse had been given in "Madarijul Nabuwwat":

"The meanings of this verse are: "You did not throw the pebbles on the enemy (apparently, you did it) but actually we did it."

معنی این آیه است که ما رمیت اذ رمیت صورة ولکن الله رمی حقیقة

From "Shawahedul Vilayet": also speaks "the real killer is Allah", then how this fact is being claimed against Imamana (As)? Particularly when Imamana (As) did not slaughter the cow but it was slaughtered by a companion. When Allah still ordains that":

"You did not kill them, but we killed them."

فلم تقتلوا هم و لکن الله قتلهم (انفال ع ۲)

In view of this verse could "a belief be formed that the killer of infidels also is Allah"?

Author of "Shawahdul Vilayet" narrates in chapter 8 that;

"It is narrated that one day Miyan Shaik Bheek (Rz) was absorbed in Divinity and he was continuously uttering the words "All is Allah" Imamana (As) went to him and asked him: "whether he was telling what was he seeing"? He replied "All is Allah". Imamana (As) advised him "knowing is Iman, and uttering is infidelity". Imamana (As) repeated his words three times then reprimanded by telling "why he was confined to the idea of an old god, go further ahead"; then he read this couplet"(Of Moulana Rome)

"Bezaram, Az'aan Khuna Khudaey ke to dari; Her Lahza Mara Taza Khudaiy deegaray husth."

I am horribly disgusted with your idea of an old god, (limited splendour), because I witness every new moment of time a new splendour of the Almighty. ("Kulla Yaumin Huwa Fish-shun" 55:29).

"Narrated that one day Bandagi Miyan Shaik Bheek (Rz) was under the ecstasy and he was telling every time that "All is Huq", on that moment Hazrat Meeran (As) went to him and asked him, "what are you seeing and what are you telling"?, he told the same thing that "All is Huq". Hazrat Imamana (As)) told that "knowing is Iman and uttering openly is infidelity". Even after Miyan Bheek (Rz) repeated the same words that "All is Huq", then Imamana told "why you are stuck to the old splendour of Allah; since every new moment creates in me the vision of a fresh splendour of the Almighty". Then he read the above Persian couplet of Moulana Rome:

"Since every new moment of time creates in me a fresh glory, a new splendour of Allah. (Continuity of splendours)"

نقـل است که یك روز بندگی میاں شیخ بهیك راجذبه حق شده بزبان شان همین سخن مکرر بود که همه حق است ، بنـاء بـر حضرت امیر علیه السلام برسر ایشان خـود تشـریف آورده فرمودند که می بینید یا میگوئید ، ایشـان هـمیـن جواب دادند که همه حق است حضرت امامؑ فرمودند آرے دانستن ایمان گفتن کفر است ایشان هـمیـن جـواب دادند کـه هـمـه حق است حضرت امام الابرار سـه بـار تکرار کرده فرمودند که چراجه خدائی کهنه مقید شدید بیشتر شوید دایں بیت خواندند

بیزارم از آں کهنه خدائے که توداری
هر لحظه مرا تازه خدائے دیگراست

In this the author had objected that: Miran (As) had said "knowing is Iman, uttering is infidelity".

1. Here the decliner had tried to create confusion. As regards "Knowing is Iman" it relates to Divine knowledge. And whereas "Utterance is infidelity" is concerned, it relates to Shariat. It seems Imamana (As) had shown favour to both. Unity and Oneness (of Allah) and Unity of Divine Manifestation are two different theories. It seems the decliner negates the Unity and Oneness (of Allah) and accepts the Unity of Divine Manifestation. To object Imamana's dictates is to negate the very concept of Oneness of Allah. There is no Sharaie accountability as far as "Knowing" is concerned. But Sharaie order inflicts on the utterances of a man or on his actions. If someone says "All is Haq", as a matter of fact, it is correct. But if say "Every thing is Haq", therefore one may start prostrating before each thing. Such an utterance is not only a fault but it renders one to infidelity.

2. Allah is One, no doubt about it, but His Splendours are countless. To Know all Splendours pertaining to Allah is called Iman. The same had been mentioned in the Verse" Kulla Youmin Huwa Fish-shun"(55:29) Meaning: In every new moment of time you will notice a fresh splendour, a fresh Glory of Allah. **But to name Allah to each of His splendour, is infidelity according to the Shariat.**

*(Note: For example, if a man weds a lady, she is known as his wife, mistress or lady of the house. When she bears a child, she is known as the Mother. If a miscreant child names her, **not as his mother, but calls her "the wife, or mistress of his father", then, his such utterance is not only rude and impudent, but stupidity**. Despite whatever he had uttered, was correct and based on real facts, but to utter this fact in such words is his stupidity and rudeness. In the terms of human relation such utterance is a fault, stupid and disrespect to a mother. Thus the spiritual relationship what Allah had created, if someone does not adhere to, it calls transgressing the Sharie limits. Thus it is called infidelity not to honour Allah's dictates. Khundmiri)*

Whoever negates the idol worship and worships Allah alone, he is faithful for all practical purposes. Thus infidelity means to negate Allah's existence. And there are so many varieties of infidelity. The negation of Shariat is different to the negation of Divine knowledge. The holy Prophet (Slm) ordained that whoever leaves prayer intentionally, he is an infidel. Then whether this kind of infidelity could become equal to the infidelity which occurs on negating Allah Himself. The Holy Qur'an also certifies this fact that whoever does not act on the Revealed Orders, he is an infidel. The point of consideration is: whether those people who do not decide according to the orders of Allah, are not they rendering themselves towards infidelity? Comparing to those who negate the very existence of Allah, the Almighty.

The real meaning is that whatever is being told about the "Divine Manifestations" must be said before persons of caliber, not before the commoners. If told before the common people, they take it otherwise in a wrong way; therefore it is a fault. The reality is that such Divine Facts should not be openly uttered before all; except before the men of the caliber who understand it. Imamana's reading of the couplet was just to say that "what attributes of Allah you imagine they are limited in your scope", because Allah's attributes are numerous and their splendour is ever changing by creating a fresh glory of a new manifestation". This is just to explain the verse 55:29 (Soora-e-Rahman) which states that "at every new moment a new splendour and a new glory of Allah is witnessed", that means to say do not be confined to an old idea and to a limited thought about Allah.

Velmi had reported bout Abbas (Rz) who advised:

"Speak to such people according to their (mental) capacity." كلموا الناس على قدر عقولهم

Further, Velmi has reported what Ibn Abbas (Rz) had said that:

""We had been ordained to speak to the people according to their caliber". امرنا ان نكلم الناس على قدرعقولهم

If it is told openly that "Everything is Divine", then how can you stop common men who thinks that if everything is part of the Divinity, then plants and stones are all the manifestation of the Almighty, then what is a harm if we prostrate before them? The decliner had objected for the word "infidelity" he is utterly wrong in his ability who misunderstood it. There are stages of infidelity. One man denies a Qazi, and another denies Allah and His Rasool. Whether both are equal? How did the decliner assume that Miyan Bheek (Rz) shall always be in the company of Godly people who enjoy the company of Imamana (As) and he would never go to the commoners for propagation of Mahdiat?

Explanation of old God:

The couplet which was read by Imamana (As) was not of his own, but it was composed by Moulana Rome (Rh). Here we have to ascertain the meanings of that couplet according to the Persian usage. Thus the words "Kuhna Khudaey" means the seeker was stuck up to that "splendour of Allah" which was already perceived by the seeker previously and he did not get any continuity in perceiving the new splendour of Allah in succession". Thus "Kuhna Khuda" means that "splendour of Allah" which the Seeker had witnessed had been solidified in his mind; and he had not progressed further. As a matter of fact the "splendour of Allah is continuing every moment of time and there is no break in it"; hence Imamana (As) said that "I am witnessing every moment of time Allah's fresh Glory, the ever changing splendour of the Almighty; a fresh view of Allah ("Kulla Youmin Huwa Fish Shun". Soora-e-Rahman 55:29) Every moment a fresh splendour of Allah is being witnessed by me."

There are certain verses which if denied infidelity is implied. Then how the decliner could object on the word "Infidelity", when it is meant in literal sense only. Therefore Imamana's assertion that "Guftan Kufr Ast" means openly declaration is infidelity. That means to say that you were unable to keep the secret to your heart and boastfully uttered openly before the commoners who do not understand the gravity of your exaltation. Thus Imamana's assertion was a sort of warning, not to tell openly. Really it is a warning and not an infidelity in real sense. This sort of explanation is in vogue in colloquial language. For example; the holy prophet said:

"I shall burn their houses if they avoid joining the group (for prayers)." لينهن رجال عن ترک الجماعة اولا حرقن بيوتهم

However, according to this tradition, punishing by burning their houses just because they had avoided to join the group cannot be justified. Further joining the Group for Prayer is ambiguous. As Sheik Abdul Haq had said that:

"There is a difference of opinion about group prayers, whether it is Sunnat, or Wajib or Farz-e-Ain or Farz-e-Kifaya?" لاتعذبوا بعذاب الله

Had the punishment for avoiding a group prayer was actually to be that much harsh, then it would not have been assumed to be Sunnat or Farez-e-Kifaya. Thus it came to light that the said tradition is just a warning. That therefore what Imamana (As) had stressed "not to openly proclaim "Everything is Divine" tantamount to infidelity, but actually it is a warning. In this connection author of "Shawahedul Vilayet" states that:

"Imamana (As) confirmed (what Bandagi Miyan (Rz) was telling) then asked (Bandagi Miyan (Rz) to describe before others just what had happened to you? So that others may also know. On that Bandagi Miyan (Rz) stated that : "My eyesight be lost if I saw Mahdi (As), actually I witnessed the vision of Allah in you." Then he narrated what he saw from the beginning to the end. Then Imamana (As) said:" Bhai Syed Khundmir (Rz) whatever you had seen is correct. "Khuda Ho So Khuda ko Dekhey" (Unless one is absorbed in the Almighty, no one could see Allah)"

"Naqliat-e-Miyan Syed Aalam" state that:

"Informed: Bhai Syed Khundmir(Rz) "Khuda Ko Khuda hi dekhta Hai."

"Hashi-e-Insaf Nama tells that:

"Narrated that Hazrat Bandagi Miyan (Rz) met Imamana (As). For the very first time, Miyan (Rz) said that: "We have not seen Imamana (As), but to Allah in you". Imamana (As) told: yes brother khundmir (Rz):"whoever immerses his entity into Allah, then he becomes Khuda, he sees khuda everywhere. (*If a drop of water merges with the ocean, then that drop becomes the ocean itself).*" In the same way. If the seeker annihilates his SELF or his ENTITY and merges into the DIVINITY, he becomes part and parcel of that Divinity, and becomes Divine himself " Faani Fillah). (Hearing this) Miyan (Rz) fell down senseless and offered three prayers being immersed in the Divinity."

حضرت میران علیه السلام فرمودند آرے تحقیق است فامابرادران بشنوند ، آنچه معامله شده است بزبان خود بگوئید بنا بران بندگی میان عرض کردند میرانجیو شکسته شود چشمے کـه مهدی را دیده باشد بنده خدائی خودرادیدم بعده تمام معامله ، مذکور سربسرپیش حضرت امام البروالبحور عرض رسانیدند حضرت میران فرمودند که آرے بهائی سید خوندمیر انچه دیدید تحقیق است خدای را خدامی بیند

فرمودند که بهائی سید خوندمیر خدائی راخدامی بیند

نقـل است بنـدگی میان سید خوندمیر حضرت میران را ملاقات کردند ، ابتداء میان چنیس گفتند ما میران رانـدیـدیـم خـدائی رادیدیم ، میران فرمودند آرے سید خوندمیر آنانکه بنده خدامی تشود خدای رامی بیند میان در آن حال ازپادرافتادند سه نماز درحال جذبه گذاردند الی آخره

These narrations inform that Bandagi Miyan (Rz) had the Vision of Allah. The words Khuda Ra Khuda Beenad" must have been pricking the mind of the decliner; but this is according to a tradition: Abu Huraira (Rz) mentioned in "Bukhari" that:

"Always my servant seeks my nearness through supererogatory prayers till I befriend to him, I become his audition through which he hears; I become his eyesight through which he sees; I become his hands, through which he holds anything; I become his legs through which he treads."	وما يزال عبدى يتقرب الى بالنوافل حتى اجبته فاذا احببته كنت سمعه الذى يسمع به و بصره الذى يبصربه ويده التى يبطش بها ورجله التى يمشى بها الى آخره

It also had been said that:

"I become his heart through which he considers; I become his tongue through which he speaks."	وفواده الذى يعقل به ولسانه الذى يتكلم به

Still there are some more like that:

"Thus he hears through me; and sees through me; and catches through me; and treads through me?"	فبى يسمع و بى يبصروبى يبطش و بى يمشى

These narrations inform that Allah becomes man's eyesight through which he sees.

When Allah becomes a person's eyesight and that person gets the vision of Allah; then if it is said: Khudai-e- Ra Khuda Beenad" (Khuda ko Khuda Dekhta Hai) what is wrong in it? Those persons object such appearance of a phenomenon when they are devoid of the meanings of the traditions. "Shawahedul Vilayet" narrates that:

"One day Miyan Syed Salamullah (Rz) complained before Imamana (As) that some persons always inquire about Imamana (As), asking "whether you are real Mahdi (As)"? The fact is that on account of resemblance to (the holy Prophet (Slm) they confirm you to be Mahdi (As). Whether Mahdi (As) is superior to Hazrat (holy Prophet (Slm)? Imamana (As) consoled him and said that Allah is greater than Mahdi (As)."?	نقل است كه يك روز ميان سيد سلام الله بحضور خليفته الله حكايت مردمان بطريق شكايت عرض كردند كه ميرانجى هر جاكه ميرويم مردم خدام رامى پرسند كه مهدى موعود همين ذات است امامر دم ذات خدام رابمشابهت مهدى موعود مى گويند مگر ذات مهدى از ذات مبارك خدام فاضل باشد حضرت ميران تبسم كرده فرمودند از مهدى خدا فاضل است

Author of "Tasviath-e-Khatemain" narrates:

"Narrated Imamana (As) that none is greater than Mahdi (As), except Allah."

نقل است حضرت میران ؑ فرمودند کہ از مہدی کسے بزرگ نیست بجز خدائے تعالیٰ

This narration is regarding Imam Mahdi (As) alone; which tells that none is greater than Mahdi (As), it is not clear on what basis objection was raised by telling that as if, it is a "disrespect to Allah"?

5. The decliner had presented this narrative: "Imamana (As) raised Miyan Syed Mahmood (Rz) and hugged him and told that "he (Imamana (As) was created as the servant of Allah". You (Miran Mahmood (Rz) too are a servant of Allah. It is easy to become Allah, but to be a servant is not that simple. Allah's mercy is that he had made us servant and made owners of our property.". But the fact is that such narration is not mentioned in "Tazkeratul Saleheen" The decliner purposely omitted a portion of the verse. The correct wording of the verse is, as below:

"Tell Oh Allah you are the king. You make king whom you like and snatch away kingdom with whom you are displeased."

قل اللّٰھم مالک الملک توتی الملک من تشاء و تنزع الملک ممن تشاء (آل عمران ع ۳)

The commentary for this verse in "Muheb-e-Alaih" is given like that:

"This kingship is prophethood, thus Nabuwwat was taken away from the Israelites and handed over to the Ismaelites". That is how Allah had deprived the Isrtelites.

ملک نبوت و رسالت است کہ از بنی اسرائیل بتیدوینی اسماعیل داد ۔

Ka'ab-e-Hammar" reports that this prophecy is regarding the holy Prophet (Slm).

"His birth place is Makkah, he would migrate to Madinah and his kingdom would be in Syria."

مولدہ بمکۃ وھجرتہ بطیبۃ و ملکہ بالشام

Sheik Abdul Haq thus commented on it:

"Kingdom means religion and Nabuwwat."

مراد ببادشاھی دین و نبوت است

Thus meaning of Imamana's assertion is that Allah had bestowed on him the kingdom of Religion and his son also gets it in succession.

Author of "Tafseer-e-Husaini" has commented that:

"Kingdom means Divine Help. Whoever gets that Help he is respected in both worlds. And if someone is deprived of such Guidance, he becomes dejected."

ملک توفیق است کہ ھر کراعطا کرد عزیز دوجھان شدہ واز ھر کہ باز گرفت مخذول دوسرائے گشت

Keeping this clarification in view, then there should be no objection to Imamana's assertion.

Now those words of Imamana (As): "It is easy to become Allah by proclaiming" Anal Huq", "Subhani" is easy; but to become servant, "Abdullah", in perfect servitude is very difficult for that servant whose characters should be according to the Qur'an which is one of the attributes of the Almighty Allah.

The decliner had also presented one more narration in which it is wrongly said that Imamana (As) had declared himself to be "the Entity of Allah" and: "I am the Sustainer of the worlds"; before Shah Nemat (Rz). But the fact is that these words were never told by Imamana (As). In fact, it was Shah Nemat (Rz) who addressed Imamana (As) as "the Entity of Allah." Which is mentioned in "Hashia-e-Sharief:

"One night Imamana (As) went to Shah Nemat (Rz) and awaken him. Miyan Shah Nemat (Rz) saw upward and told: "Miranji: "you are the Entity of Allah"."The divine Blessing is about witnessing the Divinity". Imamana (Rz) gave him glad tidings of Iman."	همـان وقـت حضـرت ميـران قريب ميان نعمت آمده بصحو رسانيدند، ميان بالانگر يستند عرض كردند كه ميرانجيـو انتـم ذات الـله هستيد نعمت براين مشاهدۀ خـدا اسـت حضـرت ميـران فرمودند كه بشارت ايمان بدهم

This narration is clear that Shah Nemat (Rz) had used those words "You are the Entity of Allah," upon which Imamana (As) had given him glad tidings of Iman. Intention of Shah Nemat (As) in telling the "Entity of Allah" to Imamana (As) was actually to describe Imamana (As) as the "Emblem of Allah" and nothing more than it. This is clear from the verses of the Qur'an, as presented by Shah Abdul Aziz:

"The voice came from a tree: I am Allah, Rabbul Aalameen."	انى انا الله رب العالمين (القصص ع ۴)
"Allah told the holy Prophet (Slm): those who are taking the oath of allegiance, actually their hands are on the hands of Allah"	ان الذين يبايعونك انما يبايعون الله (الفتح ع ۱)
""Allah tells the Holy Prophet (Slm): you did not throw, but We threw it".	و ما رميت اذرميت و لكن الله رمى (الانفال ع ۲)

Thus according to the holy Qur'an, Holy prophet's hand was said to be that of Allah; Holy prophet's action became Allah's action. From these it is proved that these are just the manifestation of Allah and nothing more. In this connection we go to the narration of Hzt. Jabar (Rz) who had mentioned in "Tirmizi" that:

قـال دعـا رسـول الـلـه صلى الله عليه و آله و سلم
عليـا يـوم الـطـائف فـانتجاه فقال الناس لقد طال
نجواه مع ابن عمه فقال رسول الله صلى الله عليه
و آله و سلم ما انتجيته و لكن الله انتجاه

"Rasoolullah called Ali (Rz) on the day of
"Ghazvai-e-Taa'ef" and discussed in secrecy.
Upon which some said: "Consultation
prolonged with his cousin". On that, holy
prophet informed that "he did not consult
Ali (Rz), but it was Allah who consulted Ali
(Rz)."

Could this be said that the holy Prophet (Slm) asserted himself as Allah? Shah Abdul Aziz
had described this sort of exaltation in these words:

پـس ایـن کـلام نـاشـی از جـذبـات حقانیه و سکر حال
اسـت کـه اولیـاء الـلـه رارومی دهد و از زبان حقیقتـه
الحقایق تکلم می کنند

" Thus such exaltation is the result of
Divine sentiments and intoxication
which occur to Godlimen who personify
themselves as Divinity".

We do not find anywhere in the classical record that Imamana (As) had personified himself
to be Allah. Even if he had said, then it may be taken as manifestation and not Divinity.
However, Shah Nemath's assertion also symbolizes Allah's manifestation only. Any such bogus
objection does not stand before Qur'an and the traditions.

7. The decliner had presented narration which states that Miran Syed Mahmood(Rz) had
denied to wear clothes purchased from the amount of ushr, while Imamana(As) had accepted
ushr for his personal use and for his family and it is said that Imamana(As) had asserted that "he
was neither born nor caused to be born". But the last two portions of this narration are not from
the Mahdavia books. Author of "Insaf Nama" chapter 9 states that:

نقـل اسـت کـه در مـوضـع بهیلوٹ بندگی میاں سید
مـحـمـود را از ار پـاره شـده بـود و میاں بابن سویت می
کـردنـد و عشـر هـم تسلیم میاں بابن بود ، روزے از ارنو
پیـش میراں سیـد مـحـمـود آوردند ، میراںؑ پرسیدند از
کـجا آوردند میاں مذکور گفت ازدرم هائے عشر جامه
خـریـد کـرده از ارکنا نیدم ، بندگی میراں سید محمودؒ
بسیار خشم شدند و فرمودند که این پوشیدن روا نیست
نخواهم پوشید که حق مضطران است

A."It is stated that in Bhelote Miran
Syed Mahmood's Pajama was worn out.
Miyan Baban (Rh) was incharge of
distribution of Sawiyet and Ushr. He
purchased a new Pajama for Miran Syed
Mahmood (Rz). Miran asked him as to
where from he had brought it? Miyan
Baban (Rh) said that out of Ushr amount
he had purchased it. Miran Syed
Mahmood (Rz) became mad at him and
told that it was not appropriate for him
to wear and thus he refused to wear,
because the amount involved in it was
meant for needy persons."

In this narration it is correct that Miran Syed Mahmood (Rz) had refused to wear pajama
purchased from ushr amount, but the other two items relating to Imamana (As) are not available
in writing in any of our books.

B. This narration had also been recorded in "Hashi-e-Sharief", but nothing is mentioned about Imamana's acceptance of Ushr amount for his use and that he said : "I was neither born nor caused to be born".

C."Naqliat-e-Miyan Abdul Rasheed" mention that:

"It is stated that Miran Syed Mahmood's pajama was worn out. Miyan Baban (Rh) who was in charge of distribution of sawiyet and Ushr, brought a pajama and gave to Miran Syed Mahmood (Rz), who asked him as to where from he had purchased it? Miyan Baban (Rh) said that it was purchased from the remaining amount of Ushr. Miran Mahmood (Rz) became mad at him and stated the amount belongs to the needy ones and not for me."

نقل است کـه میـان سید محمود درااز ار پاره پاره شـده بـود میـان بابن را عهده، سویت بود و عشر هم تسلیم ایشان بود روزے از ارنوساختہ پیش میراں سید مـحمود آوردند پرسیدند از کجا ست گفتند از میان عشـر چند درم مانده بودازوساختیم بسیار خشمناك شـدنـد و فـرمـودنـد ایں پـوشیدن روانیست حـق مضطراست (باب هفتم)

Here also nothing is mentioned about Imamana's assertion that Imamana (As) has at any time said that "he was not born to any one neither he gave birth to anyone".

D. "Tazkertul Saleheen" also mentions about the refusal of Miran Syed Mahmood (Rz), but the portion of assertion of Imamana (As) is not found in it also. Thus the four old sources of Mahdavia literature do not mention the wordings stated to have been said by Imamana (As). Therefore it is vicious, malicious and unfounded objection about Imamana (As) and through this unfounded version how one can blame the characters of Imamana (As)?

Thus all classical four sources do not state that Imamana (As) had ever told that "he was neither born to any one, nor he gave birth to anyone".(It is an allegation.)

8. The decliner had presented a narration regarding Shah Nizam (Rz) who said to have seen a dream in which Imamana (As) had eaten particles of Shah Nizam (Rz) and Shah Nizam (Rz) had eaten particles of Imamana (As). When he disclosed his dream to Imamana (As), Imamana (As) said to have stated that Shah Nizam (Rz) had the vision of Allah and that Shah Nizam (Rz) had annihilated himself into the entity of Imamana (As). This episode is recorded in "Hashia-e-Sharief" to the extent that Shah Nizam (Rz) had witnessed a dream, and told to Imamana (As), but what Imamana (As) told, was not mentioned in it."Hashia-e-Sharief's narration is this:

"Miyan Shah Nizam (Rz) came to Dairah and stated that he was immersed his entity into the entity of Imamana (As) and Imamana (As) had done the same. Then we both immersed our entities into the Entity of the holy Prophet (Slm) and then all immersed unto the Entity of Allah and Allah too had done the same and then yelled "Allahu Akber" and asked not to reveal anything before others what was said."

بعده در دائره آمدند فرمودند بنده دیدم ذات میراں ّ فرو کردم ذات ما میراں ّ ذات خود فرو کردند بعده ذات رسول ذات ما ذات خود کردند بعده ذات خدائی تعالیٰ ذات خود فرو کردیم خدائی تعالیٰ ذات بنده در ذات خود فرو کرد بعده الله اکبر گفتند و فرمودند بنده انچه می گوید پیش کسان مگوئید

The dream was seen by Shah Nizam (Rz) and was stated to Miyan Abdul Fattah (Rz) with a condition "not to reveal it to others". Here neither the dream was stated to Imamana (As) nor Imamana (As) interpreted the dream. Thus this event of the dream has nothing to do with Imamana (As), how could any objection be raised against Imamana's characters?

Whatever he disclosed the dream, no one had denied it about it, but we have to see what interpretation had been given to that dream? In this regard we have to see what the holy Prophet (Slm) had said:

"Oh Ayesha (Rz) when you interpret any dream, try to take it in a virtuous way, so that dream should turn to be a virtue to the dreamer. Thus what is interpreted it shapes accordingly to him, what you had said."

یا عائشۃ اذا عبرتم الرویاء فعبروها علی خیر فان الرویاتکون علی ماعبرها صاحبها

What Imamana (As) had said was that Shah Nizam (Rz) had immersed himself into the entity of Imamana (As). Thus that interpretation was pronounced as a virtue by Imamana (As). The decliner had unnecessarily created doubts who is not well versed with the art of interpretation of the dreams.

9. The decliner had presented another episode which states that Shah Nemat (Rz) had witnessed a dream that he and Imamana (As) were eating milk and bread. But suddenly in the dream, Shah Nemat (Rz) saw that he was actually eating kernel of Imamana's head. When he disclosed it to Imamana (As), Imamana (As) told that he was eating the kernel of Vilayet-e Mustafavi". But such episode was not found in older sources, except In "Hashia-e-Sharief" that:

"Shah Nemat (Rz) had witnessed a dream in which he had immersed himself into the entity of Imamana (As) except his head. He disclosed it to Imamana (As) who informed that Shah Nemat (Rz) would follow Imamana (As) to its entirety."

نقـل اسـت بنـدگی میان شاه نعمتؓ معامله دیدند کـه ذات حـضرت میـران در ذات مـا تمام فروکردیم مـگـر سـرمـانده است این معامله پیش حضرت میرانؑ عـرض کردیم حضرت میران علیه السلام فرمودند که پس روی بنده تمام خدائے تعالیٰ شمارا روزی کند

Here eating the kernel of a head is not reported. The decliner pointed out two things: 1. Eating milk and bread 2. Eating kernel of the head of Imamana (As). It may be pointed out that to drink milk in the dream is the emblem of Iman . As per "Kanzal Ummal"

"Drinking milk is pure Iman whoever drinks milk he is on the religion of Islam and who drinks milk with his own hands he is the follower of Islam."

شرب الـلبن مـحـض الایمان من شربه فی منامه فهو علی الاسلام والفطرة و من تناول اللبن بیده فهویعمل بشرائع والاسلام

The Holy Prophet (Slm) had narrated about Asra (Mairaj) that:

"Thus I drank milk and I was told that I was shown the way of Islam, the natural religion of Allah, the Almighty."

فاخذت اللبن فشربته فقیل لی هدیت الفطرة

Sheik Abdul Haq had commented on this tradition that:

"Whoever saw milk in the dream and consumed it, he gets direction for religion and gets knowledge and guidance."

هرکه شیر در خواب بیند و بخورد تعبیروی علم و دین و هدایت است

Thus as per the narration Shah Nemat (Rz), was on the path of Islam and eating kernel means he was getting the knowledge of Ihsan and Iman.

It was earlier told that kernel of the head as the kernel of the Vilayet-e-Mustafavi, it also indicates as the knowledge of Ihsan. Here a dream of Imam Hanifa (Rz) is presented:

"Narrated by Imam Abu Hanifa (Rz) that he had witnessed a dream in which he came to the grave of the holy Prophet (Slm) and had stolen the shroud and informed it to his teacher. At that time Abu Hanifa (Rz) was a child in a school. The teacher said if your dream is true, then you will follow the holy Prophet (Slm) and you would spread the Shariat. Thus it happened exactly what the teacher had told."

عـن ابی حنیفه رضی الله عنه انه رای فی منامه انه اتی قبر رسـول الـلـه صلی الله علیه و سلم فنبشه فاخبربه استـاذه رضی الله عنه و کان ابو حنیفه یومئذ صبیا فی الـمـکتب فـقـال لـه استاذه رضی الله عنه ان صدقت رویـاک یـاولـدی فـانک تقتفی اثر رسول الله صلی الـلـه عـلیـه و سـلـم و تـنبـش عـن شریعته فکان کما عبـرالاستـاذ رحمـه الـله تـعالیٰ و ظهرلابی حنیفه ما ظهرمن الکرامات

Khaleel Ibn Shaheen had written in his "Kitabul Isharat Fil Ilmul Basarat" that if any one steals the shroud of any Prophet (As), or of a pious man, it means that he would follow the Shriath of that Prophet or that pious man.

But the holy Prophet (Slm) had asserted that whoever steals shroud in the dream, for him paradise would be denied.

"Never he (shroud stealer) enters the لايدخل الجنة جياف
paradise."

Had this narration occurred in the books of Mahdavia, the decliner would dare to say : "See Mahdavis used to steal the shrouds from the grave of their Imam (As). Thus the objection is untenable since the decliner is not aware of the art of interpretation of the dreams.

Apart from this if we try to interpret the dream psychologically, it will create many hurdles. The holy Prophet (Slm) witnessed Allah in his dream as mentioned below:

"I witnessed my Allah in my dream, in رايت ربى فى صورة شاب موفرفى الخضر عليه نعلان
the shape of a young man whose beard من ذهب و على وجهه فراش من ذهب
was very thick and was wearing golden
shoes and golden drops were seen on
His face."

Now we dare to question the decliner, whether this dream informs the Greatness of Allah or He, as a young man?

The true dreams are of two kinds. Precisely what you saw and the other is similitude. The first kind is that whatever you saw is what you desired. Some examples are quoted here: What Allah States:

"Verily Allah had shown the truth, the لقد صدق الله رسوله الرء يا بالحق لتدخلن المسجد
dream of His Prophet (Slm) to become الحرام ان شاء الله آمنين (آلفتح ع ٣)
true: that "you will enter into the
Masjidul Haram, if Allah desired, with
peace."

Author of "Tafseer-e-Madarik" had commented that:

"It is narrated that before embarking روى ان رسول الله صلى الله عليه و سلم رأى قبل
towards Hudaibia, the holy Prophet خروجه الى الحديبية كانه و اصحابه قد دخلوا مكة
(Slm) had witnessed a dream that he and آمنين
his companions actually had entered
Makkah with peace".

Thus what the Prophet (Slm) had witnessed in the dream exactly it came true and it was a prophecy of conquering Makkah without bloodshed.

There had been a narration regarding Azaan (The Call for prayer). Abdullah Bin Zaid (Rz) witnessed a dream in which he saw a man was calling Azaan for prayers. He went to the holy Prophet (Slm) and disclosed his dream. The holy Prophet (Slm) informed him it was a true dream and asked him to teach Bilal (Rz) how to call Azaan for Salath. When Hazrat Omer (Rz) heard the Azaan, came to the holy Prophet (Slm) and told that:

"Verily I too witnessed what was shown لقد رايت مثل ماارىٰ
to Abdullah bin Zaid (Rz)."

Reported this by "Abu Dawood", "Darmi", "Ibn Maja" and "Tirmizi".

This dream was true because the way Azaan had to be called for, was shown to a man in the dream and in the same manner the Azaan started to be given from the very inception of Islam.

It was also a fact that Miyn Ameen Mohammed(Rz) had witnessed in his dream that the following words were being announced loudly by a congregation:

"LA ILAHA ILLALAH   MOHAMEDUR RASOOLULLZAH
ALLAHU ILAHUNA   MOHAMMEDUN NABIUNNA
AL QUR'AN WAL MAHDI IMAMANA   AMANNA WA SADAQANNA"

Imamana(As) informed that it was a true dream, rather an inspiration to proclaim our Creed, hence Imamana(As) made it compulsory to announce loudly after Isha Prayer and at every Religious ceremony.

In the same manner the dream of Prophet Ibrahim (As):

"Stated to his son, "truly my son I am slaughtering you." قال يٰبنى انى ارىٰ فى المنام انى اذبحك

Prophet Ibrahim (As) saw in his dream that he was slaughtering his own son, but the son was not slaughtered but in place of the son a lamb was slaughtered and the tradition of "Qurbani" started from that day onwards. Thus Allah ordained:

""And drove him off in lieu of a sublime Qurbani." وفدينٰه بذبح عظيم (الصٰفٰت ع ٣)

Finally it may be said that the decliner had no knowledge of the Qur'an and the traditions at all. (P. 587)

****

Chapter VI
Commands Of Imamana(As)
Regarding Qur'an's Consistency

Author of Hadia had uttered that some verses of the holy Qur'an are voided and abrogated; thus according to him Qur'an had become inconsistent. (P. 174 of Hadia) From the following we have proved Qur'an's consistency under the commands of Imamana (As).

Previously we have discussed how impressive had been the commentaries of the holy Qur'an in the dairahs as recorded by "Tabquat-e-Akberi", "Muntakhabut Tawareeq" and

"Mua'sir-e-Rahimi" in which the splendour of the reflection of the consistency of the holy Qur'an was depicted.

Seyuoti had narrated in "Kitabul Itqan:" that:

"Ibn ul Hassar (Rz) stated that the placing of the Sooras and verses are according to the revelations".

قال ابن الحصار ترتيب السورو وضع آلايات انما كان بالوحى

Seyuoti had also narrated that:

" Qazi Abu Baker (Rz) said that the compilation of the verses, orders, commands and preferables were all guided by Gabriel (As) who used to say "place this verse at this place."

قال القاضى ابوبكر ترتيب الآيات امرواجب و حكم لازم فقد كان جبريل يقول ضعوا آية كذا فى موضع كذا

Seyuoti had written with reference to Kirmani that:

"In this manner Qur'an was revealed according to the arrangement of the Divine Tablet as kept by Allah."

هكذاهو عندالله فى اللوح المحفوظ على هذا الترتيب

Ashatul Lamaat" states that:

"It must be known that the arrangement of Sooras and verses was accorded as and when the Revelations arrived. And whenever Gabriel (As) brought a verse according to events or circumstances, he used "to direct to keep it in that Soora after that verse" and there are many traditions in this regard also."

باید دانست که ترتیب سوروووضع آیات همه بوحی بود و جبرئیل چون آیتی از قرآن بحسب واقعه می آوردمی گفت ایں را در فلاں سوره بعد از فلاں آیت بنهند و احادیث درایں باب بسیار آمده

Ibn Abbas (Rz) had narrated about Hzt. Osman (Rz):

"Whenever any verse was revealed to the holy Prophet (Slm), he used to call the writer of the Revelations and used to dictate "to keep that verse in that Soora". Narrated in "Tirmizi", "Ahmed" and "Abu Dawood."

كان اذانزل عليه شئى دعا بعض من كان يكتب فيقول ضعواهؤلاء الآيات فى السورة التى يذكر فيها كذاوكذا رواه احمد والترمذى وابوداؤد

Whatever the holy Prophet (Slm) had arranged the verses was just in compliance of Gabriel's directions, therefore Ahmed Bin Hunbal (Rz) had reported what Osman Bin Abul Aas (Rz) had narrated:

"Informed holy Prophet (Slm) that Gabriel (As) came and commanded me "to keep that verse in that Soora."

قـال اتـانـى جبـرئيـلٌ فـامـرنى ان اضع هذه الآية هذا الموضع من هذه السورة

Author of "Ashatul Lamaat" had also said that:

"It is ascertained that the arrangement of the holy Qur'an was on the basis of the Revelations. And whatever was revealed, Gabriel (As) used to direct "to place that verse in that Soora" and there is also a Consensus."

ثـابـت شـده است كه ترتيب قرآن بوحى است و آن نيز مـنـزل اسـت و جبـرئيـلٌ دروقت انزال مى گفت كه اين سـوره را بعـد از فـلاں سوره بايد نهاد و اى آيت را در فلاں موضع بايد نهاد و اجماع نيز بر آں انعقاد پذيرفت

What more consistency can be proved regarding the Holy Qur'an?

It is a fact that in due course of time, and as remoteness increased from the period of the holy Prophet (Slm), the inconsistency started in the Qur'an. Therefore generally the commentators started to designate and point out some inconsistency in the holy Qur'an. And to substantiate their argument they say that during the period of twenty three years so many different commandments had been revealed in different periods, therefore these inconsistencies increased. But the fact is that the Revelation of the verses was revealed according to the events and circumstances; and their arrangement was made according to the directions of Gabriel (As). As regards Revelation of "**the verses which came first one were addressed and those which came later, were arranged after wards**".

(Note: However, in view of the above sentence (in Bold), we cannot and should not question the validity in designating the very first revelation "Iqra Be Isme Rabbikal lazi khalaqa" as Soora 96 and the last one as Soora 110.)

The History of Islam testifies that it was Imamana (As) who openly for the first time declared that the holy Qur'an is consistent from the very beginning to the end with a peculiarity of no verse of it had been voided, nor it had any parenthetical clause or extra sentence and not even any of the verses are disjointed or separated, or omitted, and there had been no extra alphabet nor even any repetition of the verses.

Author of "Insaf Nama" had narrated that:

"Reported that Imamana (As) never tolerated any parenthetical clause, disjointed sentences, exemptions, extermination or omissions in the Qur'an."

نقـل اسـت كه حضرت ميراںؑ در قرآن جملۂ معترضه و مستـانـفـه و استثنـاء مـنـقطع و حذف روانداشتند (باب هفتم)

In the "Naqliyat-e-Miyan Abdul Rasheed" it is written that:

"Hazrat Meeran (As) has asserted that no verse of Quran is voided, nor there is any repetition and no parenthetical clauses or exemptions and omissions occurred."

حضرت میران فرمودند که هیچ آیت قرآن منسوخ نیست در قرآن تکرار نیست و جمله معترضه و حرف زائده نیست (باب هفتم)

Naqliyat-e-Miyan Syed Aalam" states that:

"Hazrat Meeran (As) stated that any parenthetical clause, disjointed sentences, exemptions, extraminations or omissions are not available in the holy Qur'an."

حضرت میران فرمودند که در قرآن جمله معترضه و مستانفه و استثناء و منقطع و حذف روا نیست ۔

From the above it is pointed out that if we accept any parenthetical clause or sentence or any omission in the holy Qur'an it tantamount to accept inconsistency in the holy Qur'an. Therefore Imamana (As) had emphatically repudiated any such disputable items referred to above and asserted that the holy Qur'an is from the very beginning to its last Revelation is completely consistent. In this way he had repudiated the claims of those commentators who tried to stress that it is inconsistent. Some of the commentators who accept the arrangement of the Qur'an still doubt the existence of the above referred disputable items.

In this manner the contribution of Imamana (As) is commendable to emphasize and prove that the holy Qur'an has complete consistency without having any disputable literary phraseology.

The author of this book (Haz. Buzmi) had written a book under the title "Biyan-e-Qur'an" through it, it has been proved, under the guidelines of Imamana (As), that the Holy Qur'an is perfectly consistent without having any parenthetical clauses or sentences, disjointed sentences, omissions and exemptions. A few references from the said book are presented below:

Qur'an and Parenthetical Clauses:

It is written in pamphlet "Al-Jamal":

"Parenthetical clause: if a sentence occurs in between two sentences or conversation, without having any connection. For example; Stated Abu Hanifa "Rahimahulla" that intention for ablution is not necessary."

المعترضه وقعت بین الکلامین بلا تعلق بینهما مثل قال ابو حنیفه رحمه الله النیة فی الوضوء لیست بشرط

المعترضه ماوقع بين الكلامين بلا تعلق بشئى نحو

قال ابو حنيفه رحمة الله عليه النكاح سنة

""Objectionable is that which occur in between two sentences without having any connection to either of the two; for example; Stated Abu Hanifa "Rahmatullahi Alaihi" that wedding is a Sunnat."

In the first example the words "Rahimahullah" and in the second example the word "Rahmatullahi Alahi" are parenthetical sentence. Because they have no connection with either the earlier or the later words. In the holy Qur'an such sort of verses would never be found.

Some commentators have designated some verses as parenthetical, which is wrong. Some examples are presented : The "Underlined" in Arabic Text, or "Bracketed in English Text" sentence or words in the Arabic version have been designated by the commentators as objectionable under various categories, which we have repudiated their argument, by trying to justify their occurrences.

1."As to who reject Faith, (it is the same to them; whether thou warn them or do not warn them); they will not believe."(2:6)

(١) ان الذين كفروا سواء عليهم ء انذرتهم ام لم تنذرهم لا يومنون (البقرة ع١)

In this, the words "underlined" " Sawaaun Alaihim Anzar Tahum Um Lum Tunzir hum" (It is same to them, whether you warn them or do not warn them") had been said by the commentators to be a parenthetical clause which is wrong. Because these words are giving news about the infidels.

2. "They say: this is what we were fed with before. (For they are given things in similitude); and they have therein companions pure and holy". (2:25)

(٢) قالوا هذا الذى رزقنا من قبل و اتوا به متشابها ولهم فيها ازواج مطهرة (البقرة ع٣)

Here the words (WA Atwabehu Muta Shabeha "they are given things in similitude) have been said to be objectionable which is wrong, because it represents as a statement.

3. We wish indeed for guidance, (if God wills)" (2:70).

(٣) انا ان شاء الله لمهتدون (البقرة ع٨)

Here " In Sha Allah"(If God Wills") is said to be objectionable, but the word "If" is a condition for guidance.

4."And that is indeed a mighty adjuration; (if you but knew) _"(54:2)

(٣) وانه لقسم لو تعلمون عظيم (الواقعه ع٣)

In this" Lou Talemoon" (If you but knew)" is said to be parenthetical, but it is a condition.

5. But those who believe and work deeds of righteousness and believe in the Revelations sent down to Mohammed (Slm) (for it is the truth from their Lord). He will remove from them their ills and improve their condition." (54:2)

(۵) والذین آمنوا و عملوا الصالحات و آمنوا بما نزل على محمد و هو الحق من ربهم كفر عنهم سیاتهم واصلح بالهم (سورہ محمد ۱ع)

In this verse " WA Hual Haqqoo Min Rabbihim"(For it is the truth from their Lord) is said to be parenthetical, which is wrong because it supports "Revelations sent down to Mohammed (Slm)".

6. But if you cannot-and is a (surety that ye cannot) --. Then fear the fire" (2:24)

(٦) فان لم تفعلوا ولن تفعلوا فاتقوا النار (البقرة ٣ع)

In its "Walan Taf Aloo" (And it is a surety that ye cannot) is said to be parenthetical, is not correct, because it is said with certainty that you cannot do.

7. Say: I find not in the message received by me by inspiration any (meat) forbidden to be eaten by one who wishes to eat it, unless it be dead meat or blood poured forth; or the flesh of a swine (for it is an abomination). Or what is impious (meat) on which a name has been invoked other than Allah." (6:45)

(٧) قل لا اجدما اوحى الى محرما على طاعم يطعمه الا ان يكون ميتة اودما مسفوحا اولحم خنزیر فانه رجس اوفسقا اهل لغير الله به (الانعام ع ۱۸)

The words "Fa Innahur Rijsa" (For it is an abomination) is cannot be said as parenthetical clause since it informs condition of a thing.

8."They press their fingers in their ears to keep out from the stunning thunder-clap, while they are in terror of death, (but Allah is ever around the rejectors of faith). The lightning all but snatches away their sight." (2: 19,20)

(٨) يجعلون اصابعهم فى اذانهم من الصواعق حذرالموت والله محيط بالكافرين يكادالبرق يخطف ابصارهم (البقرة ٣ع)

The clause "Wallahu Muheeth Bil Kafereen" (But Allah is ever around the rejectors). This indicates that the infidels want to escape by putting their fingers in their ears, while Allah is ever around them. Therefore it cannot be said to be a parenthetical clause.

9." Allah. There is no god, but Allah . And a surety; He will gather you together on the Day of Judgment" (4:87)

(٩) الله لا اله الاهو ليجمعنكم الى يوم القيامه (النار ۱۱ع)

The words" Allahu La Ilaha Illa Hoo" are providing information. Hence it is not a parenthetical clause.

10."If any one invokes besides Allah, any other god. He has no authority therefor, and his reckoning will be only with his LORD."(23:117)

(١٠) ومن يدع مع الله الهاً آخرلا برهان له به فانما حسابه عند ربه المومنون ع٦

In this verse the words "La Burhana Lahu Behi" (No authority therefor) it denotes essential requirement, hence cannot be said to be a parenthetical clause.

11. "Follow what thou is taught by inspiration from thy Lord; There is no god but He. And turn aside from those who join gods with Allah." (6:106)

(11)اتبـع مـااوحى اليـك مـن ربك لااله اله هو و اعرض عن المشركين (الانعام ع١٣)

The words "La Ilaha Illah Hoo" (There is no god but He) denote certainty of truth; therefore cannot be said to be a parenthetical clause.

12. "And they assign daughters for Allah, Glory be to Him; And for themselves sons, they desire." (16:57)

(12) ويجعلون لله البنات سبحانه ولهم مايشتهون (النحل ع٧)

The word "Subhanahoo" (Glory be to Him) cannot be objected, because it praises Allah.

This is also not a parenthetical clause. It is their wish, against Allah.

Author of "Nahjul Adaab" had written about the parenthetical clause that:

(13)"Parenthetical clause is that which comes in between two sentences. But does not affect the meanings of the real sentence."

(13)آن جمـلـه ايسـت كـه ميـان اجزائ جمله، ديگر عـارض گشته به هيچ يكے متعلق نبود واز دورنمودن آن جمله درمعنى اى جمله خللے راه نيا بدـ

For example this sentence:

(14)"Said by Hanifa 'Rahmatullah hi Alaih' that the wedding is Sunnat."

(14)قال ابو حنيفه رحمة الله عليه النكاح سنة (اصل الجمل)

Author of "Majma-ul-Sanaaye" said that "Hashu" is an objectionable sentence which gives extra meaning. However, its existence has no value.

Its example is given in "Madarik" 'Makkata wa Zaid qaem Qur'an baladullah'. Here Zaid qaem is a parenthetical clause thus hashu misleads the meaning of the Qur'an.

Author of "Majmau-S-Sanaaye" had said that:

(15)"Hashau is an objective sentence which gives extra meanings. However, its existence has no value. The example of it is given in the "Madarik- "Makkatu wazeed qaaemun khair balaadillahi". However Hashu was not accepted in the Quran."

(15)حشـو متوسط آوردن كلام معترضه است كه زائد بـود بـراصـل مـراد مـادر سـلامت بيت نقصان نه كند و بودن و نابودن او و برابر باشد

16.Jumla-e-Mustanifa:

Mustanifa means a fresh sentence or a new paragraph it has two kinds: (1) Ibtedaiya or Muftahiha. (United or perpetrator) (2) Munqate'a or Maqtu'a are disconnected.

The first is the one which comes in the beginning of any speech or a dialogue. The other one is that which has no connection with its prior sentence. The author of "Nahajul Adab" has written that it is the one, which comes in the beginning of a speech, or statement, either in words or in mind without being in precedents.

The second kind of Mustanifa (fresh clause) is meant by the fresh clause that has been mentioned. In "Insaf-Nama" it is written that no verse of Quran is disconnected with any prior words. The examples are given here.

18."The underlined clause can be described as a fresh clause because it is either the information of the present or circumstantial state of the pronoun hidden in "Bemomineen". (2:8,9)

(18)ومن الناس من يقول آمنا بالله وباليوم الآخر وماهم بمومنين يخادعون الله والذين آمنوا (البقرة . ع ٢)

19."To say that underline clause is a fresh clause is not correct because it is a second attribute of the above said word Jannath. (2:26)

(19)لهم جنات تجرى من تحتها الانهار كلما رزقوا منها من ثمرة رزقا قالوا رزقنا من قبل (البقرة ع ٣)

20."To say that underline is a new paragraph is not correct because it is inclined to "qaala rabbuka".(2:32)

(20)اذ قال ربک للملائكة ...... قال انى اعلم مالا تعلمون وعلم آدم الاسماء كلها (البقرة . ع ٣)

21.The underline clause is not a new paragraph but it is describing about their utterances. (5:8)

(21)قالوا سمعنا واطعنا غفرانک ربنا واليک المصير لا يكلف الله نفسا الا وسعها (البقرة . ع ٣)

22.To say that underline phrase is a new paragraph, it is not a surety or certainty.

(22)لا يجرمنكم شنآن قوم على الا تعدلوا اعدلوا هو اقرب للتقوى (المائده . ع ٢)

17."Jumla-e-Maqtua": (Disconnected) new paragraph is the one which is precedent to prior clause but having no connection with the prior clause. The author of "Nahj-ul-Adab says: the second one, is the one which is precedent to the prior clause and had no connection with its prior phrase. It is also written along with the second one of the fresh clause in which the one is disconnected with the prior clause.

23. To say that underline phrase is a new beginning is not correct because it is a cause and effect phrase. (5:7,8)

(23)ولا يحزنک قولهم ان العزة لله جميعا (يونس . ع ٧)

24. This is also a cause and effect phrase not a fresh start. (6:142)

(24)كلوا من ثمره اذا اثمرو آتوا حقه يوم حصاده ولا تسرفوا انه لا يحب المسرفين (الانعام . ع ١٧)

25. To say that the underline phrase is a fresh sentence is not correct because it is either a predicate (information for "kuntum") or it is an attribute of "Khairul Ummah". (3:111)

(25)كنتم خير امة اخرجت لناس تامرون بالمعروف و تنهون عن المنكر (آل عمران . ع ١٢)

26. Say that it is a fresh sentence is not correct but it is either a circumstantial expression or a second information about "Tayefa". (3:55)

(26)و طائفة قد اهمتهم انفسهم يظنون بالله غير الحق ظن الجاهلية (آل عمران . ع ١٦)

27. Underline phrase is not a fresh statement because it is either inclined to "nuraddu" or it is a circumstantial expression of the pronoun which is hidden in "nuraddu". (6:28)

(27)فقالوا يليتنا نرد ولا تكذب بآيات ربنا تكون من المومنين (الانعام . ع ٣)

28. The underline phrase is not a fresh sentence because "Ha-ulaayi" is the meaning of "Allazeen", the word Hajajtum is related to "Ha-ulaayi" (3:67)

(28)هآ انتم هؤلاء حاججتم فيما لكم به علم (آل عمران . ع ٧)

29. The underline phrase is not a fresh sentence because it is an explained phrase. (2w:88)

(29)احل لكم ليلة الصيام الرفث الىٰ نسائكم هن لباس لكم وانتم لباس لهن (البقره . ع ٢٣)

30. The underline phrase is not a fresh sentence because it is related to a second news. (24:27)

(30)اولئک مبرؤن مما يقولون لهم مغفرة ورزق كريم (النور . ع ٣)

31.The underline words are not a fresh sentence but it is a conclusion of a conditional clause. (5:71)

(31) كلما جائهم رسول بما لاتهوئ انفسهم ٱ<u>فريقا كذبوا وفريقا يقتلون</u> (المائده . ع ١٠)

32.The underline phrase is not a fresh sentence but a new sentence hence it becomes a related or connected phrase. (27:4)

(32) الذين يقيمون الصلوة ويوتون الزكوة <u>وهم بالآخرة هم يوقنون</u> (النمل . ع ١)

33.The underline phrase is also not a fresh sentence, instead it is an attribute of Rijaalun. (7:47)

(33) وعلى الاعراف رجال يعرفون كلا بسيماهم ونادوا اصحاب الجنة ان سلام عليكم <u>لم يدخلوها وهم يطمعون</u> (الاعراف . ع ٥)

34.The underline phrase is not a fresh starting sentence but it is substituted for "Hasaba Jahannum". (21: 99)

(34) الكم وما تعبدون من دون الله حصب جهنم <u>انتم لها واردون</u> (الانبياء . ع ٤)

35.This is not also a fresh statement. It is a second object of "Waada". (5:10)

(35) وعد الله الذين آمنوا وعملوا الصالحات <u>لهم مغفرة واجر عظيم</u> (المائده . ع ٢)

36.This is also not a fresh sentence or a new paragraph but it is a confirmative or cause and effect phrase. Irrespective of this Abu-Al-Samal has read "Anna" pronounced with a vowel and "lakhabeer" without "lam" on this account it is not a fresh sentence. (100:10,11,12)

(36) افلا يعلم اذا بعثر ما فى القبور وحصل ما فى الصدور <u>ان ربهم بهم يومئذ لخبير</u> (العاديات . ع ١)

37.This is not a fresh sentence because the stop is on "fil Ilm" and "yaquloona" is a substantial expression of "Al-rasikhuna".(3:8)

(37) وما يعلم تاويله الا الله والراسخون فى العلم <u>يقولون آمنا به</u> (آل عمران . ع ١)

38 The underline words are not a fresh sentence, but the beginning words because the stop is on "sawaaun".(3:113,114)

(38) كانوا يكفرون بآيات الله ويقتلون الانبياء بغير حق ذلك بما عصوا وكانوا يعتدون. ليسوا سواء <u>من اهل الكتاب</u> امة قائمة يتلون آيات الله آناء اليل وهم يسجدون (آل عمران . ع ١٢)

39.The underline is not a new paragraph because it is related to "naseera". These words "naseeram minal Lazeena" is just like "nasarnahu minal qoum" the verse is as "Wa nasaranahu minal qoum, illal lazeena kazzabu bi-aayatina".

(39)والله اعلم باعدآئكم و كفىٰ بالله ولياً و كفىٰ بالله نصيرا <u>من الذين هادوا</u> يحرفون الكلم عن مواضعه (النساء . ع ۴)

40.This is also not a new sentence or a fresh paragraph but it is an object or a predicate. (2:2,3)

(40)ا <u>لٓمٓ ذٰلک الکتاب لاریب فیه</u> (البقره . ع ۱)

In short the commentators only seeing the word before the verse, expressed their opinion in this way as being a fresh sentence.

Had they pondered over the whole verse with the meaning, they would not have tried by accepting a new paragraph in the Qur'an, due recognition or according to the idea of inconsistency between the verses of the holy Qur'an against the traditions of the Rasool-e-Kareem (Slm).

Author of "Majmaul Sanaaey" had said that parenthetical word or clause is an added or extra word which do not change the original sense of a sentence. If you take out 'Rahmatullahi Alaihi' the meanings do not change.

Another example from "Madarik" is given:

Makkata Wa zaid Qaema Khair-e-Blad Allah." Here 'Wa Zaid Qaiema' is a parenthetical clause which has no connection either to its beginning or to its end. However in Kalamullah such words do not exist. Thus it is not possible to accept such padding or stuffing in the Qur'an.

Thus in the same manner there exist clauses like "Mustanifa, words of Qualification like "Insha Allah" (God willing) etc. or words of Exterminated or snapped words. In such words, Imamana (As) had accepted words of qualifications but not the snapped words.

Qur'an and Snapped Qualification:

Istasna (Qualification) has two kinds: Contiguous and Snapped. Example:

"Group of people came to me, but not Zaid".

جاء نی القوم الا زیداً

Because Zaid is included in the group, this Istasna is contiguous. Another example:

"Group of people came to me but the ass did not come".

جاء نی القوم الا حمارا

Here Ass is not included in the group, hence here Istasna is taken as a snapped one.

It is narrated in "Insaf Nama" that Imamana (As) never tolerated any snapped qualification in the holy Qur'an. Thus in place of "Snapped", "Contiguous" is preferable, because "Snapped" is not attached to its prior, and the Contiguous is attached to its prior. These are some examples for them:

1. ."When we asked the Angels to prostrate before Adam, all had prostrated, except Iblees." (2:35)

واذ قلنا للملّكة اسجدوا الآدم فسجدوا الا ابليس (البقره . ع . ٣)

Here the underlined words are not snapped one but contiguous one, because Iblees was from the Angels.

2. "Some of them are unlettered ones, do not know about the Qur'an, but (have) yearning."

ومنهم اميون لا يعلمون الكتاب الا امانى (البقره . ع . ٥)

Here also it is not a snapped one, because the Jews accepted what had been written in the Torah, which were according to their yearnings, as was told verbally by their scholars.

3." (Told) the emblem is that (you) could not speak for three days, except by indication."(3:42)

قال آيتك الا تكلم الناس ثلثة ايام الا رمزاً (آل عمران . ع . ٣)

Here to tell "Illa Ramza" is a snapped one but it is not correct, because conversation informs the purpose, so also the indication does the same purpose. Thus both conversations or indication are same, but the indication is silent.

4. "Thus no town (people) attained faith, although faith would have profited them, except the followers of Younus."(10:99)

فلو لا كانت قرية امنت فنفعها ايمانها الا قوم يونس . (يونس . ع . ١٠)

To say that "Al Qoum-e-Younus" is a snapped one, is not correct because town means people of the town, but followers of Younus attained faith. Therefore it is contiguous one.

5. "No useless words would be spoken in paradise except Peace."(19:63)

لا يسمعون فيها لغواً الا سلاماً (مريم . ع . ٣)

Peace means safety and security, which is not necessary for the people of paradise, therefore it is a contiguous one.

"Will never taste the coldness in water, but warm water and pus."(78:25)

لا يذوقون فيها برداً ولاشراباً الا حميما و غساقا (النباء. ع . ١)

Water or pus both are liquids, hence it is wrong to say it a snapped one.

7. "Tell them that you do not require anything except the love of being a relative."(42:24)

قل لا اسئلكم عليه اجرا الا المودة فى القربىٰ (الشورىٰ . ع . ٣)

Here also it is wrong to say snapped one, since relatives means the relatives of the holy Prophet (Slm).

8. "Verily, Angels told : we are sent towards the bad people, but Loot's family."(15:59,60)

قالوا انا ارسلنا الىٰ قوم مجرمين الا آل لوط (الحجر . ع . ٣)

Here it is wrong to say a snapped one, because the angels were sent to destroy the bad people and to save the Loot's family.

9."Thus inform them about the merciless punishment, but those who are virtuous and did good deeds, they get rewarded."(84:25,26)

فبشرهم بعذاب اليم الا الذين آمنوا و عملوا الصالحات لهم اجر غير ممنون (الانشقاق . ع . ۱)

This is contiguous one.

10. "Verily, they are enemies of mine, except the Sustainer."(26:78)

فانهم عدو لى الا رب العالمين (الشعرا . ع . ۳)

Here also it is not snapped one, but contiguous.

Thus, the commentators had erroneously accepted them as the snapped ones, just looking at the words without pondering on their meaning and purpose.

Qur'an and Omission:

According to Imamana (As) there are no omissions in the holy Qur'an. Example:

1."They deceive Allah and others who have accepted the faith."(2:10)

يخادعون الله والذين آمنو (البقره . ع . ۲)

Author of "Madarik" had stated under this verse that:

It means to say that they had deceived Rasoolullah (Slm). Thus Rasool is omitted from it before the word Allah.

As an argument he had presented the command of Allah for asking the people of the town.

However it is wrong to say that the word "Rasool" was actually omitted from the words "Yuqaadeoonallaha".

2. "And taught Adam all names."(2:32)

وعلم آدم الاسماء كلها (البقره . ع . ۳)

Here it is not necessary to give the details of those which were taught to Adam (As). Hence there is nothing omitted.

3. "Did not We find you an orphan, then provided you helper; and found you ignorant than guided you; and found you in poverty and made you contented."
(93:7,8,9)

الم يجدك يتيماً فآوىٰ. ووجدك ضالاً فهدىٰ. ووجدك عائلاً فاغنىٰ .

All three verses are about the Prophet (Slm) only, therefore there is nothing omitted.

Qur'an and Extra Words:

Some commentators have asserted that there are extra words in the holy Qur'an. But those words to whom they say are extra, they are necessary words when they are used.

The extra words are those which do not change the meanings of any sentence. Therefore

Imamana (As) never accepted that there are such words which can be called extras. For example:

1. "Neither on the path of those on whom You wraught Your calamity, nor on the path of those who had forbidden the path."(1:7)

غير المغضوب عليهم ولا الضالين
(سوره الفاتحه)

Here it is wrong to say the word "La" in" Wa Laz Zalleen" is extra; because it has come to stress.

2. "No, I swear on the day of Judgment."(75:2)

لا اقسم بيوم القيامه (القيامه)

Here La is not an extra word, but it is used to stress.

3. "Thus bring one verse like this."(2:24)

فاتوا بسورة من مثله (البقره . ع. ٣)

Here the word "Min"is not an extra word, because it is used to impress.

Qur'an and Repetition of Verses:

Allah states:

"Verily , it is our responsibility to accumulate them:"(75:18)

ان علينا جمعه (القيامه)

Whenever any verse was revealed to the holy Prophet (Slm), the holy Prophet (Slm) used to direct the writer to place it in such and such chapter and it was placed as he was directed. It was already stated that the verses were revealed in view of any incident or any event, but their placement was done according to the exigencies as directed by the Prophet (Slm) that too was done according to the inspiration only (or on guidance by Gabriel (As).

Qazi Abu Baker Baqlani (Rz) (D.403 H.) had written "Aijazul Qur'an" in which he had tried to emphasise the eloquence of Qur'an by presenting the sermons of the Arabian orators for the purpose of comparing the eloquence of the Arabic verses with those Arabic sermons. Thus the Arabian orators too had admitted that the Qur'an is not written by any man, but it is a Divine Writing.

Moulvi Shibli had written in "Nazmul Qur'an" that Shah Valiullah had opined that the Qur'an presents the eloquence of Arabic sermons.

Any point if considered to be important then that point had been repeated and this repetition is but natural. The verses of the Qur'an are just like Arabic sermons which contain many repetitions which enhances the utility of the purpose.

Apart from this the style and the material is different everywhere as written by Shah Valiullah:

"On many cases where repetition of problems had been mentioned they contain new style and new material in order to impress its venerability"

در اكثر احوال تكرار آن مسائل بعبارت تازه او اسلوب جديد اختيار فرمودند تااوقع باشد درنفوس والذباشد در اذهان

Thus such repetition which had new style and new material, it should not be taken as a repetition at all.

Author of "Qaulul Haq" had written that any topic which was considered important had been repeated frequently in the Qur'an to emphasize its purpose. And also that when a particular point was considered to be more important, then that point had been clearly repeated so that it should be scrutinized properly. Author of "Muaheb-e-ilahia" had stressed that:

"Any repetition is just to emphasise, to educate and to enhance its venerability."	گفته اند تکرار برائے دفع غفلت است وتاکید حجت وتذکیر نعمت

Kirmani (D 786) who wrote "Sharah-e-Bukhari" had maintained that those verses which had been repeated in Qur'an, actually they are not at all catogorized as repetition."

From these, it comes to light that according to Imamana (As) there are no extra or Mu'te'riza sentences in the Qur'an and there is no repetition of verses at all.

Thus if any verse had been repeatedly revealed it was just to remind or to emphasize only. Therefore it cannot be said as a repetition at all.

Qur'an and Abrogated Verses:

It is a general opinion among Muslim scholars that there are some such verses which they say that they have been abrogated. Author of Hadia had objected on Imamana (As), because Imamana (As) had emphatically emphasized that there is no verse of the Qur'an which was superseded or abrogated at all. Author of "Insaf Nama" had said in this regard that:

"Hzt. Bandagi Miyan (Rz) often informed that Imamana (As) had clearly emphasized that no verse was superseded or abrogated in Qur'an."	نقل است از بندگی میان سید خوندمیر کرات ومرات فرمودند که حضرت میراؒن در قرآن هیچ آیت منسوخ نداشته اند (باب هفتم)

On that, author of Hadia had alleged that "to say no verse was abrogated is rudeness" on the part of Imamana (As). Author of Hadia asserts that some five hundred verses had been abrogated. As against his assertion, Jalaluddin Seyouti (Rz) had stated that there are just twenty verses which are abrogated. This also had been certified by Abu Baker Ibnul Arabi (Rz). Still as against these twenty verses, Shah Valiulllah Muhaddis-e-Dehalvi had asserted that "just five verses had been abrogated". Those five verses said to have been abrogated by Shah Valiullah are narrated hereunder to examine whether his assertion is correct or wrong:

1. Legacy: "Kutiba Alaikum Iza Hazara Ahdakumul maut" which had been, according to him, had been annulled by:

1/a. "Yusikumullahu fi Auladikum" and the tradition "la wasiyata uwarisun" no will for inheriter and consensus of the Ummah.

2. Jihad: In Yakun Minkum ishroona saberoona." According to him the following verse annuls it.

3. Nikah:La Yahillu lakum mim baadi

3/a ."Inna Ahlalna laka" according to him it was annulled by "Inna Hallana Laka Azwajaka."
It is said that the following verse annuls it.

4. Najwah: "Iza Najiatumur Rasoola Faqaddimu" according to him it was annulled by the
following verse.

5. Tahajjud: "Qumil Laila illa Qaleela" according to him it was annulled by the following
verse.

But from the following it shall be proved that no verse was abrogated".

*(Note:The above five verses pertain to 1. Legacy, 2. Jihad, 3. Nikah, 4. Najwa, 5.
Tahajjud. We shall discuss about each of them and try to prove that these five verses also
had not been abrogated as informed by Imamana (As) and as represented by Hazrat
Bazmi (Rh).*

1. Legacy:

"It is prescribed when death approaches, any of you, if he leaves any goods (Legacy), that he makes a bequeath to parents and next of kins, according to responsible usage; this is due from Allah." (2:180")

كتب عليكم اذا حضر احد كم الموت ان ترك خير الوصية للوالدين والا قربين بالمعروف حقا على المتقين (البقره ركوع ٢٢)

According to Shah Valiullah, the following verse annuls this verse. But actually it does not
annul, according to Imamana (As).

"Allah directs you as regards your children's inheritance, to the male, that equals to two portions of the females. If only daughters, two or more; their share is two-third of the inheritance, and if only one, her share is half." (4:11)

يوصيكم الله اولاد كم للذكر مثل حظ الاثنتين فان كن نسآء فوق اثنين فلهن ثلثا ما ترك الٰى آخرها (النساء ع ٣)

From the first verse it becomes clear that the legacy should be distributed among parents and
near relatives. The second verse also confirms that the legacy should be distributed but clarifies
how many males and females should get. Thus how could it be said that the second verse had
annulled the first one?

2.Jihad:

"Oh Apostle: Rouse the believers to fight. If there are twenty amongst you, be patient and preserving, they will vanquish two hundred. If a hundred, they will vanquish a thousand of the unbelievers for these are a people without understanding." (8:65)

يٰايها النبي حرض المومنين على القتال ان يكن منكم عشرون صابرون يغلبوا مائتين وان يكن منكم مائة يغلبو الفا من الذين كفروا بانهم قوم لا يفقهون (الانفال ع ٩)

"For the present Allah had lightened your (task). For He knoweth that there is a weak spot in you. Therefore, if you are a hundred; be patient and preserving, they will vanquish two hundred, and if thousand; they will vanquish two thousand, if God chose or God willing; for Allah is with those who patiently preserve". (8:66)

الئن خفف الله عنكم و علم ان فيكم ضعفا فان يكن منكم مائة صابرة يغلبو مائتين و ان يكن منكم الف يغلبو الفين باذن الله والله مع الصابرين (الانفال ٩ ع)

Here also you cannot suggest that the second one had annulled the first one. Because both verses are commanded to fight thus it is obligatory on Muslims to fight against infidels and to subdue them. Just with a difference in numbers, how can you decide that the second one annuls the first one.

3. Matrimony (Nikah):

"It is not lawful for thee (to marry more) women after this, not to change them for (other) wives, even though their beauty attracts thee, except any, thy hand should possess (as handmaidens) and Allah doth watch over all things" (33:52)

لا يحل لك النساء من بعدولا ان تبدل بهن من ازواج ولو اعجبك حسنهن الا ما ملكت يمينك وكان الله على كل شئى رقيبا (الاحزاب ع ٦)

"Oh Prophet: We have made lawful to thee thy wives to whom thou hast paid them their dowers; And those whom thy right hand possesses out of the prisoners of war whom Allah had assigned to thee. And the daughters of thy paternal uncles and aunts and daughters of thy maternal uncles and aunts who migrated from Makkah with thee and any believing woman who dedicates her soul to the prophet, if the prophet wishes to wed her - this only for thee and not for the believers (at large)." (33:50)

يايها النبى انا اهللنا لك ازواجك التى آتيت اجورهن وما ملكت يمينك مما افآء الله عليك و بنت عمك وبنت عمتك و بنت خالك و بنت خلتك التى هاجرن معك وامراة مومنة ان وهبت نفسها للنبى ان ارادالنبى ان يستنكحها خالصة لك من دون المومنين (الاحزاب ع ٦)

Here the latter verse is said to have annulled the prior one. But Allah had made lawful to the holy Prophet (Slm) his wives along with the captive women who were captured in the war. The purpose of the latter verse is categorized with whom the holy Prophet (Slm) is directed to marry. Thus how can anyone suggest that this verse annuls the prior which also gives the same meanings with some restrictions. Both verses testify that Allah had made lawful to the holy Prophet (Slm) both his wives and the captive women.

4. Najwah (to speak in whisper):

"Oh the believers when you speak to the holy Prophet (Slm), then before speaking, give some charity which is good for you which cleanse you. If you are not in a position, then Allah is forgiving and merciful."(58:13)

يَاۤ اَيُّهَا الذين آمنوا اذا ناجيتم الرسول فقدمو بين يدى نجوٰكم صدقةذلک خير لکم واطهر فان لم تجدفان الله غفورالرحيم.
(المجادله رکوع ٢)

"Whether you had become afraid of giving charity? Because you did not do that, Allah favoured you by asking you to offer prayers punctually and pay Zakat and be faithful to Allah and his Rasool (Slm)."(58:14)

ء اشفقتم انتقدموا بين يدى نجواکم صدقات فان لم تفعلوا وتاب الـلـه عـليکم فـاقيموا الـصـلـوٰة واتوالزکوٰةواطيعواللّه ورسوله
(المجادله رکوع ٢)

The verse is said to have been abrogated by the second verse, requires to give charity and while the other verse requires to pay Zakat. It may be pointed out that Zakat is also a charity. Whether it is a charity or Zakat both require you to pay out something to cleanse your wealth. If the second verse stops paying charity, then the first one, could be said to have been annulled. But as a matter of fact both verses require Muslims to pay from their wealth. Therefore it does not abrogate the previous one.

5. Tahajjud:

"Oh. Thou folded in garments. Stand for prayer by night, but not all night-Half of it or a little less; or a little more; And recite the Qur'an slowly in a rhythmic tone." (73:1-4)

يَاۤ ايها الـمـزمـل قم اليل الا قليلا . نصفه اوانقص منه قليلا . اوزد عـليـه و رتـل الـقـرٰان تـرتيلا (المزمل رکوعٰ)

"Thus recite that much Qur'an which thou can recite with ease." (73:20)

فاقرء واما تيسر من القرٰان (المزمل رکوع ٢)

The verse which is said to have been annulled, on the other hand, asserts to recite clearly and the verse which said to have been annulled tells to recite with ease. Then how can it be said that it is annulling the previous one?

Thus the author of Hadia's contention that five hundred verses are annulled is negatived by Seyuthi, who informed that there are only twenty verses which had been abrogated, but Shah Valiullah's had confirmed that only five verses were annulled. Against them all, Imamana (As) had forcefully convinced others by assertuing that none of the said verses were annulled or abrogated. The same was the opinion of Moulvi Abdul Qadeer Siddiqi, previous head of the department of Religion, Osmania University, Hyderabad, who says that "He had the firm belief that no verse or any order of the Qur'an is annulled."

Thus ,which verse has been said as abrogated and annulled, it represents either the gist of that verse or clarifies it. Thus when the order persists, question of abrogation does not arise.

It boils down to say that the Qur'an, from the beginning to the end, is consistent, it does not contain any parenthetical clause or new and fresh sentence or Mustanifa, exceptions, terminated, omission, extra words and thus not a single verse had been annulled.

"Sirajul Absar" was written after fifty or fifty five years from the demise of Imamana (As). Imamana's characters were known worldwide. Therefore the author of "Sirajul Absar" did not write in detail except:

"Imamana's sublime attributes and saintly characters were so well known like the sun rays in a day. The effect of his sermons was felt by the world in depth. Even a coward, illiterate, sinful and a miser in his company became a brave, literate, worshiper and a generous one."

لقد كان اوصافه الشريفة واخلاقه الكريمة كالشمس فى الظهيرة و تاثير كلامه منتشرا فى الآفاق ولقد صاربصحبته اجبن الناس اشجعهم و اجهلهم اعلمهم و افسقهم اعبدهم و ابخلهم اسنحاهم الىٰ آخره

Before his demise at Farah, he consoled his companions who were weeping by telling:

"Asserted, if you want to weep, weep when Allah's remembrance is vanished from your hearts when I would not be among you. Whenever you will be remembering Allah, think that I am with you."

فرمودند اگرمى گريد برائے آں وقت بگريئد چوں ياد خدا از شما برود آں وقت بنده درميان شما نباشدمادام كه ياد خدائے تعالىٰ درميان شما باشد اين بنده هم درميان شما است (خاتم سليمانى)

Remembrance of Allah.

"Weep when the remembrance of Allah is gone from you."

آں وقت بگريئد كه ازميان شما ياد خدائے تعالىٰ برود

(١٤٢)

Imamana (As), for the long twenty three years, had always preached for continuous remembrance of Allah and even in his last moment of his life he asserted for remembrance of Allah only. Thus what more proof of his being commissioned by Allah, anybody would require from Imamana (As)?

Whatever doubts the author of Hadia had raised in his so called "Hadia-e-Mahdavia", they do not nullify the characters of Imamana (As), and neither they nullify the arguments presented by the author of "Sirajul, Absar".

Thus, finally we have to emphasize again that whatever the doubts the author of Hadia had raised, they have been negatived elaborately and arguably through these writings.